RUPERT BROOKE

Rupert Brooke
The Poetical Works
edited by Geoffrey Keynes

RUPERT BROOKE

A biography by

CHRISTOPHER HASSALL

There is always a living face behind the mask
—W. B. YEATS

faber and faber

LONDON · BOSTON

First published in 1964
Second Impression April 1964
by Faber & Faber Limited
3 Queen Square London WC1N 3AU
First published in Faber Paperbacks in 1972
Reprinted 1984, 1996

Printed in Great Britain by
Clays Ltd, St Ives plc

ISBN 0 571 10196 8

4 6 8 10 9 7 5 3

To

GEOFFREY LANGDON KEYNES

CONTENTS

	ACKNOWLEDGEMENTS	*page* 13
I	THE ROAD TO RUGBY	17
II	SCHOOL FIELD (i) *Junior*	34
III	SCHOOL FIELD (ii) *Senior*	64
IV	FRESHMAN	96
V	KINGSMAN	146
VI	THE ORCHARD	186
VII	THE OLD VICARAGE	247
VIII	CANNES	293
IX	THE ESTRANGING SEA	320
X	ENTER PERDITA	359
XI	A DEEP SLEEP	396
XII	ONE OF A NUMBER	448
XIII	SAILING TO BYZANTIUM	490
XIV	MAN INTO MARBLE	514
	Appendix: Poems, 1911, and the contemporary critics	535
	Index	541

ACKNOWLEDGEMENTS

There are two senior custodians of Brooke's interests, survivors of the four Trustees appointed by Mrs. Brooke, the poet's mother, Sir Geoffrey Keynes and Sir John Sheppard, who must be given foremost place in my indebtedness; and of these, Sir John knows better than anyone that his colleague holds a position which is all his own where any work on Brooke is concerned. I must not anticipate a passage in the last chapter, but Sir Geoffrey's *A Bibliography of Rupert Brooke* (Rupert Hart-Davis, 1959) and his *The Poetical Works* (Faber and Faber, 1946), the standard enlarged edition referred to throughout in my footnotes as *G.K.*, have been constantly at my side. Of even greater service to a biographer has been the collection of miscellaneous Brooke material that he has brought together over the years, some of it dating back to the time when he was a schoolboy in the same form as his friend, and of this by far the most considerable item is the collection of letters which must be something like ten times the size of anything that the late Sir Edward Marsh could have been able to draw upon when he compiled his Memoir in 1915. For making me welcome to his memory as well as to his archives, for the encouragement of his trust and much else, less easy to define, I have nothing to give him in return but the Dedication of this book. After such an active life-time, in which great matters have come and gone while the memory of Rupert Brooke still remained an object of his service, I like to think that this, the most I can offer, cannot be negligible in his eyes.

There are others whose good offices must be specified. I am most obliged to the Provost of King's College, Cambridge, for his hospitality and the amenities he put at my disposal. Dr. A. N. L. Munby, librarian of King's, proved much more than the helpful custodian of valuable papers, giving useful advice and practical assistance in matters of research; Mr. James Strachey gave me access to his correspondence with Brooke and the papers relating to his brother Lytton, and enlightened me in many ways, doing me generous service; Mr. Justin Brooke did much to put me in the picture of Edwardian

13

ACKNOWLEDGEMENTS

Cambridge and the Marlowe Dramatic Society; the late Lord Dalton kindly gave what I asked of him—a few tutorials on Fabianism and the Labour movement and the loan of relevant papers. The warmth of his encouragement and his evident devotion to my subject were heartening and of considerable value, and I honour his memory.

In one important respect the late Mrs. Cornford had special knowledge. When Sir Geoffrey Keynes put the subject of this work before me, having first enlisted me as his co-trustee, it would have been idle to commit myself without assurance that she was willing to have her say. She did more, supporting Sir Geoffrey in his proposition, and then, just as I was setting out on my researches, her death seemed to make it a bounden duty to do what she enjoined on me. I must record my gratitude to her. For the use of her letters and the memoranda she made during the First World War I am obliged to her son, Mr. Christopher Cornford.

Miss Margaret Brooke and her sister Charlotte, first cousins of the poet, have been very hospitable and helpful to me on matters of the family background, as also have Mr. and Mrs. Julian Hoare, who won my gratitude with many kindnesses. In the sphere of Brooke's old friends I am particularly obliged to Mrs. Dudley Ward for guiding me with helpful comment through her late husband's papers, and to Mrs. Sophie Pryor for making available to me the fragments of two autobiographical novels by her parents, Jacques and Gwen Raverat.

Mr. John Schroder, the collector of Brooke, has been generous with practical assistance, especially in connexion with the Marsh-Brooke correspondence and other manuscripts and relevant publications in his possession; Brooke's residence at The Orchard and The Old Vicarage, whereby he made me indebted to Miss Dorothy Stevenson and Mr. C. A. C. Neeve; the residence in Munich, for which I must also thank Professor Paul Ewald; the Brooke-Sybil Pye correspondence; the question of Swedish translation and Miss Estrid Linder; and for carrying out fruitful inquiries in the United States and elsewhere. Mr. Norman C. Kittermaster, custodian of the Temple Library, Rugby, undertook some researches for me with useful results and assisted in other ways, for which I thank him.

I am grateful for interesting and productive conversations with: Mrs. Lascelles Abercrombie, Mr. and Mrs. Ralph Abercrombie, Lady Violet Bonham-Carter, Sir Arthur Bliss, Mr. H. A. Bond of Walsingham, Mr. Gordon V. Carey, The Rt. Rev. G. A. Chase, late

ACKNOWLEDGEMENTS

Bishop of Ripon, Sir Colin Coote, Mr. Mark Arnold Forster, Mr. E. M. Forster, Mr. David Garnett, Mr. Andrew Gow, Mr. Duncan Grant, Mr. H. Noel Hoare, Mr. Laurence Irving, Lady (Margaret) Keynes, Miss Estrid Linder, Professor H. O. Meredith, Miss Cathleen Nesbitt, Mr. and Mrs. Bertram Rota, Mr. A. F. Scholfield, Miss Naomi Royde Smith, Mr. A. O. Snowden, Mr. Norman Edyvean-Walker, Mr. John Willans, Mr. Arthur Waley, Mr. Laurence Whistler, and Mr. Leonard Woolf.

For various help, chiefly by correspondence, I am most obliged to: Mr. L. R. D. Anderson, Mr. B. E. Astbury, O.B.E., Mr. Donald Bain, Commander M. S. Bradby, R.N., Mr. J. Harold Browne, Dr. Paul Cassidi, Mr. J. B. Donovan, Mr. Monk Gibbon, Commander Hew C. Hedderwick, R.N.V.R., Dr. Jan Hubrecht, Mr. Leslie Kirkbride, Mr. Percy Lubbock, Mr. H. F. MacDonald, Second Master of Fettes College, Mr. C. R. McLaughlin, Miss Margaret Murphy, Lady Nicholson, the Syndics of Cambridge University Library (for quotations from the Diaries of the late Mr. Charles Sayle), Mrs. Peggy Stott, Mrs. Rosalind Toynbee, Major C. A. G. Wingfield, Mr. Wayland Young, Mr. Peter Ward, and Mr. D. Pepys Whiteley.

To Mr. James Knapp Fisher and Messrs. Sidgwick & Jackson I am beholden, since they were the first to publish certain quotations in the Memoir by E.M. which I have been obliged to duplicate. Sir Edward Marsh made the facts within the area of truth available to him into such a proportioned little work of art that it seemed sufficient. And so it still is, within its narrow limits. If I have succeeded to any extent in showing my subject in the round, as a sculptor might do, I would rather the Memoir by E.M. were not regarded as superseded but still be turned to for its own sake, as a miniature painted on ivory.

To Messrs. Longmans Green & Co. Ltd. I am obliged in a way rather similar, owing to slight duplication with a previous work of mine, *Edward Marsh*, which they published. There are a few narrative points where that life history and this one briefly but almost exactly coincide. I have endeavoured not to repeat a quotation except where there was no evading it, and even then I trust that the very different context has given it new colour. Chiefly this applies to the last few weeks of Brooke's life. The events were news to Marsh, lived by him in the sympathetic imagination as the details came in, while here they are the very stuff of life and death. This turns out to be the only passage on any scale whose outline was given in the earlier book, but

ACKNOWLEDGEMENTS

I have made it my business to see that the sharper focus on events has refashioned a story already told.

I must also express my thanks to the Master and the librarian of Christ's College, Cambridge; the librarian of the Brotherton Library, Leeds; the librarians of Dartmouth College, U.S.A. and the University of Harvard; Mr. Robert C. Miller, librarian, Marquette University, Wisconsin; Mr. Sherril Schell for use of his portraits in photogravure; Mr. Robin Skelton, for the advantage derived from his work in assisting Sir Geoffrey Keynes on the organization of the Brooke papers; the President of Magdalene College, Cambridge, and Messrs. Hutchinson for quotations from the Diaries of A. C. Benson; the various authors and publishers of books whose names are acknowledged in footnotes; Miss Gillian Patterson, an amanuensis of critical vigilance and industry who for the second time has carried out researches on a major project, secretarially seen me through to a conclusion, and won my gratitude.

To the many correspondents of Brooke, or their executors, who have sent their letters to the Trustees, I am sincerely grateful on behalf of my colleagues. So much of Brooke's personality survives only in this impromptu form of expression that its essential contribution to this portrait must be the measure of our thanks.

C.H.

Tonford, 1962.

When Christopher Hassall so suddenly and unexpectedly died on April 25 1963 his book was finished, but no proofs had yet reached him from the printer. The task of seeing the book through the press has therefore fallen upon me as the person most nearly concerned, greatly helped by Miss Gillian Patterson and Mr. Jon Stallworthy, who has been appointed Brooke's Literary Trustee in succession to Christopher Hassall. We have tried to carry out the task in a manner which we believe the author would have approved.

GEOFFREY KEYNES

Brinkley, 1963

Chapter I

THE ROAD TO RUGBY

(1520–September 1901)

According to the muster roll of Great Walsingham for the year 1520, a certain Thomas Berry was required to furnish at need one archer fully armed. He had built himself a small but substantial house round a courtyard, just off the main road which led from the seaport of Wells to the shrine of Our Lady of Walsingham. A few yards from his door, the river Stiffkey, having passed through the grounds of the Priory close enough to carry the shadow of its tower and now flooding across the highway, conveniently provided him with a natural moat. On the other side, against the road from the sea, he put up a wall to shield his privacy from the pilgrims who must have been coming by in an almost constant stream, this being the last lap of the way to what was known as the English Nazareth.

Across the road from the garden of Berry Hall the ground rises abruptly to form a knoll; and planted on the crest, exposed, is a church, St. Peter's, a sudden projection of silvery grey stone surrounded by sky. The fourteenth-century interior is almost as bright as the world outside. Tall, traceried windows of plain glass bring the common and secular time of day right up to the altar and shine on the pew-ends with their ancient carved poppy-heads; and across the east end there runs an altar-rail of plain Cromwellian oak, massively rounded and polished again with use. Here, on November 3, 1761, there was a wedding, and the daughter of the great house over the way was the bride. She was marrying a certain William Brooke from the village of Geist which lies between Hunstanton and Norwich. Anne Parker was a young woman of quality. When the Tudors first came to the throne the family was little known outside the city of Norwich. The Parker of that day was a 'calenderer of stuffs'. It was his son, Matthew (1504–1575) who lifted the family into affluence and its name into history when he was appointed private chaplain to

17

Ann Boleyn and eventually became Archbishop of Canterbury under Queen Elizabeth, guiding the Anglican Communion at the critical time of the secession from Rome. From him was descended the John Parker of Georgian times, whose daughter Anne united her family with the Brookes of Geist. It is probable that for a time the first Mrs. Brooke lived with her husband among his clan near Hunstanton and there gave birth to her daughter, Anne the younger, who was to inherit from her grandfather Parker the handsome property opposite St. Peter's on the knoll. Anne was still a girl when she came into her inheritance, and the Brookes moved into the Hall which was to remain the family seat for a hundred and fifty years.

This heiress of Berry Hall founded the line from which Rupert Brooke was to take his descent. On August 1, 1783, there was another wedding at the Cromwellian altar rail. Anne Brooke became the wife of John Reeve, a tenant farmer at Wighton, the next village after Great Walsingham on the river Stiffkey's course to the sea. Although raised by his marriage to the level of a gentleman of quality, he continued his work on the land; but either because his father-in-law was concerned for the continuance of the family name and had made it a condition in the contract, or as an acknowledgement of what he owed to the people of gentle birth who were making him one of their number, he agreed to abandon his own surname and style himself John Reeve Brooke. Whatever the reason, by this concession or compliment to his wife the bridegroom of 1783 prevented the name of Rupert Reeve from being enrolled among the English poets.

He gave his son his own Christian name, and in due course John junior managed the farm with even greater success than his father. We hear of his prize bulls having their portraits done in oils by the itinerant painters of those days. He also did well for himself when he married into a Norfolk family called England. While Ellen England Brooke was mistress of the Hall she bore her husband two daughters and in 1821 a son, to whom she gave the names Richard England; and with him the family seemed suddenly to burgeon forth, gain distinction in a new field beyond the borders of its native county, and eventually leave Norfolk.

In 1840 Richard England Brooke was admitted as a pensioner at Caius College, Cambridge, and five years later was ordained at Ripon. During his first curacy in Yorkshire he met a Miss Harriet Hopkins of Limber Grange in Lincolnshire and in 1846 she became his wife. For several years he was Rural Dean at Hull, then in 1875 he moved to Bath where for the next twenty years until his retirement he was Rector at the Abbey, living in that sloping row of elegant houses called Marlborough Buildings, serving as Chairman of the School Board, and from his place of authority at the Abbey 'ruling Bath', as was said of him, 'with a rod of iron'. He was the father of two daughters, and four sons all of whom won academic distinction; chief among them, perhaps, the youngest, Alan England, who became Provost of King's, Cambridge. His second son was born in 1850 while he was living in the parsonage at Sowerby, and he named the boy William Parker, to commemorate the first Brooke of Berry Hall and his wife's family. Willie, as he was called at home, must have been a quiet, sensible, and rather conventional boy. He was educated first at a school in Kidderminster, and from there he went to Haileybury where he became the head of the school, captain of the first XI and carried off the senior prizes in Latin and Greek. He went up to Trinity, Cambridge, in 1869, but after a few months migrated to King's where he graduated in 1873, having distinguished himself in classics. In the same year he made college history. Up to now King's had drawn its students exclusively from Eton, its twin foundation, so that consequently its Fellows had all been Etonians. W. P. Brooke became the first non-Etonian Fellow of King's. Armed with this distinction, he at once set about to find a way of starting his career as a schoolmaster. He was extremely lucky. Only three years before, while Brooke was studying at King's, a big educational scheme for boys had been launched in Edinburgh. It had made a highly promising start and now, by all reports, showed signs of expansion.

The Governors of Fettes College, this new public school in Scotland, had just opened another house called Glencorse, and thither went one of the original masters, Charles Clement Cotterill, with his fifty boys, to be its first housemaster. Thereby he left one of the original houses without staff or students. It was already the custom for the School House to be administered by two men of equal status, and now, when one of them was moved over to fill the vacancy made by Cotterill, the master left behind found himself short of a colleague. It was this post at School House which the new man from Cambridge was to hold for the next six years.

It doesn't seem very probable that the Rev. Charles Clement Cotterill would ever have been singled out by the new member of the staff, and found especial favour in his eyes, had he not had an attractive sister. Cotterill was undoubtedly a character, while Brooke, more diffident, with a softer outline to his nature, tended to hide himself behind the modest virtues of conformity. The older man, Brooke's senior by eight years, a graduate of St. John's, Cambridge, was by comparison disquietingly self-assured. He had a harsh voice, which wouldn't have mattered so much had he not been outspoken, and his views (he was deeply concerned with social reform) must have seemed a little daring, not to say revolutionary. He was by no means a crank, but a genuine idealist, a socialist of the William Morris breed. In appearance he was clean-shaven (which showed independence in those days) tall and slim with a broad brow, pointed chin and sharp, slightly turned-up nose, and the outer corners of his eyelids drooped, adding a thoughtful look to an intelligent face. His friend Brooke was a smaller man, only five foot three in height, but of more substantial build, with a high forehead, sandy hair, wide-open blue eyes, a very clear, almost girlish complexion and the sort of moustache with a downward curve which, to the eye accustomed to fashions of a later date, seemed to give the face a disappointed look. A mild and cautious man with an occasional twinkle in his eye, Brooke was not without his own quiet brand of pedagogic humour.

A year or two must have gone by before Ruth Mary, Cotterill's sister, came up to Fettes, for she was a good deal younger than both the men, and probably came there straight from school to take up her first post as matron at Glencorse. Her father, Charles Cotterill, a native of Brigg in Lincolnshire, was the incumbent of a parish in Stoke-on-Trent where she had been born and brought up. She was in all respects a trim and elegant version of her brother, extraordinarily like him in appearance, complete with the family sag in the eyelids, almost retroussé nose, and the voice growing shrill in friendly dispute. It was a fresh, boyish face with eager regard, the light brown hair parted in the middle and drawn back tight from a clear forehead. She was pretty, and neither the very faint traces of smallpox on her cheek nor her rather stiff carriage did anything but enhance the individual character of her charm. The natural graces of a good-looking girl concealed a certain toughness whose basis was a singular strength of character even stronger than her brother's. Like him she was interested in public affairs, though her views were less radical, and she took such a lively interest in things around her that on occasion her kindly solicitude was thought to have crossed the border into mere inquisitiveness. She must know the why and the what and the how of all the boys under her roof, and one imagines visiting parents being met with a searching questionnaire.

Meeting her in a social gathering of the staff at School House at Fettes, the gentle Brooke was impressed, even, perhaps, a little awed. The only trouble about paying court to her was the thought that if it came to marriage he would almost certainly have to sacrifice his job. As yet there was no accommodation for married masters at School House. He was well placed, and he knew it, but the risk to his career deterred him less and less the more he reflected on the advantages. For one thing, whatever his situation, Miss Cotterill would make an ideal wife for a schoolmaster, providing the social front to the world which he lacked. He could safely get on with his routine of Latin and Greek while she managed the business of life. He was falling in love and, although she probably failed to show it, so was she. Throughout her life she found it difficult to give or take the affection she felt. Perhaps she had already convinced herself that any demonstration of feeling was not only unnecessary, but a little mawkish, not to say vulgar. William Parker Brooke himself was not cut out to be the hero of a lightning romance. Mutual ease in each other's presence and her brother's reassuring opinions more and more inclined Miss Cotterill toward her admirer, so that in the Spring of 1879 she allowed herself to be engaged, and began making preparations for the wedding.

In 1872 her father's brother Henry, then bishop of Grahamstown, was appointed to the See of Edinburgh. No doubt by now Brooke had been taken to tea with him and so got to know yet another of this formidable clan. The wedding was arranged. On December 18, 1879, W. P. Brooke and Ruth Cotterill were married by the bishop in St. Mary's Cathedral, Edinburgh, and Clement Cotterill signed the register as a witness.

Brooke had already made provision for their future. Fettes was ruled at this time by an amiable Dr. Potts, who was formerly an assistant master at Rugby, and knew the Head, Dr. Jex-Blake. The warmth of his recommendation was such as to make no interview necessary. Early in January 1880 the newly wedded couple were travelling to Rugby for the Easter term. The School House was having a new tutor.

II

When the Brookes left Scotland by train and alighted at Rugby, the railway station with the enormous paved platform, the longest in Europe, was still under construction, but already the wonder of the Midlands, the junction of six lines, newly erected on the site of a less pretentious halt known to readers of Dickens as Mugby Junction. Surely a city greater and more historic than Edinburgh itself must lie beyond! The plan was to begin with a courtesy call on Dr. Jex-Blake. There was no need to go house-hunting, quarters were already allotted; and now the vehicle was mounting the incline towards the town and the view was unfolding its slow surprise. The teeming metropolitan centre with its boulevards and thoroughfares packed with horse-buses, its windowed terraces, and cathedral, had either only just gone, by magic, or had never existed. Rugby station is a delusion of grandeur, or so at first it seems, an impressive and highly serviceable no-man's-land where you change trains on a journey between two places of importance.

On either side, between the intersecting roads which delivered a gust of exceptionally cold wind each time you drew parallel with one of their turnings, were small blocks of two-storey dwellings, 'workers' dwellings', with identical doors and windows, interspersed here and there with a drab little shop, and all built of that Midland brick whose peculiarly hard tone of red suggests a hot flush. And it is everywhere, for at first glance Rugby seems to have happened, all of it, within the space of about twenty years; between, say, the Reform Bill and the publication of *In Memoriam*. One imagines a sudden and hectic phase of early-Victorian development, a shifting of working-class population, and fortunes being made by manufacturers who resided elsewhere but came and supervised and went, leaving the sprawl of a red-brick, hot-looking market town exposed on the gusty northern slope of a plateau overlooking the valley of the Avon, there to catch the brunt of whatever weather there happened to be.

Severe were the problems in those early days, and some were still unsolved when the Brookes arrived. In 1845 there wasn't enough spare water for one fire-engine, and every conceivable device was attempted, including the construction of a water-tower disguised as a small medieval fortress, which looked exactly like a fortress but failed to give a satisfactory supply of water; and as for the sewage, there was a road disagreeably near the School down which no boy should venture on his Sunday walk. But by 1880 the basic advantages of civilization were beginning to come into the town by dint of tireless experiment. The streets looked pretty at night with their incandescent gas lamps, and on the outskirts several rows of more considerable dwellings, not visible to the newcomer from the station, displayed from their verandas the iron railings cast in Coventry from elegant Greek designs. These were largely occupied by what were described as 'nice people, gentle though poor', retired officers, clergy, widows, many of them having settled here because of the one unique amenity, free education in the classics at Dr. Arnold's school for the sons of local residents; and several of these roads, the haunt of polite society, were one moment provincial thoroughfares, promising to go on indefinitely, and the next mere footpaths petering out in wild flowers and bracken.

For the studious there was Over's bookshop, well stocked with the works of the Laureate and Mr. Ruskin, the latest number of *Good Words*, and assorted fiction; and the Geisha Café, as it was known in later Edwardian days, described in its advertisement as a 'pleasant rendezvous for afternoon tea', furnished with potted palms, a big iron stove, and a much-advertised oriental screen (to the kitchen) round which the waitress would manœuvre her tray. 'The shops are of a superior class and the tradesmen enterprising' we read, and one is disposed to believe it, for on closer acquaintance, and after recovering from the deception of the railway station, the town begins to reveal its true and pleasing character. Many of the gentry who watched the Tudor and Gothic developments of the eighteen-fifties made the planting of trees their recreation and, not content with the usual Victorian conifer, had the foresight to make their open places pleasant with copper beech, almond, and laburnum. There was also the pleasure ground by Hillmorton Road, equipped by the munificence of the manager of the Gas Works with a 'substantial bandstand'. No doubt a stroll to the near-by gardens and back was a most convenient resource for Mrs. Brooke when the children were small, and once arrived, there would be no temptation to loiter for the music, her family like herself being tone deaf. And often there were spruce-looking strangers to be seen passing through, riding to hounds with the Atherstone or Fernie Hunts; but on the edge of the town stood the Workhouse where, so they said, conditions were bad. There was plenty of scope here for a woman of Mrs. Brooke's vitality and public spirit; later she became a Guardian of the Poor and Justice of the Peace, but at first it must have seemed a very far cry from Edinburgh, a remote, unpromising little market centre with the look of an industrial town without the bustle and, as yet, the excuse, of industry. She would have had some cause to despond had she not known very well that in the eyes of the world the point of the town was its School, that the School *was* the town, that the headmaster ruled both with the moral authority of a Doge, and that it was no less a personage than the Doctor himself whom she was going to see.

The streets converge on the great School as if the town were making a gesture of acknowledgement that it was there first. And then Rugby prepares another slow surprise. The main building of Gothic design, though confronting the visitor with the impressive Quad Gates (which look shut fast for ever) stands back to the town, or such is the effect. This broad and massive facade of stone mullions and impregnable-looking walls is not only forbidding, but odd, for it stands sheer up from the pavement without any verge or frame of grass or paving, as if wanting to nudge the pedestrian from his path, and the great blank windows somehow give the impression that nobody ever looks out of them. And who would approach those formidable shut doors with any hope of admittance? To the left of this block stands a more habitable-looking building; short, gravelled drive, windows whose eyes are open, and a turret covered with ivy, a place to live in among heavy furniture, as once it was by Dr. Arnold; and having come this far, the visitor should go a step or two further down Barby Road (Watergate Road in the days when the Brookes lived at School Field, the big building on the right a short way down) and there at last let Rugby spring its next surprise; for at the back of the main block, already passed with a sensation of misgiving, stretches the Close—which is however in no sense enclosed, seventeen acres of green sward under the sky, surrounded but not shut in by ancient and enormous trees; on the far side a sky-line of roofs and the tops of chestnuts, like the view across a county cricket-field of almost dream-like proportions. No wonder the principal building offers its back to the town and prefers to stand looking out over the Close, where the light and the clouds are, at the distant airy scene. No more than the town itself should the School be judged by the first impact.

At the corner opposite the headmaster's lodging stands the Chapel, the work of Butterfield, built in 1872 on an Italian model that might be almost offensive were it not so extraordinarily self-assured. It is anything but modest. Should there be gargoyles protruding, high up on the hexagonal tower? There shall not only be four of them, but all four will stretch out their necks extravagantly far, and the ornamentation elsewhere of patterned brick or coign shall be no craven compromise but a forthright assertion of Italianate taste. Behind it stand the class-rooms and assembly rooms of the older school buildings, and the Close stretches flat and green right up to its buttresses. Around the Close and in all the streets nearby are related buildings and lodgings, among them a small, two-storied villa of flushed red brick, 5 Hillmorton Road.

It stands on a corner, at the junction of a main thoroughfare with a narrow lane called Church Walk: twin gables, a bay window on either side of the door, a minute pointed light—the little touch of pseudo-Gothic which must never be missed—inset between the first-floor windows to light the landing, a small front garden patch with a gate opening on the pavement, and a back-yard affording just enough room for a bicycle or two, a dust-bin, and a delivery of coal. It was obviously put up in the early fifties expressly for the purpose of housing a married member of the school staff, and built on its own, probably the first house in the row, bearing no relation to the others which are grander in proportion and later in date. It is only just not the kind of dwelling one meets with at a level crossing, and was designed, at a guess, by some builder of rural cottages who was making a first attempt at adapting his model to an urban setting.

W. P. Brooke went out early each morning, one of the two tutors at School House whose duty it was to advise the boys, direct their studies, twice a week supervise their evening prep, and take a personal interest in their welfare. In addition to this he took the Lower Vth in Latin and Greek, his own classroom being across the road from the main building, one of three small rooms beneath the assembly hall known to the boys as New Big School. It was not long before a rumour got about that whatever he might be in the classroom, he was something less than the master in his own house, and there was a story, surely apocryphal, that his wife was in the habit of sending him out into the road at night to collect horse droppings for her front garden. His day was full enough without such extramural activities. Daily chapel was at seven o'clock and the first class at 7.15, so the household at Hillmorton Road was stirring early. For a while, however, Mrs. Brooke was left with too much time on her hands. Then in 1881 her first son was born. She named him Richard England after the Rector of Bath. A second child, a girl, died in infancy, and she was desperately wishing for another daughter when at 7.30 a.m., on August 3, 1887, she gave birth to her second son. Mr. Brooke proposed the name Rupert because there was a dashing cavalier ring about it. The second name was his wife's suggestion, and one can only suppose that she put it forward so as to redress a balance. There was on the Cotterill side of the family a seventeenth-century ancestor called Chawner, a scholar in foreign languages, and according to family tradition not only a Parliamentarian but a regicide. The records prove that at least he was not tried and condemned as such, and perhaps the most we shall ever know of him is that he gave his name to Rupert Chawner Brooke.

It was rather unfortunate that Mrs. Brooke let it come out in after years how bitterly disappointed she was when she had a second son. Rupert himself knew all about it, believing quite seriously that it accounted for certain qualities of perception which could only be explained as feminine intuition. He could tell, so he claimed, the proportions of an unfamiliar room if he entered it blindfold, and similarly he would be able to say what was going on in a crowded room behind his back. Such were his odd claims. In fact there was nothing feminine in his make-up, or nothing that could be called effeminate, although the fascination that there might be, and the fear that someone might suppose there was, made him inordinately concerned not only to convince himself in his own mind, but to assert his virility in the eyes of his friends. He inherited his mother's features, more of her character than he realized, and his father's fair hair, blue eyes, and especially his skin. This was abnormally clear and smooth and at times transparent in appearance, so that the flesh seemed to shine through it, giving him an almost girlish complexion. So if he was sensitive to a stranger's opinion of his sex, he had his appearance to contend with at every turn, for masculine as it was, it was also conspicuous, and not so much handsome as beautiful. Moreover he enjoyed, if enjoyed is the word, an even rarer gift of Nature, which set off that other, so that together they affected the course of his life. Whatever his inmost, secret fears and scruples, he was born unselfconscious. He might strike an attitude in his letters, and adopt a pose in his early verses, but in his person, where he might so easily have been intolerable, he was more 'natural' than the ordinary run of men. This meant that whatever his mood or disposition might be it was always apparent, not fetched out on occasion, as with people of whom we loosely say that they are 'charming', but simply and evidently there for anyone at any time to take or leave. One felt as if in the presence of the actual, the essential, man, which is not necessarily charming, but is real. It was probably the combination of these two gifts of nature, the physical and the temperamental, which accounted for that effect on people to be called personal magnetism. It was magnetic because it was not deliberate. He was not of course unaware of its effect, but the point here is that he couldn't help it. And it means that the accident of his looks requires more than a bald statement. It was a factor in his life for good or ill, and a just account of such a man must be almost as much a record of how he looked and affected the people round him as of what he did. The life cannot properly be understood without the development of both the physical and literary gifts being followed together. Some may even think at the end that the bodily graces of the man were the undoing of man and poet alike, so necessary are they in this particular case to the record of a man of letters.

When Mrs. Brooke got out and about again, there was one obvious destination for her stroll. They were building a Memorial Clock Tower in the market place to celebrate this year of the Queen's Jubilee. She remarked more than once on the happy conjunction that the clock tower and Rupert arrived together. Her elder boy Richard would soon be going to the preparatory school run by Mr. T. B. Eden and his wife, down Watergate Road. Thanks to an aunt of her husband's, Sophia Hopkins, an agreeable marriage settlement had been arranged in Edinburgh, nothing very special, but it did mean she could afford the assistance of a maid, and a governess for the elder boy—Miss Tottenham, who would come in useful again when Rupert reached the alphabet age. In 1891, when her infant was three years old, she bore another son, Alfred. Her family was now complete. She had no daughter. Her last confinement was over just in time, for within a few months the opportunity came that her husband had been waiting for. Doubtless he had been promised a House as soon as a place fell vacant, for only on that understanding would he have accepted the tutorship in Rugby after his senior post at Fettes, but it was a surprise to everyone when School Field was suddenly in need of a Housemaster. The Houses were run almost as independent hotels, the master in charge being responsible for the food and the linen and the upkeep of the place. It was possible to make a profit. When the

Brookes moved into School Field it meant a considerable step up in the world, and although they employed a matron, for there was far more work to be done, Mrs. Brooke still wanted to do most of it herself. Now that she had three children, the increase in domestic space was providential. She took the whole management into her hands, and for a while nothing went amiss beyond a trifling detail in the first year which made her very annoyed but was soon laughed off. It was the annual custom for the boys and staff to assemble for a photograph with everyone grouped in front of the house. When the prints arrived the background was seen to be marred by a face peeping out of a ground-floor window to watch the interesting event. The inquisitive Rupert came out almost better than anyone in the foreground.

It was soon after this that he got lost. The fatal lure of the band-stand in the pleasure gardens was too much for him, an adventure which shows him almost as 'enterprising' as the local tradesmen. When he was seven his mother caught him bullying Alfred who was then aged four. 'You're a coward,' she said, 'to be hurting someone so much smaller than yourself, and if ever I catch you again I shall have to punish you.' 'Then *you'd* be the coward,' said Rupert, uttering his first recorded words.

By the year 1895 Miss Tottenham was giving Rupert his lessons, and he could write a fluent script. His mind was occupied with super-vision of some white mice, two rabbits, and a mongrel dog. Christmas always meant something exciting from Bournemouth. The Rector of Bath had just retired and had taken a house called Grantchester Dene, in Littledown Road, about a quarter of a mile from the station, and with him lived his two unmarried daughters, Lizzie and Fanny, the latter the ideal sort of aunt, her chief interest in life being to remem-ber anniversaries and despatch thoughtful gifts so that they arrived on the right day. It was during a visit to his relations at Bourne-mouth in 1896 that he discovered poetry. Perhaps the Rector was reading aloud, or there was a book at Rupert's bedside. However it came about, the poet was Browning, and the shock was profound. He had thought verse, as opposed to nursery rhymes, was merely the way they used to write hymns.

In the summer of 1897 Rupert began his school career. Hillbrow was barely a hundred yards down the road, another of those solid institutional buildings erected with alternate layers of red and blue brick, without heating of any kind, and the inevitable boring draught in stone passages that smelt of dust and the leather of down-at-heel shoes. Rupert was of course a day boy and Richard's first job of the day was to see him safely across the road. He was learning English, or whatever that may have implied, Arithmetic, and Latin. There were games, and there was gym. His first report was vaguely re-assuring to a parent, nothing specific except 'Dictation Fair' and the information that he had started learning the piano; but near the end of the term a note from Mr. Eden recommended that the boy should start learning his Greek alphabet 'since he already knows some Latin'. No doubt his father had found time to give him a flying start. The Greek came slowly, for some time later Mr. Eden went so far as to venture a positive opinion: 'He is inclined to throw grammar to the winds.'

In the Lent term of 1898 Rupert made friends with a boy who had just been moved up into his form, which was Form Three. Another boy at the school was Duncan Grant, and it was his cousin, James Strachey, the son of Sir Richard Strachey and younger brother of Lytton, through whose eyes we can catch some glimpses of Rupert at Hillbrow. Strachey had been sent here so that his cousin could keep an eye on him, and Grant had come in the first place because the headmistress was known to his people. She was a Gatty before she married, and a sister of Mrs. Horatia Ewing, authoress of *Lob-lie-by-the-Fire* and other popular works for children. Mrs. Eden herself however does not seem to have had any marked gift of her own for winning the admiration of the young. She took the principal role in the conduct of this school of about forty boys, and Strachey recalls her as 'an embittered martinet who intimidated her husband and the four assistant masters quite as much as the boys'. Her husband, known familiarly to the boys as Tommy, was by contrast apologetic and easy-going, and his approach down the corridor would be heralded by the sound of him softly humming, especially if he was about to administer punishment with a rather bedraggled and ineffectual birch which he used more as an instrument of ritual, it seems, than of actual correction. Nothing that the boys could perpetrate was so vexing to Mrs. Eden as her husband's mildness of temper.

Duncan Grant, Strachey's senior by the gulf of three years, was in Form Two, and therefore 'infinitely remote', so for the time being Strachey turned for companionship to Brooke, who was on his own inferior social plane. One of the things they had in common was their style of hair-cut, a straight fringe across the forehead. 'It had been a whim of my mother's,' writes Strachey, 'to prevent my hair from being parted at the side in the conventional way, and I found it very recalcitrant at Hillbrow when I tried to force it into a new mould.' Once an irascible master met the two boys in a corridor after games. 'Back to the changing-room, both of you,' he roared, 'and part your hair properly! You look like a couple of *girls*!'

On another occasion it was Rupert alone who was picked on. His figure was somewhat ungainly, even for a boy of ten. He was a trifle bow-legged and he would stand with his toes turned out. 'I've often had to speak to boys about not turning out their toes *enough*,' cried the instructor in charge at the gymnasium, having stopped the class, 'but I've never before seen one who turned out his toes *too much*!' In addition to this Rupert's mode of dress was a little conspicuous. In those days almost all the boys wore Norfolk jackets and knickerbockers tight at the knees. Rupert's knickerbockers were worn *loose* at the knees ('much more comfortable', Strachey reflected) and his jacket was without the usual pieces that turn back at the neck. It buttoned right up to the neck, thereby obviating the need of a tie. He was very fair and his eyes which looked small and weak were constantly being affected with pink-eye, so that he had to stay at home for a part of almost every term. 'Friendly and amusing,' Strachey sums him up, 'but as yet decidedly not glamorous.'

After his first term with Strachey in the Third, Rupert was top in Latin and French, but in English he was near the bottom, tied with his companion. By the end of the year, however, they had both pulled themselves together a bit, and were tied again, but this time at the top in English. To this period belongs a scrap of diary—'Hurrah! I found this morning a Belgian stamp in one of my pocket books. I shall swop it.' He had learned by heart the Collect for the day, was having trouble with Euclid and comparing marks with his rival. 'Aha! one more than Strachey in Latin!'—The Michaelmas term ended quite well with his performance as Portia in scenes from *The Merchant of Venice* and his winning second place in recitation for his speaking of the *Ode on the Death of the Duke of Wellington*. The first prize was awarded to another boy destined for distinction in the Arts, Duncan Grant.

In April 1899 the family went to St. Ives for a holiday. There also were Sir Leslie Stephen and his family, and Rupert played with Virginia [Woolf] on the beach. On his return to Rugby Rupert decided to found a magazine. Its only 'issue' consists of one number in his handwriting, headed 'School Field Magazine, Vol i, No 1, April 24'. It begins with a few observations on the sights he had seen, such as this of the castle at Manorbier: 'The castle is not so much of a castle as of a dwelling-place for comfort.' Then follows an item called Short Story. In this two burglars, unaware of each other, try to break into the same house; then each mistakes the other for a policeman, makes a noise in his effort to escape, which rouses the boy asleep upstairs, who rouses his father, who gets up and grabs the intruders. Then there's an article headed 'The Final War. A tale of the war for the world in 1899, by R. C. Brooke, author of *Our Burglary*, *A Race of Life and Death*, etc.' 'Before going any further,' he writes, having only just begun, 'we must introduce these people to our readers.' It is a posse of young seamen met with at sea and at a time of crisis, for 'half the Channel Fleet had sailed out under sealed orders'. The interest then shifts to London. 'Mr. Balfour in the House is announcing war between England and the Allies (France and Russia) with all its thunder and flame, its glories and sorrows.' The situation is not allowed to develop, since a sequel is promised in our next. The items are little more than a short paragraph in length; the format is clearly based on the *Meteor*, the official Rugby School magazine which must have been lying about; and there are no signs of literary promise beyond a single phrase, among the opening remarks, which describes Sunday as a day 'full of a thin impalpable restraint'.

At Brighton for the Easter holidays, 1900, whom should he chance to meet on the esplanade but Strachey, who by this time had left Hillbrow for St. Paul's. At Strachey's boarding house they played billiards until the manager stopped them on the grounds that it was Sunday, and here again, as at St. Ives, Rupert rubbed shoulders with an acquaintance who was to be an important figure in the years to come. This time it was James's elder brother, Lytton Strachey. At this age there was no significance in the encounter. Neither remembered the occasion. But the figures of his adult life were beginning to assemble. He went back to Hillbrow for the summer term.

He was now aged twelve and a member of the cricket XI on the strength of his bowling, having already played in the XV as half-back. Towards the end of the summer term there occurred the annual function known as Mrs. Eden's Match. The opposing team was recruited from the sons of local residents or masters at the Big School. Rupert acquitted himself well, and Alfred aged eight and a half showed signs of becoming the accomplished all-round cricketer whom Strachey was to admire for his 'exquisitely polished style'. Strachey himself, on the other hand, by his own report was *quite hopeless at games*' so that when, in the previous summer, he was chosen to captain Mrs. Eden's XI he could only put it down to malice 'simply in order to disgrace myself before the fashionable audience. In this I may say I succeeded to admiration.' Thus Rupert's early prowess at games was all the more impressive in Strachey's eyes, so that thinking back on his rival, in after times, Strachey was bound to admit that 'at least the markings of glamour were already there'. For the rest, except perhaps by post to his best friend, Rupert was not giving himself away. 'Quaintly solemn', someone has described him, and the boys had nicknamed him Oyster.

In the first two terms of 1900 he had made headway with his English, for Mr. Eden pronounced him 'attentive and appreciative' and his most recent report at Hillbrow declared 'He has taken great trouble with his English this term'; and somehow he had managed to persevere at the piano, if we are to believe that he 'begins to play quite nicely'. In the holidays W. P. Brooke suddenly appears in frivolous vein, inviting Miss Tottenham to tea and warning her in rhyme what to expect:

> *With puns that leave you smarting*
> *And hair that knows no parting*
> *Rupert your soul will vex.*

There was bloodshed in the Transvaal, and a pro-Boer faction held a public meeting in Rugby. Mrs. Brooke, always interested in what was going on, thought she would look in. Having sat down, she couldn't believe her eyes. Rupert was sitting aloft with the platform party. He had followed the same impulse as herself and being conspicuous as the youngest present by many years had been called up by the Chairman to demonstrate to the world that even small children were being moved to protest against the country's injustice to the Boers. When at last the eyes of mother and son met in mutual and electric glance the meeting was interrupted. Mrs. Brooke was never angry. She was merely implacable, which her boys found more difficult to cope with than an open exhibition of wrath.

On his thirteenth birthday there arrived an amusing present from Aunt Fanny: the sort of Autograph album which has a questionnaire to be filled in before you endorse your answers at the bottom of the

page. Rupert got his mother to play first. *Favourite Amusement:*
Mrs. Brooke—Cycling, watching others play games. Rupert—
Cricket, tennis, football, reading, cards. *Favourite qualities in (a)
Man (b) Woman:* Mrs. Brooke—(a) Earnestness of purpose (b)
Moral courage. Rupert—(a) Fidelity (b) Wit. As to food and drink, a
question that Rupert left blank, Mrs. Brooke had to admit 'I really
don't know'. Other entries of his show that his favourite character in
history was Gladstone; *Ambition:* 'to be top of the tree in everything',
Authors and books: 'Kipling, Boothby, Sherlock Homes', *Musical
compositions:* 'Chin-chin Chinaman', 'The Lost Chord', *Idea of misery:*
'Ignorance, poverty, *obscurity*' (his own italics).

He was often troubled with an inflamed throat, which was put
down to the dust in the passages, and half-way through the school
sports in May 1901 he was sent to bed. His earliest surviving letter,
written to a boy who had left, in facetious ye old teashoppe English,
explains how he was not only obliged to miss the sports finals, after
he had won several heats 'wherefore my temper was exceeding warm',
but was unable to sit for his scholarship examination for entrance to
the Big School. 'Wherefore an irritability of marvellous size possessed me and still possesses me . . . Forgive my letter being strange
in manner. The reason is that much trouble hath unhinged my brain;
wherein I resemble Hamlet. And if you gaze closely on my portrait
which I have sent you, you will see a wild look in my eyes, denoting
insanity.'

So without a scholarship, but with the assurance that he could sit
for his exam during the term, in September 1901 he made his
appearance as a new boy at his father's house, School Field.

Chapter II

SCHOOL FIELD

Junior

(September 1901–April 1905)

School Field was built on a substantial scale in Rugby's brand of pseudo-Gothic: the red bricks alternating with the blue, lofty gables, and stone mullions of more solidity than grace. The date 1852 picked out in blue bricks on the wall facing the road is all very well—it commemorates the addition of this land to the school property—but another date, 1567, boldly cut in stone over the front door, though it could deceive nobody, is rather more disconcerting. 'I am being informed of something important,' the visitor must often have reflected, after glancing up, 'but of what?', the next moment to be caught off his guard by Mrs. Brooke's imperious welcome. The date bears no relation to the building, of course, being the year when the Grammar School, the origin of the great institution which derives its character from Dr. Arnold, was first established in the town. It is as if the architect were so confident that his day and age were apparent in his handiwork that he could safely afford to display on the walls such pointers to other times as could only confuse the ignorant. He was right. The house is massively late-Victorian, having all the appearance of an impregnably safe place to live in. It stands back from the Barby Road, agreeably situated south east of the Close which it overlooks through the chestnut branches, and adjoining it lies that area of the sward sacred to cricket known as New Bigside.

After crossing the threshold, Mrs. Brooke's drawing-room was the spacious apartment on the left, its high and wide windows looking out over the Close to the cluster of six tall chimney-stacks on the Gothic gymnasium. Parker Brooke would retire to his study on the opposite side of the hall, his door standing at the top of a short spiral stair which led down to the boys' half of the house: the dark corridor of diminutive cells or studies where the senior boys could have their being in privacy, except for—in those bygone days—the not in-frequent mouse. Outside, below the windows, there was an area called the 'bear garden' where the boys might kick a football about in spare moments; then the dining-room, a lofty hall furnished with benches and heavy tables, a vast 'Tudor' fireplace, beamed flat roof, leaf corbels, and 'The Earth is the Lord's and all that therein is' painted round the dado in Early English characters. The feeling here is of being partially underground, for the room is lit from the Close side only and by windows so high up that the sun may look in but nobody look out. Above this, a few floors up, stands the great dor-mitory whose clover-shaped lights at one end may have reminded the senior Brookes of the clerestory at St. Peter's, Walsingham, and here each Christmas, when the Brooke boys were older, the under-dormitory maid would haul aside the beds and the floor be waxed for a dance. A pianist and a man with a fiddle came from the town for a consideration, then there was lemonade, cocoa and biscuits in the drawing-room during the intermission. From the kitchens below, the shaft of a lift went up the spine of the house with a door in the hall of the private quarters above, and legend has it that one day the bell rang, Mrs. Brooke went to open the hatch, and there, seated cross-legged in lieu of the cottage pie was one of the new boys, Rupert, with a notice pinned on his chest, 'Mother, behold thy son' —a joke which required explaining and sharp rebuke for the culprit.

A new boy must have been a little perplexed at first by the numerous regulations and niceties of difference in degree of senior-ity. There was a roll call three times a day, and, for the first year, at the shout of 'fag' you rushed to the spot and, if the last to arrive, got down to cleaning the shoes or tidying the cell of the privileged youth who had issued the summons. You must not have your hands in your pockets while walking between the house and the school, but at a later stage you might put one hand in a pocket, then both, but with your books tucked under each arm, then under one arm, according to your place in the scheme of things; and you mustn't walk on the opposite side of the road from your house, nor walk anywhere with a boy from another house; you were roused at 5.45 a.m., took your turn in the cold bath, then had a short lesson before breakfast which was not invariably up to standard (nor was luncheon, for there was once a beetle discovered in Mrs. Brooke's meat hash); then ten minutes in Chapel followed by a dash back over the Close to make toast—unless you got there first—for a praepostor (known

colloquially as a 'pre', the word, according to Rupert, being a derivation from the epithet preposterous); and your straw hat, obligatory of
course when down town, was plain or speckled, straight or tilted,
according to status. A plain straw hat, cocked at an angle, both
hands in the pockets, and all books under *one* arm, denoted a senior
swell beyond all shadow of cavil.

The headmaster now was Dr. H. A. James, nicknamed The
Bodger, a man of short stature but solid build with an ample beard
worn, like his top-hat, slightly askew, so that he always looked as if
he had just stepped out of a strong wind, an impressive figure who
taught Divinity; but perhaps the ablest scholar on the staff was
Rupert's godfather, Robert Whitelaw, who taught the class known
as the Twenty, the form below Upper and Lower Benches of the
VIth, and senior, of course, to Parker Brooke's Lower Vth. Whitelaw
was a man devoted to his subject, which was Greek, and to his art of
teaching, and by all accounts he was master of both. Perched on a low
platform before his class in the upstairs room across the old quad,
behind the chapel, he stooped over his desk and jutted the hooked
proboscis of his nose towards the boys looking for all the world like
some bird of prey about to take off from a mountain ledge. Although
very outspoken, he was never alarming, and his boys were only
frightened lest they should do anything that might give offence.
Shortly before Rupert came to School Field, William Temple, subse-
quently Archbishop, was among Whitelaw's pupils, and he remembered with gratitude the experience of slowly inching his way through
the Greek of St. Paul's Epistles with his teacher minutely annotating
and elucidating every word of the way. Whitelaw was by no means
the conventional pedagogue. Having no musical gift—which would
be evident from this story alone—he found it helped him to correct
exam papers if he hired two barrel organs to play under his window,
simultaneously, such works as the vocal gems from Verdi and
popular ditties like *The Mistletoe Bough*. Then there was H. C.
Bradby, popular for his literary teas on a Sunday afternoon. Such men
are invaluable, and perhaps even necessary, in an enclosed world of
somewhat austere routine. But to Rupert no means of respite was so
precious as the Temple Library and Reading Room, which stood a
little way up on the other side of the road from School Field. Here
was a place belonging to the school and safely within bounds, such
as any big town would be proud to boast of as its municipal library.
There was no need for a boy to play truant if he wanted to read

Milton, or consult the latest number of the *Westminster Gazette*. Whenever he could slip away, not being wanted for prep or fagging on the one side of the house nor for making conversation with a relative on the other, Rupert would run over the road to look up the book reviews or find his place in the volume of *Paradise Lost* that he was not allowed to take away.

Two thirds of the boys, Rupert among them, were on the Classical side, which meant lessons in Latin, Greek, French, Scripture, History, English, Geography, and Mathematics. With eleven hours of work a day there wasn't much free time, but you could make your leisure, as Temple did, by polishing off in half an hour the prep designed to take up two hours. In this way Temple could claim to have got through the collected works of no less than seven poets, and doubtless Rupert discovered the same resource. He had a room of his own at the top of the house, overlooking the road, with windows facing east and south and outside walls on three sides. In winter it could be cold, but it was a refuge, and he settled down to his new existence with comparative ease, odd though it was to be living a kind of double life under one roof, now in private with his family, and now in the community of a public school. They called him Bowles, because he was still rather bow-legged, as was his father, and Parker Brooke himself, so Rupert discovered, was popularly known as Tooler (which made his wife Ma Tooler) a title alleged to have been won on some occasion in his earlier days when there must have been 'a slight disorder in the dress'. He was never much in evidence on the boys' side, since the exercise of authority throughout Rugby was largely delegated to the older boys of the VIth. Notoriously absent-minded, he was in the habit of pausing on the kerb or half-way through a doorway with the forefinger of his right hand against the inside of his upper teeth, as if trying to recapture the thought which had suddenly eluded him; and one day he was caught in this posture by a hansom cab whose driver had failed to notice him in the middle of the road. He was knocked over, broke his arm, and was given first aid at home by his wife. Comfortable at last, he resumed his reverie, and, when the doctor called, asked him rather tartly what he had come for. In class he was considered a master of *meiosis*: the highest praise ever heard from his lips was 'Quite useful'.

Ma Tooler was seldom seen by the boys except when they needed medical attention. In this capacity she was both solicitous and skilled, and not unsympathetic, so long as you were doing exactly as you were told. Indeed she was inclined to be more successful in matters of health than diet. Since the house could be run at a profit and she had a head for figures perhaps there was little inducement to show much enterprise in the commissariat. Her husband's views on the management of her own department were not always welcome. There was a story of her arguing with him on the stairs, and at the end of it all he was overheard murmuring to himself, still unconvinced, 'It *is* so, all the same'. The burden of responsibility did not sit lightly upon him. 'The life of a housemaster,' he once admitted with a sigh, 'is like living on a volcano.'

'Has begun well,' wrote The Bodger on Rupert's first report. Parker Brooke had left the housemaster's space blank, so as to run no risk of prejudice. In July 1902, Rupert's first summer term, the school magazine announced that he had at last won an Entrance Scholarship. The nearest he ever got to intimacy with his father was over a Latin or Greek grammar, and he took a certain amount of pleasure in his lessons perhaps for this reason alone, for he never really enjoyed the classics. By the end of his first year he was in the House XV; and the photographs show that by the age of fifteen his gawky frame was beginning to pull itself into shape, the legs look straight, the long slim neck of his manhood is in evidence; and there he stands, one of a group, nostrils in air, the personality still in the pod, and a sports cap (surely borrowed for the purpose, it is so small) perched rather than worn on his cropped head as if it had been dropped into place from a window above.

A few months later he was promoted to Lance Corporal in the Rifle Volunteer Corps (afterwards known as the O.T.C.), and in the summer of 1903 we find him playing cricket for his house.

By 1904 two of his acquaintances had become fast friends: Hugh Russell-Smith, whose parents rented each summer Watersgreen House at Brockenhurst, and Geoffrey Keynes, Rupert's senior by four months, who settled at School Field one term after Rupert, having migrated from Dewar's house. Keynes's people lived at Cambridge where his father was a lecturer in Political Economy and a former Fellow of Pembroke College. In the summer of 1903 he had coincided with Rupert in the form called the Twenty which was presided over by Robert Whitelaw. It seems that at this time Rupert was on the Lower Bench of the VIth for classics only, since his report for the previous term declares he had made a 'good start' there, but was 'more of a linguist than a thinker'. At any rate, for his English lessons he was still in the Twenty when Keynes joined him and, curious to observe more closely this renowned Rugby character who was now his teacher, sat with furtive pencil at the ready to note down his remarks.

It was one afternoon in the Summer term of 1903. Robert Whitelaw's high desk stood on a small podium whence he could dominate the class; on his left, behind him, the blackboard fixed to the wall; on his right, the door, so that no late-comer could slip in with impunity; and one pictures him with his beak of a nose and owlish spectacles, peering to right and left as he puts his question. The subject this morning, English, is not exactly his favourite, and the boys are mostly new to him. They are shy; he is hard put to it to rouse them to any enthusiasm. And there, among the others, sit Keynes and Brooke, in that atmosphere of stunned inertia which is apt to prevail when a lesson isn't going too smoothly. The group is not being very co-operative, but the master's zeal is unflagging. 'Nobody thinks it worth while to contribute *anything*!' sighs Mr. Whitelaw, never suspecting that there's a Boswell within earshot who even now is in the very act of preserving his vexation for posterity. 'You sit there like a lot of dummies, table after table. And as for you, Podmore, you're the worst of the lot; it almost makes me ill to look at you.' Some fragment of immortal verse has failed to evoke the slightest ripple of response, one imagines, when the master goes on, 'It almost makes me sick to see how you take poetry!' Perhaps he turns away to give the blackboard a brief unseeing glance, before coming back with 'It's really inconceivable to what depths you can descend'.

And now Mr. Whitelaw applies himself to Brooke individually. The boy's answer to his question is tiresomely non-committal. 'You *do* love to have everything vague, don't you, eh?' The boy looks uncomprehending. 'You like to have it all a nice haze,' Whitelaw explains, and tries him with another question. Brooke's expression is now that of someone who feels he is being picked on. 'Oh dear,' says Mr. Whitelaw in mock sympathy, 'it *is* so tiresome, isn't it, that people *will* ask for information? Questions are so troublesome aren't they?' Brooke mumbles something or other which is promptly dismissed with 'Of course you *knew* it wasn't the answer I wanted'. Brooke then has to admit he just doesn't *know* the answer, and 'Oh dear, what *do* you know?' is followed up with 'Your mind is so inert. . . . You are determined to miss the whole point . . . You are perfectly incorrigible, you tiresome boy!' and then comes the climax of these reproaches addressed to the unawakened poet in his poetry lesson: 'You are beyond endurance. You are intolerable for sheer carelessness,' and finally, the master drawing himself up to his full height, 'I can but repeat the formula "You're losing all capacity for doing work".' It must not be supposed that the chronicler of all this spared his own blushes or got off scot free. 'I really thought you had some sense of decency,' groans Mr. Whitelaw, sorely tried, fixing Keynes with his eye, but not fixedly enough to observe the boy making a memorandum in his notebook.

And now the whole class slides back into a slough of mental torpor. A question is put for anyone to venture an answer. The silence seeps back, then Whitelaw softly speaks again. 'I hear a little indistinct murmur. Two people make a little indistinct murmur, but together they don't make a sound. Oh it's intolerable!' and then the youth that does manage to venture a positive contribution is greeted with 'How can you be so—(*long pause*)—unwise?' Soon after this Brooke pipes up again, and not wanting to be vague any more, phrases his answer with unwanted particularity. ' "At the bottom of the Adriatic?" ' cries Whitelaw, apparently echoing the boy. 'It would be more appropriate to say it's "at the bottom of the sea".' A pupil is called up to say his piece, and as Keynes's notes come to an end, it is as if, having somehow tuned-in to a school lesson of 1903, the sound at last begins to fade with the master expostulating from his rostrum, 'Would anybody believe that he had learned this by heart? Would any *living person* imagine he had learned this by *heart*?' and then to the class in general, 'It really is a *pity* you should be reading Shakespeare!' . . .

In an exercise book of this time Rupert inscribed a taunting epigram. 'Olim erat Robertus Alba Lex, Puerorum tyrannicus et saevus rex, O Bobbie horridissime!', etc.[1] Being a distinctive personality, and therefore popular, Whitelaw was much talked about, and the name for this *culte* was 'Bobbieship'. Thus at the foot of the page where Keynes recorded his teacher's expostulations during the English lesson, he wrote, as if anticipating eventual print, 'I owe much to the suggestions of Mr. R. C. B. of Rugby to whose consummate Bobbieship I am more indebted than I can say.'

The Christmas holidays began with a trip to London where Rupert

---

[1] There once was a Robert White Law, tyrannical and savage monarch of the boys, O absolutely horrid Bobbie!

saw Tree in *Richard II*, and among his seasonal gifts was a volume of Lowell's poems from Aunt Fanny at Bournemouth. 'I'm getting quite a large library now,' he wrote, and told how Richard and Podge (his brother Alfred) had been playing hockey; there had been progressive whist in the evenings, and now he was just off to a Fancy Dress Ball as Walter Raleigh arrayed in purple and yellow. 'We have found only one drawback to Christmas, and that is that Boots Library is closed for three whole days with only 6 books to read—or rather 5 because one of them is chosen by Mother and therefore not worth reading!' It speaks well for Aunt Fanny's sense of humour that he should have trusted it so far.

The fragment of a diary shows that in April Rupert's mother took him and Podge to Hastings. 'What is Hastings for if not big waves?' A week later an elderly cousin calls, and the comment is 'Why do we always know someone everywhere?' He is reading Carlyle on the French Revolution. 'The molten diction of the man!' he exclaims. Then on the 11th, 'A vivid dream this morning. I dreamt that I had a fierce dagger fight with some stranger, was stabbed by him thrice under the left shoulder-blade and knew no more—presumably dying. Afterwards I came back and haunted the house, causing much terror at a dinner party. The feeling of haunting is rather pleasing. I think I shall take it up—if it be allowed—afterwards.' A night or two later he is on the front noticing how the breakers 'look very ghostly under the white glare of the powerful incandescent (or electric?) lamps. Vast swollen greynesses heaving tumultuously and flashing out suddenly into a sheet of spray,' and then he breaks off. He had undertaken a special job for his leisure hours. He was going to have a shot at winning the annual poetry prize, to be given this year for the best poem on the subject of the pyramids. In May it was announced that the Prize was won by a boy called C. J. Stone, but there had evidently been some disagreement among the judges. *The Pyramids* by R. C. Brooke was awarded a *proxime accessit*. It was a fair compromise, for the poem showed considerable promise for a boy of sixteen and a half. Supported by the good opinion of one of the adjudicators, the Rev. J. R. Wynne-Willson, a senior member of the staff, Mrs. Brooke had the poem printed at Over's, the local bookshop, but Rupert, although encouraged by the fuss the family made over his first sustained effort, was also rather embarrassed. The idea now, he thought, was to dismiss it with a shrug, and give the minor poet William Watson (whom nevertheless he genuinely admired at this time) the credit of being his guiding influence rather than Milton. The merit of the poem lies in the way it shows the boy's intelligent understanding of the technique of *Paradise Lost*. Only the framework, the free irregular rhyme and length of line, could have come from the laureate-like odes of Watson, a safe model for an occasional piece at this time. He would have enjoyed concocting a line like 'Khufu, and Khafra, and Queen Sesostris', or describing the Sphinx as 'Voiceless, inscrutable, and grey', or devising a way of ending on a suitable note of uplift: the petty concerns of the passing moment stifle our senses, so that we cannot hear the timeless music of the spheres, nor see

> *How on the shadow of the night appears*
> *The pale Dawn of the glory that shall be.*

In the summer he played in the house cricket XI, but another infection in the throat sent him to bed in his room at the top of the house. During his convalescence he had a visitor, a local author of poems and novels such as *The Absurd Repentance* and *The Vintage of Dreams* which Mrs. Brooke cannot have read, or she would hardly have considered their author a very suitable acquaintance. No doubt Lucas had heard about *The Pyramids* and been allowed to borrow the manuscript, and on the strength of his family living close by in Hillmorton Road, had asked to call on the promising boy. His full name was St. John Welles Lucas-Lucas, and he had been as a small boy at Oakfield, a school in Bilton Road. From there he went on to Haileybury and University College, Oxford, where he had just taken his degree in Law. He was now aged twenty-five and living in the Middle Temple, London. His father was H. F. Lucas, the painter of animals and hunting scenes, who had married a Frenchwoman from Guernsey called Sarah Mordacque. Mrs. Brooke was no doubt acquainted with these neighbours of hers and the young man's wholesome upbringing, which included Parker Brooke's old school, must have recommended him to the parents as an eligible friend. Above all, he was the only real live poet in the neighbourhood, and his criticism might be of more service to Rupert than the marginal pencillings of the most enlightened schoolmaster.

When he called at School Field he brought along with him another young local writer, Arthur Eckersley, who was by way of being a dramatist and a contributor to *Punch*. Both these young men, newly arrived in the professional world of 'letters', were ardent followers of a literary vogue which was now beginning to decline, though it still held the field in certain intellectual circles, especially the universities. Since Lucas was to prove a good friend and, for a time, a powerful influence, it is necessary to give some idea of what he stood for.

He was a French scholar, soon to be engaged in editing *The Oxford Book of French Verse* which he published in 1907, so that in bringing Baudelaire to Rupert's notice he was putting him in touch with one of the root sources of the so-called Decadence in English literature, and the poems of Dowson must have been among the first books that Lucas left with Rupert for his bedside reading. The older youth provided a focus for Rupert's natural inclination to question his environment, giving it what seemed to be a justification in Art, and this more than any specific literary influence was his main contribution to the boy's half-awakened mind. He preached the aesthetic gospel of Oscar Wilde. The trial had occurred only nine years before. By the nature of his defence Wilde had seen to it that if he was going to be penalized as an erring man it would be as an aesthete and an artist that he would appear to be martyred at the hands of the philistines. In these first years of the reaction against Victorianism, a revolt of some sort was inevitable in any event, and at a time when the rift between the arts and society happened to be widening, irrespective of the trial, the creed of the aesthete was becoming a convenient weapon to hand in a social war. In a community growing more and more industrialized, where the only 'use' of anything was its usefulness for some workaday purpose, the art of poetry in particular had become increasingly and deliberately 'useless'. Gautier's ideas, at first current in Paris, had become Pater's 'art for art's sake' in Oxford, and the concern to avoid the provision of versified maxims, or quotable uplift of any sort, had led to the last somewhat overblown bloom of early nineteenth-century Romanticism, a branch of literature that in England we associate chiefly with Swinburne and the poets of the nineties—a poetry of languor, thriving on vague regret, a self-induced nostalgia for some lost forbidden love, suggesting wilting gardenias and the beer-stained plush of Romano's and the Café Royal. Late in the day, but not too late, having already a prophet in Walter Pater, the cause was given new impetus by the sufferings of a victim.

Ruskin had died only four years before. 'A few pre-Raphaelites linger still, one hears, in the remote corners of the world of Art,' wrote the author of one of his obituary notices in 1900. Ruskin, with his belief that the function of art was to 'summon the moral energies of the nation to a forgotten duty' had died indeed, or survived only in the socialist influence of William Morris and his followers who were trying more directly, through agitation for social reform, to combat the times that were out of joint. So there were now two ways of supporting the same cause: the more negative way, which deliberately widened the breach, implying in fact that the greater the gulf the better—this ranged from the flouting of convention by exotic modes of dress and the rest of the 'aesthetic' paraphernalia, to the composition of languid elegiacs on defunct courtesans. These were the people who began by sympathizing with Whistler, who had argued that the artist was answerable only to himself, and ended by mourning the late Oscar Wilde, in whose person the artist had recently been assigned by society a pigeon-hole beyond the pale. There was also the second, more positive way, a movement to strike at the root of the trouble, the basis of society itself, and narrow the breach between the artist and his industrial neighbour by transforming from the bottom upwards the world in which they had to live together.

At this stage, unaware of the larger issue, but always game for a lark, Rupert subscribed to the first of these methods, and for the three years or so in which Lucas was his mentor and Dowson his ideal, it suited him down to the ground. Beyond the writing of poems about 'lost lilies' and 'ultimate sad breaths', which he took very seriously—unaware that it would need more than the technique of a precocious schoolboy to make poetry out of a pose—his sense of the ridiculous was too much on the alert to let him go further. Only within the poetical charmed circle of literature did the aesthetic cause seem to him sublime. So in his person and his letters it was always a more candid and self-conscious pose, a source of quietly mischievous indulgence. There it was almost a luxury to know one could be extravagantly insincere with the legitimate excuse that it was all in a good cause. It showed what side one was on. He was against the Philistines. He always had been, but now he saw why, and was given a mode of action. Only a fool would misunderstand him and take what he said at its face value, and anyway only a dolt would prefer a plain unvarnished statement. He never wholly abandoned this form of affectation, for he found himself too good at it. Thus it was that in later years, a remark such as 'Have you heard that our dusky Theocritus is dying of syphilis in his native Smyrna' would at once be correctly interpreted by a friend that knew him as the simple question, 'Have you heard that Flecker is down with a bad cold in Cheltenham?' He never abandoned the cause, but the more he developed as a poet, the more he was drawn to the second, more positive mode of attack.

A sensitive boy, aware of the predicament of the arts in one form or another, and growing up in the first decade of this century, would sooner or later dimly perceive the root cause of the trouble, and a new fillip would be given to the normal desire of every new generation to show up the one before it as a breed of old fogies. The Victorians grew prosperous in a time of disquieting change which threatened to have no end. The majority looked to the arts for the pleasure of recognition, finding in a new guise what they already knew, and for the comfort of reassurance, discovering what they already believed and were determined to go on believing, even though chaos or Darwin or both should come again. The inner realities were not, they imagined, their business. There lay instability, on that darker side, so why not dwell on the side that was brighter? He writes best who best enchants us with his conviction that all will be well. Fear, well justified, led to reticence, and fearful reticence to hypocrisy, since the thing feared was reality; and that last intolerably disturbing thing was a hydra with four heads—democracy, science, unbelief, and sex. So they put up defences. Democracy, once it was regarded not as an ideal of any sort but merely as an expression of envy on the part of the lower orders, could safely be ignored; science was anyway a source of wealth and empire, and beyond that it was more convenient for the average man to stay ignorant; unbelief was simply inadmissible, being contrary to the facts as revealed by authors divinely inspired; and sex, inescapable as it was, could only be acknowledged to˜exist as a service to the community and the will of God. It had to be justified somehow, and that was the way to do it, and at the same time this appeared to sanctify the home. While Rupert was still at school, Shaw took over the Court Theatre and showed, among much else, that the sanctity of the home had its origin in a thing more elevated than an expedient view of sex. One by one he blew the defences. Because he saw them as evasions, they deserved no reverence. What with Darwin, Huxley, Swinburne, Whistler, Wilde, from every angle of thought and feeling the immense Victorian façade with all its niches filled with the busts of its civic heroes was being despoiled. In 1904, though badly scarred, it stood apparently secure, but little by little, for good

45

or ill, the work went on. Most of the intellectuals of the generation in adolescence with Rupert Brooke turned out to be irreverent. Art had become a red rag, so they waved it; religion was no longer eternal but Victorian, so they managed without it. In all this Rupert was to be what in a kindly endeavour to be tolerant an aunt of his called 'a very new-fangled young man'—in fact, a child of his time—a small figure, as he now seems, brandishing a flag among the giants, but he was there.

On that afternoon in May, 1904, Eckersley and Lucas—'a mild little man, blinking behind *pince-nez*', as Keynes has jokingly described him—left the upstairs room at School Field, having found a willing convert.

II

From time to time a girl had sat at mealtimes with the boys at School Field. She was Erica Cotterill, a daughter of the housemaster at Glencorse house, Fettes, and not very popular after she was heard to remark to Mr. Brooke at table 'That boy's got too much pudding'. It was agreeable for Rupert to have a female cousin and a pretty one who looked up to him as an adviser in matters of culture, and it was only natural that she should ask if she might borrow the manuscript of *The Pyramids*. Rupert wrote to her in May. After dealing with mundane matters such as the School XI and the weather that was 'alternately absurd and unspeakable', he went on, 'I have fulfilled one of the ambitions of my life: I have met a real live poet, who has presented me with a copy of one of his books signed with his own hand. Of course, like all poets worth counting nowadays, he is Celtic and very melancholy. Last but not least he knows George Meredith quite intimately! A most enchanting man. And—quite incidentally—his poems are often readable.' Since Lucas was not a name to conjure with, this was perhaps a more impressive way of giving news of his visitor than actually saying who he was. Like Parker Brooke, who was apt to mystify his pupils by insisting on the new pronunciation of Latin in prose but the old in verse, as being more archaic and elevated, Lucas himself reserved his 'decadence' for his prose and, when it came to the composition of verse, was singularly innocuous. In verse he affected nothing more ninety-ish than a pale echo of Housman, and in the main was all for the open road in the manner of Belloc with the difference that he packed in the colourful epithets in an effort to raise the temperature. So Rupert was now influenced by Belloc and Dowson through the fervour of the older youth's recommendation. Lucas's prose was another matter. Through it Rupert was to come under the literary spell of Wilde. It helped him, among other things, to shrug off the embarrassment of his true feelings, deflecting them, as it were, by the trick of a mannered witticism. The same letter to Erica, written during his Thucydides prep, put her in the picture about *The Pyramids*. It was not yet printed.

It's no use asking *me* about that poem, I have nothing to do with it. Mother took it from me and stowed it away in the family archives, and I have no control over it. If you don't see it first you must clamour for it on your next visit to Rugby. As a matter of fact *I*'ve disowned it long ago. It was a failure, an irredeemable and gigantic failure—nay more, it was a tragedy. I will explain. As you know, Confucius and many after him have divided tragedies into two classes, when anything intended to be humorous is taken seriously, and when a would-be serious thing is received as witty. My tragedy belongs to the first and more fatal class. I perpetrated a screaming joke. I entered for the Prize Poem a parody on William Watson in his less inspired moments, an ultra-academic, ultra-frigid caricature; and behold! it fell into the hands of the Philistines, and they thought it was meant serious, and they dug latent and unexpected excellencies out of it, and viewed it on every side, and found it good, and awarded it second prize. Such is always my fate. When I say what I mean, people tell me 'O *Rupert*, what delightful nonsense you talk!' and when I venture on the humorous, I am taken seriously and very promptly and thoroughly squashed for 'saying such strange things'. In fact I often remind myself of the hero of Miss Florence Montgomery's delightful book 'Misunderstood'—if you haven't read it, do; it is Elevating, Instructive, and generally amusing. I wept oceans of salt tears over it. He was *never* valued at his true worth by *anybody*. Everyone looked on him as a Common Boy, while in reality he was a poorly-disguised angel. Nor does the likeness end here. He also had washy blue eyes, tow-coloured hair, a habit of doing the wrong thing unintentionally, and a propensity for dying young. The Resemblance however cannot be pushed further. He expired from compound pneumonia and a broken leg: I am slowly dying of simple lassitude and a broken heart.

This was the time when he would 'let himself be found reading Swinburne' while the others went off shopping in Town; but as yet it was all in his interest to keep his eccentricities well within bounds. He read the first lesson (David's lament over Jonathan) in Chapel; was promoted to Colour Sergeant in the Corps; became a respected member of the Lower Bench of the VI, where he was glad to be joined by Keynes in October, and a strenuous half-back in the House XV. It must have been a little galling for him to be enjoying these privileges of the Establishment just when he had begun to savour the spice of social revolt. He was given his chance early in November when he was asked to write the review of *As You Like It* as presented in the Town Hall by Frank Benson's touring company. He hated it.

The article, unsigned, was his first appearance in anything resembling public print. The evening didn't begin very auspiciously. 'While the spectators were trooping in and fighting for seats, the orchestra, an old friend, gave us an overture which was greeted with hearty, albeit rather ironical, applause.' He thought it 'one of the most charming of plays, but this cast, especially the minor characters, seemed scarcely to perceive any meaning in their words and actions. At least they did not show it.' Dorothy Green as Rosalind with her 'grace of natural delivery' was the only exception. Even so, when they came to the wrestling match, we are told that 'a rather less obvious growth of affection [between Orlando and Rosalind] would have been more artistic'. Soon came the interval with 'loud music and louder hammering', then the curtain rose on the forest of Arden 'and went on for two hours'. The leaves were drab. 'As it was, the odour of "the leafy carpet" was the most striking thing—a little too striking for the comfort of those nearest the stage.' The Orlando 'like most stage heroes, seemed to suffer from an overwhelming sense of his own righteousness'. Touchstone was a total failure. 'Shakespeare's Fools are never merely fools. They are intended to do more than make one laugh.' As for Audrey '(not, as the programme hath it, Audrie) one can only say that she looked her part. Her behaviour was less bucolic than Bedlamite.' But it was the orchestra of local musicians that riled the critic as much as anything. It played with such vigour that the stage-manager had to appear from the wings and remonstrate. After this it 'relapsed into comparative harmony', but the audience then began beating time with its feet. 'The result was peculiar but scarcely pleasing.'

Since it was part of the policy of the official school magazine to 'eschew literature', Rupert and another boy, the prize winner of *The Pyramids*, had been allowed to edit a supplement called *The Phoenix*. It began cautiously, but the second issue, which came out along with his notice of the play, contained four contributions of his own. There was *A Child's Guide to Rugby School*, of which the best part was the opening address to his reader, a child who had recently overheard some lady visitor telling his mother that he was a 'big boy for his age'. 'You have read a lot of Henty, the headlines of the *Daily Mail*, and first-class cricket averages . . . You have a tall and rather weedy frame, large hands and feet spread awkwardly abroad, and a habit of shambling in a flock with nervous clumsiness up and down the gutter in High Street.' Thus the reader would be assured that the author had got his number. He is then informed that there are three classes in the social scale: the athletes—'Regard all such with immense reverence and awe; it is for them that *all* Public Schools are founded and conducted. And they know it'; then there are the masters—'part knave, part fool, but otherwise without any human attributes'; and lastly the members of the VIth, characterized by their 'wild and rabid enthusiasm for helping the rest of the school with their translation'. There was a piece of verse in the manner of W. M. Praed called *From a New Boy*, containing a racy stanza about Rugby football.

> *When first I played I nearly died.*
> *The bitter memory still rankles—*
> *They formed a scrum with me inside!*
> *Some kick'd the ball, and some my ankles.*
> *I did not like the game at all,*
> *Yet, after all the harm they'd done me,*
> *Whenever I came near the ball*
> *They knocked me down and stood upon me.*

The two other poems have more serious pretensions but, on their loftier plane, less merit. In *Afterwards* the poet is troubled with 'bitter thoughts of old delight' and is 'As one who has outlived his joy, and would forget'. What's more he 'nurses in his festered soul a slave's dull hate For this interminable Hell of Life'. The third poem is a little more promising, a well-managed sonnet on the theme that the Earth is wearied out, being 'laden with men's strife, Woe of the living—burden of the dead'. One longs for him to combine his technical ability with actual experience, no matter how simple, for as yet the impulse is merely to write a 'poem' rather than any poem in particular.

On Christmas Eve 1904 he fell ill again, and this time the doctor insisted on his having a complete change in a more grateful climate, even though this would mean the boy missing his Lent term at school. Mrs. Brooke knew of a Dr. and Mrs. Gibbons who owned a small villa about half a mile from the sea at Rapallo. Moreover there were other Brooke children going to Italy in the new year. These were Rupert's cousins Margaret and Reeve, who were soon going to a pensione in Florence. So Mrs. Brooke decided to buy a round-trip ticket which would allow for sixty days in Italy and a fortnight in France. It was several weeks before Rupert was strong enough to travel, then he set off with Alfred as his companion, his Aeschylus, the *Pro Murena* of Cicero, and the more congenial home-work of his entry for the poetry prize of 1905. The title prescribed was *The Bastille*.

He had taken the precaution of writing to Lucas for advice in the art of continental travel, and the answer was awaiting him when he arrived at the Villa Molfino, Rapallo. He had first addressed his new friend as Jack. 'Dear St. John,' began his reply of February 4, 'Is that better? I am sorry for the "blatant diminutive". It slipped off my pen, because (I don't know if you are aware of it) in that part of the "great centre of intellectuality" called Rugby you are still spoken of as Jack Lucas—I hope you don't object to being reminded of it.' Rupert was hoping to make his way home through Paris where Lucas might join him. 'I am far too ignorant to do so without some very patient and omniscient person—such as I conceive you to be— to drag me round. I should only burden you a couple of days and I shall learn many things. I might even find out something about the Bastille: for I have come away without looking it up; and my knowledge of it is a little vague at present. I have only a suspicion that it was a prison, and fell in the French Revolution: and there is no English Encyclopaedia in Rapallo. However, facts don't really matter I suppose.'

At present he did not feel equal to much sight-seeing, tempted though he was by the places that Lucas had recommended to him. 'Especially I wish to see Siena because Maurice Hewlett I think describes it as "swooning like a great tiger-moth on the rock", which makes me rather curious.' His family, however, had asked for his 'impressions' of Italy. 'I find it a vast trouble to be impressed to order; but a local guide-book has proved invaluable.'

I don't remember the 'cry of "Dijon" at two o' the morning' you refer to. It may have come during the 10 minutes' sleep I got that night; more probably it was drowned by the snoring of a Frenchman in the bunk above me, who snored all night a Gallic snore, falsetto, intermittent, and wildly exasperating. The same villain had a slimy hatred of fresh air; and thereby I got my revenge. For I opened the window by stealth in the chill early hours of the morning, when it was snowing, and froze him out. Almost the only writing I have done here has been for my deserted 'Phoenix'. I have spent many hours sitting pen in hand *trying* to be very, very funny in a high satirical line, scourging School follies with a stinging lash! But the result is not hopeful.

Your last request caused me much deep thought and ended in the production and restudy of a green notebook which I treasure. It was a rash demand, as made to one avid for criticism and help. You know not how nearly it brought on you a parcel of MSS. many feet square and weighing innumerable ounces. (I am talking—if you have forgotten what you wrote—about your mandate 'Send some golden words from Italy—and some verse!') You have had some four pages of words, gilt to the best of my power. Follows the other half which you have brought on yourself. I intend the first two for the Phoenix if my fellow Editor submits! But the third I daren't show him for fear of what he might say.

But I should like a full-grown live critic's opinion of where they are worst. Hence these, with all proper apologies.

He enclosed the sonnet which had come out in *The Phoenix*; another sonnet, *The Return*, which he was working on for the next issue, and which ends

> It may be even yet
> The old fires on the old grey altars burn,
> The old gods throng their shadowy haunted grove,
> When I can sleep, and rest me, and—forget.

and *The Path of Dreams*, a lyric which seems specially designed to convince Lucas that he had won a convert to Decadence, with its

> Sad garlands wreathed of the red mournful roses
> And lilies o' moonbeams.

Writing to Erica he complained of the German tourists who sounded like frogs in dispute. 'German, I find, sounds even worse than it looks, which is something awful,' but made no mention of his romantic surroundings except to tell a story of the butler in the house where he lived. He had put a plate under a leaking oil-lamp and next day substituted the tea-cake for the lamp and served it up to Mrs. Gibbons. 'Mrs. G. took a large mouthful of the cake. Her face was amusing.' The butler had had special tuition in making porridge. Mrs. Brooke had insisted on porridge. By way of return Rupert taught his hostesss to play Bridge. Every night the party sat at cards after dinner.

If Lucas was his link with the great sophisticated world, Keynes was his life-line with Rugby. To him Rupert complained of the intellectual desert in which he found himself:

> The only things to read this benighted place supplies are Tennyson's Poems and a London Directory of 1888. I've tried both and prefer the latter. I *did* struggle through ¾ of one of the more Victorian of the Idylls; but a severe attack of sickness and an overwhelming drowsiness compelled me to leave off. I felt as if I had consumed three basins of bread and milk with too much sugar in it.

And then Lucas acknowledged the poems. It was Rupert's first experience of professional criticism. We must infer that Lucas had picked on the lines

> *Until thy sad voice sighed through the dusk to me,*
> *Hinting of joy, of better things to be,*

and had pointed out that a voice that gave such hopeful intimations could hardly be 'sad'. His objection to the other sonnet (*Afterwards*) must have been that for so strict a form the lines were too long, adding that Rupert was trying unsuccessfully to adapt the French alexandrine to his purpose. The experiment was legitimate, and Rupert's defence of his method a good one. Lucas seems to have confined himself to questions of technique, although it was not there that Rupert needed guidance. Lucas's interest must have been a source of encouragement, but apparently it never entered his head to point out that living verse was seldom, with or without sad mournful roses, ever made out of these fabricated situations of thwarted passion. Rupert was being left to work out his own salvation. His answer from Rapallo dealt most gently with his gentle critic.

> Many thanks for the much-needed criticism and the encouragement. By a coincidence your letter came by the same post as a number of the Spectator which contained one of your 'rustic ballads'—that of the 'Ridgeway'.[1] This helped to fill me with an unwonted desire for walking; insomuch that yesterday I went up and down the highest of the innumerable hills round here; and am to-day in consequence stiff and somnolent. Nevertheless I have enough mental energy to discuss a point or two in connexion with your letter. Of course I recognize the truth of most of your criticism; but as 'there are nine and sixty ways . . .' I should like to attempt an apologia for the one I have chosen. As to the first sonnet on the whole—though a little doubtful— I think a 'sad' voice could 'hint of joy', and 'better things to be'; at least in this case. Also I cannot find a substitute, except perhaps 'low'; which would preserve most of my meaning; yet seems to spoil the sound in some inex-

[1] *Ballad of the Ridgeway*, New Poems, 1908.

plicable way. However I still waver on that point. In the second sonnet I think you have mistaken my intent. Regarding the normal line of the usual sonnet as made of 5 iambi, I have tried to build a sonnet on a line of 6 iambi, adding in short ‿ — to the ordinary line, not ‿ ‿. But of course as the line is longer, the average of the syllables has to be rather lighter than in a decasyllabic line, in order to make the thing fairly readable. In the second place they aren't my own rules that I substitute. I know nothing about French poetry, but I fancied that this form is fairly common therein: but the actual idea of using it was suggested by a delightful sonnet, 'To one in Bedlam', by the late Ernest Dowson, built on the same plan, apparently. I expect you know it: *I* saw it quoted in A. Symons' 'Studies in Prose and Verse'. I certainly think that it is a complete justification of the method!

Anyhow because the first man had a decasyllabic bent, and all others have followed him without thinking, I don't see that *that* constitutes a law. It is merely a precedent. And precedents are only made for fools and old men, I take it. The ear, I suppose, is the only judge of what is right and wrong; and I think that a dodecasyllabic-lined sonnet can give sound effects that a decasyllabic ditto can't. At least I meant by the longer line to give a feeling of weariness (don't interpret this in the wrong sense!) and dullness which I could not reach with the ordinary line.

I admit that one could not write Greek *hexameters* with an additional spondee (I got 200 lines for doing so once in Latin hexameters!); but I see no reason why Greek *heptameters* should not be a *legitimate* and quite melodious form of poetry.

These were my ideas, rather presumptuous I fear; for I really have very vague notions about technique. I generally trust to luck and put down anything that sounds all right. But the Italian winds though they may whisper many beautiful ideas in my ear, will not, I fear, teach me much about the structure of a sonnet. My faith in the 'impulse from a vernal wood' (forgive me if I have quoted wrong) does not extend to that.

I am labouring to reduce the overheavy onomatopeia in the third line.

For the rest I bow in repeated gratitude.

As for Lucas's demand for more work, he now sent 'three more victims. I don't think you would appreciate receiving "the whole green note book". Not that it's very full; but I frequently and seriously consider tearing about 8 pages out and burning the rest. For it is by now becoming outgrown. Some day soon I shall demolish it.' The three poems he picked out were written to the old formula. In the first he professed himself glad 'to bear thy load of sin'; in the second, three rather gracefully turned stanzas about nothing begin all too aptly 'What shall I tell thee of?'; and in the third, headed 'Nameless at present', he is proud to be numbered among those that have 'dared the sins that cannot be forgiven'. Condemned, and separated in death from those who, unlike him, 'never learnt to hate the Day, Nor knew the strange wrong loves we knew', he is resolved to remain undaunted 'glorying in my sin'; but were his beloved's face suddenly to appear and dwindle away again, he would know there was nothing left for him but despair. The stanza describing 'the face' suggests that the poet has been looking at one of Rossetti's paintings of Elizabeth Siddal, with 'The long chin dying in the neck's pale loveliness . . . And delicate pleading mouth that droops in weariness' and the rest. The poem is only of interest because it is the first of several attempts at expressing a somewhat Gothic idea that fascinated him: what, if there were a life hereafter, would be the effect of seeing again the most precious of one's earthly possessions—'the face'? At present, however, he is bogged in pre-Raphaelite unreality, and he ends his letter to Lucas with an ardent request for Wilde's *De Profundis* which is expected on the book-stalls any day.

To Keynes he had to admit in sorrow that he would not be seen again at School Field that term. 'Endeavour to bear up. Ere May comes I shall probably be dead and mouldering.'

I am thinking out a really humorous method of dying. One might do it quite wittily. It is an opportunity not to be lost. News takes two days to reach England from Rapallo: so you will probably hear of my decease on April 3rd. You express a very polite (and probably entirely fictitious) desire to hear what I am doing and undergoing. I don't know why. It probably won't interest you in the least. However it *can't* interest you less than it interests me so I will weary you by the account of what I do this afternoon, as an example. You can build up the other 59 days of my visit from this. I hope you find it very exciting. (It is now 6 p.m.)

(Roughly) 1–2 Lunch.

            2–3 Lie down on a sofa and read.

            3–4 Walk up and down garden trying to compose tail end of sonnet.

            4–4.30 Tea.

            4.30–5.30 Walk up and down garden throwing lemons at the cats and . . . thinking . . .

            5.30–6.30 . . . Letters.

And so on. About 9 I retire to bed with the cheerful prospect of another happy, happy day when I wake. Half the night perhaps I lie awake thinking . . . all the time I am profoundly bored. At intervals they drag me up to Genoa and round a picture-gallery; which is wasted on me. I say, 'How beautiful!' at every fourth picture, and yawn.

At the beginning of March, having run up the leaning tower of Pisa on the way, he paid his first visit to Florence, and was lodged with Margaret and Reeve in the via Bonifazio Lupi. He had raging toothache, and after an hilarious interview with a dentist, walked about the streets with a bottle of laudanum for dabbing on his gum. In spite of this he discovered he was an object of considerable interest to the Italian girls. So pointed was their admiration that he began to feel a little alarmed, and strolled about with his hand keeping a firm grip of his cousin's arm. 'Now, Margaret,' he said. 'Promise, *promise* not to let those girls get hold of me.' Duncan Grant, now an art student, turned up unexpectedly, gave news of Strachey who was now at St. Paul's School in London, and there was much talk of Hillbrow in the Piazza de Signoria. Then the obliging Mrs. Gibbons wrote to say a book (it was *De Profundis*) had arrived at Rapallo. Rupert had already found a rather patronizing notice of it in *The Times*. He wrote at once to Lucas. He was going to reserve the book for his return journey. For the present he described his adventures.

Here I am enjoying myself more than I thought I should. I have been spending much time in the galleries, trying to cultivate the Artistic Eye. But hitherto I have failed signally. I have achieved nothing except a certain admiration for Botticelli; and even that I am bitterly disappointed to find fashionable.

On Tuesday night we went out into the streets to watch the Carnival rejoicings. It was a peculiar sight full of colour and noise, and very Italian. In the distance the scene had a certain fantastic charm; but when one saw the figures at close quarters they became merely vulgar; much like a circus clown. The Piazza del Duomo was full of rather pathetic incongruity. Giotto's Tower swung upward grimly into the darkness, the summit invisible, the base surrounded by coloured lights and gay quick-moving figures and clouds of confetti. Florence attracts me rather; it has an indefinable quiet sadness; I like it best in the late afternoon. But I shall be glad to get home. I am looking forward—though I fear this is profoundly Philistine—to leaving Italy as though I were being freed from prison. A nice prison, of course, almost equal to the best American ones—yet a prison. However there are better moments. I am filled with a cruel desire to torture you by describing at length an expedition we made yesterday to Fiesole. How we had tea on the hillside and squabbled over Browning and others. How the sun began to set across the plain and beyond Florence; and the world was very quiet; and we stopped talking and watched: And how the Arno in the distance was a writhing dragon of molten gold, and the sky the most wistful of pale greens.

He was doing his best to admire the Masters, he wrote to his mother at Rugby, 'but I think I shall prefer Whistler'. On March 11 he got back to Rapallo and sent her another report on progress. 'Podge [Alfred] knows of four dead painters, one is Greuze (pronounced by him Groisy).' Maggie had discovered a new sort of chocolate biscuit; there were holes in his socks; he had left his tennis shoes in the train;

reading Aeschylus was hopeless without a dictionary; the *Pro Munera* was boring, even for Cicero; he sympathized with his father who was known 'to hate walks more than anything in the world'; above all, would she please take note that he was loth to sit with the new boys in Chapel next term. It was a somewhat tepid epistle. Perhaps her forbidding him to break his journey in Paris had dunched his spirits. She had written to say there were 'labour troubles'. There might even be riots. And so there might have been, but they wouldn't have done much harm to an English tourist if Rupert had not let on that St. John Lucas had kindly offered to show him round. All the same, Rupert was in no mood to stay abroad any longer. His mother had made a gesture, sending him the price of a London theatre ticket, to make up for the loss of the Louvre. He was frankly homesick, a new sensation, having never been a school boarder in the full sense of the term, and now a budget of Rugby news from Keynes made him impatient to be back. 'I can only quote two lines from *The Shropshire Lad* you have often heard upon my lips—a little altered this time:

> *So dead or living, drunk or dry,*
> *Keyney, I wish you well.'*

Some evening in May he would be among his friends again. It wasn't so long to wait.

I hope that evening will be a God-sent one, purple with the dying sunset and odorous with young spring: that all things in fine will be symbols . . . but I wonder. You must forgive my wild style of writing, I have been in prison for two months, warded by two Philistines. I am very tired of being grown-up: I want to laugh again, and be irresponsible and childish again, and be at School again. Have you ever been treated as an adult for 8 weeks in succession? It is a dreary experience.

Never mind. Next term I shall surpass myself. I shall be quite intolerably foolish . . . And then we shall pull the world to pieces again. You may think me impatient. But you see that is a thing one can only do while one is quite young, I take it. I have made an epigram upon it. Before the age of 25 you pull the World to pieces: after 25 the World pulls you to pieces. And we are getting on for 18, you know! . . . I sometimes think I am getting a little bald, Keynes.

There would be plenty of time for Keynes to write again, so he must collect more news of School Field. 'Nay, dear Keynaanite, think of the innumerable benefits I have conferred upon you. Have I not introduced you to G. K. Chesterton? Did I not once lend you an H. G. Wells? Have I not often made you laugh? Have I not occasionally even made you *think*?'

SCHOOL FIELD

III

In the middle of March he started home, buried in *De Profundis* all the way. Alfred had left before him, so as to be in time for school. Rupert broke the journey with a night at Milan, his very first sojourn all alone among strangers. In London he joined up with his brother Richard, and spent his compensation money on two seats for *Peter Pan*. Next day he wrote to Keynes for his birthday. 'I refrain from the usual remark. It is too banal. *But*—I really believe it is all a fraud, a deeply laid plot to obtain one of my unique letters. Obviously. Who ever had a birthday in March? Nobody.' Then came news of the next event in his literary career.

I am conscious that this illiterate scrawl is a very poor attempt at a 'birthday present', but I console myself with the thought that on Wednesday you will have a much more worthy one. I refer, of course, to the great event of the term, the appearance of the *Phoenix*. May I repeat my former words? If you (and other—more or less—*illuminati*) recognize, as in many places you will, a touch, a trick of thought or phrase, that you have laughed at of old, chuckle over it an you will but don't publish that it is mine. I am of a painfully retiring nature (as you know); and sudden notoriety is very abhorrent to me. Besides there are one or two things which look as if they might be from my august pen: but aren't. It's not a bad number, a bit uneven of course; but then you can't expect the other men to ascend to my level. One or two things are immensely squiffy, and another decidedly skippy . . . I have just realized that this letter probably will not reach you in time. It may. But what does it matter? Time is a delusion. Let us not be deluded.

Yesternight I was vastly happy. I saw Peter Pan. It was perfect. It is merely and completely the incarnation of all one's childish dreams—the best dreams, almost that one has. Red Indians, A Pirate Captain, Faeries, and all mixed up with Home . . . did you see it? If not, you must, next Christmas. It is wonderfully refreshing and never silly. And it brings out people's natures so—shows, I mean, if they are real children or no. For instance: a little way from me there was a 'grown-up' of perhaps, 10 summers, male, very blasé, and greatly bored. He obviously thought the whole thing too unutterably childish for him. Next him was a child, a white haired child of 90, his grandmother I expect. It must have been the happiest evening of her life. She chuckled and laughed all the time, with that sweetest of laughs, through which the tears shine.

Gerald du Maurier as the Pirate-Captain was perfect. You remember him at *The Admirable Crichton* I expect—wasn't it there we chanced one afternoon on each other? . . .

In early April he went to finish his convalescence at Bournemouth, where he re-read *De Profundis* in Aunt Fanny's drawing-room. ' "Nothing is more rare in any man," says Emerson, "than an act of his own," ' he wrote in the margin. 'It is true. Most people are other people. Their thoughts are someone else's opinions, their lives a mimicry, their passions a quotation.' He underlined a passage where it was claimed that Christ 'preached the enormous importance of living in the moment', also a short phrase in a passage describing the misfortune of being saddled with an artistic temperament. 'Go into exile with Dante and learn how salt is the bread of others and how steep their stairs.'

Meanwhile he conducted a facetious dispute with Keynes. The latter had started it by criticizing Rupert for not following the custom in polite circles of writing on the alternate leaves of folded writing-paper. 'Am *I* to follow the crowd?' asked Rupert. 'The reverse would be more natural. My poor conventional Keynes, you'll be defending the top-hat next. And after all the trouble I have taken with you?' Keynes retorted that he had no wish to be commonplace. On the contrary—but he did like things to be correct. To this Rupert replied that of course he applauded his friend's desire to be unusual. 'You are. But you must be thorough. I have a faint fear that still perhaps you read Dickens or even Tennyson on the sly when no one is looking.' To illustrate his point, however, Keynes addressed his next envelope to Bournemouth in a manner calculated to refute for good and all the charge of conventionality. 'I am staying with two faded but religious aunts,' wrote Rupert. 'They happened to be in when the post came, and one of them, chancing on your letter, received quite a severe shock. It's not as if she were young, either. You really must be careful!' By now Keynes had made a further criticism— that Rupert's habit of omitting to date his letters led to unnecessary trouble and confusion. Rupert replied on an undated sheet:

I bow humbly before your wrath at my omitting to date my letter. In a business correspondence it is, I admit, a low habit. But my letter was scarcely, I thought, a business one. However . . . But if you are so concerned at the difficulty which will arise when that letter is included in the 'Life and Letters', you *might* obviate it by dating the letters when you receive them. It would be, I imagine, approximately correct.

I suppose you never thought of that. Again if you are extremely curious as to the day on which I sent it, you might examine the post-mark.

I suppose you never thought of that either.

In thus anticipating one of his biographer's difficulties by more than half a century, Rupert was not being as presumptuous as it may appear. Keynes believed in him and, under all the badinage, took him seriously. Rupert was flattered, since he was never averse to a compliment, and he cherished the encouragement, for Keynes lived in a centre of learning with a distinguished father and a mother who was one of the original scholars at Newnham. Was he not much better qualified to know what was what than anyone else at School Field? But of course it could be a little embarrassing. So Rupert assumed the role of literary uncle (though Keynes was his exact contemporary) claiming to have opened his eyes to the light ('Have I not even made you *think*?') which was all the more useful as a defensive pose for its being so plainly uncalled for.

The Phoenix was now in circulation. Mrs. Brooke was not at all sure what to say, since none of the contributions were signed. 'You are very wary and generalizing,' Rupert wrote. He had banked on her making her criticisms at random, so that if she censured anything 'I might be able to write and inform you very coldly that *I* had written that particular thing. However, as you are too cautious, I had better tell you what I wrote.' He then listed seven items, making a clean breast of it.

There! And of course this is entirely a secret. To turn to a much more sordid matter, I should like to lay before you the state of my purse. I have now 10 shillings and five-pence—or possibly four-pence, I forget. My expenses here will be

3d. or so for stamps.

10s. (according to Father) for tennis shoes. And the journey and 'tip'.

He then, as was his curious custom when writing to his mother, endorsed the letter with his full signature as if he were signing a cheque.

His contributions to the third number of *The Phoenix* were either printed over the initials 'E.R.T.' or carried no clue to their authorship beyond his pencilled initials in the copy he gave Keynes. These comprise about half the magazine, and some of them may account for this being its last number. In a miniature essay called *Madness*, for example, he defines his theme as the quality of daring and originality as opposed to Sanity, which he regards as a synonym for mediocrity. It's a characteristic belief of the 'sane' man that he should 'acknowledge Shakespeare but need not have read him'; in his dress he is to be identified by 'that abomination of ugliness, a top hat', and his peculiar mode of life is to 'hunt money from morn to night'. When at last he dies 'the tattered rag that has served him for a soul flies forth to fare as it may'. So much for Sanity. It was the 'mad' man, on the other hand, who sailed forth on crusades to the Holy Land, or slew their rivals in love or perished as martyrs in the cause of their faith. 'Their madness is more glorious than his sanity. They are nearer reality. They are foolish with the folly of elemental things, the folly of Nature, with her grotesque forms of plant and animal, the folly of a little child's visions, the folly of life. And this madness shall go dancing bright-eyed down the ages, when the sane men and their sane unhealthy civilization have passed into dreams of a black past.' Then the author winds up with an impassioned appeal—'Let us throw off all feeble protests of sanity and revel in our folly . . . Why should we paint all things with black shadows of gloom and sanity? Nay, let sweet madness be our companion, and laughter our portion in life, till from our merriment we lightly turn with a smile on our lips and cheerful folly in our hearts to God's last great jest, Death.'

Another piece called *The Prevalence of the Earnest Youth* was written in the same critical spirit. Many people might suppose that the present age was noted chiefly for its Jingoism, the Sport mania, the reputation of Mr. Chamberlain, or the emergence of an apparatus known as the motor-bicycle. They would be wrong. In after years this will be remembered as the age of the Earnest Youth. This ubiquitous character behaves as if his mission in life were to make the world respectable. Given the chance he would turn England into 'one vast drab suburb'. As a scholar his style is 'a Latinized variant of Macaulayese' and his chief aim the mystification of German commentators. This is all very well, since one isn't obliged to read his works, but unfortunately he has a habit of 'discoursing with a sad superiority on the wider questions of the day' (here a rather pointed reference is made to the current issue of the School Magazine) and then he only shows that his ideas are 'infinitely nebulous' and behind the times by about a quarter of a century. The best solution would be special legislation. He must be *forbidden* to mention Ruskin, M. Arnold, Carlyle, unless he can prove he has read at least one book of each, and for his own good it must be borne in on him that 'the best way of killing a cause is to uphold it with dull platitudes and verbose ignorance'.

The third and last of the features in prose is called *The School Novel*. It begins by pointing out that *Tom Brown* and *Stalky & Co.* are thoroughly out of date. Their counterparts of today are to be found in *The Boys' Own Paper*, *Chums*, and so forth, and they all share the same peculiarly nasty sort of hero. 'He is usually of middle height, slim, but wiry—intensely wiry—and endowed with Herculean strength for use on odd occasions. He is called "a type of that healthy and clean-limbed boy who has made England what she is"; in plainer language he is an unspeakable prig in whom a painfully dull intellect is counterbalanced by a "pure and lofty" soul (not however very prominent) and a remarkable propensity for games.' So now he has a suggestion to make. What about the hero being, say, a Corporal called Reggie in a novel about a war between Rugby and Uppingham? The dialogue would go something like this:

'Very humorous,' asserted his friend Juan, 'but do you take nothing seriously?'

'Nothing,' Reggie replied emphatically, 'except of course a joke. People who take things seriously are either in the Sixth or in the San.'

'What's the difference?' enquired Juan drowsily.

'When your body needs a complete rest you go to the San. When your mind does you——'

but the chapter must end with a brief but stirring glimpse of Reggie in action; some such phrase, for instance, as 'Throwing himself off his foaming bicycle, he remarked in husky accents "All is lost!"'

One of his poems was a sonnet he had sent to Lucas. Another, *To a Cadet Officer*, begins by asking the question: What is the most ridiculous thing about him? then clears the ground.

> *'Tis naught wherewith the mere civilians taunt you.*
> *'Tis not your frown, more mocked, alas, than feared—*
> *Not even your ghastly hat (though that, I grant you,*
> *Is more than weird).*

His *voice* turns out to be the drawback. Then comes an experiment in Triolets about a boy who hasn't done his prep, and *Man*, a first attempt at blank verse, a metre he was to use very seldom, and ironically for all his distaste for Tennyson, it is *Tithonus* and the Idylls, recently read at Rapallo and disliked, which have taught him what he knows of this measure. *Man* develops the theme of an earlier poem sent to Lucas, 'Our Mother the Earth is weary,' probably his first sonnet, and perhaps because he is now using a measure seldom favoured by the poets of the 'nineties, the result is less mannered. When he writes

> *Why are our hearts so full of questionings,*
> *Of search, and passionate dreams, and vain desire?*

he gives the impression that he believes in the question he is asking.

He was to ask it again, with far more accomplishment, in 1911 when he came to write *Thoughts on the Shape of the Human Body*. For a moment he seems to have stumbled into sincerity, so that the image of an aged Earth 'Brooding upon the springs of long ago' in sombre Tennysonian cadences, and the Almighty out of compassion putting an end to it all, 'Flinging the earth into the sun's white fires', represents the earliest, faint promise of a poet. 'White' and the whiteness of things was to appear again and again until the end of his life. The poem, dated March 1905, must have been sent to the printer at the last moment, having been written or finished in the sober surroundings of Grantchester Dene, at Bournemouth. Grandfather Richard England had died here five years before, and the house was now a place of memories and retreat for the two maiden aunts. Fanny was fond of books. Still upstairs, perhaps, was the copy of Browning where in 1896 her nephew had first discovered the art that was to enthral him for the rest of his days.

Among the contributors to *The Phoenix* was the professional writer, Lucas's fellow advocate of aestheticism, Arthur Eckersley, who now sent the editor his views on the articles and poems. 'I don't think they were "wild(e)ly subtle" as you put it,' Rupert replied, 'though they were meant to combine Oscarian neatness with Shakespearian profundity—"A little more than Will and less than Wilde" in fact,' and he went on, 'I have finally given up all kinds of writing (except letters). There are only ten beautiful words and I have used them all many times—there is only one subject I can write upon, and I have written on that too often.' This was almost true, except for the threat of retirement from authorship, for he went on to say he had just embarked on a 'decadent' school novel but had got stuck. This was as far as it had gone:

Chrysophase Tiberius Amaranth sat in his study, a small pale green room, reading. From one hand an opium-flavoured cigarette circled wreaths of odorous pallid smoke among the shadows. There was a knock at the door, and the Headmaster entered. 'Ah!' he exclaimed genially, 'Studying the classics, Amaranth?'

Chrysophase laid down his book. It was French, bound in dark green, and strangely scented.

'Scarcely!' he replied, 'the exact opposite, in fact. A classic is read by nobody, and quoted by everybody. This book, on the contrary, is read by everybody—in secret; and quite unquoteable.'

'Thank you,' said the Headmaster prettily: 'I see that you have learnt one of the two duties of the modern youth.'

'?'

'To embrace the world in one sentence.'

'And the other?'

'To embrace the world in one person,' answered the Headmaster with a musical sigh.

'My dear James,' exclaimed Chrysophase, 'you are magnificent tonight! May I offer you a cigarette?'

'Thank you. I never smoke them. Their shape is so banal. But if you have some absinthe . . . Yes, just a little . . .'

Later in April he joined his mother in her hotel at Hastings having sent her a warning note. 'I haven't had my hair cut since the end of February: and it's simply grand now! But I shall have it cut today. I daren't face you as I am.' From the Palace Hotel he wrote again to Lucas. He was reading Walter Pater and trying to make headway with *The Bastille* 'so far without producing a line. It is a most distressing task to have to write about a subject which neither interests nor inspires. It lies heavily upon me like a nightmare.' He was longing for the Easter holidays to end. There was nothing in Hastings but trippers in deck-chairs reading Marie Corelli.

He was here when Keynes's view of *The Phœnix* came to hand. Although he was due to leave for Rugby next day, he wrote so that Keynes would have something to thank him for on arrival.

Your guesses at my handiwork (though you hedged a little afterwards) were astonishingly accurate. I scent witchcraft. You got a bull every time. Weren't they silly, too! . . .

The only tolerable things in Hastings are dinners at this hotel. They are noble. I had some soup tonight that was tremulous with the tenseness of suppressed passion; and the entrées were odorous with the pale mystery of starlight . . . I write after dinner, by the way. The real reason of this absurd epistle is this. I wish to warn you. Be prepared. It is this: I am writing a Book. There will only be one copy. It will be inscribed in crimson ink on green paper. It will consist of thirteen small poems; each as beautiful, as perfect, and as meaningless as a rose-petal, or a dew-drop. (These are not yet written, however.) When the book is prepared; I shall read it once a day for seven days.

Then I shall burn the book: and die.

On April 15 Mrs. Brooke and Rupert took the train back to Rugby. *The Bastille* would have to be a rush job if he was going to enter the competition on time. He had been away nearly three months. Having little visual sense, and the experience coming too soon, Italy had been almost entirely lost on him. Freedom had become irksome, and he was in no hurry to grow up. He entered School Field again with a genuine sigh of relief.

Chapter III

SCHOOL FIELD
Senior
(April 1905–August 1906)

He had reached the Upper Bench of the VIth in January 1905 and was in a state of confusion because he had neglected Aeschylus during his convalescence. He was now torn between his school work and the intractable theme of the Bastille. Then Lucas made things no easier by asking for more poems. 'What time do you suppose I have for spontaneous verse?' Rupert retorted in a fluster. However he did enclose a small piece of a dozen lines, 'but they are, I know, of a sort it is merely ridiculous for me to write'. This admission marked a distinct step forward. The new verses were on the theme of his at last turning with relief from the 'weariness of Life' to the 'weariness of dying' and were indeed, as he now had the wisdom to suspect, ridiculous. As to *The Bastille* 'I have fought the Muse for a week without the faintest success,' but he did have fifty lines in hand.

Fifteen I have had to delete as being likely to shock the lofty moral standard of the Rugby School authorities. The remaining thirty-five are the worst I have ever written. They have no ideas. They don't scan. And with the exception of two lines they are as dull and vulgar as a Bank-holiday.

In a commonplace book he was making notes on the French Revolution, none of which proved very useful in the event. Opening the pages to make a new entry he must often have been put off his academic stroke by what he found there: notes for a ballad on the Chapel choir practice beginning 'O what is that weird wild wailing? Is't the song of a sorrowful cow?'

> The noise of a dog-fight is gentle
> When compared to these heartrending groans,
> Which begin with a squeak in the treble
> And descend very slowly to moans.

—useful or refreshing maxims gleaned from Wilde, such as 'To love one's self is the beginning of a life-long romance' or 'The truth is a thing I get rid of as soon as possible'; and jottings of his own for a carol designed for use by industrialists. 'Hark, the herald angels dance. Glory to the New Finance'. All this, sorting ill with excerpts from Carlyle, would have made uphill work of the ceremonial Ode. All the same, it won the prize. The news was given in the course of an imaginary conversation sent in a letter to Eckersley. He was bored with the classics. 'Life is intolerable, a foolish gibe; the summer is a bad pun.'

[Scene. The Close in a purple evening in June. The air is full of the sound of cricket and the odour of sunset. On a green bank *Rupert* is lying. There is a mauve cushion beneath his head, and in his hand E. Dowson's collected poems, bound in pale sorrowful green. He is clothed in indolence and flannels.
Enter *Arthur*.]
Arthur: 'Good-morrow. What a tremulous sunset!'
Rupert: 'Ernest Dowson is one of the seven geniuses of this age. I am the other six . . .'

In the middle of a long speech 'Rupert' throws in the suggestion: 'On some Saturday not far away, if you secrete yourself in New Big School, you will hear me recite part of an exceedingly bad poem to a perspiring multitude. The multitude will applaud uncomprehending. It will be very funny.' Then after a lot more in the same vein:

'But come! the air is dewy and wan. On the Close, as in my heart, the sunset has faded and left all things colourless. But to the Close the sun will return tomorrow, fair and glorious as of old. Till then we will dream of dead suns and vanished evenings. I thank you for this conversation. You talk wonderfully. I love listening to epigrams. I wonder if the dead still delight in epigrams. I love to think of myself as seated on the greyness of Lethe's banks, and showering ghosts of epigrams and shadowy paradoxes upon the assembled wan-eyed dead. We shall smile, a little wearily I think, remembering . . . Farewell.'
Arthur: 'Farewell.'

The annual assembly took place on June 24 in New Big School, the great hall immediately over Parker Brooke's classroom. While Rupert was declaiming his prize poem, there sat at a piano behind him, ready to provide the interludes, Rugby's star pupil in music. William Denis Browne, a gentle spirit of great talent, was half Irish and came of a family in Leamington. He was destined to become a pupil of Busoni in Berlin and to play a role of special importance in the life of the boy who was now receiving for his prize the works of Browning and Rossetti. And then everyone went over to the Chapel for the unveiling by the Bishop of Hereford of a medallion to the memory of the school's benefactor, Frederick Temple.

With the exception of the opening paragraph, *The Bastille* is less satisfactory than *The Pyramids*. The poem opens well with the Seasons personified, imagined as offering to the grim fortress with barren alternation their several gifts of light and shade.

> *So, while the silent feet of Time sped on,*
> *It loomed tremendous, hateful in men's eyes,*
> *Tyranny's presence, for in fear firm-set*
> *Stood all the towers . . .*

He was aged nearly eighteen. He deserved the reward of public acclaim, though, of course, to Lucas he made light of it. 'The speeches were rather amusing. I am informed that my effort was one of the only two audible; and as the other was in a foreign tongue, I carry off the honours. I am also told—by a cricketer and a friend of mine— that half the audience were moved to laughter, the other half to tears. Which I regard as a compliment, though I can understand the feelings of neither half.'

The Browning was a nice thing to have, but the dramatic monologue, whether rhymed or blank, was not for him. The Rossetti was of more significance. *The Pyramids* had already shown that he had an eye and an ear to perceive the craftsmanship in a piece of verse. Then it was Milton. In the weeks to come his enjoyment of *The House of Life* was to give him through the sonnet-form a length, shape, tone, and cadence, exactly suited to the natural shape of his own thoughts. From now on all he needed, where this form is concerned, was to practise continuously and simply to grow up.

After this brief taste of literary lionhood he resumed the old routine, and on the day after the Recitation was playing cricket for School Field against the Town and being run out after adding three runs to the score. Then quite unexpectedly James Strachey at St. Paul's came back into his life. Rupert had tried 'courageously spasmodic attempts' to goad him into a correspondence. Strachey had now decided to reform, he said, and vowed to write once a week. 'I refuse to vow anything,' Rupert replied, and went on to bring Strachey up to date. Since one of his sentences has a sequel of some consequence, it should be given here in spite of the familiar facts.

'At Florence on Carnival night I quite remarkably met Duncan Grant, who gave me the latest information about you. He contradicted himself every three minutes, so the information was probably wrong; but it was very interesting and I have entirely forgotten it all.' Strachey would soon be going to Trinity, Cambridge, 'which is a pity,' Rupert comments, 'since I am for Oxford.' It is curious that the fitness of his father's college at Cambridge should ever have been in question. And then the characteristic digression:

Why at the end of your epistle do you express a hope that I shall not think you rude. Anyhow I very rarely think anyone rude. And equally obviously I think you mad. You always were; and I hope you are still. I always endeavour to be as mad as possible in this sane grey world, and I should not insult you by calling you sane.

While taking History exams at the end of July Rupert was reminded of his dismal failure in History the year before. As Strachey had just written to say how interested he was to hear that Rupert was going to be a journalist, Rupert thought he would relate his misadventure of last year. 'The first duty of an examinee,' he wrote, 'is to irritate the examiner.' Last year he had been particularly let down by a question on the Roman chronicles. 'I defined them as being as dull, useless, untrue, and far from Literature as the average Roman History. I afterwards discovered that the examiner was a wretch who had written four Roman Histories and two Skeleton Outlines and held an entirely new and original view as to which eye Hannibal was blind in.' He must now dash off to Chapel. 'They would not let me become a Roman Catholic, so I did the next best thing and joined the Salvation Army.'

After the summer term he went to the army camp for cadets at Aldershot and was allowed to celebrate his eighteenth birthday by going to London for the Rugby v. Marlborough match at Lord's. 'With advancing years I find one's thoughts turn increasingly towards the Hereafter and the Serious Things of Life.' He was commiserating with his friend Russell-Smith whose own birthday came soon afterwards. 'Did it hurt much? or did you take gas for it, as I did?' Later this month the Stracheys were moving into Great Oakley Hall, Kettering, a big house they had hired furnished for the summer. 'Why should innumerable ugly plates be hung on the walls?' asked James. 'Why should Chelsea candlesticks crowd the tables? The result is, of course, that there is no Shakespeare in the house. But perhaps the worst feature is that the church is on the croquet lawn.' Rupert was back at Aldershot, and had taken with him Swinburne's novel *The Children of the Chapel* which Strachey was also reading. 'I have not attempted it yet, being fearful that it might be as verbose as his usual prose, which overwhelms and stuns me. I imagine that by now you have been quelled to desperation, that you have quite suddenly one day run amok through your old mansion with a poker, smashing the ugly plates hung on the walls, annihilating the crowded Chelsea candlesticks, and with a keg of dynamite relieving for ever your beloved croquet lawn of its ecclesiastical encumbrance.'

Meanwhile James had brought his brother Lytton into the picture. At this time Lytton Strachey was still at Trinity, Cambridge, ending his fifth academic year at the university. James was curious to have his elder brother's opinion of his Hillbrow friend, who was now such a sprightly correspondent, so the brothers made a plan. In a short while Rupert was coming to stay. Meanwhile he would be sent a questionnaire, and his reply, together with the previous six or seven letters that James had so far received from him, would then be handed over to Lytton for analysis. So on the pretext that he was somewhat short of news, but wanted to fill up the space, James launched the enterprise with a letter, and just in case Rupert should unwittingly defeat the purpose by not giving the matter his full attention, James, as was only fair, added a footnote. 'I think these questions embrace all the Important things in life, and I warn you that you will be judged by your answers to them.' The questions were:

> Do you approve of the Royal Academy?
> What are your views on Wagner, Mr. Chamberlain, and Christ?
> Are you in favour of war at any price?
> Why are you going to Oxford?
> Does Jackson play such a good game as Fry?

Richard Brooke had recently got a job with a firm in Southsea, and Rupert was staying there with his brother when he posted his reply. He ignored the last question on cricket. As for the Royal Academy the answer was 'Yes, I approve of all forms of charitable institution'. On the University problem he was evasive: 'My father is torn asunder. Anyhow I don't much mind which.' He went on:

> Certainly I approve of war at any price. It kills off the unnecessary. As for Mr. Chamberlain I detest him. He is a modern politician, and I hate modern politicians; he comes from Birmingham, and I abhor Birmingham; he makes a noise, and I loathe noises; he is utterly materialistic, and . . .!

About Wagner I have no views. I am very sorry, but I can't help it. I have tried very hard for years, but I *cannot* appreciate music. I recognize that it is a fault in me, and am duly ashamed. In Literature, and a little even in Painting, I humbly believe I can feel the Beautiful, but I am born deaf. This is a Tragedy. For Christ—I am so obsessed by *De Profundis* that I have no other views on this subject than those expressed therein. The Perfect Artistic Temperament.

At this point Strachey must have been amused to discover that Rupert was not going to let him get away with this sort of thing scot-free. It was now his turn to stand and deliver. Rupert was retaliating with a questionnaire of his own:

1. What are the two greatest tragedies in life?
2. Show the comic side of both.
3. What is the most beautiful adjective in English?
4. When did you give up reading Tennyson?
5. What *is* the World coming to?

Before there was time for a further exchange Rupert went to stay among the ugly plates and the candlesticks. 'I hear the horses being harnessed to the fire engine which is to carry this letter to Kettering,' he ended his enthusiastic note of arrival, and doubtless the answers to his own catechism were given by word of mouth. But meanwhile the conspiracy between the two brothers developed apace. Lytton met Rupert again during this visit, but saw little of him. He would have heard a good deal about him, however, from Maynard Keynes, Geoffrey's elder brother, who was a close friend at Cambridge. Back at Rugby, Rupert heard that Maynard was expected to follow him at Kettering, so he wrote to Geoffrey, 'If your venerable brother is at Great Oakley Hall with the Stracheys, kindly transmit to him the following pieces of advice. (a) Let him not be tempted into playing croquet there: they play a mean and wildly exasperating game (b) If he is in want of anything to read do not let him attempt (as I did) *The Sorrows of Satan* by M. Corelli. It is the richest work of humour in the English (?) language . . . I am now a positive wreck . . . Lytton Strachey I found most amusing, especially his voice.' This voice of his had more significance than a mere mannerism of speech, seemingly so proper to that angular frame which, after standing a while, has been described as loosely reorganizing itself into a sitting position. The tone of voice went also with the sardonic cast of mind, an individual slant on things which was infectious among his friends, and which explains the notable observation by Leonard Woolf that 'many caught his method of thinking and thought ever after with a squeak in their minds'.[1]

For the present Lytton had the acquaintance of an hour or two and the six last letters from Rugby, including the result of the questionnaire, on which to base his analysis. James duly handed over these documents for his brother's scrutiny. By now there was a motive of more weight than simple curiosity. It looked as if Rupert might be going to Cambridge after all. Once there, he was just the sort of person who might be suitable for election to the 'Apostles', the select conversazione society of undergraduates at present adorned by Lytton himself. Was Rupert of the stuff that qualified for election to this august and exclusive body? It was a question. Lytton would know best. Evidently he first cross-examined James, and heard what there was to know, in particular of St. John Lucas and Eckersley, the two young proselytes of the literary Decadence. For some obscure reason beyond the mere convenience, Lytton gave these two men and their influence on Rupert the composite name of 'Bobbie Longman',[2] and Rupert himself he began referring to as Sarawak. There had been some talk that the famous Rajah of Sarawak was a distant relation. 'Second cousin' was the phrase, but the relationship, if any, has proved to be too slight for research to confirm. However, when at length it came to Rupert's ears that he was known at Kettering as the Rajah he promptly nicknamed his mother the Ranee, and as such from now on he always spoke of her among his friends.

Lytton Strachey had recently written, but not published, a short story in the style of Henry James. He now drew up a memorandum of his conclusions, still somewhat infected by his model, headed it with the question 'Has the Rajah read Henry James?' wrote 'The Dossier' impressively on the envelope, and posted it under the door of his brother's bedroom.

My opinion is that our view must depend upon the answer we decide to give this question.

But let us first examine some less important points. Poor Sarawak was put to a very severe test; and he didn't come up to the mark. The catechism floored him. It brought out into clear relief most of the inferior qualities which had appeared only too obviously in the preceeding letters: 1. the vile diction—'duly', 'wroth', 'therein', etc. 2. the feeble epigrams and jokes; and 3. the general aesthetic tinge. There can, I think, be little doubt that Mr.

[1] *Sowing*, Leonard Woolf, Hogarth Press, 1960.

[2] Mr. Robert Longman writes: 'The reference to "Bobbie Longman" is a complete mystery to me for I doubt if the circle in which Rupert Brooke moved knew of my existence.'

Longman must be held responsible for 2 and 3; as to 1, it would be at least charitable to account for it in some other way—as the result of youth, for instance, and a lack of power of correct expression. One other characteristic must not pass unobserved. It did not appear very definitely in the catechism, but it is to be found elsewhere; and it is somewhat irritating—a complacent egoism (e.g. the story of the history examination[1]). But I do not think we should base our theories too much upon these facts. We must remember Mr. Longman; and we must remember that the severity of the catechism test has perhaps exaggerated our vision of certain defects. We may also excuse a good deal of complacent egoism when we remember the adoration of the young Keynes, and, I presume, the whole of Rugby.

Let us, therefore, try to discover whether the letters do not show traces of some other quality, the possession of which would counterbalance the defects enumerated above. I think we ought to be satisfied if we could be convinced that the Rajah had an acute sense of character and of situation. Unfortunately the letters throw very little light upon this side of him (if it exists); but there is one passage which seems to me of the greatest importance in this connection. It runs as follows . . .[2] In the first place, can you deny that this is precisely the impression produced on one by 'Duncan Grant's' conversation? Oh! not that it's the *only* impression—but one could hardly expect an elaborate subtilty. Secondly, it seems to me certain that if he genuinely invented the phrase 'quite remarkably met' there is nothing more to be said; He has reached real heights; he has defined a situation, and understood it.

Let us add, please, to Sarawak's good qualities a general innocence, and an interest (though perhaps not deep) in interesting things. These encourage me to believe that with the wiping out of Bobbie [Longman] something might be done. But I admit the doubtfulness of it all, and I admit one other consideration, which seems to shatter my main hope—The Rajah, very likely, had not read Henry James. But Mr. Longman?

On the strength of this James must have felt it incumbent upon himself, in the interests of his friend, to undermine the influence of the egregious 'Bobbie Longman'. However, it was more than four years before he wrote to check up on the true facts of the crucial problem posed by Lytton, and then Rupert replied 'On looking up early MSS I find I wrote Henry James some years before I had read, or even handled, a volume of that impalpable, that so slightly contagious, contemporary of mine'.

II

At the end of August Rupert was 'off to a place called "the Sea" ', as he told that part of Bobbie Longman which was Lucas, explaining that

[1] See page 67, the account of the Roman history question.
[2] See page 67, the sentence beginning 'At Florence on Carnival night . . .'

it was a summer custom in his family, though 'for myself I had rather remain at home with the Close and the Temple Library than stare all day at a few pale yards of sea visible between the excursion steamers'. Early in September he was home again, doing extra work on Demosthenes and Horace, playing doubles at tennis in a wet season— 'We all stood half way up the court and patted the unrising balls to and fro with petulant half-volleys'—and catching up with his correspondence. He had so far left Strachey unthanked for his hospitality at Kettering but had thought of a good excuse. 'The wonderful and beautiful novel by Marie Corelli which I read in those three days reduced me to such a pulpy stupefaction that I am only now beginning to recover.' A big decision had been taken. Oxford was definitely abandoned. In mid-September Rupert was sent on a flying visit to Cambridge for an interview at King's—where his uncle the Rev. Alan England Brooke was now Dean—and, soon after he came back, a private tutor in classics was installed at School Field. His first glimpse of King's made no more impression on him than the sights of Italy. Perhaps he felt so small and the College seemed so vast, and the Chapel was such an overwhelming walk-over of an improvement on Butterfield's best efforts at Rugby, that all he really noticed was his uncle. W. P. Brooke, in consultation with Whitelaw, had changed his mind. If Rupert went to King's he would have to read for an Honours degree. Classics was the only possible subject, and only recently had he shown much aptitude, but it did look now as if he stood a fair chance of a scholarship, granted he took some extra tuition. Even if he failed, he was destined for Cambridge. It was pointed out to him that for a Brooke to go to King's without a scholarship would be considered something less than satisfactory. He was bidden to work. 'There is, needless to say, not the remotest ghost of a chance for me,' he wrote to Erica in resignation. 'However the idea seems to have a strange fascination for those in authority, and therefore I, as always, acquiesce patiently. It saves trouble in the end.'

The holidays were coming to an end when there was a pleasant surprise for him in the *Westminster Gazette*. This weekly journal edited by J. A. Spender ran a literary competition organized by Naomi Royde Smith. Earlier this summer Rupert had chanced on a copy in the Temple Reading Room, been intrigued by the competition page, and posted his entry. The result was that in July the literary editor published a few lines beginning 'An Evil Time came down with fateful feet' which had been sent in over the pseudonym

Sandro. They had failed to win the prize for 'the best Sicilian Octave, descriptive rather than reflective', but at least they had merited print. A month later she set another problem for her readers. They must now compete for the best sonnet about the sea written to an elaborate specification sent in by one of her subscribers. On September 16 she announced that the competitor calling himself Teragram had won, and she published the winning entry. She did not know that Sandro and Teragram were the same person, nor that both were a boy in the Upper VIth at Rugby. For several years these competitions were to provide Rupert with opportunities for technical exercise which proved of real value to his developing craftsmanship. His first winning entry, though hardly worth including among his Juvenilia, illustrates so clearly the thoroughness of his application to a technical conundrum, that both problem and solution alike deserve attention.

A former competitor named F. L. Ghey had submitted 'A Suggestion for a Sonnet entitled The Sea'. It runs like this:

The first eight lines should describe the sea as a thronged ante-chamber; the remaining six lines should speak of those who wait, entering at last into the Presence beyond.

Deep silence fills the ante-chamber, which is walled and roofed with emerald and silver; precious things lie heaped there as in a King's treasure house, but of these no man takes heed, since all wait intently for a summons from beyond. Nor do they hear those that clamour without, lamenting that the ante-chamber has closed upon their kinsfolk, so that they can no longer have speech with them.

Then, when the jewelled doors are opened at the sounding of a trumpet-blast, the pale company that enter with awe and wonder into the Presence shall rejoice, meeting again those that mourned, for they, meanwhile, shall have been let in by another door; but the ante-chamber, with its unheeded treasure, shall be left desolate.

Working on the principle 'All this has got to be got in somewhere' Rupert tidied these suggestions into a strict example of the sonnet form, using Wordsworth as his model in the octave, one of D. G. Rossetti's rhyme-schemes in the sestet, and, obedient to the last, called his finished article 'The Sea'.

> *A hall of gleaming silence, ringed by sheer*
> *Unmoving emerald water; carpeted*
> *With treasure-trove—pale pearls and coral red,*
> *And roofed with rippling silver. Far and near,*
> *Vast crowds of late-awakened souls, who here*
> *Expect and wait—the sea's uncounted dead.*
> *No sound, no stir, except when overhead*

The silver water wavers and grows clear.
Then hark, a trumpet call! The mighty throng
Sways forward, finds the unencumbered place
Wherein all who have grieved and waited long
Shall see at last their well-beloved's face.
Hushed is the homeless sea's unfinished song,
Its treasures lie forgot in desert space.

It was his first complete poem in public print, and in addition to the glory he received 10s. 6d., the first literary earnings of his life.

Soon after the Michaelmas term began he sent a copy of *The Bastille* to the Rev. J. B. Wynne-Willson, his former master of the Lower Bench of the VIth, who was now headmaster of Haileybury and had quoted from the poem in his farewell sermon in Rugby Chapel. 'You have done more with it than ever I could,' Rupert wrote, recalling his own performance on Speech Day. 'It is the common opinion that the preachers this term are a poor lot, being mostly drawn from the staff, and not the most popular part of it at that: but this is irreverent.' The Calendar for the term was now in circulation, and it was not very inviting. 'The lectures this term are even worse than of late.' His heart sank at the prospect of 'The Siege of Port Arthur, as I saw it'. There was to be no Shakespeare. 'I hope this is not caused by Benson's A Company being indignant at the *Meteor* review of last year.' He ended by hoping that Willson would continue at Haileybury his custom of reading aloud to his form some passage of English literature for one hour a week. Rupert had valued the respite.

No sooner had *The Phoenix* been suppressed after its third issue than a magazine called *The Venture* was allowed to appear and publish Rupert's verse, not his prose; the editors were playing for safety, and the October number contained *Lost Lilies*, a lyric of some length set in a 'dim languorous place Fragrant with night and roses'. Rupert's contribution was only too harmless. No doubt his main exertions were being devoted to his classical studies. Lucas received a complaint that he was growing weary of work and football, Wynne-Willson had left, leaving him to 'the mercy of several soulless dull automata, who make Beauty tedious and Life an affair of syntax', but he was growing rather interested in some of the new authors who were being put in his way. Pindar was lost on him; Propertius seemed just tolerable; Lucan was faintly pleasing but obscure, but Theocritus 'almost compensates to me for the interminable dullness of Demosthenes . . . I am wildly enchanted by him.' There was a VIth form literary society called *Eranos* and, being convinced that a little Swinburne would do it good, he had promised to read it a paper on *Atalanta in Calydon*. Since one of the masters was president of the society he thought it wise to steer clear of 'Poems and Ballads', but *Atalanta* raised certain problems. Who, for instance, was the Chorus? Lucas must please enlighten him. Meanwhile Lucas must not imagine that Rupert's own verse was being altogether neglected. He enclosed a specimen called *Vanitas* written in the vein most likely to commend it to his mentor. 'Laugh now and live! our blood is young: our hearts are high; Fragrant of life, aflame with roses'. Youth must be mindful that its hour is brief, and that not for long 'Stays the mad joyance of our golden revelry'.

Late in November he delivered himself on the subject of *Atalanta*, dealing first with the general style which he said was a compound of Greek metaphors, the double superlatives of the Elizabethans, and the language of the Psalms—and, by the way, the Upper Bench would be interested to know that this poet's elegy on Landor was the nearest thing in English to Greek poetry! But to return, the prose Argument itself was 'a most curious yet beautiful mixture of archaic English with a Greek style'. Swinburne's tricks of assonance and alliteration which were to become a tedious mannerism were featured here in this early masterpiece with freshness and beauty. The speaker read aloud the first choric ode, 'When the hounds of Spring,' and remarked, 'The music and the metrical skill of this must have struck like a thunderbolt upon the English ears of that time [1864], unused as they were to any anapaestic or dactyllic metres much more successful than the somewhat jingly melodies of Byron.' He observed that the image of fire which dominated the whole drama was foreshadowed in the very first question put by the Chorus—'But what is it that hath burnt thine heart?' He then described the characters and the action, noting that at one point half the play has gone by and nothing has happened, so gradually are the characters assembled and the situation prepared for the eventual surge forward to the tragic close, when the Chorus delivers 'a tremendous indictment of the Unknown, the supreme evil, God'. After reading aloud Meleager's dying words, Rupert concluded his first attempt at holding an audience.

And now Lucas was wanting his views on Shaw. Having just finished a sonnet that seemed worth sending, Rupert wrote:

I think I remember seeing an article on G.B.S. in a quarterly some time since; and it must be the one to which you refer. I was rather curious about G.B.S. at the time, and so started the article, but left it in the middle, with a vague conviction that G.B.S. must be very dull and foolish. I do not know quite how far Shaw is sincere, but I can accept him even if he means all he says. I find that at present (whether owing to my nature of mind or my state of education I know not) all my sympathies are intensely liberal—wide as the grave. I can enjoy and appreciate in part—or so I have the audacity to think—every kind of doctrine. I have an extreme sympathy with all fanatics, and yet am an ardent admirer of law and order! I see what I take to be the truth in the Bible, Socrates, Wilde and Shaw. No doubt I shall grow up into a rabid partisan of some extreme view; but at present I enjoy a position of great impartiality. I enjoy even Kipling.

Just now my days are passing very happily, and many beautiful things occur. I am so joyful that I fear lest the Greek idea may be true, and Nemesis fall blackly and suddenly. At present however I am plucking flowers in the sun, with this additional advantage (is it an advantage?) over my companions that I am aware of it.

Last Sunday I read a little paper on Atalanta and was mightily pleased. The usual papers we have are on such subjects as *Hood* or *Calverly*—'something to make you laugh'. Imagine the dismay of the rest of the society at being compelled to listen for three-quarters of an hour to a paper on an obscure play by an author of whom they had scarcely heard. Never a laugh from beginning to end! I saw my opportunity and took it. 'Have I not,' I said, 'many a time and oft been bored past endurance by such Philistines? Now my revenge comes; I shall be merciless.' So I prepared a very long and profound paper full of beautiful quotations and read it to them for a very long time and they were greatly bored. They sat round in chairs and slumbered uneasily, moaning a little; while I in the centre ranted fragments of choruses, and hurled epithets upon them. So they were bored for 45 minutes: and at length I ended with Meleager's last speech, quoted almost entire; and my voice was almost husky with tears: so that they awoke and wondered greatly, and sat up, and yawned, and entered into a discussion on *Tragedy*, wherein I advanced the most wild and heterodox and antinomian theories and was very properly squashed. So, you see, even in Rugby the Philistines do not get it their own way always.

The sonnet he enclosed, called *The Dawn*, was about 'the terrible sunrise of the Tomb' and how in death, though the experience may have much in it of unearthly wonder, yet for him there would be no joy were he denied the loveliest reward of all, the face of his beloved—

Nor see the pale cloud of her tossing hair
Laugh and leap out along the desolate wind.

With those lines the sestet swings to a more effective conclusion than he had so far achieved, but again the piece is no more than an artificial device. It has interest only in that it represents an advance on his previous attempt on the same theme, and imagines the situation which in three years' time, when 'the beloved' was no longer an empty phrase, he presented in his first sonnet of merit—'Oh, Death will find me long before I tire'. There once again the concluding image is suggested by the beloved's hair, but instead of a 'pale cloud' which at present is so conveniently non-committal, she is seen to turn and 'toss your brown delightful head Amusedly, among the ancient Dead'. But long before then, in a few months' time in fact, he would be trying the same idea again, and again he would fail.

He had more than his lecture to be proud of, but Lucas, one imagines, would not have been interested to know that he was now not only head of the House but in the first XV of the School. Information gleaned from the school magazine is for a change refreshingly unaesthetic. 'R. C. Brooke weighs 11 stone 12 lbs., and is a reliable centre three-quarter who, though not brilliant, is usually in his place, and makes good openings, he tackles too high.' This critical point revealed a new departure at the opposite extreme from his former practice at Hillbrow where he used to play full-back, and where he once demonstrated to Strachey his 'skilful technique of lying flat on the ground and catching the person with the ball elegantly by the ankles'. But he had more to his credit than prowess in sport. On November 29 he had delivered his maiden speech in the Debating Society, speaking in opposition to the motion 'that this House deplores the condition of the daily press'. As for sensational journalism, Rupert was all for it. 'Murders and police news are the substitute for romance. A good murder deserves two columns. *Macbeth* is the story of a murder and the *Iliad* the result of a kind of divorce case.' The speaker was nervous. Before he got half-way through he lost his place in his notes and almost his head as well. As it was, he had to skip what he considered his best jokes and confine himself to the peroration. Another speaker that evening was the boy Philip Guedalla.

Shortly before Christmas 1905 Keynes, Russell-Smith, and Brooke travelled to Cambridge for their exams and were put up in the Keynes household at Harvey Road. There was a small party one evening, and friends of Geoffrey's brother Maynard were invited, so that Rupert met J. T. Sheppard of King's, who would soon be one of his tutors in classics, and Harry Norton, who one day would carry on the good work begun by Lytton Strachey and vet him for his suitability as an 'Apostle'. On the way back Rupert went to see *Major Barbara*, the new play at the Court in London, 'a brutal, sordid play, difficult to understand and very interesting', he described it to Erica, and there was one bit of dialogue that struck a peculiarly sympathetic chord. 'One of the characters utters a scathing invective against public-school masters at which I applauded very suddenly and loudly in the midst of a dead silence.' He also fitted in a second visit to *Peter Pan*, and was again enchanted. 'In reality no doubt,' he told Strachey, 'it is very ridiculous.'

The examination results did Rugby credit. Brooke and Russell-Smith won classical scholarships to King's and St. John's respectively, and Keynes was awarded an exhibition in natural science to Pembroke. As almost always nowadays, after some special exertion, Rupert fell ill with a fever and retired to bed on Christmas Day. Being seized with a desire to read Malory's *Morte d'Arthur* he sent Alfred over to the Temple Library and was thrilled when he came back with the edition in three volumes illustrated by Beardsley. 'I never respected the Temple Reading Room so much in my life,' he wrote to Keynes. 'Yet I was insulted. I thought I knew the Library by heart: and this treasure had lurked there for such ages unobserved of me. How strange is Fate!'

You I believe were one of those who scoffed, saying 'Classics! forsooth! he got it on his Essay!' . . . But we have received my marks, together with those of the next man, and they enable me totally to refute your last calumny. I was about 40 marks ahead of him altogether, and of these I gained but 3 on the essay. Essay, quotha! It was my classics, my grammar, my history, my Cole-like[1] memory, that did it. Pray thank your brother for his letter of congratulation and for the news it contained, which was at least exciting. On the 9th prox. (!) I am going to London for 5 days—if my incipient consumption is by then departed—to witness anew the ever-wonderful-and-delightful *Peter Pan*, and whatever else happens. Shall I find you there as usual?

I have read the whole of the Elizabethan Dramatists through in 3 days.

With his position of authority in the School enabling him to feel more man than boy, he now began to let his hair exceed the regulation length, and since only black ties were allowed, the colour not the material being specified, he risked the purchase of a 'puff' tie of black *crêpe de Chine*, a somewhat insurrectionary touch with

[1] E. L. D. Cole, form-master of the Lower Bench of the VIth.

which he knew he could get away. But the new year 1906 found him still in bed. The entire household was running a high fever of its own. There was a General Election. Parker Brooke himself accompanied the Liberal candidate, Corrie Grant, when he made his deposition; Richard and Alfred were canvassing; Mrs. Brooke was having strangers to tea and converting them to Liberalism over the scones, and she was so carried away as to allow Rupert out of the house before he was fully recovered. At Corrie Grant's Committee Rooms he began editing a Liberal news-sheet called *The Rugby Elector* which—if the main contributor is to be believed, for no copies have survived—startled its readers every other day throughout the first fortnight of January with its mounting abuse of the Conservative candidate.

In the midst of the turmoil in the Committee Rooms he wrote to Keynes who was about to stay with friends in Germany. 'Isn't this absurd and delightful? We are having a ferocious fight down here, in which I am taking a great part . . . You figure me, covered with Liberal rosettes, rushing about the town . . . I have made 37 mortal enemies in 4 days. And the immense joke of the matter is that I really take no interest in politics at all.' Tomorrow the boys were coming back for the Lent Term. He was beginning to feel superannuated. 'It is terrible to feel that one is exchanging the cynicism of youth for the bright optimism of manhood; it is very sad to outgrow one's disillusions.'

Then came the climax of the political campaign, and he went down to the local branch of the Liberal Club to hear the results of the polls. 'When the result of Balfour's degradation came there was a tremendous scene,' he wrote to Erica. 'I fell on the neck of a whiskered and bespectacled nonconformist minister who stood near me and we both wept in silent joy.' He told her he was now posing as 'a rabid Socialist', though he wasn't quite sure what that signified. He did not know that this Liberal victory, repeated throughout the country, would have a profound effect on his life. From this moment a comparatively obscure movement, fostered by a group of distinguished intellectuals who were agitating for social reform and calling themselves Fabians, began to win more followers, spreading its influence through every walk of life. And already that aspect of Fabianism which will bulk so large on a later page had come into being. Shortly before Christmas, almost the last act of the Balfour government was to appoint a Royal Commission to look into the whole question of the Poor Law, and among those nominated was a Fabian, Mrs. Sidney Webb, who up to now had played no public role on the political scene.

The school Debating Society was also making him give some thought to the world at large. On January 27 he undertook to oppose the motion 'That this House deplores the growth of the Labour Party in the House of Commons'. Philip Guedalla seconded him in opposition, but nevertheless the motion was carried by 40 votes to 18. Rupert contended that it was absurd that in a so-called representative Parliament 'the working classes (five-sixths of the whole country)' should not be properly represented, and he complained that through 'ignorant prejudice and class feeling' the supporters of the Labour Party were all too often subjected to misrepresentation in the press. 'A man who has risen from working as a common labourer to being elected by his fellows to Parliament,' he said, 'must needs be an able and talented man. He is called "uneducated", but he has received the best of trainings—the experience of the hardships and problems of life . . . Liberty will make its voice heard in *some* way. We should welcome the chance of letting it make itself felt by a peaceful and constitutional revolution.' The school magazine described it as 'a very able speech'. It was the opening bar of one of the main themes in his life. It was a start, but a false start, for other concerns, more immediate, crowded politics out of his life in the months to come.

On March 20 he addressed the same society again, this time proposing the motion that the House deplored the present state of the English drama. He said he found it neither amusing nor instructive and its atmosphere was stifling and moribund. As for musical comedy it was only funny when it was vulgar; in the spoken drama the actor-manager, not the play, was the centre of attraction, and all *he* gave thought to, beyond his own performance, was the scenery. It was a pity that Rupert was not speaking from the other side of the House. He had only seen one musical comedy, *Véronique*, which hardly deserved his stricture, though without an ear to appreciate Messager's score it must have seemed thin stuff. His sweeping attack on the drama was based on the practice of Tree at His Majesty's, and the productions of Stephen Phillips in particular, one of which, *Nero*, had recently opened there. His main experience of the drama, flying visits to the Vedrenne-Barker seasons at the Court, could not possibly be brought in or he would have blown his argument to pieces and played into the hands of the opposition. Of *John Bull's Other*

Island, for instance, he would soon be writing to Keynes. 'It is unspeakably delightful. The average of acting all round at the Court is exactly four times as high as at any other theatre in London. Each character is perfect. And the play itself is exquisite, wonderful, terrific, an unapproachable satire on everything.'

The Shaw plays had first opened his eyes to the problems of social reform, but at this stage he would never have dreamed of doing anything about these problems himself. He could present a good enough case in debate, but it did not necessarily reflect his real opinions. It was purely academic. 'My present pose is as a Socialist,' he wrote to Lucas on the day before the Labour Party debate, 'and as most of the present Rugbeians hail from that "upper-middle-class" of England which regards Socialists as demons only one degree in the ranks of the Pit less wicked than Artists, I have quaint and pleasant arguments.' At present, Socialism was little more than a means, an effective weapon in the aesthetic campaign against the Philistine middle-class. It had no connexion in Rupert's eyes with anything that really mattered to him, especially the art of poetry. The two seemed worlds apart. If ever he were to discover a link between them, the game of politics might become a crusade.

Yet again he was suffering from pink-eye—'The disease comes,' he said, 'of gazing too often on Butterfield's architecture'—and advising Erica, since she had asked to be shown the light of culture, to acquire and inwardly digest 'one third of Swinburne, all Oscar Wilde, and the drawings of Beardsley'. Were it not for his *culte* of the nineties, one would describe him at this time as an ardent spirit in search of a cause, for the Decadence was beginning to wear a little thin; it was degenerating in his mind to the level of politics and becoming a lark. Early this term he dined with the headmaster, and sat next another member of the staff who had to admit he 'disliked' the work of Beardsley. Rupert retorted that he adored him because he 'caricatured Humanity', and he was amused by caricatures of Humanity. 'As I spoke I beamed on him, but he did not grasp the insult: he was merely impressed and bit his nails in wonder and perplexity.' In the same letter to Keynes he admitted that even their good friend Russell-Smith was beginning to lose patience 'because I have affected several new creeds, including the worship of Moloch and Bi-metallism. I have converted half the House to Socialism and the rest to Mormonism. I was almost lynched the other day for saying that at the age of eight I deserted the Church of England for

81

Christianity: at the age of eighteen I am deserting "Christianity" for the teaching of Christ.' This was no more seriously meant than his advocacy of the rites of Moloch. The absence in his life of any form of religion, whether organized or unorganized, indeed his rooted antipathy to it, as belonging to the Philistines, was causing a vacuum, for he had the natural fervour of a born martyr, and he was beginning to live in sore need of a sacrificial altar he could lie down on in earnest and not in playful jest. 'The pale ululation of a bell reminds me of supper,' he ends his letter to Keynes. He must give thought to his prep and 'other barbaric survivals. The Dawn has not yet come . . .' In a sense that he did not intend, how true that was.

During the first half of this year, however, there broke the dawn of a conscious poet. The first hint of it appeared in the second issue of *The Venture* printed in January, 1906. Rupert contributed three Fables, and the first of them is interesting. It tells how twelve men, poets or minstrels in an age of legend, each made 'a new song of beauty'. After they had all died, yet another minstrel came along; he heard or read the songs of his twelve forerunners 'and took the beautiful soul out of each of them and, disguising them very subtly with fair odorous words, wrought therefrom a new song'. This last poet himself then dies, goes to heaven, sees twelve thrones standing near the throne of God, and looks around expectantly to find the thirteenth, more splendid than all the others, which will no doubt be destined for himself. Instead, however, the Almighty banishes him altogether from the Presence—'for thy song was not thine own'. Rupert had learned a lesson and summed it up by writing for his classmates an allegory of special significance to his own case. From now on we should expect him to show in his verses a less slavish devotion to 'the twelve poets' who had gone before him, the *fin de siècle* heroes of 'Bobbie Longman'.

III

'Four days ago,' he wrote to Keynes on March 10, 'the Spring, violet crowned and with laughter in her eyes, danced into England . . . The English pale blue sky, the warm wind, laden with fragrances of immortal youth, the joy in the heart, have filled me with divine rapture. I am maddened and inspired to do anything. It is just such an English Spring as I wept for in the arid heat of Italy, a year ago.'

Keynes had won a money prize for an essay on Roman archaeology and was now wondering what books he should buy. Inevitably, Rupert's advice included Browning and Swinburne, but it's noteworthy that as early as this the short list should have featured Webster and Marlowe, two of the special enthusiasms of his later years. And the book-list ended with what we may guess was an expression of new confidence disguised as a joke—'Collected Poems. R.C.B. (42s. net. Printed in France. Very scarce.)'

The editor of *The Venture* had just rejected a poem of his, and, wishful perhaps to avoid any more lost lilies and the like, had asked him to 'do something funny'. The reaction to this was 'I smiled dangerously, and told them that *this* was meant to be funny. They believed, gulped twice, and expired. The lie was a good one—better than the very Wild(e) verses.' This was his first and last editorial rejection. Meanwhile he sampled every method. 'I have just written a title and I am trying to think of a book for it,' he told Russell-Smith. 'The title is *Aphrodite and the Lamp-post.*'

As was surely bound to happen, his combination of poetical and physical prowess had given rise to an awkwardness. It came to his ear that a boy in another house had asked the school photographer for a copy of his portrait. 'It appears the madman worships me at a pale distance, which is embarrassing, but purple,' ran the account sent to Keynes in Germany. 'So I wander around, taking a huge delight in the whole mad situation.' It was embarrassing because he was not by nature drawn to a romantic liaison of this kind, and it was purple because it held promise of another opportunity in the anti-Philistine war. He considered that there was a certain amount of conventional hypocrisy about such things, and this provided him with a chance to make a gesture of protest. 'It is my obvious duty,' he wrote, 'to live the aesthetic life I preach, and break the laws I loathe.' Borrowing the name Antinous from a figure in one of Simeon Solomon's paintings, and being still laid up with ophthalmia, forbidden to read, and frantic for something to do, he began to conduct an illicit correspondence. 'What he thinks of my epistles I cannot imagine.' However, he took pains to see they were written in—

good and musical English with a tendency to over-elaboration. In parts they recall the Song of Solomon—indeed they are often in imitation of that wonderful purple ecstasy. I usually address him as Hyacinth, Apollo, or Antinous, and end with a quotation from Swinburne or Catullus. I bring in odorous and jewelled phrases 'The Greek gods lived that you might be likened to them: the world was created that you might be made of gold and ivory: the fragrance of your face is myrrh and incense before the pale altar of Beauty.' I frequently add a postscript containing fifty adjectives and an exclamation mark. I don't know what he thinks of such communications; but if he has any literary sense, they must do him a lot of good.

He was not only bored, but vexed that his illness had delayed the family's departure for Italy. The large party of boys he should have accompanied had already gone ahead. However, he had discovered an intellectual distraction of sorts. He had decided to compete for the principal prize of the year known as the King's Medal for Prose. The set subject was not at first glance inspiring—'Estimate the debt that England owes to William III', so as usual he appealed to Lucas for help. 'He was a king or something, they say, of the time of Congreve and Wycherley. Of England I know nothing.' He would get the books Lucas might recommend and make them his home-work abroad.

My soul is sick for Venice. I have painted it to myself in odorous vernal words, and I think it will be more beautiful than all my dreams. I shall sit in a gondola and pour forth satires in heroic verse, or moral diatribes in blank verse. Intense surroundings always move me to write in an opposite vein. I gaze on New Big School and give utterance to frail diaphanous lyrics, sudden and beautiful as a rose-petal.

The books on William of Orange were packed and Erica received news of imminent departure.

If on Monday Ap. 9th you go to the entrance of Victoria you may soon see passing (at about 11 a.m.) a cab. On the top will be 9 large boxes labelled Venice belonging to Mother and Father, and a small parcel with my things and Podge's. Inside will be Father very irritated and excited, Mother trying to put me tidy, Podge *very* nervous at the thought of the Channel, and last, with a broad smile of vast delight,

Your patient cousin
RUPERT BROOKE

But this Italian adventure was even less satisfactory than last year's. 'Sometimes I sat in the vaporous gloom of St. Mark's,' he wrote to Lucas, 'and, gazing on the mosaics, mused on all my religions, till everything became confused, the grand pulpit changed to an altar of Moloch, the figure of Mary grew like Isis, and the fair Byzantine Christ was lost in the delicate troubled form of Antinous.' In Germany Keynes received a less highly-coloured version of these discontents.

Venice is an American colony, chiefly peopled by Germans. There is also a small Italian element in the population. It is still a little out of date, but the steamers and hotels are rapidly supplanting the old-fashioned gondolas and palaces. It promises soon to be a First-Class Popular Holiday Resort . . . I am really very grieved. They told me that I was going to a city of dreams, 'an opal betwixt sky and sea', and with my young-eyed simplicity, I believed them. We arrived at midnight and were rowed to our hotel by strong moon-light between sleeping palaces. That was lovely, and five days ago. Since then I have persuaded myself with more difficulty every day, that I am en-joying myself. Today I have finally abandoned the attempt, and confess that I hate it. It is hot and malodorous. The Venetian painters are mostly shams, more or less gorgeous. Their palaces have been turned into first-class hotels, or over-decorated. And the place is befouled by a mob of shrieking tourists. Moreover my family are extremely obnoxious people to travel with. (This evil English is brought on by an even more evil Italian brass band hard by.) I wonder if the country of your adoption is adequately represented by the specimens of it one meets here. If so, I pity you very deeply. They are very oily and guttural. But what can you expect of a country that calls this place Venedig when it might say Venezia?

After ten days the family spent a few hours in Padua and Verona, then went on to Paris. There was time for a look at the Louvre before recurrent 'labour troubles' again worried Mrs. Brooke, and they arrived back at Rugby some days before they were expected. On the way Rupert branched off to see Eckersley and pay his first visit to Oxford. 'I understand your prose style much better after seeing Keble and Balliol,' he wrote to Lucas from the O.U.D.S. club room, making a good critical point. He had no more to say of Oxford. On the way home he went to a matinee of *Don Juan in Hell* at the Court, and arrived home very late. It was the first week of May. 'I am never really happy except at Rugby in the Summer Term,' he had written from an address given as 'Margate, Italy', and he meant it. So much of his girding at the powers that be at Rugby was nothing more than a gesture to his obligations as an aesthete. He also meant what he wrote to Keynes.

The Summer Term has dawned. It is my last, and I weep. The same fan-tastic things happen, there is that strange throng of young beings, uncon-scious of all their youth and wonder. Another Spring dies odorously in Summer . . . But I am quite happy. To be here is wonderful, and suffices. I live in a mist of golden dreams. Afterwards life will come, cold and terrible. At present I am a child.

It was true. Dr. Arnold himself did not consider separation from the parents an essential part of his educational system. It occurred in-evitably where there were boarders, but in itself it was not neces-sarily a good thing in his view. One is tempted to speculate what effect this normal feature of public school life would have had on

Rupert, and to conclude that at the age of eighteen he would in some respects have been less of a child. He had been too long housed with his family and too close to it, for him to have discovered himself in that alarming freedom from family ties which is the boarder's one compensation for the ache and misery of home-sickness. Although the ordinary life of a boarding school away from home cannot be the right thing for all children, it would probably have been better for Rupert. There was nothing wrong with his school, but he should have been sent to another house. His mother had too strong a personality for him not to waste too much mental energy either deliberately agreeing or disagreeing with her, more often the latter, so that opposition of some sort was becoming almost a mannerism. It is clear that he received the criticism and was left to take the love she felt for granted. In the bosom of his family he was lonely, left to find a way of getting on without the commonplace but precious nourishment of tenderness; and succeeded, which tended all the more to make sentiment seem to him unnecessary and suspect. The release of warmth in his nature, or rather the discovery of it, both in himself and in someone else, might prove all but overwhelming, if it were deferred until his full maturity. Something in him underdeveloped and unevoked would come into being and mature within weeks instead of years, and the disturbance in a sensitive spirit inured to loneliness and capable of passionate feeling might not be a flooding sweetness but panic and unbalance. 'Afterwards life will come cold and terrible.' He was no less afraid of slipping the apron-strings for being unconscious of them. He was indeed sated with security, and he grappled his friends, especially Keynes and Russell-Smith, with hoops of steel. Lucas was an old man by comparison, and so in a different category, on the farther side of the Rubicon of adolescence. To him, in the second week of term, Rupert wrote, 'After this term is over the world awaits. But I do not now care what will come then. Only, my present happiness is so great that I fear the jealous gods will requite me afterwards with some terrible punishment, death, perhaps—or life'.

A week or two later, on his study table at School Field were lying a Latin dictionary, Baudelaire, Theocritus, and Pater, a bowl of wallflowers, and a small Venetian vase of forget-me-nots. Through the stage property lutes and rose-leaves one can detect the sincerity of a young man consciously on the 'threshold' when he sat writing to Keynes:

The gods are dealing very kindly with me. My days are filled with the sound of failing lutes and falling rose-leaves. I am beginning to value the things around me more every day, the good and the bad in them. This school-life, with its pathetic transience and immense vitality, calls to me with a charm all the more insistent that I am soon to lose it. In the gigantic game I play my part with zest, alternately 'siding' and ragging, yet always inwardly laughing, not in malice. The others are so beautifully unconscious: I am both actor and spectator.

He now added a blue ribbon to his plain white straw hat (signifying his place in the first XI), was excused certain lessons, and could take almost any liberty with the regulations, within reason, except turn up late for Chapel. After all, he had to be looked up to as an example. He was just under six-foot in height, his head, with noticeably small ears, poised well on a rather long neck. The slight upward turn of the nose, as delicately moulded as his other features, seemed to give his whole lithe frame an attitude of eagerness that matched his facial expression. The very fair hair with a reddish tinge in it looked ready to grow luxuriantly if allowed. It seemed a shame to cut it, so it wasn't, and a toss of the head from right to left, to shift the hair from his forehead, became a characteristic gesture. People in the streets of Rugby looked round as he passed. He was not so unambitious as to be sorry that he was not inconspicuous. In fact he was *very* ambitious, so why not be top in looks as well as Greek?

The *Eranos* literary society was making demands on him again. He chose as his subject not the agreeable and too much neglected James Thomson of *The Seasons*—to a loyal decadent the eighteenth century barely qualified for consideration—but the Victorian author the title of whose principal work alone was enough to win serious attention—*The City of Dreadful Night*. In June when *Nero*, the verse drama by Stephen Phillips, was a current topic, he wrote to Lucas:

I am finishing my paper on James Thomson. I have cut out all the wicked parts, but I still fear for the reception. Last week we had a paper on T. Gray. The stupendous ass who wrote and read it, after referring to The Elegy as 'a fine lyric', ended with the following incomparable words: 'In conclusion then, we may give Gray a place among the greatest poets, above all, except perhaps Shakespeare, Milton, and Tennyson.'

This lewd remark roused me from the carefully studied pose of irritating and sublime nonchalance which I assume on such occasions. I arose and made acid and quite unfair criticisms of Gray and Tennyson, to the concealed delight of all the avowed Philistines there, and the open disgust of the professing 'lovers of literature'.

I was nearly slain.

When is the novel to appear? Pray be swift to save us; or I shall think English Literature is dead, and turn my attention to writing purple poly-syllables for Tree? Did you see the bowdlerized decadent? I suppose the scenery looked extremely valuable. I dare not witness it. Nero is one of the few illusions I have left. All my others are departing one by one. I read a book recently which proved that Apollo was an aged Chieftain who lived in Afghanistan and had four wives and cancer of the stomach: and the other day I found myself—my last hope!—acting on moral principles.

In a previous letter to Lucas he had shown a sign of progress in his own verse. Denis Browne, who often deputized for the Chapel organist these days, asked for a poem to set to music. The result was a piece called 'An Easter-Day Song in Praise of Cremation, written to my Lady Corsyra'. 'I am eager to hear the music,' Rupert remarked, but it's hard to believe that he ever did, the poem being wildly difficult to set. However Browne, who has his niche in the history of English *Lieder*, may have been equal to it, in which case he was a genius indeed. It is the earliest of Rupert's 'ugly' poems, in which he is as strenuously uncompromising as he was formerly determined to evade any kind of reality, and the last two lines are the first of that metaphysical brand of wit that would characterize the best of his work in years to come. He tells Lucas that it is 'closely modelled' on Baudelaire's 'The Corpse'. In what must be a version revised in consultation with Browne the poem describes his dread of interment in the earth, and concludes with these two stanzas:

> In that unwilling bridal of the tomb
> > To lie
> Through the slow hours of stifling gloom
> In shameful, helpless agony,
> > Changed by the worm's unnatural cold lust
> > To slime and dust!

> —Rather for me the sudden flame's embrace,
> > Which clings
> Once! . . . and therewith thy perfect face
> Shall fade, the last of mortal things.
> > So for all time I'll quench my hot desire
> > In that clean fire.

Here again is 'the face' of that earlier poem called 'Nameless at present'. The face itself is still nameless, and the poem is still no more than an exercise. It is too soon, however, to assume that he has out-grown the nineties, but at least we know that the sixteenth century, where his gift more properly belonged, has come into his life by this June of 1906. 'A poet should write, for himself, for God, and for one reader—probably ideal. The poems written in the last way always seem to me the best. Is that heresy?' Rupert asked Lucas later that month. If the 'one reader' in the present instance was Browne—it couldn't have been Lucas—then the musician has the credit of having started his friend writing in what at least was, for him, a promising way.

The paper on Thomson read one Sunday evening soon after this was an ambitious piece and an important one for our purpose, for it reflected on the change in Rupert's own verse, and, looking into it, the reason why at this time the subject appealed to him is evident.

He begins by clearing the ground, dismissing with contumely the other poet of the same name. He was '18th century in date and every-thing else. He wrote "Rule Britannia", but was otherwise of a blame-less life'. So much for the author of *The Castle of Indolence*. As for this one, Rupert had counted eight second-hand book shops in Charing Cross Road, but not one of them possessed his works. Nor could he find a book about him, so his audience must put up with his own bad criticism. 'Haunted by an inherited vice of dipsomania,' he was the greatest pessimist poet in English, perhaps in any literature. He saw the world as 'an immense poison-tree of life, with its leaves of illu-sions, blossoms of delirium, apples of destruction' which could never be changed because the venom of its sap was drawn from the taproots sunk in the abysmal depths of the past. Thomson hated tyranny and, above all, hypocrisy. He wrote his poems—

> *Because a cold rage seizes one at whiles*
> *To show the bitter, old, and wrinkled truth*
> *Stripped naked of all vesture that beguiles—*
> *False dreams, false hopes, false masks and modes of*
> *youth . . .*

'Thomson, if any man, wrote from personal experience and convic-tion. . . He had the courage of his convictions, a phenomenon rare enough in England even then to be unpopular. . . His work naturally enough does not appeal to a large public: he is not often pretty, silly, or weak; among all his temptations and vices he never committed the sin of writing down to the common taste.' Although to Thomson only Death was immortal, his starkness—'Live out your candid love,' he wrote, 'hate out your hate'—and his grimness are redeemed at times by flashes of a crude and sombre grandeur

> *Though brief, each day a golden sun has birth.*
> *Though dim, the night is gemmed with stars and moon.*

Between attending his father's lessons in Homer, given in his own study at School Field, playing cricket, helping Mrs. Brooke at the garden party given in her garden, playing tennis with members of the VIth on his father's tennis court, he was soon preparing another paper for the *Eranos* group. Modern Poetry was the theme. For once he did not invoke Lucas's aid, but told him, 'I have written them a rhapsody in prose modelled on Pater's "Leonardo" and interspersed with such sentences as "Beauty cannot be moral or immoral: it is white or coloured: that is all"',' and he enclosed another variation on the theme of 'the face', not as promising as the last. 'Some day I shall rise and leave my friends,' he begins, and goes in search for his former love, and finds 'The face that was all my sunrising' not in death but in withered old age, 'And my heart is sick with memories'.

He was becoming methodical in his efforts to learn the art of poetry, and on the cover of a school exercise book had written Word Book. In this he noted new words as he came upon them in his reading: slidder, sluther, ombrifuge, extravasate, arachnoid, windlestraws, etc.; some had a more common synonym in brackets: tortive (twisted), a frippery (a shop where old clothes were sold), and he notes that 'slope' can be used as an adjective. On another page he makes a memorandum of remarks he has admired: Keats writing of an acquaintance, 'He is just spilt. He ought to be wiped up'; or Dryden— 'There are who, wanting wit, affect gravity, and go by the name of solid men; and a solid man is, in plain English, a solid, solemn, fool'; on a loose leaf tucked in the cover, waiting to come in useful one day, is an isolated sentence of his own, part of a parody, perhaps, of Lucas's jewelled prose—'Strange night-creatures twittered the epithalamium of day and darkness, and the Occident was scarlet with hymenaeal flames.' There are several quotations from Shelley's letters to Peacock and John or Maria Gisborne, such as 'Some of us have in a prior existence been in love with an Antigone, and that makes us find no full content in any mortal life.' It may be that these prose entries were made at a slightly later date, as also the only word in the Word Book which ever came into his poems—'Arval-bread = baked meats'.[1]

On Speech Day he mounted the platform to receive the King's Medal for Prose. His essay on England's debt to William III had achieved its end. After him, one of his friends, A. D. Schloss (Arthur Waley) was called up to receive the Latin Prize. The prize essay was an accomplished piece of prose, though it began by stating that setting out to portray the monarch in question 'one needs the sombre dirges of Elizabethan blank verse for full comprehension'. In him we come up against 'the intolerable gloom of Puritanism'. The author had been to the National Portrait Gallery to have a look at him. 'Immediately he strikes one as being a stranger. His narrow cold face contrasts strangely with the sneering artificiality of James and the German complaisance of Anne.' Then follow observations of the kind an examiner would enjoy, such as 'But William was far from being a second Galba'. If another Stuart had succeeded to the throne instead of William 'Canada, the most satisfactory part of our Empire would certainly now be French, and perhaps India also'. Rupert ended by pointing out that the lesson of the revolution of 1688, which brought absolute monarchy to an end, was a lesson that every nation must learn. 'France learned it a century later; Russia is only now beginning to learn it. The price of it must always be paid in human lives and suffering, and it is our peculiar glory that we of all nations have learnt it most cheaply and most endurably.'

Rupert was never very strong in health for long at a stretch, and the illness was hard to specify. He nearly missed the great day of the prize-giving owing to what is influenza in one letter, hay-fever in another, and ophthalmia in yet another, which may be summarized at a guess as the inevitable pink-eye and a temperature from the effort to get the essay done in time. And now he was due to read his last paper to the *Eranos* on what would be the last Sunday evening of term. He was conscious that it would be his last appearance as a schoolboy. He complained to Erica that he already felt gnarled with age. She had the grace to protest, 'As to your pretending to think I'm not old,' he replied, 'I laugh! Age is not a matter of fact, it is a

---

[1]
> *I shall not hear your trentals,*
> *Nor eat your arval bread;*
> *For the kin of you will surely do*
> *Their duty by the dead.*

from *Lines Written in the Belief that the Ancient Roman Festival of the Dead was called Ambarvalia*, written in 1910. G.K., p. 92.

matter of soul. I am forty-seven. Of course I *pretend* to be young occasionally just to amuse people.' And then the bell went for supper. 'I go to nibble petulantly at a biscuit. I am starving myself in an effort to become ethereal.'

When the last Sunday evening came, Whitelaw, Parker Brooke, Alfred, and several others not eligible for membership of the *Eranos*, joined the boys of the VIth in Old Big School for Rupert's farewell appearance with his paper on modern poetry. 'We know that when the last oracle had been uttered,' he began, 'and the old shrines deserted, the gods, having no worshippers left, went out into the world and took service under the new order of things, each choosing, where possible, some congenial occupation.' As for the Muses they were many of them now alive in England. 'And if you hear a man deny it (unless it be a poet in a moment of despondency) you will know him for a poor pedant, blind and deaf.' Melpomene, for instance, has a walking-on part at His Majesty's, and Erato is a barmaid at Euston station. Anyway, his audience could judge of their continued existence by the variety of living poets he would bring to them this evening. He had found only one comprehensive book on the modern poets. It was by William Archer and the most that could be said about it was that it weighed 2 lb. 12 oz. Though Swinburne was still alive, there were no great figures active in poetry, but that was no excuse to despond.

Do not listen to my quotations with a sneer in your souls because they are 'minor poetry'. People who speak disparagingly of minor poetry are either stockbrokers and lawyers and rich practical people who don't understand, or reviewers in the Press, who are always young men fresh from a university with souls so stuffed full of intellectual pride that they might as lightly speak of minor roses or minor sunsets.

First he took the poets of what he called the material, modern world, and chief of these was Kipling. He traded in blood and victory 'and other sentiments that came to a head during the late Boer War'. He agreed with the critic who said that turning over the pages of Kipling 'one feels as if one was sitting under a palm tree, reading life by flashes of superb vulgarity'. Then there was Henley, who stood for what was best in imperialism. 'One may hate, as I do, the *way* in which he loved England, but one cannot deny the sincerity of his love and the power of his expression of it.' He then read the whole of 'What have I done for you, England, my England?' also 'The Last Post' beginning 'Blow, you bugles of England, blow'—the theme on which one of his own war sonnets would be a variation. Henley's themes were Speed, the Sword, Wine, Passion, without any curious question of their value. With him Rupert associated William Watson, who was more patriotic than imperial, a more accomplished craftsman than either Kipling or Henley, and one who had the good sense to oppose the Boer War, but unfortunately 'too often his style is that of the art that reveals art and conceals inspiration'.

Then there were the poets of the Celtic Revival, the Irish poets of hope and failure. 'They belong to a weak nation, part of a great empire, but they cannot accept the imperial spirit; their ideals are not of material wealth; they weary of modern industrialism, so they revive the old mythologies. . . And in their thin half-forgotten mythology, their vague symbolism, the misty loveliness of their language and their measures, they endeavour rather to hint at than attain the secrets of beauty beyond precise conception.' Yeats was the best of these. Although he seemed these days to have given up verse for prose, he was essentially a poet, and Rupert read aloud, 'Had I the heaven's embroidered cloths'. Having quoted Yeats, he wanted to make a transition to the more characteristic poets of the nineties, and his first thought was to clear the mind of the bogus decadence, before coming to the real thing. On second thoughts he cancelled the passage, but it should be given here for its evidence that the speaker knew what was false—'true' decadence, he calls it— when he saw it.

It is quite natural and suitable that an ordinary modern should write and read verse with far-sought epithets, strained meanings, and intricate harmonies. The true decadence comes when the dweller in cities revolts against his civilization, puts on a smock over his frock-coat, and goes out into the country, hoe in hand, singing unnaturally simple harvest songs.

Instead of this he led straight in to that other school of poets which was not, he said, unrelated to the Celtic Revival, but it was English and in his opinion of much greater interest. The key-note of this poetry was modern, but also timeless.

It whispered indeed through the poetry of every age, but of late the whisper has grown into a cry insistent and very plaintive. It is one of the key-notes of modern art. From Botticelli and da Vinci this secret has passed into the tired beautiful faces of Burne-Jones's women and the sad mystery of modern landscape-painting. It is the Spirit of Autumn, of weariness, of decadence.

They are pale and listless because they have seen the face of Death between the roses. By far the best of these poets was Dowson who died only six years ago. 'With a body ruined by sin and intemperance and the soul of a poet,' he created a new sigh, as when Victor Hugo said to Baudelaire, 'You have created a new shudder'—bringing a sigh or a tear 'as near to faint music as speech can come'. With this the speaker read aloud the poem to Cynara and remarked:

When you have listened to the great poets and their gospels, and grown weary of the hot splendour of their passion, the high majesty of their genius, or when, with some other moderns, you have explored the abysses of your own soul and return sick and frightened, it is pleasant to find refuge in such poetry as this, that strives not for the eternal verities, but deals in faint exquisite words of a man's vision, being full of 'a pathos too young and too frail ever to grow old'.

He then talked of the French influence, first evident in Swinburne and Rossetti and all those poets of the decadence who were 'neither popular nor morally improving'. It was a characteristic ingredient of modern verse. 'With much that is beautiful it combines an exotic deadly charm.' But why was this? Or, rather, how? 'It is the music of perversity, sensuous and mystical, telling of evil secrets and haunted twilights, finding a sudden beauty in ugliness, terrible harmonies out of discord. At times, like heavy incense, it wearies one with an almost physical oppression.'

In contrast with these there were a few poets who achieved their effects through simplicity. Chief of these, in the lecturer's opinion, was one whose name would probably be new to his audience—A. E. Housman. 'I wonder how many have heard that name as a poet's.' He was best known, perhaps, as the editor of Juvenal. About twenty years before he had published a few poems in a little book, but nothing since. They did not merit their obscurity.

Their matter is nothing much out of the ordinary, little countrified songs in a vein of pessimistic but healthy quietism. In form they incline towards doggerel, being generally of the utmost simplicity of phrase and metre. Yet through them all there is a very undeniable ring of poetry.

He had no time to do more than mention Meredith, who must be shelved, literally, as a classic, and 'through mere prejudice I have omitted such established "minor" poets as Theodore Watts Dunton and Robert Bridges'; he threw in the names of John Davidson and Wilde as poets who had revived the ballad form, and if the clock were not showing signs of impatience he would have read aloud a deftly turned trifle or two by Austin Dobson. He came abruptly to his peroration, which began as an apology for the number of his readings—

Many of them must have failed, for poetry read or heard for the first time can only convince if the moment be in tune with it. So one should read *A Shropshire Lad* on an autumn morning when there is a brave nip of frost in the air and the year is sliding quietly toward death.

Perhaps his readings from Dowson, though, stood a better chance with his hearers.

These surely are in tune with an evening like this, when the light is fading and the air is cool with late rain, and the roses, with the Summer Term, have almost come to an end.

A few days later the school broke up. Last term there had been a family row over his report, his contention being that he had already done his job by winning a scholarship. It was unreasonable to expect any more of him, academically, for the present. This view was not shared by Parker Brooke, but now the headmaster's report for the Trinity Term, 1906, was to hand and considered, as Tooler would put it, 'quite useful'. Rupert's place was ninth in the Upper Bench of twenty-one boys.

His work is more uneven than that of any boy in the form; he either dislikes details or has no capacity for them. But when he is good—on the purely literary side of his work and scholarship he is capable of very brilliant results, and in English composition he *must* make a name. Always a delightful boy to work with. I am very sorry to lose him.

He had been very happy, but now he was not only downcast but conscious of a deep disquiet. Keynes, back from Germany, joined him at School Field, which somewhat restored the situation, and the two of them travelled up for the annual Rugby v. Marlborough match at Lord's where Keynes watched his friend bowl to good effect, making two good catches, but score a duck.

From his private window overlooking Barby Road, Rupert watched the departure of luggage and excited children. The small boys looked so much smaller than he could ever have been himself. It was absurd to want to stay among them any longer. In two days' time he would be nineteen—and lamenting to Russell-Smith that 'Father Time has turned yet another leaf in that Great Book which has no plot and very little local colour'—but it was something bigger than merely leaving school that he had to face. The thought of Cambridge was not so much a dread as an enormous and vaguely forbidding blank. He must also leave home.

Chapter IV

FRESHMAN

(*August 1906–March 1908*)

'At school friendship is a passion,' wrote Disraeli in *Coningsby*.
'It entrances the being; it tears the soul.' In the same vein
Rupert wrote to Keynes from the unearthly quiet that prevailed at School Field where he had just moped away his nineteenth
birthday. 'It is not fashionable to feel these things deeply. But this
deserted Rugby is Hell, and I am a pale ghost who has lived, and can
now only dream.' So he packed and went off to stay with the Russell-
Smiths at Brockenhurst. At Watersgreen House there was a young
family of brothers and sisters, a tennis-court, a hammock, and the
Browning he had been reading in the train, and he was in no hurry to
rejoin his own family circle that seldom made light of things and was
given to such long silences at meals. He was enjoying himself, but
Lucas must be given a more 'aesthetic' impression. 'This New
Forest is sad with the prescience of Autumn; and at sunset and dawn
the little hollow places are full of sudden white mists; and the earth is
covered with dead brown leaves, and the pines shake with many
tears. The stillness and solitude here frighten me, for there are
memories and visions, and one hears other voices whispering in the
heart. I should like to be in London, in the crowds and the noise,
where one can be silent and alone. Write to me.'

Within a few days he was off again to the Rugby Home Mission
Camp at New Romney, where boys from the impoverished back areas
of Notting Hill were taught to observe the rules of cricket and read
something a little more improving than *Chums*. Lucas had announced
he was going to France. There lay his chance of a longer reprieve. It
was that or Rugby, and he wanted to avoid being there, hanging
about, when the boys came back. 'I had rather be anywhere else in the
world. In Touraine I should be very disagreeable and quite silent,
but I might be useful for carrying things.' In the meantime there was

nothing for it but to go home after his three days of duty at the Camp.

It looked as if he were going to be taken on a shopping expedition to Cambridge. 'You will come with me,' he appealed to Keynes, 'and help curb my fantastic family's taste for suburban furniture and puce wall-papers.' He was afraid, he said, that his last year as Head of the House had left a permanent mark on his character and qualified him for the melancholy epitaph 'In trying to be respected he became respectable'. The Cambridge jaunt, however, was somehow evaded and an invitation extracted from the convenient aunts at Bournemouth. Lucas was ill, so that way of escape was blocked. 'I had dreams of dying quietly in France . . . my few conscious moments soothed by you reading Baudelaire. But now alas! I shall expire vulgarly at Bournemouth; and they will bury me on the shore, near the bandstand.' He was bored and listless, and wrote asking Erica if she was still alive. 'I suppose you are? Do you like it? I have rather forgotten the feeling. Come and lay a few lilies on my grave soon, it is rather bare.'

He was now at Grantchester Dene where, having just ploughed through *Sordello*, he got down to a serious study of Baudelaire. He always seemed to have the most unsuitable books with him at Aunt Fanny's. Not long before it was *De Profundis*. Now he was seated between his aunts on the promenade reading *Les Fleurs du Mal*, or drafting a parody of Lucas's next romantic novel which he had seen in manuscript and was due out in September. 'It begins with my famous simile about the moon,' he wrote to Lucas, 'but soon gets much more lewd.' This simile, in which the moon is likened to 'an enormous yellow scab on the livid flesh of some leper', was evidently not tried out on Aunt Fanny or she might never have given him the cushion for his room at King's, a substantial bolster covered with pale green 'plushette'.

Keynes had contributed some Beardsley reproductions, and Erica also sent him a picture. The kindness of the thought was more apparent than the actual theme depicted.

The long green sky will give my rooms that air of placidity and restfulness which I generally so lamentably lack; and the mauve but magnificent sheep have a bucolic charm of colouring and gesture that quite captivates my rustic soul. You must come to Cambridge and see it in position on the bright yellow walls that grace my future abode. By what title to call the Picture I have not yet decided. Can you help me? Suggestions have been made: 'Cattle ranching in the Pyrennees', 'The Intense Shepherd', 'Gadara', 'A Posture in Puce', 'Mr. Tree as David watching the sheep in the first Act of S. Phillips' new play *David*' or 'A Tale of Old Palestine'—and others.

The plan was to go home, collect his luggage and a parental blessing, then leave for Cambridge. He was still at Bournemouth on October 6 when his last letter as a schoolboy was posted to Keynes.

I shall see you within a week. I expect to turn up early on Tuesday morning, if I have not, ere that, killed myself in the train that bears me from Rugby. I have been in this quiet place of invalids and gentlemanly sunsets for about an hundred years, ever since yesterday week. But tomorrow I return to Rugby for a few gloriously ghastly days. I shall be wonderful there, laughing wonderfully all day, and through the night wonderfully weeping. Then—leaving the people I have hated and loved I shall throw off, too, the Rupert Brooke I have hated and loved for so long, and go to a new place and a new individuality. I shall live in Cambridge very silently, in a dark corner of a great room, clad perhaps in cowl and scapular. I shall never speak, but I shall read all day and all night—philosophy or science—nothing beautiful any more. Indeed I have forsworn art and things beautiful; they are but chance manifestations of Life. All art rests on the sexual emotions which are merely the instruments of the Life-force—of Nature—for the propagation of life. That is all we live for, to further Nature's purpose. Sentiment, poetry, romance, religion are but mists of our own fancies, too weak for the great nature-forces of individuality and sexual emotion. They only obscure the issue.

So our duty, Keynes gathered, was to propagate the species and quietly await our physical dissolution, 'heeding as little as possible the selfish and foolish greed for personal immortality, or the incomplete love of an individual'. Shaw, Wells, Nietzche, they were all at one in this. 'It is rather grey, but quite logical and scientific.' However, there was a character he had come across in a play by de L'Isle Adam who said, 'Science will not suffice. Sooner or later you will end by coming to your knees,' and his companion asked, 'Before what?' and the other replied, 'Before the darkness!' Keynes must have wondered with some misgiving in what mood his old friend was going to descend upon King's Parade.

So long as he keeps an eye out on the right side of the train, a freshman to the Isis can tell at a glance that he is about to arrive. Tom tower, St. Mary's in the High, the Radcliffe Camera, and a cluster of pinnacles, too many and too jumbled, as it seems, to be identified at once, suggest a page of an illuminated manuscript where the tops of buildings jostle together within the compass of their city wall. At Cambridge, however, you alight at a railway station, then start down a long straight stretch of road in search of the first signs of a university. The difference is important. Oxford is compact, its manner brisk and formal. Cambridge is an academic town of grey brick, enclosing colleges of old red brick and stone, which has grown up where there was more elbow-room among the flat meadows by the side of its placid stream. There are no bluffs or rises except the Gog-Magog and Castle hills, and of these it has been said that they appear to have been supplied by Nature for the express purpose of relieving the neighbourhood from the charge of undiversified flatness; and the Cam, if not mistaken for an ornamental water, is a river which has apparently come thus far too soon, and so can afford to take its time for the rest of its way to the sea. It lingers, looking like a moat against fifteenth-century walls and the fringes of great lawns, passing under small Palladian bridges, seeming to flow, not always onward, according to the direction of the wind. And by comparison with a graduate from Isis, a man of the Cam might be distinguished by a certain casualness of manner and a deliberate but halting mode of speech, with pauses for thought and now and again a vowel humorously drawled, as it were to italicize his point.

On the first day of term about fifty hansom cabs were drawn up in the station approach. The young ladies of Girton were met and escorted to their destination in a growler without being given the least opportunity for association with the youths, and although Newnham was a little more closely integrated with the university, its students were subject to a surveillance no less strict. The male and female communities lived apart; or the chaperone presided where they briefly met. Elsewhere shrewd mothers might arrange the tennis or water-party; here there was practically no common ground. There was a saying: 'To be seen alone with a man in a four-wheeler spells doom.' Many of the young men never danced, so that even the balls in May week relied on the exertions of a few stalwarts in the art, who had the good nature and the stamina to take the floor for one waltz after another. Nor was there educational any more than social or political equality between the sexes. Higher education for women in polite society was still looked upon as just a trifle common, and 'I say, don't let on you're learning Greek', would be a not unnatural piece of brotherly advice to a sister before a social gathering at home.

Two trams with one horse apiece plied to and fro on rails between the station and the centre of the town, one branch ending at the Senate House, and the other opposite Christ's College. The streets were quiet and almost empty; foreigners of any sort were seldom seen; and most of the undergraduates were somewhat dowdy in appearance, it not being quite the thing to look smart. Cloth caps in winter, straw boaters in summer, would be in evidence, and bowler hats on a Sunday; walking-sticks and gloves being essential appendages for visits to Newmarket or Lord's. Almost all the young men, many of whom were destined for the ministry of the church, wore grey flannel trousers, stiff collars pitched rather high under the chin, and Norfolk jackets; and the roysterers would talk of 'lashings of beer', (a phrase from Kipling) while to others, more restrained, the situation would be 'awfully jolly'. 'I say, what a simply rippin' frock!' was a safely modish form of compliment in May week, if a gallant were moved to be gushing; and at a tea-party in college when at last the chaperone lifted her veil, it would be understood as the signal for the host to relax, show new animation, and have leave to remark, glancing from one lady guest to the other, 'May I fill a pipe?' Old friends still addressed each other by their surnames, a custom soon to die out, and walked and talked with an air of privilege; the shops, their windows less spick-and-span than today, had counters graced with more courtesy; the streets smelt wholesomely of horses and leather and even of the surrounding greenness of the fields.

Early in October 1906 a new generation arrived and dispersed towards its various colleges, among them a new wave of agitators in the anti-Victorian revolt. Trinity, twice as large as any other college, absorbed the greatest number, and about fifty went to King's, where there were already about a hundred men who were now no longer freshmen. As the hansoms drew up at the cobbled approach to the entrance gate, obsequious porters ran out, pushing small barrows, with 'adroit familiarity' wheeled in the baggage, and, taking charge of the valise with things for the night, conducted the new arrival to his appointed set of rooms. Among the newcomers, Brooke climbed to the top of Staircase A in Fellows' Buildings and was shown into Room 14. The Head Porter then directed the freshman to his first interview. The Tutor at this time was W. H. Macaulay, great-nephew of Lord Macaulay, a somewhat austere but amiable figure who supervised the work of about thirty assistant tutors and a hundred and fifty undergraduates. For the most part the dons were young, and over none of them had fallen what Charles Tennyson has called 'that glass dome which separates without hiding the married couple from the rest of the world'. Moreover they lived in college, so that by sharing the life of the place it was easy for the senior and junior member alike to come to terms and be friends. It was a predominantly male society and, in a sense, enclosed; the small world of the college meaning far more to the kingsman than the university as a whole. King's was his world, not Cambridge, and the scholar in classics was fortunate indeed to have assigned to him as his friends and mentors such men as then were Fellows: Henry Sills, Nathaniel Wedd, the authorities on Greek and Roman History, J. T. Sheppard the youngest of these, a lecturer of dramatic power, Walter Headlam, who thought and composed in Greek like a citizen of ancient Athens, and Goldsworthy Lowes Dickinson the gentle, unassuming spirit whose work and influence through his books, such as *The Modern Symposium*, which he was now writing, and *The Greek View of Life*, extended far beyond his room at the top of Gibbs's Building in the front court. Among these Fellows in residence the first to be visited after the Tutor was Nathaniel Wedd. He advised the classical student on his reading, taking care never to lay down the law. Faced with a list of likely books, the freshman was invited to make his own suggestions, then Wedd would make his comment on the choice. The extraordinary contrast with the way things were done at school could be disconcerting at first. The tutor was now an equal, man to man, who gave his junior colleague to understand that over and above the immediate business of exams, the aim and end of studying the classical authors was the enrichment of life through close acquaintance with great minds.

At the head of King's, Dr. M. R. James had already held the office of Provost for a year. He was rumoured to know all the ghost stories of the last thousand years; to have ready the answer to any problem relating to the apocryphal books of the Old Testament; and to take his leisure in the field of obscure hagiology. He was said to have made his own translation of one of the gospels from the original Coptic and sent it to Queen Victoria while he was still a boy at Eton. The Dean was none other than Uncle Alan (known locally as 'Brookie' which irritated Rupert) whom the freshman was instructed by the Tutor to wait upon next morning. But first he must get himself a gown. This, it was pointed out, was not only the proper dress for calling on the Dean, but in general use it would save him the embarrassment of being mistaken for a tradesman.

The Dean would apprise his caller of the regulations: how he must not stay out after midnight, and was expected to attend Chapel not less than four times a week and once on Sunday or, having some valid reason, must sign out with the Head Porter. After Chapel at eight, the day's work began at nine (technically, that is; one's conscience was free to make other plans) and since this particular visitor, one of many, happened to be a nephew, it was agreed that Brooke should call on his uncle for tea on Saturday afternoons. The next courtesy visit was to the Provost's Lodge. It was the first Sunday of the term when Brooke paused on the front steps, finding he had coincided with another freshman who was to share the interview. He was very tall, with somewhat sloping shoulders, a benign, almost ecclesiastical expression, and, judging by his genial greeting, a voice of command for the declamation of Milton. Hugh Dalton, the son of a tutor to the royal family who was now a Canon of Windsor, had just arrived from Eton and settled in rooms out of College on Peas Hill. Walking away together after the interview, Brooke and Dalton discovered they had a good deal in common. Like Brooke, Dalton had first discovered Swinburne through *Atalanta*; he knew all about *The Shropshire Lad*, and was glad to discover that they shared a good opinion of Belloc and Henley. And then there was politics. Although Dalton was the quicker to take the actual plunge into Socialism, both these freshmen only needed the influence of a strong personality to tip the balance. He was there in the great college down the street, a History scholar of Trinity, now awaiting, so to speak, to come into their lives. For the present Dalton and Brooke decided to found a society of like-minded kingsmen, and they called it the *Carbonari* (the charcoal burners) as a tribute to the revolutionary group of that name in nineteenth-century Italy, and they picked their associates with care. At their second meeting Brooke read aloud his poems, but that was in the weeks to come. The first thing was to get accustomed to these new surroundings, buy books, second-hand if possible, sort clothes and crockery, and plant Aunt Fanny's cushion on the sofa which matched the new curtains dyed a shade of 'sorrowful green'.

The day began at seven: the bells of Great St. Mary's by the market-place would be heard chiming the hour, the gyp (manservant) opening the window and making the best of it with his observations on the weather. At the beck and call of several masters, a gyp could be counted on to borrow extra forks for a special occasion, deal shrewdly with creditors among the local tradesmen, and pack the picnic basket for Newmarket. More important was his female counterpart, the bedmaker, an elderly party in black bonnet and shawl, clasping an ample hand-bag for stowing her perquisites. She needed cash to buy muffins for the tea-party, a stiff broom, a duster or two ('This place fair *eats* dusters'), and she unstrapped the box of household goods from home, wagging her head over the omissions. 'What, no cruet, Mr. Brooke, sir? Well, fancy. We won't get very far, you know, without a cruet.' So this was adult freedom. Brooke was not exhilarated, nor was he even comfortable. The door which had been shut from birth now stood so wide it made a draught. No longer were there looks of recognition at every turn. He had entered a community where he was no one in particular. And then there were the extraordinary mornings that were merely there for you to do what you liked with them; no scramble downstairs for roll-call, no summons of any sort beyond your own conscience and, very discreetly, and not too early, the Chapel bell.

Outside, massive iron railings, each prong topped with a *fleur de lys*, and a strip of lawn spanned the width of the college, shielding the pseudo-Gothic screen from the carriages of King's Parade; and in the centre of the screen, the work of Wilkins in the eighteen-twenties, the Gatehouse which has been likened to a magnum of brandy with soda bottles. The pinnacles in attendance, erect on either side, reflect the ornamental motifs of the Chapel, whose lofty east wall terminates the screen at its northward end, so abruptly, and so vastly out of proportion with the surroundings, that at first it can go unnoticed, for the stranger's eye is not accustomed to looking for masonry where it would only expect to see the heavens clearing up or clouding over. A cobbled approach, a dark entry with its notice boards, and then the front court opens on the view (an enormous square of untrodden-looking sward) with the figure of Henry VI in weathered bronze, the modest founder, surprisingly small, dwarfed by the space and scale of things, presiding over his gentle fountain in the centre. To the front, ahead, Gibbs's Building, an eighteenth-century block, distinctive for the silvery greyness of its classic lines unruffled in their Gothic setting; a spacious arch in the centre, framing treetops and passing clouds beyond, and popularly known as the Jumbo Arch for no ascertainable reason, unless someone, astonished by its proportions, may once have thought it a convenient shelter for the college elephant. At left, a less conspicuous block which incorporates the Hall, again the work of Wilkins in the spirit of the Gothic Revival, but discreet and suitably subdued, as well it might be in the presence of what dominates the Court on the opposite side—a sudden precipice, pale with the pale brownness of dry sand above the watermark, elaborate in contrast with the grey simplicity of Gibbs's.

Ruskin has described the Chapel as a billiard table with its legs in air, and anything will serve so long as it evokes an image as familiar in the mind as the dome of Paul's. 'Ah!' many a visitor must exclaim to himself, seeing the real thing at last after all those engravings, and though brief the comment, and hardly adequate, there is little more to say. Certainly, it is loftier than we thought and narrower, suggesting the fragment of some master plan which was never carried further than this splendid cliff, as indeed, we learn, was the case. Tall windows seem rescued from collapse by recurring buttresses whose elegance and strength combined just save this side-view from the sheerness of a cliff. Within are seen heraldic beasts, diadems, and the giant fungus of the Tudor rose on a scale to dwarf a sunflower; for after a century of political delays, the structure was finally accomplished in the reign of Henry VIII, and the prodigious emblems of his royalty usurp the credit of a Plantagenet foundation and even, perhaps, a little of the Almighty. The State of England is here affirmed as confidently as the hope of Zion. If one cannot agree with A. C. Benson who remarked that it was 'no more holy than the Union Jack . . . altogether it won't quite do,' yet we see what he meant. But what with the stone cobweb of the fan-vaulting above the antechapel; the organ case like the poop of *The Great Harry* jutting midway into an indoor sky; the tapers burning at evensong, remote, in the Choir; and by day the subdued dazzle of tremendous windows—Elijah rapt to heaven and letting fall his scarlet mantle of prophecy, Christ walking in the Easter garden and 'holding a spade as if to give colour to Mary's mistake'—inexorably, and with a slow magnificence, the balance of sacred and secular is overtipped and the pomp of things terrestrial forgotten. Ever since Henry Sidgwick had resigned his Fellowship of Trinity in 1869, because he could not in all conscience subscribe to the articles of Christian dogma, it was easier for a don at Cambridge openly to combine scepticism with learning and still adorn his post. At Trinity and King's the intellectual climate was agnostic; and for many, Brooke among them, who came to King's already disenchanted with organized religion, the Chapel, whose physical presence dominated their daily round, was no more than a colossus surviving from a vanished age of giants, a place to visit in deference to custom, a presence taken for granted as though it were some earth-bound feature of the weather.

In the obscurity of his sitting-room, Brooke began to put himself in order. 'I try not to notice the wallpaper,' he wrote from staircase A in his first letter home. The green curtains were answering, and for four guineas he had managed to get a sofa which was big enough to lie full length on and prop one's head on Aunt Fanny's cushion. A week later he had attended a concert 'by a man called Kreisler', had been called on to play full back as odd man for his college football team against Caius, learned how to make coffee which could be drunk without grimaces, and was experimenting with a pipe and tobacco. His bed-maker had unpacked the crockery from Rugby and found only five cups, and the book-shelves looked rather bare. The report was lacklustre. Nothing except his meals out of Hall with Keynes, Russell-Smith, or Andrew Gow of Trinity, another Old Rugbeian, moved him to the slightest show of enthusiasm. He was happier harking back than wondering on things to come. To Erica he was outspoken: 'I do not know if it's the climate or the people: most probably it's neither, but my cantankerous self. But for some reason I find this place absolutely devoid of interest and amusement. I like nobody. They all seem dull, middle-aged, and ugly.' He was thoroughly ill at ease, . . . 'In fact, I suppose I'm "growing up".'

Within a week or two he was back in Rugby on the pretext of playing football for the Old Boys. The experience only showed him that he had already outgrown his old surroundings and he belonged nowhere. And now, according to his letter to Lucas, Cambridge people were still as ugly as they were last week, but had become tiresomely young.

This place is rather funny to watch; and a little wearying. It is full of very young people, and my blear eyes look dolefully at them from the lofty window where I sit and moan. Innumerous people I knew on the other side of the Styx come in to see me. They talk vivaciously for three minutes and I stare at them with a dumb politeness, and then they go away. My room is a gaunt *Yellow Book* wilderness with a few wicked little pictures scattered here and there. The book-shelves are enormous and half empty: But it was rash in you to inquire about books I needed. I had thoughts of sending you a list of all the evil books I really should like. I want, for instance, to complete my set of the three great decadent writers (Oscar Wilde, St. John Lucas, and Rupert Brooke). Of the last and most infamous of the three I possess most of the works but of the other two I have less. But perhaps these would have a too bad influence on me.

When Lucas sent him his poems and the latest Dunsany to furnish the shelves, Brooke was still out of sorts, but he was becoming a little more realistic.

At certain moments I perceive a pleasant kind of peace in the grey ancient walls and green lawns among which I live; a quietude that does not recompense for the things I loved and have left, but at times softens their outlines a little. If only I were a poet I should love such a life very greatly, remembering moments of passion in tranquillity; but being first and chiefly only a boy I am restless and unable to read or write.

In 1906 the Greek Play Committee was planning to repeat the success it had had with the *Eumenides* of Aeschylus some twenty years before. C. V. Stanford had composed the incidental music, and the production, arranged for six performances at the New Theatre in early December, was in the hands of Walter Durnford, one of the senior dons at King's. In an idle moment Brooke had wandered into the A.D.C. theatre in Jesus Lane, and sat down to watch a rehearsal. A. F. Scholfield, a kingsman in his fourth year, was rehearsing the leading role of Orestes in the forthcoming Greek production, and Justin Brooke of Emmanuel, who had the part of the Pythian Prophetess, was in the stalls. He had already met the Brooke of King's, discovered he was at a loose end, and asked him to come along. It was then that Scholfield happened to look into the stalls and wonder who the newcomer might be. He asked to be introduced, for the young man was of striking appearance and he might be willing to help. 'You won't get much out of him,' said Brooke of Emmanuel, in an aside, 'He's very shy,' then he called his new acquaintance to his side. He had to explain that he was no relation, although, oddly enough, he had a brother who was also a Rupert Brooke. The form of class distinction most strictly observed in the University was the seniority of second-over first-year men, and since Scholfield was in his fourth it was not thought surprising that he had not met the visitor, though they were both in the same college. Brooke of King's was game for anything. He agreed to play the Herald. He had no lines to learn. All he had to do was look statuesque, and put a property trumpet to his lips and appear to blow while 'a villain in the orchestra,' as he put it to Lucas, 'simultaneously wantons on the cornet'. He reassured his mother. 'The part is not difficult. The rehearsals are very amusing.'

At this stage he was invited to lunch with the Fellow of ripe years and distinguished but chequered reputation who occupied the set of rooms at King's immediately opposite his own. The episode is only of interest to mark the point where legends cross. Oscar Browning, the History don, was what a bed-maker who could not be expected to perceive his finer qualities, would have called 'a card'. Opposite the freshman's rooms of 'sorrowful pale green', his apartments were glowing with dull gold wall-paper and tastefully overfurnished; he was huge, 'swollen with uncooked knowledge', English yet Oriental in a way too elusive to define, overflowing with kindness and anecdotes involving persons of exalted rank, touchy with petty pride, and given to not very skilled bouts of Beethoven or, less haltingly, *Off to Philadelphia in the morning*, on his continental harmonium: 'a character in a lost play of Shakespeare's,' as Nathaniel Wedd once described him. Brooke might have taken to him, if only that he was a fellow agnostic. When asked why he had a crucifix on the wall of his ante-room his answer was, 'To fwighten the agnoggers'. But Brooke was perhaps too young to appreciate such exuberant eccentricity. Apparently the O.B. did not favour him with one of his unforgettably odd remarks such as 'I awoke at five and read Coventry Patmore slap through'. The occasion was hardly a success. 'He was rather quaint to watch,' Brooke wrote to his mother, 'but I did not much like him. He was so very egotistical,' and thereafter no doubt he heard but little of his neighbour beyond the muffled and uneven strains of the Eroica symphony from across the landing.

It was characteristic that the next thing Lucas heard (in a letter addressed from King's College, Upper Tooting, Hell) was that Brooke was on his way up to town 'to see Mr. Tree about the production of my next tragedy', when in fact he was only going to Dulwich to play football. As for the Greek play, a ticket had been arranged, and 'I wear a red wig and cardboard armour and luckily am only visible for one minute'.

At the opening performance, on November 30, Brooke made his first appearance on a public occasion. A. C. Benson wrote in his diary, 'A herald made a pretty figure, spoilt by a glassy stare'. Percy Lubbock took note of the Herald's curious hop to the right or left, each time, before lifting the property trumpet to his lips. The herald of the immortals with the grace of a Ganymede was half a faun. Also in the audience was Edward Marsh, a civil servant from Gray's Inn, who was present as the guest of his former tutor, A. W. Verrall of Trinity, author of the English version of the play which was being sold in the theatre. Some years after Marsh recalled how 'the radiant, youthful figure in gold and vivid red and blue, like a Page in the Riccardi Chapel, stood strangely out against the stuffy decorations and dresses'. . . . When the performance was over Brooke made new acquaintances. Some of them were important. The characters in his life story were assembling. One of the play committee was F. M.

Cornford, who was working as a junior classics don with Verrall at Trinity; another was Jane Harrison, the authority on primitive Greek religion, a don at Newnham. It was she who overheard Brooke remark 'Nobody over thirty is worth talking to', and borrowed it as a text for one of her lectures.[1] From the audience came A. C. Benson; Charles Sayle, an under-librarian of the University Library, brought George Mallory, destined one day to win renown on Mount Everest; Dr. Verrall brought Edward Marsh; and, prominent among those in the cast, needing more introduction, was Justin Brooke, who brought into Rupert's life another aspect of the Victorian revolt and confirmed his interest in the drama.

This undergraduate of Emmanuel was a son of Arthur Brooke, the founder of Brooke Bond's tea business. Although born in Chiswick, he had been brought up on his father's estate near Leith Hill in Surrey, and was essentially a man of the country. By comparison with him, the Brooke of King's was town-bred. This difference between them had its influence on the character of the younger man. Justin was now in his third year of reading for the Law, having come up from Bedales, the progressive school now in its heyday. The influence of Bedales was strong in the new Cambridge group that was coming into being during the latter half of this term. Those places will be obvious where the 'aesthetic', Bedalian, Fabian, 'Bloomsbury', elements in the anti-Victorian revolt shaded off into one another, but each was distinct at the core, and all four, one after the other, went to the making of Rupert Brooke. The headmaster of this leading co-educational school was J. H. Badley. One of the principal differences between his system and that of the public school was the importance in his curriculum of music and literature and especially the acting of Shakespeare. The school was modern, but opposed to much that modern industrial society stood for. A characteristic of the Bedalian was a love of the open-air, not only indulged at given times of the day in the form of organized games, but adopted as a way of life, walking and camping out; but they did not take it in bad part when others in Cambridge, who were not of their persuasion, called them the 'dew-dabblers'. In their enlightened but unfashionable pursuit of music they fostered the cult for newly discovered folk-songs, noting with dismay that when the social season was over more than half the

---

[1] 'Crabbed Age and Youth,' delivered this term to the Trinity Essay Society. 'I had more than one conversation with the utterer of the doom,' she said, 'which I had in my folly felt to be worth while.' Nevertheless, she rather agreed with him.

audience at concerts and at Covent Garden were Jews, who went there, of course, solely for the sake of the music. And together with all this there was the attitude to sex, which in its ̃ulsion from those Victorian taboos which insisted on arbitrary limits to the topic of conversation, was rather an absence of attitude than anything more positive; but it was part of the new feminist movement to break down the prejudice which disallowed a woman the right to exert her intelligence in public affairs, confined her to the sphere of the domestic virtues, and set her up as an idealized figure on an *art nouveau* pedestal. In an age when more and more political power was being transferred from the landed interest to the Liberal industrialist, a whole stratum of society in the middle station had begun to decline. The son and heir might launch out into a new field, change with the changing times, if he had the wits, but the unmarried daughter, no longer in her first youth, and left with a competence that enabled her to go on living more or less in the style she was accustomed to, had no prospect before her but a life of retirement in the polite obscurity of a room in Bayswater. She was one of a growing multitude which came to be known as 'the chaste surplus'. To the Bedalian of 1906 there could be nothing comical in the music-hall figure of a maiden aunt. She was an object for compassion and protest. Above all, her niece of today, they thought, must be saved from suffering the same fate, and this, unlike their forebears, was what the Bedalian meant by worse than death.

The protest embraced a whole way of life based on outworn custom. It was widespread in the younger generation outside Bedales, where it took other forms. For some the social world of the 'enemy' might be symbolized by the minutest details: the customary visit to the stables after morning Church on Sünday, the image of the *pater familias* with his Bible at breakfast, the rustle of petticoats on a gas-lit landing, the smell of household soap. While for others it would be revealed in the usual answer given to that inevitable question among freshmen—'Where do you come from?' The reply was practically never 'London', for although the upper classes owned houses in the metropolis, occupied during the London season, they could not be said to 'live' there. While the lower orders, on the other hand, were notorious for having never lived anywhere else. If you wanted to give the right impression, therefore, you were careful what you said. At Bedales there was religious instruction, but the advanced young person elsewhere seldom went to church except when he had to; he would rather sacrifice sentiment altogether than risk the charge of being sentimental; he did not gloss over the truth in deference to custom; while unmarried he lived chaste, not so much out of principle or for propriety, but because it seemed to him sensible—and in social behaviour he was, by the old standards, often studiously ill-mannered. The 'enemy' had a code. This too must be, not exactly flouted, but ignored. What the conventional would call lax manners were the hall-mark of the free-thinking man or newly emancipated woman. Thus it was a subtle compliment to a woman not to show her those little attentions that were once her due when she was all frailty and mystery and the goddess of the hearth— a 'compliment' such as the older generation would rather be spared. There was no need to stand aside that a lady might enter the room before you, or rise from your seat when she came in; no need, if the topic was not of your choice, to take part in general conversation out of a sense of social obligation. At the risk of being thought insufferable, you were 'natural', which satisfied your conscience, if not the needs of the generality. As to the eternal questions, Science, and Darwin in particular, had provided a kind of skeleton-key to them all. The rest was progress in the light of reason along the 'ringing grooves of change'. But one did not admit to a knowledge of Tennyson.

Justin was the chief representative of Bedales, but he was not alone. A school friend of his had recently come up from the Sorbonne (where he had graduated in mathematics) as an advanced student attached to Emmanuel, and the two of them were now sharing rooms outside college. Jacques Raverat was a Frenchman of considerable character and culture. His father's country house was the Château de Vienne at Prunoy in the department of Yonne. It must have been soon after the *Eumenides*, that Justin arranged a tea-party in his rooms for the Brooke of King's to meet his old friend. Among his papers Raverat left the fragment of an autobiographical novel in French, in which he described his first encounter with Brooke. He was slumped in a chair, and at first his voice seemed disagreeably harsh.

He was undoubtedly extremely beautiful, but with a childish beauty of undefined fluid lineaments, as if his mother's milk was still in his cheeks. But one could already foresee another kind of beauty which he was to have a few years later. His forehead was very high and clear, his chin and lips admirably drawn; the eyes were small, grey-blue and already veiled, mysterious and secret, and with a jerk of his head he constantly tossed back his overlong hair as it fell over his face. It was the colour of tarnished gold and it was parted in the centre. In order to humanize a little his Apollonean beauty I should add that his nose, with its delicate nostrils, was slightly turned up, which gave his face a humorous expression—an expression which he would have preferred to conceal at this period of his life. When he smiled, the corners of his mouth made his expression even more humorous, and it was this that finally overcame my prejudices, so that I soon allowed myself to fall under the charm of his conversation.

Raverat and Brooke took to each other at once. They spent the rest of that day browsing in bookshops, and Raverat remembered Brooke telling him how 'one night under a solitary lamp-post he had seen a working-class woman in the arms of her lover with her pale ordinary face transfigured by the aura of love' and had felt 'sick with envy'.

The *Eumenides* was an excitement soon come and gone. The term's work was not seriously interrupted. He was attending the lectures of J. T. Sheppard, studying Greek history with Henry Sills, and twice a week he visited the room with the Oriel window in Bodley's Building and read Aeschylus with Walter Headlam. The floor was littered with strips of paper (book-markers which had come adrift) notes of possible emendations of the text, reproductions of paintings by G. F. Watts and faded back-numbers of *The Sporting Times*. Headlam, aged forty-one, stood before the fire and read aloud an Elizabethan lyric or declaimed in Greek the speeches of Agamemnon with dramatic zest—nervously pulling at his pipe, now going into a small room adjoining for more tobacco, now striding to the bottle of ale on the piano to fill his glass. He lived with intensity in a world of pure scholarship, cricket, and music, oblivious of almost everything else. 'He never knows,' Nathaniel Wedd remarked of him, 'He never knows what time of the year it is unless it snows, so be careful not to tear up paper near his rooms or he will go away on a Christmas holiday.' When Sheppard and he were asked to desist from playing croquet on a Sunday morning, Headlam exclaimed, 'I deplore a faith so fragile that it trembles at the click of croquet balls heard on the way to Chapel'. He was an ardent admirer of the Elizabethan dramatists, infected Brooke with a passion for the plays of Webster, and found him an easy convert to the poetry of Donne, the major poet who was generally regarded then as little more than a crank.

The scope of the Classical Tripos had recently been enlarged to include more literature, philosophy, and art, and the examination for the first part was then taken at the end of the third academic year. It was in three parts, consisting of a translation, a composition, and a general paper; a preliminary college examination, in translation and history, was taken at the end of the first year. Brooke worked, or tried to work, but even his tutorials with Headlam consisted more of Donne than Aeschylus. Sheppard was a lecturer who aroused his flagging enthusiasm; Wedd was a wit: when Brooke, having over-slept, apologized for his lateness, he was told not to worry—'I never get up before Thursday'—but still he could not settle down. He enjoyed a meeting of the *Carbonari* when he read aloud a new poem, *The Song of the Beasts*, and a sonnet in alexandrines, called *The Vision of the Archangels*, an incident in a dream or fantasy in which the Cherubim are seen to be 'Bearing with quiet steps, and great wings furled', a child-sized coffin containing the ashes of a defunct Almighty and letting it slip over the brink of space. He was still an apprentice poet, a schoolboy at large, without a school. But there was a gleam of hope ahead. He was homesick, and the Cambridge term was due to end a fortnight before they broke up at Rugby.

With a visit to *Man and Superman* at the Court Theatre on his way through London, where the posters were promising *Candida* for January, he hurried home to find his mother so ill with influenza that a nurse was in charge. A Christmas illness of his own had almost become a habit, so of course he caught the infection, providing the nurse with another patient, and missed the beginning of his next term at Cambridge. 'She cannot understand my permanent look of resigned melancholy' he wrote to Erica of the new member of the household. 'I tell her it's my broken heart, and sigh.' He had been reading Shaw's *Plays Pleasant* for a second time and felt 'more cer-tain than ever that *Candida* is the greatest play in the world'. Doubtless he had seen himself in the character of the young poet Marchbanks and envied his love for an older woman who treated him with all the tenderness and forbearance of a mother. The play was about something he dimly understood, although he had never met with it himself outside his fantasies. 'I think,' he wrote to Erica, 'when I have lost all the vain knowledge I ever had I shall go to London or Paris and live for one year a life like a great red flame,' and part of the process, he said, would be to 'drink the purple wine of beauty from the polished skull of some dead Archbishop'. He en-closed his latest sonnet about the Archangels and had another dream to tell.

I once dreamt I was in the Gardens of Heaven walking between great odorous beds of helichrys and asphodel. Turning a corner I met the present

Headmaster of Rugby School in his shirt-sleeves. He was digging up all the beautiful flowers. I hit him severely on the nose, and asked what he was doing. He said he was uprooting the useless flowers and planting vegetables for food instead. I told him that in Heaven one subsisted entirely on beautiful thoughts. He replied that he would starve; and continued to dig, muttering. He began to swell as I gazed, and, still grunting 'Cabbages and Onions', grew so big that he blotted out all the sky . . .

To make up for all this bosh, I shall copy out for you the wonderful sonnet of the Century. But if you show it to respectable people they'll kill you.

Keynes was the first of Brooke's friends to show signs of losing patience with his *fin de siècle* brand of Byronic melancholy, or at least the first to register a protest on behalf of sincerity. Brooke had only recently introduced him to 'Bobbie Longman'. He was trying to get his own back on Keynes when he wrote from a bed of sickness, 'Arthur Eckersley was tremendously excited about you. He said you had the most decadent face he had ever seen; but then he writes for *Punch*. I told him that you were a notorious evil liver and that your distinguishing feature was your sincerity, and he was very pleased.' All the same, the point had gone home, and it warranted a straight answer.

I have thought over your idea of my at length giving up the pose of discontent and taking to optimism in my old age. I think not. The change might be refreshing, but I scrape along very well as I am; and the pessimistic insincerity pleases *me* at any rate, which is the main thing.

And a week today I shall return to Cambridge! And there I shall find all the witty and clever people running one another down again. And I shall be rather witty and rather clever and I shall spend my time pretending to admire what I think it humorous or impressive in me to admire. Even more than yourself I attempt to be 'all things to all men'; rather 'cultured' among the cultured, faintly athletic among athletes, a little blasphemous among blasphemers, slightly insincere to myself.

However, there are advantages in being a hypocrite, aren't there? One becomes Godlike in this at least, that one laughs at all the other hypocrites.

The sonnet, *To my Lady Influenza*, 'probably the work of Oscar Wilde, at least of his school,' was an excellent piece of nonsense in which the Disease was imagined riding through the Streets of Rome like Isis—'while monstrous eunuchs yapped in obscene glee', or like the Sun-god—

> *Phoibos, in all thy pale pink nudity;*
> *Or She (wearing a fillet on her brow*
> *And absolutely naught else) from the sea*

FRESHMAN

> *Rising, an argent dawn! so cometh now*
> *My Lady Influenza, like a star*
> *Inebriously wan, and in her train*
> Fever, *the haggard soul's white nenuphar,*
> *And lily-fingered* Death, *and grisly* Pain
> *And* Constipation *who makes all things vain,*
> Pneumonyer, Cancer, *and* Nasal Catarrh.

To Erica he described how at the Court before Christmas he had
'laughed little hollow laughs when Shaw mocked at all that other
people worship . . . Will you come to Cambridge? It's a morbid
thing to do, but if you appeared there in the middle of some gaunt
term you might save the reason of your desperate cousin.'

It was now the second week in January, 1907. He was packing for
Cambridge, already late, when there was an urgent summons from a
doctor in Southsea. Dick, his eldest brother, was ill with pneumonia.
Parker Brooke left at once, and was with the young man when on
January 13, after an illness of only a few days, his son died. Richard
was a youth of keen intelligence and charm but some deep-seated and
nagging sense of inadequacy must have played on a flaw in his
character, leading him to drift into a habit of intemperance which had
weakened his constitution. As the frailest of the family he had been
cherished with an especial poignancy, and the blow to the father was
almost overwhelming. When he got home, he found Rupert was up
but Mrs. Brooke only just off the danger list herself. The boys
were about to come back from the holidays, Rupert offered to
stop and help, but the parents wisely preferred that he should be out
of the way of their grief. And now, on the day of the father's return,
a letter arrived from a director of Richard's firm of engineers. The
news had not reached him. He said the young man had been doing well
and was being considered for a better job. 'It's the sort of ironical
coincidence one reads in a book and winces at,' Brooke wrote to
Lucas, and left behind him a note for a boy he had hoped to see before
he went: 'I am very glad to get away before you all return. This
sounds rude. But I am feeling terribly despondent and sad, and I feel
that I could not face everybody. The only thing was if I could help
Father and Mother by staying, but they say not, and I do not think so.
And if I stayed I know I should break down. There is an instinct to
hide in sorrow, and at Cambridge where I know no one properly
I can be alone . . . I hope you'll be gentle to my pater at first. He has

had a terrible time, and is very tired and broken by it.' Soon after his return to King's he called on Sheppard for a tutorial and in the middle of the lesson suddenly broke down and sobbed bitterly.

Crippled by borrowed boots, he soon gave up his afternoon exercise of football; even Headlam introducing to him the Odes of Pindar failed to divert him; yet eager for distraction he called on the editor of the *Cambridge Review* and offered himself as a reviewer. He also showed him a new poem which, though unsigned, provided on February 14 his debut in Cambridge print. *The Call*[1] shows a rather sudden advance, and its rhetoric conveys a real emotion. At first glance it looks as though it were just another of those pieces dedicated to some imaginary friend or paramour who has died in youth, but the genuineness of the passion is something quite new, leaving no doubt that he was venting his feelings by fancying a reunion with his brother. The poem ends:

> *Your mouth shall mock the old and wise,*
> *Your laugh shall fill the world with flame,*
> *I'll write upon the shrinking skies*
> *The scarlet splendour of your name,*
>
> *Till Heaven cracks, and Hell thereunder*
> *Dies in her ultimate mad fire,*
> *And darkness falls, with scornful thunder,*
> *On dreams of men and men's desire.*
>
> *Then only in the empty spaces,*
> *Death, walking very silently,*
> *Shall fear the glory of our faces*
> *Through all the dark infinity.*
>
> *So, clothed about with perfect love,*
> *The eternal end shall find us one,*
> *Alone above the Night, above*
> *The dust of the dead gods, alone.*

He also revived his interest in the *Westminster Gazette*, and sent them a curious little prose poem called *The Five Knights* which his mother didn't understand. It meant nothing 'except what it said,' he explained, not very helpfully. 'It was merely a kind of idea I once had.'

[1] G.K., p. 164.

She was free to regard the knights as representing five continents or five planets, if she pleased. She was particularly interested, however, because for the first time he had signed a printed piece with his own name; but this, she imagined, was due rather to caprice than the author's pride. He also sent up *The Beginning*, one of last year's poems, because it happened to fulfil the requirements for a competition. It was printed, though it failed to get the prize. He was more successful competing for the best version from the German of 'Liederbuch der Gottheit' by Christian Wagner, done from a literal translation provided by Geoffrey Keynes. Sending the result to Keynes, he enclosed 'A Comment'. 'I fear it's not very literal.'

A COMMENT

God gives us, in earth's loveliness,
    His own great song-book, it is stated.
We stumble through (and have to guess
    To whom or what it's dedicated!)

On first perusing, how we yearn to
    Mark every song! but soon, my friend,
The only page we want to turn to
    Holds two best words of all, 'The End'.

But since we've got to read it through,
    Let us, as true philosophers,
Sit down, and critically review
    God's very minor book of verse.

One poem I've underlined—the best—
    (There's all sorts in God's poetry-book!):
But of the lot I most detest
    God's vulgar lyric 'Rupert Brooke' . . .

Lucas was given news of a more important venture, his first essay in criticism.

I am rather wretched and ill. In my 'literary life' I have taken the last step of infamy, and become—a reviewer! I have undertaken to 'do' great slabs of minor poetry for *The Cambridge Review*. I have read volumes of them, all the same, and all exactly the stuff I write. I frequently wonder whether I have not written several of them myself under a pseudonym, and forgotten about it.

The editor struck out the more scurrilous remarks, but left the authors bitterly discouraged. One of them was informed that he was a 'feeble echo of Richard le Gallienne—which is as though one should speak of imitation gilt or London milk diluted', and half-way through the article Brooke made his transition with 'It is a relief to turn from the merely silly to the merely dull'.

On March 24 he was in Rugby again, reading a paper to his old friends of the *Eranos* Society. On the way through London he saw *Peter Pan* once again. 'Ever since that wild day,' he wrote to Lucas, who had been his host, 'I have gone about as one in a dream, quoting to myself all the gorgeous fragments of *Peter Pan* that I can remember . . . As I stroll through Cambridge, Trinity Street fades and I find myself walking by the shore of the Mermaid's Lagoon. King's Chapel often shrinks before my eyes, and rises, and is suddenly the House in the Tree-tops.' But before the end of this term matters of much greater moment had arisen. They were slowly to transform his life. Hugh Dalton became a Fabian Socialist, and one evening he took his fellow Carbonaro to meet the man who had finally won him over.

Frederic (Ben) Keeling, who was a year older than Dalton and Brooke, and now in his third year, had rooms in the top of one of the turrets overlooking Trinity Great Court. Over the chimney piece hung an enormous poster depicting the workers of the world surging forward with clenched fists, and the legend 'Forward the Day is Breaking' inscribed beneath.[1] He would explain that the picture was inspired by William Morris's *News from Nowhere*, and Brooke must have noted the title, resolving to read it as soon as it came to hand. Keeling was already a Fabian when he came up as a freshman and found that the Cambridge branch had six members, only one of them being an undergraduate. Throughout 1905 and much of the following year they would meet above a dairy in Bridge Street, and seated on grocery boxes plan the reconstruction of society; then the Liberal victory in 1906 gave new hope to the waverers and suddenly the Fabian membership began to grow. It was in the Spring of 1906; Brooke must have been preparing his last paper for the *Eranos* in Rugby, his discourse on modern poets, when the heartened Fabians in Cambridge held a meeting in the Chetwynd Lecture Room, presided over by the first two Fabian undergraduates, Keeling of Trinity and Richard Coit, a freshman of King's; V. H. Mottram,

[1] This drawing gave Brooke the idea for *Second Best* (G.K., p. 144), his only Socialist poem, containing the lines 'Yet, behind the night, Waits for the great unborn, somewhere afar, Some white tremendous daybreak', often in after years quoted by Dalton in his political speeches.

a physiologist, was elected President. As a gesture to the fair sex, however, it was decided to adopt a female treasurer. This was Amber Reeves, but before long her post was filled by Katharine Cox, a girl from Newnham in her first year. J. C. Squire was the Secretary. The Cambridge University Fabian Society was founded. This was the first undergraduate society to admit members from Newnham and Girton. Among them was a daughter of Sydney Olivier, a founder member of the London Fabians. Keeling himself, whose personality dominated the group, has been described by H. G. Wells as 'a copious, rebellious, disorderly, generous, and sympathetic young man'. He had been brought up near Colchester in such a way as to make him put high on his list of reforms the liquidation of the conventional family unit. He laughed immoderately, talked volubly with an infectious idealism, and abominated sentiment; he was gay, Rabelaisian, outspoken on sex, and acknowledged to be the spear-head of the anti-Victorian league. There was, of course, opposition. Earlier this month it had come to a head on what was known as Keir Hardie Night, an incident which had finally won over Dalton to the cause. It was a nine days wonder, and Brooke, wide-eyed with admiration, listened to Keeling's own version of the affair.

Hardie had recently come back from India and made bold to criticize the British Administration. When the Fabians began to advertise his visit to Cambridge, there was a general girding of loins. Keeling's bed-maker was an ally. She let him know that the men who lived below him on the same staircase were hatching a plot to screw up the door of his room while Hardie was having a bite before the meeting. At this Keeling ordered a dinner from the College kitchens, loudly stating who it was for, and talked everywhere of the coming event, even letting slip, with apparent naïveté, the time of Hardie's arrival at the railway station. Meanwhile he arranged for Hardie to come by a different train and be met and taken to Coit's rooms in King's. On the day, two counterfeit Keir Hardies created a diversion in bewildering succession. The first, in characteristic hat, beard, and red tie, stepped from the train and was pursued by a cabful of Tories to Trinity. There, simulating panic, he ran past John's, turned sharp left, the enemy hot on his heels, until at Magdalene he turned in triumph and snatched off his false hair. The second, who was Mottram, the Fabian president, even more convincingly made up by the A.D.C. costumiers, alighted at the same spot by Trinity, and was escorted across the Great Court to Keeling's rooms. Keeling himself then slipped out, and ran round to the Guildhall where a body of trade unionists, in some need of reserves, was holding the platform against a reactionary mob. Meanwhile, Mottram-Hardie and his companions 'kept up the fiction of a great feast in my rooms', pretended not to notice the sounds of furtive carpentry, and allowed themselves to be screwed up and triumphed over with jeers and hoots of derisive laughter through the key-hole. At eight p.m. one of the bogus Hardie group let down a mountaineering rope into Trinity Lane and the whole party quietly made its escape, having taken care to leave the lights on. By this time some £40 worth of damage had been done at the Guildhall, but the genuine Keir Hardie was met by Hugh Dalton, smuggled into King's where he met the two Counterfeits, congratulated them on their appearance, and gave the talk he had come to deliver in comparative peace. But that was not the end of these disturbances. Three weeks later there was a demonstration in Trinity Great Court with the crowd murmuring, 'We'll wash Ben Keeling'. Again the bed-maker, whose name should be inscribed in the annals of social reform, gave due warning. This time Keeling smeared the treads of his staircase thickly with margarine, and for his second line of defence had his windows and inner door protected by a network of electrified barbed wire operated by a press-button device in his bedroom. Here he had decided to make his last stand, if by unlucky chance he should fail to electrocute the Tory opposition. It was looking like bloodshed, and Keeling was ready to carry out his last ditch manœuvre, when the Dean put in a timely appearance at the foot of the staircase and dispersed the marchers. That was the end, 'though,' as Keeling remarked, 'we *thirsted* for battle.'

Brooke listened to this saga with feelings of awe and respect. He was at one with his parents in their Liberal sympathies, but he was still cautious about what seemed like taking the plunge into Socialism. At home it would be thought going *much* too far. To register full membership one signed a document called the Basis. This he was in no hurry to do, although powerfully swayed by Dalton's example, and impressed by the glamour of Fabian prowess against the Philistines. For the present he went no further than accepting Keeling in person as a new force among his friends, and allowing himself to become an Associate. This was a new invention of the Fabians devised for easing the waverer by easy stages over the border. Since the recent General Election you could put your name down as an Associate, which was at least an act of good will for the time being. Brooke thought he would see first what effect the Basis had on Dalton. Anyone who had the right ideas about Swinburne and Henley must have got his head and heart in the right place. As for politics? Well, there were books to read, and he must do a lot more thinking.

Curious to sample Justin Brooke's open-air existence he planned to go a long walk with Russell-Smith when the term was over. From Rugby he wrote to fix the details. 'I have never been a "walking tour" (damned word) before . . . Describe to me the satchel I shall bear. A sort of leather thing, or bag thing . . . But oh! but ah! I forget the *crux*, the *summum bonum*, the *ne plus ultra*—on my head, what? A cap, I suppose . . . And within the napzak, what?—ah! I know you told me, but I have forgotten; something about an invisible helmet, and 7-league boots, and a sword of righteousness . . .' First it was Deal where they were to meet and set off, then his companion made a better suggestion. 'Folkestone? Yes, yes. I applaud Folkestone,' came the reply from School Field. 'It hath I know not what of democracy and a monolith it shall certainly remain.' So they met and sallied forth, accoutred strangely, through Amberley, Petworth, and Arundel, and since the internal combustion engine was not yet in command of the country byways, walking the roads was not only a safe thing to do but a refreshing pleasure. On the road to Market Lavington he wrote to Lucas, 'I am terribly Fabian; which in our family is synonymous with "atheistical", "Roman Catholic", "vulgar", "conceited" and "unpractical". I try to write Fabian hymns; but ah, my uncles weep.' Less often now were his spirits suddenly quelled by some reminder of his recent loss, as when he ended his first letter to Raverat, 'England is full of the shade of dead Springs and the mockery of a living one'.

There had been a plan for the whole family to go abroad, but Parker Brooke was a sick man, still unable to rally after the blow, so the boys went alone, Alfred using Rupert's stomach as a pillow in the train to Florence where rooms were awaiting them in the Pensione White off the Piazza Cavallagieri. The place was alive with elderly English ladies. 'All the sitting rooms are so full of them that Podge and I are terrified of going in.' The parents were resting with the aunts in Bournemouth, so the news was couched in terms appropriate to the breakfast-table as a whole; there must be tactful restraint on the subject of elderly spinsters. One of them, however, who could safely be said to be 'rather a discerning old person', not to say clairvoyante, 'asked me if I came from a public school. I said, "Yes". She gazed at me for a minute, and said, "Rugby". I was terrified at her wisdom!' A week later the aunts were glad to hear of Rupert's resource in dosing Alfred with ammoniated quinine, and interested to learn that the younger boy had the greater capacity both for Florentine paintings and chocolate cake.

At the present moment Podge is being very pleasant about pictures to a lady (aged 50 or so) a few yards off. He has picked up a good deal, and very cleverly pretends to about three times as much knowledge. I recognize one or two second-hand remarks of mine! The lady is frightfully impressed. My book on Florence (which I think the aunts gave me) is very useful indeed. Weather today glorious, yesterday rather poor and rainy. Today I went in state with an armful of flowers which I placed on Landor's and Clough's graves. I felt I represented Rugby, and ought to! I also spared one rose for E. B. Browning.

From Florence they went to Siena, and thence to Milan, arriving on April 15. When Rupert scribbled a letter to Lucas he had been travelling all night 'so it is nearly forty hours since I slept. I feel insane, and shall go to bed.' Before reaching this point, he had declared, 'I have made the final and irrevocable discovery that I hate and am perfectly blind to all painting and sculpture.' To the parents he was less depressing. 'Love to the aunts. Tell them we are revelling in Botticelli.'

Early in May the boys were in London, visiting the Max Beerbohm exhibition, and *Patience* at the Savoy. With these exceptions the metropolis was a dead loss. 'Elsinore without the Prince is nothing to London in your absence.' Lucas was gratified to be told. 'Rosencrantz and I found it inconceivably dreary.' Back at King's he picked up a letter from Erica written unwittingly in support of Keynes. She was contending that her cousin extracted 'unreasonable misery from art'. This, Brooke retorted, was 'all bosh. Art isn't the thing that makes one happy or miserable: it's Life. Art is only a Shadow, a second-rate Substitute, a refuge after Life—real Life.' She was urging him to abandon his melancholy pose and look on the brighter side, but the letter was inadvertently first opened by the wrong hand.

I live on a landing opposite Oscar Browning; a man of bad character and European fame. Your last letter got mixed with *his* morning's post by mistake; and he opened it, naturally. As there was no ordinary beginning, he may have got some way before discovering his error. I still laugh to think of him trying to grasp your highly ethical and valuable advice.

Brooke went on to explain how when last his cousin had seen him he was in the vein to talk flippantly of death and separation. 'Now I have known them, and it hurts, and I'm puzzled and tired, and there's nothing to be done.'

He was in the middle of the May exams, aware that he was doing badly in Greek and worse in Roman History, when an invitation from Keynes to meet Belloc at a meeting of an undergraduate society in Pembroke was so exciting that he spent a sleepless night; nor were there prospects of lying in when exams were over, for the Chapel clerk had called with instructions to read the Lessons at eight o'clock each morning all the next week. For this reason he began his letter home, 'I write feeling a little depressed,' all the same, there was news worth telling. The three old Rugbeians, Keynes, Gow, and himself, had attended the meeting at Pembroke. The day began with an auspicious breakfast.

Today I have been mingling with the great! R. S. Durnford gave the annual 'landing' breakfast—i.e. for all on this landing of this staircase, the two Durnfords, myself, and the 'O.B.'. The last was in great form, talking of what he was going to do when his 'old friends', 'Curzon and Campbell-Bannerman', came up to receive honorary degrees this week, and so on. And at lunch I met Belloc. For him I must begin at the beginning. On Friday I went and heard him read his paper on History in Pembroke. Gow was also there: I had introduced Belloc's works to him and he is very keen on them. Belloc (in the intervals of discussion) drank beer all the evening: his paper and replying was all magnificent to hear. Afterwards Gow who is a person of consummate conceit and 'unabashedness' got into conversation with Belloc, and invited him to lunch for today. Hence my lunch: for of course I went, too. After the paper on Friday Gow and I were coming away when I remembered that Belloc was not staying in Pembroke, so we turned back to see if we could escort him home. We met him coming out of Pembroke and discovered he was staying about a mile away, and had no notion where it was. There was no cab to be found, so we showed him the way, and walked there with him. He was excited after the discussion on his paper and talked absurdly—rather in the *Path to Rome* style—all the way. And at 4 p.m. today I met him again in the street and, finding he was still hazy as to the best way to his house walked there with him again. So altogether I feel rather pleased with myself!

The last event of term was a meeting of the Carbonari at King's when Brooke repeated the talk he had given at Rugby earlier in the year. The title of a book 'The Vagabond in Literature', by Arthur Rickett, had set him thinking. He said there were two kinds of vagabond, of the body and the soul, and the second was far the more interesting, for it suggested 'a rebellion against the safeties and little confines of our ordinary life'. It comes unexpectedly, this wander-thirst of the Spirit, like an odour on the Wind, more compelling than any other kind of summons. 'There are few who have died so early in life that they do not run some risk of hearing thus suddenly Pan's flute in the distance and falling victim to the divine madness' . . . The speaker almost stumbled into a foreshadow of Freud when he went on to say, 'When industrialism has swamped the earth men will turn and look into their own souls and there find many perilous paths and unlit darknesses'. Judged by his standards of vagabondage 'Shelley was a somnambulist, Byron a tourist', and then of course there was Dowson, who was always craving for the impossible, and seemed to Brooke like the two men he once saw in a drawing of Blake's (entitled 'I want. I want.') who were propping their ladder against the moon. Then as for Cunningham, Grahame and Belloc, 'surely it was their wildest wanderlust of all that led them, at different times, into the House of Commons!' He spoke of Villon, Borrow, Stevenson, Gérard de Nerval who went about leading a lobster on a string 'because it neither barks nor bites and it knows the secrets of the deep'; all these men in their several ways were blessed with the gift of 'quicksilver in the heart'. 'Your typical vagabond of the spirit', said Brooke, breaks through the laws an alien world has made 'with a half hysterical defiance'. He is neither for God nor His enemies. 'It is his punishment that in the mire where he wallows the stars are reflected: his punishment and his reward.'

He did badly in the May examinations, having no head for classical or any other kind of history, but there was still time to recover lost ground. Before term ended, his brief appearance as an ornament in the *Eumenides* had led to another theatrical venture. It proved to be of much more consequence, and it deserves tracing from the first beginnings. It all began when Hugh Wilson, a third year man at King's, was having tea with Justin Brooke. The topic was the drama, and Wilson remarked that the set play for the Pass degree that year was Marlowe's *Faustus*. He had just been reading it with admiration, but one couldn't get much out of a play by reading it to one's self. Couldn't a play of that calibre ever be *seen*? 'Why not?' asked Justin; the query was echoed, and after further talk there seemed to be no good reason why not. Justin was fired with a sense of opportunity. Perhaps this could be a start. The Irish Players from the Abbey Theatre had been in Cambridge on their first visit to England. They brought with them the plays of Lady Gregory and Yeats, and the actors were mostly humble people from Dublin. The vitality of the acting, freshness of the dialogue, the air and gesture of poetry, had more than ever convinced him that the climate of the English theatre was languid and in dire need of the vigour of poetry. Marlowe, surely, was the answer. And why not offer the brainwave to the A.D.C.?[1] It was in the audience at an Irish play that Justin had met Charles Sayle, the under-librarian, who had first put him in touch with the A.D.C. In vain Justin had begged its committee to risk a little Shakespeare, but they were wedded to farce. This he regarded as better than nothing—which it was, but by only a narrow margin— so he became its regular leading lady. But now, with *Faustus* in mind, there was nothing for it but to found a new group with a special mission of its own. Wilson himself was half-way through his exams; he would soon be going down, so Justin first roped in Rupert, who shared his enthusiasm for the Irish Players and needed no converting to Marlowe, then at his suggestion both called on Andrew Gow of Trinity. It was Gow who won the consent of the Vice Chancellor and, conscious that the good will of a senior member was necessary to lend the project weight, he brought in one of his own tutors in classics, Francis Cornford, whose rooms were in Nevile's Court. Dr. Verrall, Professor Henry Jackson, and the Provost of King's promised their support; the Greek Play Committee began to re-form for a new purpose. Cornford enlisted the help of his senior classical colleague at Newnham, so that the *Dr. Faustus* enterprise was said to be 'fathered by Cornford and maiden-aunted by Jane Harrison'. The production would be neither frivolous entertainment nor a part of the curriculum. Coming under neither head, it looked like being a distraction from more legitimate pursuits, so the new dramatic group needed all the academic weight it could collect.

The parts were allotted, and rehearsals were to begin at the Victoria Assembly Rooms as soon as the long vacation was over. Justin himself was Dr. Faustus, and there were four young men from Rugby: Rupert as Mephistophilis, Geoffrey Keynes, The Evil Angel, Denis Browne, Lucifer, Russell-Smith as Gluttony among the Seven Deadly Sins; with Gow active in management. Then there were George Mallory (The Pope), Cosmo Gordon (The Cardinal), and Clive Carey (Chorus). There were, of course, no women in the cast (the comely youth A. R. Marshall played Helen of Troy) and

[1] The University Amateur Dramatic Club.

there were to be no names on the programme. The Bedales and Rugby elements had come together for the revival of the classical drama in Cambridge.

Moved to learn more of the Irish Players, Brooke began investing in their works, *The Pot of Broth*, for example, and *Cathleen ni Houlihan*, and carried them to Bournemouth for the beginning of his long vacation. 'This came to me as I was sitting by the sea the other day,' he wrote to Russell-Smith from the promenade. 'I don't know what it was—perhaps it was the rhythm of the waves. But I felt I *must sing*. So I sang:

> *'I love a* scrabbly *epithet,*
> *The sort you can't ever forget,*
> *That blooms, a lonely violet*
> *In the eleventh line of a sonnet.*
>
> *I know one such; I'm proud to know him.*
> *I'll put him in my next GREAT POIM.*
> *He plays the psack-butt very well:*
> *And his Aunt was a Polysyllable.'*

The night is purple with a weariness that is older than the stars; and there is a sound of inevitable tears. R.

Last Easter, in the train between Bologna and Milan, he had got the idea for a sonnet which he called *Dawn*[1]—'Opposite me two Germans snore and sweat,' the first of his poems (unless we were correct in connecting his brother with *The Call*) to be drawn from actual experience. At any rate, the pose of the 'decadence' has vanished from his verse with dramatic suddenness. He had indulged in one last fling half-way through last term, with *Ante Aram*, which was published unsigned in *The Cambridge Review*; the last line—'Or the soft moan of any grey-eyed lute-player' he was himself to parody in an amusing piece of nonsense ending 'Or the soft moan of any bed-maker'. So the King's magazine *Basileon* where *Dawn* appeared, has the credit of publishing the first poem of substantial promise. There was another piece with it, opening hopefully 'They are unworthy, these sad whining moods' then lapsing into rhetoric, as he discovered for himself, for he never republished it. But *Dawn*, the sonnet from the Italian train, makes no effort to force the issue into poetry. Sensitive to a situation, and staying true to his own feelings, he finds an image to evoke them.

[1] G.K., p. 162.

FRESHMAN

A wan light through the rain
Strikes on our faces, drawn and white. Somewhere
A new day sprawls . . .

At Grantchester Dene, Bournemouth, he was poring over a map, looking for somewhere to go with his books and a friend or two, when he came upon the improbable word *Mupe*. 'Have even *we* made a better name?' he asked Russell-Smith, having at length picked on Lulworth, half a mile from the Mupe Rocks. He had Plato with him, but wanted Demosthenes, Marlowe, Shelley, Whitman, Keats, and, through the influence of Headlam, Donne. Then he found the missing book. He was, of course, with the aunts. 'I have spent the evening reading Marlowe when they aren't looking.'

He took rooms for himself and his companion above the Post Office of West Lulworth. It would cost thirty shillings a week for them both, and five shillings extra for attendance. He was by now converted to the open-air life and was going immensely long walks by himself reading Lucretius 'an author whom Arthur [Eckersley] declared yesterday, with an high strange laugh, to be *dear* at any price'.

His performance in the May exams was so notorious that he was getting letters of sympathy. It was said that his 'flippant remarks' in the History papers had caused offence. As to the results (a poor second), 'It is a subject,' he said, 'on which many views can be, and are, held; some, I regret to say, with partisan fervour.' He succeeded in persuading a new friend, Dudley Ward of John's, to join him, and sent minute instructions. 'From Wool one bicycles 4 miles to Lulworth Cove. Does the road wind uphill all the way? No, not quite to the very end, in spite of Miss Rossetti.' Lucas, meanwhile, was given an insight into the life at Grantchester Dene.

My Evangelical aunts always talk at meals like people in Ibsen. They make vast Symbolic remarks about Doors and Houses and Food. My one aim is to keep the conversation on Foreign Missions, lest I scream suddenly. At lunch no one spoke for ten minutes! Then the First Aunt said '. . . The Sea? . . . The Sea! . . .' And an Old Lady Visitor replied: 'Ah?'

So he made his way to the Post Office by the sea, and lost his keys, and had to break open his trunk with a pick-axe, ate ill-advisedly and was very sick 'throwing up, indeed, all I had eaten for weeks and also my immortal soul and several political convictions', he wrote to Keynes. 'Today I am weak but cheerful. I can sit up and take a little

Plato.' He was soon fit and in good spirits, and he sent Keynes an imaginary report in the local paper of the distinguished visitors arriving at Wool station. 'The rain was mainly in two sharp showers from 6 a.m. to noon and from noon to 6 p.m. The ardour of the crowd was undamped, and about 4 p.m. the cry went up "They are on the point of effecting their ingress into the station!" Lightly as boys the Pair leapt from the train, The Old Thing [Russell-Smith] being slightly in front and a good deal behind.' Meanwhile, outside the station, the massed clergymen of the diocese sang a hymn, followed by the undenominational schoolchildren's rendering of an anthem specially written for the occasion:

We welcome Them as They issue from the station, etc.

Carried away by the fantasy, Brooke then gave the local reporter's account of their appearance.

NOTES ON DRESS
by our Lady Correspondent

The Old Thing was looking very chic and a little piqued in a plain pink travelling dress with bodice to match. The chiffon cut-away was neatly worked in with trimmings of fleur-de-lys rosettes down the side, the whole being smartly taken up by valanced double-couplings of mouse-coloured mousseline. The skirt was cut low and full and got clear away over the hips, but was caught up by a neat flounce of cream plush. A small bunch of imitation cherries on the left shoulder completed the *ensemble*, which, though quite *tout fait* for July, must be held a little hard on the tonal values.

B. was wearing his *coiffure* full, but rather low, and a little to windward.

There follow a brief interview with a local worthy, the notable prognosticator, 'at his well-appointed residence in Mupe Lane,' and an ode to Lulworth of which the last fifty verses are omitted but described as 'still simmering'. In less frivolous vein he wrote his poem *Pine Trees and the Sky*.

An incident at Lulworth well illustrates his custom of adopting a manner appropriate to his correspondent. He wrote to his mother:

One day we were reading on the rocks, and I had a Keats in my pocket, and it slipped out, and falling into a swift current, was borne out to sea. So we leapt into a boat and rowed up and down the coast till we espied it off some rocks. But the sea was rather rough and we could not land on that rocky part, or get near Keats. So we landed half a mile off on a beach, and came over the rocks to the Keats; and we found it, I stripped and went in after it and got it. It is indeed quite spoilt: But it only cost two shillings to begin with.

Then Keynes was told the same story:

On Tuesday we sat on seagirt rocks and read J. Keats. When I leapt from rock to rock J.K. fell from pocket into swirling flood beneath; and, ere aught could be done, was borne from reach on swift current. We rushed to the harbour, chartered a boat, and rowed frantically along the rocky coast in search of it . . . At length we spied it close in, by treacherous rocks, in a boat we could not get to it alive. We beached our barque (at vast risk) half a mile down the coast and leapt lightly over vast boulders to the spot. At first we re-saw it not. Then Hugh's small but acute left eye saw it in the midst of a roaring vortex. There was a Pause.

With a hurried misquotation from Diodorus Siculus I cast off my garb, and plunged wholly naked, into that 'fury of black waters and white foam'— Enough. J.K. was rescued, in a damaged condition. All (except my Stomach) is well.

At this time he did not know of an association which he discovered four years later. He was reading the Letters of Keats.

Oh, I've read Keats and found the most AMAZING thing. The last place he was in was Lulworth. His ship was becalmed outside. He and Severn went ashore and clambered about the rocks all day—his last fairly happy day. He went aboard and wrote, that evening, his last poem—that sonnet. The ship took him on to Italy, coughing blood and suffering Hell because he wouldn't see Fanny any more. Fanny sat in Hampstead with Mr. Brown. It was at the end of Sept. 1820.

He celebrated his twentieth birthday with the Russell-Smith family at Brockenhurst. 'I am now in the depths of despondency because of my age,' he wrote to Lucas. 'I am filled with a hysterical despair to think of fifty dull years more. I hate myself and everyone.' After some days in Rugby he was arranging to stay with the Keynes family in Cambridge so that he could see about getting himself a new set of rooms in college. 'What I chiefly loathe and try to escape,' he explained, 'is not Cambridge nor Rugby nor London, but—Rupert Brooke. And I can only do this by rushing suddenly to places for a few days. He soon overtakes me.' Geoffrey Keynes had taken the recklessly progressive step of investing in a 'loco-motor-bicycle', the first to be seen in the purlieus of Cambridge. Brooke thought he should ride it to School Field. 'You will find a choice of some fifty beds'. Sayle was told of Keynes's resolve 'to snort over here and break our old-world serenity . . . While he sleeps I shall steal out and prick his automobile-bicycle all over and remove many screws and ungum the best bits. Then he will mount it on Monday and die.' Rugby was duly astonished by the vehicle, and the intrepid rider survived the journey home.

On September 8 the whole family left for Belgium and found rooms in the Place Louise at Brussels. Rupert admired the Rodins, enjoyed watching the steam trams from his window, or drinking absinthe with Alfred in out-of-the-way cafés. From one of these he wrote to Erica. She had asked for news of his writings. He was too busy with dead and decaying languages, he said, to dream of original composition. 'I am afraid you, in common with the rest of the impatient world, will have to wait, at least for some years, for the divine products of my inspired pen. I am sorry for the world.' His new friend Sayle heard from him. 'This ink is essence of charcoal filled with the decomposing bodies of Flemish flies and German waiters. All evening we have been sitting at an evil café sipping thunder-coloured coffee from glasses.' He saw *Les Troyens*, the opera by Berlioz, and it was totally lost on him. 'They all sang very well, I am told. But I do not understand noise music.' More entertaining was the architecture of the Palais de Justice, erected in 1876 and 'quite good, in the old Assyrian style'. He imagined a madman mistaking it for an antique erected long before the Christian era, making it the subject of an epic poem, discovering his error, and throwing himself under a tram. 'What of the East? Who stand where Sargon stood?' might be a line from his posthumous masterpiece, or 'The grey dust that was Asshur-banipal'.

Rupert and Alfred went on alone to the Hotel de la Paix at Antwerp. 'This evening,' he wrote to Gow, 'I have sat in a café—sipping an exquisite pale green liquor that tasted like a half-ripe hyacinth and smelt like an Italian cesspool and looked like the waves that murmur around Lesbos. The city was white with innumerous lamps more startling and brilliant than many of my best jokes.' He did not share Alfred's conscientious passion for sight-seeing, and the thought that he was now writing to Lucas added an appropriate melancholy. There were labour riots, and street fighting had occurred.

Last night I sat for hours in a café . . . The painted void faces of those that passed filled me with dull horror. I prayed that some great archangel would smite suddenly, blazing down the street, and blast the crawling maggots. The English are the only race who are ever clean and straight and beautiful; and they rarely. I shall never go abroad again. In England of an evening the sun god used to be crucified in beautiful agony on the red places of the west: Here only a suppurating sore is opened afresh and the hot damp air grows damper and fouler. When I get back from here I have to work frantically at Cicero to make up for lost time and then, very soon, go back to Cambridge. Go back to Cambridge for my second year and laugh and talk with those old dull people on that airless plain! The thought fills me with hideous *ennui*.

'I am weary of days and hours.' I am going to drag my tired body out (I have been in nearly all day) in the faint hope of finding a riot.

'The sight of fire and street-fighting might soothe my seared soul,' he added. The next time he was in Antwerp the 'faint hope' was fulfilled. It was not soothing. At Bruges, having rejoined the parents, he posted his parting shot.

> *From too much love of Memling,*
> *From John van Eyck set free,*
> *I swear, without dissembling,*
> *They don't appeal to me.*
> *Rubens is far too clever*
> *Vandyck and Teniers never*
> *Could captivate*
> > *Yours ever*
> > *Profoundly*
> > *R.C.B.*

Exigencies of metre and rhyme dictate the frigid haughtiness of the close.

In late September they arrived home. A parcel was awaiting him, forwarded from King's. It contained *The Marble Sphinx*, a prose fantasy by Lucas, who had just brought out *The Oxford Book of French Verse*. The latter was reviewed by Brooke in *The Cambridge Review*, where he riled the editor by observing 'Some may complain that Prudhomme did not die sooner'. The prose work is important. Brooke had read the manuscript early in his last year at school. Not only did it give new impetus to the 'decadence' just when it was beginning to wane, but the influence of this study in the grotesque can be found in Brooke's poems as well as his letters. His first poetical effort under its influence was *The Beginning* (1906) 'Some day I shall rise and leave my friends,' in which a lover goes in search of a lost paramour and 'seeing your eye and ashen hair, I'll curse the thing that once you were'. While still fascinated by Lucas's theme of beauty corrupted and humiliated by the passage of time, he wrote the twin sonnets *Menelaus and Helen* (1909) which are derived directly from a passage in *The Marble Sphinx*. Not only beauty in decline but domesticity is there reviled, and Helen in age is depicted as a wrinkled matron, 'haggard with virtue', a tribute in verse to that aspect of overblown romanticism that Lucas celebrated in his fantasy and which had sunk deep into the mind of the adolescent Brooke.

In *The Marble Sphinx* Alexis, a young cup-bearer, has been beaten
by Nubian slaves and left at the roadside 'with his open hands half
hidden in the long grass'. He is rescued by an old man and a girl who
come past, carried in a litter, and taken along with them to the feast
of Thanatos. The description of the two in the litter gives a fair
impression of the general style, and warrants our attention for more
than one reason. Within a few months, early in 1908, Elroy Flecker
came up to Cambridge as an advanced student in Oriental languages
attached to Caius, and began his acquaintance with Brooke. He
would certainly have been told all about *The Marble Sphinx* and if he
bought or borrowed it he would have discovered a writer of 'jewelled'
language who was intrigued with sadism and the idea of a gross and
corpulent man associating with a girl of delicate youth and beauty
such as, not long after, Flecker himself was to portray with more
artistry in the love of Hassan for Yasmin. Alexis saw that within the
litter 'two figures lolled'—

the one a very corpulent old man with a flushed and hideous face and a bald
head that was crowned with roses; the other, a pale girl with lips of
startling scarlet and strange painted eyelids. A golden lantern hung above
them, illuminating the diaphanous rainbow-hued raiment of the woman and
the loose coils of flesh in the man's throat and neck. He was drinking tawny
wine from a cup that Parrhasias himself had painted, and ever and again he
caressed the white shoulders of the girl with his blotched and scaly hand.

At the feast a girl dances a Salome dance in a ring of skulls. She
picks up one, the skull of Helen, 'the breath of whose hair once
drove men mad. But she grew old, and her bright hair became grey
and thin: yea, Helen, the desire of Heaven, became a bald and
withered hag who was fain even in summer to crouch over the fire . . .'
and then she holds up the skull of 'Antinous, the fair Bithynian', and
others who fell at Marathon. At length the dance is interrupted by
the thunder of drums, and Zeus is seen approaching, an old wretch
in filthy rags, leading the gods of the East astride elephants and
tigers. 'The hideous bulks of a thousand idols rocked stupidly to and
fro', and then come the lesser Olympians, all degraded and defiled,
among them Aphrodite who has become an ageing courtesan. At the
climax appears the Marble Sphinx, a supernatural creature let loose
by Pan to avenge the gods, that wreaks havoc among the guests but
cannot prevail over Death, who is master of the feast. Eros, however,
has one arrow left. This kills Thanatos, and Love and Pan, alone of
the immortals, survive the massacre. In the eyes of Alexis the figure

of Love and the Christian Saviour seem to be identified, and the fantasy ends with this hint that the tale was an allegory. But only those, we feel, who have suffered the romantic agony can possibly find the key.

Mrs. Brooke was reported as 'definitely not liking it'; Corrie Grant, the M.P. for Rugby, who happened to be in the house, read it, and confessed himself baffled; Keynes, the week-end visitor, was impressed. As for Brooke himself, he had long since paid Lucas the compliment of adapting to his purpose some of his extravagances of thought and style. Even so, it now struck him afresh. 'It has coloured my dreams for nights,' he wrote to the author. 'I love and loathe it more than ever.' Some time before he had drafted a parody. It was a vampire priestess who lived in a temple. 'In pallid vestments on the altar steps slept two acolytes, white-visaged and satiate of interminable vigil, lit by the grotesque palpitation of the seven guttering altar-tapers.' But he came nearer to Lucas in imagery with the sentence 'It seemed that as the strong sun creates life in decaying food, so the moon's cold flame had generated in this lonely corner a mass of huge maggots.' They were victims of the priestess. There is no record of a comment by Lucas. A pity.

He was laid up with a bad leg, having been knocked over and kicked on the knee in a game of football. 'It is as swollen and strangely green and black as your prose style, but not nearly so pleasant . . . I only walk when Mother has gone out and cannot catch me on my feet. Then I rush up and down to relieve my feelings. Rugby is full of the next generation. It is raining.'

On October 7 he arrived back in what he called 'the mephitic unhealthiness' and occupied new rooms at King's, Room One on E Staircase, on the ground floor of Gibbs's buildings, at the corner further from the Chapel. Lowes Dickinson lived at the top of the building. In his work, he now left Henry Sills, started going to Nathaniel Wedd for History, but remained with Sheppard and Headlam for Greek and Latin composition. Arthur Schloss (Waley) was a welcome freshman from Rugby and a newcomer to the Carbonari, but Raverat whom he had hoped to see, was still on the Continent, a sick man. It was nearly two years before he reappeared in Cambridge. A note from him in France prompted Brooke to try and rally his spirits.

I am, indeed, villainous not to have written. Only when I returned to this miasma did I know you were not to be up this term. And since then this tinselled booth we call life has been filled with flaring torches and shouting and the scarlet of trumpets and squeaking of the puppet-show. I spend my hours in seeing vain and shadowy people; and even so I can never flee myself. And my soul is an eremite; and rebels.

And you—why should you wish to be in this swamp, pilgrim? Where are you? A man ran swiftly, like a sudden flame, at midnight, and cried that you were at Venice. Then there was silence. Do you indeed glide in sombre silence down fantastic canals, where the gloomy houses on either side spring into the night sky, and from invisible windows overhead strange voices whisper to one another hot, wild endearments, or wail out once, and no more?

Cambridge is a 'wilderness', uneventful except when Keynes makes his weekly foray down King's Parade on his 'smell-machine'. The only substantial piece of news is the progress of *Faustus*. 'Justin is excellent; Geoffrey and Mallory both bad.'

Rehearsals had begun at the Victoria Assembly Rooms within a few days of the beginning of term. Justin combined the leading role with function of producer and stage manager, by virtue of the fact that he alone of the group had any experience of theatrical presentation. Gow assisted him. Even before the curtain had gone up on the first production, there was talk of making this the inaugural event of a new society. They issued a fly-sheet which announced that 'should this performance prove successful, it is intended to form a Society in Cambridge for the production of other Elizabethan plays'. Justin had special aims: to get the players to speak the verse as verse, and not as stilted prose—(since most of the cast had read the Lessons at school, there was a general tendency to lapse into a parsonical monotone); to persuade the players to remain anonymous; to try the innovation of the female parts being taken by women; and to make it a rule that the senior member of the society, whoever it might be, should never have control of the policy. It must be an undergraduate enterprise with the senior member on the committee giving weight to its deliberations and representing its interests in places of authority. No one minded being anonymous, but the proposal to include girls from Newnham and Girton in term-time productions was an un-dreamt-of departure from university custom. It would be some while, several years no doubt, before such a daring move was authorized, but when Justin and Cornford came to draft the regulations of the society they expressed them in such terms (and such was their optimism) that no word of their articles would have to be altered in the event of the ban being lifted.

Within a few days there was a crisis. Andrew Gow, a founder member, who had furthered the cause by persuading Cornford to take an interest in it, turned up at rehearsal and told Justin that as he wanted a First in his Tripos, he must withdraw; moreover he contended, no doubt quite rightly, that he could not be the only one of the company who was having to give too much time to what was after all only a form of recreation. The whole affair was developing out of proportion. He thought the production should be cancelled before it was too late. This seemed a legitimate point of view, so the two men decided to put it to the assembled cast and abide by whatever they said. Justin posed the problem, and an ominous silence ensued. 'Well,' said Rupert at last, for no one else seemed ready to take the initiative, 'since we've got so far, it seems a pity to give it up'— hardly an adequate reason for continuance at the risk of everyone's hopes of academic distinction, but it was enough. There was no dissent. Gow himself withdrew his objection; the rehearsal went on, and the infant dramatic society that was still without a name survived its first crisis.

There were days taken off from rehearsal. Brooke called on Lucas at Goldsmith Building in London and was taken to see Sarah Bernhardt in *Phèdre*. One afternoon he staged his first tea party, and Rose Macaulay, just down from Somerville College, Oxford, whose family lived not far away at Shelford, came with her mother and sister to the new room lit by Japanese paper lanterns. There were desultory sessions with Headlam, who was himself more interested in the progress of *Dr. Faustus* than the Greek matter in hand, and a football match against John's. 'King's are weak this year and need my services,' he wrote to his mother while tidying up after the tea-party.

There were misgivings about *Faustus*. Some said, 'It isn't a play, anyway,' others, 'Why don't they get someone to coach them?' At the dress rehearsal J. W. Clark, an out-spoken official of the university, whom the A.D.C. had silenced by electing to their committee, was heard to exclaim—'A set of incompetent amateurs mumbling rubbish in the dark!' When this came to Justin's ears, his last fears were dispelled. He knew they were all right. Then on November 11 at the A.D.C. Theatre in Jesus Lane *Dr. Faustus* was given the first of two performances.

FRESHMAN

The curtain was delayed a few minutes by the arrival of Prince Leopold of the Belgians and his retinue. In the audience was E. J. Dent, the musicologist and don at King's, who was just back from a long absence on the Continent. He noted first the programme, a single sheet with the list of Marlowe's characters (and no names of the players) on the one side, and on the other nothing but a quotation of two lines:

> Most highest of all their fires but one
> Our morning star, sole risen before the sun.

And then the curtain went up on the first production by the group that would soon be calling itself *The Marlowe Dramatic Society*. There was no music, no scenery save dark green hangings, no footlights, and the performance was punctuated with frequent black-outs. Of the two Brookes, Faustus 'looked absurdly young', and Mephistophilis (Rupert) spoke in a 'thick and indistinct voice' with his head concealed in a cowl and generally half turned away from the audience. It was crude, Dent thought, but the dramatic incidents were curiously compelling and the whole evening seemed to be suffused with what he could only call the 'spirit of poetry'. It was like nothing he had seen before, and he was so moved to learn more about this venture that he went back-stage to meet the Brookes. He found Mephistophilis 'silent and uncommunicative'. However, the show had gone well, and the management had £20 in hand. A leaflet distributed in the auditorium announced that should the performance prove a success, it was intended to found a society. There were no newspaper critics present, but everyone *felt* it was a success.

Charles Sayle then gave a supper party for the principals at his home at 8 Trumpington Street. A month before Rupert had dined with him alone. 'He is so full of art and poetry,' Sayle wrote in his diary that evening. Three days after the last Marlowe performance, Rupert called again and found him out. It was late in the afternoon. He decided to wait. That night Sayle made another entry in his diary:

I did a little shopping, and came home. Standing in my hall in the dark, and thinking of other things, I looked towards my dining-room, and there, seated in my chair, in a strong light, he sat, with his head turned towards me, radiant. It was another unforgettable moment. A dramatic touch. A Rembrandt picture. Life.

Elsewhere he was making an impression. Although he was still no more than a cautious Associate, Hugh Dalton and himself had been

135

elected to the committee of the Fabians. On the day *Faustus* opened Brooke had written to an Old Rugbeian at Oxford to say he was coming over with 'an indecorous, atheistical, obscene set of ruffians called the Fabians . . . I look just like a Socialist'. They were all going in workaday cloth caps, Norfolk jackets, and flannel bags. Brooke was put up for a night at Trinity—and got back to Cambridge in time for an important Fabian occasion attended by Shaw and Granville-Barker. Shaw devoted his remarks to his scheme for the formation of a 'middle class' party in Parliament. 'I preferred the funny bits,' the new committee member confessed in a letter to Erica. Granville-Barker spoke on 'Socialism and the Drama' and dined afterwards with the undergraduates' committee. 'I sat next him!! I neither spoke nor ate, but sat still watching his face. The profile is one of the nicest things in the world. And his voice!' Brooke had not yet attended a meeting of the committee. Most of his colleagues, he had heard, were 'Newnhamites, strange wild people, whom I shall infuriate by being utterly incompetent. I am greatly looking forward to it.'

When he wrote to Erica he had just got back to his rooms after taking part in another theatrical performance, mounted by the frivolous A.D.C. For three nights he appeared as Stingo in *She Stoops to Conquer* with Justin Brooke, who had for some time now reigned unchallenged as the society's leading lady, playing Miss Hardcastle. The faithful Sayle watched a performance, and shortly afterwards recorded an odd scrap of conversation. The topic was occasioned by a visit from Steuart Wilson, the musical brother of Hugh, the Marlowe founder. Both the Wilson brothers were uncommonly tall. 'I am exactly six feet,' said Brooke, 'which is the exact height I wish to be,' then, on being asked why, he went on, 'Because there is a legend that Christ was exactly six feet, not a hair's breadth more or less.' Sayle asked him where on earth he had got this improbably precise information. 'Somewhere in Yeats's prose,' came the reply.

Rupert and Alfred had arranged to join a party of thirty at Andermatt on the Gotthard Pass, Switzerland, so when term ended he went home to pick up his things, then filled in the interval before sailing with the convenient aunts at Bournemouth. His unsuitable reading this time was a new publication of mildly revolutionary character called *Human Justice for those at the Bottom from those at the Top* by none other than Clement Cotterill, his uncle, who after leaving Fettes had become headmaster of a school in Liverpool and now lived in retirement near Godalming. The thesis of the book was a plea that since both rich and poor alike owed their condition to the same cause (the commercial system that dominated modern society) the affluent should voluntarily come to the aid of those in need. Cotterill based his appeal on the innate goodness in human nature, and maintained that his scheme was only not in operation already because the upper-classes, having more money than imagination, needed a pamphlet of this sort to put the idea into their heads. The only alternative, in the author's opinion, was the catastrophe of civil strife. Reviewing the book in a Cambridge magazine some months later, Brooke declared its pages were imbued with 'a splendid atmosphere of faith and idealism'. From Bournemouth he wrote to his uncle acknowledging the book and describing his own position.

I am an Associate (not an actual Member) of the Cambridge Fabian Society, and have lately been coming across there a good many Socialists, both of the University and from without, as well as unattached sympathisers like Lowes Dickinson. I wish I could get more of these, especially among the Fabians, to accept your definition of Socialism. Most of them, I fear, would define it as 'Economic Equality', or, the 'Nationalization of Land and Food Production' or some such thing. In a private way I have some influence among some of them, and have been trying to urge on them a more human view of things; I shall be able to do so a good deal better and more clearly now. Socialism is making great advances at Oxford and Cambridge just now; but its upholders are too apt to make it seem, to others and to themselves, a selfish scheme of economics. They confound the means with the end; and think that a compulsory Living Wage is the end, instead of a good beginning. Bernard Shaw came down last term, and made a speech that was enthusiastically received, in which he advised a state of things in which each 'class' had its own party in Parliament fighting for its own hand. The whole thing was based on selfishness. It was not inspiring.

Of course they're really sincere, energetic, useful people, and they do a lot of good work. But, as I've said, they seem rather hard. Must every cause lose part of its ideal, as it becomes successful? And also they are rather intolerant, especially towards the old order. They sometimes seem to take it for granted that all rich men, and all Conservatives (and most ordinary Liberals) are heartless villains. I have already, thanks, in part, to various words of yours, got some faith in the real, sometimes over-grown, goodness of all men; and that is why I have found your book so good, as a confirmation rather than a revelation. And this faith I have tried to hammer into those Socialists of my generation I have come across. But it's sometimes hard. The prejudices of the clever are harder to kill than those of the dull. Also I sometimes wonder whether this Commercialism or Competition or whatever the filthy infection is, hasn't spread almost too far, and that the best hope isn't in some kind of upheaval.

Both the aunts were in bed with colds. This meant that Rupert was at liberty to read at meals and put butter on his potatoes, as he told his mother. She had threatened him with a knitted waistcoat. 'I do not hold with waistcoats,' he wrote, firmly declining the offer, 'they are bad for the chest or something.' Calling and coughing through the closed door of her bedroom, Fanny had sent messages to Rugby, time and again calling her nephew back, having had an afterthought. Rupert was unable either to convert her to Socialism through the key-hole or put his ear to it the better to catch her message, since she had stuck the key in on the other side to prevent the germs from seeping on to the landing. But it was most necessary for him to give a trustworthy report. The aunts at Grantchester Dene, especially Fanny, were easily intimidated, and Mrs. Brooke's kindly interest in their well-being was something they did not have the courage to say they almost preferred to do without. Besides it was so well meant. 'May says I ought not to have a fire in my bedroom,' said Fanny to Lizzy, wistfully, one cold morning when May (Mrs. Brooke) was staying under their roof. Lizzy looked exasperated. Was Fanny incapable of learning from experience? 'Why,' she asked her sister in an impatient undertone, 'Why did you ever *tell* her you had a fire in your bedroom?' There was another occasion when May came back to the drawing-room from one of her incursions into the kitchen. It was at a time when the two maiden ladies were feeling rather satisfied with a new cook. 'Where did you get that cook?' May inquired. No answer, so she went on, 'Don't like her face.' Mrs. Brooke had recently become a local magistrate at Rugby. 'It's the sort of face,' she explained with a grimace of mistrust, 'I'd expect to find looking down at me from the dock.'

By Christmas Brooke was at Danioth's Grand Hotel, Andermatt, learning the part of Algernon in *The Importance of Being Earnest* which some of the party were going to present in the ballroom. The party was a Cambridge medley. 'They are nearly all Socialists,' he wrote to Erica. 'Even the Newnhamites and others of their sex and age are less terrible than they might be.' At least two of his Fabian Committee were there, the new young lady Treasurer, whom everyone was calling 'Ka', and Margery Olivier, accompanied by her sister Brynhild with whom Brooke thought he was in love for at least four months, until, that is, he met the youngest of the family. For the moment he was dazzled by Bryn, and sullen with the onset of his manhood. 'I'm a bad person to be one of a party of merry people like these. I'm too dull and sulky,' was all that Erica was told. There was much ski-ing and tobogganing. 'I am fat and red and my nose has no skin.' For some reason Erica had got it into her head that he worked too hard. 'You are quite wrong. I may fall ill of a broken heart or of perpetual misanthropy or, certainly, of the Cambridge climate—but of overwork, never!'

It was now the year 1908. Early in January he was in Cambridge taking exams, seated beside a notoriously conscientious candidate. 'He looks so wise all the time that he gets on my nerves.' His uncle Alan, the Dean, was also on his nerves. Habitual non-attendance at Chapel on the one side, and on the other the feeling that there was nowhere on earth where there wasn't a blood relation to get into his hair, led to sparks and the line 'Intolerable consanguinity' on which Brooke constructed a lively sonnet[1] which appeared (anonymously of course) in a local paper. James Strachey was his companion. He had also come up early. 'He has sojourned in Mentone of late and was sorry. He tried to get into the gaming-rooms at Monte Carlo but was turned out because he was too young! So does tragedy border upon farce.' On the 23rd Brooke attended his first Fabian Committee meeting, and the Marlowe Dramatic Society was now formally constituted with himself as President, Geoffrey Keynes as Secretary and Cornford Treasurer. In that quarter there were already new developments.

During a tutorial Headlam had pointed out that the Tercentenary of Milton's birth was due to fall in the summer of this year, and he suggested that the masque of *Comus* might make an appropriate sequel to *Doctor Faustus*. Only a few days later Justin called and discussed under the paper lanterns a new enterprise for the Marlowe Society. Dr. A. C. Shipley, Master of Christ's, Milton's college, was proposing to mount an Exhibition to celebrate the Tercentenary, and he also had conceived the idea of a production of *Comus* in the college garden, near the mulberry trees planted, according to tradition, by the poet himself. He had asked Justin to call on him, and they had talked of ways and means. One of the Fellows of Christ's, Sir Francis Darwin, botanist and author of the life of his father, Charles Darwin, had an 'artistic daughter', as the Master put it, who was a private pupil of the painter Will Rothenstein. She lived with her father, a widower, in the Madingley Road and might be persuaded to help with the designs.

[1] *In time of Revolt*, G.K., p. 1.

And so it came about that early in February the two Brookes called at 13 Madingley Road. Frances Darwin, aged twenty-one, had recently come back from a spell of convalescence in Switzerland. Her mother, Ellen Wordsworth Crofts, a great-niece of the poet, had died suddenly in 1903, and her only child had been slow to recover from the shock. Mrs. Darwin was one of the original students at Newnham and the particular friend of Jane Harrison. She had been brought up near Bolton Abbey where her father was the Rector, together with a brother Ernest, who made a name for himself as a painter. The daughter she left behind was an omnivorous reader, but her books and even her lessons in draughtsmanship with Rothenstein were not enough to engross an active mind, so that the prospect of working on designs for *Comus* came at a providential moment. The two Brookes were almost taken aback by her eagerness to do what she could for their scheme. They never suspected that she was as ardent a devotee of poetry as themselves. Already she had begun writing little pieces of her own, which ended almost as soon as they began, drawing their poetic energy from a single word, or two at the most, which seemed to colour their surroundings and hold them together with the compactness of an epigram. She became the first contemporary poet to share Brooke's art with him, and through that fellowship and his trust she was to exert an influence on his life.

Her father's only child by his second marriage, she was of middle height, with long dark hair, brown eyes deep set, and the blunted features characteristic of the Darwins, which could change in a trice from an almost masculine strength to a peculiarly feminine softness when they smiled. Her withdrawn and slightly quavering voice, which at first might give an impression of affectation because of its Cambridge drawl, gave utterance to the thoughts and feelings of a nature unaffected and unassuming almost (but not quite, being, as it were, sophisticated from birth) to the point of naïveté; a nature easy of access, and therefore vulnerable, wide open to the trend of the moment. As befitted a Darwin, her life was sustained by the relish of a curiosity never satisfied. 'Oh, Mr. Brooke! A production of *Comus* in the garden of Christ's! . . .' then, never entirely carried away, the note of down-to-earth detachment. 'But suppose it rains!' She had a point there.

It now struck the Brookes as unreasonable to suppose that the English climate would reform out of respect for Milton. They would persuade the Master to entertain his guests at the New Theatre after their Tercentenary banquet, then perhaps there could be a public matinée next day. Miss Darwin was not at all sure she could undertake the entire responsibility of the dresses. She had a cousin, she said, of greater promise in draughtsmanship than herself, in fact there was talk of her becoming a student at the Slade next year. For the scenic designs Will Rothenstein, Miss Darwin's own art master, would be consulted by the next post, and as for the two young impresarios, their next step should be to call on the cousin at Newnham Grange beyond Silver Street bridge.

Gwen Darwin was a year older than her cousin in Madingley Road. Her father, Sir George, an elder brother of the Fellow of Christ's, had been Plumian Professor of Astronomy since 1883, and he lived in a larger house with a wife and family of children. Gwen, the eldest, agreed to collaborate with Frances on the costumes; Jane Harrison enlisted young ladies from Newnham for the cast (this was irregular, but since the performance would be given in the long vacation they would be offending only the spirit rather than the letter of the law) and among them there was Ka Cox, who agreed to be one of the four dancers in the Pavane and to work with the Darwin cousins, helping to execute their designs. E. J. Dent was to arrange the music from Lawes and Purcell; and Albert Rothenstein, William's brother, promised to look after the scenery, and was given a budget of £15 for the purpose. It was altogether a most elaborate enterprise. After the Brookes had called at Trumpington Street to outline the developing scheme, Charles Sayle wrote in his journal that night, 'It fairly took my breath away'.

In mid-February Sayle, Mallory and Brooke were invited by Geoffrey Keynes to hear H. G. Wells give a talk on Socialism at Pembroke. On his way back to King's, Brooke gave Sayle the proofs of his poem *The Song of the Pilgrims*, his first poem submitted to the *Westminster Gazette* for its own sake, independent of a competition, and signed with his own name, and he asked Sayle to check the punctuation. Perhaps he had already got the idea from Frances Darwin, who was in the habit of inviting her friends to 'contribute the commas' to her poems. Brooke's new piece was nothing special— (the sentence 'The fires we left are always burning On the old shrines of home' was probably the origin of Lena Guilbert Ford's catch phrase in the First World War, 'Keep the home fires burning') —but Sayle by now was captivated by the personal magnetism of the young man. 'I do not know in what language to moderate my appreciation of this great man,' he entered in his diary. 'The world will learn to know him later on. It has been mine to know him now.'

While Wells was still in Cambridge he accepted an invitation from the *Carbonari* at King's. They arranged a debate on the subject of 'the family' in Brooke's rooms where Wells was the principal speaker. Lowes Dickinson was there and Ben Keeling of Trinity; Gerald Shove, a new supporter of the *Carbonari* who had come up last term from Uppingham, a dark man with high cheek bones and a mordant wit, more stable in temperament than the unpredictable Keeling, but like him pledged to the liquidation of Victorianism; Arthur Waley, and of course Hugh Dalton; and the whole occasion seemed to Brooke to represent his arrival at last as someone acknowledged among things and people that mattered. 'Wells is a very pleasant little man,' he wrote to his mother, 'insignificant in appearance and with a thin voice (he has only one lung) and slight Cockney accent ('thet' for 'that'). He is rather shy.'

Near the end of this Lent term the *Carbonari* met again, and Brooke read his paper on the modern poets which had provided his last word as a schoolboy at Rugby. It seemed a very long while ago, and turning up his notes, it must have been borne in on him that he was no longer quite the same person. His opinions about the poets had not altered much, but there was an air of nostalgia in the paper which, since he had no time to do any rewriting, nevertheless needed some explaining. So he wrote a new opening, telling his listeners how the essay first came into being as a kind of farewell speech to the Upper VIth at Rugby—

—people I had grown rather fond of, and whom I felt I was going to see only a few times more in this world—and even then I was a little doubtful about the next. And anyhow I was very sad at the whole thing. I had been happier at Rugby than I can find words to say. As I looked back at five years I seemed to see almost every hour golden and radiant and always increasing in beauty as I grew more conscious, and I could not (and cannot) hope for or ever quite imagine such happiness elsewhere. And then I found the last days of all this slipping by me, and with them the faces and places and life I loved, and I without power to stay them. I became for the first time conscious of transience and parting and a great many other things. So in this paper written at such a time you may find a tone of sentimentality, weakness, sorrow, or what you will. At least you know why it's there.

He also contrived a new ending, and tried to answer the complaint that modern poets seemed to ignore the progress of science such as 'the nebular hypothesis of evolutionary theories'. In so far as these ideas concern the human race as a whole, his poets did indeed remain unmoved, but wherever they touched the individual's hopes and fears 'then they affect every poet very deeply, for it's a tendency of the poetic nature to find the feelings of the individual more important than anything else.' Disbelief in personal immortality, for instance, runs through most of modern verse. The only faith nowadays is a conviction that 'human love, though temporal, may be so great that eternal death is a little thing: one perfect moment outweighs unending darkness; it is worth while.' And then there was the poet's place in the revolt against industrial society. As for the man who objected to poetry on the grounds of its 'uselessness and irrelevance', what could one say to him?

I'd like to show him that poetry expressed in words is an easy, reasonable, and sane affair, as natural and pleasant as good eating, or exercise, or sleeping; and that Poetry itself is a thing neither he nor anyone else could possibly do without. It is life. It's the spirit of gloriousness in things, the only thing for which anybody, whether mooning poet or 'sensible Englishman' lives, the Crown and Explanation and Justification of the Universe.

Perhaps it was on this occasion that an unconverted *Carbonaro*, pressing his case, elicited from Brooke the remark which Dalton overheard and never forgot. 'There are only three good things in the world. One is to read poetry, another is to write poetry, and the best of all is to *live* poetry,' and he said he was beginning to have glimpses of what poetry *really* meant—how it solved problems of conduct, settled all questions of value, and, through its unaltering freshness, 'even kept one young'. This acceptance of youth as an absolute good was part of his aesthetic faith. The essential man could only be as old as his sensibilities. If only he could prevent his perceptions from growing blunted or the lustre of his enthusiasm dim, he would never be without the most precious aspect of his youth. One evening Brooke and Dalton were sharing a window seat overlooking King's Parade. They had been discussing the nature of Beauty, a common topic in those days when the philosopher, G. E. Moore, was making everyone think afresh about the nature of the good life. The discussion had already lasted for an hour or so when they were disturbed by a party of young men going home, whooping and whistling under the window, having dined too well. 'Those fellows,' said Brooke, 'would have thought us very old if they had been in this room tonight, but when they go down and sit on office stools they will grow old quite suddenly, and, many·years hence we shall be talking and thinking about this sort of thing, and we shall still be young.'

The Lent term was at an end. He had opened his mouth on the committee of the Fabians; he was the only undergraduate on the governing board of *The Cambridge Review*, 'I am very pleased with myself about it,' he wrote to his mother; President of the *Marlowe Dramatic Society*; a host in his rooms to Wells and Lowes Dickinson. He was also, at last, an initiated member of the Society, or the 'Apostles', whose custom was to meet on Saturday evenings. Having for some time been a candidate or 'embryo' he was now 'born', in the parlance of what was called for short 'the Society', an exclusive body which had flourished since the days of George IV. When Tennyson and Hallam were members, it was imbued with a high sense of social responsibility, and its effect on the Victorian poet was to give him that lofty sense of a mission which accounted for a didactic element in his work, an element now found to have lost all trace of poetic life. Under the influence of Moore, or rather that section of his philosophy which most appealed to the young men of his time, providing them with what almost amounted to a substitute for a religion, the Society was concerning itself in the main with the individual and the relative value of his states of mind. It profoundly affected Brooke long before he actually read a page of the book from which this climate of feeling was derived. Indeed it was not until 1910 that he at last came to open *Principia Ethica*. But for a member of the Society there was no need to read the book. One was infected by it through one's friends for whom it coloured every mood and opinion. Moore's attitude to life was the bond between Dalton (not himself an Apostle) and Brooke in the window-seat when the late night revellers lurched below, and at a stage when Brooke has grown more closely acquainted with it, there will be need to examine what he found. That is not yet. It is enough to know that to him it was somehow incomplete and left him unsatisfied. He needed to complement Moore with some philosophy which linked him more closely with his neighbour. The strength and indeed the nobility in Mrs. Brooke was her Puritanism. It was there hardly less in her son, where, in that divided nature, it could create a conflict under stress and so might even become a source of weakness. So far, however, there was no trace of discord, and the solution he sought was under his nose. If Moore and his disciples revealed to him so much of the true, the beautiful, and good, as concerned the private individual, there was already to hand a complementary faith for a man who could not indefinitely give second place to his moral obligation to his neighbour. He was, almost, a Fabian Socialist. If he signed what they called the Basis, then the principles by which he might be able to conduct his life would be all assembled.

His ideas had begun to clarify. Friends were entering his life, sorting themselves out, and taking up their positions as if for the opening of a drama. He had met Sidney Webb at breakfast, and given another tea-party in his rooms for the ladies of the Fabian committee, Margery Olivier and Ka Cox, chaperoned by Ka's stepmother. Until recently he had still felt a freshman, always inclined to hark back to a smaller world where everything seemed so very much more safe and simple and himself so much more important. Within the last few weeks these things had changed. He had just been to Oxford again, 'to tell them what I think of Socialism. Very good for them,' he wrote to Raverat who was still abroad, and on the way back the whole party had listened to a debate at the House of Commons as guests of Corrie Grant, the member for Rugby. He was enjoying Cambridge at last, so he could afford to disguise his true feelings in terms of extravagant insult, and in the style of *The Marble Sphinx* (which he no longer took very seriously) for he was now writing, he explained, not from what Henley meant by 'England! my England!', no, but rather from—

the Hinder Parts, the *faeces* or *crassamentum* or dregs, the Eastern Counties; a low swamp, a confluence of mist and mire, a gathering-place of Dankness, and Mud, and Fever; where men's minds rot in the mirk like a leper's flesh, and their bodies grow white and soft and malodorous and suppurating and fungoid, and so melt in slime.

I have a cold.

Chapter V

KINGSMAN

(*April 1908–June 1909*)

It was early April, 1908, and he was writing to Hugh Dalton from seaside lodgings in Beacon Terrace, Torquay.

Under the influence of
    (a) Talks with the wee, fantastic, *Wells*.
    (b) His books.
    (c) Fabian tracts.
    (d) Private meditation and prayer.
    (e) Arguments on the other side.
    (f–z) Anything . . . etc. . . . .

I have decided to sign even the present Fabian Basis, and to become a member (if possible) of the central Fabian Society.

The former part, I suppose, may wait till next term; as I have no Basis with me. Spiritually, the thing is done (not without blood and tears). But the latter—is it possible, and what steps can I take, even now? Where write? What say? . . . Tell me . . . I am eager, as a neophyte always is, for action.

On the way through London he had met Wells at the National Liberal Club. The book of his that moved him was the one just out, *New Worlds for Old*; the tracts were numerous, the meditation no doubt prolonged, and the 'arguments on the other side' picked up in dispute with his parents at home. Under 'Anything' one must include *In Peril of Change*, a collection of essays by Charles Masterman, the Liberal M.P. who had won his seat in the general landslide of 1906. Brooke and Dalton were regarding him as the leader of the Radical-Socialist wing of the Liberal Party which they hoped would eventually join forces with Labour and 'so form a real Socialist Party in Britain. And then, of course, there was *News from Nowhere*. 'I'm not your sort of Socialist,' he had said to Dalton last year. 'I'm a William Morris sort of Socialist.'

Brooke's notes and marginal jottings show that he had traced

Keeling's political faith back to its first beginnings. He discovered, perhaps first of all, that when Darwin published his theory of evolution in 1859 he made the young generation of that time look round at the world and man's condition afresh. Nothing could be taken on trust from those who had grown set in their ways before the dawn of the new age. Already current was the philosophy of Comte which, under the name of the Religion of Humanity, set out to cleanse society of superstition and inequality of wealth and reorganize it on the basis of what was considered pure reason. But like the Christian churches the Positivists, as they were called, were content to moralize capitalism, and soon there were many who began to search for some method of reforming industrial society which was at once more radical and more sure. Among English thinkers it was John Stuart Mill who first suggested that there was, or could be, an alternative to the capitalist system, and it was his argument of the case which converted William Morris. *News from Nowhere* came into Brooke's hands in the long vacation of 1907, some eight months before he decided to sign the Basis. Brooke was staying a night at Godalming with his cousin Erica and her father. 'I found *News from Nowhere* in my bedroom,' he wrote to Clement Cotterill, 'and read it on and on all through the night till I don't know what hour! and ever since I've been a devoted admirer of Morris, and a Socialist, and all sorts of things.'

He was allowed to keep the copy he borrowed. It is dated July 11, 1907. This political fantasy had first come out in 1890, and was cast in the form of a dream of a remote future, a pastoral Utopia: no foreign trade, no central government, no inequality of wealth or class, or surplus goods, no slavery to money or power, and the pleasure men take in their work is the most they ever ask to get out of it. Anarchy is too drastic a word to describe the principle governing the economy of this earthly Paradise, and Communism too simple. Asked whether he accepted Marx's theory of value, Morris replied 'To speak quite frankly, I do not know what Marx's theory of value is, and I'm damned if I want to know.' He had tried to take the science of political economy with the seriousness that was its due, but 'much of it appears to me to be dreary rubbish'. He was drawn to Socialism by the spectacle of wasted life seen with his own eyes, and in an act of poetic fantasy, he destroyed industrial society as if it had never been, and then supposed an England that his mind and conscience could inhabit at peace. Brooke had for long admired *The Story of Sigurd the Volsung*. In the work of Morris, Poetry and Revolution seemed to have joined hands and found a single voice. But the 'news' had come from 'Nowhere' beyond the ferment of a poet's brain. Brooke wanted practical ways and means.

In his copy of the book he noted down his thoughts—'Greek city states—the medieval guilds—different kinds of mutual aid.' And then he thought of the Swiss cantons, 'valuable instances of the way in which mutual support springs up directly it is allowed,' noting that in Russia since about 1880 there had been a movement towards village communities. He copied out scraps from the book—'individual men cannot shuffle off the business of life on to the shoulders of an abstraction called the State'; phrases illustrating the gap between riches and poverty (the gap that must be closed before any form of popular art can flourish): then, in bold letters, 'Education towards Revolution—our policy'. And among his loose notes 'how often it consoles me,' he writes, 'to think of barbarism once more flooding the world, and real feelings and passions, however rudimentary, taking the place of our wretched hypocrisies . . . I used really to despair once because I thought what the idiots of our day call progress would go on perfecting itself: happily I now know that all that will have a sudden check—sudden in appearance I mean—as it was in the days of Noë.'

Looking back, in these days after his discovery of Morris, Brooke would have learned that for many, dissatisfied with Comte, Christian Socialism was the solution, the Fabians not yet being in the picture; but not every would-be reformer was a Christian, and for these it was no use turning to Ruskin with his pious preoccupations and a gospel of art that was lost on those to whom art meant little at the best of times. Then in 1883 Thomas Davidson gave his series of lectures under the heading *The Fellowship of the New Life*, and at first his supporters thought of founding a community abroad, which must have reminded Brooke of a similar plan that Coleridge had toyed with many years before. At Davidson's second meeting it was resolved to form an association 'whose ultimate aim should be the reconstruction of Society in accordance with the highest moral possibilities'. Then in January 1884 one of their number proposed that the new society should be named after the commander Fabius Cunctator of ancient Rome, famed for his policy of awaiting the psychological moment before striking hard. These people were pledged to combat the competitive system of economy and 'to reconstitute Society in such a manner as to secure the general welfare and happiness'. It was another two years before they realized that

Socialism was the only word that could adequately express their aims. These early Fabians, however, were only an offshoot of the New Life supporters, many of whom continued as they had begun, among them Parker Brooke's friend, Corrie Grant, M.P. for Rugby, who was also linked with the young Brooke of King's through his enjoying the financial support of Justin's father, the managing director of Brooke Bonds.

When Shaw joined the Fabians in 1885, and wrote the second of its Tracts (Brooke collected a complete set of these pamphlets) he made their deliberations at once more sprightly and more acidulated by introducing the issue of conflict between the classes and even within the family, in the hope that 'every child may have a refuge from the tyranny or neglect of its natural custodians'. He also contended that men 'no longer need special political privileges to protect them against women' and that the established government 'has no more right to call itself the State than the smoke of London has to call itself the weather'. Next year William Morris attended the first Fabian Conference, and spoke as a delegate of the Socialist League, the group of reformers who familiarly addressed each other as Comrade and would admit no compromise with capitalism at any price; and by contrast with this and the New Life the character of Fabianism now appeared more clearly defined. Pledged to radical reform, it was non-revolutionary, neither anarchist, like Morris, nor Communist, like so many of the League, who, carried away by their ardour, had swallowed the analysis of Marx and somehow managed to survive. By this time two colleagues in the Colonial Office, Sidney Webb and Sydney Olivier, had been enrolled as Fabians, and they with Shaw and Graham Wallas worked together to establish the movement, not as a political party, but as an intellectual faith with power to influence public opinion. Throughout the nineties it seemed, to that fraction of the outside world which took any notice, almost hopelessly Utopian, even incomprehensible, or if not, then there were circles where Socialism became a rude word. H. G. Wells joined in 1903, and then, at the General Election of 1905–6 when the Liberal Brookes at School Field were so active and Rupert rose too soon from a bed of sickness to canvass for Corrie Grant, no less than four successful Labour candidates and three Liberal turned out to be Fabians confessed.

But Brooke did not support the movement on the strength of its present character or growing success. He went back to the time before ever it began, when Davidson was lecturing, copied out Davidson's remarks, and stowed them in a box file: two sentences on the meaning of meaning—'The acorn does not explain the oak but the oak the acorn. The *meaning* of the acorn is revealed in the oak,' and 'The true meaning of teaching is to create a new heaven and a new earth in the souls of your pupils'—and he copied a passage in which the lecturer rallied his listeners to react against their environment and heredity—'In the face of an act of real will, heredity counts as nothing . . . It is utterly debasing to be bullied by heredity. The belief in its power "shuts the eyes and folds the hands" and delivers the soul in chains to the demon of unreality.' At the same time Brooke was reading Giddings' *Sociology* and again making copious notes. 'That only is the perfect life in which action is good in itself, and its reaction is happy because life-saving,' and especially a passage where Giddings explains how the properly organized social being 'returns to Society with usury the gifts wherewith he has been by society endowed: and this truth will be the starting-point of the ethical teaching of coming years'. Thus Personality, says Giddings, need not perish with the individual life. 'It goes forth into the everlasting life of man. And so, little by little, age by age, society which has created man is by man transformed.'

Brooke was at Torquay for ten days, reading Greek for Headlam, reflecting on his decision, impatient to sign the Basis. Dalton assured him there was no hurry. 'Many thanks,' Brooke replied. 'The first strange fever flickered and died, and I am content to sit quietly till next term. So I have left Pease [secretary of the Fabian head-office] in peace. "Pease, perfect Pease," as the hymn says.' He was overwhelmed with trying to fathom the works of Aristotle. 'By next term I shall be able to sit up and take a little Webb-and-milk . . . Your remarks about the Licensing Bill are strangely like a passage of Ibsen. They haunt me.' Then fuel was added to the fire when Erica wrote to say Bernard Shaw had given her father two tickets for the opening performance of *Getting Married*. Brooke accepted, but with misgiving. 'Mother will swoon if she hears.' (She was insisting on his giving more thought to his Tripos.) 'Only you are to behave and *not* "clutch my arm at thrilling moments". If you do, I shan't lose my head, but I shall lose my temper. Bring an umbrella and clutch that if you *must* clutch. I shall need all my wits and attention for understanding the line of thought of a new Shaw play . . . You must be very good and patient and only speak when you explain the jokes to me.'

To Keynes he was writing from the promenade, Torquay. 'As a Socialist you should be careful about facts, even in a peroration. I am not a poet: I was, that's all.' But in fact the reverse was true, for he had been drafting a sonnet which for the first time was a piece of verse which could only have been conceived by a natural poet. The signing of the Basis was a decision only reached after months of painstaking preparation. There is an air of gravity about the new poem, as of a young man just emerged from adolescence and conscious of the responsibility and the mystery of human existence which lie before him. Entitled *Seaside*[1] it expresses without a trace of ninetyish affectation, what is almost nothing, a moment of awareness in a commonplace situation, impossible to paraphrase beyond baldly stating that it is night at a seaside resort, and the band is playing on the promenade. The poet goes down to the rustling edge of the water where it is very dark and seemingly timeless but where the trivial sounds from the bandstand are still just audible. The first section, or octave, setting the scene, was apparently written without much trouble, and by the end of it nothing worthy of note, poetically, has happened. A scene has been set. No more.

> *Swiftly out from the friendly lilt of the band,*
> *The crowd's good laughter, the loved eyes of men.*
> *I am drawn nightward: I must turn again*
> *Where, down beyond the low untrodden strand,*
> *There curves and glimmers outward to the unknown*
> *The old unquiet ocean. All the shade*
> *Is rife with magic and movement. I stray alone*
> *Here on the edge of silence, half afraid,*

The revisions in the manuscript make it possible to piece together the process which enabled these unexceptional lines to become part of a poem of subtlety and curious beauty.

Six lines remain. And now, with the sestet, difficulty begins, for he must enter the heart of the matter, and for a sonnet there can only be these six lines more. He seems certain, at any rate, that 'Waiting a sign' should begin the next line which carries him into the sestet, for that, in simple terms, is why he is half afraid, standing on the edge of immensity, his mind overshadowed, not only by the night but by some eternal and indefinable question. So he proceeds, opening a new sentence, 'In the heart of me'—no, perhaps better, 'in my heart's deep', then he goes on:

[1] G.K., p. 152.

> *The blackening waters surge to greet the moon*
> *And all the tides turn seaward: here's the choice!*

No, the last three words are too abrupt and dramatic. They break the atmosphere. Instead, prolong the action of the waters with 'lightly leap'. 'And all the tides turn seaward, lightly leap,' followed by:

> *. . . sudden and clear*
> *My vision's back to that forbidden dream*
> *I slew long since*

But this whole 'dream' idea distracts from the elusive present moment he is trying to catch. The poem has taken a wrong turning. Let the 'dream', whatever it was, be left to hang about *behind* the poem. Better forget it, and go back to the 'sign' at the point of transition into the sestet, rough out the remainder, and see what happens.

> *Waiting a sign. In the deep heart of me*
> *Black swaying waters surge to greet the moon*
> *And all the tides set seaward. From the band,*
> *Sudden and careless, the throb (or snatch) of an old tune*
> *Leaps lightly forth, and blows along the sand*
> *And dies between the sea-wall and the sea.*

Assuming that he looked at the end first, the most important part, there's something peculiarly satisfactory about this last line. The repeated 'sea' is useful as a sound, as if the throb or snatch of an old-fashioned tune were eventually lost among the sea-sounds of the shore; but then while 'leaps' is certainly better for the tune than for the 'waters' where it first appeared, 'Leaps lightly forth' suggests too brisk and elegant a movement for what must be made to seem a paltry and frivolous little scrap of sound as compared with the sound made by the sea, the symbol of Death and Eternity; then 'blows', though not bad, is perhaps too violent and not enough of a preparation for 'dies' in the last line. In fact, 'leaps' would be all right, granted it came earlier, and was followed by something else which took the elegance and dignity out of the sound before it finally 'dies'. This will need space, so moving up a line, he comes to 'Sudden and careless' which looks inessential in a place where he could, if he wished, put 'leaps'. He does this, and now he must fill out the line which has probably anyhow got to end in 'tune' because of the rhyme. He writes 'Leaps the gay fragment of a mocking tune', and gets his 'trivial' effect by putting 'That tinkles and laughs' where 'Leaps lightly forth' was before; and as for 'blows', it would start the dying effect earlier—making it more gradual—if he substituted 'fades'. The last three lines are now in order, and the poem sinks slowly into the sand as do the waters and the sound of the tune.

> *Leaps a gay fragment of some mocking tune,*
> *That tinkles and laughs and fades along the sand,*
> *And dies between the seawall and the sea.*

Turning now to the beginning of the sestet, the first line may be let stand for the moment—it may turn out to be all right—but there's more than one thing wrong with the second. If one epithet could do the work of 'Black swaying' it would be stronger; 'surge' is again too violent, almost too small, for a movement which has got to seem cosmic in scale; 'greet', too, is small in the sense that it personifies the sea. So 'black swaying', 'surge', and 'greet' are scrapped, and this second line eventually becomes 'The sullen waters swell towards the moon,' and the poet is left with one more line to tinker with—'And all the tides set seaward. From the band'. This band is safely planted in the first line of the octave, so it's redundant here. Providentially, 'From inland', which he substituted, preserves the rhyme, and keeps the poem at the sea-edge, at a distance from the 'friendly lilt of the band' where the whole thing started. He is now left with 'And all the tides set seaward' which is the climax of a phrase which began with 'In the deep heart of me,'; 'the' (tides) is the third definite article in one and a half lines. One of them should go. Whether for this, or for some other reason—perhaps owing to the personal touch of that 'forbidden dream' which was long before dismissed from the surface of the poem, but must still be as it were haunting the back of it—he risks (with a 'my') making the tides personal to himself, and at once a beautiful phrase appears, a romantic sort of poetry takes charge of the poem as a whole, which is now complete, so that the final sestet reads:

> *Waiting a sign. In the deep heart of me*
> *The sullen waters swell towards the moon,*
> *And all my tides set seaward.*
>
> > *From inland*
> *Leaps a gay fragment of some mocking tune*
> *That tinkles and laughs and fades along the sand,*
> *And dies between the seawall and the sea.*

II

From Torquay he went to the Green Dragon, an inn at Market Lavington on Salisbury Plain, where Geoffrey's elder brother, Maynard Keynes, had arranged a gathering of the Society. There was G. E. Moore, playing his own accompaniment as he sang in high baritone the songs of Schubert, singing 'with his whole body', till the sweat stood on his forehead; R. G. Hawtrey, the economist, R. C. Trevelyan, Desmond MacCarthy and, among others, a character descended from Voltaire, Lytton Strachey. 'Of course it finally destroyed me,' Lytton wrote to Virginia Stephen, 'the coldest winds you can imagine sweeping over the plain, and inferior food, and not enough comfortable chairs. But on the whole I was amused.' Then he talked of his companions, who included someone he seemed, or pretended, to forget he had met before, 'a young undergraduate called Rupert Brooke—isn't it a romantic name? with pink cheeks and bright yellow hair—it sounds horrible, but it wasn't.' Miss Stephen replied that she had 'seen R.B. once leaning over a gallery at Newnham'. She was now living with her brother Adrian in Fitzroy Square, and the death of Thoby, another and beloved brother who was an especial friend of Strachey's at Trinity, was drawing Lytton and herself into a closer bond of friendship. Sometimes Virginia Stephen would stay with the Darwins of Newnham Grange when she visited Thoby or Adrian; her father Sir Leslie Stephen's portrait was on Headlam's wall, and a frequent topic of his conversation—these points are not as irrelevant as they may seem, for one must picture Brooke at this time encountering almost at every turn what was later known as the 'Bloomsbury group' and being drawn into their orbit. And now, with Moore and Strachey, he was at its fountain-head:

Lytton, who 'looked like a new variation of *Homo Sapiens*' as Frances Darwin described him, 'slightly Mephistophelian yet with human and lovely brown eyes'; Maynard, one of Moore's most ardent and accomplished supporters, described by that same observer as having 'a long nose, slightly retroussé, and this, together with his full underlip, made him look as if Circe had attempted to wave her wand over him but had dropped it for ever at one glance from his formidably amused and brilliant eyes'; and then there was E. M. Forster, a slightly older man, who would often come over from Abinger and stay with Lowes Dickinson at King's after a Saturday evening with the Apostles. He alone of these writers had already declared himself in print more substantial than a literary review. His second novel, *The Longest Journey*, had come out the year before this gathering on Salisbury Plain, and his story *The Celestial Omnibus* was folded in Brooke's pocket at the time. Above all, there was Moore, 'the greatest living philosopher. It is terrible to move in the best society,' Brooke confided in his mother.

Moore taught informally, by the give and take of conversation, and his ideas circulated, or rather percolated, from lip to lip rather than on paper bought or borrowed. If his passion for exactitude makes his philosophy rather dry reading, he was agreeable to listen to and modest in his manner, never asserting or gainsaying, so that his attitude to life and his ideas were present in the air like an effluence wherever he was in chosen company. Brooke, responsive to friendship, was easily infectible.

What matters most in life, he gathered, are good states of mind independent of any action or consequence that may follow. The relative value of your states of mind can only be assessed by considering in each case the state of affairs as a whole, or what is called their organic unity. In love, for instance, the value depends on the worth of the person beloved and the degree of reciprocity. Good is indefinable; a property in things as indescribable to someone who has never perceived it for himself as the colour yellow to a blind man, but it may be found most often in beauty, truth, or a beloved companion, so that in the creation and enjoyment of beauty, the pursuit of knowledge, and the fellowship of human intercourse, especially in all these when combined, may be discovered the greatest good, the state of mind, that is, of highest consequence. Pleasure, however, is not necessarily a part of a good state of mind. To know *exactly* what one feels is the prime duty, avoiding all ready-made and traditional wisdom, habitual response or convention, basing one's judgement strictly on the exercise of reason, each man his own severest judge in his own case. Feeling without the check of reason is suspect; general principles of conduct, of course, such as the Victorian sense of duty, are anathema, and religious dogma is not merely untrue but unnecessary. In the light of reason we must judge things afresh, hence comes what Maynard Keynes called 'comprehensive irreverence' (as towards those things formerly held sacred, such as sex, the family, civic duty, etc.) and his own reluctant criticism of the system when he wrote that on occasion it could lead to a certain 'thinness of feeling'. Loosely applied, it could also lead to egoism, casual indifference to one's neighbour which was at least a-moral, and a brand of self-sufficiency or self-rightness (if not exactly self-righteousness) which could result in contemptuous criticism, for instance, and an intolerant disdain for the unconverted. There was of course no need for 'belief' of any kind to come into it. Absolute confidence in the rightness of your own perceptions counter-checked by reason took the place of dogma, and, incidentally, there was always the profound Cambridge conviction that if you *want* to believe in a thing it is probably untrue.

Henry Sidgwick, who created the precedent for agnosticism in positions of authority in Cambridge, as we have seen, was elected to the Society in 1856 and was still its foremost personality when Bertrand Russell and Moore himself, both of Sidgwick's college, were elected Apostles in the early nineties. In 1900 Sidgwick died. The year before that, Lytton Strachey and Leonard Woolf came up as freshmen; then in October 1903 people began reading Moore's newly published book; moreover he was present in person, gradually assuming Sidgwick's influential place. Absolute candour was already the only rule the Society demanded, sincerity, that is, but not necessarily gravity, or even consistency. And so the cult of the timeless moment, the perfect state of mind, took hold, and the extraordinary freshness of its freedom from all convention, its reference back all the time to nothing but what you yourself possessed, your reason, struck young men such as Maynard Keynes, when he went up in 1902, and Brooke in 1908, with the force of a revelation. So Brooke found himself admitted to the society of his seniors, enjoyed the privilege of admittance to an intellectual aristocracy as august as, and far more exclusive than, Fabianism where he found his social ethics. With these two systems in parallel he fancied he had put his house of life in order. In the spirit of 'comprehensive irreverence' Strachey was destined one day to create a landmark in the art of biography; and Virginia Stephen (Woolf), bringing her genius to catch the timeless moment 'when the beauty and terror of life are reconciled', as she said, was to write *The Waves*. And Brooke? The cult of the aesthete picked up from St. John Lucas was now absorbed in the cool and serene air of a magnificent Ideal. Once only did he perceive the very thing he had heard so much about—an organic whole—and, while still aware of a 'state of mind' that was so evidently 'good' that it seemed suspended out of time, begin and achieve a poem, modest among those grander master-pieces, but belonging to their company, *Dining-Room Tea*. That was not yet. The liquidation of Victorianism, which had begun as a lark at Rugby, was now an intellectual passion and his mission in life, and his programme was complete. From Market Lavington he went to Cambridge for the Easter term, and with Ben Keeling and Hugh Dalton, the president and president-elect, as his sponsors, he signed the Basis.

III

The form was in two parts (i) a declaration of assent and the terms of the Basis (ii) a summary of the aims: to free land and industrial capital from individual and class ownership, to do away with Rent through the abolition of private property—'Rent and Interest will be added to the reward of labour', hence 'the idle class now living on the labour of others will necessarily disappear', and equal citizenship for men and women. By coincidence this opening stage of Brooke's Fabianism came to a climax before the preparations for *Comus* turned his mind to other things. On May 10 Keeling gave a supper party for more than twenty guests at his rooms in Trinity. The guest of honour was Sir Sydney Olivier, who was now governor of Jamaica. Wells arrived late and had to sit in the window-seat with his plate on his knee. Lady Olivier sat on Keeling's right, and three of her daughters were present. Brooke found himself beside Margery; and the youngest daughter, Noel, a dark haired girl of fifteen and a half, sat opposite. Olivier then addressed the Fabians, and afterwards the guests of Keeling's supper-party reassembled for coffee in Cornford's rooms. The lecturer's youngest daughter must have been feeling younger than ever in such distinguished company when she let slip the small green coffee cup which was being handed to her—one of a valuable set—and would have been seriously put out of countenance but for the intervention of a young man, who ran over to reassure her and pick up the pieces. Noel and Rupert were talking to each other for the first time. When the Oliviers left, Wells hung back and took charge of the conversation. Brooke wrote to his mother that evening. 'He argued in his thin little voice for a long time, in a very delightful manner.' A few days later Brooke was writing to Raverat in France.

Cambridge is as ever; but now speciously arrayed in a pretence of heat and light green buds. Really, of course, it is a swollen corpse, and we buzz on it like flies. And yet . . . and yet—there has been a stirring. My long dead life thrills strangely and opens its eyes. The golden age may yet return—or

has a letter cheated me?—Pah! I riddle. The night awaits me—and this
letter.

He had been fascinated before now, but for the first time in his life his
heart was touched. He had written to the youngest of the Olivier
daughters, whose family was staying in Cambridge.

Then the saga of *Comus* began with a letter from Frances Darwin.
Who was to teach the steps of the pavane? Charles Sayle knew of an
admirable Mrs. Fletcher. She would have to be paid! 'There is no
scene-painter in Cambridge,' Brooke complains in the course of his
reply. 'To hire one would cost about £5.' The manager of the theatre
is being awkward; Benson's company is occupying the scene dock.
The only thing to do is forget it and go and play tennis with the
Macaulays at Shelford. Then Miss Darwin invites him to meet Max
Beerbohm. 'We have never met him in our lives before, which is
rather alarming.' Brooke goes and finds both the Rothenstein brothers.
As for Max, he is 'a quaint little person', he tells his mother; then
Max and Albert Rothenstein, wearing bowler hats and pepper-and-
salt suits, are observed being rowed by Margaret Darwin in the
Newnham Grange boat. On May 22, 'I wonder if I'm right in thinking
that the sonnet in this week's *Cambridge Review* signed R.B. is by
you?'[1] wrote Frances Darwin. 'If so, please don't think it impertinent
of me to say how much I like it.' In his letter home Brooke had to
confess that he was not only rehearsing *Comus* but the part of Major
Kildare in *His Excellency the Governor* which the A.D.C. was presenting in May Week. This would give him a good excuse for not
attending any of the balls. He still couldn't dance, he explained to his
mother, and he loathed standing around exchanging pleasantries.
Francis Cornford had invited forty men from the Working Men's
College at St. Pancras, and persuaded him to entertain a party of them
in his rooms, and he had found them all much against the observance
of Empire Day. Not until June did he reveal that he was playing a
part in *Comus* as well as stage-managing the production, and even
then he thought it wiser to let it come out later that he was learning
one of the principal roles, the Attendant Spirit.

The first reading of the masque took place one morning on the
dusty stage of the New Theatre. Everyone was there. A. Y.
Campbell of John's, a scholar and future professor of Greek, read the
Elder Brother, Dorothy Lamb, sister of Henry Lamb the painter and
follower of Augustus John, took the part of Sabrina, rising from her

[1] *Failure.* 'Because God put this adamantine fate.' G.K., 147.

'glassy, cool, translucent wave'. None of it was very promising. The part of Comus was eventually given to Francis Cornford, who, apart from being a don, had previously been debarred from taking part by what was considered to be his 'great age' of thirty-three. The two Brookes were there. Justin was going down, so he could only stand about and look wise, but Rupert, as the stage-manager, thundered at cowed Newnhamites that they must be punctual at rehearsals (the head of School Field was reasserting himself) and in the circle of chairs happened to sit in the only direct beam of daylight which shone through an open window, high up at the back of the circle. It caught the light on his hair, and Frances Darwin, seeing him now for the second time, and taking him as a representative figure of her generation, which was, she felt 'magnificently unprepared for the long littleness of life', began working out an epigram beginning 'A young Apollo, golden-haired'. She was not attempting a portrait of someone she hardly knew, yet long afterwards her opening line became a catch-phrase to describe a legendary figure which had never existed in such simple terms.

Many of the choice souls of that Cambridge day and age were gathered there; Brooke was head and front of the enterprise, and the unusual presence of young women made every mustering of the company an occasion of social consequence. They were like young people thrown together, as if at random, for the duration of a sea voyage, and perhaps because he feared these special circumstances might lead to the kind of romance which is regretted when voyagers make the shore, Brooke took it upon himself to assume a role among them like that of the King of Navarre in *Love's Labour's Lost*. He invited his companions to join him in taking an Oath that no one must get engaged to be married within six months of the last performance, and it may have been on the evening of the vow (to which everyone submitted) that Frances Darwin took part in a conversation that stuck in her memory. She was talking with the two Brookes.

Rupert: When I marry I shall settle absolutely everything in my own house. My wife must completely obey me.

Justin: (*taking him seriously*) Oh Rupert, I should hate that! I *do* want a wife who can stand up to me.

Rupert: No. I shall settle *everything*.

Miss Darwin: But may she never have her own way even about the children?

Rupert: I suppose she may just settle little things about them when they are quite small. That's all.

Miss Darwin: For instance, if she thinks they need a change, mightn't she just mention that?

Rupert: No, I shall come down to breakfast one day and thump my fist on the table, and say 'We will go to Margate tomorrow'.

Miss Darwin: And mayn't she even say, 'I think, dear, it would be better to go to Eastbourne in three weeks'?

Rupert: Well, she might just *suggest* that. And perhaps I would consider it.

It was the custom for the *Comus* committee to meet over tea at Newnham Grange, and all progressed smoothly until Frances Darwin suffered a relapse in health, and was taken off by her father to Brides-les-Bains. Cornford and Jane Harrison also retired from the scene, Justin went down early, and Rupert was left in sole charge, with the designer Albert Rothenstein, his guest in college, showing an almost wanton reluctance to get up in the morning. In the end Brooke hired three college porters to hoist him bodily from his couch, only to find that the theatre manager was forbidding Rothenstein to do any painting of scenery under his roof. 'He is forcing us to use his filthy scenery, a fate too horrible to contemplate,' Brooke wrote to Miss Darwin, and then again 'I frequently tell my friends nowadays that an actor-manager's life is a dog's life and advise them not to take it up. It irritates them,' then later, 'I am going to compose a threnody on Redfern [the manager] (whom I poisoned this morning) and so to bed.'

The Master of Christ's removed these obstructions by taking over the whole theatre himself until his Milton celebrations were over. Brooke was now making lists of stage-properties, running errands, stirring buckets of paint, assisting Rothenstein back stage, consulting books on stage construction at the University Library or a copy of the Trinity Milton facsimile, so as to check doubtful points in the text, or looking in at the Grange to see whether Ka Cox and her sister seamstresses were making headway under the guidance of Gwen Darwin; anything, in fact, other than such activity of thought as might be required of him by the instruction 'Give an account of the political aims and achievements of Epaminondas', scribbled on his list of stage props. The costume for Comus and Brooke's own were being made by a new friend of his, Sybil Pye, whose family lived at Priest Hill near the Olivier family at Limpsfield. She was a pupil of Ricketts and a bookbinder, and with her sister Ethel, a sculptress, adorned the circle of Limpsfield neighbours which included the family of Edward Garnett and whom Brooke would soon be getting to know.

'It is impossible not to feel bitter at the thought of the paint being slodged on without me,' wrote Frances Darwin from France, but she was back in time for the last minute turmoil. From June 22 the theatre was entirely at their disposal, and Brooke and the two Miss Darwins got down to painting the back-cloth a deep midnight blue, while Noel Olivier made herself useful carrying paint-pots and washing brushes. This sky-cloth caused trouble. It was Rothenstein's idea to have gold sovereigns sewn on to it. They would catch the light, he said, and give the effect of stars. Brooke was alarmed at this, as also was the manager of the theatre, especially when Rothenstein proposed to erect a number of scaffold poles to represent the forest in the tangles of whose 'nodding horror' the Lady and the younger Brother had to lose their way. Brooke objected to the sovereigns, saying they were too realistic, worse, they were vulgar, and, not at first getting his way, fell into such a pit of smouldering dejection, which rendered him speechless for the whole afternoon, that Miss Darwin suggested a compromise of half-crowns, though one wonders how she made out that reducing the exchange value would make a difference. The number, however, was eventually reduced to three, a great concession, and Frances Darwin swore she would sew them on where they wouldn't be seen. And so it was. They were never visible. The night lacked moon and star. Rehearsals grew more intensive and obliging ladies, working late, sat about in the stalls among swags of material, executing Gwen Darwin's designs. Among them Ka Cox, with better cause to be flustered than anyone, for she was taking her Tripos, was observed sewing or embroidering in the stalls, or 'quietly averting many small practical catastrophes,' as Frances put it, or when Dent arrived, laying aside her needle and thread to rehearse the pavane with Margery Olivier. 'She looked too big and heavy compared with the other, slender, long-necked girls,' wrote Miss Darwin, recalling Ka at this time. 'Her own especial qualities didn't come out.' Nor, where the acting was concerned, did Brooke's. He was unable to conduct his limbs with any show of naturalness when made conscious of them, and he found it difficult to forget them. 'Shall I hold my hand like *that*?' he asked of whoever was within earshot. 'Shall I put these three fingers *together*?' He was no actor and, according to Dent, an indifferent speaker of verse with a harsh voice, somewhat constricted in the throat, and a defective sense of rhythm; and yet by all accounts his delivery in private was of an altogether different order. 'He read verse in a small company better than anyone

I have ever known,' was Dalton's view. Brooke seems to have found it difficult to project his voice in public without loss of naturalness, but even this limitation did not greatly matter. Dent, his severest critic, goes on to say it was 'his passionate devotion to the spirit of poetry that really gave *Comus* its peculiar and indescribable atmosphere'. There was some danger that Brooke's reverence for 'the spirit' might lead him to ignore the value of those cruder theatrical virtues which are necessary to make any production effective as a public show. One evening after rehearsal he was at Madingley Road, reading aloud the last pages of Malory's *Morte d'Arthur* to Frances Darwin and her father. 'Why do certain things in literature really stir one more than anything else in the world,' he said, having closed the book. 'There are books, sometimes, which I can't take down from the shelf without my hand trembling to think what is in them.' This, he said, always happened when he turned to Milton.

Comus was bringing him good friends, but at this juncture he suddenly lost one, and the shock made him angry and afraid. A week or two before, Walter Headlam had amused Brooke by describing a rival theory on a problem in Greek as 'a wind egg hatched in a mare's nest'. Now he was dead in London. He had gone up to town for a cricket match at Lord's, was taken to hospital, and within a few hours died at the age of forty-two. 'One gets so *angry* at that sort of thing,' Brooke wrote to Rugby. He felt ill and miserable.

The papers made very little of it—it's odd to compare the fuss they made when Jebb died, and Headlam was a far greater man than Jebb. He published so little that outside people didn't know much of him. But his friends and we who were his pupils, knew his great genius. I don't know how much of him they will be able to rake together from his papers. But all the great, ripe, splendid works we all proudly looked forward to him achieving—which we knew he might consummate any time he gave himself a few months—have died with him, can never be made. That's the terrible thing. Even in Cambridge many people knew of him most as a brilliant 'scholar', i.e. emender of Greek texts. But he was also about the best writer of Greek there has been since the Greeks. And what I loved so in him was his extraordinary and living appreciation of all English poetry, modern and ancient. To hear him repeat it was a delight. He was an excellent poet himself; and had perfect taste. He first inspired me with a desire to get *Comus* done, a term or two ago, and has often talked about it since. I had made up, in my mind, a little list of things about which I was going to ask him, large and small points, in *Comus*, to make certain that we should interpret and understand it in the best way possible; but I put it off till too late . . . the whole thing makes one so rebellious; to think what the world has lost . . .

The death of Headlam added to the strain. On July 9, the day of the dress rehearsal, he was in a state of nervous collapse and spent the afternoon sitting in Dent's garden, motionless for hours, while his mother in lodgings off Bene't Street was entertaining James Strachey and Frances Darwin to tea. 'He *seems* to have good manners,' she was saying of Justin, whose fashionably off-hand manner she had observed was even more conspicuous than her son's. She was fond of Strachey, but when Rupert looked in to ask how she had got on he was amused by the way she expressed herself, not entirely at one with him in his high opinion of her guest: 'One wouldn't call poor James *clever.*' Miss Darwin warmed to her, and was struck by the beauty of her skin which, however, was marked by innumerable tiny wrinkles, and she 'sat like a man' she noticed, with legs straight out and her body slumped in the chair. 'She gives the impression of nobility,' was Miss Darwin's summary of this remarkable woman. Meanwhile Brooke managed to pull himself together for the last rehearsal and the supper afterwards at Sayle's house.

Next day, July 10, the Master of Christ's gave a banquet, and *Comus* was performed before his private audience of Fellows and guests. Alfred Austin as Poet Laureate sat with his host in the front of the stalls. There also were Thomas Hardy, Edmund Gosse, hugging his hat and umbrella, and Robert Bridges who slipped out before the end, having lost patience with what he saw and heard. (He had his own theories on the delivery of Miltonic verse.) The two Miss Darwins were selling programmes. Frances showed Mrs. Brooke to her seat, and was handed a coin. 'The mothers of celebrated actors don't have to pay for their programmes,' she said with a smile. 'He is *not* celebrated,' said Mrs. Brooke with unexpected vehemence. When the curtain rose, the Attendant Spirit was discovered; the Lady and the Brothers appeared, then Comus in disguise; the story in honour of Virtue unfolded, ending with a pavane and a galliard danced by four Cavaliers and four young ladies in full satin gowns.

After the show Sayle brought Laurence Binyon back-stage, and Darwins were in evidence at every turn. 'So at last you've heard *Comus*,' someone remarked to Gosse as he was going out. 'I have overheard it,' was his comment.

Next morning Brooke, accompanied by Ka Cox, went again to Trumpington Street. Sayle had invited them to breakfast with Thomas Hardy. 'He was incredibly shrivelled and ordinary,' Brooke wrote to Raverat, 'and made faintly pessimistic remarks about the

toast.' Then in the afternoon of that day the second and last performance was given, this time to the public. There were, of course, no
names in the programme.

The Academy noted that the players 'spoke the lines with a nice
regard for the values of austere and stately English'; the gestures
were 'immature', but it was 'all very reverent and sincere . . .
Unquestionably, though, the greatest individual success, in this and
other respects, was made by the player of the Attendant Spirit, whose
voice and comely presence were of enormous help to the scenes in
which he figured.' The *Cambridge Daily News* wrote of the same
player whose gestures were 'somewhat stilted'; the *Cambridge
Chronicle* declared that 'by an exceedingly clear delivery of the opening lines, he made quite plain to everyone, even the very few unfamiliar with Milton's work, the sort of person we were to encounter
with Comus', while the other local paper, the *Review*, told how Brooke
seemed 'thoroughly to enjoy his part—a marked contrast to the
Brothers, depressed presumably by the priggishness of the sentiments they must utter'. The critic of *The Times* thought that the
sense of an august occasion had been allowed to detract from the
drama. The rout of monsters attending upon Comus himself, for
instance, were 'rather subdued in behaviour'. What seemed almost
a religious spirit pervaded the performance. The canvas back-cloth
representing the 'gloomy wood' of the first scene was not much
admired; the second scene of 'green hangings with here and there a
splash of red', lit by limes from the wings alone, and the stage bare
but for a reproduction of the Ludovisi throne where Comus would sit
in state, was thought impressive and to represent an innovation in
stage lighting. According to the *Athenaeum*, although some of the
cast were 'a little too inclined to fixed postures' the Attendant Spirit
was 'the best of the performers and a better reciter of blank verse
than we have heard anywhere'; and one London newspaper went so
far as to refer with bated breath to Newnham—'whence, said a
whisper, came some of the players'.

An article by Lytton Strachey in the *Spectator* of July 18 was more
expansive. It found the performance 'happily devoid of those jarring
elements of theatricality and false taste which too often counterbalance the inherent merits of a dramatic revival', and it showed that
those responsible had held before their minds 'a high ideal of artistic
accomplishment'. We learn that the scenery was 'quite unobtrusive,
as all scenery should be', as also were the costumes. This was a

doubtful compliment. The text itself lacked dramatic interest and this was 'rendered peculiarly obvious at Cambridge owing to the studiously undramatic method of declamation adopted by the actors'. There should have been more contrast of tone, and not all the players were fitted by Nature for their parts. Was it not 'unfortunate that the figure of Comus himself was almost as lean and sallow as the abstinence which he decries?'

One of the few phrases in the whole masque which seem to have caught something of the fire and intensity of the great Elizabethans occurs in the splendid passage in which the Attendant Spirit describes how, as he was sitting in the wood, he heard the Lady's song—

> *I was all ear,*
> *And took in strains that might create a soul*
> *Under the ribs of Death.*

That is not only beautiful, it is exciting; but, as it was enunciated by the actor, one felt the beauty of it and nothing more. However to have accomplished thus much is no small achievement. How infinitely rarely does one hear, in any theatre, the beauty that is blank verse! From this point of view, the performance at Cambridge was indeed memorable . . . The existence of such a body of able and enthusiastic lovers of poetry and drama must be welcomed as at least an augury of a better state of things.

To those who took part themselves the production was chiefly remembered for two performances: Cornford as the dark sorcerer 'moving in his panther skin of glistening robes with a strange and disembodied grace', and the Attendant Spirit, 'shining against the dark wood,' and speaking the final benediction:

> *. . . Mortals, that would follow me,*
> *Love virtue, she alone is free,*
> *She can teach ye how to climb*
> *Higher than the Spheary chime;*
> *Or if virtue feeble were,*
> *Heav'n itself would stoop to her.*

After the public performance there was a dance at Newnham Grange, the whole cast being still in costume, Brooke wearing a 'short spangled sky-blue tunic' so short and tight he dared not risk the manœuvre of sitting down. He stood, leaning against the wall for most of the evening, introducing his mother to the rest of his Cambridge friends, among them the youngest, Margaret Darwin, younger sister of Gwen; and many of the folk who frequented Newnham Grange and were now sweeping around with the grace of Van Dyck countesses or the elegance of velvet Cavaliers, no longer characters in *Comus*, now that the play was over, but the real-life figures of an Edwardian *Love's Labour's Lost* dancing in masquerade.

IV

Mrs. Brooke was worried by her son's exhausted condition, and persuaded him to accompany her back to Rugby. 'The fun being over, I sneaked away on Monday and left you all to clear up the mess—the dresses for all of you, the accounts for poor Comus, and so on,' he wrote to Frances Darwin, who had written, supposing he was still at King's. 'My mother (I can plead) packed me up and snatched me here to sleep and recover . . . I felt a deserter; but I can always adduce the week when the committee went to the seaside and I faced the World and Albert's Artistic Temperament alone.'

He was now scheming to lure Margery Olivier to Rugby, in the hope that she would bring her youngest sister. A friend of Mrs. Brooke, who when asked whether she knew the Oliviers, exclaimed, 'My yes. They'd do anything those girls,' had not helped. 'Mother (whose "*any*thing" is at once vastly ominous and most limited) is, and will be for two months, ill with foreboding. She pictures, I think, Margery climbing the roof at night, or throwing bread about at table, or kissing the rural milkman.' But the scheme went awry. 'All my dreams are dead. Ghosts of old hopes get into the ink and make it blotchy.' He pressed Keynes to come and stay for a while. There was nothing to do, 'but in any case it will be amusing for you to glow exquisitely against the scrofulous wallpaper and autumnal curtains of this lazar house.' And in this mood he came of age on August 3. He was alone with Alfred and his parents. No less than seven people, not counting relations, wrote to congratulate him. Geoffrey Keynes sent him the latest edition of Blake; Sayle ordered a bunch of roses from the garden at Chalfont St. Giles, where Gray had composed his Elegy. 'How it doubles the value of a gift (as of a prose style),' Brooke wrote to him, 'when it is "exquisite" and fetched from far with pains!'; his parents gave him a cheque for ten guineas which he decided to spend on a John drawing when next he was in London. 'The rumour about my age was quite true,' he wrote to Dalton, who was uncertain of the date. 'I did it a fortnight ago. Leaving my unprofitable youth and its fancies, I stepped across the Threshold of

Manhood, jauntily, manfully, leaving a company of dancing children behind. I stumbled a little on the step, which I did not perceive.'

Dalton and Keeling were going to visit School Field on the way to the Fabian Summer School where Brooke was to join them later. 'I told my mother,' he wrote to Dalton, 'that the chief end of life was Pleasure, and she burst into tears. My uncle the Dean will be here. No matter. It will add to the comedy. But Ben must be not-blasphemous. I told the family a lot of people would be lunching here that day. "Who and What kind of?" they said. "Oh, All right," I vaguely smiled at them, "practically Liberals—there's Dalton, son of a Canon . . ." ' Dudley Ward was already at School Field, coaching Alfred in history, and becoming a close friend of the elder brother. One day there was an excursion to Stratford-upon-Avon where they sat in a punt reading aloud Meredith's *Modern Love*. Brooke lent him *The Symbolist Movement in Literature* by Arthur Symons. 'He read it, very earnestly,' ran the sequel reported to Sayle. ' "Do you know" he confided to me as we sat reading in the garden, "I can't help thinking these fellows are rather *dangerous*. You know when a man begins seeing things that aren't *there* . . . well, I mean, he may see *anything*, one feels." He beamed at me patiently through his spectacles. I did not know what to say; so turned the conversation to fluctuations in unemployment, and his storm-tossed spirit was at ease . . . But Ward is an excellent person. He, Alfred and I read *Sigurd* aloud at nights, round and round till our brains sleep, and we only hear the great plash of the wave-like verses.'

Dalton and Keeling arrived at Rugby, picked up Ward, as ardent a Fabian as the rest of them, and started off for Wales, having fixed a rendezvous where Brooke would join them. Dalton received an administrative postcard.

I shall debouch at Leominster or some of those neighbouring places about 5 or 4 or so on Wed. I shall expect to find that you have secured a place for me to sleep in for a night without darkness and the death-hour rounding it. Leave your address at all stations and places within ten miles. I am sorry you are so old. I bring a blanket, chocolate and 19 books, all in a bag.

R.B.

They were a party of seven. James Strachey, Arthur Waley, Shove, and the contingent from Rugby all stayed with Beatrice Webb *en route*. She was on holiday in a farmhouse near Leominster. 'You don't have breakfast in bed, do you?' she inquired with the inflexion that makes a statement out of a question. She was impressed with

Keeling, also Dalton, whom she entered in her diary as 'an accomplished ecclesiastical sort of person'. The others struck her as rather commonplace, though 'perhaps Dudley Ward was a little over the line of medium capacity'. Brooke she actively disliked for his having regaled her with a 'super-conceited lecture on the relation of the university man to the common herd of democracy'. She discovered on a later occasion that this cocksureness was by no means confined to Brooke. After visiting the site of the first performance of *Comus* in the ruins of Ludlow Castle, the party went on into Wales.

The school occupied two houses and their outlying buildings at Llanbedr, a village near the sea between Barmouth and Harlech, and the course lasted about ten days. It was August 30 when the Cambridge party arrived and took up their quarters in a converted barn. There was much fooling about and shouting, and grotesque mimicry of the Webbs. There were thirty students on the course, and they were offered lectures on Tolstoy, Shaw, the Poor Law, rambles, and dances of an evening. All tastes were catered for, from devotees of Swedish drill to students of the Russian novel, and the prospectus had promised all vegetarians a table of their own. Granville Barker, if heard aright, lost a few points in the course of a debate when he declared that in the Socialist state of the future 'all women will have dresses of the same material and wear them for the same length of time'. 'He actually said that!' wrote Brooke to Erica in stunned amazement. Even so, he came away from Llanbedr more Fabian than ever.

On his return to Rugby there was a letter awaiting him from Comus in person. It was as if Berowne should write, making a humble confession to Navarre in the middle act of this *Love's Labour's Lost* in which they were living. 'Have you heard of the great and signal disgrace which has befallen us all, even all who played in *Comus*?' Cornford began. He had broken his vow. 'The full extent and savour of the disgrace will gradually come home to you when you learn that the other offender is Frances Darwin. O Rupert, we despair of forgiveness, and shall never look you in the face again.' The Darwins were now in Ireland. Cornford had committed his proposal of marriage to the post, and his first intimation of a reply was a telegram from Sir Frank—'Letter received. Think you will like answer', but the erring Comus had not as yet divulged these details. He was contrite. Brooke of course was only too pleased to learn that the Vow had been taken seriously, and it was 'more honoured in the breach than the observance' if it brought about the union of two such cherished friends.

But I shall hold a meeting of the *Comus* people and pass a vote of censure on you both. (I feel that Brierley will second it.) You are really very disgraceful. I'm glad you're ashamed. I think the beasts will tearrr you both to pieces. That their leader should forsake the palace and the *absinthe* in the flower-vase, for an assistant dresser—something less than a stagehand—one to whose bullying and cozening in the matter of changing the *caste* Justin [Brooke] too can witness, one who (I fear you must have forgotten) *wanted to cut out part of the text*!

Yet as Stage-Manager, as Patriarch and Head of that Body of the Elect who were concerned in Comus, I can almost forgive the infamy. It would be so dreadful to think of any of the Elect breaking away outside——

But oh! I wish I'd all of them here now that we could add our joy at the news, and rejoice. I go about alone in this desert, in the most absurd state of elation about it, as if I'd done something splendid myself! I felt, when the great time of Comus was over, that somehow the glory was incomplete, a thirteen-line sonnet. And now comes the perfect crown of a perfect summer. You observe I regard the whole thing from the point of view of the joy it gives *me*!

Before term began Charles Masterman, Dalton's hero, was actually coming to speak at Rugby and stay with the parents at School Field. 'Rugby is hideous but you need not notice it,' Brooke added to his invitation. 'I can't promise that you'll be able to talk a lot with him because there may be a lot of filthy Liberal provincial politicians hanging about. But at least we'll have him more lonely at breakfast.' Dalton accepted, and was shown the Chapel. 'Do you see that spot,' said Brooke, pointing to a bare bit of wall beside the memorial to Clough. 'They are keeping that for *me*.' Then he packed for the Michaelmas Term, and on the way through London stayed with Dudley Ward, who was now one of his intimate friends and rabidly Fabian. 'But don't be there to welcome me. I would not prevent you preaching in Hyde Park all afternoon. I will sit on the doorstep, and read Kant in the original Hebrew till you return.'

It proved to be a very social term; he declined a meal with the Darwins of Madingley Road because 'I have pawned all my boots. Why? TO BUY JOHNS. This does not refer to the College; but to drawings of Augustus John.' On the advice of Albert Rothenstein he had added a good deal of his quarterly allowance to the birthday money to buy two drawings. Not satisfied with the excuse, Frances Darwin replied 'Come to tea in your socks. You will be welcome.'

Brooke and Dalton had been invited by Lowes Dickinson to join the discussion society which bore his name and met in the rooms upstairs. There A. C. Pigou, the new King's don in Political Economy, read a paper on 'Recent Results in Psychical Research'. It fascinated Brooke, and years afterwards it was the theme of a mature sonnet.[1] Brooke's own view was that he had no grounds for supposing he had an immortal soul, nor did he wish it.

One night everyone stayed on late at the *Carbonari*. When the meeting broke up, and men were dispersing to their rooms round the front court, Brooke and Dalton hung about at the entrance to the staircase, continuing the debate. The topic was the soul, and their voices were raised, when a head crowned with a night-cap appeared at a high window of Gibbs's Building. It was Lowes Dickinson. 'I wish you'd go to bed!' he called out, testily, 'I can't sleep.' Next morning the two *Carbonari* went up to apologize and were asked what they were talking about. 'Immortality,' one of them replied. 'Oh,' exclaimed Dickinson, seeing the incident in a new light, 'now if only I'd known that, I would have come down and joined you.' Dickinson was a being as rare for the breadth of his tolerance as for his learning, and when he was offered the Khan Travelling Fellowship, the main purpose of which was to widen the Fellow's mind, Brooke exclaimed, 'If they widen Goldie's mind any more, it'll break!'

There was tea with A. C. Benson at Magdalene to meet Gosse and with the Verralls, where were Virginia Stephen's sister Vanessa and her husband, Clive Bell; and Saturday meetings of the Society brought Eddie Marsh, an Apostle of the nineties, down from London. At this time Marsh was a Civil Servant at the Colonial Office, an eager young socialite in his early thirties, who had also read Classics when he was up at Trinity with Moore, and seemed to have an uncommon knowledge of French and English poetry. He had no idea Brooke himself ever tried his hand at verse before the first breakfast *à deux* when he was shown *Day that I have loved*, and pronounced it an accomplished exercise in the metre of Dowson's *Cynara*. Brooke would also have shown him his latest winning entry in the *Westminster Gazette* competitions, *The Jolly Company*, published this month as the 'best new and original poem about stars'. The poem drew a letter from Frances Darwin. 'I hope you will go on writing poems . . . I can't imagine it having been written to order however spontaneously—which is proof that it's poetry and not verse, I think.'

[1] *Sonnet (suggested by some of the Proceedings of the Society for Psychical Research)*, G.K., p. 40.

Brooke was afraid she might be thinking the worse of him for having invoked the Muse for the sake of a cash reward. 'Of course I think it's an excellent thing to write for 2 guineas or more, whenever possible,' she replied. 'I haven't really got such a sentimental ideal of a poet as you seem to basely suspect me of!' The first Westminster Problems Book was just out, containing six pieces by Brooke (one wrongly attributed). 'It is horrible to find forgotten things knocked off in a hurry, solemnly resuscitated in cold blood,' he wrote to his mother. 'I hate it, in spite of the pleasant fact that the book is almost entirely written by Rose Macaulay, Lord Curzon, and myself!' Whatever he might say, the *Westminster* provided him with an unusual opportunity to practise his craft, and the financial inducement was not to be ignored. He was living on an allowance of £150 a year paid in quarterly instalments, a figure which remained unaltered for the rest of his life. He had recently spent most of his cash savings at the sale of Headlam's books, so the *Westminster* competitions were more than a pastime.

He read two papers this term: one was *Political Satire in English Verse*, where he quoted Rochester and Marvell as first having the requisite 'amused disdain', talked of Butler's *Hudibras*, Dryden (a master except in *Annus Mirabilis* which was 'dam bad' because the metre didn't suit him) and Swift, and Hilaire Belloc, already a big influence in Brooke's life, and about whom the speaker evidently grew somewhat heated. 'I am thankful for such robust people, thinking of the swarms of decadent and immunized maggots that now swarm over the putrescent corpse of English literature. We moderns are like invalids sitting in a darkened room, afraid of our own shadows and speaking in Maeterlinckian whispers. I thank God when someone shouts or laughs or swears aloud.' He praised Belloc for his satire and quoted from *Emmanuel Burden*, 'To see him open his umbrella was to comprehend England from the Reform Bill to Home Rule.' The phrase had given Brooke an idea for the *Carbonari*, a satire on the English middle-class in the person of a figure whom he decided to call John Rump, which would do well, he thought, for a meeting next term.

His correspondence was another obstacle to his progress in the Classics. Erica was still at school and relying upon her cousin for enlightenment on subjects outside the curriculum, such as Socialism, sexual ethics (a book translated by Ashley Dukes was recommended) and the definition of certain useful terms. Brooke's homily on 'asceticism' gives a fair example.

It means by derivation 'training'. In Greece an *ascetic* was one who trained his body for sports. So it got to mean one who denied himself little ordinary bodily pleasures like eating Turkish Delight for the sake of strengthening his body—'training' in fact. Then it was used under Christianity for men who denied themselves pleasures of this life for the sake of the next. That's more or less what it means now—denying the body for the sake of the soul. The 'Lent' idea. Denying yourself some little luxury because you think there's a virtue in self-denial. Some people will define it as denial of little pleasures for the sake of a greater one. But this makes it too wide. Anyone would come under that definition.

He had just made his first speech at a political gathering. 'It was bad, and I frightened,' he told his mother, so when at last he got down to answering Erica's letter asking for advice on how to speak in a debate, he was less sure of himself.

I suppose your debate is long past by now, and all the valuable advice I might have given, from the depths of a twenty-one years' experience of the world, useless, for that occasion at least. I wonder what you did. I don't think anything I say is much good, for I often think I don't know how the mind of anybody else works—certainly of you. My own point of view is this. *How* one says things is very important. For, I often find, when I have something in me I want to tell people, I fail through being unable to find the right words, and so *I* give people the wrong impression. The great thing is to *make other people understand what one means*. So merely to blurt it out and understand it oneself, does not do, I find. So, for myself, I always go very slowly and carefully; telling a little every now and then, picking my time. And this is because I have to feel my way. I know neither how other people think, nor how to express my own thoughts, at all well: so I go slowly. This, of course, won't suit you in the same way. You instinctively think it rather dull and crawly. But it is a point of view worth considering. This is the difficulty which makes me very rarely speak to a lot of people at once, and, when I do, say almost nothing important; because, as crowds are stupider than individuals, and I am bad at public speaking, I cannot feel I make them understand. I prefer talking to one or two people, or, better still, writing, as one can think and stop and change words, then. I think it is good to shock people a little, and speak out to them, but one must be careful to do it gradually, as a rule, so as to get them accustomed by degrees. Only, I think, if one really feels 'inspired'—feels it *absolutely necessary* to tell out some burning thing—if one is sure of this feeling, to speak out is right at all costs. It is a matter to settle with one's own conscience, I think.

His conscience was a little uneasy. He had done hardly any work this term, and he was wanting to spend Christmas frivolously in Switzerland. There was a party going for eleven days. The hotel and journey there and back would cost eleven guineas, he told his mother, asking

her consent and making out that he was in need of a change. He overdid it, though he won his point, then wrote again.

> I am afraid I may have written rather dismally. What I meant about the
> holidays is this. It is quite true that I have plenty of opportunities for resting.
> But I always feel that I oughtn't to, and I can't do nothing. There are so
> many things I must learn and do; and there is not too much time. My brain
> *must* be working. And so the only way (I find) I have a real holiday from *my*
> work, is on a walking-tour or in Switzerland; times and places where it is
> impossible to think or read for more than five minutes. In a way such things
> are a waste of time. And I can't imagine anything I should hate more than a
> long holiday like that, of more than a week or ten days. It would be in-
> tolerable. But, I think, just a week's mental rest strengthens a mind for some
> time. This sounds rather priggish; but I'm really very much in earnest about
> reading and writing.

The party included Dr. Verrall's daughter Helen, Herbert Samuel,
Godwin Baynes the Socialist rowing blue and student of medicine,
who had done the Fabians good service on Keir Hardie Night; and—
the main reason for his needing a change at Klosters, in the Engadine,
rather than anywhere else—Noel Olivier, now at Bedales, and her
sister Margery. The party arrived on December 18, and began
writing and rehearsing their own show for presentation on Boxing
Day, *From the Jaws of the Octopus*.

'Armour and Explosives by the entire cast', says the programme.
Although the text of the melodrama was as much the work of Helen
Verrall and Carey as of Brooke, perhaps we may detect his brand of
humour in the wistful remark, 'I sometimes think you love me for my
cardigan vest alone,' or in the villain's opening address to the world
at large. 'Again, as for so many winters past, I find myself in this
hotel disguised as a servant'—in unflattering terms he refers to the
heroine and goes on—'Even now I have bound her to the rails before
the oncoming express and she belike is crushed to atomies. (*Whistle,
scream, and voices without*) Ha ha! 'Tis done. Perchance 'tis *well* done.
But hist! One comes (*returns to back stage and polishes boots*)'. The hero,
Eugene de Montmorency (played by Brooke) now enters, utters the
same speech word for word with the slight difference of one syllable
which reveals that he has *un*tied the heroine, and so on. Asked how it
all went, 'I parodied my *Comus* gestures and voice,' Brooke replied.
'No difficult matter.' And then with tobogganing and hilarity the
New Year 1909 came in at Klosters.

The peace of the vacation at Rugby was marred by a row with his mother which lasted two hours, and since James Strachey was complaining of his off-hand manner, Brooke, back at King's, began to wonder whether his ill-humour was not developing into a trait. He felt he owed Strachey an explanation. 'You must remember I (how pleasant it is to write about oneself always!) live more transiently and without noticing than is your standard . . . I have a theory of loving all things, but a practice of hating, or being violently irritated with, almost everything. More especially of late, people and sounds. Partly I have evolved a naif but passionate desire to be educated, and have been trying to get to work to remedy the barrenness of my education. That happened a lot. And always, in the evening, people *came in* . . . You do not conceive how I love my own company and thirst for knowledge.' He was soon making his casual callers an excuse for his neglected work. 'If I had a room on the second floor, instead of the ground!' Now it was Dent looking in to discuss the music of *The Silent Woman* (the Marlowe Dramatic Society's next venture) now Ronald Firbank, leaning against the chimneypiece and looking witty, and now it was the poet Flecker, looking swarthy, who had dropped over from Caius. It was maddening.

In February Brooke appeared as the Prologue in *The Silent Woman* produced by Reginald Pole of King's, and the *Carbonari* met in Brooke's room for their third annual dinner. There were seven toasts: the King, the *Carbonari*, the World the Flesh and the Devil, Our Better Selves, Life, Death, and the Great Unknown. Death was proposed by Waley; and Brooke responded to the last. His gyp, who served at table, was disconcerted by the proceedings. He also looked after Pigou, who next morning asked his manservant how the feast went. 'Well,' said the gyp, with a crestfallen expression, 'they drank the King's health, sir, but not with much loyalty.'

There were eventful meals these days. Another was the Sunday breakfast given by Maynard Keynes, who had recently resigned from the India Office so as to accept a lectureship in economics at King's. Both the Strachey brothers, Sheppard, Shove, Harry Norton, all members of the Society, were present when Brooke found himself attacked from all sides for upholding his admiration of H. G. Wells. 'Finally, Lytton, enraged at Rupert's defences,' Keynes wrote to Duncan Grant, 'thoroughly lost his temper and delivered a violent personal attack.'[1] Soon afterwards Sheppard was the host, Shove the victim, and Brooke the leader of the attack 'for calling himself a

[1] *The Life of John Maynard Keynes*, R. F. Harrod, Macmillan, 1951.

Christian when he isn't one'. On February 9 it was Brooke's turn to entertain the Apostles. He introduced them to a visitor from the great world and gave a dinner-party in his room which lasted over three hours, chiefly owing to a monologue over coffee delivered by Hilaire Belloc, the principal guest.

While Belloc was still in everyone's mind, Brooke read a paper in Dalton's rooms called 'The Romantic History and Surprising Adventures of John Rump', a satire in the manner of Belloc's *Emmanuel Burden*. Under the title was a motto, a quotation from a sermon delivered in Rugby Chapel in 1904. 'It is character we want, not brains.' There is a verse Prologue set in Heaven. 'Very far away one can see the Universe, a point of yellowish light swaying uneasily in the blackness.' The creator addresses what is as yet only potentially Rump, asking it to choose between remaining unborn 'in timeless incomplete serenity'

> *Or in the world to be a man, and grow*
> *Subservient to space and time, though changeless*
> *Bowing to change, spirit to matter wed*
> *In mystical conjunction, there to live*
> *Blind in the dream, the folly of what seems,*
> *Transient, incarnate, unremembering.*

The soul chooses birth, and the reflection follows that 'the whole clanging Universe has laboured to this end. Star dust, gases, and movement, protoplasm, and the great hammer of Evolution, have one crown and completion, the seventy years of his being. Each man is unique. The one life of each is infinitely important, an immense chance for god-like success or chaotic failure.'

Rump's father was a retired master of a house in an English public-school. The satire waxes bitter. 'Like all incompetent hotel-keepers, they are continually being tempted to make up for unbusiness-like and wasteful organization by lowering the quality of food and accommodation.' His wife Violet suited him perfectly, being 'a peculiar mixture of irritable discontinuous nagging and shrill incompetence'. John grows up, learns of Hell fire from his nurse, and is 'put off' religion for life, all emotional subjects are carefully avoided, only sport is allowed to be taken seriously. Attaining manhood, incomparable dreariness sets in. 'He entered the living-room ("walking," he told himself, "as one in a dream") and greeted his tepid breakfast with a mirthless smile.' His life passes in unrelieved mediocrity, and his death is described without compassion. One assumes that Brooke's listeners must have thought it daringly realistic and refreshingly irreverent, for Rump's only fault, as far as one can see, was that while 'he might have been a thousand splendid things' it was enough for him to be genteel. So the soul makes off towards its Creator, and the angels in semi-chorus sing a Swinburnian stanza or two of mounting expectation, then the Deity speaks.

> I do espy him like a fretful midge,
> The while his wide and alternating vans
> Winnow the buxom air. With flight serene
> He wings amidst the watery Pleiades;
> Now Leo feels his passage, and the Twins;
> Orion now, and that unwieldy girth
> Hight Scorpio; as when a trader bound
> For Lamda or the isle of Magadore,
> Freighted with ambergris and stilbium
> and what rich odours . . .

The remaining '127 lines', we are told, are lost in the hubbub of Rump's arrival in top-hat, frock-coat, and umbrella. He is examined. All he can say in defence is that he was an English gentleman. God reproaches him, and gives judgement: 'Perish eternally, you and your hat!' Rump does not even wince. 'You long-haired aesthetes, get you out of heaven!' he declares

> I am John Rump, this is my hat, and this
> My umberella. I stand here for sense,
> Invincible, inviolable, eternal,
> For safety, regulations, paving-stones,
> Street-lamps, police, and bijou residences
> Semi-detached. I stand for Sanity,
> Comfort, Content, Prosperity, top-hats,
> Alcohol, collars, meat. Tariff Reform
> Means higher wages and more work for all.

At this the Deity, the angels, Heaven itself, dissolve, while Rump remains, leaning on his umbrella, swelling in stature until he blots out the stars. The English middle-class and its religion, with an affectionate smack at Swinburne and Milton *en passant*, have been ridiculed for several pages, and the *Carbonari* have rejoiced.

Meanwhile Fabian affairs were engrossing more of his time, now that Hugh Dalton had taken over from Keeling the office of President. He had persuaded Ramsay MacDonald, Chairman of the Independent Labour Party, to come and speak, and Lowes Dickinson had promised a series of four lectures on the Ideals of Democracy. As a member of the committee, Brooke attended these events, and, warned by Keeling's example, he prevailed upon his bed-maker to pass on to him any sinister rumours she might overhear while tidying up for the Tory opposition at King's. When Shove's rooms were turned upside down while he was out, Mrs. Brooke wrote asking for a full report on the outrage (the Fabians had printed a leaflet of the facts) and thereafter she must have been expecting every post to bring news of her son's immersion in the founder's ornamental fountain.

Before term ended he met the senior Tutor, W. H. Macaulay, to discuss his future, for in a month or two he would be leaving Part One of his Tripos behind him. G. C. Macaulay, Rose's father, was advising that he should give up the Classics and concentrate on English Literature in his fourth year. The Tutor supported his brother in this, as well as in his warning that Brooke should decline an invitation to take over the editorship of the *Cambridge Review*. He strongly recommended that he should not only live out of College, but out of town, so as to make it a little more difficult for callers to drop in for a chat. Finally he suggested that he should submit an essay for the Charles Oldham Shakespeare Scholarship that year—which would help him to turn his thoughts from Latin and Greek toward the academic side of his new subject.

All this suited him well enough, and the prospect of finishing with the Classics was so attractive that he expressed himself a little too strongly in a letter home. 'I didn't *really* intend to burn my classical books!' he wrote again in haste, for his parents were taking him too literally. The question of living out of town, and in lodgings, was something he could not, and need not, face at once, so he went to stay with Strachey at Manaton in Devon and read the new book on prosody which in a letter to Marsh he called 'Poor Professor Saintsbury's latest'. 'What a good name for a play,' Marsh replied. 'I shall suggest it to Barrie.' 'I said *poor*, partly because he is a Professor,' retorted Brooke, 'partly because he will die of swallowing his false feet. He has a passion for feet. It sounds horrible.' Health was the order of the day, frequent cold baths, and a pulley for developing the biceps. From Manaton he went to a gathering of the Apostles at the Lizard in Cornwall. Moore himself was there, James Strachey, and

Desmond MacCarthy, and it was early April and warm enough to bathe, but even the philosophy of the 'organic whole' could not divert Brooke's mind from the adventure he was planning by post with Dudley Ward as his accomplice.

It had cropped up, in correspondence with Margery Olivier, that at Easter her sister Noel and herself might be taking rooms in a cottage in the New Forest. Dudley was a natural diplomat, a man not to be suspected of subterfuge, so he must somehow discover the details, and work out a plan for what would appear to be a chance encounter. The party in Switzerland had given Brooke an opportunity for seeing more of the youngest of the family and just as he feared, or rather hoped against hope, he had succumbed, and was now in love with a schoolgirl younger than himself by several years, and whose poise and air of detachment only enhanced her charm. But Noel was so young that she was in no sense ready for the perturbing ardours that would always be in the air when either Brooke himself or yet another postcard or screed of his was in the offing. In the absence of her parents, who were now in Jamaica, Margery was the chaperone and alive to her responsibility. Brooke soon got the impression that Noel was hedged about with family surveillance as well as by the circumstances attending on her youth: her withdrawn way of life as a girl still at school, and the mantle she wore of her own unawakened calm, which he could not, and partly dared not, come near; yet for which—quite apart from the brown hair, gravity of expression and grey eyes—he fondly loved her. If it was all in his interests to give her family no grounds for mistrust, it was equally important to make sure that his people at Rugby were given no cue for reflections inconveniently parental. He was financially dependent, of course, and might have to remain that way for long years to come, and although he might be said to have vanquished, or at least dismissed, the Victorians as a whole, his life-long habit of filial respect and duty had so far left their authority quite unshaken in the enclave of School Field. Besides, the Ranee too was on the alert, although she suspected the wrong one of the four sisters. Rupert had work to do, examiners to satisfy, a niche in life that he must secure. Were not his Fabian extravagances enough for his more responsible self to contend with? To Brooke himself all this, though a grievance of a kind, only added spice. So for the present nothing jarred the idyll, and walking at Manaton he was in high spirits. 'On one side,' he told Raverat, 'were woods strangely coloured with green and purple by Spring; and on the other great purple moors. The Sunsets were yellow wine. And the Wind!—oh! there was never such a Wind to take you and shake you and roll you over and set you shouting with laughter!' Meanwhile it was imperative that Dudley should find out the family arrangements for the New Forest, and casually let it be known—

that we shall be passing their door. I do so because (a) I've been writing to Margery about once a week since January, and she'll be about sick of me, (b) I daren't do it, (c) I have no time: and you have plenty. So you must settle. But oh! be tactful, be gentle, be gently tactful! Perhaps they will hate us? Horrible thought! Do not intrude! apologize! apologize!

I must think of other things; and be calm. One thing is that all must be settled by tomorrow (Monday) week—all, I mean, about the place of meeting and starting. Another is this: very important. *You must not breathe a word!* Nobody must know where I am in those four days. It must be a profound, a profound secret. I am cleverly deceiving my family about it all. I have been obliged to tell Hugh R. Smith that there *will* be this *lacuna* of half a week. But he knows not why. I have told him I am going to 'seek Romance'! He believes I am going to wander through Surrey disguised in an Italian *sombrero*, with a guitar, singing old English ballads for pence! Ho! ho! But remember, a profound secret. It adds *so* much to the pleasure of it all. To vanish utterly for four days, and on *such* an errand. Be wholly discreet! If you have told any, deny it. Be mysterious!

A day or two later it was 'I hope you are thoroughly perfecting all plans'. Dudley was being indefatigable. Then Brooke met Maynard and Geoffrey Keynes and Ka Cox who were walking over Dartmoor from Tavistock. They all had a picnic lunch. Was Geoffrey interested in Ka? he faintly wondered. Certainly Jacques Raverat was. They had been corresponding ever since the illness which had kept him in France. That was the best part of two years ago. Ka happened to remark that he was now convalescing in Corsica. But this was of no consequence. What Dudley must do now is find an address where letters can be picked up, 'for if I am going to join my people at Sidmouth (the bloody latest!) on Tuesday morning, pretending to have arrived from Cornwall that moment, I must be up on their last few letters to me. That you may understand how everything stands, I will draw out programmes of my movements as various people believe them.' Then follows a chart with columns leading up to one headed 'You, I, and the Almighty' and at the bottom, at the latest date shown, having re-entered the great world everyone, not only the Almighty but the Russell-Smiths no less, are shown as sharing in common the knowledge that he is at Sidmouth. 'I shall be in disguise on Friday, and you will fail to recognize me. Look out for one in a black beard, and an eyeglass: with a pink rose in his button-hole, and waving a scarlet handkerchief.' This elaborate network of subterfuge, and the adventure itself, cost Dudley the advance payment of £2 7s. 0d. Brooke at the moment of departure for the rendezvous, was so excited that he forgot to leave a tip for the maid, and the nuisance of despatching it by post with a suitably misleading postmark (to put Russell-Smith off the scent) came near to wrecking the scheme at the outset.

According to the secret chart, and the Almighty's column, the days April 10–13 were spent in 'Arcady', which on maps more mundane is known as Bank, in the New Forest. The cottage where the Olivier sisters were staying was a discovery of Keeling's. It stood on a knoll among beech trees and was the home of a Mr. Primmer, a retired butler, and his wife, who had also been in private service as a cook. The food was unusually good, and Mr. Primmer waited on the young people at table. In the day there were walks and rides on New Forest ponies, and in the evenings Brooke read aloud. The sojourn at Bank was happy and without event, except for the death of Tolstoy reported in the newspaper, and an account of the funeral of Swinburne, on which Brooke was soon to make his comment. 'Cornwall was full of heat and tropical flowers,' he wrote to Raverat in Corsica, 'and all day I bathed in great creamy breakers of surf, or lay in the sun to dry (in April!); and all night argued with a Philosopher [Moore] an Economist [Shove] and a Writer [MacCarthy]. Ho, we put the world to rights!' Then he had left to carry out the first stage of Dudley's scheme.

But then, after the Lizard, oh! then came the Best! And none knows of it. For I was lost for four days—I went clean out of the knowledge of anyone in England but two or three—I turned, and turned, and covered my trail; and for three-four days, I was, for the first time in my life, a free man, and my own master! Oh! the joy of it! Only three know, but you shall, that you may from your far islands, picture to yourself what a strange place was our England for four days about Eastertide. For I went dancing and leaping through the New Forest, with £3 and a satchel full of books, talking to everyone I met, mocking and laughing at them, sleeping and eating anywhere, singing to the birds, tumbling about in the flowers, bathing in the rivers, and, in general, behaving naturally. And all in England, at Eastertide! And so I walked and laughed and met a many people and made a thousand songs—all very good—and, in the end of the days, came to a Woman who was more glorious than the Sun and stronger than the sea, and kinder than the earth, who is a flower made out of fire, a star that laughs all day, whose brain is clean and clear like a man's and her heart is full of courage and kindness; and whom I love. I told her that the Earth was crowned with wind-flowers and dancing down the violet ways of Spring: that Christ had died and Pan was risen: that her mouth was like the sunlight on a gull's wings. As a matter of fact I believe I said 'Hullo! isn't it rippin' weather?'

As for your request for a letter about me, 'my doings, feelings, dreams,' etc.—what am I to write? Some doings, and feelings, I have told you. I am not unlike the R.B. you used to find, as you say, learning Ernest Dowson by heart. And yet different. From being sad I have travelled far; to the same goal as you, that of laughing, at times—often—for the joy of life; and by how different a route! I find all things—the sum of things, at least—admirable. Splendour is everywhere. I have come out of the Night; and out of the Past. There are many great poems and paintings in the world, and I love them; also there are the sun on the sea, and flowers, and people's faces. I am intensely happy; and not with that *Maeterlinckian* happiness that always fears the gods' jealousy. For I feel certain that the happiness is abiding. At least, I have had it, and known. Nothing can take that. So I dwell, smiling. The world is full of tremendous hopes. I am going to be a 'failure' in my Tripos. And they all curse me for wasting my career. I smile at them. Never was my conscience so serene. I know more than they.

It will be remembered how often at school he had tried to write a poem about a face that was either glimpsed in dreams, or recognized again in some future existence; but the piece was never more than a boyish exercise, for the idea was only an idle fancy. In this month, and probably during these days, he wrote the sonnet about 'your brown delightful head,' beginning 'Oh Death will find me, long before I tire Of watching you,' and two years afterwards, well knowing how much better it was than anything else he had done of this kind, and why, he placed it foremost among the poems arranged for his first published collection.

On the Esplanade at Sidmouth the parents had taken rooms often favoured by Beerbohm Tree and his family for a seaside holiday, and here Brooke finished his sonnet and received more guineas from the *Westminster Gazette*, having won a competition for the best poem bearing the title *The Voice*;[1] the original interpretation of the given title and the merit of the piece illustrate the value to him of these competitions. It was the first of four prizes won in succession and he followed it up with an ingenious exercise in the manner of Edward Lear. Such were his literary recreations in Arcady. Among the events which had occurred while he was retired from the common light of day was the burial of Swinburne like a Christian. This was a blow to Brooke's atheistical pride. He was enraged on Swinburne's behalf,

[1] G.K., p. 132.

and wrote to Dalton, 'Did you see that, against his desire, the bloody parson mouthed Anglicanisms of blasphemous and untrue meaning and filthy sentimentality over him?' Apart from this brief eruption of prejudice, his way of life had been, as he said, 'as uneventful and as perfect as a bird's'. Nor did the prospect of increased activity among the Fabians disturb his calm. 'Are you going to attempt Cambridge again,' he asked him, 'now when the little trees are green and white and the Socialists are singing all down the backs?'

On April 23 he spent the first of many nights in Marsh's rooms at the top of a stone staircase at Raymond Buildings, Gray's Inn. The walls were covered with drawings by Girtin, Cozens, and Sandby, for Marsh had not yet begun his patronage of the younger painters of his day, and where there were no pictures there were books. Marsh seemed to live closer than St. John Lucas to the professional world of letters; his frequent anecdotes of the *beau monde* and apt quotations must have made Brooke feel he had found a link with metropolitan culture, as indeed he had, but it was difficult to take Marsh seriously. He seemed like a caricature of the Trinity Apostle. From Gray's Inn Brooke went back for his last term in College, and so as to pick up the threads with his Cambridge friends (the dew-dabblers, not the Apostles) he set about inviting them all to come together for a May-day celebration.

It was on May 2, long remembered by them all for its enchantment; a grey cold day with a little watery sun in the afternoon. Justin was on the scene again, although he had gone down, driving a large open motor-car of German manufacture called an *Opel*, an object of wonder and envy and withal a most unusual convenience. Very early in the morning he picked up Geoffrey Keynes from Harvey Road, Gwen and Margaret Darwin from Newnham Grange, and Ka Cox and Dorothy Lamb from Newnham College. 'Ka is Senior Student and has a conscience,' Brooke had told Gwen, so 'another passenger' was included for the sake of respectability, and they all packed in and drove out to Overcote on the banks of the Ouse, not many miles away. On the road Justin was struggling to get his arms into his Norfolk jacket when the vehicle swerved out of control over the grass verge, heading for a pile of stones, and Justin was talking and laughing so much he didn't even notice until Geoffrey cried 'Look out!' and an abrupt swerve in the nick of time averted disaster. The crab-apple was in flower where they opened their baskets on the edge of a meadow, and a nightingale, almost too good to be true, was actually seen at close quarters singing intermittently in the hedge as everyone spread their coats on the damp grass and lounged, leaning against each other—a group ready to hand for an Edwardian Watteau—and Brooke read aloud Herrick's poem *Corinna's going a Maying*—

> *Come, let us goe, while we are in our prime,*
> *And take the harmlesse follie of the time.*

One of these merrymakers, recalling the alfresco breakfast half a century later, and looking, perhaps, a trifle shamefaced yet happy in the reminiscence, declared, 'I regret to say we made wreaths of apple blossom.' Another recalled the chains of cowslips and daisies.

At tea that day with Sydney Cockerell in Cambridge, Brooke met another poet of the older generation, Wilfrid Scawen Blunt. The 'harmlesse follie' of that early morning must have already seemed like a dream of long ago. It was a most genial Spring, and one night Dalton, Arthur Waley, and Brooke sat under a tree down by the river at the back of King's, and read Swinburne aloud to each other by the light of a bicycle lamp; and once Brooke, Dalton, and another, slept out there the whole night and the head Porter, spying their prostrate forms from a distance, reported to the Dean that 'two men and a woman' were lying asleep under the limes, so seldom these days would Brooke submit his long hair to a barber. And it continued somnolently warm throughout May as the time of the Tripos drew near, and Brooke was more than ever beset with distractions. One of them was the Winchester Reading Prize, a competition held in the Senate House. Brooke entered, reading aloud Keats's *Ode to a Nightingale*, but could not prevail against the sonorities of Dalton declaiming Milton.

In recognition of this year of Charles Darwin's centenary the *Carbonari* demanded of him an appropriate paper. For text Brooke chose a pamphlet by Oscar Browning which had been printed privately in 1905, and called 'The Evolution of the Family'. Brooke called his talk 'Endogamy', defined by Browning as marriage within the family or clan, and exemplified by Artaxerxes who was said to have married both his daughters. Brooke used the idea to illustrate the impossibility of a real 'marriage of true minds'. How could man ever relieve his solitude? 'Our best success is only to perceive by a glimpse the vague outlines of another wanderer in the fog . . . What's the use of howling ourselves hoarse if almost all we get is indistinct cries from a distance? . . . When I see you and talk with you, observe your jerky marionette movements and mobile terrifying masks, hear you pouring out unintelligible noises, I am led to do the same, to shout and gesticulate in a vain frenzy for understanding . . . And then I wonder if it's a sickening nightmare from which I shall awake, screaming, in a more perfect solitude. Sometimes, in conversation, I suddenly want to scream, to wake myself.' Now and again, he went on, there was an illusion of communication, but it was only born of delirium. It was better to resign oneself to loneliness. 'It is something to possess your own soul.'

In the same vein he wrote to Scholfield who had suggested their sharing rooms out of college.

There are various reasons. I am passionately enamoured of solitude; and as a.housemate I cannot imagine myself as anything but wildly irritating. I am still uncertain, a little, whether I may not continue in King's and achieve complete solitude here. If not, I am going to try to get rooms in Grantchester, or further, even. I passionately long to shut myself wholly up and read only and always.

Grantchester was a small village on the Granta some three miles from the town. If you glanced back, the top of King's was visible between the trees almost all the way. There was a mill there and a secluded spot where the water was deep enough for bathing, and tea-gardens on the river bank that Brooke and Geoffrey Keynes had visited on several occasions at the end of a local stroll, for the route known as the Grantchester Grind was an acknowledged Sunday walk, with a rest in a garden at the end and a cup of tea served at this time by Mrs. Stevenson, who lived at a riverside cottage called the Orchard.

He sat for the Tripos in May, then went to stay with the Cotterills at Goldalming. Naturally only Dudley was informed that the chief attraction was not cousin Erica but the proximity of Bedales.

Oh ho! the South! The Lakes of Surrey! They call me! And I shall possibly see Noel in the distance! The air and sky is full of noise about it! Tremendous sensation in the heavens! The earth wildly enthusiastic! Life is splendid. I am king of infinite glories. Tra! la!

And then to have to pack a bag! And even that is a ritual of infinite joy and calm splendour. All things are romantic as means. This piece of paper has come to an end.

R.B.

When he got back to Cambridge in June he began seriously to negotiate for rooms at the Orchard. He was offered a sitting-room at the front, looking out towards the church, a bedroom immediately above, free use of the river garden, and all meals, for thirty shillings a week. This seemed reasonable, so he began to move his belongings. Then the results of the Tripos were made known. His name was among those in the second class. Stricken by his failure to get a First (though he could not have been altogether surprised), he went straight to Frances Darwin, who had now become Mrs. Cornford, and was living with her husband in Chesterton Road. 'The colour was drained out of him,' Mrs. Cornford observed. '*I* don't care,' he remarked, 'but it's my people.' He went and came back again an hour later. 'This is for you,' he said, and handed her a facsimile of the Shakespeare first folio. Was it his mother, she asked, that he was so concerned for? He said it was. 'How glad I am,' he declared, 'How glad I am that mother isn't just a nice old lady!' He did not know that F. M. (Comus) Cornford was one of the examiners, and that it had been debated whether his papers did not more properly belong to a lower class than Second. The term was over, and he was angry with himself.

Mrs. Cornford followed him with a letter. 'You always seem to me to lead such a splendid "living" kind of life up here, and that is the one thing that really matters. And I think everybody who cares about you must feel that too . . . You mustn't be sorry.' It was now all the more important to redeem his academic name by winning the Shakespeare scholarship which Macaulay had proposed. He chose the subject of the Elizabethan dramatist John Webster, bought Florio's *Montaigne*, Sidney's *Arcadia*, and any relevant work he could lay hands on, dismantled the Japanese lanterns at Gibbs's Building, and took a hansom to Grantchester, leaving the trunks of books and clothes to be sent on.

Chapter VI

THE ORCHARD

(*June* 1909–*December* 1910)

The Stevensons observed their new lodger going about in a blazer and bare footed or, suddenly emerging, transmogrified, with a bowler hat, gloves, and umbrella, for a trip to London, and coming back very late and saying that he had dived for a tin marked Chocolate Biscuits only to find it was full of flour; or calling out to greet his friends who were shouting under the bedroom window. 'Well, what do you want? Some grub, I suppose.' The Stevensons were a little perturbed by the bare feet. 'This is a divine spot,' their lodger was writing to Dalton. 'I eat only strawberries and honey. If you're ever house-hunting there's an admirable ruin near, with a sundial and no drains.' This was his first reference to the place next door, the Old Vicarage.

'Between the bridge and the church,' he explained to Eddie Marsh, who was coming to stay, 'accessible from the river.' Did he think his guest was coming by canoe? Perhaps he should not risk arriving in time for dinner, 'though if you'd face bread and water *I* don't mind.' By the time Marsh was there, Augustus John and his family had arrived in two caravans and were encamped in the neighbouring field. He was painting Jane Harrison's portrait, and Marsh and Gilbert Murray were among Brooke's guests who were taken over to meet him. This was hardly the academic solitude which Brooke had come to seek. He was as busy as ever. One sentence declining an invitation from Geoffrey Fry in the most serpentine manner of Henry James is evidence enough.

Do you know, I am so certainly and prominently an entertainer of so many various and possibly not continuously compatible young people, at the date you indicate—the 7th, in short, that I, very gratefully, dare not (happy, too, as I am, if I may say so, ignobly comfortable at least, in the benediction which the not-to-be-broken industry of a Shakespeare scholar bestows, in this fluttering crisis, upon the cowardice of a so easily lured butterfly), play Proserpine to your fiery, your regal, your too abductive chariot?

There was a special reason, which Fry would have appreciated, for the implied reference to Henry James. The great man himself had just been visiting Cambridge as the guest of three admirers whom he had never set eyes on before. One was Geoffrey Keynes, another Charles Sayle, who provided the bed and breakfast at 8 Trumpington Street. On June 12, after Sayle had shown him round the University Library, Henry James was the guest of honour at a small luncheon given by Keynes in his rooms at Pembroke. Brooke walked over from Grantchester in a fever of awed anticipation to complete the party. All went smoothly, and next morning James breakfasted with Maynard Keynes at King's. A few years later, having breakfasted in the same company (with the addition of Bertrand Russell) D. H. Lawrence declared, 'They made me dream of a beetle like a scorpion'. James did not go as far as this, but it was evident that he came something short of enjoying himself, and, as Geoffrey Keynes has recorded, he was 'bewildered by the scintillating conversation that eddied round him'. He asked whether the young man who was his fellow guest at Pembroke the day before was thought of as a good poet. Someone answered in the negative. 'Thank goodness,' said Henry James. 'If he looked like that and was a good poet too, I do not know what I should do.' Desmond MacCarthy's version of the remark was, 'Well, I must say I am *relieved*, for with *that* appearance if he had also talent it would be too unfair,' and the inquiry, addressed to himself, had opened with, 'Who is the long quiet youth with fair hair who sometimes smiles?' MacCarthy also asked Brooke what James had talked about and was told, 'He gave me advice; he told me not to be afraid of being happy'; but since the setting of MacCarthy's account is more fantasy than fact, as Keynes has shown,[1] perhaps the sage's advice too was fictitious.

Brooke was not at the breakfast. Instead Sayle asked him and Mallory in for coffee after luncheon at Trumpington Street. James talked of the ballet and the frontispieces in preparation for the new edition of his works. Next day Brooke suggested giving Henry James the experience of a punt on the river. Sayle dropped the pole as he was pushing off, and it glanced off the novelist's head, but no

---

[1] *Henry James in Cambridge*, Geoffrey Keynes. The London Magazine. March, 1959, vol. 6, No. 3.

damage was done, and Brooke took over control of the navigation, standing at the bow in a white shirt and white flannel trousers and every so often lunging into the water with his pole. It was a halcyon day, and the hour too sweet for conversation as they glided at ease under the small Palladian bridges, by Tudor walls and limes in leaf, probing the chequered shade. Long afterwards recalling the occasion when he 'very unforgettably met him', Henry James conjured up in his mind an image of this quiet interlude on the water. 'He reappears to me,' he wrote, 'as with his felicities all most promptly divinable, in that splendid setting of the river at the "backs".' And thus it came about that a few days after the river party, Brooke, infected by his august acquaintance, felt obliged to inform his young friend that he could not come, that indeed he was unable to play Proserpine to his fiery, his regal, his too abductive chariot.

While Brooke was settling in at the Orchard, James Strachey was also in process of moving out of college. He was going down, and sorting papers. 'I found a great many more documents in the final disruption,' he wrote, 'So I most unwisely wrapt them in brown paper and ordered the Nightingale [the porter at King's] to put them in your rooms. They'll certainly be lost, or sold by that person to the Press.' A prompt reply came from the Orchard—'A brown paper parcel! My God, you are a devil. All is lost. I shall leave England. Rupert.' Strachey was giving news of the play *Press Cuttings*, which had been written by Shaw for his sister in support of her cause of Women's Suffrage and forbidden by the Censor. James had just had a session about it with the dramatist himself. Brooke had nothing of such moment to report. James Elroy Flecker of Caius had been over to the Orchard, and they had met again in Cambridge. 'Lunch with Flecker today was simply Hellish—old cold bloaters, sardine paste, and the relics of your gooseberries—oh, and dirty! hairs in the butter! soot in the cream! Why does he creep so!'

July was very hot, and the joy of it enhanced by the return of Raverat after an absence of nearly two years. Brooke arranged for him to be put up at the Old Vicarage, for he was curious to know what the ramshackle place was like inside. Raverat noticed that his old acquaintance no longer parted his hair in the centre, chewed the end of pencil while writing, never smoked or drank alcohol, and ate no meat. One of Raverat's first good offices to Brooke was to take him along to his old school, Bedales, in the innocent guise of a friend in tow. Noel, at an upper window, was amazed when she caught sight of them crossing the yard, but she was unable to fall in with their plan of taking her out to tea. But words were exchanged, and by way of return, Brooke promised to foster Raverat's courtship of Ka Cox. As a member of the Fabian Committee, where Ka was still the Treasurer, he was well placed for putting a word in her ear. With Raverat gone, Brooke thought it was time to let Erica know of his new and delightful situation. He was settled, he said, in—

a sort of a cottage, with a dear plump weather-beaten kindly old lady in control. I have a perfectly glorious time, seeing nobody I know day after day. The room I have opens straight out onto a stone verandah covered with creepers, and a little old garden full of old-fashioned flowers and *crammed* with roses. I work at Shakespeare, read, write all day, and now and then wander in the woods or by the river. I bathe every morning and sometimes by moonlight, have all my meals (chiefly fruit) brought to me out of doors, and am as happy as the day's long. I am chiefly sorry for all you people in the world. Every now and then dull spectacled people from Cambridge come out and take tea here. I mock them and pour cream down their necks or roll them in the rose-beds or push them in the river, and they hate me and go away. The world smells of roses. Books? pah!——

He appended a book list, headed, of course, by the philosophy of G. E. Moore. Now that the theory of states of mind had become a part of his life, he could afford to make fun of it, as in his letter to Dalton, after finishing with Fabian affairs.

I have made a *very* good Anti-Nature Poem to Railway Lines on Which I Suddenly Came When Walking on the Edge of Dartmoor; Being Tired of Irregular Things. It begins

'*O straight and true! straight and true! . . .*'

and further on there's a verse

'*For no Laws there be in Sky and Sea,*
And no Will in the wayward Wood;
Nor no States of Mind in the Gypsy Wind,
—The which alone are good.'

It halts a little, perhaps.

It was still July, and the Olivier sisters, Bryn, Daphne and Noel, were camping out near a weirhouse over the River Eden at Penshurst, and David Garnett, their neighbour at Limpsfield, and Godwin Baynes had pitched their tents near by when who should turn up but Dudley Ward and Brooke. Once more, no doubt, Dudley had got wind of the family arrangements. Brooke walked with Noel along the river, and they were picked up by Dudley and Daphne in a boat and were rowed home. After supper somebody suggested bathing by the light of a bicycle lamp propped up in the grass by the edge of the water, and they all went in, and again next day, to the admiration of the villagers, as they laughed and dived in the weir. 'Rupert,' said Garnett, 'taught us the trick of fast and loose,' and, feeling drawn to him, he observed him closely.

His complexion, his skin, his eyes and hair, were perfect. He was tall and well built, loosely put together, with a careless animal grace and a face made for smiling and sudden laughter. As he ate in the firelight I watched him, at once delighted by him and afraid that his friendliness might be a mask.[1]

And then there were trips to the summer season of the London theatre, breakfast for twelve at the Orchard, with Mrs. Stevenson amiably trying not to be at her wits' end, tea parties in punts under the willows, journeys to Cambridge by canoe, and bathes above Byron's Pool near Grantchester Mill; and Gwen and Jacques and Ka and Geoffrey and Dudley and Justin (Frances, the wife of a don, was now, perforce, a little withdrawn from the circle) were seldom out of each other's company. 'We used to loll in armchairs and talk wearily about Art and Suicide and the Sex Problem,' wrote Gwen in the fragment of an autobiographical novel which she left among her papers. 'We used to discuss the ridiculous superstitions about God and Religion; the absurd prejudices of patriotism and decency; the grotesque encumbrances called parents. We were very old and we knew all about everything,' and she too did her best to record her impression of Brooke's physical presence.

Perhaps the most obvious thing about him was his beauty. He was not so beautiful as many another man has been, and yet there was something in his appearance which it was impossible to forget. It was no good laughing at him, calling him pink and white, or chubby, saying his eyes were too small or his legs too short, there was a nobility about the carriage of his head and the shape of it, a radiance in his fair hair and shining face, a sweetness and a secrecy in his deepset eyes, a straight strength in his limbs, which remained for ever in the minds of those who once had seen him, which penetrated and coloured every thought of him.

But more valuable, because even more fugitive than a visual image, is Gwen's memory for that audible quality one can only call the texture of speech and there are passages in her fragment which are of such a convincing fidelity that they enable us to overhear Brooke and

[1] *The Golden Echo*, David Garnett, Chatto and Windus, 1953.

his companions in the act of casual conversation. 'Your hair's too long,' says Jacques, suddenly, *à propos* of nothing. Brooke protests that it isn't much longer than his.

'It's miles longer than mine.' Pulling it down, 'Mine only comes to my eyebrows and yours could go into your mouth.'

'Anyhow, it's very beautiful.' One had to have it like that, he says, if one was a poet.

'Rot. Look at Shakespeare.'

'Well, that was the bitterest thing in his life, his hair all coming out like that.'

'Why don't you grow a beard too.'

Rupert says he probably will, the moment he starts writing blank verse. For the present he's the clean shaven sort that confines itself to brief lyrics.

'I wonder *why* poets have to have long hair,' says Jacques.

'Because they are so beautiful. And that's because they live evenly all over. Brain, body, heart, legs, liver, all in perfect order, instead of living only in their brains, or only in their bodies, like most people. Now it would be absurd for a mathematician to have my hair.'

On another occasion Brooke declares there ought to be rules for one's conduct with relations, and launches into a monologue:

Parents, now: you kiss them sometimes, and send for them when you're ill, because they are useful and they like it; and you give them mild books to read, just strong enough to make them think they're a little shocked, but not much, so they can think they're keeping up with the times. Oh you ought to be very kind to them, make little jokes for them, and keep them awake in the evening, if possible. But never, never, let them be intimate and confidential, because they *can't* understand, and it only makes them miserable.

'The worst of it is,' says Jacques, 'Parents don't like being brought up on Rupert's plan.'

'No, they don't, but it's all for their own good. Why, they'd die if they knew what we were really like.' And Rupert goes on to say, 'Calmness and firmness are no good with my mother. She's so much calmer and firmer than you are yourself.' He says the dread of intemperance is a common topic with his parents, and Jacques remarks that people aren't really qualified to talk about the effects of drink until they've been drunk themselves. 'Wouldn't it be fun to see all those people getting drunk so as to qualify for a temperance meeting!' then Rupert chips in with, 'They'd do that sooner than not talk about it!' which leads him to the subject of Decency.

Decency is a very odd thing. Supposing we four, each of us, agreed to wrap up our little finger in a bandage, and when anyone asked us why, we'd blush and look uncomfortable and laugh in an embarrassed way and say 'Oh, well, it's a thing we don't generally mention.' I feel sure it would take on very soon.

'Ears would be better,' says someone. 'They're so indecent anyhow.' One evening Jacques was depressed. 'I don't know why I'm alive,' he moaned. 'What's the good of living?' 'I don't know,' said Rupert, 'unless you happen to enjoy it. I do, just now.' 'And I think it's bloody,' said Jacques. Rupert looked him up and down. 'You're better than most people. Anyhow you're conscious. Mostly they're blocks. Wood. Stones. No eyes. No ears. No brains. Nothing but stomachs and reproductive organs.'

The others are lying about on the grass, secure in their antediluvian world, or in winter eating muffins by the light of the fire. Jacques can't bear the thought of turning out second-rate, 'publishing a little green volume every five years that someone on the press calls "promising" and people say What does he *do*? . . . Oh he writes poetry.' Brooke sees no cause to worry. 'That's probably what they've said about every poet that ever was.' 'Well, it's not good enough for *me*!' 'You're too dam proud,' says Brooke. 'I like a little fame, and a little money as well. Not but what I'm not going to write a million times better than I do now. You just wait and see.'

The circle was beginning to widen its circumference. Raverat was moving into lodgings in Chelsea so as to study printing at the Ashendene Press; Gwen would soon be an art student at the Slade; James, secretary to the editor of the *Spectator*; Geoffrey a student at St. Bartholomew's Hospital; Ka supervising and generally mothering all who came within range of her ready sympathy from a flat in York Street, Westminster. Brooke at the Orchard, and Frances and her 'Comus' by their domestic hearth, still kept the group, at least in spirit, centred on the University.

Late in July Brooke, Dalton and Margery Olivier attended the Fabian Summer School in Wales. They listened to a series of talks given by Beatrice and Sidney Webb on what was called The National Minimum, a theme defined by Mrs. Webb when she declared 'The universal maintenance of a definite minimum of civilized life becomes the joint responsibility of an indissoluble partnership in which the individual and the community have reciprocal duties.' To understand why these words rang in Brooke's ears with the motive force of a battle-cry one must glance back a short while, to April of this year, in the New Forest. When Brooke succeeded in being lost to the outside world he took with him into 'Arcady' not only his Shakespeare and the works of Aristotle but a volume which the Fabian Society had brought out in February, entitled *The Minority Report of the Poor Law Commission*.

The Royal Commission set up by the Balfour government to inquire into the Poor Law had been at work since 1905 under the chairmanship of Lord George Hamilton, and by the time its Report was ready for publication, a small group on the committee led by Beatrice Webb, unable to approve the methods or subscribe to the conclusions of their colleagues, had drawn up their own Report based on their own researches which recommended their own system of reform. This was published in one volume as a sequel to the Report of the Majority, but as there was some doubt whether it would win enough attention this way, Sidney Webb, who had drafted it in collaboration with his wife, succeeded in proving that the work was not Crown Copyright but his own, and brought it out by itself in an edition available to all Fabians and the public at large. For two years it engrossed Brooke's mind, and most of his energies were given to the campaign for the spread of its ideas.

The Poor Law that the Webbs were agitating to abolish dated from 1834, a time when it was necessary for the government to oblige men under threat of penalties to work in the expanding factories of the north. It was based on the notion that a man's poverty could only be his own fault. If wealth was the proper reward of con-scientious work, then poverty was the price of idleness. It was there-fore needful to force the idle to exert themselves both for their own good and for the benefit of society. Charity was inevitably a form of poor relief given at the cost of those who had made the effort to work, and by encouraging the destitute to breed it only increased the num-ber of hungry mouths. So Charity was looked on as a private affair to be discouraged by the State, while relief of a sort was officially pro-vided in the form of The General Mixed Workhouse where all varieties of destitution, the sick, the aged, the mentally defective, were given refuge, without regard for the nature of their distress or concern for the cause which had brought it about.

The first concern of The Minority Report was to promote what it called the 'Break-up' of the Poor Law, so that poor relief would not only be administered locally, but lose its name, and the Poor Law thereby lose its stigma; it would be 'broken up' according to the various categories of destitution, each having its own department of Health, Old Age, Employment, and so on, thus ensuring 'to the workers by hand and brain steady progress in health and happiness, honesty and kindliness, culture and scientific knowledge, and the spirit of adventure'. The Report afforded a minutely documented picture of social life on its lowest level, suggested a programme for the creation of social services which then seemed revolutionary, managed to remain extraordinarily 'human' in its approach, and readable in spite of the dryness of assembled facts and figures, and above all it implied a moral code—an obligation to serve, which worked both ways as between the individual and the community. If through a sequence of some thirteen Acts of Parliament, extending over nearly forty years of legislation, from 1908 (Labour Exchange Act) until 1948 (Children Act), the Minority Report has been justified piecemeal, this last feature, the spirit which informed the whole—what Mrs. Webb referred to as an 'indissoluble partnership' and 'reciprocal duties' when she spoke at that Summer School in 1909 —has somehow got lost by the wayside. The consequences, of course, are not our concern here, but it was this moral factor, not the massive evidence alone (although it came as revelation) which in Brooke's view gave the Report the nobility of a cause worthy to make it a complement to the philosophy of Moore. They fitted perfectly. The 'good' state of mind in this social context was now to be adjudged in relation to one's neighbour in misfortune, and the 'organic whole' embraced one's nation as a whole.

Early in 1909 the Webbs founded a Society within the Fabians known as the National Committee for the Prevention of Destitution, its aim being to arouse the public conscience and explain the need of the 'break up' of the Poor Law. Brooke, Dalton, and Keeling were among its first members, and throughout this summer they planned a campaign for the Michaelmas Term. Sidney Webb himself was booked for October 21, when Brooke would succeed Dalton as President of the Cambridge Fabians; Dalton agreed to the next date, when he would deal with general principles—and Ka Cox, the Treasurer, five days later was assigned a rather cumbersome subject, 'The Machinery of the Minority Report and a Criticism of the Majority Report'. The latter was made her especial province; she was to study the two reports in parallel and be ready to answer questions so as to expose the weaknesses of the 'Majority'. As it bore sixteen signatures, and the 'Minority' only four, challenging questions were inevitable. The arrangements ended with a talk by Clifford Sharp, who was soon to become the first editor of the Webbs' weekly magazine, *The New Statesman*. Leaflets were piled under the table at the Orchard. Brooke got onto his bicycle and distributed them round the neighbourhood from door to door; a new kind of visitor began calling at the Orchard, Will Crooks, the working-class M.P. who in 1903 seized Woolwich from the Conservatives; and Webb himself stopped for the night of his lecture; while the exchange of notes with Dalton mingled grave policy and farce. How were they to pay for the hire of the Assembly Rooms? 'The Treasurer (a fool),' writes Brooke, 'may refuse to pay out of her own pocket.' The Treasurer was a butt for their jests. Brooke had just glanced through her lecture notes. ' "We are not much interested in the treatment of the aged and infirm—we don't want to study *them*—we want to find out what's wrong with the whole damned Poor Law." (That sentence, I grieve to say, fell from the Treasurer's lady-like pen.)' Dudley had just been staying at School Field. 'Departing, he waved a careless hand and bade me tell you that Politics was a game for clever children, women, and fools. He vanished, lit up by the flash.' Mrs. Brooke was a little anxious lest Alfred should be infected by his elder brother's example, so Rupert was studiously casual on the subject, knowing that in the end Alfred's curiosity would suffice to work his undoing. 'Alfred said to me, shyly, "Can Associates of the C.U.F.S. go to meetings and so on?" "Oh yes," I was cheerily off-hand, "they can do everything almost. The only thing is they are all Conservatives. The Liberals are all full members," I had him there!'

The Webbs, it was noticed, had been so tactful as to avoid all use of the inflammatory term 'Socialism' in the course of their Report. It was a matter of Fabian policy to be equivocal. So the Cambridge meetings were not *ostensibly* planned in the cause of the Minority Report. Drawn to hear about the proposals in the 'Majority' the audience awoke to their position only when it would be rude, or too much bother, to get up and walk out.

At the end of August Mr. and Mrs. Parker Brooke rented the vicarage at Clevedon, Somerset, a Victorian house with many bedrooms, and spacious grounds which included a tennis court. The number of spare rooms gave the Ranee the hospitable idea of getting Rupert to invite his friends. James must come, he thought. 'There are a lot of books here that you'll like. The *Dictionary of Religious Anecdotes* is good'; and Dudley Ward: 'Bring any volumes of Synge you can lay hands on, also Yeats, and *Atalanta in Calydon*. You can ransack my rooms, and Dalton's. Use your discretion which to bring. We can always fall back on Shakespeare,'—and Granville Barker's plays were due out on Friday! There must be play-readings under the trees; then again to Dudley, a day or two later, with more urgency, having been ill, and claiming that his only way of keeping in touch with 'life' was playing tennis barefoot: 'It's not so effective as living in a tent by a river with three Oliviers: but it annoys the family. I am becoming eminent (no thanks to them) but detestable. The family atmosphere is too paralysing. I am sinking. Save me, or I die!'

On August 26 the look of welcome on the parental faces must have been a little forced when the station brake rolled up the drive filled with the most extraordinarily miscellaneous Cambridge assortment: Gerald Shove, Dalton, Francis Birrell, Gwen Darwin, A. Y. Campbell, two of the Oliviers, Eva Spielman, who had been with them in 'Arcady', Dudley Ward, etc., and later Maynard Keynes dropped in for a while, and Eddie Marsh was driven over by Edward Horner. ('I cannot read the name,' Brooke had replied to his postcard, 'Horner or Homer? Not *the* Homer, dare I hope, the writer?') Descending on the vicarage where peace had reigned since 1860, or at least for the last fortnight, they proceeded to go their own ways, coming in late for meals, not changing in the evening, or dressing casually and omitting to linger in the dining-room after dinner to pass the time of day with either of the parents. Twenty minutes after the gong, Mrs. Brooke would sweep into the dining-room with tight lips and ring the hand-bell for the food to be taken away and kept hot. She did not conceal her feelings.

'I prefer Miss Cox,' she would say, in Gwen Darwin's account, 'her wrists are very thick and I don't like the expression of her mouth, but she's a sensible girl. I can't understand what you all see in these Oliviers; they are pretty, I suppose, but not at all clever; they're shocking flirts and their manners are disgraceful.' Or if Rupert put in a good word in someone's defence the pendulum promptly swung the other way. 'I can't understand what you all see in Miss Darwin. She's not pretty at all, or attractive. On the whole I prefer the Oliviers; at any rate they are good looking.' One day she drew Gwen aside. She was anxious about Rupert's friends, and Gwen gathered that there had been trouble in the past with Richard. 'He's so much influenced by his friends. Poor Mr. Shove now. I always feel sorry for him, he seems so very unsteady. One could place no reliance on him, and I don't think he has a very happy nature. And with that sort of character one *never knows*. Now with Mr. Dalton I always feel safe; he's so very prudent in all respects. Though I wish he were not consumptive, poor boy.' It was no use saying he was *not* consumptive. She had made up her mind.

One day Rupert confronted his friends in the garden. 'I say, I wish you'd try to be nicer to my mother. Of course I know it's all nonsense about that sort of thing, but, well, I think she'd like it. She's old, you know, and minds about these things.'

'Haven't we been nice?'

'How dreadful. I'm sorry. Didn't I say good morning?'

So they decided to reform. They would take it in turns to be sociable, but they were so long deciding who should begin that they were all late for dinner.

At last they went, and everyone declared the occasion a great success, and the Ranee, asked what she thought of Maynard, observed evasively, 'I have never met so many brilliant and conceited young men'. Brooke, however, had felt the strain. He was writing to Ka Cox, arranging a new 'Minority' campaign, when he had to change the subject and confide in her. Ka always seemed to understand one's troubles. 'Oh, poor Mother's Experiment of having some of my Acquaintances in a House in the Country this Summer! They've come and gone, singly and in batches. And the Elder Generation couldn't stand *any* of them! O Ka, it was dreadful, and most harassing to my tactful organization of the day, how they strangely didn't like . . . *anybody*! Most painful: and a little amusing.' Bryn Olivier, for instance. 'She (very innocently) preferred to be, and *did* be, alone or with anybody, in the garden, rather than in the drawing-room with Mother, and plunged up mountains all day. In 1870 it was quite invariable to be in the drawing-room . . . And so they're both quite right and wrong—should be the verdict. But what *does* one do with Nymphs, with quite inexplicable sparkling people?'

The rest of the vacation was spent at School Field, planning to go straight to Cambridge for the Michaelmas term though in fact making for The Champions, Sir Sydney Olivier's house at Limpsfield. But the scheme was beset with hazards. Naturally, Dudley Ward was his sole confidante, and now, September 8, a letter of his was to hand. Brooke replied:

I got your letter this evening at dinner. I was very sick; because I was waiting for another: on TENTERHOOKS. I answer yours now because I'm a trifle lonely, to tell the truth; and I've had a damn bad week: but just now my irrepressible thoughts of SPLENDOUR have bubbled up again, and in spite of my people, my work, and my troubles, I am defiantly sincerely and vastly hilarious. Not my meagre mother's nightly anti-Olivier lectures do more than momentarily inflame to wrath my bumptious joy.

For one thing he was incapacitated by an injury sustained at Clevedon, and none other than Ward himself had inflicted it, as Brooke explained next day, when his mood had changed.

I'll tell you; and why I'm this morning in the worst temper I've ever been in. (Lord! I've had a scene with Mother! She *crept* out of the room, at the end—which was brought on by my choking with rage, and being therefore unable to continue.) It begins 16 days ago: when you and I and admirable people were charging ridiculously down a far hill in the dark. You with the gay childish *abandon*, which is indeed your most lovable characteristic, ran up behind me and kicked my left ankle with your heavy boot, laughing the while with high hysterical delight. The hole you made was poisoned by a sock, and, they say, inflamed by tennis: and changed into a sore that grew wider and deeper with incredible rapidity. When I got home the doctor examined it. And I have been on a sofa with my left leg in bandages ever since. The wound slowly diminishes. But if I 'go about on it' before it's well, the elderly, shifty fraud who is my doctor, says it will turn to an abscess and eat the bone of my leg. *Then* I shall be a bit of a fool at wooing dryads.

Well, the creature, damn him! stopped my going to 'Cambridge' to-morrow. But I thought Wednesday would be all right. And when a letter from Margery came this morning, suggesting Wednesday, I sang Easter Hymns in bed for half an hour, till Mother came in to dress my foot. She was a bit startled. But she was more startled, when, at my careless mention of Wednesday, she pooh-poohed the idea, and I broke into invective, I made such a good speech of concentrated fury, that she was brought to admit that Wednesday would probably be all right. But I've still the doctor to face. If he flatly forbids, they've got me in bandages, moneyless, and without luggage: so I'm pretty helpless. But if he *does*, when he comes on Tuesday— this house, from then till I *do* go, will be laden with an inspissated gloom to which the Egyptian darkness was a positive *glare*.

There was some straight speaking mixed with the invitation from the elder sister, only acting in the interests of someone who could not be expected as yet to fend for herself. But it was lost on Brooke, who was in no mood to make the effort of putting himself in someone else's position. Truth was they both had a tendency to dramatize, and Brooke's helpless predicament at the moment did nothing to restrain him, as he showed in his letter to Ward.

I (not as an individual, but as a Young Man) was to be shut out of Noel's existence (except at Limpsfield). Lady O's New Educational Scheme. Then Margery added seven pages of damn plain speaking of her own. All about my 'wild writing', 'looking ahead' and a thousand things. A great fierce blazing kind sermon. But my God! she said some dreadful things, about women, that made me hate her. I *won't* believe them. Love, for a woman, she said, destroyed everything else. It filled her whole life, stopped her developing, absorbed her. 'You'll see what I mean if you look at women who married young' she grimly adds. 'No woman should marry before 26 or 27' (why *then*? if it kills them). And later 'if you bring this great, terrible, all absorbing thing into Noel's life now . . . it will stop her intellectual development', etc. It's a bloody theory, isn't it? The logical outcome is that one must only marry the quite poor, unimportant, people, who don't matter being spoilt. The dream of any combined and increased splendour of the splendid you, or the splendid I, with the splendid X—that's gone. We can't marry X. At the best we can, if we try to marry X, marry her corpse.

It's very cheering, isn't it? One pictures Margery sitting in that dining-room, in front of the Motto 'Love is enough' . . . and commenting on it, from woman's point of view. It's funny.

But I'll not believe it of Noel. All the same, I was torn by mistrust of myself, fear, perplexity, and despair, all that night. I didn't get to sleep till 6; having gone to bed at 11. The next night three a.m. saw me awake, thinking. My dear, I've had an *awful* time. I don't know what to do. 'Wait!' was the burden of her letter. 'Go away if you like! But don't tell her! Wait! for her sake!' And I'm still perplexed; as to what is best for Noel. There were other upsetting things in the letter: of all kinds. I quote. 'Are you sure this is final? . . . If it were not, and you went on now so that she came to love you, have you thought how it would be with her? (I think I would find a way to kill you.)' I loved her, then. Lord, how they love each other, that family! They make me feel rather mean and solitary. Then, in another place there was a sentence: 'She is so reasonable about you now. Let her remain so! . . .' That was painful. I didn't imagine she *wasn't*. But to have it rubbed in! Oh! of course I am delighted! I wave my hat with pallid enthusiasm: And say in a high voice 'Hurray, hurray! Just what she should be—reasonable about me! Excellent, excellent!' *Reasonable*—Lord, what a word!

Before term began a magazine containing four of his poems was on sale in Rugby. It provided a digression in his letter to Ward.

The *English Review*[1] is mentioned every time anyone comes to a meal here. 'Do you ever see the *English Review*, Mr. X?' leading gracefully up to 'Rupert had a lot of poems in it the other day!' (That's Mother.) Then the family all cheer. Alfred tries to look solemn and giggles: the servant does a step-dance in the background: I turn brick-red: the visitor gives a start,

---

[1] Vol. III, No. 2, September, 1909. *Finding, Blue Evening, The Song of the Beasts, Sleeping Out: Full Moon*, all included in Poems, 1911.

says 'Really? how interesting! Let me see, what name did you say? *English Review?* for September? yes! I must get one immediately!' and jots down something on his shirt-cuff. (He thinks it'll be 6*d.*, or 1*s.* But it's half a crown.) And I make some ghastly jape about mentioning my name to the publishers. Then it's over till next time.

None of these four poems were characteristic. Only two had been written this year, and perhaps the best was the latest, written in May after the Arcadian adventure with Dudley. It ends:

> *Her passing left no leaf aquiver.*
> *Pale flowers wreathed her white, white brows.*
> *Her feet were silence on the river,*
> *And 'Hush!' she said between the boughs.*

It was inferior to the sonnet of the same date. The subterfuge of turning his love into a dryad in order to write about her has nearly, but not quite, overlaid the genuine emotion with the conventional graces of a pre-Raphaelite painting. His nonsense verse or parodies, however, occasioned by the *Westminster Gazette* competitions, had proved consistently successful and won him several prizes. In the same month of May he published over a pseudonym a sonnet on the proposed title *To Two Old School Friends* and, as requested, attached his own critical comment. For his entry Brooke may have recalled the impact of his first encounter with Justin, in whose eyes he had seemed so excessively urban.

> *What! make you mouths, O twain mad dreamers, yet,*
> *You of the woodland, of the city you?*
> *Still mock you at me as 'between the two',*
> *As 'torpid, dull, suburban'? You forget;*
> *The soul is its own place. And mine is rife,*
> *Even mine, in spite of all that mother says,*
> *With wine, and song, red night and sunless days,*
> *And life! Life amorous! Even in Balham, life!*
> *Know you of Nature? . . . Down our street there grow*
> *Trees, iron-fenced! whose names I do not know.*
> *Of Art? . . . My wall-paper is greenish grey,*
> *And all my ties of a sad umber shade.*
> *Of Life? . . . Upon the landing, yesterday,*
> *I suddenly kissed the under-parlourmaid.*

There is Poetry. The *images* are clear and fascinating; the turns of *phrase* individual; the *idea* not blatantly obvious, but subtly important; the *metre* boldly licentious and utterly successful. No monotony there! Look at that eighth line! See how the first swings you gloriously into the subject, and the sixth is full of pathetic simplicity, and the last two gloriously crown, in sense and metre, the whole! How subtly the unexpressed character of the speaker is vividly revealed! This is clean, good writing, all of it. What virility! what music! What *verve*! I have not faltered in my wonder and admiration of this poem for weeks, not since May 9, the day I wrote it.

He had begun the month with deservedly winning the 'Prize Poem' in the manner of some minor poet of a past age. He chose Robert Greene and called his piece 'The Shepherd Doran His Dumpe: A Pritty Lamentable Ditty of Love's Flighte (attributed to Ro. Greene)'.

> *Mine Harte, that like to Salamanders burn'd*
> *Is now growne Colde;*
> *Mine Eyes, that wept for Love Unkinde, are turn'd*
> *Even to Stones, that have no Lust for Seeing;*
> *Cupid, that in my Brest to Dwel was bolde,*
> *Is Fled, and my Sadde Songs pursue him Fleeing:*
> Ah Love: swete Love, whose prettie Torments erst did shake me,
> False Love, ah Love, alas! if thou wilt now Forsake me!
>
> *Saméla, her that was mine Onely Deere,*
> *I seek no more;*
> *Nor doth her Beautie move mee, tho' so Cleare*
> *It shines, not Venus' Selfe I holde Above her.*
> *I love her Not, who Loved soe wel before,*
> *And what's her Beautie, sith I cannot Love her?*
> Ah Love, swete Love, whose prettie Torments erst did shake me,
> False Love, ah Love, alas! if thou wilt now Forsake me!
>
> *Thus I, long time that Groned in Cupid's Thrall,*
> *May now Goe Free*
> *Yet of my Freedome take no Ioie at all.*
> *My Praier being Granted turnes to mine Undoing,*
> *And that I love not More Tormenteth mee*
> *Than ever Love didde, or my Vain pursueing:*
> Ah Love, sweete Love, whose prettie Torments erst did shake me,
> False Love, ah Love, alas! if thou wilt now Forsake me!

In the following week he won the prize for the best review of an imaginary book. For this purpose *The Last Dragons* by G. K. Chesterton came into being, in which, we are told, 'Mr. Chesterton has suddenly developed a long observed tendency and lapsed completely into Mr. Henry James's style.' He did nothing more in this kind until Clevedon when again he won the prize for 'the best report upon the results of a competition for an original eight-line poem'. He began by saying, 'Dear Herrick would have won this competition easily', and concluded:

A song is a static poem, a poem without growth, or movement. The first line gives you an emotion, the last repeats it. You don't, aesthetically, get anywhere. Now, an eight-line poem—that beautiful hybrid between a lyric and an epigram—should contain an ideal (I don't mean tell a story) which lives, moves, smiles clearly on you, and takes you captive in exactly eight lines.

It was late September, and he was still at School Field, planning the Fabian campaign with Dalton, wanting to get back to the Orchard and be the host again in his own rooms by the river. Dalton was writing an article on him for the series *Those in Authority* in the *Granta*. 'You might put in that my real life began since I went to live at Grantchester,' Brooke told him, 'that I have a pet cow called Betsy, that I can play country tunes on a pipe . . . I don't think there's anything to be left out except that I know Latin and Greek.' In his article, which was unsigned, Dalton (remembering Brooke's remark to him at Rugby) wrote 'There is a vacant place reserved for him between Matthew Arnold and Arthur Hugh Clough in the Poets' Corner in Rugby School Chapel', and told of his playing tennis barefooted and being able to pick up the ball with his toes. (Brooke's prehensile toes were remarkable. He could take a match from a box and light it, and one occasion in Gray's Inn some years hence, on being challenged by Stanley Spencer, he executed a detailed drawing of a house and signed it with his right foot.) Brooke's free-and-easy ways had caused much comment, and it was true that it caught on in King's and from there spread through the university. 'He is sometimes credited with having started a new fashion in dress,' wrote Dalton, 'the chief features of which are the absence of collars and headgear and the continual wearing of slippers.'

Meanwhile the Strachey brothers were in Stockholm. 'I gather Lytton's corresponding with you about a house in Grantchester,' wrote James. 'Would you hate anyone being near you? though I suppose you both dislike one another too much to meet often.' There was no vestige of dislike on Brooke's side, although Lytton had once attacked him rather stridently at breakfast. Nothing special about that. Sooner or later everyone among the Apostles was singled out for his share of hilarious contempt. Brooke welcomed the idea of such a neighbour.

Dear Lytton,

My knowledge of the house at Grantchester is oddly fragmentary; and I'm doubtful which part you'll want. But I'll lay it before you.

My landlady told me about it, recommended it for a place to stay in, and gave me the address: which I decipher as

Mrs. Neeve,
The Old Vicarage,
Grantchester.

The Neeves are 'working-people' who have 'taken the house and want lodgers'. (Beware of that plural.) So far they have been singularly unsatisfied. Mr. Neeve is a refined creature, with an accent above his class, who sits out near the beehives with a handkerchief over his head and reads advanced newspapers. He knows a lot about botany. They keep babies and chickens: and I rather think I have seen both classes entering the house. But you could be firm. The garden is the great glory. There is a soft lawn with a sundial and tangled, antique flowers abundantly; and a sham ruin, quite in a corner; built fifty years ago by Mr. Shuckbrugh,[1] historian and rector of Grantchester; and *most* attractive. He used to feast there nightly, with . . . I don't know whom. But they still do, spectrally, in the evenings; with faint lights and odd noises.[2] We of the village hate passing. Oh, I greatly recommend all the outside of The Old Vicarage. In the autumn it will be very Ussher-like. There are trees rather too closely all round; and a mist. It's right on the river. I nearly went there: but I could find no reason for deserting my present place. It's only the inside of the house I don't know about. I put Jacques there for a week (James will tell you who Jacques is) and he seemed happy. But he's very wild. The cooking mightn't be *good*. But I think they're cleanish and docile. I go to Grantchester on Thursday: so if you'd like me to talk to them, I will, or I can give you a bed at my Orchard, for you to reconnoitre.

Lytton Strachey spent a night at the Orchard, and was observed to have a habit of sitting with his back against the book-shelves, reaching a hand over his shoulder, and bringing forward without looking the first book he touched, reading a snatch of it, putting it back, and grabbing another, all without turning round, or so E. M. Forster was

---

[1] Actually Samuel Widnall, author and printer of several topographical books, and pioneer in photography; he was never ordained but affected the appearance of a clergyman, and in 1853 erected a Folly at the bottom of his garden, the ruinated fragment of what might be a medieval nunnery.

[2]
> And spectral dance, before the dawn,
> A hundred Vicars down the lawn . . .

The Old Vicarage, Grantchester, 1912.

told, the guest who succeeded him in Mrs. Stevenson's spare bed at the Orchard. Forster had come to read a paper to the Society. The term had begun a fortnight before, and Forster's host had been elected the third President of the Cambridge Fabian Society. Dalton, touching up his article, his own term of office having expired, wrote his friend's new claim to distinction at the head of his tribute in the *Granta*. The President of two Societies, founder of the *Carbonari* (whose new member this term was none other than 'Podge', the freshman) model of the new informal undergraduate dress, public speaker, reviewer, poet, Brooke had become a figure as remarked in King's Parade as ever he was in the Close at Rugby. Passing the porter's lodge as the freshmen were arriving, 'Do these young men make you feel old?' Dalton asked him. 'No,' said Brooke. 'Not old. Only tremendous.'

II

At the Orchard (which he described to Marsh as 'golden and melancholy and sleepy and enchanted. I sit neck-deep in dead red leaves'), he put the finishing touches to his campaign in support of Beatrice Webb's scheme for reforming the Poor Law, and with the help of his committee, consisting of Margery Olivier, F. M. Cornford, Ka Cox, and Shove, began planning a further campaign on the theme 'University education and modern news' to be launched in the new year. His academic work was confined to his essay on Webster which won him the Charles Oldham Shakespeare Prize in December, and an effort, less productive, to get ready a collection of his own verse for a private edition supervised by Jacques Raverat. 'I love seeing my little things in print,' he wrote. 'And I can torture people I know with them more easily so.' But whereas Raverat wanted the material at once, Brooke favoured a delay. 'I could make a better, and more generally hated, show, then, I feel.' For the moment he was writing round to his friends, laying a plan which seemed more important than the publishing of verse. In fact he had evolved what seemed a better scheme for immortality. The idea had originated during a walk at Clevedon. In return for Raverat's offer to print his verse, here was another proposal, an opportunity available only to the elect, among whom, for Raverat's sake, Ka Cox was included.

I meant to 'make an offer'—or rather propound a scheme to you. But there were always so many people . . . I will do so now. But it is, whatever your answer, *a secret*.

It is difficult. I begin thus.

The world is, in certain ways, rather bloody, at present. It is a good world, but imperfectly organized. One fault, one great fault, in it, is that its inhabitants grow old.

Examine this. I don't mean in *years*—that's inevitable, and not necessarily bad—but in *spirit*. Now, there are two classes, I am certain, of people; and very splendid people in both. The first *naturally* get old in spirit, as they get old in years. They are quite happy in it—it's not necessarily a blemish—only a shortcoming, a pity. Many good splendid people are such. Geoffrey, I should think, might be one. There are many.

The other class doesn't *naturally* grow old. It does so, in this present world, because of the bloodiness of arrangements. But it needn't. And if people of that class *don't* grow old they are—my God how splendid! Just sometimes they don't. You are of this second class. So am I. So are many people I know and you know. At this point you object 'But, Rupert, *we* shan't grow old!' My dear Jacques, we're very admirable and we youthfully lead splendid lives—with Art and Friendship and the great blusterous beautiful world about us—now. We are twenty-something. In 1920 we shall be thirty something. In 1930 we shall be forty something. Still running to and fro—London, Petersfield, Cambridge. Still in a country where one *has* to know so many dull stupid grey lived sleepers. Still going to the last play, reading the last book; passing through places we've been in for twenty years; talking to rather fat, rather prosperous, rather heavy, married, conservative, suspicious people who were once young with us; having tea with each other's wives; 'working' 10–5; taking a carefully organized holiday, twice a year, with Ruskin, luggage, and a family, to Florence, disapproving of rather wild young people.

My dear Jacques, think of 1940, 50! . . . We *shall* become middle aged, tied with more and more ties, busier and busier, fussier and fussier; we *shall* become old, disinterested, peevishly or placidly old men; the world will fade to us, fade, grow tasteless, habitual, dull; and at x̄y years, in a stuffy room, with *all* our relatives, wife's relatives, friends, servants, and medical attendants, around, we shall swollenly stupidly and uninterestedly—*die*!

There've been other people in other generations who swore not to get old, who found Life as good as we do, and vowed to keep it so, to stay young and clean-eyed.

Where are they now? Dead. You meet their bodies walking the streets of London, fat, dead, top-hatted, ghosts, haunting the civilization that was their ruin . . .

Oh, never fear, we'll get old, you and I and the rest, and dull, as all the others did. It is certain.

You'll say you've had these thoughts, as all of us have. We who *could* keep young to the end, will grow old. It is the age's fault.

Suppose that a band of the splendid young people in the past had formed a scheme to escape the great destroyer, to continue young, and suppose they had succeeded—wouldn't *that* have been a *wonderful*, an unequalled triumph? a splendid example for the world? and a glory for themselves?

So far theory: stale, you may think. But poignant enough for me. Be patient: and hear now History.

In the beginning of September I was walking on a cliff top with four splendid people, Dudley Ward and Margery and Bryn Olivier and Hubback. The world was before us, sun, rain, wind, the road, and each other. We were filled with joy and youth and ecstasy. We talked as we ran and swung along, of Davidson[1]—quoted (you know it?)

> *Out of time and out of all*
> *While others sing through sun and rain*
> *'Heel and toe, from dawn to dusk,*
> *Round the world and home again.'*

we were the 'others' then. We should die, as he had died; and there'd be others . . . and others . . .

Had he died? we wondered (the body'd not been found then). I drew a picture of the poet, married, with grown up sons, hampered, driven to write, poor, worried, fettered, walking out one day from it all, changing his name and appearance and facing the world anew, reborn, tasting every drop of life with the keen sense of youth and freshness and the added relish of experience. It couldn't last long perhaps, twenty years or so; but twenty years of that is worth an immortality of—the other. It wasn't true: But it might have been.

The idea, the splendour of this escape back into youth, fascinated us. We imagined a number of young people, splendidly young together, vowing to *live* such an idea, parting to do their 'work in the world' for a time and then, twenty years later, meeting on some windy road, one prearranged spring morning, reborn to find and make a new world together, vanishing from the knowledge of men and things they knew before, resurgent in sun and rain—

We determined to be those people.

Will you join us? Will you, in twenty years, fling away your dingy wrappings of stale existence, and plunge into the unknown to taste Life anew? There'll be many, I hope—not too many, though! We choose people we all agree on. Some people are obviously right; some not. We're going to ask Ka. You'll suggest others. It's the greatest grandest offer of your life, or of ours. You'll accept! I'll explain the conditions.

On the 1st of May, 1933, at breakfast-time, we will meet on Basle Station. Did you ever hear of so splendid a place of meeting? We may have parted, lost sight of one another for years. But on that spring morning, in that mad place, whiskered and absurd and unrecognizable, we'll turn up. And then? . . .

Then, Life! What else matters? Details elsewhen.

In *April* 1933 R.B. will be a greying literary hack, mumbling along in some London suburb.

In *May* 1933 the offices, muddy drawing-rooms, hatchet-faced middle-aged fools, and snivelling newspapers that knew R.B. will be dully wonder-

[1] John Davidson was drowned near where they were walking.

ing what the devil . . . The newspapers will talk about suicide . . . one or two people, left in England, in the know, will smile and be silent.

And R.B. will be fishing for tunnies off Sicily or exploring Constantinople or roaring with laughter in some Spanish Inn or fitting up a farmhouse or two, with some friends, in America, or rushing wild-haired through Tokyo pursuing butterflies, or very sick on an Atlantic tramp. What does it matter? Only—he'll be *living*.

This is an offer. A damn serious and splendid offer. Take your time and consider. The Oliviers, Ward, Hubback and I are going: also Baynes and one or two more: and others we're going to ask. All splendid people. We'll select, all of us, people—the right people—slowly and surely. If, at the last moment, any person daren't do it, he stays at home, holds his tongue, and only he is the worse. Details later. All can slowly be worked out. Some are in favour of going once and for all; some want there to be an option of returning to the old things at the end of . . . three? five? ten? years. It is possible. Few would return: and those returning would never be as if they'd never gone. They'd have changed everything. They'd have taken the Step: made the Choice. Consider all these things: you'll find reasons for them. Supply details. They may all be altered or filled in. The great essential thing is the Organized Chance of Living Again: THE SCHEME.

It has made me wholly happy about Life. Life is beyond words *good*. And now, by this, it *will be*: always to the end. We shan't have to murk and spoil this flaming gift of God—these few years out of Eternity—this great chance that is Life. We'll take and live it to its full extent—be glorious at fifty! We'll be children seventy-years, instead of seven. We'll *live* Romance, not *talk* it. We'll show the grey unbelieving age, we'll teach the whole damn World, that there's a better Heaven than the pale serene Anglican windless harmonium-buzzing Eternity of the Christians, a Heaven in Time, now and for ever, ending for each, staying for all, a Heaven of Laughter and Bodies and Flowers and Love and People and Sun and Wind, in the only place we know or care for, ON EARTH.

RUPERT

Jacques accepted, and after canoeing back to Grantchester from a Fabian meeting Brooke seized pen and paper to welcome Raverat as the newest associate of the ever young.

Your great letter was like an April day in the Autumn. We shout hilariously of youth to each other across the skies—while the little grey people mumble down to death. It is splendid to meet or hear from other people who are Going. They have an halo round them. We smile to each other. Margery Olivier writes, it may be, that she has had three weeks' rain in Surrey, 'but it will be fine on Basle platform in 1933'.

He was in the same exalted mood when he read to the Carbonari Society a paper called 'From Without', signifying his reflections from without the town. He was by now fully converted to a rural way of life. The origin of his paper was a talk he had recently had with Noel while taking her back to Cambridge in a canoe after a party at the Orchard. 'We of the country abide, perdurable, slow of brain, with hearts that change from glory to glory, like a pool at evening.' By contrast there was his audience, 'you little people, you noisy, quick-witted, little, dark, shifty-eyed, bitter-tongued, little men of the city —you think that peace is ignoble, dull and dulling, a thing of sloth . . . I am an alien here, and homesick and shy, reading my rough words with an archaic Arcadian burr, with all your clever bright eyes, glittering round me, and your whirring brains—What is that minute pervasive ticking in the room?—evolving your next joke but two.' Only two miles away, in Grantchester, there were better things to be concerned about, 'and the white bed and the open window with the dark coming in'. Then he launched into a fantasy. He was bathing at night, 'I stood naked at the edge of the black water in a perfect silence. I plunged. The water stunned me as it came upwards with its cold, life-giving embrace,' then a figure appeared, some local deity or naiad of the stream, and they talked and more than ever was he con-vinced that it was futile to think of any existence beyond the here and now. 'Paul died daily. We *live* daily. It is a new thing.' His strange companion talked of mortals and their transitoriness.

It is so important to realize, and so difficult, how little time there is. If they could only grasp it in their imaginations, for how short a time they shine with their odd gifts, on the scene: how long the before and after probably are, and how dark: what an adventure it all is! Not feverishly, for then you lose all; not languidly, for then you lose half . . . There is no time to reason, and still less to hate. We must feel and be friends. We must seek in art and immensely in Life for the end here and now. To pass from emotion to emotion, radiantly, for a few years, and then vanish.

Brooke went on to talk of the state 'beyond the grave'. These, he said, were idle words. 'Oh they sound silly in this hot room. But out in the woods—you've no idea how meaningless they are there. That, she told me, was the use of the country. Among trees or by a river you cease to find it interesting or meaning anything. You go by bushes with dogroses, or over the long grass, and there is the per-petual voice of the wind in the trees, and the calling of the birds, turn-ing homeward with the light; and through it all and beyond it all, dimly, but, I swear, truly felt, something which was not indeed per-sonal, but—I stammer in my speech—I think other words or another language was used then—but an unity, a wholeness . . . We have inherited the world. Why should we go crying beyond it? The present is amazingly ours.'

THE ORCHARD

In another paper this term, read to the Society, and called *Eggs in Moonshine*, his aim was to discover whether truth was less important as a means (the end in view being a good state of mind) than was generally supposed, and he brought up the differences between Moore and Bergson, whom the former had declared was 'not only stupid but wicked'. Brooke tried to demonstrate that there was no absolute truth. 'Shelley felt himself rather noble, and the human race rather noble. He had many more good states of mind than if he had realized the truth.' Indeed truth was not necessary to the good life. 'Any fool, who discovers Jesus suddenly has states of mind as good, perhaps, as Moore's when he discovers some great truth. Keats in discovering the *un*truth about Beauty probably had better.' Brooke certainly demonstrated that absolute truth, supposing there to be such a thing, was an unnecessary ingredient of the 'organic whole' which conduced to a good state of mind, and for a moment we wonder how he had the nerve to expose the limitation in Moore's system, possibly in Moore's presence, until we realize that in Brooke's mind he was doing no such thing. To someone like himself who has rejected transcendental belief there is no truth beyond what seems to be true, and, as he says, 'truth does not depend on itself but on the believer, be it true *or untrue*'. Since discussions turning and turning about on nice points of this kind were Brooke's delight on so many Saturday evenings in term-time over three years, they cannot be ignored. They seem curiously detached from practical affairs, and even from reality as many would understand it. Perhaps they seem so remote because they assume an extraordinary stability in society, an assumption which, of course, was natural and proper then, and nowadays would be ludicrously bizarre. Maynard Keynes may well have heard this paper which Brooke read to the Apostles at Trinity, and in after years he wrote of his associates in the Society, 'We were not aware that civilization was a thin and precarious crust erected by the personality and the will of a very few and only maintained by rules and conventions skilfully put across and guilefully preserved.'

In another Society address of this time, Brooke supposes a talk being given by his grandson newly elected to the Society 'solely on the strength of his name and yellow hair', on April 29, 1948, in which the youth invites his listeners to look back on their predecessors of 1909. 'Tremendous, across forty years, they loom! . . . The photographs we have in the Book of the Stracheys, Shove, Sheppard, Greenwood, and Keynes, representing them as middle-aged, plump and strangely bald, whiskered all, were taken much later—shortly, in fact, before they all committed suicide.' This lamentable end of so many budding intellects was due to their proving false to their own principles. 'They could not—it was, perhaps, the superfluity of their spiritual and intellectual health—they could not—though indeed this very inability often led them into the most exquisite bypaths of phantasy—they could not say what they meant.' The young speaker, 'gulping quietly', then describes how these thoughts came to him when, going through the rubbish in his late grandfather's desk, he came upon the script of a typical paper of 1909. The talk then becomes a satire on formal education, which is considered worthless, 'whether the best things be taught or the worst—English or Classics', as against education unconsciously through the influence of environment and by intuition where alone, not in so-called 'education', lies the only real education of the mind. At any rate, Brooke Senior asks at the end, having killed himself off in 'the brilliant and witty period of the twenties', what *will* the Society be debating in 1948?

Throughout a term of meetings, political and philosophical, his residence at the Orchard did little to reduce the number of his callers. The pleasure of a walk into the country was only an added inducement to his friends, and often they called for breakfast before he was up or even awake, and Mrs. Stevenson would hear cries of 'Rupert' in the lane and then, through the dividing wall, only the response of a grunt, and the casement window thrown open for the start of another day packed with talk and the dashing off of last-minute postcards. Among the articles written at this time was a criticism of Ezra Pound's *Personae* for the *Cambridge Review*. Brooke found this new poet 'blatant, full of foolish archaisms, obscure through awkward language not subtle thought, and formless; he tastes experience keenly, has an original outlook, flashes into brilliance, occasionally . . . When he has passed from stammering to speech, and when he has more clearly recognized the nature of poetry, he may be a great poet.'

At the end of the term he went for a few days to Rugby, where he at once began firing off letters at Gwen Darwin. She was organizing a party of seven for the fancy dress Ball at the Slade Art School, and they were all to go as the winds or leaves of Shelley's *Ode to the West Wind*. Brooke himself was to be the wind of the title, clad in his Comus costume of the Attendant Spirit.

Isn't it giving me too good a job? I see that the leaves are 'yellow and black and pale and hectic red', so there's some choice! I may point out though (of course, I'm a very literary person, you know, well-read, etc.) that the West Wind conducts Clouds and Waves as well as Leaves (vide P. B. Shelley). Ka would be a very good wave—she'd have to be blue and large, and lie down and roll up and down the Slade . . . and then break in foam. Could she break in foam? She might come out all over white frills periodically and snap and roll her eyes. I'd thought out a lot of *seven* ideas, in case the leaves fall through. We might be the Seven Branched Candle-stick, or the Seven Virtues (Honesty, Hypocrisy, Faith, Respectability, Stupidity, Charity, and Monogamy) (I'd be Faith in my blue dress, with a silly smile) or The Seven Seasons (False Spring, Spring, Summer, St. Luke's Summer, Autumn, Winter, and Fog) or the Seven Rays of the Spectrum, or the Seven Seas. But we could go as these at the last moment.

The talent for practical detail recently lavished on the Minority Report was now as alert as ever in the service of Carnival. 'Jacques'll be a jolly good dead leaf,' and as for James, 'It's a pity he can't come as a DEAD TWIG,' and then in mounting excitement:

I foolishly quite forgot, and had my hair cut this morning. However I can fluff it out, and get some man to arrange it with silver—or without. I might have a WAND.
(I don't believe Shelley thought of the W.W. as blue and white.)
As for St. George's, is a separate room ordered for us? I wonder if I shall dress after; or come in a compromise. Dare I rush about London in the middle of the afternoon with bare legs? My *largest* overcoat only comes down so [to the knee]. My dress is *so* sky-roby, wove by Iris, that it affords special difficulties. (By the way, I hope so much leg won't offend the Slade?) Is there a room at the Slade, where we can all arrange each other's drapery and hair?
I guess my Comus dress isn't very heavy. But if you don't send it here, will you take it to London and deposit it with Jacques, Justin or somebody?
It's lucky I don't dance. I shall be able to sit out all the time near a stove. Is there any record of what Spirits wore in Winter? I suppose a jolly fur-rug wouldn't be allowed?
What's a Dead Leaf like?

At the same time he arranged a night for himself at Gray's Inn. 'I hope you've evaded the Suffragettes so far,' he wrote to Marsh. 'What do you do when they fling vitriol at you? Is an umbrella any use?' Marsh was told nothing of the revels at the Slade. The picture he was given was a thought more sober.

I sit here and read the Drama and study the Poor Law. Tomorrow night my father is going out to dinner, and I have to take House Prayers. Imagine it! I am immensely excited. I shall recite the admirable phrases of Edward VI's Prayer-book to 54 pink and white cherubs. I may perhaps extemporize a notable 'prophesying'—or isn't that Anglican?

And then again to Gwen, for now the Ball was imminent.

I shall have a large brown rug with me. So I shall wear that if I'm cold.

May *non*-dancers dispense with gloves? However proper at a dance—I feel they'd be wrong for a wind. (Moreover I hate them.)

It is very young and impudent of Margaret [Darwin] to be a *green* leaf. Shall I wither her with a look? As a dead leaf one is very nice colours I suppose. Do you have brown paper instead of a face? And all the ends and edges of you ragged?

Then came the late December afternoon when they all foregathered in the house of Gwen's uncle, W. E. Darwin, at Egerton Place, and that evening at the Slade; Maynard Keynes disguised as a cook was standing with his brother Geoffrey (an ancient Briton), Max Beerbohm, Rothenstein, and Wilson Steer, when the Leaves and Winds, all strangely arrayed, made their entrance together, as if 'driven' by the West Wind, and were drawn into the measure of the waltz, the friends who had celebrated May Day, Gwen, Margaret, and Ka, Jacques, Justin, Rupert, and on this occasion, James. And the revel lasted until the small hours.

Soon after Christmas, some of the Winds and Leaves were together again at the Hotel Schweizerhof, Lenzerheide, in Switzerland, and Brooke was among those that set about devising another performance for the New Year. Ka was missed from among them, so four of the young men, headed by Raverat, signed a postcard. 'We passed thro' Basle this morning while you slept. Ha, ha!' The new show was *The Super Ski*, in which Raverat was a polar explorer, Dudley Ward an evil deity called Thaw, and Brooke again the unctuous hero, Sir Galahad Bere de Bere. We detect his hand in the parody of Meredith sung to the tune of 'The Honeysuckle and the Bee', beginning 'Under yonder archway, brooding o'er the doormat' and containing the lines, 'Valet! But he is what my heart first waking Whispered a Duke was, more than duke is he.' No one will ever know (perhaps it's a good thing) who perpetrated the lyric 'If I should spread the butter of a kiss On the Swiss roll of your heart . . .' As Brooke could not sing he mimed and an *alter ego* at his side, who was given a name (Vernon) all to himself on the programme, delivered the musical numbers.

They began the journey home by sledge, skimming down the valley for two hours, keeping just ahead of the dawn, to the nearest railway station. Eventually they reached Basle, admired the Holbeins, then while awaiting the midnight train to Paris Brooke ate what he afterwards recalled as 'green honey', quoting, very aptly, a line from a sonnet by Wilfrid Blunt, 'I have eaten honey and behold I die'. In the Louvre at Paris he fainted, and by the time he reached Rugby it was thought he had typhoid. 'I lie here, my face bright orange,' he wrote to Geoffrey Fry, 'I subsist on Tapioca. My tongue and mouth and throat and stomach are raw where that accursed stuff touched them. The skin peels off like bad paper from a rotten wall.' He read *Prometheus Unbound* and touched up a poem drafted at Lenzerheide after a rough crossing. It was called at this stage 'A Shakespearean Love Sonnet', but as *A Channel Passage*[1] its outspokenness was to provoke more comment than any other of his early poems. He also finished *Dust*, which he had begun in December: a sonnet 'I think if you had loved me when I wanted', and on January 11, the very day he wrote a trifle called 'The One before the Last', his family entered a time of serious trouble.

Parker Brooke's sight began to fail, and he complained of acute neuralgia. Dalton and Maynard Keynes were coming to stay and make speeches at the General Election, and they were not put off. Alfred played the host, and himself spoke at a public meeting. 'I don't do these things,' Brooke told Erica, 'I can't speak slow enough.' The Ranee was becoming gravely concerned for her husband, who was now afflicted with depression and lapses of memory. Already it was clear that he would need help in the coming term, and Rupert was the obvious person for the father to turn to. 'I've got to live here and help run things,' he wrote to Ka as a member of the Fabian committee, 'for my father's eyes have temporarily gone, and he has neuralgia. "Duty to one's family," Ka, that you sometimes, and so solemnly mention! That is what is dragging me from the place where I am happier than anywhere (*no*, not Cambridge—Grantchester!) . . . But I'm sorry and sad for my father and mother.' Ka was finding him a sympathetic repository for her own troubles. 'Your account of your states of mind,' he commented, 'amused and terrified.' And now he would have to miss the Marlowe's important production of *Richard II* with Reginald Pole, his fellow Kingsman, as the King, and Dalton must take over the campaign for the Minority Report. More important in the sequel was his correspondence at this time with Frances Cornford.

'Do you know,' she had written in November, 'after Xmas, some time, I am publishing (at a humble little publisher at Hampstead) a volume of 30 small poems. Do you think that very minor poetry is

[1] G.K., p. 113.

disgusting I wonder?' Brooke evaded the question, declared he was most excited at the prospect of being the friend of a poetess, and added, 'To show you you aren't *everybody*, I may say I'm also having a volume printed in a month or so! Mine however is privately printed, I think, and in Chelsea, a far more respectably artistic, if less up to date, locality than Hampstead. Are you also Tortured by the impossibility of selecting more than about five poems you can still bear?' When Mrs. Cornford replied, she was acknowledging a wedding present, a John sketch, given by Rupert and Ka among a group of her friends. 'I long to have a house where people will come in naturally when they want, and find a little shelter and friendliness and a few beautiful things to look at.' A new house that was to be called Conduit Head was being built off the Madingley Road for this very purpose. 'You must help us prevent our house turning into a dead suburban castle with a smell of repulsion and distrust in the hall!' There was no fear of that, but the house was to be a place of refuge and important decision in time to come. She wrote again from Dorset.

Do PUBLISH your poems and not have them privately printed. Francis went back this morning to vote, but he charged me to tell you from him that he thinks it is cowardly and anti-social only to be printed privately! I know really it is a kind of perverted modesty, but I am sure you are wrong. It is so much nicer to feel like the smallest boat on a real open sea than the hugest and most precious vessel on a sugary private river. Indeed I think there is a touch of preciousness about private printing, which is *the* thing one should seek to avoid. People will write to you humbly and beg for copies because of their great admiration etc. But if you publish, then they can just go and buy it cleanly and simply, if they do care sincerely. And then it would be so good if some quite unknown person happened to see them and like them and write to you. It would be the kind of compliment worth having. And it is quite possible it would reach people who would care and might never know otherwise. And then reviews would be good fun—squashing or otherwise.

To this Brooke replied from School Field:

I had never thought of people *writing and asking* me for the book. The idea makes me white with terror. I am writing to urge on Jacques Raverat to sell the thing at a low price in all the shops in Chelsea. But they will review us together. *The Daily Chronicle*, or some such, that reviews verse in lumps, will review thirty-four minor poets in one day, ending with

Thoughts in Verse on Many Occasions
by a Person of Great Sensibility
By F. Cornford

and

Dead Pansy Leaves: & other flowerets
By R. Brooke

and it will say 'Mr. Cornford has some pretty thoughts; but Miss Brooke is always intolerable'. (They always guess the sex wrong.) And then I shall refuse to call on you. Or another paper will say 'Major Cornford and the Widow Brooke are both bad: but Major Cornford is the worst'. And then you will cut me in the street . . .

Mrs. Cornford's arguments, combined with his own dissatisfaction with the meagre collection which was the most he could put together, decided him to decline Raverat's proposal after all. J. C. Squire, first secretary of the Cambridge Fabians, was working for a publisher called Stephen Swift. He looked in that direction first, but again drew back, unsure of himself, and his poems remained uncollected for another two years. Meanwhile, Mrs. Cornford's enthusiasm had brought a new literary hero into his life. She was concluding her former letter from Dorset.

We went on Friday to see Thomas Hardy. He was the most touching old dear I have ever seen. We started in terror, but as soon as he entered the room we discovered that he was much more frightened of us than we of him. He wouldn't believe that anybody could possibly come to see his Dorset plays in Cambridge . . . he seemed under the impression that everyone there would be shocked at his poems. I want you badly to write about *Time's Laughing Stocks* in the Review. I should like to be able to send it him and show that we do, some of us, appreciate him. I know it would be a real pleasure to the old man. I never saw anyone so modest, or so needing appreciation. And in any case it's a thing that *ought* to be done. The poems are such splendid real things. They are haunting, and people don't appreciate them enough. Lines out of 'The Trampwoman's Tragedy' go round and round in my head.

Since January 11 Parker Brooke had groped about the house or sat for hours despondent. A week later he went to see a specialist in London. 'At this hour (noon) precisely' Brooke wrote to James Strachey, 'the interview begins. It is supposed the specialist will say he has a clot on the brain. Then he will go mad by degrees and die . . . And it is more painful to see mother, who is in agony . . . What does one do in a household of fools and a Tragedy? And why is Pain so terrible, more terrible than ever when you only see it in others?' Later that day he wrote again. The report was vague. 'That we may have another term's profits from the house we're going to beg the new Headmaster to let us stay on. We'll be thrown out at Easter.' On that day he also wrote to Dudley, grieved and alarmed. 'He's a very pessimistic man, given to brooding, and without much inside to fall back on—in the way of thought.' The doctor had called it neuralgia. Then he said he didn't know. 'And then there was a time when we all talked of other things and Mother and I kept looking at Father, and at each other, and nobody dared to say the things they thought, and there were words floating in the air and in the brain and in the middle of conversation and one suddenly saw them and felt unable to speak.' And now the sufferer was the Ranee. Her hope had been slowly going. 'She suddenly broke down with me tonight: and prayed he could die quickly. He had left the room . . . We keep it all pretty dark (which for God's sake do you) but the old servants got to suspect, and creep about sniffling; and I am full of self-pity.'

Geoffrey Keynes was asked to keep an eye on the Marlowe Society; Mrs. Cornford was told he must resign his part in the production of a play by Yeats that she was promoting. 'Oh, and I'm so sad and fierce and miserable not to be in my garden and little house at Grantchester this term. I love being there so much—more than any place I've ever lived in . . . I'd thought of being there when the spring was coming, every day this winter, and dreamt of seeing all the little brown and green things. And I always hate being at home.' The suspense while awaiting the report on his father had been a waking nightmare. 'It inspired me with thousands of little Hardyesque poems about people whose affairs went dismally wrong, or frightfully detestable persons I couldn't help falling in love with, or interviews with the Almighty in which he turned out to be an absolute and unimaginative idiot.'

On the 23rd he was at the Orchard, picking up books and mail, and he had a ticket for the Marlowe Society's *Richard II* when a telegram recalled him to Rugby. Alfred and he took it in turns to sit and watch at their father's bedside. 'Death's horrible,' he wrote to Raverat. 'I've never before seen it. But death's kind.' On January 24, 1910, William Parker Brooke died at School Field, aged fifty-nine, and was buried on the very day his fifty boys came back for the Easter term. Rupert was unable to help. He had caught influenza at the funeral, attending the ceremony which he had resented so fiercely on Swinburne's behalf. 'There are things,' he wrote to Dent, 'pieces of folly, or bad taste, or wanton cruelty—in the Christian, middle-class way of burying the dead that make me ill,' and he added, 'I've always felt so especially unlike and separate from both my parents—in good and bad qualities alike.' For five days he sweated in a fever.

III

After a week he found himself as Housemaster of School Field, and Aunt Fanny came from Bournemouth to assist the Ranee in her work as matron. 'I work like a Professor and feel the Spring in my bones,' he reported to Marsh, having been ill and for days 'subsisted on milk and the pieces I could surreptitiously bite out of my thermometer'. Now he was rather enjoying a novel experience.

A bare two days at Cambridge to collect absolutely essential books was all the devil of a Headmaster would allow me; and that barely. So I sit and grind my teeth to hear of live things moving in the world beyond my cave. I take no form-work; so I am free to do my own work. Being a Housemaster is in a way pleasant. The boys are delightful; and I find I am an admirable school-master. I have a bluff Christian tone that is wholly pedagogic. Also, they remember I used to play for the School at various violent games, and re-spect me accordingly. Every night at 9.20 I take prayers—a few verses of a psalm and one or two short heartfelt prayers. I nearly had to prepare the lads for Confirmation, but I, rather pusillanimously, wriggled out of that. But a certain incisive incredulity in my voice when I mention the word God is, I hope, slowly dropping the poison of the truth into their young souls.

He was starting work on an essay for the Harness Prize at Cam-bridge, his full title being 'Puritanism as represented or referred to in the early English drama up to 1642'; and enlisting the help of Geoff-rey Keynes with his knowledge of German in the new Westminster competitions. 'If you will send me a prose translation of this, by Saturday or Sunday, I will give you 2s. 7d. of what I get as a prize,' then later, 'My lines were exquisite and slate coloured,' and then, accounting for the success of their collaboration, 'It's the alteration of the little words that makes all the difference between Poetry and piddle.' Raverat came to stay. 'Bring *Tristan* and read it to me, and if it's perfectly dreadful I will read you some of my notes on the Poor Law at the same time,' and he wrote again to Keynes while super-vising house prep 'The inky babes are splashing each other. I must rise and cuff them . . . My love to Cambridge.' His friends in turn were told of his changed circumstances. 'Occasionally they bring me difficult sentences in dead languages and ask help in translating them. And when I fail they hate me.' Ka Cox was regaled with, 'Lots happening. Gibson is still in the Sanatorium with swollen glands. Bacon mi has got his *Gym XX*. House mile on Saturday and Confir-mation on Tuesday. No other news.'

When Strachey came to stay at School Field and look in again at Hillbrow and Mrs. Eden after all these years, a somewhat quarrelsome phase of his relationship with Brooke had just come to an end. It had opened with Strachey's asking him what he was like as a companion, and Brooke beginning his reply with 'Well, chiefly, I suppose, you're intelligent, interesting, and witty, compared to other people,' but he continued, 'On the other hand, like the sea in Mr. Chesterton's poem, you sometimes leave nothing but a mood of ironic gloom . . . My "Kindness" is, yes, due to old age, but partly to feeling it, gently, a pity you don't seem to enjoy things for the moment.' Strachey replied that Brooke always seemed not only ashamed of showing his own feelings, but curiously uninterested in other people's. Brooke snapped back, 'My way of disregarding people's emotions seems to me superior to going all squashy about them as you did . . . Really, of course, I don't disregard them. Being immensely egotistic, I am as delighted to see other people suffer when I am suffering as any of your common selfish sentimentalists. I can't really agree that it's a high emotion. But I am most proud if it really gives me a claim to have a "heart".' To this Strachey retorted 'How wonderfully you can penetrate the human heart! You really are most fearfully good at psychology. Does your amazing flair enable you to foresee the exact moment when I shall "go" melodramatic and cut your throat?' and he closed his side of the controversy with 'I think it's hard that you should have erected the preposterous convention by which no one may ever be serious unless he's satirical, for fear of being considered "squashy" or "sentimental".' The influence of the Society, and Lytton Strachey in particular, had worked so strongly on Brooke that nowadays he was apt to be cynical to a degree excessive even in the eyes of Lytton's own brother. James was drawing attention to a quality in his friend's character worth registering at this point for sake of the sequel, a *volte face* so extreme that it cost him the friendship of Lytton and James alike. For the present this exchange of home truths did no harm, and Strachey was put up in the attic at School Field. 'You must not,' says Brooke, 'laugh when I say grace.'

During the spells of leisure in his father's study he read Elizabethan plays, and a new book of poems which had arrived bearing the inscription *To Miss Brooke with the respectful compliments of Major Cornford*. 'They stir and live in this place where to me sometimes everything seems dead' he wrote, and made notes at her request for a confession of his View of Life, a task he never accomplished beyond a few observations in a letter. 'Life, as it appears to me, is a chain of sensations and experiences (thoughts and colours, wind, food, and talk) . . . I care not greatly if they "exist", if they are only the "appearances" of some strange "realities", or if the whole is only my dream or another's. All I know is these sensations and experiences, I cannot prove that I know them . . . That other people are in a similar way seems to me likely, and it certainly pays to act as if they are.' He was too busy making notes on the Puritans. 'Something had to happen to start or help the plot,' he noted down about the Eliza-bethan drama: 'There was no bosh about motives. The thing hap-pened. The king was jealous, etc.' and again, 'To make a language rich and living is an effort of *Will* on the part of the living writer.'

At the end of March the half of School Field that was a private residence began to be dismantled, and a man came round to offer his price for the fittings and odd pieces of furniture piled in the hall; Parker Brooke's papers were burned, and after fifteen years the Brooke régime came to an end in a state of melancholy confusion. Mrs. Brooke had rented a detached house of three storeys in the Bilton Road, with a grey stucco front, a patch of front garden, and an entrance porch at the side approached down a short gravel path; a quiet road, for a hundred yards or so further down it petered out in a foot-track through bracken and briars. The drawing-room at School Field was now in disarray, and Tibby the cat, aged sixteen, was given the quietus of poison in her milk. Mindful of the Arcadian adventure last Spring, Brooke scribbled an impromptu in verse for Dudley who was now a correspondent on the staff of the *Economist* in Germany.

> *Easter! the season when One had rebirth*
> *Whom some call Ishtar, some call Mother Earth,*
> *And others Jesus, or Osiris. Now*
> *A certain subtle magic on the bough*
> *And a bright strangeness in the wind (a sort*
> *Not known in Germany or here) has brought,*
> *These hundred centuries past, the bloody rotters*
> *Who lusted, raped, and (knowing not) begot us*
> *—In fact, our Fathers, from remotest times—*
> *To sing in company, make foolish rhymes,*
> *Lust more than ever, dance, drink wine, eat bread,*
> *To greet the jolly spring. And they are Dead.*
> *(And lately—since the Greeks—they've spoilt the feast*

With morbid superstitions from the East.
E'en now small boys at chapel down the road
Munch little morsels of a Jewish God.)
Easter, you bloody man! And a full moon!
And so I think of you; and write.

                                    Oh, soon

The little white flowers whose names I never knew
Will wake at Cranborne. They've forgotten you.
Robin, who ran the hedge a year ago,
Runs still, by Shaston. Does he remember? No.
This year the ways of Fordingbridge won't see
So meaty and so swift a poet as me
Mouthing undying lines. Down Lyndhurst way
The woods will rub along without us.

                                    Say,

Do you remember the motors on the down?
The stream we washed our feet in? Cranborne Town
By night? and the two inns? the men we met?
The jolly things we said? the food we ate?
The last high toast in shandy-gaff we drank,
And—certain people, under the trees, at Bank?

It was a crude exercise in a style he was to try once again, in very different circumstances, and with more success. He was glad to be released from his filial duties at Rugby, but, surprisingly, it was quite a wrench.

I meet my freedom quietly. I get
A certain pleasure from the fifty dam
Young fresh-faced mindless scamps to whom I am
Father, and mother, and all their maiden aunts.
I feed their minds. I satisfy their wants.

It was April 6, and he was about to leave for Lulworth Cove, where Lytton and James Strachey were going to join him in lodgings. He saw the Ranee established in her new house, then left for Dorset. At Gray's Inn Marsh received the acting Housemaster's last word on the subject.

For the rest of Eternity my stable address is 24 Bilton Road, Rugby. School Field, that palatial building, will know us no more. And henceforth I shall have to play on other people's Tennis lawns. I wept copiously last week in saying good-bye to the three and fifty little boys whose Faith and

Morals I had upheld for ten weeks. I found I had fallen in love with them all. So pleasant and fresh-minded as they were. And it filled me with purpureal gloom to know that their plastic souls would harden into the required shapes, and they would go to swell the indistinguished masses who fill Trinity Hall, Clare, Caius, . . . and at last become members of the English Upper, or Upper Middle, Classes. I am glad I am not going to be a schoolmaster for ever. The tragedy would be too great.

He had sent a few poems to *The Nation*, and was telling Keynes that the Editor 'was so astounded by them that he has preserved an awestruck silence ever since', when the mail at Lulworth brought a surprise. It occasioned his first letter to Bilton Road.

Did you notice an 'Urgent' letter you sent on to me? It was from the *Nation* about one of two or three poems I sent them. They wanted me to change two or three phrases, which they thought. generally, 'too strong'. I was very angry; and went round to see the miscreant—it was signed 'for the Editor'—and then some initials. It turned out to be Nevinson, who is editing the paper for a fortnight while Massingham's away. He said he liked the poems very much. I convinced him about one or two of the suggested alterations; but there were still two or three more he said the public wouldn't stand—though, he added, if he were sole Editor himself, he'd print them, because he liked them. It's all nonsense. But I said I'd try to think of some alternatives. He said he expected that several of the poems I sent in would come out in the *Nation* at intervals. So I'll keep my eye on it and let you know. It's not worth while taking it in: because the intervals may be a month or two. Nevinson asked me if I was a don!

It was the beginning of his difficulties arising from the so-called 'ugly' poems. He had probably included *A Channel Passage*. *The Nation* eventually published *The Goddess in the Wood*, the only poem written while he was Housemaster at School Field, but the main interest in the episode is Henry Nevinson's own impression of his visitor.

Suddenly he came—an astounding apparition in any newspaper office. Loose hair of deep browny-gold; smooth, ruddy face; eyes not grey or bluish-white, but of living blue, really like the sky, and as frankly open; figure not very tall, but firm and strongly made, giving the sense of weight rather than speed, and yet so finely fashioned and healthy that it was impossible not to think of the line about 'a pard-like spirit'. He was dressed just in the ordinary way, except that he wore a low blue collar, and blue shirt and tie, all uncommon in those days. Evidently he did not want to be conspicuous, but the whole effect was almost ludicrously beautiful.[1]

Brooke visited Nevinson on his way back at last to the Orchard. Staying the night with Marsh, they saw a performance of *Trelawny*

[1] *The Nation*, May 1, 1915.

of the Wells, then went on to one of Lady Ottoline Morrell's Tuesday evenings at her house in Bedford Square. Ottoline Morrell, a sister of the Duke of Portland, was a character of eighteenth-century distinction and a mind in no way subject to the conventions of high society beyond those which happened to suit her or the young artists who frequented her salon. Lady Ottoline's drawing-room was perhaps the only plot of common ground where Edwardian Bohemia and polite Society could meet on equal and easy terms. In being admitted to her circle Brooke was aware that he was entering an aristocracy of letters as exclusive as the Apostles of Cambridge, in fact the leaders of the one were ornaments of the other, for here again were Lytton Strachey, Bertrand Russell; here too were the daughters of Leslie Stephen, together with an element unfamiliar to Brooke, the young painters who had won special honours at the Slade or were disciples of Augustus John, among them one, the artist of a now famous portrait of the elder Strachey, whom Eddie Marsh had recently mentioned in a letter to Brooke at School Field. He was describing the Tuesday salon, hoping to take Brooke with him when the Rugby term was over, and naming the guests he talked with, some of them new to his acquaintance. From those he singled out 'one Henry Lamb, a painter, do you know him? he was in a rough brown suit, with tails, shaped at the hips, and had a red handkerchief round his neck, but looked far more elegant and fashionable than any of the men in faultless evening dress. I'm afraid he didn't take to me much, and I'm told he has a cold and selfish nature.' Brooke had no reason to be interested in the man or his nature until eighteen months afterwards, when the name cropped up again.

A huge May-day breakfast party which taxed the resources of the Orchard to the limit, began a spell of comparative peace in his village of Grantchester. He made Thursday his day in Cambridge, and on the first of these he kept an appointment with Macaulay, Tutor of King's, and Tilley, the don in charge of the Modern Language tripos. The topic was a Fellowship. 'Apparently my last chance for sending in a dissertation would be in the December of 1912. They think *two* shots is much the best thing. So that probably I had better send in something in 1911.' Tilley said he had read Brooke's articles in the *Cambridge Review* (his recent contributions were on *Richard II* and a new biography of Shelley) and advised a subject which involved research and literary criticism. He also strongly advised that he should learn German so as to read the critical works in that language.

He spent that evening with Flecker. 'Have got to learn the entire Russian tongue tonight,' wrote Flecker on his card of invitation. 'Pray for me. Your brother in Poesy.' Then the month of May passed agreeably, with Lytton Strachey coming to tea on the day Pudsey Dawson, the Orchard bull-terrier, murdered a cat; and dining with A. C. Benson and George Mallory at Magdalene to discuss 'whether all poets were really saying the same thing'; sitting at Newnham Grange and being drawn by Gwen Darwin and Frances Cornford; working on the Puritans in the University Library; facing a crisis among the Fabians caused by a left-wing discussion group at Peterhouse deceptively called The Sex Society, where someone had made an improper remark about the monarchy and was assaulted by rowing men with sticks; withdrawing again into his retreat, and writing to Marsh, 'The apple blossom and the river and the sunsets have combined to make me relapse into a more than Wordsworthian communion with nature, which prevents me from reading more than 100 lines in a day, or thinking at all'; canoeing into Cambridge to address the Apostles on the subject of Intolerance. He seemed to believe that a certain amount of it was necessary. 'If you think steadily of the human character you'll find, alas, it requires both love and hate to keep it healthy. Only to love generates sloppiness, just as only to despise acidulates.' Writing his notes, he must have recalled the recent dispute with James Strachey. Somewhat in the same way as Darwin, who at the end of his working life found he had forgotten how to appreciate poetry, so curates (the improbable villains in this absurd serio-comic discourse) 'in decrying all that they don't like themselves are unable to appreciate good of almost every kind'. At this stage of his life, Brooke himself was more intolerant than he can have realized, but one feels he was nearer the mark when he suggested one should 'always *recognize* faults in, say, a poet, while enjoying, giving one's time and imaginative sympathy to, his *virtues*', and he showed there was hope that he might one day grow out of his own intolerance alike for Jews and Christians when he declared, 'I should attack intolerance on this ground, of the utter impossibility of really understanding the infinite complexities of another person's character.'

In June he was camping out with Geoffrey Keynes, thirteen miles away at Overcote, where there was nothing but an inn, a ferry across the Ouse navigated by pulling yourself across on a chain, and wild birds, duck and snipe and herons. 'I became quite expert at cooking,' he told his mother, 'especially fried eggs . . . I slept out, and Geoffrey slept inside the tent,' and when not bathing or talking of this and that, Brooke wrote a review of his friend Flecker's new volume called *Thirty-Six Poems*, and made an effort to live up to his views on tolerance. Flecker, he thought, 'too often seems to have been inspired with a few good lines and completed the poems with a few dull ones,' but at best, on almost every page, he found 'the healthy human vulgar man's vulgar and mixed emotions made, somehow, beautiful by the magic of poetry'. He meant it as high praise, and assigned Flecker to the more flattering category when, not afraid to over-simplify, he said 'Now the chief division of poets, probably, is into those who can handle metre and those who cannot'. Works by poets of the former kind gave one, as did Flecker, 'an unaccountable and almost irrational pleasure in the reading'. For this reason, perhaps, Brooke was unable to appreciate the greatness of Whitman, and continued to the end wedded to the resources of traditional technique. Flecker, who must have been gratified by these remarks (both poets were now conscious of a rivalry) had a habit of shooting off exclamatory postcards. One arrived at the Orchard a week or two after this. 'Yah, Wordsworth! I'm *much* more famous than you. I have written a splendid poem on Don Juan!'

His essay on the Puritans had to be submitted for the Harness Prize when it was still unrevised. He preferred to go up to London as leader of the Cambridge delegates to the Fabian Conference. 'It was great fun,' he told Dalton, chiefly because the female delegates were all out to make Women's Suffrage the main issue at the expense of the campaign for Poor Law reform. 'The Northern delegates were superb men. They lashed the Women with unconquerable logic and gross words. There were most frightful scenes, and the women gibbered with rage . . . Old Shaw popped up and down; and a man from Manchester and I conspired democratically in a corner. But vainly.' The conference was opportune, for he had begun to plan his own main effort in aid of the Cause, a tour of the south-west in a caravan with Dudley Ward, speaking at open-air meetings at street corners and on village greens. A bill was being printed for the harangue at Poole in Dorset on July 26. '*Poole High Street, close to the Free Library. Principal Speaker MR. BROOKE. Questions invited. In Support of Proposals for Poor Law Reform. Sponsored by the N.C.P.D.* Hugh and Steuart Wilson of King's were lending their caravan, and presumably it was also their horse, Guy, whose maintenance for the twelve days of the tour, reckoned at two pounds and three shillings, was being paid for by Ka Cox, out of her Society funds. Gwen Darwin was designing a poster. Even if they didn't speak in every village they happened to pass through, they must 'display the poster', said Brooke in his instructions to Ward, 'look Wise, and scatter pamphlets'.

In the new parental home at Bilton Road he sat among Fabian tracts, the Minority Report at his elbow, prepared his speech, and wrote constantly to Ward. The only serious distraction was the family finance.

My dear,
    I begin this in a Lawyer's Office. My mother started to explain some of her finance to me last night; and I was (of course) so extraordinarily clear-headed that I found two errors and an omission and cleared up the whole tangle of my father's affairs. So this morning she has entrusted me with the task of explaining to the Lawyer. Ultimately we have to pay the Government £30 more. I was adamant about it.
    My letter, which crossed yours, explained some things. The Wilsons rather insist on the 28th. So I have suggested they find us on the afternoon of the 28th: we all feast and sleep round the caravan that night, and they drive off on the 29th leaving us at the nearest railway station. That will at any rate get rid of the horse and cart.

Then follows a list of things—Primus stove, plates, spoons, cocoa, salt—that Dudley must please pick up at the Orchard; all the tracts and posters to be waiting at Stockbridge station by a certain date— 'Horse £1 a week maximum, Cart 5s. Horse very quiet'; then another letter of numbered paras: 'I think you'd better write postcards about the price of the horse, if we leave it till 16th Wilson *may* hold out for more!'; surprise that Ward had arranged a meeting in Corfe Castle— 'Hurrah for Mrs. Bestwish [Cavendish Bentinck] of Corfe. Will it be an assembly of matrons in a drawing-room? My extensive obstetric knowledge (derived from the Elizabethan drama) will tell,' and so on, ending with 'I don't know what you mean by saying my career's "simple", damn you'. On another day it was a list of books he was bringing, nineteen volumes, from Marlowe and Donne, through Mary Coleridge and Saintsbury to the Webbs, and 'We want, besides, *special local information* about the counties we pass through— about Poor Law etc. Where can we get it?'

The winding up of his father's affairs was not the only source of interruption while he prepared his harangue. A party of fifty German students was coming to Cambridge in August, and a feature of their visit was to be a repeat performance of *Doctor Faustus* by the Marlowe

Dramatic Society. This time Cornford was to play Faustus, and Brooke wanting less to learn, and having laughed off the suggestion that he should be Helen of Troy, agreed to make a brief appearance as the Chorus in a scholar's gown and black skull-cap. During this Fabian summer his liaison with the project (until such time as Justin should have arrived back from abroad) was Mrs. Cornford, whose urgent postcards, especially on the difficulty of finding ladies who were at once suitable and willing to play any of the Seven Deadly Sins, kept breaking in on Brooke's political meditations with farcical regularity. One lady presented a special problem. 'We did not specify her Sin, but on plotting it all out today Gwen and I thought she would be *much* the best Lechery.' She might, however, gib at the idea—will Rupert consult her?—otherwise they'll have to settle for Envy, and again, 'If you know a likely Sin I should be very glad to hear of her on a p.c.' and then, rather wistful, 'Oh dear, the Sins are beginning to drop off in the usual way and develop parents and things!' Hearing that she was having trouble with a certain member of the cast, Brooke wrote to say that he had discovered an 8th Deadly Sin— the Artistic Temperament. But all somehow worked out, and, under pressure, Ka settled for Gluttony, and at last Justin, little suspecting what effect his example would have on Brooke's future, came back with travellers' tales from Canada. Brooke asked Raverat to confirm the rumour.

> *Is it true that our Justin's appeared?*
> *Has he come, as we all of us feared,*
> *Not the Justin we knew,*
> *But Western, but new,*
> *With an Accent, a Soul, and a BEARD?*

Armed with the text of his speech, answers to probable questions, and a bundle of books, he at last set off from Rugby for the rendezvous with Ward at Stockbridge. The caravan, Guy, his head in a nose-bag, Dudley on the box with the reins, the pots and pans from the Orchard, were all in readiness according to plan. They rattled through Bournemouth in disguise, for fear of being recognized on revolution bent by Aunt Fanny. And before the serious work began, they looked in for tea on Edward Thomas, who had obligingly invited Noel to come over from Bedales. But in spite of all distractions the plan of campaign went ahead, and if the standers-by had ever heard an orator more accomplished, which was very probable, they could never have listened to a speaker more fervently sincere.

His notes show that one of the most common objections to the idea of reforming the Poor Law was the fear that social insurance of any kind would soften the moral fibre of the working man it was supposed to benefit, so the burthen of Brooke's speech was that it's all very well to be so piously concerned for the moral character of the poor—what about the moral fibre of the nation as a whole and its responsibility towards its citizens in need? Experience in previous meetings had taught him the wisdom of airing these moral considerations right at the start. He referred to a leaflet that Ward had probably distributed among his listeners (it showed that the speaker's aim was to 'abolish the workhouse and provide properly for the aged, the sick, the children, and the unemployed') and explained how the only instrument that could achieve his end was the document in his hand, the Minority Report. Did it ignore the moral factor? Let another question be answered first—Was it justice that everyone requiring public assistance should be held to blame and penalized by conditions which prevailed in the General Mixed Workhouse? If not, then should we not first make a distinction between those who are destitute through no fault of their own and those who should be condemned for idleness? Only to the able-bodied could the existing laws be applied with any shadow of justice; but even so, how much better it would be if, instead of throwing himself on the State only when he was near starvation, he were encouraged to do so *directly* he was out of a job? The moral factor worked both ways. The fight against destitution was the joint responsibility of the individual and the State. 'When we are in trouble or danger from other people,' Brooke said, 'we throw ourselves on the State in the shape of the policeman or the law court. This "loss of independence" does not weaken the character; it leaves men free to use their energies more profitably. For a working-man to spend his time in unaided, individual, encounters with thieves, disease, and the devil of unemployment, certainly may (if he is always victorious) foster and widen his sense of personal responsibility and self-reliance, but it is still more certainly a *ridiculous and sentimental waste of time and trouble* . . . It is not possible, as Society is organized, for every man to get work. It is not possible for every man to avoid more than a certain amount of illness. The monstrous error that these things *are* possible was at the bottom of the Report of the 1834 Commission and the whole of our Poor Law since. Thousands of lives have been sacrificed to it, and untold Wealth.'

Having established the need for reform, he argued the necessity for the break-up of the Poor Law. Between two and three millions, he said, were destitute in Britain. 'If the whole population were under the command of one sane man, the *first* thing he'd do would be to feed those millions so that they could contribute towards the production of wealth.' He was here this afternoon that his listeners might realize what was happening. 'If through flood or earthquake three million were rendered destitute, everyone would scrape and contribute. It's only because the destitute and needlessly suffering millions are *here all the time* that people won't notice them!' Two things were therefore essential. The governors of this country must alter the machinery of their law, and England herself must undergo a change of heart.

He related various anecdotes which he had picked up from Sidney Webb's address to the Fabians last October, and ended by returning to the existing laws, exposing the folly of their underlying principle. 'You cannot "punish" the sick, infirm, or aged.' That there should ever have been legislation which made it possible would surely be 'one of the grimmest jokes in history if it were not one of the ghastliest of errors'. Questions were invited. One imagines a noisy debate, with Ward chipping in, to quote chapter and verse of the Report, then the congested peace of the caravan and the Primus stove from the Orchard roaring under Mrs. Stevenson's kettle.

For twelve days they moved from town to town, and spoke on the green or in the market and handed out their leaflets, and the only letter Brooke found time to write was addressed from Wareham. It was to Erica, telling her how best to spend the present of a pound on modern poetry. 'Francis Thompson, and especially Thomas Hardy are both very modern and very good.' Flecker and Frances Cornford, of course, were included. 'I'm glad you've been among people who live for Art. It must be very good for you. I live for Art myself; especially in the evenings. But why are you not a Fabian? Which kind of non-Fabian are you? the feeble-minded or the emotional?'

His opening address was designed chiefly to combat ignorance and moral prejudice, the prepared notes for question time show that he needed ready-to-hand rejoinders for those who were entrenched in complacency. 'Nowadays people are sure, not that their opinions are true, but that they would not know what to do without them,' must have come in useful, also 'Supposing your opinions to be true. If they cannot be argued about they will be held as dead dogmas not as *living truths*. If your true opinion is held independent of argument, this is not *knowing* the truth, it is clinging to a superstition which is

accidentally true.' And to the mistaken patriot who might contend that
there could be little wrong with the laws which have 'made England
what she is', he had ready: 'Our only energy now is in commerce.
We are only collectively great; we today compose a State which
neither built up England nor will prevent her decline'.

The caravan was handed back to the owners at Winchester. Guy
took it upon himself to gallop away up a hill. However, the Wilsons
were left to deal with that untoward event while Brooke went on to
an hotel near Buckler's Hard, Beaulieu, where there was a camp, and
Noel, one among the many camping out. His policy of snatching
moments of her company had been none too successful this year. In
March, merely because she was passing through the railway station,
it had meant contriving the pretext of an appointment with a dentist
in Birmingham.

I got a card from N. to say that she might get to B'ham at 12.10; or
missing that, at 1.45. I leapt out of the 12.11 directly it touched B'ham: and
saw the extraordinarily inexpressive behind of the 12.10 sliding westward
out of the station. Nobody seemed to know if she had been in it—or, really,
to care. I felt if she *had*, she'd have had her head out of the window. So I
waited cheerily for the 1.45. I searched every carriage in that train. She was
not there.

Nothing else *very* funny has happened lately.

At Beaulieu several of the Cambridge friends were under canvas:
Sybil and David Pye, Jacques Raverat, Godwin Baynes, Ka Cox, and
Bryn Olivier and Eva Spielman with the young men to whom they
were now engaged, Hugh Popham and Bill Hubback, and the talk
was often of the new production of *Doctor Faustus*. Ward had got the
impression that the Oliviers were planning to go abroad in August,
'to place the sea and several ranges of mountains between Noel and
my sinister self', as Brooke interpreted the news. Whether or not this
descent on Beaulieu was an effort to catch her before she left the
country, it is evident that on Brooke's side, though his feelings might
not alter, for they were real and deep, this the tenderest of his relationships was becoming a trial of patience, that very one of the
virtues which he only had in limited supply. He was so free to do as
he pleased in every quarter of his life but this. He had never put his
feelings into words, not for Noel to hear at any rate, and now he was
suspecting that this day or two in camp might prove to be his last
opportunity for some time to come. So he chose a moment when Noel
and he were separated from the others, gathering sticks for a fire,

made a declaration of his love and, finding it not rejected (as he must have known would happen, for his feelings had been apparent for so long, though unexpressed) he turned to run and spread the news. She restrained him, and there was no announcement. All the same, he could not disguise his happiness, and the reason for it was soon common knowledge among his friends in camp. In the event, Noel did not go abroad, but was soon to be understudying Envy, one of the Vices in *Faustus*. As for Brooke, he could have had no cause to regret that he spoke out when he did, but his action was to have its effect on his future in a way that he could not have foreseen.

It was early August when he got back to the Orchard, only to find that there had been some muddle about the rooms. So he had to be put up next door, at the Old Vicarage. Rehearsals for *Faustus* had begun. At his suggestion Reginald Pole who had done well as Richard II was taking the part of Mephistophilis. Brooke was the Chorus. Sybil Pye and her sister Ethel (one of the Deadly Sins) Brynhild and Noel Olivier, were all put up at the Old Vicarage, and Sybil wrote an account of her stay. She recalled how Brooke would read aloud of an evening. *Antony and Cleopatra* provided one of his best performances. 'Our sitting-room was small and low, with a lamp slung from the ceiling, and a narrow door opening straight into the dark garden. On quiet nights, when watery sounds and scents drifted up from the river, this room half suggested the cabin of a ship. Rupert sat with his book at a table just below the lamp, the open door and dark sky behind him . . . His type was, I suppose, entirely English, but when he spoke, and especially when as now he read aloud, there was a clearness in his diction, an expressive freedom in the movement of his lips, that one associates with races to whom speech comes quicker than it does to us . . . I believe an eye unpractised in such things could often have read what he was saying merely by watching his mouth.' It was Donne or Swinburne generally, and passages of *Modern Love*. She remarked 'the quite unforced variety which distinguished his reading voice. He would drop from an airy lightness to a sombre, deep emotion with a suddenness and grace that made us catch our breath.' Sometimes they came back late from rehearsal, when the night was very dark, and he paddled the canoe for the three miles of river to Grantchester, and although the water was overgrown and the visibility nil, he avoided the hazards, knowing every yard of the way by heart. 'He would know, he said, when we were nearing home, by the sound of a certain poplar-tree that grew there: its leaves rustled faintly even on such a night as this when not a breath seemed stirring.' And there was an afternoon when he sat with Noel and Sybil, high up in the branches of a great chestnut tree, and read aloud from *Paradise Lost*.

Sybil found his public performance disappointing. 'Whether an audience irked him, I am not sure, but it is certain that we missed at the performance all the charm of those rehearsals of his part, with lovely gestures, which took place daily on the Vicarage garden. In mad mood he would choose as audience for these the fat bull-terrier that belonged to the house—and whom he had renamed Mr. Pudsey Dawson, in reference to a supposed former owner. Standing under a briar arch, with bare feet and shirt thrown open, he would appeal with passion to this person, giving chance observers all the joy an official audience was to lack.' There were games of Up-Jenkins, a play-reading from Shakespeare with Brooke as Antony, and one night they bathed by moonlight above Byron's Pool by the mill, and after coming ashore he climbed a young poplar tree to dry himself, and with the bough bending down with his weight he hung there a while upside down with his hair and the leaves almost brushing the long grass— a trifle Miss Pye remembered because she happened to remark that the spectacle put her in mind of one of Blake's wood-cuts, and she recalled the sudden look of almost childlike pleasure in his face. 'Among all his freedoms, this absence of self-consciousness was perhaps the most remarkable,' for with most adults there was generally a line dividing one stage of development from another, but with Brooke, she thought, there was no such division, so that at times he was at once both man and boy 'and we seemed looking at the very gestures of the child he must have grown from'.

The performance was given on August 17, and the small audience of German students was flattered and impressed. Some of them were surprised by the irreverent scenes of horse-play involving the Pope, which, they said, would never have been allowed on the stage in their country. After the show there was a gathering—it was really a house-warming party—at Conduit Head off the Madingley Road, the new house into which the Cornfords had just moved. Brooke feared the black scholar's gown that he wore as the Chorus might cramp his style, so he brought along his old sky-blue and tinselled costume as the Attendant Spirit and donned the many-pointed crown of a player king. Then all the Vices and Virtues, with the Pope and Faustus, still in their costumes, and Dudley Ward (the call boy), and several of their German audience, piling into a horse brake, drove off to Conduit Head, with Helen of Troy (Bryn Olivier) following on her push bike. Gwen Darwin and Jan Hubrecht, another of the company, cycled alongside. The beer and cheese consumed, Hubrecht suggested a torchlight procession along the road back to town, so they formed up behind Helen of Troy, a radiant figure with gold powder in her hair, Brooke at her side, in the wagging light, and they all moved off in a rout down the Madingley Road until they drew level with the Observatory where they turned and retraced their steps. Having come back to the relics of their feast, they threw down their torches in a burning circle around Cornford and his wife, their host and hostess, dancing wildly under the night. Sybil Pye was observing Brooke. 'Outside the ring of lights the night was as dark as his dark dress, and his figure—preternaturally tall in such a guise—rapidly melted into it; but the fitfullest gleam from the bonfire would catch and run up the tall points of his crown, giving it and his head a sort of ghostly detachment from his body, and marking vividly the peculiar golden quality of his hair. This hair, escaping from under the crown, flapped and leapt as the dance grew wilder: and all the while one was aware of that strange anachronism—the lighted eyes and serious face of a child's complete absorption, and again the detached watchful intelligence . . .'

He carried with him some of this elation to Rugby. The Ranee was in bed, having been knocked down by a horse, but her condition was not such as seriously to affect his state of exaltation. 'Life is splendid. I cannot contain myself at meals. They suspect me,' he wrote to Dudley Ward. 'I roll about and gurgle inside. Life, Dudley, Life!' and a day or two later it was 'It is absurd to say the world is dull. It is superb . . . *superb!*' and to Sybil Pye, 'Since Monday I have read 11 plays, 3 novels, a book on Stocks and Shares, and *Principia Ethica* besides all the current magazines and papers. How gorgeous it is to work! Ha!' In this mood he paid a visit to the Fabian Summer School at Llanbedr, bringing his own blankets, and sharing the floor of a stable with James Strachey. 'We have had interesting and useful talks with these young men,' Beatrice Webb wrote in her journal, 'but the weather, being detestable, must have made the trip appear rather a bad investment for them, and they were inclined to go away rather more critical and supercilious than they came.' 'They won't come, unless they know who they are going to meet, sums up Rupert Brooke [who must clearly number Mrs. Webb among his failures] . . . They don't want to learn, they don't think they have anything to learn . . . The egotism of the young university man is colossal. Are they worth bothering about?'[1] Mrs. Webb would organize immense uphill walks which prompted Brooke and Shove to found an 'anti-athletic league' whose members swore not to walk more than three miles a day. 'There was a remarkable scene,' Strachey has recalled, 'in which Rupert and I tried to explain Moore's ideas to Mrs. Webb while she tried to convince us of the efficacy of prayer.' Neither side made much headway.

Brooke enjoyed himself a good deal more than Mrs. Webb supposed. On September 11 he wrote to Lytton Strachey:

We all loved Beatrice, who related amusing anecdotes about Mr. Herbert Spencer over and over again. She was very inquisitive, too, about the Society . . . She'd a long story about handing *Principia Ethica* to Mr. Arthur Balfour, who skimmed it swiftly and gave it back, saying 'Clever, but rather thin. The work of a very *young* man.'

'You ought to go once there,' he told Ka, 'to learn a little about Life, and to teach them—what? Anyhow, it's not so bad as you think . . . and I was acting on my Conscience in going there, instead of reading peacefully. And acting on one's Conscience is always rather fun.'

There was a new feeling in his letter to Ka, and rather more of idle gossip about himself and the world, less concentration on the Fabian matter in hand. Ka was turning to him, becoming more than an acquaintance, and in his sympathy for her in a time of trouble, he was discovering that she on her part seemed blessed with a warmth of mature understanding that was beginning to be precious to him. Since his return to England after nearly two years of illness abroad, Jacques Raverat had tended to move away from Ka, whom everyone had taken it for granted he was going to marry, and during these past months in Chelsea, while he worked at the Ashendene Press, and Gwen Darwin lodged with her uncle in London, pursuing her studies at the Slade, he had undergone a change of heart. In the course of time the name Gwen Raverat would be added to the chronicle of British wood-engraving.

The engagement was announced. Ka Cox was by no means destitute of admirers, but it was useless trying to conceal the blow to her pride, and no one understood her position better than Mrs. Cornford, whose letter telling Brooke the 'tremendous news' had probably

[1] *Our Partnership*, Beatrice Webb, Ed. Barbara Drake and Margaret Cole, Longmans, 1948.

come to hand at Rugby during the preparations for the caravan tour. She was overjoyed at the prospect of adding Raverat to her family, but concerned for her friend.

I saw Ka this morning. She is absolutely sure of the rightness of it, though it has moved her, more than she would have guessed beforehand I think. They've all three had a pretty hard week of it. Her soul is puzzled and wrenched and somewhat hurt still, but her mind gets on the top of it and sees it all quite simply and wisely and in the most completely noble way, only it's so natural to her you don't stop to think how noble it is. I feel I should be sentimental if I tried to say how much I love her. Jacques I haven't seen yet, only Gwen, and she's alight. It is glorious. I've come to the conclusion that it's terribly easy for men and women to love each other with some parts of themselves—but to find two people who answer each other from the top to the bottom of the piano, so to speak—like Gwen and Jacques, is the rarest and I truly believe the most splendid thing in the world . . . Lord, how quickly Life goes! . . . She does slash about her puppets with her great hands so unexpected and quick. Think of all us innocents in *Comus* year.

And now there was an invitation to hand for Rupert, Noel, Ka, as well as Gwen, to stay at Prunoy, Raverat's country home in France. Noel crossed the Channel, escorted by Ka who was handsome in a French cloak of military blue. Brooke felt he could not accept, not with Ka there, who he well knew was still unable to renounce her love for Jacques, and with whom his own relationship was undergoing a change. His Platonic friendship for Ka, now three years old or more, was becoming disturbingly self-conscious. He dreaded the atmosphere of emotional imbroglio at Prunoy, which was certain to be quite intense enough without the addition of his own disquiet. Even now, whatever 'rightness' she may have done her best to see in this latest engagement among her Cambridge friends, Ka had by no means given up hope that Raverat might wake up one morning with the realization that he was making a mistake. For Brooke it was rather a coincidence that Ka should be drawing attention to her need of someone to confide in just when he himself was wanting the same thing and finding it all too easy to take from her as much as he gave. She was an orphan, looked up to by her younger sisters almost as a parent, so that she gave the impression of one who lived behind no family stockade, an independent and up-to-date young woman, as accessible as ever she might choose to make herself, and of a warm and open nature, a combination of qualities he had not met with before. Yet he saw her in a light which seemed to make no difference whatever to his sentiments for Noel. This warmth for Ka was of a different order, affecting, or rather supplementing, his relationship with the Ranee more than with anyone else. Ka seemed so much older, as she was in many ways more mature than he. She was a woman in whom he could confide about anything under the sun, including the Oliviers, for instance, when she had finished deploring the irrational behaviour of the Darwins. But there were several young men in her life who would be only too glad to listen to the same tale. For Rupert, on the other hand, she was a discovery, the more strange for having been this long while under his nose; the more precious for being the only one of her kind.

IV

It was late September, and the news came that the Harness Essay Prize at Cambridge had been won by the entry bearing the motto 'Charged with an Axe nigh in the Occiput'. This was Brooke's entry on the subject of the Puritans, and his success, following the Charles Oldham Scholarship, which had brought him £70, not only helped his funds but considerably offset his disappointing performance in the Tripos. It was a curious, and not entirely satisfactory essay, arranged in four parts not really distinguished from one another except by their numerals, and after giving the Puritans their place in history, the author became more and more exasperated with them until he lost his detachment. A letter from A. W. Verity, one of the judges, showed that this flaw was not unnoticed. 'I think our feeling was,' he wrote, 'that in some of your references to the supposed immorality of the Puritans, your *expression* was rather unconventionally direct, and might be toned down a little, especially as you seemed to leave it open whether the charges were applicable to all Puritans alike—and whether they might not be true.' But the essay is a considerable work, enlivened with remarks such as—to the theatre audience of 1632 'a Puritan country cousin must have been the ultimate conceivable boundary of idiocy'; rather startling judgements, such as that *Measure for Measure* is a study in Puritanism in which the only difference between Angelo and Isabella is that the former succumbs to temptation and the latter does not—'Ben Jonson would have made Angelo a lecherous buffoon'; and a great many amusing quotations from unfamiliar plays which show extensive reading. Of these Brooke's favourite was a short speech by a lady of fashion embarrassed by a maid of hers who affects the Puritan zeal:

> *Yesterday I went*
> *To see a lady that has a parrot: my woman,*
> *While I was in discourse, converted the fowl,*
> *And now it can speak naught but Knox's works,*
> *So there's a parrot lost.*[1]

He gave pride of place to the Puritans in Ben Jonson's comedies and summed up the character as 'a long, lean, snuffling man, who speaks through the nose and in a strange, ignorantly biblical jargon. The more open joys of life fly before that darkening presence; but there is the glint of the goat in his eye. Lying, fawning, foolish, hypocritical, gluttonous, he crawls swiftly along a dusty road, pursuing gold and his own salvation, hurrying in tight black clothes, with pursed lips, between unnoticed meadows.' One hopes that the occasional touches of light relief were not lost upon the examiners. After speaking of the Puritan distaste for the church organ, which they termed 'Babylonian bagpipes', the author tells of the Puritan chandler who in his excessive zeal 'thought any man in a surplice was the ghost of Heresy, and was out of love with his own members because they were called organs'.

At the end of September Brooke was still with his mother at Bilton Road, and although there were problems to face, nothing as yet had occurred to change his hopeful view of the universe. Ben Keeling, however, now a protégé of Beatrice Webb, and at work in London, seemed to be losing something of the splendid ebullience which had carried him through Keir Hardie Night. He wrote to tell Brooke of his new-found pessimism, an admission which moved Brooke to send him a letter that must be quoted in full.

Dear Ben,

I've several times started to write you a notable and rhetorical letter. But my life has been too jerky to admit of much connected thought lately. So the letter always fizzled away and was not. I'm sorry I didn't write sooner. But I wanted to be able to write down a great attack on your pessimism, in abundant reasoned language. And such a thing takes time and thought. Also, I may agree with you. What is pessimism? Why do you say you're becoming a pessimist? What does it mean? He may (I say to myself) mean that he thinks that the Universe is bad as a whole, or that it's bad just now, or that, more locally and importantly, things aren't going to get any better

---

[1] *The City-Match* (1639), Jasper Mayne.

in our time and our country, no matter how much we preach Socialism and clean hearts at them. Is it the last two? Are you telling us that the world is, after all, bad and, what's more horrible, without enough seeds of good in it? I, writing poetry and reading books and living at Grantchester all day, feel rather doubtful and ignorant about 'The world'—about England and men, and what they're like. Still, I see some, besides the University gang. I see all these queer provincials in this town, upper and middle and lower class. And God knows they're sterile enough. But I feel a placid healthy Physician about it all. (Only I don't know what drugs to recommend.) This is because I've such an overflowing (if intermittent) flood of anti-pessimism in me. I'm using the word now in what is, I expect, its most important sense, of a feeling rather than a reasoned belief. The horror is not *believing* the Universe is bad—or even believing the world won't improve—on a reasoned and cool examination of all facts, tendencies and values, so much as in a sort of general *feeling* that there isn't potentiality for good in the world and that anyhow it's a fairly dreary business, an absence of much appreciation and hope and a somehow paralysed will for good. As this is a feeling it *may* be caused by reason and experience, or more often by loneliness or soul-measles or indigestion or age or anything else. And it can equally be cured by other things than reason, by energy or weather or good people, as well as by a wider ethical grasp, at least so I've found in the rather slight temporary fits of depression I've had in exile and otherwise lately—or even in an enormous period of Youthful Tragedy with which I started at Cambridge. I have a remedy. It's a dangerous one, but I think very good on the whole; though it may lead to a sterile but ecstatic content, or even to the asylum. In practice I find it doesn't—or hasn't yet—made me inefficient.

I am addressing an Adult School on Sunday. I have started a group for studying the Minority Report here. I am going to Cambridge in a week to oversee, with the light of pure reason, the powerful energies of those who are setting forth the new Fabian Rooms; and later, to put the rising generations, Fabians and otherwise, on the way to Light, all next term. The remedy is mysticism, or Life, I'm not sure which. Do not leap or turn pale at the word Mysticism. I do not mean any religious thing, or any form of belief. I still burn and torture Christians daily. It is merely the *feeling*—or a kindred one—which underlay the mysticism of the wicked Mystics. Only I refuse to be cheated by the *feeling* into any kind of *belief*. *They* were convinced by it that the world was very good or that the Universe was one or that God existed. I don't any more believe the world to be good. Only I do get rid of the despair that it isn't, and I certainly seem to see additional possibilities of its getting better. It consists in just looking at people and things as themselves—neither as useful nor moral nor ugly nor anything else, but just as being. At least that's a philosophical description of it. What happens is that I suddenly feel the extraordinary value and importance of everybody I meet, and almost everything I see. In *things* I am moved in this way especially by some things; but in people by almost all people. That is, when the mood is on me. I roam about places—yesterday I did it even in Birmingham!—and sit in trains and see the essential glory and beauty of all the people I meet. I can watch a dirty middle-aged tradesman in a railway-carriage for hours, and love every dirty greasy sulky wrinkle in his weak chin and every button on his spotted unclean waistcoat. I know their states of mind are bad. But I'm so much occupied with their being there at all, that I don't have time to think of that. I tell you that a Birmingham goaty tariff reform fifth-rate business man is splendid and desirable. It's the same about the things of ordinary life. Half an hour's roaming about a street or village or railway station shows so much beauty that it is impossible to be anything but wild with suppressed exhilaration. And it's not only beauty, and beautiful things. In a flicker of sunlight on a blank wall, or a reach of muddy pavement, or smoke from an engine at night there's a sudden significance and importance and inspiration that makes the breath stop with a gulp of certainty and happiness. It's not that the wall or the smoke seem important for anything, or suddenly reveal any general statement, or are rationally seen to be good and beautiful in themselves—only that *for you* they're perfect and unique. It's like being in love with a person. One doesn't (nowadays, and if one's clean-minded) think the person better or more beautiful than larger than truth. Only one is extraordinarily excited that the person, exactly as he is, uniquely and splendidly just exists. It is a feeling, not a belief. Only it is a feeling that has amazing results. I suppose my occupation is being in love with the Universe—or (for it is an important difference) with certain spots and moments of it. I wish to God I could express myself. I have a vague notion that this is all very incoherent. But the upshot of it is that one's too happy to *feel* pessimistic; and too much impressed by the immense value and potentialities of *everything* to *believe* in pessimism, for the following reason, and in the following sense.

Every action, one knows (as a good Determinist), has an external effect. And every action, therefore, which leads on the whole to good, is '*frightfully*' important. For the good mystic knows how jolly 'good' is. It is not a question of either getting to Utopia in the year 2,000, or not. There'll be so much good then, and so much evil. And we can affect it. There—from the partly rational point of view—is the beginning and end of the whole matter. It oughtn't to make any difference to our efforts whether the good in A.D. 2000 will be a lot greater than it is now, or a little greater, or less. In any case, the amount of good we can cause by doing something, or can subtract by not doing it, remains about the same. And that is all that ought to matter. Lately, when I've been reading up the Elizabethans, and one or two other periods, I've been amazed more than ever at the way things change. Even in talking to my Uncle of 70 about the Victorians, it comes out astoundingly. The whole machinery of life, and the minds of every class and kind of man, change beyond recognition every generation. I don't know that 'Progress' is certain. All I know is that change is. These solid, solemn, provincials, and old maids, and business men, and all the immoveable system of things I see round me will vanish like smoke. All this present overwhelming reality will be as dead and odd and fantastic as crinolines or 'a dish of *tay*'. Something will be in its place, inevitably. And what that something will be, depends on me. With such superb work to do, and with the wild adventure of it all, and with the other minutes (too many of them) given to the enchantment of being even for a moment alive in a world of real matter (not that imitation, gilt stuff, one gets in Heaven) and actual people—I have no time now to be a pessimist.

I don't know why I have scribbled down these thin insane vapourings. I don't suppose you're still as desperate as you were when you wrote in June. When are you coming to Cambridge? I am going to Germany for the Spring Term. But if you can get over next term, are you coming out to stay at Grantchester? I lead a lovely and dim life there and have divine food. Hugh [Dalton] is going to be in London, and Gerald [Shove] is old as the hills and withered as a spider, and I am the oldest Fabian left (except Tram[1] who is senile) and I dodder about and smile with toothless gums on all the gay young sparks of the Fabian Society, to whom I am more than a father. So you might tell me if you are going to shake off for a day or a month the ghastly coils of British Family Life and of Modern Industry that you are wound in, and come to see the bovine existence of a farmer.

In the name of God and the Republic

Rupert

He posted this letter on the way to the New Bilton Adult School, where for the first time Mrs. Brooke heard him address an audience. The subject was Shakespeare, and she made a mental note of his concluding remark: 'I would advise a friend to read Shakespeare in the spirit in which I would tell him to visit Rome or play Rugby football or eat, if he can afford it, that very fine pudding called *Poire Melba*.'

He stayed on in Rugby so as to speak at several Minority Report meetings, but by October he was back at the Orchard, in time to receive a series of visitors. First there was Edward Thomas, who had put him up at Petersfield, before the caravan tour, at his cottage conveniently near Bedales. 'I have never been in Cambridge,' Thomas wrote, 'and if you don't think it's too late in life for a first visit, I shall very gladly come after an invitation such as yours . . . What are you doing now? Verse or "only prose"?' Then there was Dudley Ward who wanted to show Cambridge to two beautiful young German ladies, Annemarie von der Planitz and her younger sister Clothilde, who was dancing in a Reinhardt production at the Coliseum. They were lodged at the Old Vicarage, Dudley having received a warning: 'I've had dreadful scenes with the Stevensons. The village "talked" because of bare feet. So they *must* keep their boots on. Otherwise they mayn't stay. This is true'; and E. M. Forster, glad to come 'though I cannot fly or swim and have no bicycle and it is certain to rain'. Brooke wrote to his mother, 'E. M. Forster the

[1] V. H. Mottram.

writer has just been staying here two nights. He's a very charming person—an old King's man of 27 or 29. Get his new novel *Howard's End*. It would interest you. Can you send me some more money for the year? I have still a fair amount to receive, and the University won't pay me my second half of the Oldham. And I want to pay some bills.' She had inquired about his poems. Was not Raverat going to bring them out? 'I haven't even found a publisher yet,' he replied, 'though machinery to secure one is in motion. The real difficulty is that I want to finish off a dozen more before I print, and I can't do it. At least, I do it very slowly . . . Perhaps it *is* best not to talk about it much in Rugby until everything is settled and announced.' Raverat had lost his patience. So had Squire.

Brooke was now writing to Rugby from Wick Green, near Petersfield, where he was staying again with Edward Thomas. Mrs. Thomas was away, so the two men were cooking and managing for themselves, and the elder, who had not yet discovered his own rich vein of poetry, listened, and no doubt criticized, as the other read aloud. Brooke's latest poems were *Flight*, *Dust*, possibly the excellent and curious 'Ambarvalia' poem, containing the lines which Marsh thought not unworthy of Coleridge—

> *And the air lies still about the hill*
> *With the first fear of night.*

and four sonnets[1] of which the most recent ended, 'I thought when love for you died, I should die. It's dead. Alone, most strangely, I live on.' Brooke as observed by Edward Thomas deserves notice. 'He stretched himself out,' Thomas wrote, 'drew his fingers through his waved, fair hair, laughed, talked indolently, and admired as much as he was admired. No one that knew him could easily separate him from his poetry . . . He was tall, broad, and easy in his movements. Either he stooped, or he thrust his head forward unusually much to look at you with his steady blue eyes. His clear, rosy skin helped to give him the look of a great girl.' In his moods Thomas noticed that he ranged between a Shelleyan eagerness and a Shelleyan despair. 'It was characteristic of him,' he remarked, 'to apply the Shelley epithet "swift" to a girl's hair.'[2]

Edward Thomas must have given him food for poetical second thoughts, for when Brooke got back to the Orchard he put everything

[1] *The Goddess in the Wood*, 'I think if you had loved me,' 'I said I splendidly loved you,' and *The Life Beyond*.
[2] *The English Review*, June, 1915.

aside to work on his poems. He complained to James Strachey '*You've* probably never tried to write poetry for three weeks and failed. Even if one succeeds, it's wearing'; and to Dalton, 'I have lost the Art of writing Poetry: but acquired the immense serenity of the Cow . . . Human life is a fretful thing. But I have developed the Foreknowledge of Death, since my last birthday.' He had an address to prepare on a subject which had been neglected since 1888 when the artist Walter Crane published a Tract on Socialism and the Arts. In the course of sorting out his ideas he made only one trip to Cambridge. A. C. Benson had invited him to dine at Magdalene with Percy Lubbock, and once again the impression made was put on record. According to Lubbock, Benson the copious author was a man 'constrained to make himself agreeable by a sort of doom of courtesy which he could not escape', so Brooke would not have noticed the scrutiny he was being subjected to. He had been offered a lectureship in English at Newcastle, as a preliminary step to a Chair at a University, and no doubt this was a topic of conversation. Perhaps Benson was responsible for advising him to decline the offer and concentrate on working for his Fellowship of King's. For this purpose Brooke decided to submit two related works, his essay on the Puritans which had already won him the Harness Prize, and a dissertation based on his Charles Oldham scholarship paper, 'John Webster and the Elizabethans'. The latter was to be his main undertaking for the coming year 1911. He had just been writing a critique of the *Cambridge History of English Literature*, Vol. 5, which dealt with his chosen subject. He found the dry academic style intolerable. 'It's like trying to smell flowers through a blanket.' Saintsbury's chapter, alone among the rest, stood out 'like a hippopotamus in an expanse of mud, clumsy and absurd, but alive'.

At Magdalene on November 9 the talk ranged wide and free, and Benson was pleased, and a little surprised, to observe that for all his local fame and popularity, Brooke was neither egotistical nor self-regarding, showed no conscious desire to create an impression, seemed 'easily pleased, and preferred that the talk should wander where it would'. Then Benson turned his attention to the physical appearance of his guest:

He was far more striking in appearance than exactly handsome in outline. His eyes were small and deeply set. It was the colouring of face and hair which gave special character to his look. The hair rose very thickly from his forehead, and fell in rather stiff arched locks on either side—he grew it full and over-long, it was of a beautiful dark auburn tint inclining to red, but with an underlying golden gleam in it. His complexion was richly coloured, as though the blood were plentiful and near the surface; his face much tanned, with the tinge of sun-ripened fruit. He was strongly built, but inclined to be sturdy, and even clumsy, rather than graceful or lithe; his feet and hands were somewhat large and set stiffly on their joints; the latter had no expressiveness or grace and his feet were roughly proportioned and homely. Nor did he sit or move with any suppleness, but laughed, rather huddled, in his chair; while though his glance and regard were frank and friendly, his voice was far from beautiful, monotonous in tone, husky and somewhat hampered in the throat.[1]

Hector Macpherson's *A Century of Political Development* had proved useful when making notes for the caravan tour. It was now again at Brooke's elbow, as he prepared his lecture *Democracy and the Arts*. ' "That, therefore, which, whom" . . . What a sentence!' he scribbles in the margin, more respectful of the matter than the style; and 'All a man's actions affect others,' he jots on a slip of paper. 'How does any man become one of sound judgement? By keeping an open mind,' and 'There is rarely any religious tolerance: only religious indifference'. Two years before, at the Summer School in Wales, he had listened to a lecture on Social Reform and the Drama given by the translator of Ibsen, 'a keen, able, solemn, whiskered, well-meaning man, Mr. Archer,' whose thesis was that Art depended for its subject-matter on the lives of leisured people in a society of the kind where a certain amount of social injustice was inevitable. Social reform on democratic lines, Archer contended, would mean the end of Art. Brooke reserved his rebuttal of this for his scornful peroration. 'I am not going to rhapsodize about the Spirit of Democracy as dawning in the operas of Wagner or the anarchic prose of Whitman or Carpenter,' he began. ' "Brotherhood" will not be heard of in this paper. Neither comrade nor cumrade shall be mentioned by me. I would detain you *this* side of the millennium'; nor would he talk of the artist 'under Socialism', because that phrase, regrettably, tended to 'drop the pink gauze of unreality over the whole issue'. It was December 10. He was addressing the Cambridge Fabians for the last time as their President, and was in deadly earnest.

'Democracy,' he said, trying to arrive at a definition, was 'the ordering of the national life according to the national will'. This meant an increase in collective control. 'Observe the situation, and remember it's a real one, not one in a book. 1, Art is important. 2, The people

[1] *Men and Memories*, A. C. Benson, John Murray, 1924.

who produce art at present are, if you look into it, nearly always
dependent on unearned income. 3, We are going to diminish and
extinguish the number of those dependent on unearned income,' so
the State must find a way of giving back something of what it takes.
Next he defined Art, and rejected William Morris for saying that
'all poetry ought to be of the kind a man can make up while he is
working at a loom. Much of his own was. That may be why a lot of it
is so dull'. This led people to the idea that a man could, and should,
earn his wage by day and work as an artist of an evening. Nothing
could come of this but a culture of amiable amateurs. No less abhorrent to him were those who talked of the 'art of the people', or of
'expressing the soul of the community'. This was dangerous nonsense. 'The Community hasn't got a soul; you can't voice the soul of
the Community any more than you can blow its nose.' The main
business of art was an individual affair.

'I saw—*I* saw,' the artist says, 'a tree against the sky, or a blank wall in
the sunlight, and it was so thrilling, so arresting, so particularly itself, that—
well, really, I *must* show you . . . There!' Or the writer explains, 'Just so and
just so it happened, or might happen, and thus the heart shook, and thus . . .'
And suddenly, deliciously, with them you see and feel . . . Discussion is
merely one of the means, not the end, of literary art. You are in the midst
of insoluble problems of temperance reform and education and organization.
The artist, as artist, is not concerned. He leads you away by the hand and,
Mamillius like, begins his tale: 'There was a man—dwelt by a churchyard'—
it is purely irrelevant.[1]

Democracy will insist on universal education. 'This change in the old
conditions, this breaking up of unity, this multitude of opening minds,
may bring complexity and apparent confusion of standards; but also
(I say it soberly) the chance of vast, unimaginable, unceasing additions to the glory of the literature of England.' There was an argument that the lower classes, growing literate, would prove coarsely
devoid of taste. 'If the washy, dull, dead upper-class brains this idea
haunts were its only home we could leave it. But it lurks in the Victorian shadows.' How *could* the ignorant be expected to distinguish
between false and true. 'It is the future—their future fineness—we
work for. It is only natural that the taste of the lower classes should be
at present infinitely worse than ours. The amazing thing is that it is
probably rather better.' He mentioned a group of poor and ill-
educated Cockney writers he had met in London. 'Their poems give

[1] *Democracy and the Arts*, Rupert Brooke, with a Preface by Geoffrey Keynes. Rupert
Hart-Davis, 1946.

fuller value when pronounced as they thought and felt them.' There was more hope in them, he thought, than in 'the old-world passion and mellifluous despair of any gentleman's or lady's poetry'.

We must learn from the past. 'It is impossible to know how much more Milton and Marvell would have given us if they had had enough money to live on . . . Tom Hood, a great writer, both comic and serious, was, artistically, ruined by the continuous flood of jokes he had to pour forth all his life.' And having indulged these reflections, he considered the artist living today. The dead are past our help. 'But the living, them you can stir or warm and enable to work, and work at their best.'

Do you think this unnecessary, slightly insulting? Is anyone muttering, 'But we *are* modern and up to date. Nietzsche is our Bible, Van Gogh our idol. We drink in the lessons of Meredith and Ibsen and Swinburne and Tolstoy . . .' They are dead, my friends, all dead. Beware, for the generations slip imperceptibly into one another, and it is so much easier for you to accept standards that are prepared for you. Beware of the dead.

It isn't that Art is 'immortal'. On the contrary 'If you write a poem on Tuesday it begins to die on Wednesday. Some take longer dying than others. That is all.' What matters is its value here and now. 'There is something in almost all Art that only a contemporary can get—only one who shares with the artist the general feeling for ideas and thoughts and outlook of the time.' Coming to practical measures, 'There is nothing, I suppose, to be *done*, except indirectly by smashing smugness and propriety, and encouraging enthusiasm rather than criticism in the World.' To the future Socialist Government he recommended that a panel of thirty members should administer a fund which would award thirty creative artists an allowance of £250 a year each. In this lecture Brooke clarified and examined the problem of the artist in what we now call the Welfare State, anticipating by more than thirty years the social problem which during the Second World War gave rise to the body which eventually became the Arts Council of Great Britain. He ended his address by showing that Archer was sadly mistaken in thinking Art was inconsistent with social progress. Neither Tragedy nor Comedy can die out while there is Death and Fools. 'Though we perfect the marriage laws it will still be possible to fall in love with the wrong person or with two people, and still be painful,' and there will always be some elderly critic, black-whiskered and perplexed, telling the young that Art is being ruled out of life, 'a recurrent figure of most excellent comic value'.

It was a noble valediction to the Fabians, and at the same time he wrote a Circular to Freshmen, which was printed and distributed by the Fabians in every college. 'From being the Society to which individuals with a lust for martyrdom turned, it has become the most popular of the political institutions of the university.' In Brooke's year as President new Club rooms were opened in Trinity Street, with a librarian (A. L. Bacharach) and the membership rose to 105 signatories of the Basis, and 142 associates. It was gratifying, but for Brooke it was Poor Law reform alone which had really provided the impetus for all his exertions since early in 1909 when the Minority Report was published; and now, in that quarter, there was a distinctly cold wind blowing. No doubt the public conscience had been stirred, but the prospects of the Minority Report itself were looking dubious. Within a fortnight of Brooke's lecture on the Arts (it was significant that even he was no longer giving priority to the old cause) Beatrice Webb was making an entry (December 10) in her private journal: 'Sidney and I are both feeling weary and somewhat dispirited. In spite of all our work the National Committee does not seem to be gaining new members and our friends are beginning to melt away. One wonders whether we have not exhausted the interest in the subject . . .'[1] She was going to continue the campaign for another six months, then both the Webbs were due to leave the country for a world tour. In February, 1910, Lord George Hamilton, Chairman of the original Royal Commission, openly declared his opposition to the Minority proposals; and within a few months Lloyd George and John Burns brought in the Insurance Act 1911–12. The difference between their measures and those put forward by the Webbs seemed to many people hardly worth quarrelling about. But to the Fabians the difference was enormous and vital. What they considered the root of the evil was still untouched, indeed the abominated Poor Law of 1834 with its Workhouse system was destined to remain practically unaltered for another eighteen years, until the Local Government Act of 1929. For the Act of 1911, while certainly relieving the hardships of unemployment by compulsory insurance, could do very little, if anything, to prevent their recurrence, and the idea of 'reciprocal obligation', the moral factor so important to the Webbs, being overlooked or ignored, the Fabians of Brooke's persuasion could only foresee the encouragement of malingering and a general disinclination to work. 'This,' John Burns was overheard to remark,

[1] *Our Partnership*, Beatrice Webb, Ed. Drake and Cole, Longmans, 1948.

when the Bill was passed, 'has dished the Webbs.' The Minority Report remained as a massive record of social history. The Webbs began to build again, elsewhere. So did Brooke.

He would endeavour to win his Fellowship, learn German, study Webster, and manage another poem or two, if possible. His poetry was the only serious distraction, now that the Fabian dream was over, and already the present of A. H. Bullen's anthology of Elizabethan lyrics was turning his thoughts that way. 'I read them when I ought to be learning German,' he wrote to Geoffrey Fry, 'and I writhe with vain passion and envy. How did they do it? *Was* it, as we're told, because they always wrote to tunes? The lightness! There are moments when I try to write "songs", "where Lumpkin with his Giles hobnobs", but they are bumping rustic gaffaws.' He was going abroad for his German. There was a room booked in Munich.

In a few years you may come and stay with me in my villa at Sybaris or my palace near Smyrna or my tent at Khandahar or my yacht off the Cyclades. But you will be a respectable lawyer. You will waggle your pince-nez and lecture me on my *harem*. Then a large one-eyed negro eunuch will come and tie you up and pitch you into the sea. And I shall continue to paint sea-scapes in scarlet and umber.

Such was the fantasy. The fact was that Mrs. Stevenson was handing over her lodger to her neighbour Florence Neeve. The agreeable Mrs. Neeve, who lived with her husband at the Old Vicarage, was anxious to give her son, now aged about fourteen, an education proper to a youth who was aspiring to become a Congregational minister. Mr. Neeve kept bees in the spacious and somewhat neglected garden at the back which led down to the river. The honey from his hives, always sold in the comb at sixpence a section, was of unusual quality and popular among visitors to the Orchard tea-gardens. But the income was modest. A reliable tenant, willing to take over half the small house and settle down, seemed better than counting on undergraduates who were here today and gone tomorrow. So a few days before Christmas Brooke walked to and fro from the Orchard with armfuls of books, and staked his claim. He was off to Munich, he said, and would be back in May.

Chapter VII

THE OLD VICARAGE

(*December 1910–December 1911*)

Christmas at Rugby was a season of modified good will among men, owing to the elections. The Tories had commandeered all but twelve of the motor-cars in a constituency comprising ninety villages, so that Brooke, in charge of Labour 'conveyances', was obliged to leave voters stranded at the roadside, and for the next day or two forlorn expostulations were arriving at Bilton Road. 'We was waiting in the rain for three hours for that motor.' Delivering leaflets on the doorsteps where formerly they had deposited 'charity' was another mean Tory advantage that drove Brooke to vent his spleen in a report to Ka.

It is not true that anger against injustice and wickedness and tyrannies is a good state of mind, 'noble'. Oh, perhaps it is with some, if they're fine. But I guess with most, as with me, it's a dirty mean choky emotion. I HATE the upper classes.

The relationship with Ka had come to that stage when mutual sympathy for the awkwardness of their friends was an emotional bond which any moment might draw them to look solely at one another. Brooke was now suspecting that Margery's protective guard over Noel was rather less altruistic than had at first appeared, and he was forced to admit to himself—and to Ka—that he couldn't help thinking her 'wicked. Not very judicially, but I do. And what's to be done if you think a person you know so well is wicked?' As for Ka's own perplexities: 'Don't be black. Give me your blackness: it won't be noticed.' Both Gwen Darwin and Raverat were her guests on Christmas Day, then the whole party went on to Cove Cottage, Lulworth, where Brooke joined them, and on January 1st, 1911, wrote his poem 'Sonnet Reversed' while Raverat drew his portrait. Then occurs a trifling incident, the first of a series which sets a pattern for the future.

THE OLD VICARAGE

It isn't clear what happened, but suppose a bookshop near Lulworth, Christmas over, and Ka determined to give Rupert a belated present. He is on edge. Perhaps he cannot be bothered to make up his mind what he wants, for in fact there's *nothing* he wants in sight, but being pressed, he gestures vaguely, and a little ungraciously, towards a crowded shelf, as if to show, for the sake of peace, that any of those would do, for after all it's the spirit of the gift that counts. So what does it matter if he's landed with yet another copy of, say, *The Light of Asia*? Now there seems no doubt that in compensation for her lack of the more superficial qualities of her sex which take the eye and heart of man, Ka was one of those women on whom Nature has bestowed a sure instinct to perceive just when and how to raise the temperature of a situation, drawing towards herself a beam of emotional regard. Normally the book would be bought, for instance, after some hesitation of choice, and the bell at the shop door tinkle briefly at their casual exit. But on this occasion Brooke happened to be indecisive, and he was too casual, and her look, one hurt glance, might be enough to make him disgusted with his ingratitude, so that by the following day he would be running a fever of self-reproach. With Ka, we suspect, there was no temperate and golden mean. It was either the frigid detachment of a discussion on the seating arrangements for Sidney Webb's lecture next week, or the sub-tropical climate of what she called an 'H to H', the abbreviation she used for a heart-to-heart talk. The exercise of this faculty was probably not conscious (or it could hardly have been so effective) and in justice we must not attribute either the good or the ill that came of it to her character alone. It takes two to create a recurring pattern of behaviour, so that together they might almost be said to compose a third person: in this case a being acutely sensitive, fearfully unsure of itself, and the fringe of hysteria its native place. Brooke wrote from Rugby where he was picking up his luggage.

We drifted away, I all the time too (somehow) lost and shy and perplexed ever quite to seize a chance of saying one or two things that I was on fire to say. I wanted passionately to know that you were painless and vacuously cheery. All yesterday and today (though—do *you* find it?—half a day and eighty miles are all time and space for the veils they hang between oneself and one's yester-self) I'm red and sick with anger at myself for my devilry and degradation and stupidity. I hate myself because I wickedly and unnecessarily hurt you several times. (I don't mean that I'm sorry—for my own sake—for all that happened; or that I'm an atom changed from what I said and suggested. That stands.) But I hurt you, I hurt you, Ka, for a bit, unforgiveably and filthily and infamously; and I can't bear it; I was wild to do anything everything in the world to *undo* the hurt, or blot it out (but what could I do? I waved my arm in the bookshop at thirty books—but that'ld have meant nothing).

Three days later, when she had replied, it was, 'Oh all right, I'm not sad. You can't stop me being ashamed. But so long as you're not hurt, the world's very fine.' He was off to Limpsfield. There too he was in difficulties with his conscience about Margery. 'She says she never interfered (after a momentary impulse). Noel agrees.' He told Ka. 'Ecco! Where am I? Perhaps the Archbishop was right; and 2 + 2 hardly *ever* makes 4, except occasionally in the evenings . . . But apologizing to Margery is a little thing; finding oneself in a mere Chaos of disconnexions is the horror . . . It's horrible being partly responsible for other people's souls. One feels so timid.' And then came the departure for Munich, Ka met him for supper at Victoria station, and it happened again. From the Pension Bellevue he wrote, 'Oh, Ka, be it noted (for future reference) that the supper was a mistake . . . I don't mind giving way to emotion if there's nothing else to do. When I'm seen off anywhere in a train, I always cry in a corner of the carriage as it steams away—even if it's only Aunt Fanny I've left standing on the platform. But where there is something else to be done—Oh, it's too *gauche* and wasteful to be overcome by the situation . . . But I'd made myself rather hysterical.' He had only walked away a little too abruptly, making the break, not properly saying good-bye. Anyone would suppose they were in love. They were not, but if it continued this way, Brooke might find it hard to forego the emotional stimulus, whether of pain or pleasure, which he was finding nowhere but in this closer relationship with Ka. He had called at Limpsfield and withheld nothing from Noel. 'One *has* to be open,' he had written to Ka just before leaving England. There was no harm, Ka must have imagined. Wasn't it only natural that Rupert should be turning to a confidante who was at once mature, unattached, and easy of access? There was no question of her usurping Noel's especial place in his affections. Rupert must explain, and Noel would understand.

He began his life at Munich by taking lessons in German with Professor Schick and going around with a fellow student who wanted to pick up some English. Ludwig Dellefant was an agreeable youth and 'luckily for me, very meek . . . he submits to German all the time, quite placidly'. They sat in cafés and walked and talked, and one evening Dellefant took him to an undergraduate club for students in modern languages. 'The Germans consume an enormous amount of beer, but they didn't get drunk in the same way that English undergraduates do,' he explained to his mother, 'and every so often they burst into song.' It was an extraordinarily far cry from the Dickinson Society at King's. 'All Munich—all Germany—is highly excited about *Der Rosenkavalier*, Strauss's new opera. It was first performed in Dresden on Thursday.' He saw it later in Munich and his interest in the libretto gave new impetus to his struggle with the language. There was also an Ibsen season, acted in Dutch. One play in particular enthralled him. 'Do you know the play of *John Gabriel Borkman*?' he asked Raverat. 'Therein is a youth who will fly from his mother in order to LIVE (it happens in Norway also).'

Every morning he called at a certain café to read *The Times*, and it was there that he read of A. E. Housman's appointment as Professor of Latin at Cambridge. In that same week Brooke had won a *Saturday Westminster* competition for 'the best new and original letters to live poets'. Before leaving England, with Lascelles Abercrombie in mind, he wrote the rhetorical parody ('We never knew blank verse could have such feet') beginning, 'Sir, since the last Elizabethan died'.[1] Now he had another idea, '*A Letter to a Shropshire Lad*, apropos, more or less, of a recent appointment' which he copied out for Geoffrey Keynes.

> *Emmanuel, and Magdalene,*
> *   And St. Catharine's, and St. John's,*
> *Are the dreariest places,*
> *   And full of dons.*
>
> *Latin? so slow, so dull an end, lad?*
> *   Oh, that was noble, that was strong!*
> *For you'd a better wit to friend, lad,*
> *   Than many a man who's sung his song.*
>
> *You'd many a singer's tale to show it,*
> *   Who could not end as he began,*
> *That thirty years eats up a poet,*
> *   And the muse dies before the man.*

[1] *A Letter to a Live Poet*, G.K., p. 87.

THE OLD VICARAGE

Such gave the world their best—and quickly
  Poured out that watered best again,
—And age has found them, tired and sickly,
  Mouthing youth's flabby dead refrain;—

Or lived on lads whose song's long ended,
  Who will not blush for all they say;
Or damned the younger songs and splendid;
  —Oh, lad, you chose the better way!

Let fools so end! Leave many a lesser
  To blot his easy-bettered page!
But play the man, become Professor
  When your ailment is your age!

You turned where no tune yet is clinging,
  Where never a living song was sung;
E'en Greek might tempt a man to singing,
  But Latin is the lifeless tongue.

You may stir that dust to laughter.
  The lonely wreath that once you made,
—Unsmirched by feebler song born after—
  We have it, where it will not fade.

Those who don't care for song now hear you
  In curious, some in languid rows.
Undishonoured, clean and clear, you
  Teach and lecture, safe in prose.

For, lads of harsher voice or sweeter,
  They'll all together find one crown,
And hold their tongues from wagging metre
  In this—or in a dustier town.

No lad has made a song-book
  To please the young folks there,
No living tongue is spoken,
  And it's little one will care.

And there's time enough to dawdle in,
  And there, there's plenty o'dons,
And it's drearier than Magdalene,
  And a long way duller than John's.[1]

[1] *Saturday Westminster*, May 13, 1911.

Life in Munich did not become really enjoyable until he used an introduction from E. J. Dent and called on Frau Ewald, the painter, and her son Paul, a student of Physics, who lived in München-Schwabing. Early in February Brooke changed his lodgings so as to be near their studio apartment in Friedrichstrasse and was often with them for a meal. 'Rupert!' Frau Ewald would exclaim, 'Take that yellow hair of yours out of the jam'—for he had a way of sitting at an elegantly laid table, his chair pushed back, elbows spread far apart, and his chin cupped in his hands. These friends were the first to hear his new poem *Fish*, sketched out in his rooms at Ohmstrasse; and his company was welcomed and his flounderings in German patiently endured, but they found him insular to a fault, and either unwilling or unable to throw himself unself-consciously into the new life around him. Paul Ewald therefore decided to broaden his acquaintance, and first he took him round to meet Paul Leuba, a Swiss from Geneva, studying singing in Munich; a shortish, stout man in his early thirties, well versed in the French poets, an admirer of Maeterlinck whose plays he would declaim with histrionic fervour, and in spite of his generally somewhat derisive attitude towards the English (whom he considered primitive and underdeveloped) he warmed to Brooke, and for a while they were fast friends. With Ewald they walked one Sunday from the Worthsee to the Starnberger See, swapping quotations, for all three were lovers of poetry, most especially of Baudelaire. Then Paul Ewald introduced Brooke to a far more notable figure, Karl Wolfskehl, patron of poets and the modernist painters who 'go pilgrimages to all the places where Van Gogh went dotty or cut his ears off or did any of the other climactic actions of his life. They are young and beetle-browed and serious. Every now and then they paint something—often a house, a simple square bordered by four very thick black lines. The square is coloured blue or green. That is all. Then they go on talking.' Wolfskehl was tall, with a long pointed beard, slightly cross-eyed and short-sighted, his claim to distinction being that he belonged to the privileged circle of disciples around the poet Stefan George who rarely deigned to show himself in public. On the first Thursday of every month at his grand saloon in Leopoldstrasse, Wolfskehl kept open house for the painters, writers, and musicians of Schwabing; velvet waistcoats with jewelled buttons were in evidence; men with hyacinthine locks and women cropped like men, and most conspicuous of all, except Wolfskehl himself, Sacharov, the dancer, with his face made up violet, and no one in his vicinity looking in the least surprised. When all were assembled and refreshed, and Sacharov had arranged his limbs on the *chaise longue*, the lights would be dimmed, and Wolfskehl, holding the text an inch from his nose, his black beard jutting to the fore, would start intoning the latest oracle from the pen of Stefan George, 'the words,' in Ewald's phrase, 'ebbing out in beats like a bell when you stop hitting it with a hammer.' Then silence, everyone too deeply moved to speak, and sometimes too bewildered, for the poems were apt to be impenetrably obscure, and if anyone should venture to confess that the light had not yet dawned or that they were anything other than irresistibly swept away, the prophet would become inarticulate with vexation, the wineglass in his hand, or the back of the chair that supported him, snap suddenly, and he would have to retire to the next room in order to re-compose himself. He could not tolerate the slightest criticism of what was called Georgian poetry. (The hardness of the g's should represent a world of difference.) Earnest seeker of the truth, why should Wolfskehl eventually shave his beard and emigrate to New Zealand, as he did? Briefly and strangely he crosses our path, in appearance like a Bavarian Lytton Strachey, with his beard and his short sight and his utterance pulsing like a bell when it has been struck with a hammer. One hopes that Brooke rose to the occasion, and that his own recital of Swinburne, when Wolfskehl gave him the floor, was suitably attenuated and obscure. This was surely an even farther cry from the Dickinson Society.

'And what if I'd not met the lovable Mr. Leuba,' wrote Brooke to Frances Cornford, 'or Dr. Wolfskehl who is shy and repeats Swinburne in large quantities with a villainous German accent, but otherwise knows no English.' What could have made him give the impression of shyness, we wonder. Was it perhaps a touch of Hesse-Darmstadt courtesy which softened his manner to a young poet from the land of Swinburne? He fades out, clean-shaven, into the mists of the Antipodes, and Brooke is again alone. Indeed there was much of the day when Ewald was at his studies and there was little to do but sit in a café and indulge his habit of introspection. It provided him with the opening of his letter to Mrs. Cornford.

The worst of solitude—or the best—is, that one begins poking at one's own soul, examining it, cutting the soft and rotten parts away. And where's one to stop? Have you ever had, at lunch or dinner, an over-ripe pear or apple, and, determined to make the best of it, gone on slicing off the squashy bits? You may imagine me, in München, at a German lunch with

Life, discussing hard, and cutting away at the bad parts of the dessert. 'Oh!' says Life, courteous as ever, 'I'm sure you've got a bad Soul there. Please don't go on with it! Leave it, and take another! I'm so sorry!' But, knowing I've taken the last, and polite anyhow, 'Oh no, please!' I say, scraping away, 'it's really all right. It's only a little gone, here and there—on the outside . . . There's plenty that's quite good. I'm quite enjoying it. You always have such delightful Souls! . . .' And after a minute, when there's a circle of messy brown round my plate, and in the centre a rather woebegone brown-white thin shapeless scrap, the centre of the thing, Life breaks in again, seeing my plight, 'Oh, but you can't touch any of that! It's bad right through! I'm sure Something must have Got In to it! Let me ring for another! There is sure to be some in the Larder . . .' But it won't do, you know. So I rather ruefully reply 'Ye-s, I'm afraid it *is* impossible. But I won't have another, thanks. I don't really want one at all. I only took it out of mere greed . . . and to have something to do. Thank you, I've had quite enough. Such excellent meat and pudding! I've done splendidly . . . But to go on with our conversation. About Literature—you were saying, I think . . . ?' and so the incident's at an end.

And then your letter came! So many thanks. It made me shake with joy to know that Cambridge and England (as I know it) was all as fine as ever. That Jacques and Ka should be sitting in a café looking just like themselves— oh God! what an incredible lovely superb world! I fairly howled my triumph down the ways of this splendid city 'Oh! you fat muddy-faced grey jolly Germans who despise me because I don't know your rotten language. Oh! the people I know—and you don't! Oh! you poor things!' And they all growl at me because they don't know why I glory over them. But, of course, part of the splendour is that—if one only knew it—they, too—these Germans —are all sitting in cafés and looking just like themselves. That knowledge sets me often dreaming in a vague, clerical, world-mystic, spirit over my solitary coffee in one of the innumerable cafés here in which I spend my days. I find myself smiling a dim gentle poetic paternal Jehovah-like smile—over the ultimate excellence of humanity—at people of, obviously, the most frightful lives and reputations at the other tables; who come presently sidling towards me. My mysticism vanishes and, in immense terror, I fly suddenly into the street . . . Oh, but they're a kindly people. Every night I sit in a *café* near here, after the opera, and read the day-old *Times* (!) and drink—prepare to hear the depths of debauchery into which the young are led in these wicked foreign cities!—HOT MILK, a large glassful. Last night I spilt the whole of the hot milk over myself, while I was trying to negotiate the *Literary Supplement*. You've no idea how much of me a large glass of hot milk can cover. I was entirely white, except for my scarlet face. All the people in the café crowded round and dabbed me with dirty pocket-handker-chiefs. A kindly people. Nor did I give in. I ordered more hot milk and finished my supplement, damp but International.

Oh! no! Cambridge isn't very dim and distant, nor [E. J.] Dent a pink shade. I somehow manage, these days, to be aware of two places at once. I used to find it wasn't worth while; and to think that the great thing was to let go completely of a thing when you've done with it, and turn wholly and freshly to the next. 'Being able to take and to let go and to take, and knowing when to take and when to let go, and knowing that life's this—is the only way to happiness' is the burden of the Marshallin in the *Rosenkavalier* (the rage of Germany just now!). There's some truth in it. But sometimes, now, I find I can weave two existences together and enjoy both, and be aware of the unique. things of each. It's true that as I write, there's an attitude of Jacques' or a slow laugh of Ka's or a moon at Grantchester or a speech of Dickinson's, that I'd love, and that I'm missing. But there'll be other such, no doubt, in May and June——

He had been seeing more of Ibsen's plays. 'I'm old-fashioned enough to admire that man vastly. I've seen five or six of his plays in four weeks. They always leave me prostrate.' The news of his poems was that he still had hopes of being published by Dent's who, nevertheless, 'is now wanting me to leave out "some too outspoken" poems! I am taking a Dignified line.'

I finish this tourist's effusion at 2 o'the morning, sitting up in bed, with my army blanket round me. My feet, infinitely disconnected, and southward, inform me that tonight it is freezing again. The bed is covered with Elizabethan and German books I may or may not read ere I sleep. In the distance glimmers the gaunt white menacing Ibsenite stove that casts a gloom over my life. The Algerian dancing-master next door is, for once, quiet. I rather think the Dragon overhead (the Dragon = that monstrous livid-faced screeching pouchy creature of infinite age and horror who screams opposite at dinner and talks with great crags of food projecting from her mouth: a decayed Countess, they say) is snoring. I have this evening been to *The Wild Duck*. It is not as good, I thought, as most. Do read 'John Gabriel Borkman'! . . .

Oh, I sometimes make up a picture of Conduit Head, with Jacques in a corner and Gwen on other cushions and Justin on his back and Ka on a footstool and Francis smoking and Frances in the chair to the right (facing the fire) . . . It stands out against the marble of the *Luitpold Café* and then fades . . . But say it's true!

Ewald was right. Brooke would have been getting more out of his experiences abroad if chronic homesickness had not kept him so stubbornly detached. However in *Fasching* or Carnival time he made a distinct effort. The idea was attractive enough, he explained to Raverat, but somehow the reality fell short of expectation.

The theory's all right. But these smooth, baggy, tired faces in the streets with the watery obstinacy 'It is *Fasching*. We are enjoying ourselves' in the eye . . . I, anyhow, felt I'd like to be Gay, Young, a Part of it, lightly taking and leaving Joy, like a Greek. So I took off my clothes and went to a Bacchus-Fest, where all was roses and the apparel second century A.D. The young lay around in couples, huggin' and kissin'. I roamed round, wondering if I couldn't, once, be even as they, as the animals. I found a round damp young sculptress, a little like Lord Rosebery to look on. We curled passionate limbs round each other in a perfunctory manner and lay in a corner, sipping each other and beer in polite alternation.

The night, as the saying is, wore on. 'We became more devoted. My head was in her lap, she was munching my fingers, when suddenly I became quite coldly aware of my position in the Universe.' It was mutual, and 'we very solemnly and pathetically kissed each other on our quiet intellectual lips and hugged a space and so parted: she to her mother . . . I to seek the Nubian who had thrown oranges at me'. It was almost dawn as he wandered home down Ludwig-strasse. 'There were nine dustmen, me as a Greek, naked and cold, and a crapulous moon. I felt rather tired.' The detached observer had recovered himself. Then news from home made him long for the familiar faces and the life they had shared.

Yes: I must write about it. I live such a—somehow—flat life in München, away from people I know, that it is rather fine to think of you as living highly. That's rather what I meant by *elevation*—the way it struck me. I find it gives me something to live on—fills the trams and streets and the fat German faces with certainty and life. The white and purple lamps down *Theresienstrasse* in the dusk—I saw them, in such a queer coloured evening, the day Ka and Gwen and Frances wrote. The street hit me violently, being so lovely, and I flung out arms and gulped. Angels were walking in it. But it seemed to stand alone and signal to all the other beauties or realities in Europe, beacons winking at each other above the world. So are good things in touch. I fantastically thought of the great people I loved in England burning then so amazingly. 'Jacques . . .' I informed a prostitute. 'Gwen' I added, to a policeman. Neither seemed to grasp my point at all. But I was dancing. For a part of such things—a part that appeals to solitaries in Munich, though it's secondary on any real scale of values—I speak as one who adds a little apologetically, that the altogether so glorious landscape is, also very notable for its cabbage-bearing proclivity—is that it provides one (viz. the solitaries, the, in the hypothesized case, *un*central) with a firm-ness in life. I sit on you. When—it is part of the game that it comes oftener here—I realize my vileness, I can reflect that, even without me, the world has its points. It is pompously evident that we are all, rather vaguely, carrying Banners of it's never quite clear what Causes against very dimly realized Enemies with great enthusiasm and very probably—in no quite intelligible way—Upward . . . And solitaries who had previously thought themselves lonely umbrella-stands of Banners, scramble up from the mud they relapsed into, and hurry after the retreating dust cloud and the shimmer of what startling drums! . . .

In a word, Rupert, in München, scores more heavily off God than ever.

A variation on the same theme, conveyed in syntax less involved, was sent to Geoffrey Keynes.

I'm in Munich. Did you ever feel, when you were a child, about once every six months, a sudden waking, and a knowledge that you were, somehow, on a higher level, and that all the rest of the time you'd been thinking you were living, but really asleep. There were two grades of life, A and B, and the A periods signalled to each other across the valleys. But it was only in A you really knew the difference. So one feels here. I more than exist; I live. Good and bad things happen: and I'm not at all wanting to return to England. Only . . . there's the suspicion that it's all just not very interesting —that it's B. Or do you remember 'stopping out'?[1] One was there, alive and conscious.

One's whole personality was there—only, somehow, without the point. One was curiously *uncentral*. So, you see, I'm here; only—England central. And I feel rather on the edge.

All the same, there were moments, vivid, fraught with a vague, grotesque significance. Was he present at the Burial of Prince Carnival? He was. And the celebrations on the ninetieth birthday of the Prince Regent? There were illuminations in the evening and brass bands, and at midday a man flew over the town and dropped flowers over the *Residenz*. 'Personally I sat in a café reading Keats. And, let's think, what else?'

Yes: it *was* Munich in Carnival. I came late home from a café one night, and round the corner of a deserted street came a Pierrot and a Pierrette, a harlequin, a Negress, and a Man in a Top Hat, all in Indian file, stepping in time, very softly, toes pointed, and finger on lip. Whence they came and whither went, I don't know. But it was wonderful.

The Ranee heard tell of a ten-mile walk to Grünwald with Leuba, and his failure to induce a German acquaintance to join up with them. 'Their idea of an enormous walking-expedition is four miles in a greatcoat and a bowler.'

There is no other news except that the German wash has shrunk my best flannel shirt literally a foot. It is the most amazing thing I've ever seen. I don't yet see how it's possible.

Meanwhile in London there was a fancy-dress ball, to which Virginia, Vanessa, their brother Adrian, Clive Bell, and Roger Fry, had gone as figures in the paintings of Gauguin. James Strachey was also there, and overheard a conversation about Rupert which he passed on to Munich. 'He has just come through the stage,' someone was saying,

[1] In the sick-room at School Field.

'when he sits all alone in a darkened room with a picture by Botticelli . . .' 'And has *reached* the stage,' another voice put in, 'when one
hears the World throbbing like a violin string.' There was talk, it
seems, of his apparent unsuccess in affairs of the heart. 'I'm not surprised people don't fall in love with Rupert,' someone declared, 'he's
so beautiful that he's scarcely human.' 'Oh, yes,' said James, dryly,
'*temperamentally*, no doubt.' The gossip gave Brooke a laugh at
breakfast. He was writing to Ka. 'I feel so old and unwise; as one who
ran (a little cursorily) through the whole of Life six years ago. It is
metaphysically true that everything is worth while. But (on alternate
days) I feel quite flat. It turns out—did I tell you?—that I am No
Good. Otherwise everything is all right.' He had dropped a hint that
she might come out and join him. 'I meet the English trains every
day, just in case . . .' She did not come.

II

On April 8 he arrived in Vienna to stay with E. P. Goldschmidt, a
Fabian and a Trinity man, who had a flat in the Heugasse area. The
plan was to go walking in Dalmatia, where there was still a chance
that Ka might catch up with them, but news came that Alfred was on
his way to Florence with Robert Whitelaw, the now aged Rugby
schoolmaster and godfather of Rupert, newly a widower and unused
to travel abroad. He needed an escort. So if Alfred brought him out
and settled him at the hotel Berchielli, Rupert must bring him back.
By then it would be May, 'so the only "foreign town" you could
"wander into" then to find me'll be just "dear old Cambridge",' he
wrote to Ka, disconsolate. 'Oh, Ka, you should have come sooner!
Lord, it would all have been otherwise!'

During these past weeks the Marlowe Society had presented *The
Knight of the Burning Pestle* in Cambridge, and Brooke's article on
the play had brought to a climax his published remarks on a favourite
topic which has a bearing on his work as a poet. It had become a
hobby-horse which he missed no opportunity to ride, and when he
left for Munich in January 'two articles were waiting to come out in
the *Cambridge Review* while he was away.[1] The first was a review of
the *Cambridge History of English Literature*, Vol. vi, which dealt with
the drama up to 1642. What raised the issue was Brooke's conviction

[1] *Cambridge Review*, January 19 and February 23, 1911.

that *'Tis Pity she's a Whore* was Ford's best play. The History gave another opinion, and the reviewer maintained that this was only one instance of a prevailing flaw in the attitude of his contemporaries to Elizabethan literature. 'The irritating and, in both senses of the word, impertinent habit of judging Elizabethan plays by moral standards—the flabby and disgusting moral standards of modern upper middle-class drawing-rooms—spreads far . . . Indeed the Elizabethans were unrefined, their stories were shocking, their thoughts nasty, their language indelicate. It is absurd to want them otherwise.' No one seemed to understand that the vitality of these writings was inseparable from their alleged 'coarseness'; it was ludicrous for people to complain that their realism should be mingled with indecency. 'True realism, they think, is a fearless reproduction of what real living men say when there is a clergyman in the room.' It was the same sort of mentality that endowed Elizabethan comedies with a synthetic charm he called 'quaintness'. Having exposed the false vice of 'coarseness' in the tragedies he went on in his second article to expose the false virtues which some people might be attaching to the play by Beaumont and Fletcher, 'as happens with such literature and other antiquities as time has robbed of all good and vigorous qualities, and given only a pathetic second childhood, which the young, in desperate veneration, value under the name of "quaintness". There are a few places in this play where the decay may have set in, if we are not careful . . . But quaintness, which swathes dead books as sentimentality swathes dead people, has little hold on the living.' From Vienna he wrote to E. J. Dent, 'I hope you appreciated my remarks about "quaintness"—which some people have attacked.' He was afraid the Marlowe might be losing its pristine character, and sent his view to Dent at King's.

We've drifted into a habit of electing only actors: and actors are apt to be *geschmacklos*. So that I'm terrified of the whole thing getting out of reach, unalterably controlled by a circle of people who are utterly delightful in themselves and wholly dead collectively. A company of perfect gentlemen delightfully acting the romantic comedies of three hundred years ago—is that anything different from a Twentieth-Century A.D.C.? Isn't it our duty to be unpopular, at length? 'An audience composed of Heads of Houses' gives me the sudden chill consumptives have when they strike a match and find blood on the pillow. Do you remember the description of Keats doing that? But I've a plan for next year I'd like to discuss when I get back, which is, A Triple Programme. It was suggested to me when I saw a Schnitzler one-act play called *Die Letzten Masken* in München. It will exactly suit us—

only one female part and that easy, middle-aged and unimportant. It's a quite good (tragic) psychological piece. Some of us could translate it. (It's in *Lebendige Stunde*, which I possess.) Another piece might be a medieval mystery: and the third farce or comedy. It seems to me a scheme that'd get us out of the rut we're in, without being too risky, and would also give a lot of light for the future.

He was not exactly attacked for his two articles, but among others Geoffrey Keynes remonstrated. 'Yes, I am quite ready to attack the antiquarian and the bibliophile,' Brooke replied. 'Only I did not.' Brooke recalled, no doubt, that Keynes himself was already in process of becoming a Bibliographical authority on Blake and Donne, so he had better make a nice distinction. 'I was not thinking (e.g.) in what *edition* you read Donne: but whether you read him for poetry or "prithees" and "quotha's". A different question, eh? Ask Dent what he thinks about people who like 17th century music for its "quaintness".' Whether coarse or quaint, falsely vicious or virtuous, both these factitious qualities, he argued, were fatal to the essential life of literature. Because of the 'coarseness' in certain of his poems, this ardent belief lost him the patronage of more than one publisher. It remained to be seen how he would fare with Frank Sidgwick.

After ten days in Vienna he went to Florence and was gentle with Whitelaw, the sad old scholar. What crowded years had gone by since that first English lesson in the Twenty room. Whitelaw had become something more than a godfather, and Brooke never mentioned him but with especial tenderness and respect. They pottered around picture galleries, lingered over coffee, gazing into space. The person on Brooke's conscience was Marsh. Last winter Marsh had gone to great lengths, expounding the character of a novelist whose latest work he was recommending. It was St. John Lucas. This habit of living his life in separate compartments, each ignorant of what was going on in the other, had now led to another embarrassment in the same quarter. While Brooke was in Vienna, Marsh had called at the Orchard, expecting to find him in. Obviously Marsh must be the first to know of his present whereabouts.

Here I live in a pension surrounded by English clergymen and ladies. The pens they use are abominable. They are all Forster characters. Perhaps it is his *pension*. But to live among Forster characters is too bewildering. The 'quaint' remarks fall all round one at meal-time, with little soft plups like pats of butter. 'So strong,' they said, next to me, at the concert last night, of the Fifth Symphony, 'and yet so restful, my dear! Not at all what I should call *morbid*, you know!' Just now the young parson and his wife, married a fortnight, have been conversing. 'Are you ready to kick off?' he said. How extraordinary! What does it mean? I *gathered* it merely meant was she ready to go out to San Lorenzo. But does the Church talk like that nowadays?

So I am seeing life. But I am thirsting for Grantchester. I am no longer to be at *The Orchard*, but next door at *The Old Vicarage*, with a wonderful garden. I shall fly from Florence, which is full of painstaking, ugly pictures. But before I go, I've got to settle the question, 'Shall I lay a handful of roses on Mrs. Browning's grave? and, if so, how many?' These literary problems are dreadful. And the English Cemetery is so near!

He had little to show for the weeks in Munich. 'I spent two months over a poem that describes the feelings of a fish, in the metre of *L'Allegro*. It was meant to be a lyric, but has turned into a work of 70 lines with a moral end.[1] It is quite unintelligible. Beyond that I have written one or two severe and subtle sonnets in my most modern manner—descriptions of very poignant and complicated situations in the life of today, thrilling with a false simplicity. The one beginning "I did not think you thought I knew you knew" has created a sensation in English-speaking circles in Munich.' Such German culture as he had sampled seemed to him suspect. 'It has changed all my political views. I am wildly in favour of nineteen new Dreadnoughts. German culture must never, never prevail. The Germans are nice and well-meaning and they try; but they are SOFT. Oh! They ARE soft. The only good things (outside music perhaps) are the writings of Jews who live in Vienna. Have you heard of Mr. Schnitzler's historical play? They act an abbreviated version which lasts 7 to 12. I saw it.'

Talking with Whitelaw in Florence of his christening, Hillbrow, School Field, and Willie Parker Brooke, provided a sobering interlude. More than a year had passed since the death of Parker Brooke, and now, after Whitelaw's forty-two years of married life, here was the good old man left with practically nothing but his love of Greek. To Brooke it was all a random process of mere Chance. All the beliefs that posited an unfolding pattern or governing principle of life seemed to him futile. Here was Gwen Darwin, for instance, in a letter just to hand, perhaps the most unsentimental and clear-sighted of all his women friends, talking of a three-cornered heart-to-heart between Jacques Raverat, Ka Cox, and herself, and implying, apparently, that she was slipping from the ranks of the rationalists, for the way those three had been first drawn together into a triangle of friendship and then split asunder, with Jacques and herself on the one side, more

[1] *The Fish*, G.K., p. 78.

close than ever before, sharing the prospect of marriage—it all seemed to her like the predestined steps of a ballet in which they moved obedient to a superior will. This was apostasy. Brooke could not let it pass.

I thought your letter was red with crime and dark with forebodings. You said you'd all three felt, that week, as if you were in the hands of some external power, rushing you on. External Power? What? God? The Life-Force? Oh, my Gwen, be clean, be clean! It is a monstrosity. There is no power. Things happen: and we pick our way among them. That is all. If only you'd been at Camp last year, you'd have learnt that one can sail eight points *into* the wind. To be certain of it is the beginning and end of good behaviour. Oh! Oh! I implore you to extend the flickering fingers of derision at the sky. Did that vapid blue concavity make Brunelleschi build the Pazzi chapel? No! no! Derision's for God. But if it's really that madder horror, the Life-Force, that you're so anthropomorphically female to, even derision won't do. Laws do not wince. When you jeer, they wear the set, tired smile of a man who politely listens without hearing what you say. It only remains to cut them—cut the L.F.

But there aren't laws. There aren't. Take my word for it. I saw—I lifted up the plush curtain and looked behind—nobody, only dust and a slight draught from the left. (*Dust and a little draught* rhymes with *laughed* in the metrical version.) There are no laws; only heaps of happenings, and on each heap stands one of us and crows—a cock on a dung-heap or a beacon on a hill (in Lord Macaulay's poem) according to taste.

So!

It wildly embraces life when one realizes one's free-will (psychological *not* metaphysical). 'Realizes' not intellectually, but again psychologically, as one does with generalizations and moral rules. You learn them till they're so much part of your mind that you've forgotten them. You unconsciously regard or disregard, just as you aren't nowadays aware of disregarding the telegraph-wires in looking at a landscape. So you aren't saying all the time 'This is the only time in all Eternity I shall be in Verona in the Spring' but your nearly-unconscious awareness of the fact heightens all your staring at the Scaligers. Pfu! And so you aren't always only thinking 'I *can* choose which street I go down'; but the background knowledge of the choice deifies the street you do go dancing down. It's queer that *all* the important things somehow partake of the same nature—metre, moral rules, meandering, and all—in involving a well-lit individual thing on a background of unconscious consciousness. The Puritans dimly try to build up the background: the hedonist flaps inconsistently for the thing. *We* go for both; we join up Puritan and Hedonist: we have (once more) only connected.

Well, as for Life. (It's the beginning of summer: and you're making a great splash: So I may as well tell you.)

The great thing about Life is to realize three qualities in things: (1) this controlability I've mentioned; (2) Uniqueness; (3) Transience. All things are so; pins, moments, paramours, letters, intimacies, lamps, spinach. I saw

THE OLD VICARAGE

Giotto's tower with the sun on it this afternoon. *I* saw *Giotto's Tower* on April 28, 1911, with *6.0 p.m. sunlight* on it. I needn't have done it. I splendidly came out of all the ages, I hurtled out of the darkness to do it. It was half a second—it changed as I looked; and so did I. It and I and the light won't be quite the same again.

If you let the principles fairly sink in, and begin to realize Life, it leads to fainting in Restaurants, screaming before a wall-paper pattern, and madness in the end . . . You have no conception of the depths of horror of the mean and egoistic human heart. One day—when you are seventy and famous and referred to in the papers as the 'Rosa Bonheur of latterday England'—I will tell you the Whole Truth about the Average Human Heart. And you will die.

But perhaps you've already discovered the Great Secret—the Horror—that joy's as incommunicable as sorrow. Loneliness. Crying alone is bad enough: but that's an old story. It's when one suddenly discovers that one must always and for ever laugh alone . . . That's one of the things that, two by two, people sooner or later learn, and never tell for the sake of the young . . .

It's so late: the stars over Fiesole are wonderful: and there are quiet cypresses and a straight white wall opposite. I renounce England: though at present, I've the senile affection of a godfather for it. I think of it, over there (beyond Fiesole). Gwen and Jacques and Ka and Frances, and Justin and Dudley and Dr. Verrall and the Master and Lord Esher and Mr. Balfour . . . good night, children.

RUPERT

England was renounced, but a return ticket was in his pocket, and early in May he brought Whitelaw home to stay with the Ranee at Bilton Road. Then he left for his new lodgings near Cambridge.

III

The Old Vicarage was a long, ramshackle, three-storeyed house of red brick, with attics and dormer windows in a high roof; at the back was a veranda, sagging in places, and canopied all along with virginia creeper, and a profuse, overgrown, sweet-smelling garden with random trees, mostly ancient chestnuts, enclosing the demesne; a lawn ending in long grass, giant trees, and briars on the river bank where the water flowed four feet deep; and here and there stray relics of the nineteenth century—on the lawn a cement sundial in the form of a book lying open on a lectern, a cement basin with a fountain in the centre, and the sham Gothic ruin in a far corner, overhung with branches; and to one side stood Mr. Neeve's orderly beehives, concealed among the thickets. A five-barred gate, always hooked back among the bushes, stood at one corner of the gravelled approach, giving access from the road; the whole property was shut in by trees entangled with ivy, and the nearness of the river filled the air with the smell of dampness. Brooke rented three rooms; at the top of his part of the stairs there was a low wicket gate, for his bedroom had been a nursery, and he would tell how on going up late at night it was almost as if the ghosts of Victorian children plucked at his sleeve; beneath it was the living-room, a round table in the centre littered with books and letters, and a glass door with yellow panes of *art nouveau* design which, he said, gave him the illusion of sunshine on a wet day, shadowed by strands of creeper from the veranda roof beyond, led out on to the lawn. The branches of an old box-tree also darkened his garden window.

It was a small village in these days, yet august in origin, having grown up on the site of the Roman settlement which first brought civilization to the area where Cambridge came into being, three miles further down the river. There was one shop, kept by Sabina Hockley, the village postmistress (her husband delivered the mail) and a hansom cab could generally be found for hire in its place by the churchyard wall. It's unlikely that Brooke ever entered the church, and he certainly could not have checked his watch by the clock, which throughout these years was a local joke for its erratic performance; nor did he make any acquaintance in the village; even the Neeve schoolboy, who lived in the other half of the Old Vicarage, only spoke to him once. The hand-bell rang a little after midnight, and being still up the boy went to answer it and found the lodger struggling to do up a parcel and unable to find any string. He had no idea of the time, he said, and regretted the disturbance. Apart from this the young Neeve only caught sight of the lodger in the garden, usually in white flannel trousers, bare feet, and a polo-type sweater. On one occasion, peering from a back window, he espied a bit of white shirt sticking out of a hole in the seat of his trousers. Brooke always seemed to have friends with him, who had dropped in unexpectedly, and never enough cups and saucers, and they would lounge about in a circle on the grass, and there would be a murmur and a burble of somebody reading aloud—'poetry, I suppose'.

The Neeves had occupied the Old Vicarage for three years when Brooke came as their first semi-permanent guest and was given the use of his three rooms and full board for thirty shillings a week. It was a bargain. Florence Neeve herself was a most amiable woman, and her apple pies made from her own fruit were thought of so highly that a specimen was always to hand in the larder. Back late from the Diaghilev Ballet, which was now astonishing London, and which Brooke saw fifteen times this year, he would make for the larder, and take a slice of cold pie upstairs through the wicket gate to eat while going to bed. For breakfast there was neither jam nor marmalade, but Mr. Neeve's own brand of honey, then Mr. Hockley would arrive on his red bicycle and deliver another postcard from Gray's Inn, or from Ka at Woking, or a prize guinea or two from the *Westminster Gazette*.

Often the day had begun long before this, for a crisp early morning was the best time to bathe. You went out of the garden into the lane where the thick white dust shifted and slipped under the sandshoes, over the bridge in front of Grantchester Mill, across a meadow still sopping wet with dew and into the river above Byron's Pool, to bathe naked in the dark water smelling of mint and mud. The water was held up above the Pool by a dam with grey sluice-gates (now replaced by a weir) marking the site of Chaucer's Mill at 'Trompyngtoun', as described at the beginning of the Reeve's Tale. At the dam was the gathering place of deep waiting water, where you plunged in for the bathe. Below was the Pool, from which a placid reach of the Granta moved away northwards by yellow flags and trees bordering the farmlands of the Trumpington Hall estate. From a point above the bathing-place flowed the leat leading to the Grantchester Mill (burnt down in 1928), the water gushing out, cold and swirling, from beneath it into the Grantchester pool, broad and deep—to one side a meadow, to the other the tremendous chestnuts on the edge of the Old Vicarage garden. A short distance below the garden the two streams, from Byron's Pool and Grantchester Mill, united; then, to the north, the prospect opened out, and over there, between the willows and across a flatness of intervening fields, were the distant pinnacles of King's.

Brooke never learned how to dive, but all the same he enjoyed the abandoned gesture, starting with the correct stance, then hurling himself into space and falling with a flat splash. Pudsey Dawson, the bull-terrier, followed suit, and there was a puppy called Laddie that also threw itself in, or slept on Brooke's feet at night, and had a way of expressing ecstasy by 'seeming to turn right round inside its skin'. Following Dawson's example in other things, it ate frogs, which at times were very plentiful in the Old Vicarage garden. Sybil Pye was only one of the visitors who noticed Brooke's peculiar concern for the frogs, how he would break off a sentence or even the delivery of one of his own sonnets, gently to steer away from Dawson's insatiable jaws another hopping mouthful. The observant Miss Pye stayed a day or two next door, and was taken trips in the canoe, Brooke having first chucked in an armful of books; then he would keep the paddle going with his left hand, and with the other make pencil notes on Webster, steadying the text against his knee. Sitting on the bank, they played a game of awarding academic degrees to the poets. To Wordsworth Brooke awarded a First, but only grade three. His friend protested. Surely Wordsworth had written the most beautiful two-stanza poem in the language? 'Support that with quotation,' demanded Brooke, and having spoken from memory 'A slumber did my spirit seal' she noticed that 'the whole air had changed', all extravagance and mocking laughter were suddenly quite gone from her companion's face. She had won her point. And then they were gliding home again, once more lighthearted, and the line of his jaw when he laughed was like a lion on an Assyrian frieze. He was wearing a black flannel shirt and a red tie—the same as last year, she remarked. Didn't he ever worry about his clothes? 'No,' he said. 'I find it quite easy to dress on three pounds a year.' Back in the garden, she exclaimed at the splendour of the madonna lilies. Brooke couldn't share her enthusiasm. He said they made him feel rather uncomfortable, 'as if the angel Gabriel might pop out from behind them any moment and announce something'.

When the talk was general, she was rather surprised to observe his unexpected 'docility and gentleness . He rarely said much, but looked in silence from one speaker to the other, then, with a deepening interest in his look, abruptly put a question. If he felt obliged to disagree 'he had a way of working the last speaker's opinion into his own in such a way that any dissent he felt appeared as merely a comment'. On the night Raverat came to stay, he found Brooke kneeling with a lighted candle, trying to track down a flea to its supposed lair between the floorboards. 'There's always flea powder, you know,' said Raverat, looking on. 'It's advertised a lot.' 'It's no good,' said Brooke, who was stark naked, and in a bad mood. 'They rather like it. It just excites their appetite.'

Another visitor this summer was David Garnett. In the garden room there was an atmosphere of business and 'unhurried leisure', he felt, and next morning he was roused early by friends from Cambridge who had come for a bathe, among them Geoffrey Keynes, 'eager, lean, and in a hurry'. That night Garnett and Brooke dined with Lowes Dickinson at King's and came back by canoe. Their dinner host was expected to lunch with them at the Old Vicarage next day. They waited. An American guest, who was more punctual, proposed holding hands round the table and lowering heads by way of grace before meat, otherwise there was no incident of note until after the meal when Lowes Dickinson at last turned up, sorely discomposed and caked with mud. He had decided to have a quick bathe on the way, not in Byron's Pool, but further down the river, on the edge of Grantchester. Leaving his clothes on the bank, he stepped in naked, and was on the opposite side when the voices of young ladies in a punt were suddenly heard coming closer, so there was nothing for it but to conceal himself among the reeds until they had gone by; but instead the punt came alongside and was moored, and the young people proceeded to settle down to a picnic luncheon while the gentle philosopher subsided further and further into the ooze. There was the stigma of nudity, not to say indecent exposure, to be reckoned with, as well as the shame of eavesdropping. But his clothes were on the other side, and he was helpless. He could not make out the faces of the intruders, and somehow their voices were not reassuring, 'so there he stayed, having finally reached the bottom, and felt himself slowly congealing'.[1] At length the party moved off, Dickinson retrieved his trousers, and arrived at the Old Vicarage in a palsy of cold as the coffee was being cleared away. Brooke ran for a blanket and hot milk, and the smiles were more or less under control until the good-natured American expressed his profound relief that none other than Goldsworthy Lowes Dickinson himself had luckily escaped from a predicament so compromising that who knows but it might even have led to the resignation of his Fellowship. At this their grave concern for the discomfiture of their guest of honour gave way to paroxysms of laughter.

Soon after this Brooke and Garnett were together again for a week, sailing on the Broads with Brynhild and Margery Olivier, Godwin Baynes, and Dr. Rogers, the obliging chaperone. They shared a cabin and talked into the night, or bathed from the dinghy which they had in tow; Brooke would sit in the sun, his back against the mast, still making notes on Webster, (for the dissertation for the Fellowship

[1] *The Golden Echo*, David Garnett, Chatto and Windus, 1953.

had to be submitted at King's before Christmas); then some of the party continued the holiday at Limpsfield, the young men in tents under the pines. Brooke related a tale of mystery and imagination about a woman who received a supernatural visitor. He gave her instructions on how to build a machine that could only be operated by dint of her own intense prayer, but once it was set in motion would like a marvellous dynamo generate animal magnetism. The story develops with the machine accomplished, standing ready on the top of a hill, then peters out, the remainder gone from memory as if grown inaudible from the soughing of the pines and the many years between. It was like this the whole unusually serene and halcyon summer, when the pressure of petty events had relaxed in every quarter of Brooke's life, and there were long consecutive hours of reading and mooching around at the Old Vicarage, and one cannot distinguish one day from the next because of the calm like a summer haze; but now, for a week, we catch him sitting under a sail on the Broads, or concocting a yarn at midnight under the trees, and now he is back in the Grantchester garden, writing to Ka, 'There is no wind and no sun, only a sort of warm haze, and through it the mingled country sounds of a bee, a mowing machine, a mill, and a sparrow. Peace! And the content of working all day at Webster. Reading and reading and reading. It's not noble, but it's so happy. Oh, *come* here!'

In July we glimpse him at Covent Garden watching *Schéhérazade* with James and Ka; then again he reappears at the Vicarage. 'Come. We'll be wholly frank!' he writes to Ka, pressing her to be his guest. 'If you don't understand quite—nor, you know (don't tell anyone) do I. We'll explain and discuss, discover and guess, everything. Pride's irrelevant. Come!'

It's nice of Aunt Annie to remember me. But I wonder what she'd say if she heard how we talk to each other—the things we relate or propose. What'ld even Frances say? . . . What a hidden, distressful world it is, where people don't know what others do, or might do, and say, and be! O my dear, we'll, in any case, be so intimate, so *damned* intimate.

That's what's called a *cri de coeur*. Oh, how I'll try to cut off all the outside, and tell you truths. Have I ever seemed to you honest? That was when I got one layer away. There are nineteen to come—and when they're off what? Patience! patience! I grow cleaner, perhaps.

What drivel! But it's better than thinking on the old round—'How many people can one love? How many people should one love? What is love. If I love at 6 p.m. do I therefore love at 7? If . . .' Pah! if you were here, and I, that's all; and then all's clear. Isn't it damn silly to destroy anything by thinking?

You *must* come this week-end. Then we'll talk: and laugh. You'll have thought by then. Oh come, come! Never mind Aunt A.

But she cannot get away. Instead he dashes up to Manchester where she is looking after her aunt. Then Jacques and Gwen, newly married, call at the Old Vicarage, and are off again, leaving him 'drooping in front of the Old Vicarage and very sentimental and jealous . . . But afterwards I've been so lofty and so full of thoughts about Immanence and Transience and the Larger Outlook and so—occasionally —selfless—in a word so very like Ka, for an hour . . .' He was overcome with a sudden access of energy.

Mourning and moping—*Lord*! How damnable that one should ever do it. The time that's wasted! The time that's wasted in *anything* except tasting passionately! God, I'll never be flat again. As for last Wednesday and Tuesday, I was too despicable. Never mind, at least you've learnt something. The wise Ka has discovered what a Man of the World's like when he's tired. Or did you know even that before? Or—No: I was too despicable—to collapse on you. Oh! Why do you invite responsibilities? Are you a Cushion, or a Floor? Ignoble thought! But why does your face invite one to load weariness on you? Why does your body appeal for an extra load of responsibilities? Why do your legs demand that one should plunge business affairs on them? Won't you manage my committees? Will you take my soul over entire for me? Won't you write my poems? . . .

But it's—or something's—cured me. Worse thought than ever!—if spiritual valetudinarianism's to be the rule! Better to marry for health than to use Ka as a remedy for tiredness—or are we to face even *that*? Why not? Perhaps it's even the Ultimate Compliment: After all, if ever you get much fatter, some one of your friends'ld have to cut your toe-nails: which is the same sort of thing. So you might be that as well as everything else—and nothing anywhere be lost . . . After all, whatever we find each other, I'm better than Galahad, you than Beatrice. So, once a year, as a pat of butter (this weather) plops on a plate or (in Mr. Swinburne's lovely words) as night sinks on the sea, I'll sink on you, flabbily, and you'll be a moment's Atlas: and all will be well—as long, Ka, as you don't believe in it at all.

But just in case she takes that too literally, he risks a graver note. 'Oh but I want to see you. Just now I'm scribbling this merely to say that I think you're a most lovely and splendid and superb and loved person. Ka. What can I give you? The World? a slight matter . . . But do hurry to Cambridge, or I'll to London *soon*. Damn your aunts!' He stayed a night at Newnham Grange with Mr. and Mrs. Jacques Raverat and, conscious afresh of the blow that Ka had sustained, overdid for her sake his own telling how he could not help but suffer 'the ignoblest jealousy mixed with loneliness to make me flog my pillow with an umbrella till I was exhausted, when I was shut into my lonely room to read myself to sleep, and they went roaming off to tell each other truths. Oh, it's too damned irrelevant! But we might convalesce together . . . So I *must* meet you, and we'll settle each other's business. I've got the rest off my hands! I've told Jacques about Marriage and Dudley about Women and Gwen about Babies and James about Wisdom, and I've brought Cambridge up to the level in European culture. Now for you! Besides, we'd mitigate each other's loneliness.'

So she came at last and stayed two nights on Mrs. Neeve's side of the house. From the first she had known of the especial relationship with Noel. She understood and respected it. There was never a thought in her mind to do otherwise. Lytton Strachey dropped in for luncheon and Lowes Dickinson for tea, and the Cornfords came over from Conduit Head, and Brooke was at ease in his favourite place among the usual familiar friends, but there was an exhilarating newness among them and in the air; or so it must have seemed, though of course it was nowhere but in his own mind. It was no longer possible for him to deny that reluctantly, but none the less desperately, he was in love with Ka.

She was born in Albert Place, Kensington, four months before Brooke. Her father, Henry Fisher Cox, a son of the Rector of Luccombe, was at Trinity, Cambridge, where he made a special study of the literature of the early nineteenth century, especially Hazlitt and Blake, and then became editor of the *Examiner* when John Stuart Mill was one of the contributors. Much of his time was given to improving the conditions of the agricultural labourer, on which he wrote a book of importance in his day, then, rather unexpectedly, in association with a college friend, he started a firm of stock-brokers in the City, prospered, and eventually bought himself eight acres of Hook Heath near Woking, where he built a house, fixing a tablet in the hall which commemorated the name of every man who had taken a hand in the work, not omitting the labourers who had dug the foundations. By his first marriage he had three daughters, and since his wife was for a long while an invalid who died when the children were still quite small, Katharine, the second, shared with her elder sister, Hester, the responsibilities of house and family. She acquitted herself with precocious good sense, maternal affection toward her sisters, and almost wife-like solicitude for her bereaved father, so that even when he married again, they continued to hold a special place in each other's affections. He offered her a choice: the cost of keeping a horse or a

University education. She chose the latter. His sudden death in 1905 was a blow which left her secure in worldly goods alone. Emotionally she found herself in a state of deprivation which seemed to grow no easier with the years.

Although born in town, she grew up in the Surrey home and at her school in Southwold, as a country girl, always at her best in the open air with a scarf round her head and wearing homespun clothes (most original in her day) with an unconscious swagger like one of those peasants in tight bodice and heavy skirt falling in many folds, which stand about in the drawings of Augustus John. Being rather heavily built, these plain stuffs well became her, and she never gave thought to passing fashion. When she appeared at a ball in her first year at Newnham, someone asked her why she wore a man-sized pocket handkerchief tucked into the neck of her mauve evening gown bordered with silver braid, and she replied it was just in case her partner should break his leg. 'She might have been described as ugly,' one of her friends has remarked, 'but no one ever thought it of her.' She carried her strong shoulders bent slightly forward, habitually in the stoop of a woman nursing a child; her light brown hair was soft and long and gathered back, and her eyes, small and grey, were short-sighted, so that she had to wear *pince-nez*; her nose, rather turned up, was curiously flattened at the tip, which gave it peculiar character and her full and expressive mouth would hang open a little, showing her very white teeth, when she was slowly thinking; her complexion was very smooth and clear, and her low voice made one believe that she understood everything with a profound, almost maternal comprehension. 'Everything about her,' wrote Mrs. Cornford among her notes of this time, 'her hair (which curled in the novelist's "delicate tendrils" at the back of her soft neck) her skin, her simple and woman-like dresses, which generally in those days seemed to have the colours of flowers, were pleasant and fresh. There was not one touch of strain about her anywhere. To be with her was like sitting in a green field of clover ... She accepted everybody without criticism, as she did the Weather, and then gave out, not knowing how much she was giving.' Gwen, Jacques, Justin and the others would congregate in her sitting-room at York Street, sit on the floor and talk by the light of the fire and the street-lamp shining through the window, and according to Gwen's account it would be 'Ka, where's the best place to buy sofa cushions?—Please, this Arab costume is too small for me, will you make it longer so that I can go to the Slade dance?—How does one send a parcel to Germany?—What do tortoises eat?—What does Mrs. Smith do to my coffee to make it so nasty', and so on, while Ka, patiently attending, 'sat with her white hands in her lap'.

She 'minded being plain', it seems, and her father, aware of this, tried to make it up to her, though indeed she had no cause to worry. There are subtle advantages in the unobvious. Some young man might be reflecting how good it would be to be loved by her, and only after a while would it dawn on him that he could fall in love with her himself, and then he would notice her listening so attentively, and be touched by her evident understanding, and eventually come to realize that what he valued more than anything else in the world was precisely what she could give—the balm, the luxury, of her solicitude. But with that native calm of hers she could be slow, slow to perceive the finer point, slow 'as a bear' Virginia Woolf (who called her Bruin) used to say, and she could absorb the atmosphere of places and people, unconsciously, 'like a vegetable', Brooke once remarked, not meaning it as praise; and so her kindness, sometimes lavished by instinct of the heart without scruple of the head, could prove a source of trouble in the end, as much to herself as to others, for simply by being herself she risked the consequence of some deliberate act of choice when in fact she was intending no such thing, had only gone her usual good-natured way, been neither good nor bad particularly, nor this, nor that, but as natural and blameless as a fruit.

Small wonder a woman of her looks and unconventional ways was popular among the artists. John himself, and his younger followers, several of whom she met at that Gauguin ball in February while Brooke was away, saw in her at once the embodiment of an idea of womanhood (derived by John, perhaps from the peasants of southern Ireland) and asked her to sit as their model and share for a while the free-and-easy life of the studio. The Bohemian artist, however, living and working under the eye of the master, was as much a type of Edwardian aristocrat in his own way as the man or woman of letters who belonged to the group that was taking its name from Bloomsbury, and Ka was a welcome figure in both, moving from one to the other with ease, yet never belonging to either. The ultra sophistication they shared was not required of her. She was Ka. That was enough.

Brooke was at home among the writers. He knew them all, but among the painters Duncan Grant was the only one he could call a friend. Possibly he met a few more when he went with Marsh to Lady Ottoline's salon, but no doubt by now he had forgotten their names, though he knew from Ka how much she enjoyed the fuss they made of her, none with more flattering attention than Henry Lamb (the artist that was to achieve a masterpiece with his portrait of Lytton Strachey) who would already have asked her to sit for him, had not Duncan Grant come along with the idea first. This proposition, now that Rupert had entered her life on a more confidential plane, gave rise to a situation that was, Ka thought, a little delicate, not to say awkward. The portrait by Grant was bespoke for Geoffrey Keynes. The Lamb alternative would have been a simple matter, but Geoffrey happened to be such an old friend of her new admirer. What would Rupert think, or, come to that, what would any of his Cambridge acquaintances deduce, were they to find a portrait of herself displayed on Geoffrey's walls? The last thing she wanted was to make Rupert jealous or come between friends. So she demurred, consulted Rupert by letter, not suspecting that he was so sure of himself that the notion of Geoffrey or anyone else upsetting a relationship of his had never entered his head. To her surprise, therefore, he was almost angry. 'Is it again this unpleasant side of you one occasionally splashes into, this English Ladyhood? Are you for ever playing for safety?' he wrote, wondering how she could have become so unaccountably prim of a sudden, mistaking her motive.

Why shouldn't Geoffrey have a picture of you by Duncan? Why wouldn't it 'do'? What *would* people say? (I omit, in writing, you see, your half of the dialogue.) That he's in love with you? Let them say it. Perhaps he is. And when they *have* said it—or said that you're engaged—what then? What follows? Nothing. Nothing. Frightfully nothing.

Oh, come. The group of people we're part of may be awfully honest and genteel and chaste and self-controlled and nice—but at least we're far enough ahead for that. We don't copulate without marriage, but we *do* meet in cafés, talk on buses, go unchaperoned walks, stay with each other, give each other books, without marriage. Can't we even have each other's pictures?

'But for God's sake don't refuse on the "It wouldn't do" ground, nor, on that wildly irritating one which almost crept in—"can't think what you see in poor little *me*"!' The knowledge of what her mere existence now meant to him, the new and almost incredible acquisition in his life—the candid admission to himself of his love for her—the knowledge, too, that he had declared himself and she had not discouraged him, all contributed to an extraordinary access of energy and exaltation; but it was no use pretending any longer that these latest developments were a secret between themselves. She had stayed at the Old Vicarage. It was, in fact, entirely innocent, but who was to know that for sure? Anyway, and in any case, what did it portend? A note from Dudley, who was still in the dark, showed that Virginia had apparently been talking to James. No harm in that, but Ka had better know what people were saying. After an exceptionally crowded day, Brooke ended up with the Ranee at Rugby, and from there he wrote to Ka.

Yesterday I got up at 4.30—bathed above Oxford: worked in the Bodleian, went to the Grafton Galleries, saw *Schéhérazade*, called on Geoffrey, talked to James, and caught the midnight train down here. At 2.30 I walked up, strung with bags, this mile and a half. It was incredibly hot. I crept into bed at 5.30: after a cold bath, and claret and soda. Living is sheer ecstasy. How one packs things!

Your letter—it's half castrated by your punctuation; but I made out some of it.

Ka, they've been Talking, about You and Me. Talking! Awful. If you only knew what James said Virginia said So and So said . . . ! These mediate ignorances! But your repper, my dear, is going. Oh, among the quite Advanced. I, it is thought, am rather beastly; you rather pitiable. How otherwise, you see, can a situation be explained where two people have, in no *Morning Post*, 'arranged a marriage'? Isn't it too monstrous? They gibber night and morning, teleologically. 'How will it end?' They impudently ache for us. There are, you must know, only two 'endings' for this or any other case. (1) Marriage. (2) Not. (1) is entirely good, (2) entirely bad. And the goodness and badness are *ever* so retrospective . . . They live for the future like Puritans and judge by the end like Parsons. Is there no SIGN to give them, that each minute is final, and each heart alone? Sonnet? I'll sonnet ye!

> *Marriage was on their lips and in their eyes.*
> *Churches they scorned! their hearts unshackled stars*
> *Scurrying, fearless down bewildered skies*
> *To Love's own sanctuary, the Registrar's.*
> *The kind souls trust that "all will end all right":*
> *"No painful sequel" hope the timid souls:*
> *Two good friends wed is the dear souls' delight.*
> *Not for the game they play, but for the goals.*
> *"Will Ka and Rupert marry? Let us pray!"*
> *If Ka or Rupert loves, they hardly care;*
> *Whose morrows lead to—our least yesterday!*
> *Who pray for day all day, till night is there.*
> *"The Means! How will it end?" And all the while*
> *The Eternal End goes by: We love, and smile.'*

Hurried dreariness. We will talk. Do not fret. That's hardly worth the saying. We are covered from sight by a blazing veil of rightness.

The 'blazing veil' did not entirely conceal the thought that was beginning to weigh on his conscience. The understanding with Noel reached at Buckler's Hard was no childish or casual thing to be lightly brushed aside. Ka was taking it as seriously as he was himself, and inconsistent as it might seem to be with all that had happened since, he was determined still to honour it, though what precisely it could still signify must have been rather hard to say. He was perplexed and, between the hours of heedless exhilaration, growing more troubled every day.

In the eyes of Raverat, who alone of those closest to Brooke has left an impression of Noel at this time, she had 'a square, brown, hard face, with wonderful grey eyes', and she gave him the impression of accepting Brooke's devotion with 'a calm, indifferent, and detached air, as if it were her due', as if in her eyes her admirer were 'too "young", too visionary, too absurd'. Although no doubt he oversimplified, for the indifference must have been only skin deep, it is clear that the two friends, Noel and Ka, were of sharply contrasted natures, and that it was the difference between them which gave Brooke's predicament of this year its peculiar character: the one reserved, as much by nature as from tender age, secure in the bosom of her family, and not so much detached as relatively self-sufficient; the other an emancipated young woman of her time, not only averse to reticence but generous with her feelings and, owing to her loss of the father she had once relied on for affection and security, in perpetual need of that boosting of assurance which comes most readily from pride in the possession of a man's regard. Brooke met this with his corresponding need, but beyond that their ground in common came to a stop with a contrast even greater, perhaps, than the difference between the two young women of his choice. However much of a realist he might be in every other respect, when it came to a Cause, whether the Minority Report or a girl who touched his heart, he was first an ordinary sentimentalist and then, as the infection grew, a passionate idealist. And a Cause he must have or languish. Ka was not made that way.

In spite of worries, it was the most placid summer of his life and, off and on, the happiest. At the end of July he was still at the Old Vicarage, reading the Elizabethan drama, comparing the styles of Heywood and Webster (for he had evolved a theory that *Appius and*

Virginia was by Heywood, not by Webster among whose works it
appeared) and for a while he never left the house except to look in on
the Cornfords at Conduit Head. Frances was in the last stages of
writing a Morality Play, *Death and the Princess*, and often Brooke
called after supper to hear the progress. 'I can't imagine him using a
word of that emotional jargon in which people usually talk or write of
poetry,' she has recorded. 'He made it feel more like carpentering.'
Sitting on the floor (he said he 'couldn't think rhythmically sitting
up') biting the end of his pencil, and jotting notes in the margin of her
manuscript, he would say, without looking up, 'I like that,' or 'That's
good'. They held each other's poems in severely qualified esteem, she
criticizing him for what she called his 'over-grand' manner, he calling
her habitually brief lyrics 'the old, old heart-cry business' with a
quick sidelong glance, in case he had gone too far. Sometimes, when
there was no graver matter to discuss, they would amuse themselves
by composing rhymes, each in turn providing a line. An example
copied out by Brooke gives no clue to the details of authorship.

> *Ah, would I were in Bavarie,*
> *Alone and with my bellamy,*
> *What time the blossom is on the tree*
> *And the geese fly home.*

> *A petticoat of striped wool,*
> *An earthen jar with cider cool—*
> *An April lad was ever a fool*
> *When the geese fly home.*

One day she said, ' "Now the tulips all are out And the fields I go
about," were my first lines ever, aged seven. What were yours?' He
described how he was once taken to the seaside after chicken-pox.
Someone at school had just told him of 'a thing called blank verse',
where the line, so he understood, must have five feet with two beats
in each. Just as he was thinking of this a huge wave broke over
the promenade, and he started to work out a line on the given recipe.
No one had mentioned anything about long or short accents, so he
was in the dark in the small matter of rhythm. But at length he
achieved—*One day Poseidon grown strong will conquer*—which seemed
to fulfil all the requirements, with a feminine ending thrown in. This
confirmed Mrs. Cornford in her impression that he was born a
'deliberate' writer, contriving with conscious artifice, not capable of
the unaccountable, 'given' phrase, such as 'Come unto these yellow

sands', but liable instead to arrive at a felicity like 'I heard the thin gnat voices cry Star to faint star across the sky',[1] which she would always quote as characteristic of him at his best. But they talked of many things, and she recalled his once remarking that the reason he knew 'what women felt like from inside' was that his mother had wished for a daughter before he was born.

Mrs. Cornford added to his portrait some touches of her own. Not the contours of his face, she thought, but the steady and candid look in it, so hard to define, was the secret of his appearance. 'There was a deep-seated generosity in him, at once sensible and tender. I used to think that the real reason why the charm of his face struck people so greatly was because its clearness and fairness were not simply a happy accident of youth, but the expression of qualities innate in his spirit . . . There was something dateless in his beauty which makes it easy to picture him in other centuries, yet always in England.' She couldn't help rather resenting it when others used of him the word 'beauty', for it 'somehow managed to give a quite wrong impression of him' she wrote, 'and yet it was an essential thing about him, how "lovely and pleasant" he was to look upon'. He was well aware of his boyish appearance, and they used to pretend that he traded on it to charm the elderly and eminent. 'So of course you were frank and boyish?' asked Mrs. Cornford, on hearing he had just met Henry James. 'Oh yes,' he said, 'Of course I did the fresh, boyish stunt, and it was a great success.' But she was concerned chiefly to leave on record some idea of the general impression he made, rather than the external features of a portrait. 'It was a continual pleasure,' she recalled, 'to look at him fresh each day—his radiant fairness, beauty of build, his broad head with its flung-back hair, deepset frowning eyes. The clear line of his chin and long broad-based neck on broad shoulders were so entirely beautiful that he seemed like a symbol of youth for all time . . . To watch him putting on his boots, frowning and groaning, with the absorbed seriousness of a child, with which he did all practical things—he would look up with a pink face and his pleasant hair tumbled and his sudden sharing grin which always had the loveliness of a child's.' In his nature he was, above all, both puritanical and romantic at once. 'It seems to me now symbolic of him that I first knew him when he was acting in *Comus* . . . Deep-ingrained in him, and handed down to him I should imagine through generations of English ancestors, was the puritanical spirit. I remember how

[1] *The Jolly Company*, G.K., p. 139.

clearly it showed when he spoke the Chorus in *Faustus* in some sort of Puritan scholar's dress. And nobody could miss it, whoever saw the scorn and sternness in his face when he spoke of things that he hated, things corrupt and unclean.' She was touching on an element in his character without which his story in the chapters to come would be incomprehensible. If Mrs. Cornford first attached to him the idea of a 'young Apollo', an attribute which caught on as the years passed until she sorely regretted it (for she soon came to realize it was only a particle of the truth), one should add to it here the evidence of his fellow Apostle, H. O. Meredith, that he always gave the impression of a man of the land. Some quality about him of an English yokel, a frankly bucolic being, was no less conspicuous than the loose grace of a gangling Apollo.

When neither out at Conduit Head, nor working on the Elizabethans, the business of the day was twofold. The Chaplain of King's had recommended him to a Swedish girl at Newnham who was translating two plays by Gustave Collijn of Stockholm and wanting a collaborator to help her with her colloquial English. Estrid Linder, forewarned by letter 'Don't expect too much of R.B. at first,' arrived on her bicycle at Grantchester, and thereafter was a regular visitor for tea, going over the scripts of *Dust* and *Bland Vassen* (Amid the Reeds) which Brooke revised, rearranging the stage directions, readjusting the dialogue. Even more than the prospect of a professional fee, he valued the discovery through Miss Linder of the plays of Strindberg. Alone of all his dramas, *The Father* was then available in English, but in return for advice on *Bland Vassen* Miss Linder helped him to try his hand at translating specimen pages from the other works, finding him an apt pupil, eager to learn as much as he could about the great dramatist with whom Collijn himself was associated in Sweden. The other preoccupation was his own verse. This was of more consequence, and eventually it ousted Webster, Collijn, and even Strindberg.

The correspondence with Frank Sidgwick, an acquaintance of Lytton Strachey and a native of Bilton Road, Rugby, had begun on June 13, when in answer to Brooke's overture, he wrote from Adelphi Terrace suggesting a meeting in his office at noon on the 14th. 'I am sorry to have to limit you to that hour,' he wrote, but he had good reason. The morrow was his wedding day. 'I imagine you know that hardly any poetry pays its way.' Brooke called, and Mr. Sidgwick took the poems with him on his honeymoon. 'We think they are all worth publishing, and would get a good deal of attention in the Press; but it is very difficult for us to take a risk of such a volume, small as it is.' Knowing that Brooke was prepared to carry the cost himself (in fact it was the Ranee who had promised to subsidize the venture) Sidgwick offered to issue the book on a commission of fifteen per cent on the copies sold. He thought the total expense would work out at about £9 or a little less. Then followed the hitch that Brooke was anticipating. 'We want to suggest the elimination of the Seasick Lover [*A Channel Passage*] for which you might substitute . . .' and then he named an innocuous rhyme which had appeared in the *Westminster Gazette*. Brooke protested, of course, but he met with more forbearance than hitherto. It was probably under pressure from Sidgwick that the title 'Shakespearian Love Sonnet' was dropped. But the poem remained. Sidgwick, however, felt bound to issue a further warning. The contract arrived at the Old Vicarage with his letter of July 28. 'As to the "Channel Passage" we feel bound to advise you very strongly to omit it, as we have no doubt that the majority of your reviewers will pounce upon it, to your disadvantage. But if you still wish it to remain, we should recommend its being hidden away at the end of the book.' He was perfectly right about the reviewers. They pounced.[1]

The final costs for an edition of 500 copies were £9. 17s. 6d. This was more than the Ranee had allowed for, so Rupert must make sure that he was not parting with his copyright. Mr. Sidgwick was reassuring, and now all that remained was delivery of the material, but the prospect of publication at last was acting as such a stimulus to the Muse that for several weeks no manuscript was forthcoming. He wrote to Ka.

When I got your letter—midday, yesterday—I was fairly on my last legs. I'd been working for ten days alone at this beastly poetry. Working at poetry isn't like reading hard. It doesn't just tire and exhaust you. The only effect is that your nerves and your brain go. I was almost a mouthing idiot. I couldn't think or sit still or stop eating. I had reached the lowest depths possible to man. You just saved me. I worked out that you'd not be accessible till Saturday, and then only with babies and probably Ethel. So I wired for James. He is reading about Prisons on my right, now. Dudley, from London, is expected any moment. He wired last night!

I've not dared to write again yet. I've been talking and playing. But I'm going to risk half an hour at a sonnet after tea. I am made of wet paper, and

[1] See Appendix.

I'm longing to walk or camp. Oh! oh! I wish you were here. I'm not so damp as I've been. But I'd like to sink back.

Hush! I must write business. I am a Man. Your letter was almost impossible to understand. Virginia comes here (I'm rather nervous) on Monday till, say, Friday. By the following Tuesday I start for Camp.

It was the end of August. Justin was making arrangements for Camp. Meanwhile Virginia Stephen arrived at the Old Vicarage, and occupied Ka's bed on the other side of the house. The garden room was strewn with scraps of Strindberg, pages of *Bland Vassen*, and fragments of verse. Probably the guest had brought with her an early chapter of *The Voyage Out* to revise while Brooke was reading or writing stretched out on the grass. One warm night there was a clear sky and a moon and they walked out to the shadowy waters of Byron's Pool. 'Let's go swimming quite naked,' Brooke said, and they did. Then there was an afternoon during that week when they were both at work in the shade of the chestnuts. Brooke was revising the end of his poem *Town and Country*. 'Unconscious and unpassionate and still, Cloud-like we lean and stare as . . .' what could it be? It must be something in Nature that was absolutely dazzling with a 'staring' brightness. He pondered, and was at a loss. 'Virginia,' he called out, 'What's the brightest thing in Nature?' She reflected a moment, then suggested, 'Sunlight on a leaf.' 'Thanks!' he said, at once convinced, and the line became 'Cloud-like we lean and stare as bright leaves stare'.[1] She noticed that he would sketch a poem, establishing the rhyme words in their sequence, with another word here and there as guidance for the later process of filling in. This was a more accurate as well as more charitable way of putting it than Raverat's exclamation one day when all the friends were together. 'Have you seen Rupert's note-books, with all the first drafts of sonnets with blanks left for the Oh God's?'

Having succeeded in persuading Virginia to join him at Camp, he left Grantchester and called on Ka, who now had a cottage of her own near Woking, in the hope of persuading her to accompany Virginia. She agreed, and on August 27 he arrived at a meadow near Clifford Bridge, on the banks of the River Teign, five miles from Drewsteignton, Devon. A party of Old Bedalians had pitched a camp there, and Justin had arranged that they should leave their tents and tackle in place, so that his friends from Cambridge could move in. Among the men of the party were Justin, Rupert, James Strachey, Geoffrey and,

[1] *Town and Country*, G.K., p. 124.

for a time, Maynard Keynes, and a new character, Paul Montague, a zoologist and musician, who had made his own gittern and could sing Elizabethan songs at the camp fire in a pleasant tenor voice. He lived near by at Crediton, and he passed on from his mother a general invitation to tea. The ladies were three of the Olivier sisters, Daphne, Bryn and Noel. Ka and Virginia had not yet arrived, so it must have been soon after taking over the encampment that they all walked over to Crediton and called at a house named Penton, which stood on a hill, overlooking the town, the home of Colonel Montague in retirement, an officer esteemed in his Victorian day as a writer of farce. He was not at home for the invasion, but since the party was unusually large, Mrs. Montague took the precaution of giving orders for dining-room tea. Since it was on August 30 that Brooke at last posted his manuscript to Frank Sidgwick, he probably got rid of the package this afternoon, at Crediton, on the way to tea.

They talked on round the table as the day drew in, and 'happiness crowned the night', until Mrs. Montague proposed they should all go to Crediton Fair, for the barnstormers had pitched their tent and announced that they would present a version of the popular drama called *The Lyons Mail*, and the best seats were only a shilling. The tea-party from Penton took up the whole of the front row. As was the custom, having memorized the plot, the players gagged their dialogue, which required a certain amount of verbal resource, especially in the emotional scenes. 'Curse the woman!' cried the heavy lead. 'She makes me (*long pause*) uneasy.'

At the Fair they all remarked on a curious sight—a girl, the living image of Ka, leaning against a booth. At that very moment Ka was, in fact, laboriously making her way on foot from the station in company with Virginia Stephen, who was audibly complaining, having so far covered only about five of the eight miles to Clifford Bridge. 'They'll have a wonderful tea ready for us,' said Ka, making the best of it, although it was past supper time. 'They'll all be there to welcome us.' But they were not. There was a note pinned to the flap of the cook tent. It said nothing about food. Perhaps the others had expected to be back before this. Anyhow, the late arrivals, reconnoitring in ill humour, happened upon the remains of a blackberry summer pudding, the handiwork of Justin, and had they but known, prudently put aside by him, but unfortunately not yet thrown away. By now, while Ka and Virginia swallowed several mouthfuls of purple mould before growing aware that it had 'turned', the party from

Crediton Fair had started home, and were standing in a row at the top of the valley, looking down on the tents and a gleaming curve of the Teign which moated them about on two sides. It was an unusually still, moonlit night. And then, no longer talking, or only with voices hushed, they walked down into the picture they had wondered at from above. The 'skin of the day' had been cast into the hedge. But something, a memory, remained. Brooke was starting a new poem as he walked down towards Ka.

The mornings began early at Clifford Bridge. At five-thirty Justin and Ka rose to put on the porridge and do the chores before breakfast. One early morning they were surprised to notice what seemed a mound of old clothes under a gorse bush. On closer inspection it turned out to be James Strachey wrapt in a blanket. He hadn't slept. Willing to be a martyr to this open-air craze, he had made up his mind to watch the sunrise. 'I'd always heard the dawn was a very wonderful thing,' he said, shivering more than the leaves around him, 'and I'd never seen it,'—a wistful episode, which Brooke memorialized in a couplet over his breakfast bowl.

> *In the late evening he was out of place,*
> *And utterly irrelevant at dawn.*

Strachey did not care to sample a second night under the stars. But the days passed in extraordinary, autumnal peace, diversified by trivial though consistently delightful events. Lytton Strachey, writing his first book *Landmarks in French Literature*, was in lodgings now accompanied by James at Manaton, not far away, and they all went over to tea; there was a walk to Yestor and back, nearly thirty miles in all, and on the journey home they decided on a man-hunt, one of the party breaking away and trying to get back to Camp without being caught. The lot fell on Brynhild Olivier to be the quarry, and she outwitted and outran them all; there were play-readings, chiefly Justin and Rupert sharing the parts, while Virginia and Ka and Noel lay around under blankets, listening; Justin was stung by a wasp and Rupert sucked out the poison; there was a conversation around the fire about the dramatists when Rupert said there were three years in Webster's life that no one knew anything about. He quoted the line of Webster's about Paris and the goddesses, 'and they dancing naked before him,' and followed it with Synge's phrase in *The Playboy* 'and he with the great savagery to kill his Da!' and remarked 'Clearly, Webster must have gone to Ireland for those three years and caught the Irish turn of phrase,'—for in those days it was a fashionable kind of joke which brought in reference to the Irish Players who were still the talk of London; or Brooke sat apart from the others, in the middle of a meadow where there was no shade from the sun, revising his dissertation, or reading the letters of Keats to Fanny Brawne.

During these few days following the party at Penton on the hill, and ever since the walk home down into the valley with Noel and the others, towards Ka in the camp below, Brooke had been working on his poem *Dining-Room Tea*,[1] in the same measure as *The Fish*, written in Munich and Vienna. Apart from the traditional form of sonnet, octosyllabics were from now on his favourite vehicle. A year before, he had described how 'Life one eternal instant rose in dream Clear out of time,'[2] but that was only a passing fancy in the course of an indifferent sonnet. At Penton he experienced another moment of awareness, almost too elusive to describe, like that evening at Torquay in 1908 when he took the momentous step of signing the Fabian Basis and was alone on the seashore at night within earshot of the band on the promenade.[3] On this occasion the presence of someone he loved gave the 'moment' something of the tenderness of a love experience that was innocent of passion. 'How could I cloud, or how distress, The heaven of your unconsciousness?' All the ingredients of the moment, even the element of love, composed a Platonic Idea—the theory whereby things on earth are seen as the mere projections or shadows of realities existing out of time, a notion he would have met with in working for his Tripos, and in his reading of Pater's *Plato and Platonism*. From now on he was to make play with it in the best of his verse—*Tiare Tahiti*, for instance, and *Heaven* in which he recast *The Fish* as a satire on religion to make a much more successful poem. *Dining-Room Tea* marks a stage in his development that should be looked at a little closer, even at the risk of seeming to overlay a modest and simple thing with exposition.

In his Muses Library edition of Donne Brooke had marked two lines of *The Exstasie*. 'All day the same our postures were, And we said nothing all the day.' Perhaps the Penton experience would have been lost on him as a poet (in that he might have let it pass as altogether inexpressible) had he not already been made aware of such unsuspected areas of feeling through his studies of a poet who had

[1] G.K., p. 110.
[2] *The Goddess in the Wood*, G.K., p. 99.
[3] *Seaside*, G.K., p. 152.

known them before him and managed to preserve them in a shape of speech. Like *Thoughts on the Shape of the Human Body*, written a few weeks earlier, the Penton poem suggests the cast of thought, not the expression, of Donne. It may seem invidious to speak of such a masterpiece as *The Exstasie* in the same breath with Brooke's light-weight piece, but he was clearly aiming at nothing more profound than what he precisely and, for the first time consistently, accomplished. In an Edwardian domestic setting; in circumstances far less intense, and then only for a moment, the indoor light seemed to be falling 'on stiller flesh, and body breathless'. One can understand why Flecker called Brooke 'our Donne Redivivus', although in the end it was not Donne, but a lesser figure of the same school, whom Brooke most resembled when his poetic lineaments were fully evolved. If *Dining-Room Tea* is nourished at the root by a classical education, it owes its virtue to something more than the marriage of his poetic nature with his Tripos. He was conditioned, as we say, to be susceptible to an experience of this kind by another aspect of his Cambridge life, the philosophy of Moore and the climate of thought and feeling among those who lived under his influence. The party at Penton may be said to have induced a good 'state of mind', complete with what would be considered a satisfactory 'organic whole'. The theme of Virginia Woolf's *The Waves* is the moment when 'the beauty and horror of life are reconciled'. Elsewhere she asks, 'What is the thing that lies beneath the semblance of the thing?' and in *A Room of One's Own*, speaking of reality, she says, 'Whatever it touches it fixes and makes permanent. That is what remains when the skin of the day has been cast into the hedge.' The timeless moment was found to be a source of significance in the visual arts as well. Roger Fry, for instance, writing of Chardin (as if of the group at Penton) remarked that 'the way that people took their place in the space of the room had at moments some special meaning which he was quick to seize'.

Dining-Room Tea was a new beginning in Brooke's verse. It also marks an end. After these many May-ings, cross-country man-hunts, play readings, productions, hi-jinks in the Swiss Alps, and discussions on the Beautiful and the Good, this social concoction of young people, so oddly yet so delightfully harmonious—compounded of Rugby and King's and Bedales, laced with Bloomsbury—was beginning to dissolve. After James, Ka was the first to leave; she baked an enormous cake and sent it to the friends she had left behind at the river side.

After Camp Brooke stayed at Manaton with Lytton and James Strachey, then on the way through London attended a Beethoven concert with James. At the National Liberal Club, Dudley passed on a rumour that Ka was ill. She had left the Camp some days before— not 'whole months' as Brooke's letter of extravagant concern implies. Was she testing his defences? How *could* she be ill?—

What with? how ill? Why are you so damned far off? Oh, come down to England! And this evening, during a Bach thing, it suddenly came on me you were drowned (trying to save Frances). I felt certain for five minutes. And then Dudley's tidings brought it all up again. I knew it was a telepath. You've died of typhoid. Woman, you're lying dead now. I've thought it all out, all the damned details. Oh, Lord, Lord! You're not to be dead; it won't bear thinking on. I *will* sleep . . . I can't help thinking of the idea of that funny slow strong body having stopped. Oh God, it's madness to figure your eyes. But think (I'll be sane) how extraordinarily confident of immortality we slip round corners and away for whole months. And any silly tangle of chance may do for us. That you stopped loving me, or I you— that'd be a little thing. But that we'd never more for all ages know that queer lovely laughing absurd craning peering wrinkled wise kindly Christian clever old slow thing called Ka—it's a devilish unmentionable monstrous idiocy that only comes to tired fools like Rupert.

I'm foolish tonight. I'll write better tomorrow.

By then he was at Grantchester. 'The garden is immeasurably autumnal, sad, mysterious, august,' he wrote to Mrs. Cornford. 'I walk in it, feeling like a fly scrawling on the score of the Fifth Symphony.' The rumour about Ka turned out to be false, but she was tired. So was he, and ashamed of it.

It's so maddening not to be able to keep up to the liveliest level always, when one knows there's no *reason* why one shouldn't. Why isn't the brain always dashing about after new ideas? Why isn't one always tasting very consciously? And what'll one say in the $\begin{cases} \text{gutter} \\ \text{grave} \\ \text{vase (if cremated)} \end{cases}$ when one remembers how things were wasted—opportunities—on that day, and that——

To have such Mondays and Tuesdays, and to be grumpy on Wednesday; oughtn't I to be wiped up? And I spend my time in thinking I'm putting others on their right paths. An Influence. What a comic figure!

I'm determined to live like a motor-car, or a needle, or Mr. Bennett, or a planetary system, or whatever else is always at the keenest and wildest pitch of activity. When you see me foolish pinch me and go away to sensibler things! I shall always object to you wasting your time in being too often charitable to other people: but I'll kill you if you waste it being charitable to me.

THE OLD VICARAGE

Oh, I *will* startle you. I'm going to be so damn intense. I'm going to crowd more into every remark I make to you or bite I give your finger than even you have in a whole fat day. I'll make more out of roll and butter in this A.B.C. (it's morning now, and breakfast) than you'll ever get from your eggs and fruit and home-made jam. I'll liven you!

You're so fine.

But I'll wake you up a lot yet. And I'll tell you all the secrets of Hell: and you shall tell me unmentionable things.

Nothing matters except the moment.

RUPERT

Meanwhile a correspondence, somewhat lugubrious by comparison, had been going on with Sidgwick. He happened to be away when some new material arrived for incorporation in the manuscript of poems, and now he was worried to discover among the additions, 'a sonnet entitled *Lust*—which we think we must ask you to omit,' he wrote on September 18. 'If it had been good, we should not have raised any objection; but as it is, we think, not more than not bad, we should recommend its omission.' On the same day Brooke was at the Old Vicarage, writing to Erica, 'I have developed into a ferocious man. I live a dark, passionate, sudden life, compounded of scholarship and tragedy. I often shout suddenly and leave the room . . . All the summer—

I alternated between seeing the Russian Ballet at Covent Garden and writing sonnets on the lawn here. This is a deserted, lonely, dank, ruined, overgrown, gloomy, lovely house: with a garden to match. It is all five hundred years old, and fusty with the ghosts of generations of mouldering clergymen. It is a fit place to write my kind of poetry in (exactly what, and how frightfully modern, it is, you will learn in October or November if you have sufficient money to buy, and intelligence to understand, my book).'

On hearing from Sidgwick, he wrote to James Strachey, telling him that his publisher thought *Lust* 'not good as poetry and not decent as idea. Do you agree about the first? I'm so despondent about the value of the whole book that it may have to go—the sonnet. But I'm pretending to be firm.' Strachey was moderately reassuring. 'I think I thought it was a good one—though obscure, you recollect.' So on September 20 Brooke answered his publisher's letter. He should have attached his articles on the 'coarseness' of the Elizabethans.

Is the objection to 'Lust' only that it's bad as poetry, or also that it's shocking as morals? I can't see that it's any worse as poetry than the rest of the book (except one or two poems). Technically it's not much, I admit; but any fool can write a technically good sonnet. And I hoped that the newness of the idea might counterbalance that.

If it's thought to be improper, it must be sadly misunderstood. It's meaning is quite 'proper' and so moral as to be almost untrue. If the title's too startling *Libido* or Ἐπιθυμια could be substituted; tho' I'm afraid that would only make it more obscure.

My own feeling is that to remove it would be to overbalance the book still more in the direction of unimportant prettiness. There's plenty of that sort of wash in the other pages for the readers who like it. They needn't read the parts which are new and serious. About a lot of the book I occasionally feel like Ophelia, that I've turned 'Thought and affliction, passion, hell itself . . . to favour and to prettiness'. So I'm extra keen about the places where I think that thought and passion are, however clumsily, *not* so transmuted. This was one of them. It seemed to have qualities of reality and novelty that made up for the clumsiness. The expression is only good in places. But the idea seemed to me important and moving. I know a lot of people who like my earlier work better than my present. They will barely notice this sonnet. There are others who prefer my present stuff. I've shown the sonnet to some of them. They thought it good (by my standards, whatever they may be!). And they weren't, I assure you—though they were of all ages and kinds—shocked.

I should like it to stand, as a representative in the book of abortive poetry against literary verse; and because I can't see any aesthetic ground against it which would not damn ¾ of the rest of the book too, on any moral ground at all. If your reader has misunderstood the sonnet I will explain it to him. If you really think it finally ruins the chances of the book, I suppose it ought to go. If you think it will only decrease the sales, we could make some additional agreement about the number sold within the year, or something. If it's too near the beginning, it can be buried.

The poem in question was hardly worth the struggle, but doubtless in Brooke's mind a principle was involved. After the usual, almost daily budget of gossip about James and the rest, Ka heard the outcome.

P.P.P.S. Correspondence with Frank Sidgwick over the sonnet entitled *Lust*. Did I tell you? He wanted it left out. Said a woman's smell was an excrement. I wrote an *immense* letter, saying it was the only serious poem in the book, and a million other things. This morning he's come down like a shot possum. Compromise: It's to be printed, but called *Libido* (Latin)! Let us Pray.

III

The problem of finishing the dissertation on John Webster in time was now critical. His best chance of a Fellowship depended on it; he was still determined to offset his disappointing performance in the Tripos, and the special appendix on *Appius and Virginia* alone demanded all he could muster of accurate and painstaking scholarship. There was less than three months in hand, and when the Michaelmas term began in October, the stream of visitors to the Old Vicarage would start again. He must go to London, not only to be safe from temptation, but so as to be near the British Museum. For this purpose, Lady Strachey was the required 'householder' who vouched for his character on the card of admittance to the reading room, and Maynard Keynes, who was going away, offered the use of his room in Fitzroy Square till he should find a quiet place of his own. 'My only passion,' he confided in a friend, 'is a slight lust for the British Museum.'

The only recreation he planned for himself in London was singing lessons. E. J. Dent recommended Clive Carey, so Brooke appealed to his old friend: 'I've come, lately, to that period of life at which every young man stops short and looks round. I have turned the corner. I am on the way downhill. In short, I am twenty-whatever it is; I forget for the moment. And it seemed to me I ought to learn to control my voice. With death so near there isn't a moment to lose.' He wanted, if not exactly to sing, then at least to be able to listen and understand, or, failing both of these, to acquire a 'more manageable reading and speaking voice'.

On October 14 he walked into 21 Fitzroy Square, and the routine began of reading in the Museum, trying to sing (forlorn enterprise) and going back to Grantchester for the week-ends. He was working at full stretch. Small wonder he took care to avoid being caught up in the aesthetic and social vortex of Gray's Inn, where there would be a free bed, certainly, but little free time. After about three weeks he wrote to Maynard Keynes, thanking him and adding that at least his tenancy had served to remove some of the squalor. Ka had found him a cheap room at 76 Charlotte Street. After getting him settled, she omitted to pick up from the table an essay she was writing on the Russian novelists, a much discussed work in progress that she was stubbornly refusing to let Brooke have sight of until it was finished. Next day she got it back with a letter addressed, so it was alleged, from the Athenaeum!

Dear Miss Cox,

It was more than kind of you to let me see some of your work. I need hardly say how much I was interested in it. Your thought seems to me elevating and restrained: your style subdued and dignified. It is obvious that you have studied with profit the masterpieces of our great stylists. You have shown me a work of indeed notable promise; and I have spent many happy hours with it. If I say that, with all its merits, it seems to my ears, unused, I know, to modern fashions, a little *unfinished*, I hope you will not put me down at once for an 'old fogey'!

I hope very much you will go on steadfastly in the path you have chosen for yourself. The profession of a woman of letters is an arduous, sometimes even a *dangerous*, one. But I feel sure you will, in old age, be able to look back with contentment, feeling that your life has not been altogether ill-spent. And you will always have the satisfaction of knowing that you have chosen for yourself the walk of life for which your aunt has always destined you. I need say no more: But remain

Yours very sincerely
RUPERT C. BROOKE

P.S. I must add that the unassuming and silent way in which you left your little essay among my papers, to catch my eye when it might happen, has touched me as being so delicately and tactfully what only *you*, if I may say so, could have done.

During these weeks there was a momentous walk on Hampstead Heath when Dudley, tripping, at that moment, over a cat, broke the news that he was engaged to be married. Frances, Gwen, Jacques—now Dudley. One by one his friends were withdrawing each into his enclosed world. 'Into one of the privatest and most frequent shrines in all my chapels, with a pink light ever burning therein, the deity himself threw such a bombshell!' he told Jacques. 'I felt so awfully lonely.' Of course there was consolation in Fräulein Annemarie joining the circle. 'I really like her so *very* much. She's the nicest stranger I ever met, almost'—but his bachelorhood was becoming more and more frigidly conspicuous in his eyes. Ka wrote often enough, but somehow she never said much, or at least never said quite what he wanted. 'Oh I did like your letter. Though there were bits—notably a passage on *unconscious idealists* and *undergrowth*—I could make *nothing* of . . . I can't answer that sort of letter when I'm working.' It would take 'time and emotion', he said. He was ploughing through the plays of Chapman. There were times nowadays when he was so dog-tired he could barely lift his head. Something might crack, he thought, if the knowledge of her love were not sustaining him. If only she were not so fatally accessible to all her friends, he reflected. No wonder she tired herself out. He wrote again, insisting that she must stay at home at least four days of the week and read or write her 'slipshod feminine prose. Your damned hangers-on can see you *there*.' Perhaps this was a little presumptuous of him, he must have thought, so to soften the blow he then bade her remember that she had 'the most adorable eyes, mouth, and neck, in England, that your nose would be on the same level, if it weren't for a place at the end that's *too* ridiculously Ka to be taken *quite* seriously; that your body's strong and antiquely divine; that you've an affectedly drawling laugh that puts several pounds on a sick man's weight, even down 85 miles of telephone; that if one sees you swing (*exactly* like yourself) across the street, the world's on the instant radiant and immortally good.' And now she could be the first to read his poems. He happened to be in Rugby when the proofs arrived. He sent them on to the flat in York Street.

I wonder if it *is* very degraded—or very annoying—to send you this. Not annoying, I think, because you after all needn't look at them. It rather pleases me, sending them. If you've time and pleasure, look at them. I really want (but not badly) advice about corrections. If you do look through, say what you think about *Capitals*, and *Italics*. And special points. Or say nothing. You may touch anything, from commas upwards. And you may write or draw on the proofs. These don't go beyond me.
'Town and Country' *may* be rewritten.

To oblige Dent and Carey, his music teacher, he had agreed to walk on as a Slave in a production of *The Magic Flute* at Cambridge; so for the last week of November he was at the Old Vicarage, and Ka received much happier news of progress on the dissertation.

I worked till 1: and then ran nearly to Haslingfield and back before lunch, thinking over the next bit. There was such a clearness and frosty sun. Some men under a haystack, eating their lunch, shouted how fine a day it was. I shouted back, it was very cold; and ran on. They roared with laughter and shouted after me that with that fine crop of hair I oughtn't to be cold . . . It was wonderful and very clean out there. I thought of all you Londoners, dirty old drivellers. Now I'm come in to rehearse my nigger part and to work. I've realized that taking part in theatrical performances is the only thing worth doing. And it's so *very* nice being an intelligent subordinate. I'm a very good subordinate—it's such a test. I'm thought not to dance well: but my intelligence and devotion have brought me rapidly to the front. I am now the most important of 7 negroes.

A day or two later there was a domestic alarm and excursion. The dissertation, and the next letter to Ka, were almost incinerated. (Wallis was an official on the Labour Exchange who also lodged at the Old Vicarage.)

This letter was interrupted, in the middle. Do you smell soot? I've been the last half hour with my arms up a chimney. The beam in the kitchen chimney caught fire. 'These old houses!' we kept panting. It was so difficult to get at, being also in part the chimney piece. Only Mrs. Neeve, I, and Mr.

Wallis at home. Mr. W. dashed for the Brigade on his motor-bike. An ever so cheerful and able British working-man and I attacked the house with buckets and a pickaxe. The bowels of the chimbley are now on the kitchen table, charred but out. And, worst horror, the Brigade's somewhere crashingly on the way. I was masterful at the always slightly wrong minute—but gave very decisive directions for the rest of the day.

Chapman now.

You on Wednesday.

RUPERT

P.S. There are a lot of men in such *wonderful* clothes in the kitchen. Taking the rest out. I admire them *so* much. One is so beautiful, shining . . . Mrs. Neeve says: 'There is no doubt we were all Lying in Danger last night.'

Mrs. Stevenson says: 'Thank Goodness it's morning and not night, now!' And I—I see—was so dreadfully irrelevant all the time. Oh!

The Magic Flute, conducted by Cyril Rootham, was performed at the New Theatre on December 1 and 2, a notable event in the history of Mozart in Britain, but the 7th Nubian Slave spent every spare minute writing his dissertation in the dressing-room. On December 4 the house of Sidgwick and Jackson published *Poems*. There was no dedication. He had offered it to Noel. She declined, but he arranged the book in two sections, one written before their meeting at Trinity the other afterwards, and in the foremost place, out of the chronological order, appeared the sonnet written in that 'Arcady' of 1909— 'Oh Death will find me long before I tire Of watching you'. Before the year was out the costs were covered and nearly three pounds profit in hand.[1]

Poems, 1911, began its astonishing career very quietly. But apart from absorption in his last minute revisions of Webster, Brooke was in no fit state to be as exhilarated, or even interested, as he should have been by the long deferred appearance of his first book. He wrote hopefully enough to Sybil Pye. 'Huh! I shall write much better things in the next year or two, now I've time to practise the thing seriously and continually,' and to another friend, in the old vein, 'I have to leave England, because of my book. It is too Pure. And my Godfather and seven other Rugby masters cut me in the street yesterday,' but there are no comments on the reviews, if indeed he looked at them, and one is conscious of a vaguely muffled tone in place of the usual resonance of his affairs. He was uneasy about Ka—nothing definite; he was merely ill at ease—wishing, for one thing, she wouldn't be seen about so much with the painter Henry Lamb. There was no mention of him in a letter. What could he have said? but there is no

[1] Thirty-seven impressions were printed up to May, 1932, totalling 98,855 copies.

doubt that at this time of strain and overwork he was beginning to feel a slight chill of insecurity, and to make a deliberate effort to convince himself that nothing was going wrong.

Some days later he got ready to join his mother at Eastbourne. The plan was Rugby for Christmas; the usual reading party to see the New Year in at Lulworth, then a week or two with the Ranee in Cannes before going on to learn German in Munich. Anyway, it was bound to be some while before he could settle again at the Old Vicarage, so he tidied up the garden room, the pages of Strindberg and Webster and Chapman, and the note-books of poems and odd phrases left over: 'A presage marked as Memory hurries by'; and bits of a curious satirical hymn where geometrical expressions are treated as Platonic Ideas—'Eternal Rhombus strong to save', and 'The Oval is a deathless Oval there And the Great Square eternally a Square', and, more promising 'the Eternal Curve Jostles for ever the eternal Line'; and other stray scraps:

> *All night I went between a dream and a dream*
> *As one walking between two fires.*

>   *. . . like the moths.*
> *But do not love as they do,*
> *With a strange feathery soft inhuman love.*

> *And there is sorrow in the leaf,*
> *And in the flower forgetfulness*

> *The soul, like a thin smoke, is spread*
> *Crying upon the air.*

He said good-bye to Mrs. Neeve, and left Cambridge for a last night in Charlotte Street. There he gave up his room, settled with the landlord, and went on to Eastbourne. He couldn't sleep.

Chapter VIII

CANNES

(*December 1911–February 1912*)

From the Beachy Head Hotel at Eastbourne he started organizing the reading party at Lulworth. Justin and Ka had promised to repeat their administrative performance at Clifford Bridge; Maynard Keynes was now asked to bring Duncan Grant; Norton and Shove were coming, also Gwen Raverat, and a young Hungarian poet from King's, Ferenc Békássy; 'Virginia *may* be turning up any time,' and he also dropped a line to Lytton Strachey, holding out as inducement the efficiency of Ka Cox. He also busied himself with sending off copies of his poems to friends. In his jaded condition the Russian Ballet alone seemed to be an art worth pursuing. 'They, if anything, can redeem our civilization,' he wrote to Sybil Pye. 'I'd give anything to be a ballet designer.' Then he turned back to his work on the Elizabethans.

The dissertation was finished at Eastbourne, and getting back to Bilton Road by December 20, 1911, he threw himself into an armchair in his upstairs room and slept round the clock. The letter awaiting him from Marsh must at least have aroused in him some stirrings of pride. 'I had always in trembling hope reposed that I should like the poems,' wrote Marsh, 'but at my wildest I never looked forward to such magnificence. . . You have brought back into English poetry the rapturous beautiful grotesque of the 17th century,' and he went on to pick out this poem and that for technical criticism or praise. Then came the difficulty that Sidgwick had foreseen. Marsh was more tolerant than some of the professional critics. Even so . . . 'The *Channel Passage* is so clever and amusing that in spite of a prejudice in favour of poetry that I can read at meals I can't wish it away—but at the risk of your thinking me an awful borjois (as the man says in St. John Lucas's story) I must protest against the "smell" line in

CANNES

Libido[1] . . . there are some things too disgusting to write about, especially in one's own language.' Brooke answered this on December 22, having shaken himself out of his long sleep.

Your letter gave me great joy. It was good of you to write. I horribly feel that degrading ecstasy that I have always despised in parents whose shapeless offspring are praised for beauty. People are queer about my poems. Some that I know very well and have great *sympathie* with, don't like them. Some people seem to like them. Some like only the early ones—them considerably, but the others not at all. These rather sadden me. I hobnob vaguely with them over the promising verse of a young poet, called Rupert Brooke, who died in 1908. But I'm so much more concerned with the living; who don't interest them. God! it's so cheering to find someone who likes the modern stuff, and appreciates what one's at. You can't think how your remarks and liking thrilled me. You seemed, both in your classing them and when you got to details, to agree so closely with what I felt about them (only, of course, I often feel doubtful about their relative value to other poetry) that I knew you understood what they meant. It sounds a poor compliment—or else a queer conceitedness—to remark on your understanding them; but it's really been rather a shock to me—and made me momentarily hopeless—that so many intelligent and well-tasted people didn't seem to have any idea what I was driving at—in any poem of the last few years. It opened my eyes to the fact that people who like poetry are barely more common than people who like pictures.

I'm (of course) unrepentant about the 'unpleasant' poems. I don't claim great merit for the *Channel Passage*; but the point of it was (or should have been!) 'serious'. There are common and sordid things—situations or details —that may suddenly bring all tragedy, or at least the brutality of actual emotions, to you. I rather grasp relievedly at them, after I've beaten vain hands in the rosy mists of poets' experiences. Lear's button, and Hilda Lessways turning the gas suddenly on, and—but you know more of them than I. Shakespeare's not unsympathetic—'My mistress' eyes are nothing like the sun'. And the emotions of a seasick lover seem to me at least as poignant as those of the hero who has 'brain-fever'. 'Whatever', I declare simply and rather nobly, 'a brother man has thrown up, is food for me.'

The 'smell' business I don't really understand. Four hundred poems are written every year which end 'The wondrous fragrance of your hair': and nobody objects. People do smell other people, as well as see and feel them. I do, and I'm not disgusted to think so.

Surely the truth was that he had outgrown his early affectations in the manner of Rossetti's 'He would feel faint in sunsets and at the sight of stately persons' or even Browning's 'dear dead women, and such hair too', and was now self-consciously entertaining 'unpleasantness', cultivating that astringency which, as someone has said, 'we

[1] G.K., p. 127.   *Your mouth so lying was most heaven in view*
And your remembered smell most agony.

associate with ammonia in the bath', as a protest against prudery. It was also—though he would have been as shocked to hear it as were those others by his 'smell'—a last flicker of the by now defunct movement of the Pre-Raphaelites who, scorning standardized beauty, insisted on 'seeing things as they are', so that in the words of a critic in the *Athenaeum* of 1851, they were both acclaimed and abused for their 'singular devotion to the minute accidents of their subjects'. Perhaps Brooke's best defence would have come from the Pre-Raphaelite apologist William Rossetti, who in 1901 wrote in his Preface to the facsimile of *The Germ*, 'A writer ought to think out his subject honestly and personally, not imitatively, and ought to express it with directness and precision: if he does this, we should respect his performance as truthful, even though it may not be important.' But the virtue of this truthfulness unsupported by critical selection has as little to do with Art as the virtue of selection by itself, exercised for an attack on prudery or for any other social purpose. A fair answer to both Brooke and Sidgwick-Marsh may be found in John Bailey's monograph on Whitman. Some of that great poet's work was marred, according to his critic, by the 'rather silly pleasure he took in shocking the respectable . . . But there is of course no more sense in spoiling a poem or a novel in order to annoy Mrs. Grundy than in spoiling one in order *not* to annoy her.' Indeed the good lady should be kept out of the picture altogether. But Brooke, as we have seen, risked his position in polite society, for sake of a principle. His gesture, so moderate by comparison with what we have since grown accustomed to, was regarded in its day as a swashing blow of defiance. It was a Cause.

Marsh was now private secretary to the First Lord of the Admiralty, Winston Churchill. 'I suppose you don't edit a magazine,' Brooke ended his letter of counter-criticism. 'I might review Elizabethan books at some length for *The Admiralty Gazette* or T.A.T. (*Tattle Among Tars*) or whatever journal you officially produce. At least I hope you'll issue an order to include my poems in the library of all submarines.' On an earlier page his reference to the dissertation was despondent. 'As I had a Soul Crisis as well as Insomnia and other things, I couldn't do it at all well. I came to London in a dilapidated condition after it was over.' He might join his mother in the south of France, he said, before going to Germany. 'I want to stay out of England some time. 1, I don't like it, 2, I want to work—a play, and so on, 3, I'm rather tired and dejected.'

It was probably while tidying up at Charlotte Street that he asked Ka to meet him in Germany, and she positively declined, conscious of the understanding with Noel. If that was the only reason, well and good. Somehow Ka didn't seem the same these days. But maybe he was only tired and jaded and imagining things. They would talk it all out in Dorset. On Christmas Day he wrote to her about the books they should have at Lulworth: *War and Peace*, Milton, Donne, and, as if prescribing a dietary regimen for an invalid, 'Possibly Browning, Ben Jonson, a little Keats'.

On December 27 he arrived at Lulworth. There was a room for him at a place called Churchfield House. There too Lytton Strachey was staying. Others were at Cove Cottage. Henry Lamb was at Parkstone with Augustus John, and from there, two days later, on Saturday 30th, he telegraphed to Strachey, announcing his arrival at Wool station, shortly after four that same afternoon. It must have been Lytton who let him know that Ka was at Lulworth, and offered to put him up at Churchfield House if he should decide to come. He arrived. Unwontedly, Brooke kept himself aloof from the others, and was observed going off by himself, quiet, uncommunicative; yet Ka was in high spirits, much as she was on that last visit to Lulworth a year before when Gwen observed her. 'She pulled on great boots and laughed in the wind,' she wrote. 'I remember her, standing on the very edge of the cliff, her crimson skirt whirling in the wind, her head tied up in a blue handkerchief, and the gulls screaming below.' And for much of that Saturday evening Ka was lost to the others, somewhere on the shore, it was supposed, with Strachey's friend.

It was still the year 1911, if only just. So not more than a day and a half could have gone by since Lamb's appearance on the scene, before Ka sought out Brooke, found him alone, and took the opportunity of telling him in her usual calm and gentle way—for these two were always quite open with each other—the very thing he had been suspecting for the last month or two. She thought, she said, that she was in love with Lamb. Among other things, she added that he had got the same Christian name as her father, and she was particularly glad of this. Surely that was a happy omen? But now the slow strain of the past few months, too suddenly redoubled, became too much for Brooke to bear.

It was natural for idealistic love, poisoned by jealous fears, to ascribe the motives of a libertine to its prospering rival. So whether or not the waves of nausea and disgust which now overwhelmed him in his dejection had any origin outside his own jaundiced fancy is immaterial. He grew desperate, and the pain of jealous rivalry enflamed his love into a passion. He was suddenly at the point when he must either retreat or try to snatch an advantage. There was no question which he would choose, so he tried, and failed. Injured in her pride that he should be asking her, imploring her, to marry him straight away, only now, when he was driven to it by panic (the additional factor of a sort of puritanical horror was, rather naturally, incomprehensible to her) Ka saw no alternative but simply to refuse. She felt shocked and humiliated, as did Brooke himself, not only that he should be rebuffed (which he must have half expected) but that he should be feeling as much disgusted with himself as with anyone else, for every scruple of his tender regard for Noel had been swept away, it seemed, by his infatuation for Ka. She meant what she said, but the trouble lay in that she was as incapable of a forthright decision between her two admirers as was Brooke on his part in the case of Noel and herself. If ever she had wanted to try her hand at the old and normally harmless game of playing one man off against another, it had got disastrously out of control. She grew alarmed, Brooke was beside himself, begging her not to see the painter any more, or at least for a while, to which she could only reply that she would promise no such thing. Why should she? What's more she was hurt afresh, angry to discover that apparently Rupert was no longer trusting her to look after herself. But more than anything, she was perplexed in the extreme by the irrational ferocity of his revulsion, so that when he tried a new opening, and argued that if she would not marry him, could she not at least come out and be his companion for a while in Munich— just as it might have been in January last—and when, moreover, she heard him declare, 'I shall go mad if you don't come,' she consented, if only for the sake of peace and sanity, giving him gentle assurance that all might still be well. He was clearly a sick man, and she alone was in a position to help.

Monday came, the first day of 1912, and James Strachey, who had come for the week-end, and found himself a puzzled spectator of Ka's bewilderment and Brooke's distress, was on the point of leaving for London when Brooke suggested accompanying him on his journey; and they walked all day by hill and down and along the top of the Purbeck Hills as far as Corfe Castle, where James caught his train and Brooke walked on the further mile or two to Studland. After only four days at Lulworth his objective was the comfortable fireside of the

Raverats. They were greatly concerned for the state of his mind. The problem was more than they could manage on their own.

Somehow the Raverats got him to London, and to a nerve specialist in Harley Street, Dr. Craig, who recommended mental rest, special foods (for the patient had lost a stone in weight in the past two months) and the sunshine of a place like Cannes, where he happened to be going anyway. But he must leave sooner. In fact he must go at once. They telegraphed to Paris, where Elisabeth van Rysselbergh, a daughter of the Belgian Impressionist painter and a young friend Brooke had known in Munich, was asked to meet, feed, and put him on the train for the Riviera. Meanwhile Brooke felt he must speak to Noel, who for some months now had been a medical student at University College, London. He found her at Limpsfield. He was concerned for Ka's well-being, he explained, and Noel must have been no less concerned for his. His visit gave him a brief respite, for there were no recriminations to face up to, nor disharmony there, whatever he must have felt within his own mind. He rejoined the Raverats in London. They saw him off at Victoria, and a line he had underscored in his Donne best serves to describe his state, stricken in mind—

As gold falls sick being stung with mercury.

II

His train pulled into Paris very late. He was met by Fräulein van Rysselbergh, and at her apartments in the Rue Laugier he slept for eight hours while she changed his money, reserved a seat for him in the train to Nice, and wired Mrs. Brooke. By the fire he glanced through a manuscript of André Gide's which he had borrowed from Raverat, and wrote to Ka.

I want so to turn altogether to you and forget everything but you, and lose myself in you, and give and take everything—for a time. Afterwards— doesn't matter. But I'm so wanting that security of Heaven. I'll make myself so fine for you. And I'll find and multiply all the many splendours in you.

In three weeks he would make himself fit for her. 'If the carriage is hot and horrible tonight, I shall think of your eyes and hands and mouth and body and voice, and sleep instantly and happily.' Her reassurance was the only tonic.

It's so funny the two things combining—that I'll give you things you never dreamt of and you'll make me the wonderfullest person in the world, *and* that you've those funny blue infantile eyes that almost shame one. That you should be at the same time both everything in the world *and* Ka. I love you so. I kiss your lips.

That evening he found himself in a railway carriage with a talkative Duchess and her maid, and Bonnard, the painter. At Nice he was met by Mrs. Brooke, Alfred, and a mound of luggage. Perhaps the wire from Paris had been a little too disturbing. At any rate Mrs. Brooke had decided that there was nowhere in Nice suitable for an invalid. Rupert must be taken straight to Cannes. She had already booked a room with a balcony at the Hotel du Pavillon. They took the next train. 'It's all so precisely what I expected,' Rupert was writing to Ka next day. 'The Ranee pushing my book in the English portions of Cannes, and bawling English with incredible success to crumbling foreigners. She has also entirely subdued eight solitary and separate maiden ladies in this hotel.' There were tropical palms below the window, a fountain playing, and many orange trees. He couldn't read for more than two hours a day. 'Patience and water-colours give me occupation. Why aren't you here to teach me knitting?' He went on:

I find myself—what *is* this degradation?—wanting you at each moment, to tell you exactly what I think about what I'm reading or about some person. The pleasure of telling you about things is so extraordinarily great. What does it mean? Keeping telling you everything would, it seems, make such a wonderful and golden background for everything else between us. I've such a longing to get out of myself, my tight and dirty self—to put it all out in the sun, the fat sun. And it's so hard to tell the truth, to give one-self wholly away, even to you. So one wants to chatter and pour everything out . . . and then perhaps truth may slip out with it.

Oh, I lie and am placidly stupid; and I'm hardly ever touched by that uneasiness. I've put everything away, and I'm concentrating on getting well. Two dangers I see. There's the danger of writing too long letters to you, every day. I *will* be continent. And there's the danger of too great vitality and avidity. Sometimes as I lie and pant like an overfed puppy, thoughts of you and Munich and—I don't know what, storm so irresistibly in; and I can't help feeling such amazing energy and life in all my limbs and mind, that I'm racked to be up and off to meet you at the Hauptbahnhof. You go burning through every vein and inch of me, till I'm all Ka; and my brain's suddenly bursting with ideas and lines and flames, and my body's all for you. 'Sh-sh.' I hold myself in, and wait, and grow fatter. But I'm certainer than ever that I'm, possibly, opening new Heavens, like a boy sliding open the door into a big room; trembling between wonder and certainty.

He was aware now of the roots of his unease throughout last year. Not having the strength of will to break away from either of the two women he loved, he had wronged them both. 'I couldn't give to either of two such people what I ought, which is "all".' But now he seemed to have found a 'sort of peace'.

I'm more sane, a little, about the world. Oh, far from sane: but better. I'm convinced that sanity is the most important thing there is. I'm so hampered and spoilt because there are things I dare not face, and depths I daren't look into. The sane person can go anywhere and imagine and write anything. By God! *you're* sane, with your splendid strength and beauty. But I've been half-mad, alone. Oh, it's all mixed up with this chastity, and everything's a whirl, and still I'm mad and tiny and frightened. But I'm clambering up to sane light. You've given me such sanity already—sometimes when you didn't know it. But you will give me more. I'll be able to do everything and look at everything, if you'll give me that strength. Oh, give it me Ka! It'll be for a time. Afterwards you may give what you've made of me out to the world; and anything may happen—, no harm can, then.

For some days he was too weak to write much or read. By Wednesday she would be installed in the Nikolai Platz at Munich, but on this Sunday evening, as he sat writing again, he imagined her at the play in Oxford. 'It *is* funny that you should be in that great dark building listening to *Œdipus*, and I in a bedroom over the Mediterranean.' Had she ever written a paper on the Greek dramatists? he wondered. He could just imagine what it would be like, not the actual words, 'but the furry atmosphere of your inconsecutive ideas,' and would her generosity of spirit find excuses even for Kreon? 'And would you find Kreon "nice"?' Then came Monday 15th when he ventured out for his first walk, leaning on Alfred's arm. At about the same time, he knew Ka was being seen off by Justin at Victoria.

He was feeling stronger. 'You should see my hands! They're so plump. I'm almost indistinguishable from you, in your most careless days, round and jovial.' About twice a day he had fears that he might never be able to drag himself to Munich. 'I couldn't bear that. I'd die, really,' but for most of the time he lay wondering what they would work on together when they met—a book on Socialism and Marriage, or better still, a play—'We solemnly sit down (in my fancy) at a neat desk and discuss scenarios'—but he mustn't forget that this letter would be awaiting her in Munich. She should go and see *The Seagull* at the *Lustpielhaus* and *Der Rosenkavalier* should be bought and read before it is seen. 'Later, we'll go together,' and then about getting on trams: 'it's so important. The gate *lifts*. You might have an accident.'

Sometimes he felt curiously trapped in the present moment. 'I can

scarcely remember back before a fortnight ago. And often—generally
—I can't see forward more than a month. I want to look beyond; but
your breasts and neck and voice are in the way.' And all the while his
reliance on her grew more complete. 'Loving you implies a geometrical progression.'

One gets worse and worse. You grow on one, so. It's a pervading, irresistible thing, 'Ka'. It's like having black-beetles in the house. 'I've got Ka
in the body . . . My dear, I've tried *everything* . . . Put down carbolic. My
dear, *Yes*! . . .' So, I tell you, I get frightened. Where's it to stop? Am I to
plunge deeper and deeper, for ever? Damn you! And it's so nice to—sometimes nice even if you don't care and won't have anything to do with me
(save pity). That's queer. I'm happy; but also I'm frightened, Ka.

You and your letter! One of the reasons, I always suppose, I get deeper
and deeper in, is that I *know* you—what you're like, and the whole good
truth (=facts) of you. And then comes along something quite unexpected,
that I'd never conceived to be in you, some queer corner in that round.
And I'm tumbled over. Who'd have thought that you had a prose-style that
was a superior combination of The Old Testament and poor Mr. Wilde.
'Virginia was more fantastic than an army of apes and peacocks.' What an
image! *What* a mind! God! I wish I could write like that!

I shall finish this tomorrow morning. I've a faint idea, oh! less than a hope,
there may be a card or note from you tomorrow: crawling round through
Nice or somewhere—though you *have* stupidly lost my address. *Die unfähige
Ka!* Oh, I don't really expect one tomorrow—posted, it'd have to be,
Saturday evening (and you tired). I thought it out, that you might send me
news from your retirement at Woking, writing comfortably on Sunday . . .
posting perhaps on Monday or via Nice . . . I shall get excited—oh, infinitesimally—at the approach of the Wednesday posts. I expect nothing till
Thursday morning.

Oh, and you, Devil, were tired on Thursday night! I wish I knew how you
were now. On Friday night I think you were being tired, somehow. I had
the horrors, then; so I think may be something was happening to you.
Were you . . . But I had the horrors. And again čuriously, this afternoon
(but that may be because I dreamt, horribly, all last night, about you—no,
not altogether horribly; only some. But you were at Woking, asleep).

After her first day in Munich he wrote as if his *alter ego* had been
her travelling companion across the Channel. 'Being asleep, I
couldn't know if you were sick; but I thought you looked greenish as
you stood waiting to land. I looked in on you from time to time as you
crashed through Germany.' He scribbled his thoughts, and as the day
wore on, the sense of tension, as of repressed hysteria, which he had
experienced at Lulworth, came slowly back. There had been no letter
from her for some time. He left his own unsealed, so as to go on with
it next day, and retired to bed after what seemed an endless afternoon

of gathering depression. He woke early next morning, unaccountably frightened, and resumed his letter.

Friday morn.

Damn! A Bad Night. It followed on Depression yesterday. For five hours yesterday I was convinced that it was all something right inside the head, and that I was either going to have a stroke, or else going slowly mad. It may be true: and one's so damnably helpless. Any other illness, one can suddenly shut one's teeth and one's hands and throw off. One can say 'I'm *not* going to be ill any more' and one isn't. But madness—means that it isn't up to 'one' to say anything. And yesterday (and part of today) I felt a cloud in my head and about me that seemed to mean it too certainly . . .

Again he left the letter open, thinking, perhaps, that later in the day he might have better news to send.

Friday even.

In Munich and in health these plaints sound silly, I guess. But here it's always raining, and I'm alone, in a way, and I'm fighting such a bloody slow hopeless sort of fight, and there's a long time in the day that it feels entirely one of the credible things—like fine weather tomorrow, or 30 seats on the second ballot, or anything ordinary—that I am going mad. Oh, my dear, I find I'm still so ill and weak. And oh! I'm so far from you.

I'll write other things. For there's many hours in the day when I'm cheerful—knowing I will get to Munich, whatever happens, so that something, oh, my God, and perhaps all—will be all right.

I went to a Classical Concert at the Casino: this afternoon. Music, you know, has more of a nervous appeal than most things—directly in a queer way—even for the *unmusikalisch*. So at first I nearly gave in. But I stuck it out—it's part of a long scheme to hoodwink the Ranee. And the after effects are that I'm brighter than the rest of the day. You know it's *doing* things—mildly—and not thinking that may pull me out in time. Damn the rain!

He had slipped out during the afternoon and spent hours searching for a Munich newspaper that might give him some idea of the plays or concerts she could be going to. The only morning post was a fan-letter forwarded from his publisher. Someone had been so intrigued by the harsh criticism of the poem *A Channel Passage* that she had bought the book so as to form her own opinion and found that her money was well spent. But there was nothing more from Ka. Perhaps she was at a loss to know how to answer. 'Do not consider yourself bound to write me at equal length,' he assured her, 'I desire very short, but not too infrequent statements of your existence and happiness.' The thought of their one day having a son had never crossed his mind until she had mentioned it. 'Why do I imagine his arms unusually long? Pince-nez; Damn! Do you know, I lie for *hours* trying to put the walk, the gait, together. I *can't* quite imagine it.' And he added a few lines after supper. 'I'll not do much more tonight. I sniff a letter from you nearing Cannes.'

He was right. The morning brought another of her 'kind cold letters'. It did him small good. He was no better, and there was Ka quoting Gwen Raverat's comforting opinion of him and reminding him of 'the young Apollo, golden haired' in Mrs. Cornford's epigram, which had come out in her book. The irony of this compliment must have tasted bitter.

You and your permanent thinking. I *don't* understand, of course. But I'm still mad and scary, incapable of any impersonality. Oh, Ka, I wanted to come so strong and clean and sane and well to Munich and to pay back a bit by helping you—in both ways, by common sense and the other subconscious business. I could. But I'm not getting better. I'm only just what I was 10 days ago: and 10 days more'll see the end of January. And I don't want to come ill and foolish and beastly as I was, to weaken and worry you and sponge on your strength. And yet I *can't* keep always away and let everything drift by and get worse and worse, for not seeing you. What shall I do? I think the sight and presence of you might put me right again in a day or two. It's so ghastly lying here, struggling and thinking, fruitlessly, while these gray days go by; and nothing but your tired, kind cold letters to stay me. Oh, my dear, I'm sorry. I know we're waiting and you're thinking and I oughtn't to bother or complain. I've no faith and no strength. If only you were with me an hour, I'd get both; if you were with me a day, I'd be well again; a year, and I'd be the most wonderful person in the world.

Gwen once thought me 'sane' did she? I've always enjoyed that healthy, serene, Apollo-golden-haired, business. But, my dear, our relationship's based a bit deeper! My face—do what you like with it. But you, and only you in the world, understand my horrible nature. It's so importantly my humiliation and my—safety, joy, what is it called? I may be, and shall be, perhaps, sane and everything else one day. But, the dirty abyss I am now—I've let you see. Don't pretend you don't know me, fool.

I suppose I oughtn't to post this. I think I shall. I'll write better, tonight and tomorrow. I think, soberly, I am a trifle better today—if it matters.

It was Saturday the 20th when at last he posted his long serial letter. It ended, 'Does one still say "with love"?' and by that evening he had realized that once again he might have frightened her, even forfeited something of her esteem, by unloading his misery on her with such abandon. 'I'm just writing for half an hour this evening to put myself in a better light.' So now he was sick with self-abasement.

You have been so wonderfully nice, your presence has been so cool and happy to me, these weeks when I've been a devil to you—I'm ingratitude, dirty, dirty, dirty—

One changes so, if one's ill and on a rainy Riviera. Two nights ago I had (after German consultation with Evelyn) a Hot Bath. I was so radiant, getting out of it. I almost rushed to you. I looked at myself, drying, in the glass, and I thought my body was very beautiful and strong, and that I was keeping it and making it splendid for you. And I knew that if I rested a night on your breasts, and then caught fire from you, my mind and heart too would be able to give you a million things that only I in the world knew of and could give. I was so happy. I was happy thinking of Munich . . .

And then at other times I lie and *ache* to twist my thoughts on to Shakespeare, a poem—anything; and they always go back to the blackness, till I can't bear it and from thinking of suicide then, think of it immediate, to cut the thing clear and set you free from a fool.

Eh, I *do* want your presence, you know, to keep me fine and sane, just now.

But tonight I *know* I shall get to Munich. I can see the Ranee thinks she's going to keep a hand on me for a month or six weeks. But I give her ten days at the outside. I shall have to be beastly to her, I suppose.

At such a time as this it was odd that another review of his poems should turn up, and one that came near to striking home. 'Ineffectively ugly and unpleasant'? Perhaps, but the critic also said that it was 'enormously to his credit that he has managed to stagger free from convention'. He went on with his letter, quoting: 'But if he is content with the merely—

'surface freedom of speech and manner; if he is content with his present Puritan ignorance of passion and his own body, and pursues the phantom of sensation, his power of concentration will gradually leave him, he will stagger back into the conventional fold, and eventually, sick of "mad magenta minutes", be received into some great hospital (Rome?) for men's souls . . .' He may, on the other hand, it appears, turn out a Poet. There's a lot more; Yes. It's what a gentleman in the *Observer* thinks about

> Your lover
> RUPERT

It was probably at this point that he wrote to James Strachey. 'I thought I was mad for two days. But it's now doubtful . . . It seems incredible I should ever be in fair health again.' He tried to explain.

The Ranee mixing my Ovaltine was alarmed to see me get out of bed a few minutes past ten last night and stand hands folded and head bent, and my lips moving—ruby—buzz—vacuum—they framed. She made no comment. It's part (I've discovered) of the Treatment to pretend that nothing I do is out of the way. Dare say I often get out of bed at the worser moments.

He was obviously in better spirits. 'How vain, most adorable creature, is the pursuit of pleasure in the absence of an object to which the mind is entirely devoted,' begins a letter to Ka written in the same artificial vein throughout. 'I am always desirous to be alone; since any sentiments for Katharine are so delicate, that I cannot bear the apprehension of another's prying into those delightful endearments with which the warm imagination of a lover will sometimes indulge him, and which I suspect my eyes then betray.' One may as well cut to the concluding paragraph.

Can I tell you with what eagerness I expect the arrival of that blest day, when I shall experience the falsehood of a common assertion, that the greatest human happiness consists in hope? A doctrine which no person had ever stronger reason to believe than myself at present, since none ever tasted such bliss as fires my bosom with the thoughts of spending my future days with such a companion, and that every action of my life will have the glorious satisfaction of conducing to your happiness.

Speaking in his own voice, he began another letter on the same day. 'You are quite the nicest person in the world, and absolutely right. And I am a beast and a toad.' He was delighted with her account of life in Munich. 'I did it all, so exactly, you know, a year ago. That Post Office business—well, well! Reflect, when the panics come, on the figure of me suffering likewise, only more gauntly—very red in the face; consider me conscious, in Cannes, of your paroxysms, and giggling . . .'

Oh my dear Ka, Ka with that particular hair and head and neck, and a certain walk, and a special way the clothes have of going down over the hip, and strong hands, and a hundred other things, Ka peering about and saying 'Hoo!', Ka whom I know so very well, and whom I've been so beastly to, and whom I love so, I wish I could see you, red streamers out and head a little forward and solemn-eyed, Ka-ing down past the *Siegers-Thor* and the Library and eyeing the *Residenz* and noting the ladies in charge of the streets and round with joy at four Bavarian privates doing the goose-step salute past an officer (is that still to come?) and finally poking [in at] *Theatiner-strasse* and tentatively buying soap—a laborious 'Wie viel?' and then the tender of 10 marks to be changed, to cover your ignorance of their reply. I wish I could see you.

She had met someone, she said, who confessed she had been in love with him a year ago. 'So she and "all Munich" are still in love with me? Can it be?' he replies, 'A whole year. These things must last longer in Deutschland. I'll endeavour not to feed their passions. I've developed an extraordinary monogamy of soul-tone lately—a pathetic and belated offering, my dear.' He advises her on what to say when she comes up against the *avant garde* intellectuals—'pour out a few names, Van Gogh, Cézanne, Matisse, Derain . . . Wonderful the effect'll be, and the result cheap at the price. Try it.'

He held this letter over until next day. 'A little sun this morning. And this afternoon we go to tea at the California. Mr. Arthur Balfour, Mr. and Mrs. Arnold Bennett, the Ranee, myself—England in a nut-shell.' There follow some rough ideas for plays they might work on together, and, after an interval 'I've been weighed at Mrs. Ginners. I've put on 7½ pounds in 12 days. Glory! . . . Each letter from you puts on a pound.' Then, harking back to his alleged old flame of last year, he can barely conceal his irritation.

Damn Joanna and my cheeks. I never even let her kiss them. Why am I old and dead and ugly, and why do they think me a lovely child. The Rev. W. Christie on Wednesday thought I was twenty-one. And old Mrs. Woolaston (of whom more later) thought Alfred and I were twins aged eighteen, she confided in mother in the *Salle de Lecture* after I'd tottered to bed. 'He has a skin like a girl's—He looks very like a girl . . . in his *Face*' put in Miss Barclay.

God! God!

On Monday there was nothing from her by the usual post. Of course she was busy, enjoying herself, making new friends. He began to grow aware of a very slight unease at the back of his mind.

My dear, with your resting and your work, you can stand solitude a bit; so, Ka dear, *don't* get mixed up and dutifully socially entangled with a lot of people. Say you've a *devilish* lot of work to do. They'll all be freezing on to you, because you're so divinely the nicest person in Europe, these Grahams and Poultons and things. And then, when I come, you'll always be con-scientiously disappearing, '. . . besides, they're really quite nice, you know' —Ka dear, *don't*, for God's sake! Let's have those few days—apart from work, etc., for laughing over Munich. We'll descend on a German or two, out of our fastnesses; but let's have each other. So don't, for once, be so wicked and unfeeling and unimaginative, as to be soft. You've done enough harm with your tolerance.

He pulled himself up in time, catching sight of the tie she had given him, on the way to Victoria.

Indoors (resting).

I'm really getting on very well: my body ('nerves'). But I wish you were here to look after my soul. It'd pay the Ranee (if only the poor dear knew!) to pay you to telegraph, say four times a day; once 'I am very well; and you?', and once 'Goodnight', and once 'Munich is so very nice', and once, if you cared, perhaps 'Noch lieb'ich dich'. She could balance the cost by knocking off my extra milk and baths: and I'd be 15 stone in no time.

We get on very well, the Ranee and I. Half the day she spends in reproducing to me verbally her conversations of the other half. She's only still a little sore about my tie. She says it is 'so conspicuous'. I pretend it is my only one. And it is understood that (a yellow like that!) I bought it at Liberty's on my way through.

Having rested, he went out, leaving his letter unfinished, and when he got back there was a telegram from Munich. He was taken completely off his guard. The news that Ka had just read his letter of last Friday, the one written in a slough of despond, had taken fright and decided to leave at once for Cannes, was altogether much too much of a good thing. For the next few days the developing situation tottered precariously on the border-line of farce. A passage in his budget to Munich of a few days later describes the opening episode.

Oh, I am a beast.

We went up to a distant hotel that afternoon, Monday, to tea. We successfully saw Mr. Balfour! Returning, we found no train, so we had to walk a long way. We got back here at six. The Ranee solicitous. I was to lie down till dinner. But your telegram was waiting. (I don't know when it arrived.) I stared at it—it required some taking in. 'Nothing'—I answered, '—er—from James, you know: about a thing . . .' We both talked to Mrs. Digby a minute. Then I slid swiftly to the door, muttering vaguely 'Just answer it, you know . . . take a tram.' The Ranee was half in tears. But I'd gone. There weren't any trams. (It's only half a mile.) I thought and thought, as I walked.

I'd provisionally settled the Ranee, if you did come. It was to be that you were on your way from England to Italy and had so kindly come a rather longer way to see if I wasn't better. What simpler?

While Mrs. Brooke was left wondering what in heaven's name this frantic to-and-froing of urgent correspondence was about (if indeed she did not suspect the simple facts of the case already, for by now there should be no need to state that she was no fool) Rupert dashed round the corner and despatched a telegram:

Telegram partly unintelligible for heavens sake don't come on account of me or my letters was mad and wicked other letters on way am much better if however your own business can meet any train love.

This accomplished, he could only return to the hotel, praying that he had not acted too late, and go on with the letter he had left in mid-air when the moment came to leave for tea with Mr. Balfour.

Just back to find your telegram. And now from telegraphing; I must send this tonight, in case you don't come: as I hope.

For I diagnose that my beastly letter upset you. I'm worthy of treading to death in dung. I *was* ill, and am a bit; but I'm much better. I *will* get to

Munich in a week. I'm really all right: only very rarely morbid. I'm so sorry. If it's other business, to tell me some best or worst—But it can't be.

This he posted, then in bed next morning started again. There was always, of course, the faint possibility that it wasn't so much his 'desperate' letter which had prompted her telegram as something else, unknown to him—or a combination of both. He was worried.

Oh, Ka, my dear, I wish I knew what has happened. I suppose I shall know tomorrow or the day after. You see, it may be that you've something sudden to tell me—I can't see that as between you and me anything so sudden can have happened, but you may be affected in some other way from outside, so as to affect us . . . Or it may be, as I think, my letter, which you'd get this morning.

If it's that, you see, I've tried to stop you . . . The journey's 32 hours or more: and a damn awkward one. And if you suddenly appeared there'd have to be such very difficult explanations with the poor Ranee: which might tie our hands rather— Oh, you see, it all wouldn't do, when one's like this and in this place. My dear, I solemnly swear I *will* come to Munich, whatever happens (short of your forbiddance).

Then follow minute details of the alternative routes to Munich. She is advised to buy a continental Bradshaw as a supplement to his suggestions. Genoa—Milan—Verona—Brenner Pass—Innsbruck—Munich—32 hours at the least. He could never do it without breaking his journey for a night. What about her meeting him half-way? 'Innsbruck, or over the top to Verona! Ka, you can pop into a train at Munich *Hauptbahnhof* at 8.45 in the morning and be in Verona at 7.41 that night, or Milan at 11! Or Munich 20 minutes before noon and Verona at 11. Or if you'd rather sleep than read Dostoevsky and see the Pass and the Alps, you get in at 10.40 at night, you meet Romeo at 10 next morning! Ka! we'd meet in Verona and I'd show you the Scaliger tombs and the Amphitheatre (Venice only two hours off!) . . . It'll cost you £2, which I shall pay . . . *Do* do it. You can. You must!' Then back to the possible consequences of Friday's fatal letter. 'I can see, I fancy, it all working up: as your letters come, and I'm helpless to stop it, because it's really 48 hours ago . . . But to have worried you—I ought to go off and never let you think or hear of me again. I'm too foolish and mean for you to spoil yourself about.'

Tuesday afternoon, and still no answer to yesterday's wire. Expecting any moment to see Ka bursting in with a look of grave anxiety on her face (only matched by the corresponding look on the Ranee's) there was nothing to do but fill in time and paper-space with news of the day.

No: I don't give readings, or even talk cricket. I'm not known as a poet.
Mother let out one evening, after I'd gone to bed, that I was going to take
up 'writing' as a profession. But it hasn't been referred to. And old Miss Fox,
who is so fond of me, thinks I look like William Poel, whom she's also *so*
fond of, knows his family. She took me aside, in fact, and said she knew all
about William's married life 'which has been very strange, yes, and interesting'. I was highly excited; listened attentively for 40 minutes. All she could
tell me was that he had had two children (one died) and his wife is a great
invalid. I professed enthusiasm.

As one Fabian to another, the opinion of the lounge on Keir Hardie
might be worth relating. Then followed a summary of the day's
routine.

And there aren't many Colonels. One Anglo-Indian (old Hullar) but a
very progressive one. 'That fellow, *Keir-Hardie*, now, you know. Of course,
what he says is poison. Poison, Sir! But there's a dear old friend of mine,
old John Simple (Sir John Simple) (one of the best chaps), who has a province out in Bengal; and, y'know, he had to entertain the fellow—Keir-
Hardie. He didn't like the idea, one bit. But, you know, he told me afterwards, that he really wasn't at all a bad chap, just like anyone else, quite a
decent chap to have stay with you. Really! 'Straordinary, isn't it? Oh, I'd
like to get to know some of these Labour Leaders, as they call them. I
sometimes think perhaps we don't hear both sides of the questions, down at
Cheltenham, you know.'

The Ranee gets madder daily. She now runs the whole Hotel. I am lost in
wonder: and more determined than ever that she must marry Gerald. I have
never met two people so made for one another. He will be Prime Minister
in 1922.

It will give me extraordinary pleasure to tell you my whole day.

At about 8 I wake. Till nine I drowse. At 9 there is a knock and the Lift-
boy brings a letter from you. I kiss it dimly and put it unopened in the bed
(the shutters are still shut, against mosquitoes) and murmur, in a rather
maudlin way, about you, till 9.10. Then Evelyn appears with hot water: and
hurls the shutters open. I remark in German that it's still bloody weather.
She agrees with immense vivacity. At 9.15 Fritz appears with

> Chocolate
> Four Rolls
> One Egg.

As he vanishes I get out and wash and produce the Ranee's private jam
from the wardrobe. I return to bed, search it for your letter, and open letter
and egg together. Funny about ritual. I eat and drink very slowly; laughing
slightly. Your letters are so *very* like you, you know. And I can visualize it
all. Also, it's so extremely nice that you really were writing to me two days
ago.

It's gloomy coming to an end of one of your letters. But then one reads it
again; or yesterday's for a change. And there's such a quantity of acute

pleasure to be got out of them—your letters. I get very pleased and well, and swallow great cups of chocolate, saying (in a mixture of frightenedness and triumph) 'She does, you know, love me. Ka! It *will* be all right!' . . . etc.

At 9.45 I'm towards the end of breakfast. The Ranee knocks. I conceal your letter and make out I'm reading *The Dynasts*. She enters in a magenta dressing-gown and brings yesterday's *Continental Daily Mail* (which appears with her breakfast). For an hour I alternately read the Mail and lie thinking.

11. Ovaltine and milk mixed by the Ranee who finds me writing to you and rebukes me for writing so much.

I write till 11.30; get up: and totter down to the front. Once in seven days it's not raining, and then I watch a lady of seven dressed as a Turk, in exquisitely baggy trousers. She is white and scarlet and digs the sand in a delicate, unEnglish manner.

Déjeuner opposite the Ranee 12.30–1.15. I eat enormous quantities of flesh. She tells me what Mrs. Woolaston has been doing.

(This is all so very dull, I find. I'm sorry. You see, I'm kind of hung-up. Are you on the way here? What's happening? I don't know what to write.)

1.15–1.45.	General conversation in the lounge. (Prices and weather and that Lloyd George.)
1.45–3.	(or less) totter out.
3–4.	Rest (writing).
4–5.	We make Tea in here and read the *Daily News Précis* of Mrs. Woolaston.
5–6.	*The Times*, alone, in Salon.
6–7.	Write.
7–8.	Eat.
8–9.	Read the Dynasts.
9.	Hot Bath.
10.	Goodnight.
12 or 1.	Sleep.

By God! it is dull and mean: now I look.

10–12 p.m. is the dangerous hour: you know.

That's how I've lived these later, well, days. I'm really so very much better; and ashamed of myself. I feel so very well and strong. I keep fairly well off the horrors—because I only think of Munich and seeing you again. And I've a sort of shaky, misty, convalescent confidence that all's come right.

There were two days when I had to fight every second during an hour's dinner to prevent myself fainting, and then come up here afterwards to lie and think I should not get to Munich, that you'd go back to London, and——

I should never see Ka again, you see.

But I'm all right now: healthy and happy. And I'm *going* to come. And I'm not going mad, anyhow till after I've seen you, which is all that matters. Verona, you've written about that?

Tuesday evening and still no acknowledgement of his wire. 'I'm afraid you've ridiculously started. If you suddenly appear, I know I shall cry.' And he ended his long letter: 'Hope. Do you know about it?

A drunkenness. *That* once kept me from sleeping. Goodnight. I love you so'—then Alfred ran out to post it and send yet another telegram.

But by Wednesday morning, although there was a letter posted long before, there was still no evidence whatever that he had succeeded in preventing her making the journey to Cannes.

And here's your letter; and no telegram. And I don't know if you're at Munich, Verona, Paris, Genoa, Marseilles or just outside my door.

Nor do I know what the Ranee'll make of it. Oh God, I wish I could have a telegram. You see, if you *didn't* start you ought to have wired in answer to mine; if you *did* start, you ought to have wired *en route* to say when you were coming. ('Ought' not *moral*, my dear; but sc. 'by the laws of Causation'.)

As evening came, the suspense grew, and he found himself more than ever in the paradoxical situation of living in dread of the sight of the one person he longed to see.

(You make me feel horribler than ever.) I sit and wonder which of these carriages you're in.

You may come by the 1.12 (from Genoa) or the 1.50 (from Paris).

But I shall post this, in case; and to fill this post.

I've been to Cooks to find out about trains to Munich. I *think* I shall have to go by a *train de luxe* as far as Milan or Verona. Verona noon (preferably) or midnight. And then you! (unless you're round the corner!)

I'm such a mixture of feelings, just now. This may get to you after you've been four days in this hotel!

He had just got back from posting this when at last her telegram arrived. She was safe and well in Munich. That much he knew long ago. The crucial part of the message was if anything more tantalizingly obscure than before. 'Corresponding with English telegrams between France and Germany, my dear, is a Symbol of All Human Communication. I've been working at it . . . "Did give a ten mark piece for the soop". That's hard.'

'Give' I thought must be 'owe'. You owed me, or I you, 10/– [i.e. Ten shillings] for these telegrams. True, but pointless, you know. Then I thought of it in your silly writing. 'Give' of course. 'Did give a ten mark piece for the soop.' Interesting. But I felt something underlay it. Suddenly, in a conversation with old Mrs. Fox, I involuntarily said 'I'd!' Very loud. 'What?' said Mrs. Fox. 'The Ides of March,' I stammered. 'Shakespeare, you know—but please go on, Mrs. Fox, what did *you* say, when *she* said *that*?'

It was hilariously frustrating to be alone with the knowledge that Ka would give ten marks for the soop. 'I've such a feeling of baulked tenderness. I feel sure it's sure to be something very nice; and that I should love you more than ever if I knew. The soop. Too recondite.

I've tried similar words. Soot. Poop. Shop . . .' However, the wire had succeeded in conveying to him that she would come and fetch him if he were too ill to make the journey himself, so he now felt the moment had come to start preparing the ground for his departure.

At lunch I plucked up my courage and tackled the Ranee. My dear, an awful scene. Where had I been? it carelessly began. 'Walking' . . . I was so uninterested.

'To the Hotel de Ville?' She is always relentless for facts.

'Further . . . to Cook's.' The words were, rather than became. Her agitation was suddenly manifest. What *could* I want there? I was looking up trains. 'Trains?' 'For Munich.' She didn't know I wanted to go straight on there. I oughtn't to go there for at least two months.

I was pretty despondent. I couldn't say 'But, my good woman, Ka's got a bare *four weeks* from today!' I felt the old helplessness before authority creeping over me: and wished you had emerged from the morning train. But I aped cold astonishment and colder reserve. And she began to crumble. I conveyed that I hated Cannes, her, the sea; that I should rest superbly in Munich, so quiet and healthy.

So battle's joined. She wants to wire Dr. Craig for a forbiddance. By God, I *will* come.

There was still some uncertainty. 'The poor Ranee's perhaps right that I ought to have two months more. But, you know, circumstances make it impossible! I've got out of the abysses fairly well. I'm up and down, 'twixt a certain despair and immense vitality.' Her recent letters had sustained him. 'I felt so sure you loved me as I did you,' and he was drawing strength from the knowledge of her concern for him. 'I lie (or sit) and find that it's when we (in my brain) swing inwards, turn round and in, towards each other, and the complications and distant views and hypothetical next-year-but-ones and the world are shut away, that it's so wonderful.' His reliance on her was absolute. 'Be kind to me the first day or two we meet. I'm wanting to run to you, being tired, and, restored, hide in you for a bit, helpless and unthinking. I can't really rest, you know, anywhere else.'

The day passed in a state of lull after suspense, with Bridge after dinner, his mother presiding, then before bed the writing of a report on his condition. 'It's like ski-ing. One doesn't know how far down one came: till one starts plodding up again.'

You know, when I write, just nowadays, I find myself not wanting to do anything but write your name, again and again, as I $\left\{ \begin{array}{l} \text{whisper} \\ \text{call} \end{array} \right\}$ it, and write that I wish we were together, and that I love you . . . It's absurd. I love you in so many ways, in a day, now. One after the other. Not all, you know, tired—whining. Don't believe me only that beaten thing you could only pity, that December evening.

Madness: yes. I think I've got over that idea. It seemed to account for everything so perfectly; and there were things—I can tell you everything, when I'm with you. You're the only person in the world, Ka, I can tell everything to. It's an amazing feeling. I've never told anyone anything, hardly. 'Secretive.' I've a curious feeling of safety. If I show you the whole of me, I can scarcely show you worse than you've seen. I think I've said all this before in another letter.

I don't really know, even, how ill or well or mad or sane or good or bad I am till I'm with you again. All's waiting now. In a few days . . .

He left the letter open, and continued it in bed next morning. 'It's mad, mad, mad, that we shouldn't be together; *now*, and continually.' She still hadn't decided between Verona and Milan, so Bradshaw was again resorted to, and her spare time in either place prior to his own arrival, organized; if Milan, the cathedral; if Verona, booking rooms in an hotel. Then a postscript.

One thing, wherever you come to meet me, *bring a German postcard*: I shall immediately write on it and enclose it to Munich to be posted. You must find someone for me to enclose it to. Hugh, perhaps.

It was convenient that Hugh Russell-Smith of his remote boyhood at Rugby, happened to be in Munich. His presence there was already planted as the pretext for a trip to Munich. There was no need to say that it was neither the only attraction nor the principal one.

It was now Thursday, January 25. He did not write until after dinner.

Very little tonight. This'll reach you Sunday morning—with luck it may be my last letter that gets you!

I'm such a coward, when I'm like this, you see. I sit opposite the Ranee with things on my tongue, and just daren't utter them; because it'd mean five minutes' row. But I *will* put it to her tomorrow 'Sunday' I shall say, 'Sunday night', and if there's too *awful* a row I'll yield hour by hour and day by day. But Monday or Tuesday or Wednesday morning I shall be seeing you.

She must be sure to bring a ruck-sack stuffed with clothes and Dostoevsky. He is going to eat a lot. He must. The Ranee *did* write to the nerve-specialist he had seen in London. 'Your son,' he replied, 'was obviously in a state of severe breakdown when I saw him. He was hypersensitive and introspective. He must not recommence literary work for some months yet.' How was that possible? Rupert asked. 'And I've such a damn good poem rustling away under the bracken, in my head. Introspective. Ha!' At about this point a telegram was delivered, saying she would meet him half-way, 'any hour, any place,' no details; and he must at once have dashed off a note and posted it before finishing his main letter of the day. 'There's only two seconds to write in. You see your telegram's come. I don't know what to do. I'm afraid I shall laugh all dinner-time: or sing . . .'

Once I meet you, I'm in your hands. I give up responsibility. You may do what you like. So choose *precisely* which you like; and wire on Saturday. 'Verona' or 'Milan': or if you've some additional details. Then I'll sometime wire the day. We meet on either station.

Ka! It will be good. I shall be infinitely gay and well. I look Italian. You look merely German.

Oh! but to see you again and touch you!

We shall be splendid.

Then an interlude while the Ranee bustles around, setting things in their place for the night, Alfred hovering at the door—he must have been sent out with the note that was just finished—then again Brooke is alone, feeling more sure of himself and Ka, more confident than ever that he was approaching hourly the blessed consummation of a long and slowly developing acquaintance.

It's Ka I'm going to see. You're going to make me so amazingly strong and fine. And I'm going to give you undreamt things.

When each hour and feeling, lying in front, is black and strange (only black with strangeness): it's so wonderful walking into them with another person, in this way, to talk to. That, damn it, doesn't express. I'm thinking about Companionship, when it's there as well as everything else.

One does get further and further in with you: as I've said. It's all very queer: looking quite remotely backwards. We toiled up the Andermatt toboggan-track together the second day. When we, alone, got to the top, you sat on the toboggan, looked out to your left (to the pass to Italy) and said, rather self-consciously, I thought, 'Damn!' I looked at you, and pondered what your (or any young woman's, but, then especially your) mind was like.

Then there was an evening in the late autumn of 1910 (I think then; anyhow before the first Lulworth). I know precisely where you were standing: by the curtain that screens the Door (in the Flat), your back to it and to the wall-edge, facing West. There were probably other people there: Jacques perhaps. You'd for some reason, got on a low dress. I looked at the firm and lovely place where your deep breasts divided and grew out of the chest and went down under the dress: your columnar neck rising above it, and Ka somehow behind or in it all . . . and I was suddenly very giddy, and physically hit with a glimpse of a new sort of beauty that I'd not quite known of . . .

'I wondered if you knew what was happening in those few seconds.'

When next they meet, what a difference. 'You're to be the Ranee and Dr. Craig and everything else! Good-night, dear. In a few days——' He turned out the light. She must now be to him both everything and everyone.

Next morning there were two letters from her at breakfast. One of them, unstamped. 'Dear old Ka! So the Ranee's had to pay 50 cents.' Once before this month he had had deliberately to subdue a slight sensation of disquiet. Here it was again. He couldn't altogether conceal it from her. Nor did he wish to. Or was he being unreasonable? All the same—

I'm bothered about your Wednesday ball. It's so likely that it'll clash with Verona, I see. Oh, Ka: I don't want to stay here two or three days longer than I need. And I don't want to make you not go to your ball through duty to the engagement for meeting me. And I don't want to hurry through Verona and get back to send you in bright yellow to a ball while I spend my first evening in solitude in an hotel; being jealous of you at a ball, with so many naked men there. Virgins like you, you know, give in immediately if they see a naked man.

Now he came to think of it, she hadn't yet made her decision about Verona. There was nothing about it in these last two letters. As for the ball, perhaps, on second thoughts, it didn't really matter much, either way.

I'll be very happy anyhow; so if you'd rather not break some Munich engagement, ball or other, you're to wire when you get this, if you haven't done, and if there's time.

I'd even wait at Verona! I've set my heart on it—on Italy—you know.

I expect I shall write a little by the next post. I ought to get up and go out now. A concert this afternoon: Mendelssohn and Mozart, Ravel and Saint-Saens. Very Cannes. I want to write you such great flaming letters. I know how mean and dull these are; and how little they're what I want to say. But I'm not really up to it yet; writing down things. It's so difficult and requires such power. Only don't think I'm as flat as I sound. And don't think I'm going to be as flat as I am. Health, you know, makes a great difference in those things . . . Even now, I know I love you more and more over-whelmingly than anyone ever can or has or will. There's a lot in me, I'll tell you, Ka. My strength all goes out to you. I blaze out more to you . . . Everything seems to be coming back. The other night, in the rain, a man was singing between my window and the sea. And suddenly I felt that shiver; and romance (the keenness and darkness and life) came back. I knew how dead and flat I'd been, how long. And walking home in the evening from the *Californie* on Monday (your telegram was waiting for me) I suddenly smelt. I hadn't smelt little things—trees and rain and the sea and wet gravel—for ages. It all goes for fuel.

CANNES

My God, if you'd stay with me, somewhere down on the coast by Venice, while the Spring woke: on and on! What we'd be, there! (Oh, there's cafés in Venice—Florian's in front of St. Mark's.)

I can see myself going up and up, these days and weeks in front. There's no stopping and with you in the Universe, and nearby.

While posting this he also sent a telegram—*Tuesday morning Milan or Verona wire dont sign come only if dance lets you oh my dear Verona*—and while still out took the opportunity of buying a ticket, although the point where he would break his journey to join up with her was still unsettled. He wrote again.

Friday night: in a hurry.

Awful scenes with the Ranee. But, as wired, I'm coming. At first she was horrified. Then in wild despair she came down to only a week. But I've bought the ticket!

I get into the train Monday evening (as you do).

I shall write tomorrow. My last letter.

My dear, it's so splendid.

I'll know tomorrow where we meet. I think the arrangements are obvious and fixed. I don't want you to wire too often: for suspicion's sake. *Anyhow* don't wire after 1 on Monday. The dance—I explained. I don't want you to miss it: and I don't want us to have to start Wednesday dawn for Munich. Que faire? But you'll decide—have decided. I'll be happy anyhow.

I'm rather tired—it's so beastly hurting people, as I do the Ranee. But it's got to be done. You'll 'look after' me so, when I tiredly fall into your arms in Italy. I wish I could tell her that. Three days from now I start. Within 90 hours I see you. My god! Italy!

Oh my dear; I must stop: and go to go on fighting. But all's so very well: because I'm to be seeing you. Everything leads to that.

—and before settling down for the night he began again:

My last letter to you: I think. Hands and lips, next. Only invalids know what time is. A hundred years have gone over since I saw you at Victoria. I've forgotten you, so. But I know that I'll find something so extraordinarily kind and lovely and comfortable. I've that long-ago feeling of a 'lap', a place you hid your face in, and shelved responsibilities. All's confused and tiring, and unimportant for a bit, in front: and then you! It's like the last ten minutes in a muddy House-match; or the last two miles on a long walk.

These things go on round, the Casino, and walking back in the rain, and Miss Barker on Mendelssohn, and Mrs. Digby on India, and Mrs. Fox at Bridge, and Ovaltine. But in 85 hours I'll see Ka. Tomorrow morning I shall get your letter written after hearing about Verona. I'm so excited. Friday night, I wonder what you're ridiculously doing now: reading German grammar, or at a theatre.

Oh my dear I'm going to rest so wonderfully these three days. And be so finely strong as I prance down the platform. You know, it would be too absurd for us to keep apart a second longer. It's been monstrous we've kept apart so long. I've even thought I ought to have hushed it all up (my 'nerves') and rested ten days in England and come straight to Munich. Only there were depths I got into, I couldn't fight in. And I, even I, was a little ashamed of trading on your strength and goodness. Even now, I feel at moments a bit, a bit ashamed—but, I think—know, that's irrelevant, nonsense, wicked even, between you and me. Isn't it?

Tuesday! I wonder how you'll find me? As much better as you thought? Will you be pleased or disappointed? I'm really so much better, I think, than three weeks ago: and yet something short of what I'll be.

'S! But we'll talk and laugh.

Oh, Ka, I *won't* be a bother to you this time, a whining baby on your hands. Please look forward to it only with happiness—and not a sigh too, that you've the great load of me to carry.

Oh, my dearest, it's so splendid in all the hurry and the doubts and the incompletions, and mistrust and funking, and sham to find one thing that stands out clear and certain and great. One thing clear in all the tangle. By God, it's good to have one thing you can take and shake in God's face, with 'Here's one thing that, without "ifs" and "mights", *is*!'!

I'm lying in bed now in this funny room (no, it's not very large). When I shut my eyes and whisper your name over, I can feel your hands and face and hair above and about me. Oh, you must be thinking of me now. You must know. I think of you in a million ways. I know just how you'd like one French family in this hotel better than any one else in the place, for a certain quality—I do, too. And I think of your eyes when you say something. And I think of your gentle strong soft body—my thoughts are entirely indecent and entirely clean. I see you with your head thrown back. I put my bare arm round your bare back; and my arm's infinitely strong and the curves of your back are the loveliest things in the world.

It must have been in the small hours of the morning when he started to play with the wild idea of Ka throwing up her responsibility for Hester (her elder sister and her principal tie in England) and following Munich with a tour of Greece and Spain, then eventually settling down in 'some English hut'.

We'd be able to then, with a good thing behind us. You'd have given me the strength and sanity, and I'd have given you—oh God, *something*! But that, now, for it's clear and good. Oh, Ka, we'll know even better soon, in Munich: and talk. But I know it! I know it! I know it!

Dearest, it's so late. I must sleep. I shall do so, happily and well. I'm all cool-burning with love for you. I know you so. Oh, I wish I could write—I couldn't even say it. But touching does. If you were here!

I kiss every inch, every inch of you and every thought of your heart.

Goodnight.

Next day the Ranee, a subdued figure, as she seems among all these fervent communications, quiet in her dignity, vexed and baffled, her relationship with Alfred becoming ever closer, one imagines, as Rupert is carried ever further away from her comprehension on his intermittent gusts of hysteria, comes at last to the conclusion that further obstruction—even for his well-being as she conceives of it—could only do more harm. She must have been afraid for him, and even, by now, secretly a little afraid *of* him—as he had always been of her, knit closely, both of them, in that most profound of all relationships, yet somehow dumb from the very start with the ache of incommunicable love. What else but just this, at the childhood root of the trouble, was driving her to distraction and her son to the borderline of insanity with the craving for he knew not what, although to him, no doubt, it must have seemed to be the simple agony of desire and nothing more?

Saturday morning. No news of Verona. But there were letters. 'The woman writes page after page,' James Strachey once wrote of Ka to Brooke, in the tone of voice that regards it as an endearing trait, 'but she tells one *Nothing*.' All this abundance of mail! It was rather sad, Rupert seems to have reflected, that if the Ranee were suspecting an entanglement with some young woman or other, she was almost certainly not only suspecting the wrong family but the wrong member of it. Her gently disparaging observations on Bryn Olivier fell wide of the mark.

He was going on with his page of the night before:
Saturday morning.

Ach! it's been so beastly. The Ranee was dispirited, and generous over money, and the rest. She's entirely given in. I suppose you're disliking me for it all. But what could I do? What would you have done?

Your letter of Wednesday night—Thursday morning, this morning. And one from poor Mr. Masefield. His writing's so far more feminine than yours. Your envelopes may be seen by the Ranee; she thinks they're from Hugh. But if she sees his—oh! she'll think it's the old story. Bryn, you know. Did I ever tell you that Hester's not the only one who knows the truth of my tragedy? Each time I get a telegram (and what with you and the Apostles there's a lot) the poor Ranee thinks that Bryn's so brilliantly (one can see her) going to swoop down and carry me off.

Well: in half an hour I go to be weighed: and get the Ranee's money. (I'll enclose my weight in a postscript.) So I'll end off. The Ranee's leaving for England on Wednesday: so we may dodge the postcard. But you must bring one, an envelope for it, and prepare someone to dispatch it from Munich.

Your duty's so very simple. You get into the 10.40 p.m. (having discovered from Cook's if it goes) on Monday night (I'll be at Nice·then) at Munich. Then we commence rushing towards each other. I suspect both trains'll go just a little faster than usual. If you settle on Verona: you get out at 10.0 Tuesday morning and go for 115 minutes stroll, then you return and I fall out of a carriage into your arms. If you've wired 'Milan' you (perhaps) change at Verona, and get to Milan at 12.25 p.m. There you'll see me waiting. We lunch hard by the Duomo. And if you decide not to come; you can be on the Munich platform at 10.14 Tuesday night.

But you are coming! I'm upset about the dance. But I'm leaving all to you. You *did* wire 'any day and hour'!

And then again a moment's shadow of that vague unease. 'You don't mind my letters, do you?—I mean it's so hard sometimes, to know how other people are feeling. Oh, but I know it's all right.' Perhaps she was going to muddle the date.

Everything's so very right, with you ahead. This next Tuesday, the 30th. Don't make any damned mistake of a week.

He had barely written his name at the foot of the page when the porter brought him a telegram. She had at last chosen the rendezvous. Verona! but he had just been weighed, and the thoroughly disappointing result was forcing the last protest out of the Ranee.

Damn! Weight only ⅛lb up, in a week. Ranee sicker than ever.

Your telegram has just come. (Ranee intercepted, but didn't read, of course. She's sure something's UP.) All's right, then. You'll get there at 10, wander till 11.55 and then meet me Verona. Tuesday.

From noon on Tuesday you're in command.

Auf wiedersehen!

Oh, if you *don't* appear I shall sit in the station, eating, till you do: or till a message does. You likewise.

You'll know all about hotels— You're to travel with a RUG, because the Brenner's *cold*.

Till Tuesday.

    R

I kiss you.

The plan worked. Just before noon on Tuesday, January 30, the train from Cannes pulled into Verona station. Rupert had his head out of the window. Ka was there, standing at the opposite end of the platform. He got out and ran. She saw him.

Chapter IX

THE ESTRANGING SEA

(*February 1912–September 1912*)

Scaliger tombs, the amphitheatre, as arranged; and at last each other's company, almost as imagined, but not quite. Something was missing. While Mrs. Brooke at the hotel, misunderstanding and misunderstood, cancelled her rooms for the next three weeks—she had bargained for a longer family sojourn by the sea—and packed for Rugby, her son, released from the necessity of having to put a face on it and contend—as gently yet as firmly as could be—with her opposition, lapsed from the perfervid and highly practical adventurer into the almost helpless apathy of an invalid. It was just such a state of passive indulgence rather than the ardours of a philanderer which he had really been longing for throughout those days of hectic correspondence. It was enough to be nursed with tender concern in an atmosphere free of restraint; nor would Ka on her part have been conscious of any anticlimax. The warmth of her nature, and her ready sympathy, which made it easier and more natural for her to afford the refuge of a mother rather than a lover, only encouraged him to do what most he wanted, give way and be a burden to her, the sort of burden that such women live to carry and would be lost without. He had her all to himself. Nothing else mattered, not even, after all these protestations, his continued chastity, which had once seemed to him to be the root cause of his collapse. Prostration of body and spirit, now that he had let himself go, some lingering vestige of respect for the old conventions (such as he would have denied with contempt) and, curiously, the sudden absence of the need, combined to bring these two without the least privation to the state of peace that others only reach through passion.

These reasons would be enough on Rupert's part, but on the other side there was another factor, something which he knew nothing of, and at present he was in no condition to be told. They sat at pavement tables and watched the passing show, or strolled the byways, wanly admiring the architectural splendours of Verona. She bought him boxes of pills and little bottles of lurid-coloured tonics, tried every means to rally his spirits, gossiping, planning local jaunts, and archaeological sprees, skilfully managing the modest funds. He watched, complied, and followed in her wake, wanting nothing but what he was enjoying there and then, the solace of her presence. At Munich they went to the Carnival ball, and he stood at the side, still watching, feeling the pride of possession, as she waltzed by in her hired fancy dress and mask. There were concerts and picture galleries, and on February 9 they arrived at Salzburg, where he passed through some kind of crisis, unburdened his mind of many things he longed for her to know, lay awake in a fever, and she sat up all night in his room, hoping to infect him with her calm. It was now that these two close friends began living together as lovers. After two days he seemed to be a new man, suddenly restored, almost his old self, and on February 13 he wrote his first letter since leaving Cannes. 'I really rather believe she's pulled me through,' he told James Strachey. 'As the flood subsides I totter round, picking up the jetsam. There's not much that a man may save. A broken blossom I have. There's a blob in the near distance that may turn out to be a ruined rhyme . . . I see England, queerly, through such a double glass . . . It is like hearing Orpheus through the waters of Lethe.'

They returned to Munich. For a week he was rallying every day, and with the experience of Salzburg behind them, suffered and won through, thanks to Ka's tender ministrations, they were now on a new plane of candour and understanding. He still could not concentrate for long enough to read or write, but he was happy. The same cannot be said of Ka. While he was recovering something of his old vigour and lightness of heart, her sense of strain increased and felt all the worse for her having to conceal it from him. She must have been wondering how soon, and in what circumstances, she could be as open with him as he had with her, and at last rid herself of what was becoming an unbearably false position. She was not in love with him. More than that, she was in love with someone else. She could not respond to his letters from Cannes in quite the same vein, fond of him though she was, and the more he let her watch the image of her growing in his imagination, and the more of himself that he not only offered but positively flung down at her feet, so much the more she must have recoiled, bewildered and embarrassed by the power over him that he was thrusting into her hands. At the same time she was torn, reluctant to lose him altogether (having so recently lost Raverat), and since she was also afraid of his growing dependence on her, now that illness had made him more sensitive than ever, there was nothing for it but to temporize, get him really strong again, and having earned his gratitude, tell him the truth. She too, of course, belonged to a generation in revolt against Victorian hypocrisy. They regarded the virtue of candour as absolute. Rupert could only respect her for acting on principle, for being so considerate as to wait until he had recovered his health and sense of proportion. Was someone as free as the wind to act as she pleased to confine her affections to a single object? And was *she* to blame for his tumbling headlong in love with her? Surely Rupert would understand that he might not be the *only* person who lived in need of her? Whatever his own opinion of Henry Lamb, he was hardly in a position to judge with fairness, nor was it—let it gently be said—his business.

By the end of the week they had decided to visit Starnberg by the lake, and booked two rooms at the hotel. They left by an after-dinner train on Saturday, February 17. It was at the railway station in Munich, before boarding the train, that Ka chose her moment, or she may have been rushed into it by the way the talk was going. More likely the distraction and bustle of a crowded platform was offering itself as a convenient setting in which to drop a remark whose effect might with luck be a little diluted at first by the jostle of passers-by . . . She had been meeting Lamb while Rupert was in Cannes, either in the company of Lytton Strachey or at a house-party, possibly at Lady Ottoline Morrell's country home near Henley, where she was a guest with Lytton and certain others of the Bloomsbury circle of writers, and especially of painters whose names at least Rupert would know. By the time Sunday came at Starnberg, Ka was more alarmed than ever she was at Lulworth just before the New Year. And now she had no one to turn to.

Part of the trouble was that Brooke could not get himself to believe in either the genuineness of Lamb's regard for Ka or in hers for him. To Brooke, for all his brilliant promise as a painter, Lamb was no more than 'Sir Smile', as Leontes says of Polixenes in the play, a plausible philanderer about town moving in a circle of dazzling but rather raffish acquaintance that was notoriously easy-going in its attitude to sex. And from the flattering society of these people, Ka, by comparison a naïve child of Nature, was acquiring a veneer of false sophistication, false because second-hand, and liable to corrupt, because its values were borrowed from a view of life which had never been her own. So in Rupert's eyes the mainstay of his life was in peril of squandering herself on the passing whim of someone who probably found her tedious enough, except as an episode to beguile the dull hiatus between one mistress and the next. Such was his dread, and something worse, for it cannot be doubted that he tumbled to much more than ever she intended to convey, was afflicted in particular by the thought of her being at the house-party, and having received another injection of the jealous poison, his conclusion was—again in the words of Leontes—'To mingle friendship far, is mingling bloods. I have *tremor cordis* on me—my heart dances. But not for joy—not joy.'

He considered himself responsible for her. At least *his* eyes were open, he would contend, if hers were not, and to the anguish of an acute and baffled sense of responsibility were now added feelings of isolation, betrayal, and utter dismay. She had admitted that she had only come out to Munich because he seemed desperate, and she was afraid for him. She owed him the truth. Was she to blame if he couldn't stand it? She was only meaning all for the best. 'She did not have it in her,' a friend of hers has remarked, 'to conduct a passion.' The trip to Starnberg was a miserable fiasco.

Back in Munich they stopped calling on his old acquaintance. Frau Ewald alone they went out of their way to visit. She had built herself a small house by the lake near the village of Holzhausen, about twenty miles from town. Brooke, she observed, was being regaled at intervals with pills and medicated drops and looked in pitiable shape. He was sinking back into the state of collapse which had overtaken him at Lulworth. On top of that he now caught cold and ran a fever. Ka was distracted, and at once began organizing their return to England. She could not unsay the truth, but she could redouble her efforts to undo the harm, and little by little she succeeded, or so they both believed. By some freak of the human climate, everything began to show signs of relenting and righting itself. Touched by her concern, Brooke repented of the hard words he had let fly in his bitterness, while she for her part, came near to yielding the very position she had been at such pains to defend on that black Sunday in Starnberg —her freedom to meet and admire whom she pleased. Perhaps she gave way under duress, or simply in order to give him enough spirit to face the journey home, or from a pathetic need to feel that she had not altogether failed him—the sense of failure, of course, was mutual —and yet the sequel shows that if at first there was something of all these in her mind, beneath them lay another factor, of which she was not yet fully aware.

They were going home earlier than was planned. Somehow, they thought, this enforced separation, due to illness, must be discounted. They would try again, come back in a few weeks and recapture the atmosphere of Salzburg, as if nothing had happened in between.

On February 21 they started back, three weeks after their reunion in Verona. He was to regain his strength at Rugby, and some day near the end of April, go back to Germany, meet Dudley Ward, now Berlin correspondent of the *Economist*, and use his flat in Charlottenburg as a base for exploring the surrounding country for some spot where Ka could join him. Only this time they would be together on more auspicious terms, neither as nurse and invalid, nor mother and child, but simply as man and woman, soon to be man and wife.

II

'You've heard Ka brought me back?' he wrote to James Strachey from Rugby. It was the last week of February. He and James were planning to spend a long week-end together at the Mermaid Club, Rye. Brooke had come back to give his mother evidence of his continued existence, deal with neglected correspondence, and take breath before going off again. The most urgent thing was to write to Eddie Marsh. A long article on his *Poems* in the *Poetry Review* had lain for too long unacknowledged. Marsh was not of his own generation. He belonged to Brooke's 'public' life, or his professional life, if he could be said to have one. There he occupied an especial place, but the turmoil of his private existence Brooke reserved for his coevals who shared it. Marsh, he suspected, might not even understand it, and at all costs his invaluable friendship must not be alienated. So he skipped the details.

Your letter found me in Munich. I was at Cannes for two or three weeks, Munich two or three more, and now I've unexpectedly come home.

Alas! your tidings of me in rude health at Cannes were far from accurate. I find I was getting ill through the autumn and winter—and I don't know how long before—with work and things. The final rush for my incondite and incomplete dissertation finished me. I went to Lulworth after Christmas for a 'reading party'. There I collapsed suddenly into a foodless and sleepless hell. God! how one can suffer from what my amiable specialist described as a 'nervous break-down'. (He reported that I had got into a 'seriously introspective condition'! and—more tangibly—that my weight had gone down a stone or two.) I tottered, being too tired for suicide, to Cannes, not because I like the bloody place, but because my mother happened to be there. I flapped slowly towards the surface there; and rose a little more at Munich. I've come here for a month or two to complete it. After that I shall be allowed (and, by Phoebus, able, I hope) to do some work. My cure consists in perpetual overeating and oversleeping, no exercise and no thought. Rather a nice existence, but oh God! weary. I detail all this to account for my recent silence and my present lumpishness and banality, and to illuminate any future reports you may hear of the dead and doltish remains of the shipwreck.

Your letter and review gave me immense and slightly pink-cheeked pleasure. It is absurdly kind of you to face the terrors and pangs of parturition (at, you report, so advanced an age for a first confinement!) for me. Either innate and long-hidden genius or else the continual and earnest study of the masters of English (me and Trollope and Crashaw and the rest) has given you, though, a finished and practised wit and clarity of style that'll fairly prick the honest stammerers who neighbour you in the Poetry Review...

I liked the review very much from my own point of view, and of course felt passionately in agreement with it. But one feels so distorted and uncertain and obvious about one's own work, that I'd rather, in any case, offer only thanks and not comment. I've an insistent queer feeling of having got rid of poems I've written and published—of having cut the umbilical cord—that they're now just slightly more anybody's concern than mine, and that everybody has an equal right and a faintly greater opportunity of understanding them. But with this reservation, and in the spirit of two *Philologs* discussing some musty classic, I'd like to make two suggestions. One is that there wasn't any intention of having 'the beloved' at the table in that Dining-Room. If she was (as I'll confess she happened to be on that imagined —or generalized—occasion), it was rather in her capacity as one of a few very close friends, than as anything more intimate—and more disturbing. If you think the situation demands a central figure, all right. But it seemed to me to be a group.

Then there's *Town and Country*. The point is, what time of day do they go off their heads? You suggest midnight. 2.30 p.m. was rather my idea; with all the horrible stillness of hot sunlight. But that's again rather a matter of choice . . .

London sounds rather bright just now. But I don't think I shall be in it for more than half an hour for weeks and months. I'm going to grow fat and serene here. Anyway, I've got a turn against London just now: against England as a whole, rather . . .

I'm very glad Gosse and Austin Dobson liked the book. Wasn't it perhaps your skilful advocacy? I've always had a sort of respect for Gosse, in spite of an almost irresistible tendency to despise anyone who was writing about English Literature before 1890. He seems to keep an unusual

combination of sanity and vitality in his taste, or outlook. Does he think my
Muse one of those 'Decaying Maenads in a throng' who 'shout a startling
and indecent song', that I seem to remember he recently wrote about? . . .

Oh, yes about *Dead Men's Love*. You're entirely right, as to the meaning
of it; in all ordinary meanings of the word meaning. I suppose it was just
an idea—that they only found out they were dead by discovering the absence
of bodies in that way, and that Hell just consists in such absence of bodies.
But if anyone, realizing that the point of Hell is that you have precisely
similar desires in the absence of the means of satisfying them, can't help
thinking of cis-Stygian embodiments of the horror—let him! I say. For a
poem is essentially, I take it, tended by millions of strange shadows, just
as poor Mr. W. H. was; and I'll not deny this was one of the shadows. But
it was only a shadow: not in any way the substance. So I hope your elderly
friends'll be assured that I've not the smallest doubt they'll still for a long
time be able to say with Ovid

> *Decepta est opera nulla puella mea.*
> *Saepe ego, lascivae consumto tempore noctis,*
> *Utilis, et forti corpore mane fui—etc.*[1]

I think there's no news to tell you. Mrs. Cornford tried to engage me in a
controversy over the poems—she and her school. They are known as the
Heart-criers, because they believe all poetry ought to be short, simple,
naïve and a cry from the heart: the sort of thing an inspired only child might
utter if it was in the habit of posing to its elders. They object to my poetry
as unreal, affected, complex, 'literary', and full of long words. I'm rewriting
English Literature on their lines. Do you think this is a fair rendering of
Shakespeare's first twenty sonnets if Mrs. Cornford had had the doing of
them?

TRIOLET

> *If you would only have a son,*
> * William, the day would be a glad one.*
> *It would be nice for everyone,*
> *If you would only have a son.*
> *—And, William, what would you have done*
> * If Lady Pembroke hadn't had one?*
> *If you would only have a son,*
> * William, the day would be a glad one.*

It seems to me to have got the kernel of the situation, and stripped away all
unnecessary verbiage or conscious adornment.

Jacques and Gwen Raverat came to Rugby for a night, and were the
first to be told the full story of Cannes and Munich. Then they all
left together, Brooke making his way to the South coast. During the
three days with Strachey at the Mermaid Club, Rye, he wrote to Ka

---

[1] *Amores* II, 10 26–8.
> No girl has been beguiled through my doing.
> Often after a night spent in dalliance,
> I rise in the morning with no slackening of my body's vigour.

five times. 'One's almost further from you among the upper classes than elsewhere.' But the surroundings were not unpleasant.

My dear,

We're in a Smoking Room. They're all in evening dress: and they talk—there *are* these people in the world—about Bridge, Golf and Motoring. They're *playing* Bridge——

I've been feeling a lot better to-day. I got a morsel afraid Jacques or Gwen'ld. attack you—worry you. But I guess, you'll allow for (it's not unknown in you) their love——

Jacques, my dear, was extraordinarily nice to me. It seemed a comfort—when one had (I feel, you know) spued it out—that he was there, one's friend, loving (you and me) meaning well, suffering—in the world. The Universe seemed to oscillate less than it has.

Then the plans for next month. 'You've, dear, a lot of thinking—quiet—to do: about arrangements in Berlin. *What's* to happen, and how . . . About rooms—the number and situation. I can always give my address as Dudley's you see'—and so on, punctuated with ejaculations overheard from the neighbouring card table. 'My hand was *mud*!' 'MUD, sir?' 'MUD!' . . . 'It's a question of minutes till they ask James to make up a four. You've *not* taken quite all the joy out of the world, Ka,' then back to his own thoughts, 'I'm loving you so extraordinarily—one pulls the barriers, and it comes full flow.'

Thursday I shall see you—it'll be nice.

I want, I extraordinarily want—it's too degraded—to *work* for you. Do a lot of hard things—a Treatise on Prose Rhythm—a Play—An Epic—and watch you read them. Then if each made a thousand pounds and I gave you 2/3. Damn!

But Happiness is defined as you reading my proofs.

Next day he tells her he is going to the Oliviers at Limpsfield before coming on to her at Woking. 'Oh, I know what I'm doing, it's all right! I admire her rather extraordinarily.' Then in an impulsive postscript. 'You'd better marry me before we leave England, you know, I'll accept the responsibility. And the fineness to come.'

Brooke and Strachey spent much of the next day in Winchelsea, looking for some new place for a reading party in April. He was tired, glad of the companionship of this oldest friend, but a little disquieted that, nevertheless, James was the brother of someone who had become his *bête noir*—and a little ashamed of having to admit it. 'He loves you, but it may be it's only his love for you that matters to him, not *you*. You know how the Stracheys feel? James *is* better than the rest . . .'

One tires, still away from you. (Oh, I'm *much* better!) People wrangle. 'You want *Company*', 'You want *Peace*'—But the answer never given, is always that in solitude one frets to illness, in company one talks . . . and then gets tired and collapses. 'There's only *Ka* to be with: then all goes straight —will go straight . . .'

I wonder if to send this to Woking or London. I suppose you'll come down late evening. Tired. Or will you put it off till Tuesday? You're a bother of a Ka.

After dinner they paid, or tried to pay, a call.

James and I have been out this evening to call on Mr. Henry James. At 9. We found, at length, the House. It was immensely rich, and brilliantly lighted at every window on the ground floor. The upper floors were deserted: one black window open. The house is straight on the street. We nearly fainted with fear of a Company. At length I pressed the Bell of the Great Door—there was a smaller door further along, the Servant's door we were told. No answer. I pressed again. At length a slow dragging step was heard within. It stopped, inside the door. We shuffled. Then, very slowly, and very loudly, immense numbers of chains and bolts were drawn within. There was a pause again. Further rattling within. Then the steps seemed to be heard retreating. There was silence. We waited in wild agonizing stupefaction. The House was dead-silent. At length there was a shuffling noise from the Servant's door. We thought someone was about to emerge from there to greet us. We slid down towards it. Nothing happened. We drew back and observed the House. A low whistle came from it. Then nothing happened for two minutes. Suddenly a shadow passed, quickly, across the light in the window nearest the door. Again nothing happened. James and I, sick with surmise, stole down the street. We thought we heard another whistle, as we departed. We came back here shaking—we didn't know at what.

If the evening paper, as you get this, tells of the murder of Mr. Henry James—you'll know.

'It's better here, you know, than at Rugby. Oh, partly the situation's better: but mostly, one doesn't think think think, unendingly and blindingly, alone, with nothing to do.' In this letter he at last abandons himself totally to his infatuation. The horrors of Starnberg might never have existed. The last vestige of reserve has gone. 'You, Ka,' it ends. 'Nothing else means anything.'

You, oh you. You fill one's horizon—one's narrow horizon—and one's life. Ka, and her dresses, and her walk—it comes round and over one. I think of living close to you for long, knowing and being known, seeing a child: knowing your mind, knowing your ways and thoughts round me. Taking things, strength and rest and love—and giving love and a thousand things—the great things I'll do.

But in an aside he remarks, 'Oh lord, I'm so sick of not seeing your handwriting on a letter. Not since Saturday morning—and a slight postcard then.'

From Limpsfield he goes to Ka at Woking, where they decide that it's not possible to put off any longer giving Mrs. Brooke an opportunity of making Ka's acquaintance on her own ground. It was only prudent, since thoughts of matrimony were in the air, and somehow only fair to the Ranee—not that she would necessarily see it in that light. There was no knowing how little or how much she had already pieced together. Were she to have deduced that Ka was the cause of all the disturbance at Cannes, Miss Cox would certainly not be *persona grata* at Bilton Road. But the risk had to be taken, and for everyone's sake, the sooner the better. Brooke was at Bilton Road again by about March 7, having come from Woking. After a day or two he declares, 'I'll tackle the Ranee', and proposed the 15th. They must do the thing properly; she must come on the Friday and stay until the Tuesday. Will she please answer about this? Her letters of late, though few—'Only one letter so far, and that a scrap'—have shown that she was having a peculiarly sharp attack of tantalizing obscurity. When Ka at last confirmed the date, it was then up to Brooke to procure and transmit an official invitation from her hostess. That wasn't so easy. After the interval of a day or so he could no longer put off sending her at least a report on progress.

It is hard to be certain, looking back on it. It was a Victory, I feel pretty sure. But possibly a Pyrrhic one. Anyhow, there's an acerbity, a sense of incompletion and a possibility of future unrest, hanging in the atmosphere of this lonely and hideous drawing-room.

The war began last night.

10.30 *p.m. Wednesday.* I lay in my bath and thought very carefully (I have thought at intervals the whole fortnight) just what form of words to use. It would be wearisome, and, I trust, supererogatory, to illustrate and emphasise the large variety of openings, and the importance of making the right choice. One might lead the Ranee to comment that next week-end was empty, and then with a feigned hilarious surprise, 'Oh!' one would cry, slapping one's thigh, 'then we'll have Katharine Cox' (suddenly inspired) '—yes! and James with her! They're great friends, you know!' Or one might almost boredly announce 'I thought of asking Ka Cox down for the week-end, and James at the same time. Do you mind?' Or one might quietly say 'I've been thinking, Mother, and I think you'd *like* Katharine Cox. She's so *different* from the Oliviers!' (put a little less baldly perhaps)—'I thought of asking her here etc.' Or again, 'I've just—so delightful!—heard from—who but— Katharine Cox? She says—(a lot about James, Virginia, Suffrage, etc.)—and she's—being turned out of her flat—forlorn and homeless, the loveable creature!—just wandering in London . . . I thought it'd be a kindness to ask her here a week-end . . .' (There was a variant in which Winifred had got Scarlet Fever, so you couldn't go home.) And a million others.

I chose the simple direct (you know my diffidence) and dried. I put on my pyjamas and dressing-gown (ha! you don't know *that*, *Gott sei dank*) and sailed out (10.45 *p.m.*) *en route* for my room, *via* the Ranee's, to say goodnight. She was a little sleepy, and a little wan. I suddenly remembered I was tired. It seemed such a *dead* hour to fire it off. 'Supposing she pretended not to hear that I was speaking at all!' I suddenly thought. I was overcome with Terror. We talked gently about Alfred and a million things. There were several pauses: in each I *tried*, slightly, to say the words. Nothing happened —not a sound came. At length I suddenly kissed her and fled. (11.0 *p.m.*) I felt defeated, almost disgraced. I was panting and exhausted. Luckily the victor (I'm persuaded) was unconscious. This morning (11.15 *a.m.*) the same thing happened: (3.15 *p.m.*) on a similar scale. (5.15 *p.m.*) And this afternoon, before tea and after. A dreadful mist, a nightmare feeling of impotence, hung over the whole day. I thought I was under a spell. At 5.30 a very nice letter came from you. It shook me into consciousness. I sat up in a chair and looked round the room (I was alone). I took a long breath, and swore a terrific oath this evening should see it done. (I was picqued, too, by your assuming I hadn't done it. Damn you!)

Dinner started at 7.0: for the Ranee goes to a meeting on Welsh Disestablishment at 8. Each time the maid was out of the room, I assayed: and (7.40 *p.m.*) each time failed. At length dinner was cleared away (my appetite had given early on). Five minutes remained before she would go to put her things on. The torture was supreme. I wheeled my chair into action (so that my face was in shadow), and made a titanic effort. My being shook to the depths of my penis. A voice I hardly recognized, dry, hoarse, inhuman, croaked 'I think I should like—etc.'. There was a pause. The Ranee did not start or change, only shrank a very little into herself. She appeared dreadfully old. It was obvious she had been reading my correspondence when I was out —or some of last year's letters. She stared at me and merely asked '*when* did you think of them coming'. 'Oh. The week-end after this one.' 'But Alfred'll be here—does that matter?' Then I realized my fatal error (my head is affected, you know). I'd written to the man, found out he was probably not going to be here, and not told the Ranee. I blundered more by saying 'Oh! he won't be here till the Monday.' How did I know? 'He'd—er— told me so: written.' When? She didn't know I'd had a letter from him. Had I *asked* him? *She'd* asked him this question three times, and had no reply! Why hadn't I told her? . . . It flooded on. For, you see, it became apparent, even by the rules, almost (which don't allow letter-reading—like yours, dear!) that it was a deep-laid plot. All seemed lost. Genius inspired me to a step which enabled me to take a breathing-space (in which, precisely, I write) and retire after the engagement, with loss rather than defeat. For I muttered that I'd written about reviews of my book in local University papers, and that he'd answered dates incidentally. I added if he *did* come back for the week-end, I shouldn't mind (which isn't true). The Ranee headed off on the Review-track—pausing, in her queer, abrupt way, to say

'Of course' (partly it was her way of assenting) 'if Alfred's here, I can put, if you like, you into the big spare-room with . . .' 'With?' I said, without moving a hair. 'with *James*,' she sighed. And I had won the cavalry-engagement. Then her mind hopped its usual Knight's move backwards, her nostrils expanded, and she started 'I *wrote* to Alfred about those Reviews . . . It's too bad of him . . .' Then I imperceptibly looked at the clock. It suggested to her—all unconsciously—Time. She was in danger of lateness and fled to put her hat on. In two minutes she clattered down and (7.47) out of the front door—without looking in. That showed—I thought—that the battle was not ended. At 9.30 I go out to Mr. Whitelaw: till 10.30. So I shall only see her a few minutes tonight. There'll be sparring then: but I've got the advantage that *she's* got to attack every time, henceforward. Lord! Lord! It's an exhausting world. I shall never dare to tell her about you being in Germany. If I *can*, I shall hint at a few days. But be prepared for the worst.

I think she suspects you a bit. But she always does. You, I, she, James: what a tangle of cross-motives and dissimulations it'll be! We'll want our clear heads. But it'll be fun.

Oh, it will be nice seeing you. A week tomorrow. By the 2.0 please: if it runs. You couldn't motor? . . .

Jacques tomorrow early: I hope. I shan't write a bit while he's here. People do *notice* so! I *may* scribble a note in bed one night.

Next day there was a lull before the second round.

The Ranee was so excited about Disestablishment last night, that she forgot you. And this morning, so far, she's lain pretty low.

I sit here like a weather-beaten mariner, thinking of the stormy sea. Do you know it's less than three weeks since we were at Starnberg? The things— the adventures, Ka, we've been through together! It's quite certain no other two people in the world could have done it. I'm so old and proud and strong . . .

An Interlude. The Ranee entered from the rain, screaming 'Here's Mrs. Bullock'. So I winked and put my tongue out; and the Ranee, as Mrs. Bullock entered behind her, jigged and grimaced and shouted, in a stage whisper, 'You'd better go upstairs'. So here I am, upstairs. We don't like Mrs. Bullock. But the Ranee's sorry for her, and helps her.

The Ranee, I'm glad to say, has given up the lost-child craze. At one time she used to wander the streets accosting all small, lonely, tearful children. With infinite patience she used to discover they came from the other end of the town. Determinedly the Ranee would grip the lost baby, and march it back two miles to its hovel. Sometimes she'd meet an upper-class acquaintance bound in the same direction. 'Mr. (or Mrs.) Bradby's going in your direction. How fortunate!' the Ranee then roars to the amazed baby. Then to the sky, 'It *says* it lives in Paradise Court, and it's name is Wilkins.' She would press the dirty small hand into the clean large one; and rush in the direction of the next small lonely creature: leaving a hot-faced wrathful young master or master's wife, and a hot-faced frightened baby to tread their joint paths in silence. But generally she followed it out to the end, scolded and made friends with the Mother, and adopted the whole family . . .

I cease. It will be very nice when you come. *Do* behave, though. Will you remember *not* to call me 'Dearest'? Think it. I think it continually. I'm very well; and loving you very much; and quite happy, and only thinking that these days are going by, wasted a little, when one's well and twenty-four, and you're in London.

Go on resting—and loving. You are very splendid.

How he achieved the final stage is not on record. 'I must not know too much about your life,' he wrote, adding that he *had*, however, planted the fact that they had recently chanced upon each other in Munich. The only drawback about the week-end they picked on was the knowledge that during it the news might arrive that he had failed his Fellowship. He had small hope of success, and he was aware that the electors were due to meet and vote on March 16. Meanwhile he could polish off his arrears of letters. To Dent, who had begun his book on Mozart, and might soon be seeing Frau Ewald in Germany, he tried to account for his long silence, giving him news of his collapse in January. 'I spent a week or so in the most horrible kind of Hell; without sleeping or eating—doing nothing but suffering the most violent mental tortures. It was purely mental; but it reacted on my body to such an extent that after the week I could hardly walk.' To Virginia Stephen (now soon to marry Leonard Woolf, who had come back from Ceylon the year before) he was more expansive, knowing she too had been suffering in much the same way.

Virginia dear,

I'm told—in the third-hand muffled manner I get my news from the Real World—that you've been, or are, unwell. It's not true? Let me implore you not to have, as I've been having, a nervous breakdown. It's *too* unpleasant—but you're one of the few people who, of old, know what it's like. ('Hypersensitive and Introspective', the good doctor Craig said I was.) I feel drawn to you, in this robust hard world. What tormented and crucified figures we literary people are! God! how I hate the healthy unimaginative hard shelled dilettanti, like James and Ka.

It was a pity you couldn't come to that House Party long, long ago, at Lulworth—not that you'd have enjoyed it: it was *too* horrible. But you might have made all the difference. I fell into an abyss there. Bruin Cox (who, robbed of her offspring by the authorities, was diverted into being general wet-nurse for the ricketty gathering) pulled me out and dispatched me to the South of France. There, among Mr. and Mrs. Roberts, Miss Barker, old Mrs. Woolaston, Mrs. Paxton, Colonel Hullar, old Miss Fox, and the two Americans, I rallied a little. (One day I shall tell you their life-histories.) But it was Munich that brought me in sight of shore: and Ka that brought me to Munich. I showed her life there—i.e. Carnival. She took

a slow but intense part, and hugged several men of her own size in mid-
street. She even went to several costume-balls, disguised as a human being.
She waltzed—I watched her—with slow relish: the gay petticoats only
rarely whisking aside and giving a glimpse of furry pelt beneath . . . She
talks Deutsch now as if it were Urse.

It's nice being in a foreign town—the irresponsibility of it. It's like standing in the wings after you've done your scene, and watching the next performers. Other people's lives are in the centre, instead of your own. It's as
good as being old.

I'm not really in England. It's only an interim between two ½-periods
abroad. One gets into the state of mind for being abroad. I've carefully
got into it for a period of twelve months. I happen to have come to Rugby
for a month in the middle, in order to get my health back. It doesn't really
interfere, or break the abroadness. I *am* abroad, and I generally put 2½d.
stamps on my letters. I stay out here, on the Continent, for a year perhaps. So,
unless you could escape England and come out I shan't see you again; which
gives me a great deal of pain. A year = for ever. It would be horrible not
to see you at all in 1912. If I'm in Germany in July, couldn't you represent
the Daily Press at the Mozart and Wagner Fesspiel?

Rugby is not very interesting. I drink stout all the morning, and slumber
all the afternoon. My mother occasionally brings in tales of the devastating
cyclone they call Life in these parts—tales in her usual vein. Would you
like to hear of old Mrs. Enticott (the ex-gardener's wife), and the operation
on the Lower Part of her Stomach, in a Public Hospital, and how they pulled
the stitches out too soon, and what the other patients said to Mrs. Enticott,
and how Mrs. Enticott said to the Nurse, every two minutes, 'Please, Miss,
do you think you could just let me die? I think I'd rather die'? . . .

There is no really exciting news. I was present at a rehearsal of the first
Act of an undiscovered Gilbert and Sullivan opera, last night, in my dreams.
But I have forgotten the tunes.

Drink stout—it is the only way. I have a deal more to say to you, but I
can't think what it is. Maybe I shall one day see you. I hope so.

Ever

RUPERT

Ka came to Rugby, and somehow Time didn't stop, but brought the
following week-end of March 24. Eddie Marsh turned up for a night,
and they went a long walk into the open country, and Geoffrey
Keynes brought over Hugh Wilson to dinner. Life wore the semblance of normality. 'Mention *nothing* connected with my life,'
Brooke had impressed on Keynes, 'no names, nothing, for the Lord's
sake. Relations between the Ranee and me are peculiar. And one
must be very cautious.' Marsh believed him when he accounted for
his low spirits by saying he was fighting off an attack of influenza and
that the walk had made him feel much better. Even Keynes could have
had no opportunity to hear what was really the trouble. 'I say, I

must get away from here!' was the appeal to Strachey, the day after Marsh had gone.

The truth was that Ka had come the week-end before, as arduously arranged, but had gone, long before Tuesday, probably after only one night. While Mrs. Brooke was out, her drawing-room at Bilton Road had become as it were the departure platform for Starnberg, the tension between them until then rendered unbearable by the necessity for restraint. The guest was off again, when she had barely unpacked, and with heaven knows what garbled excuse. Whatever she may have said this time, we know that it was the bitter violence of Brooke's reaction which made the situation impossible. He held himself entirely to blame, and this was an added source of misery and remorse.

The Ranee, for whom it was the more disquieting in that she may have had no notion of what it was all about, must at last have begun to feel concern for her son's mental balance. As for him, in this the worst of his agonies to date, he was alone with someone frantic to give what help she could, but in whom, for her sake, he could not confide. And now the letters to Ka became a Cannes-like stream, all on the same hectic pattern. The night she left he fainted, with the dissertation on Webster in his hands. The news he anticipated had come.[1] Writing again, he had to break off because of a curious tingling all over the skin of his face and a sensation of burning in his head, so that he had to lie down. Then day after day the same recriminations and regrets go aching round and round: she is driving him mad; he wants her to die, not so as to have her dead, for that would be the end of the world, but for the sake of peace; a more sure way were his own death, and he has visions of the Ranee at her tea-table with her neighbours trying to console her after his suicide. What other way out could there possibly be, since for him there is only Pain or numb Absence of Pain, never peace, for she is in both? She is cursed with such a fatally 'kind' view of the world that the least breath of influence on her warm and undiscriminating heart can incline her this way or that. And always her replies, it seems, are unreproachful, for always his rejoinder begins with a word or two of tender compassion, and perhaps the brief acknowledgement of a 'nice' letter, but again he is carried away as he proceeds, obsessed with the pity of it all, until he has quite forgotten his more rational self of a page ago and is doing the very thing he began by saying he was so anxious to avoid, writing

[1] Hamilton Hartridge, Professor of Physiology at London, had been elected by thirteen votes to one.

such words as could only inflict another wound. Again he is stricken
with remorse to hear of the pain he has caused, and now he is almost
pleased, for how could she be suffering if she did not love him? He
would gladly endure the Hell of hurting her yet again rather than
have the knowledge that he had irresponsibly let her go her own
feckless way. With his love and the keen pangs of it he is isolated in
time and space; she is *not*, yet she will not admit it; at any rate she
must keep a 'fierce and militant cleanness', nothing else matters. He
cannot understand people, 'if they value cleanness, not fighting for it';
he longs to vent his endearments, but always they are choked back;
he reviles and cherishes, spurns and clings, and still she cannot or will
not understand, entrenched in a position where she frankly cannot
share his point of view; she cannot see it, and try how he may, he
cannot adequately define the thing that maddens him; a kind of un-
scrupulous candour is the ferocious instrument they wield against each
other, she only in defence, not only living up to their anti-Victorian
principles with a vengeance but coming perilously near to dying by
them with absolutely nothing but more anguish gained. And so it
goes on for upwards of three weeks.

By early April he was again at Rye, then among the Oliviers at
Limpsfield, and from there, on the same itinerary as before, he went
to Ka at her cottage. 'You're both very good,' he wrote to Gwen and
Jacques Raverat. 'You stand when most things rock and slide'—

I'm going to leave Ka alone till she's rested and ready for Germany. I
found her (I came yesterday) pretty bad. To rest, as far as she will, is the
best thing for her: (and for me). She sees—anyhow—what other people
think. It can stay there for a bit. Time starts——
I went to Limpsfield a few days. I talked to Noel. She was astounding.
Being there—and she—gave me extraordinary rest and strength: I found.
I feel all ways vastly stronger——

The extraordinary gift for reconciliation that Brooke shared with
Ka had come to the rescue again and won for them another respite, but
not for long. Brooke went to stay with James Strachey at Bank,
Lyndhurst, where Mrs. Primmer, renowned for her 'wholesome
cuisine', looked after their creature comforts, while Brooke read
Samuel Butler or tried his hand at translating Swinburne into German.
He did not realize that for Ka and himself the roles were being re-
versed.

But so it was. Now it was Ka who was becoming over-anxious;
Rupert, if anything, almost indifferent. The moderation in the last few

letters she received seems to have struck her as a little too good to be true or, in another sense, not nearly good enough. She was now in fear of losing him. The buffeting of the last few weeks, in which Brooke had unquestionably put himself in the wrong, however she may have erred herself, had had what only a few weeks ago he would have welcomed as the consummation most devoutly to be wished. She had not been shocked out of patience by his verbal assaults, nor had she given him up in disgust. On the contrary, even now, and at last, she was falling in love with him, when it might be too late. It was. She had the good sense not to show the resentment she must have felt at his visits to the Oliviers at Limpsfield. There was no talk of their return to Germany being abandoned; but the sudden lull, though a balm of sorts, was a deal too sudden and serene, and the more she reflected the more she must have wondered, while it dawned on her that she was deeply in love with him and him alone.

A letter from Maynard Keynes at King's brought criticism that was constructive and real hope of Brooke's winning his Fellowship with the second try that he was entitled to, if he chose to make the effort. Brooke was heartened, but his reply could not conceal his weariness.

My poor mind isn't at all what it used to be (all of you, of course, think that a trifle: but, Lord, it was all I had!) When it has recovered—if ever it does—I shall write a short play, before the End. My next year's dissertation will have no more facts but ninety pages more epigrams, so *that* won't take long.

Hugh Dalton had seen the Fellowship announcement and written to commiserate. After all that had happened of late, it seemed like the proverbial voice from a remote and happier past. 'You were good to write to me,' he said, recalling the Fabian adventure.

Friend of my laughing careless youth, where are those golden hours now? Where now the shrill mirth of our burgeoning intellects? and by what doubtful and deleterious ways am I come down to this place of shadows and eyeless pain? In truth, I have been for some months in Hell. I have been very ill. I am very ill. In all probability I shall be very ill. It is thought by those who know me best (viz. myself) that I shall die. Nor do I greatly want to live: the savour of life having oddly left it, and my mind being worn and flabby, a tenth of anything it used to be.

I do nothing. I eat and sleep and rest. My thoughts buzz drearily in a vacuum. I went in January to a slightly American nerve-specialist who said I was deplorably unwell. He made me drink stout and swallow the compressed blood of bullocks. In consequence I am now enormously fat. Boys laugh at me in the street. But that is partly, also, on account of my manner. For I am more than a little gone in my head, since my collapse.

I go back to Germany soon. They are a slow race and will not know I am stupid. I shall never appear in England again. I shall never write poetry or limpid prose again.

From Lyndhurst to Limpsfield again, where he wrote his only surviving letter to James Elroy Flecker, now in the consular service at Beirut.

I, as another poet once, have fallen on the thorns of life and have bled bucketsful. And I am far too poor to give you the copy of my poems you indecently ask for. Damn you, go down to your local Bowes & Bowes[1] and order it and have the cost put down to the Government, like a gentleman and a Pro Consul.

Also, I do not like the book. It is misprinted, and it recalls the golden days before the Crash.

Oh, yes, the Crash came. Precisely at the beginning of this year. I galloped down hill for months and then took the abysm with a leap, like Decimus Somebody. Nine days I lay without sleep or food. Monsters of the darkest Hell nibbled my soul. They nibbled it away and therein that noblest part of it which men name the intellect. I am sodden and soft and dead, a don but less learned, a dotard but less energetic. I almost write prose-poems. Since January the ninth (portentous date) I have been forbidden to work or run. I drift from place to place and eat enormously and sleep. I am utterly degraded and shall never climb from this morass. Why has God thus visited me? I am going to Germany (where my kind abounds) in a day or two. Thence into the Ewigkeit. If you see, any day, marching into the great portals at Beyrut a fat bald man with a slobbered red beard and a scaly eye put him into some quiet asylum for it will be me. I have obtained a divorce from my Muse (the decree is shortly to be made absolute): she is thought moreover to have committed some slight bigamy. I live on stout and modern English fiction. Among the bards I am a very hodmanclod.

You are married. Why are you married? Never mind you will be dead soon and why do the Italians shoot at you so? I saw it all in the Times. Perhaps you are dead already.

My swarthy friend Elroy, my golden-tongued and lax-metred Orpheus, you would never let me teach you how to write Poetry; but it does not matter now: and you are a fine fellow. When you read in the East Levant Gazette that I've taken the last step, weep once, and then lay up the whole thing (with the moral) in your heart and tell it often to the young. What the moral *is* I shall not tell you. But you may warn them never to be Good *and* Wise. It does not pay.

Pray for me
Thine

RUPERT

Felicitate your wife from me: but beat her, lest worse befall.

Within a few days he was back in London again, staying at the

[1] The Cambridge booksellers.

National Liberal Club. Ka happened to see him through the window of a bus, and she suspected that he was no longer keeping her informed of his movements. Her anxiety brought on the next crisis in their mutual distress, which was described in a letter to Raverat.

My letter to Ka did *not* get her in time at Woking; and my covering note to Harley Street was confiscated by Hester. So that Friday she only knew I was, silently—she thought—in London. At lunch she looked out of a window and saw me on a bus-top. It was the final stroke, for (it appeared) she'd been thinking of nothing but me for four days ever since her letter. She telephoned in the afternoon to the N.L.C. that she *must* see me. We met for half an hour—in Trafalgar Square and the Park. When we met she collapsed and had to lean behind a lion, against Lord Nelson's pediment, till the crying was over. I think she thought I'd suddenly decided not to bother about her at all: and it brought her round with a jerk. Next day (oh, I missed Friday's train, of course) she'd had my letter and that had put her back up again, a bit. But she seemed really relieved we were going to proceed with the German visit, I thought. Her revulsions are queer. I've not heard from her since. So we tug and jerk. But (in a callous moment) I thought the weather seemed to be clearing . . .

Having no funds for another continental trip, he was financed this time by James Strachey who saw him off, wondering what on earth would be the outcome.

III

By April 25, 1912, he was installed in a pension near Dudley Ward's flat in Charlottenburg, Berlin. Annemarie von der Planitz and her mother were in the city, and often in the flat, for she was to be married to Ward in Munich on May 11. Ka was urged to come out and see them before they went. Meanwhile Brooke went off house-hunting, and on the last day of April he began a letter, sitting at the roadside half-way between Ketzür and Brandenburg, armed with his Baedeker, the poems of Donne, and a *Manchester Guardian*. 'But this part of the country is too flat.' So were his spirits, though he did his utmost to delude himself with a semblance of enthusiasm. He wanted desperately to make amends.

I am here because I love Ka and she is coming to Germany and we are going to live in a house together, and I must find one, and this looked a good place on the map . . .

I am here because at Fettes, in the seventies, Willie Brooke and May Cotterill got thrown together. And then they had a son and a daughter, and the daughter died, and while the mother was thinking of the daughter another child was born, and it was a son, but in consequence of all this very female in parts—sehr dichterisch—me.

It none of it seems to hang together.

I've just seen a smaller crested wren.

Two soldiers are bearing down at the double. On! on!

The train again.

I can see that one will get fond of the country round here very quickly. The woods and small hills and great sunsets and the lakes. This particular region probably won't do. It's nice enough. But I can see the others'll be nicer. The villages are rather lovely. I don't know what German rooms are like in the country. I want slightly bigger hills.

There's five such silly men with me in the carriage: and a placid baby in the corridor.

I shall go these expeditions every alternate day till you come: God with me, and a decent amount of sleep given.

You, you'll come, I know, and bring colour and things with you. There'll be all that, I can see. You do want me a lot: and I you. And we know a great deal.

I'm just passing through Potsdam. I've a fancy you may be, just now, in Grantchester. I envy you, frightfully. That river and the chestnuts—come back to me a lot. Tea on the lawn. Just wire to me and we'll spend the summer there; with Goldie to tea every Saturday and a fancy dress ball on Midsummer night.

And then 'Just here we pass through miles of pine forests: and under each pine tree there is a paper bag.' The river and the chestnuts at Grantchester were indeed coming back to him. So far this year he had not even set eyes on them. Having posted the letter on his return to Berlin, he went to a performance of *Frühlingserwachen* by the contemporary Frank Wedekind, and for months to come he was blowing hot and cold about translating that author's plays into English. The description of an inn at Neustrelitz in Mecklenburg had satisfied him as a place fit for Ka, so he now sat back and awaited her arrival.

His favourite haunt was a table by the window at the Café des Westens, a place of rendezvous frequented by artists and journalists, which stood at a cross-roads near the station in Charlottenburg called the Zoo. There were the usual marble-top tables and chairs on the pavement under a maroon-coloured awning, but the establishment was distinguished by its unusually wide windows where the patrons could sit out of the wind and watch the world go by. A waitress brought the coffee, and a boy the glass of water to go with it—the single cup entitled you to sit and read the newspapers for as long as you liked—

and here were all the English journals whose Berlin correspondents were regular patrons of the café; here Ward always looked in after posting off his latest article for the *Economist*; and it was here that some journalist acquaintance of Ward's told Brooke of an incident which had actually happened last year somewhere in Lithuania—a man who had run away from home when he was thirteen, came back after many years, but made out he was only a passer-by, seeking shelter for the night. He was going to spring a pleasant surprise on his family next morning, for he had saved up and brought with him a gold watch and a wallet stuffed with money. During the night he was murdered by his own sister, egged on by the avarice of her parents, who had no idea who the man was until a villager called to congratulate them on the return of the prodigal. On this theme Brooke began to write a one-act play in the bare prose of Masefield's early dramas.

The episode is worked out deftly, the nearest thing to a character being the simple-minded daughter, who plays the role of an illiterate Lady Macbeth to her brother's Duncan, while the yokel who unwittingly calls at the crucial moment to make love to her, heightening the suspense by seeming to relieve it, somewhat resembles the Porter. That same plot had been used by George Lillo in 1736, who in turn may have got it from the Welsh Ballad called 'The Black Monk', is nothing against it. In more recent times Darius Milhaud has used the story for his one-act opera *Le Matelot*, and perhaps (failing Elizabethan rhetoric) music is the best kind of dress for the bare bones of this improbable anecdote. Given a group of illiterate boors and an astounding coincidence, anything may happen, and if there is only one rounded character in a group of pasteboard types, the aim had better be farce. Brooke chose to take it seriously, for the peasant setting must have reminded him of the Irish Players. The play he called *Lithuania*—itself a pointless label unless that country were notorious for breeding homicides (one might as usefully start calling *Macbeth* 'Scotland')—opens in sullen gloom and ends in a catastrophe which, though strong, is not in the least tragic, since the victim is no more than a cog in a plot-spinner's machine. It is an exercise in melodramatic irony, and half a page of stunned dialogue immediately after the murder suggests a dramatic gift which deserved a better opportunity. Perhaps in plotting out this savage curtain-raiser at the café-table Brooke found some relief, putting to an artificial use one or two corroded pieces of the iron which had entered into his soul. Of more consequence to the world at large was his other employment at his table by the window in the Café des Westens. He was still awaiting Ka's arrival in Berlin.

By the look of the manuscript in a pocket account book which had been given him by Maynard Keynes, it was an impromptu, copied out later with very little variation from the first draft. 'I've a fancy you may be, just now, in Grantchester' he had written to Ka. 'That river and the chestnuts—come back to me a lot,' and perhaps, what he afterwards told her was the germ of the poem, had already occurred to him:

> Ah God! to see the branches stir
> Across the moon at Grantchester!

The piece was dashed off in the same serio-comic vein as the rhyming letter to Ward of 1909—it probably began as a verse letter to Ka— but was enormously helped on this occasion by his shortening the line by a foot. The Fish shows he had already mastered the craft of octosyllables. It was becoming his characteristic measure, as it was of Andrew Marvell whom in many other ways, and on a smaller scale, Brooke resembled. If in a literary guessing game, confronted with 'Annihilating all that's made To a green thought in a green shade', some player should answer 'Brooke' he would lose a mark, and perhaps the game, but he would be no fool.

In the margin he writes a list of villages near Cambridge to be got in, and eventually Comberton gives place to Trumpington in 'And worse than oaths at Trumpington' so that the former village is the only one of the list to be left out.

> And is the river running still
> Beneath the mill, beneath the mill?

becomes—

> And laughs the immortal river still
> Under the mill, under the mill?

There are four lines describing the people at Grantchester which are omitted in the fair copy;[1] the clock at the end first stood at half past, not ten to, three, and beyond two or three more verbal changes of less interest, the poem first called Home, then Fragments of a Poem to be entitled The Sentimental Exile, then, a few months later, The Old Vicarage, Grantchester, still stands as it stood in the pocket book

[1] And so at General Elections
They have the strength of their convictions
The atheists vote Liberal
And many do not vote at all.

at the Café des Westens. For most of the year 1911 the church clock *had* stuck, but at half past three (so the poet took only forty minutes' worth of licence!); the honey which might or might not be still for tea (the very natural question implies the hope that Ka, who may be there, will answer in the affirmative), was of course the produce of Mr. Neeve's hives which normally appeared at breakfast; and even 'The sly shade of a Rural Dean' was the poet's way of incorporating a local tradition. This fine poem, frankly sentimental as the original title suggests, and which at first glance may seem a little too whimsical, is nevertheless curiously factual, and its sincere feeling is only shrugged off, disguised in playfulness, because it was written by a typical Englishman in Berlin who was feeling sentimental about Grantchester, rather than by a German in London indulging a similar nostalgia for, say, Feldberg. The German lyric would have been earnest to the point of mysticism.

The quality which by this time has become peculiar to Brooke is a combination of wit and sincere feeling, not alternating, as in Byron, but inextricably at one, so that the conception of the poem, as well as each of its details, is a witticism. The quality is of course what we have come to know as 'metaphysical'. In *The Old Vicarage* the gravity makes fun of itself, the levity takes itself seriously. '*Is* he sincere?' we ask, anxious—for sake of our self-esteem as critics—not to be taken in, not to be 'charmed' from the straight and narrow path. Does he honestly want to know what's going on at Grantchester, or is the whole thing no more than an ornamental gesture? Charm? oh yes, but is it native or self-conscious? And while we are speculating, the poem has quietly come and gone by, not staying for question, like the ghost in *Hamlet*. What we did manage to catch, if we missed the oblique sincerity, was an undersong of simple, careful, yet somehow 'easily', measured music:

> To smell the thrilling-sweet and rotten
> Unforgettable, unforgotten
> River-smell—

or the felicitous image

> Unkempt about those hedges blows
> An English unofficial rose.

The charm, if that is the word for it, is as natural and 'open' as the comeliness of its author's face. An effortless poetry is arriving on the page 'as easily as leaves to a tree', in the only lyric way it could come, if Keats is to be trusted; a way rarely possible in our more critical age when the purity of the poet's impulse is so easily repressed or diverted by the *angst* of circumspection. Perhaps it would be easier for Brooke's posterity if he were not *quite* so engaging. The quality is always suspect. From our distance in time we are suspicious of the Georgian self-consciousness in the presence of an audience—and true it is that the writers of that age were eminently sociable—and the impression is that the poem was posted when the ink was hardly dry, and forthwith delivered on a salver in the drawing-room, or is it the dining-room where, contrary to usual custom, tea is laid? At any rate it is a formal and a gracious age, too close in time to enjoy the privilege of being 'historical', too remote in spirit to be properly understood. It is in fact (as are the poems it produced) 'old-fashioned'. The pride, the amplitude, the air of stylish leisure, the rooted hopefulness, the large assumption that society was destined to continue in some shape or form—all these are gone . . . 'and all the immoveable system of things I see round me, will vanish like smoke,' Brooke wrote to Keeling. 'All this present overwhelming reality will be as dead and odd and fantastic as crinolines or "a dish of tay".' But this poetical improvisation, although inevitably a little 'odd and fantastic', is not dead, except among those who are unaware how easy it is to do old-fashioned things injustice and blandly suppose their modernity to be a lasting virtue. *The Old Vicarage* has even survived the ordeal of being popular.

And it was, as a matter of fact, sent off 'when the ink was hardly dry'. The editor of *Basileon*, the King's magazine, had written in hope of a contribution for the issue in June. The dead-line had gone by, but the printer was asked to hold his hand, for Brooke had sent a telegram—'A masterpiece on its way'. He wrote to Mrs. Cornford, 'I scrawled in a café a very long poem about Grantchester, that seemed to me to have pleasant silly passages'; and, writing after a long interval to Lucas, he confessed he hadn't 'written *anything* since August', that is just before he sent in *Lust* and *Dining-Room Tea* to Frank Sidgwick. In the same spirit Sullivan would have claimed for his credit the magnoperatic *Ivanhoe*, while omitting to throw in a reference to *Iolanthe*, such is the tendency of the English genius to feel put out in the presence of the slighter thing it does best. *Lithuania* is forgotten, or only remembered because its author wrote more modest things which are still alive.

THE ESTRANGING SEA

Perhaps a way of warning Ka that she would find him an indifferent companion was to let her know his present outlook on life and the human condition. A real marriage of true minds was an impossibility . . . 'if you take a calm view, everybody's a pretty lonely figure, drifting in the gloom; and even the people who think they're, wonderfully, in pairs—there's not much difference between them and the rest,' then he wanted to quote Matthew Arnold's poem on the inescapable solitude of man, but couldn't . . . something about 'echoing straits', was it?—and human beings like islands in 'the unplumbed salt estranging sea'.[1] Anyway, here was Annemarie, for instance, going off to marry Dudley. Brooke had bidden her good-bye and pressed her hand—she seemed so happy—'She didn't notice the sea, hear the murmur of the billows, spy a white flutter on the horizon. She thought it was Berlin.'

Soon after Ward had gone to Munich for his wedding, and Brooke had seen them off, Ka arrived, and they went on to Neustrelitz. After two days they started wandering. For a few days they settled at Feldberg. He tried to work up some enthusiasm without letting Ka notice either the effort or its failure. 'The crux is that that absolutely dead feeling I had when I was in Berlin before she came, hasn't vanished,' he told Dudley. 'I was afraid, beforehand, I might—when I saw her—be dragged down into that helpless tortured sort of love for her I had all the first part of the year, and had just crept out of. The opposite. I remain dead. I care practically nothing for any person in the world. I've anxiety, and a sort of affection, for Ka—But I don't really care. I've no feeling for anybody at all—except the uneasy ghosts of the immense reverence and rather steadfast love for Noel, and a knowledge that Noel is the finest thing I've ever seen in the world, and Ka—isn't. But that doesn't come to much.' In a letter to Strachey he tried to account for his peculiar deadness of emotion. It couldn't be understood, he said, from small details. 'But it's the irresistible false fondness of the whole that pins me shrieking down.'

[1] *Who order'd that their longing's fire*
Should be, as soon as kindled, cool'd?
Who renders vain their deep desire?
A God, a God their severance ruled!
And bade betwixt their shores to be
The unplumb'd, salt, estranging sea.

(To Marguerite)

They managed to live in the present, avoiding all mention of things past. Brooke continued to do his utmost to conceal the numbness which had come over him, and he must have succeeded, for Ka, now very unsure of herself, was nevertheless almost happy. 'Only—there's some mud wall between us,' he wrote to Raverat. 'Or rather, my faculty for loving her got cauterized too far.' They spent the days out walking and found a lake with sailing boats for hire. Brooke was able to tell Raverat that he was 'as certain as I am about anything that I could make her promise to marry me within a month. Only I'm still dead'. As to the recent days of waiting in Berlin, 'I'd not have cared if the whole lot of you'd had your necks broken'. But Ka soon fell ill, and Brooke himself was afflicted with one of his fevers, so they made their way back to Berlin and Ward's new apartments in the Spickernstrasse. It was agreed by now that the question of marriage could not properly be faced until they were both fit. At least there had been no recurrence of the Starnberg horrors. There was no passion of any sort whatever. They lived like brother and sister on holiday, or with the indifference of an elderly married couple. There was utter calm. To Brooke it was a state of stupor; with Ka it was chiefly caution, but such was her love, she 'knew' it would all come right. They agreed to part for the time being. He must be alone to think things out. She understood. Her sister in trouble, recalled her to England, providentially for all concerned. It had been a strain. She went with the knowledge that before long he would have sorted himself out and either ask her to marry him or finally tell her it could never be.

'I'm going back to rest in Grantchester,' he told Raverat, ' "Marriage or Murder", you say. Well, we've tried both, in a way. I don't at all want either. Though it's true, I don't want anything else.' He was staying behind for another week or two. 'I think really,' he went on 'my love for Ka was pretty well at an end—poisoned, dead—before I discovered she was after all in love with me: before, that is, I came to Germany.' His mind was clearing. 'I feel so extraordinarily now as if I'd been asleep—or delirious—for six infinite months. Nothing's real . . . She writes to Dudley that now she's, anyhow, glad it all happened. That's something (if it's true). I envy her; and want to let it rest at that.'

It was the middle of June. In writing to Lucas, he must have been glad of an excuse to talk nonsense.

Inscrutable, hideous enigma; old as the Sphinx and thrice as passionless;

how are you? It was even rumoured that you appeared in Rugby to celebrate—as usual—the holy feast of Quinquagesima, that you saw your
grotesque father, your twisted and malicious step-brothers, and even the
debonaire, the Satanic, the Hellenic, the infinitely beautiful Arthur—
and were too stony-hearted to come and sit awhile by my heated bed. Pfui!
Why is this? What have I done to you? has it got round to your ears that
I called you a mingy and coprologous Oxford poetaster. It is true. But you
should not have believed it. Or are you envious that my anapaests were
livelier and lither than yours? Or did you loathe my too intricately modern
poems, Nestor, so much that you swore to abjure me? Or do you only detest
all my friends—but that should hardly be a cause for division, for I do,
too.

He was now alone in Ward's flat, keeping the place warm until the
couple came back from their honeymoon in Venice. 'Please, please,
Ka, rest and wait,' he wrote as he grew again distracted and depressed. 'Hadn't we better fix a date? The end of July? Would that
do? It's madness for me to make up my mind, now: isn't it? I can't
rest till I know you're quiet for a bit.' He worked on *Lithuania*, read
Thus Spake Zarathustra, marking passages such as 'Ye say it is the
good cause which sanctifieth every cause. War and courage have
done more great things than charity.' (The combined influence of
these two occupations were hardly such as to raise the drooping
spirit.) Ward came back from Venice, and after seeing his wife off on
the train to Munich, Brooke and he left Berlin for an hotel in Cologne.

The chief attraction was a Van Gogh exhibition, and for Brooke it
was the first stage of the journey home. He was again in the depths of
despondency. 'I was dull and low enough with you,' he wrote to Ka,
'but lively compared to what I've been without you. These two weeks
have been horrible. Thank God I'm on the way back to England. Oh,
be happy that you've got the downs and sea and clouds of England.
These railways and streets and hotels and unindividual meals are
deadly . . . I wander in a dull fierceness from thing to thing. There's
nothing in the world: Oh God I hope I find rest and peace and kindness in England, and then some strength or life. I feel as if all
strength or all good were burnt out of me . . .' Nothing seemed to be
left, he said, but 'mechanical dull driftings through the days'. In this
despondency he wrote to Geoffrey Keynes, who had not only seen the
poem on Grantchester in print but passed through the village itself.
'It relieves me to know that my description of Grantchester is true,'
replied Brooke. 'The mind of man decays and grows uncertain with
disease and the quiet lapse of time, and I had become more than a

little doubtful if it had ever happened that I was in such a place, or if I had but dreamt it . . . I may be there next week-end—shall we bathe? I haven't bathed since November. There's a lot to wash off.'

Keynes was now working as a medical student in London, one of the few friends of his who had in no way been involved in any of the sorrows of this year and was as yet largely ignorant of them. 'Have you any cure for syphilis of the soul?' Brooke asked. 'I have tried several injections of spiritual 606.' To him, despondent in Cologne, news from Keynes seemed like a voice from a lost age of innocence that might somehow, even now, be rediscovered, and Brooke warmed to him. 'I have no emotions. But my indifference to the universe seems to diminish infinitesimally when you swing into view.' All might yet be well. 'It may be there is a herb growing at the bottom of the river just above the pool at Grantchester, and that if I dive and find it and bring it up—it will heal me. I have heard so. I do not know. It seems worth trying.'

As Dudley left Cologne for Berlin, James Strachey arrived and went with Brooke to the Van Gogh exhibition. They then travelled to the Hague where they shared a room at the Hotel des Indes. Strachey had brought out from England the new book by Belloc. His first reading of *The Four Men* proved to be one of the most important moments in Brooke's life, but many months must pass before the effect of this unassuming little fantasy, illustrated with not very good photographs of rural Sussex mounted on brown paper, comes to the fore in Brooke's mind and so qualifies to be registered as an event. From the Hotel des Indes the two friends walk out in search of the great paintings of the Hague, then stroll back for another chapter of *The Four Men*, or to scribble a note to Ka. 'You seem in some ways better. I'm glad of that. Please never think of me at all.' Unfortunately he could not help thinking of Noel.

In the course of writing to Mrs. Cornford it was brought home to him that there was much more than Ka's well-being on his conscience. There was Noel. Mrs. Cornford, he thought, had misjudged her, and he was angry in her defence. 'It's when one is conscious of having given them evil and wrong in return for fineness—that you can't *stand* other people wronging or badly misjudging them . . . Among a hundred horrors I had been so wicked towards Noel, and that filled me with self-hatred and excess of feeling seeking some outlet.' Throughout these past months Noel had been largely withdrawn from the actual field of events, so that only her image, the idea of her and what she stood for, rather than her self in person, was all along a factor in the imbroglio. Only now, when the worst seemed over, did she reappear in Brooke's view as a figure as closely involved as anyone. Whatever her sense of shock may have been, Noel accepted, or seemed to accept, the news he gave her from time to time with a dignity he may at first have taken for granted, not realizing what it cost; but when at last, no longer self-absorbed, he began to imagine the price he must have made her pay, there was nothing he could do for her but grieve. And now he had been fierce in her defence with Frances Cornford, the only person who might prove of real help to Ka, if she could win her confidence. 'I suppose it was weak and fretful of me,' he wrote, apologetic. He must go gently now, for Frances was becoming his last hope.

But don't misjudge her. She's very fine. Ask even Jacques, who knows her a bit. He's the only person in the world who knows her well. I can see her faults and virtues (and everyone else's) with an absolutely clear and cold eye, as dead people do see. I'm very grateful to her; for she's given me a great deal of good and very little bad, and, in the end, that's fairly high praise for a human relationship. That's all. Don't be angry at my having written this, Frances.

It was the end of June. Brooke and Strachey sailed for England. Whichever way he turned, Brooke's life seemed ruined either by mismanagement or mischance; and if ever he had thought to blame this person or the next, it was nothing to his self-disgust.

On his first evening in England he went with the Cornfords to the pit at the Court Theatre where two short Irish plays were making a double bill, and in the interval met Eddie Marsh who took him back to Raymond Buildings. Next day they both attended a London gathering of the Apostles, and E. M. Forster, R. C. Trevelyan, and Brooke were together at Gray's Inn for the night. As the junior, Brooke slept on the sofa sustained by the comfort of a letter which had arrived that afternoon. There were several friends he could talk to freely, but only one who could help Ka. Today's letter was most opportune. Mrs. Cornford did not have to be asked. 'All yesterday,' she wrote, 'I tried dumbly to say (so hard that I couldn't properly attend to the play) that I know you are pretty miserable—if ever in the future, any time, I could be any possible good or help, tell me, and I'd do anything . . . I don't believe really one can help one's friends, except by just being there and being fond of them, but I had just to say this once to relieve my mind.' Mrs. Cornford's intervention was to have far-reaching results.

He stayed another day at Gray's Inn before leaving to call on his mother at Rugby. When Marsh got back on the day Brooke left he found a note on the table. 'I was so angry at the amount of books here I wanted to read that I've taken one. *The Charwomen's Daughter*; having first made sure it wasn't a presentation copy.' Mrs. Brooke must have been relieved to see him. The Ranee had heard practically nothing of him for about three months. And now there can have been very little about himself that he could say.

By the first week of July he was at long last installed again at the Old Vicarage, Grantchester. 'You see?' said Mrs. Neeve, bringing in the tea-tray on his first afternoon at home, 'there *is* honey still for tea!' Brooke was amused to discover she had seen his poem in *Basileon*. He now sent a copy to Marsh. 'Here's this hurried stuff,' he wrote, and returned the latchkey of Raymond Buildings which had been in his pocket for ten days. His old rooms were still vacant, but not entirely unoccupied, as his first letter shows. It was to Maynard Keynes.

Dear Maynard,
    There are two things—no, three. One is that they *will* fall into my bed and get in my hair. The hot weather brings them out. They climb the walls and march along the ceiling. When they're above me they look down, see with a start—and a slight scream—that there's another person in the room, and fall. And I never could bear wood-lice. Mrs. Neeve sprinkles yellow dust on my books and clothes, with a pathetic foreboding of failure, and says 'They're 'armless, pore things!' But my nerve gives.

He confided in James Strachey that he dreaded being alone, 'You *must* throw off the horrors,' Strachey adjured him in reply, and was then rewarded with a fuller account of the other inmates.

My God, James, they've begun. Last night it was awful. There must be between three and four hundred thousand of them. They emerge, at 10 p.m. punctually, from two caverns by each window. Their survey of the room is (as the Webbs said of India) 'a stupendous example of British amateurishness'. The old ones, vast and potbellied, stay in meditative raptures near the night air. The babies trot in and out between their legs. The middle-aged travel. They dizzily climb the walls. They turn triumphantly along the ceiling—its glades and peaks are extraordinarily romantic to them—above the bed they become uneasily aware that Something's Up—they look down —then agonizedly perceive 'There's someone else in the room'. They lose their heads. I watch them reel and totter. With a slight scream they fall, and then there's a new wood-louse chase through the bed-clothes for me.

Strachey was therefore in two minds whether to accept the kind invitation to stay.

News of *The Sentimental Exile* had first reached Marsh from Lowes Dickinson, who had of course found it in the King's magazine. As Marsh was now supplanting St. John Lucas as Brooke's private critic in chief and adviser, his reaction to the poem was heartening.

It's *lovely*, my dear. I see why Dickinson likes it best, and I think I agree with him, it's the most human thing you've written, the only one that has brought tears to my fine eyes. You say it is hurried. I do hope you'll polish it up just a little and make it perfect . . . I showed it to my two old pundits Gosse and Dobson, they were enraptured! and begged me to assure you of their continued admiration. Austin Dobson said they were the best octo-syllables since Shelley I think it was. Gosse very much wants you to leave out the couplet in brackets about shooting themselves, which he thinks silly and out of key. I don't much like it. Also he says why Satanic? why make them evil spirits when it's much nicer and more fun to think of them as good ghosts of good clerics? and he says if the clerics are Satanic, Byron, Chaucer, and Tennyson, must be so too. Well, it's a lovely poem. I'm not sure the line I like best isn't 'From Haslingfield to Madingley'. You certainly have the art of using proper names. *Never* write anything so good again without my knowing. I should never have heard of it if G.L.D. hadn't mentioned it in a postscript—and then where should I have been?

Having recently had him to stay for three nights, Marsh was puzzled that in all that time Brooke had apparently not thought his poem worth a passing mention. Perhaps it was too intimately connected with a period of misery that he wanted to forget. Certainly the poem was a painful reminder. He had done it, and there was an end. He couldn't face revising it. A German colloquialism was given its correct form; he substituted a 'between' for a 'betwixt', and at Marsh's suggestion he changed the title. This was perhaps a pity, since the poem lost its clue to the key in which it was pitched. As for the recommendations passed on from Gosse, the ghosts (including Tennyson) remained Satanic, and the elders of the village continued incontinently to shoot themselves.

At the end of July he joined Maynard and Geoffrey Keynes and others, including Noel, at Eversleigh where there was a house-party, with much good talk and readings from Jane Austen by Maynard after supper. 'Did you catch that, sir?' Maynard would bawl in James Strachey's ear. It was the new joke to pretend that James was more deaf than he actually happened to be at the time. 'Eh, eh?' said James, cupping a tremulous hand to his ear, playing up. But the pleasantries were lost on Rupert. He was taking strong sedatives to make him sleep. There was a solemn task before him. Justin Brooke was staying close by together with his famous *Opel* automobile. To him Rupert confided that he had promised by now to have made up his mind about marrying Ka. He must meet her somehow. Justin offered to put himself and his vehicle at Brooke's disposal, but considered the suggestion of a café in Oxford, the proposed rendezvous, a bad one, for Ka would have to travel too far. Instead, Justin suggested putting Rupert down at the roadside near Bibury, then fetching Ka and leaving them together to wander away into the woods.

This plan was put into operation. It was August 2, a day of intense heat and stillness all over the coloured counties. When the two had walked away through the fields, Justin waited at the wheel of his car a little further down the road. He sat there, wondering, for three hours, and in all that while no vehicle came past, and there was only one passer-by, a farm-labourer who touched his cap and genially remarked in broad countryman's burr, 'The corn's gett'n ripe,' as he walked on. There wasn't a breath of wind. At last they appeared, leaning against each other, but only at one in the pain they shared. Nothing was said. Ka was holding the pieces of her broken *pince-nez*.

They drove her home, then Justin and Rupert spent the night at an inn near Witney. Brooke had insisted that she should tell Mrs. Cornford her own version of everything before he spoke to her himself. This Ka had done shortly before they met at the roadside. 'I remember her,' wrote Frances Cornford in her random reminiscences, 'leaning her head right back against the wall while tears poured down her fair skin, and saying, "You don't know how awful it is when one has broken down that wall of separation that one lives in and let another human being come right in, to have to live alone again." She pushed out her big hands as if she was trying to push away the wall that had closed round her again. This was the most dramatically expressed thing I've heard her say; generally she was as quiet as a tree in suffering or joy.' Ka could not have failed to 'notice the sea, hear the murmur of the billows'.

It was now as if Brooke were trying to hand back to the friend, who alone could help—since she loved them both—the person who but for dire mischance should have been his wife. At Witney, on the night of the worst day he had ever known, he began a letter to 'Comus' and his wife at Conduit Head.

You'll anyhow have gathered from what of the story you heard (and you didn't hear it all, if only that Ka doesn't know it all), that we were waiting to get clear a bit—It seemed useless to prolong the strain—I know it's all no use—So today I went, *en route* for Rugby (I missed a train, and am stranded here), with Justin, in his motor, and saw Ka for four hours; and told her. I can't love her, you see. So now it's all at an end. And she's passed out of my power to help or comfort. I'm so sad for her, and a little terrified, and so damnably powerless.

Oh Frances, it was Hell. Ka, whom I loved, whom I love so still, is in such hopelessness and agony. My God, it was awful. When one's seen people in pain like that, one can't ever forget it. Oh, to hurt people one loves, so. I feel as if I can't go on loving, for the despair of it all. I feel like a criminal (though I know I'm not). She spoke wildly—one does at first, I know—it was terrible. I'm aching so for her.

She was so fine. It's so easy to be bitter and mean, especially after a strain; I've been bitter and tiny often these months; she has, sometimes; but she wasn't bitter—only nakedly bare and true, simple, she was fine.

She's in such agony. No one can comfort or help her. It tears me so, to think of her.

Next morning he added another thought—

You might write (saying I've told you that we're ended) and praise her. Don't discuss it all. Just say what you think of *her*, as herself—tell all the truth of how great you think her, and then lies. Pile it on, it doesn't matter if it's true—love and praise. It's the only sort of thing that helps human nature in these bloody moments. It sounds silly: but it's true. Not that anything'll do much. And it's impudent of me to write in this way. I'm all exhausted and worn with the pain of it.

—then finished his letter on the platform at Oxford station as he awaited the train to Rugby. He had promised to celebrate the happy day with the Ranee.

It is incredible that two people should be able to hurt each other so much. I expect I shall see you.

RUPERT

I'm twenty-five today.

After three nights he made his way to Cambridge and Conduit Head, anxious to hear what solace Mrs. Cornford had managed to give, and eager to lay before her his own account of the troubles. She was ready with a plan, having noticed that the only time in recent months when he had seemed at peace with the world was when he was occupied in painting an awning in her garden. She recalled the image of his absorbed attention and believed it was a clue to the sort of cure that might restore his balance of mind. He must go away, as far as possible from England, and undertake the simple task of a man who labours with his hands for a weekly wage. The place she picked on was California, and for some reason the notion became fixed in her mind that the ideal occupation for him, once he had arrived on the coast of the Pacific, would be something connected with oranges. Whether he should pick or cut or, more feasibly, *grade* oranges, she could not at this stage particularize beyond the species of fruit. The orange became a symbol of spiritual therapy, and in both their minds 'California' acquired the significance of the one spot on the face of the globe sufficiently remote from Woking and Limpsfield (the two focal points of his disquiet) to render his menial task effective. But chiefly, he must quit not only the country but Europe. Ka was given similar advice, and within a few months she was over the German border into Poland. As for Brooke, he saw the wisdom of a complete break, but he was slower to act. It needed an effort of will, and he had lost the power of decision.

From Cambridge he went to stay with Gilbert Murray and his family at Overstrand, Norfolk. Rosalind Murray (whom Mrs. Cornford had introduced to Brooke during the rehearsals of *Comus*) was now a trusted friend and another source of help; but unhappily no one succeeded in preventing the two who had become inseparably locked in a relationship of love-hatred from exchanging letters. They would not leave each other alone. 'Read *that*!' each in turn would exclaim, throwing down the latest communication on Mrs. Cornford's table; each with the same words, brusque tone of voice, and even the identical gesture. From Overstrand he sent Ka news of Mrs. Cornford's suggestion that he should go away for a year 'before deciding where I am . . . I suppose I might as well go. I feel more inclined to kill myself. I thought Frances very good and fine. Of course she doesn't understand what males feel or want. But she seemed better than anybody else . . . At present my mind has about as much chance of deciding about going, or anything, as a river has of deciding where it shall run into the sea,' and he admitted the revival of his love for Noel, adding by way of comment that she herself of course had grown sick of him long ago.

James Strachey came to Rugby for a night—it was still August—and hearing the long and lamentable history over again, maintained that his brother Lytton was altogether unfitted for the role of Pandarus that Brooke seemed to be assigning him, and was innocent of any such thing; and he defended his brother's friends, among them Ottoline Morrell, from the imputations that were put upon them. For now the whole group that lived in Bloomsbury and borrowed its name for their circle—even including such an old acquaintance as Duncan Grant or so cherished a literary companion as Virginia Woolf—were all tainted in Brooke's mind with the same baleful influence, described for Raverat as 'the subtle degradation of the collective atmosphere of the people in those regions—people I find pleasant and remarkable as individuals'. Strachey at Bilton Road must have been almost speechless in the face of this wholesale attack, except to say bluntly that it was nonsense. But on this one subject of the influence of Bloomsbury as a whole Brooke would not tolerate an opinion contrary to his own, nor could he endure for long the presence of any person who could entertain such an idea. There was nothing for it but to break with Strachey, who left the house prematurely, as Ka herself had done in March. The dispute continued a while, neither yielding an inch; the one growing more strident as the other stuck to his more discriminating view; and now it was Brooke's misfortune not only to have lost his oldest friend but to have sent him packing. They met, briefly, dutifully, once or twice more. They were never reconciled.

After this interval of time it would be idle to inquire more closely into the rights and wrongs which lay beneath the sufferings of this year, nor is there need to try. What must not be overlooked is their effect on Brooke himself. By now, mid-August, it was growing clear. Within the compass of this one topic which brought about the break with Strachey—an emotional complex of love, hate, jealousy, recrimination, disillusion, self-reproach, and austere moral judgement— Brooke never lived to regain that wholesome objectivity and balance which restores the sense of proportion after a phase of breakdown. The injury had gone too deep. His condition remained—in this one sphere of memory and association alone—what scientists who chart the mind would have us call paranoiac. On the broader and more conscious plane the shock was such as to transform his anti-Victorian zeal into a respect for much that he had formerly despised and brushed aside as needless. Since no one can define normality, and since there are wise men who have said there's no such thing, it may at first seem peculiarly unilluminating to remark that from now on just this was high among Brooke's values; but within any given *order of society* the word does have an aura of meaning, and it can do service here. Mrs. Cornford gives evidence that he began to think differently about the accumulated knowledge of truth which underlies the elementary conventions, whose observance is the average man's first step towards security, or at least stability, in his private life. It was a *volte face*, whether or not we regard it (as he himself would never have done) as a return of the prodigal to the social values of the Victorian middle-class that were his by birth.

After Strachey's last and final visit to Rugby, Brooke went to stay with John Masefield and his wife at Great Hampden in Buckinghamshire. By then Ka had replied to the agitating letter she had received from Norfolk. As so often before, she was aiming to give nothing but calm, but by now she had little to spare. 'I sit in front of the cottage writing,' Brooke started, in hopefully casual vein. 'Mr. Masefield is inside, singing old sea-shanties to the baby.' Her letter was to hand. 'It seemed very wonderful and beautiful. There's that—if you want to know the good that one's got—seeing the great beauties in you.' He can give her, for what it's worth, the comfort of assurance that Noel will never marry him now—'she rather dislikes me, and always will'. Soon, though, he is carried away by an upsurge of the bitterness he can no longer keep in check, for now he cannot get himself to cross the Atlantic, as he admits would be the sensible thing, because he dare not leave Noel behind unguarded; she is still unspotted by the world and happens to share with Ka the same friends whose influences he dreads. In this, the letter which touched the lowest depths, and which need not be quoted at length, he echoes her own words which lie on the paper to hand. 'I "make the world a horror"? I must "trust people"? But, child, the world is a horror. You know it is. And you know it's "nonsense" about trusting women—Oh one can't go into it again.' She had obviously expressed her sense of outrage at the idea of killing himself (as he had hinted in his letter from Overstrand) for no just reason that she could possibly see. There could never be an adequate reason for such a thing, she seems to have contended, and in countering her argument he plumbed his misery. A few lines are enough.

'Suicide'—oh, it's not because I've messed things with you. I'm too selfish for that. It's, as far as it goes, not for any rational reason—but because I'm finished. It's merely the feeling—I'm no good; there's despair—the days bring a sort of pain and nothing else; and I think I'm a little mad. My dear, it's nothing to do with you—I'm somehow rotten. And I guess it'll be better if I don't leave children—people like me—behind.

It was fortunate that Brooke was at Great Hampden, in the company of Masefield, an older man of robust and noble spirit, but there was little that any friend could do. For some reason he now went to Clapton to see the body of General Booth lying in state. A dull, heavy silence reigned in the hall. 'Hysteria,' said Brooke to his companion, under his breath, 'Hysteria gone stale in the air!' On August 21 he wrote from Rugby to Sybil Pye. 'I crawled here a day or two ago with ghastly headaches, in collapse.' He was off again before the end of the month. Harry Norton, the Cambridge Apostle, called and drove him away to the remote peace of Moffat in Scotland, where he slept long, ate little, and hardly spoke beyond what courtesy required. From Scotland he wrote to Raverat, who would be seeing Ka. 'Don't worry her with all your bright intellectualist explanations, generalizations, and theorizings about what Should and Shouldn't have been, about her Nature, about mine, about Woman . . . Love me, if you will, for suffering . . . but I think it's foolishly romantic to honour one for it. Suffering's a dirty business. It only weakens and destroys at best—and worst, poisons. Nor do I at all love life.' On edge he wrote to Mrs. Cornford, who was afraid she might have upset him by her criticism, for she had done some straight speaking.

You are so stupid. Isn't the situation clear? I have, and Ka has, been through a bad time, and we're both, more or less, for the moment, in a bad way. One's friends may help—who else can? You can't expect the Sultan of Turkey or Mr. Balfour to take much interest in us! One's friends are limited in number. Knock out, for the purposes of the present, those who haven't grown up. Knock out those who aren't good. There's a handful left . . . What can one do but take their love? . . . Oh, don't you see? Let's have no more of it. You're good; and you understand things—more or less, as human beings can. That's all. You can't, now, make me 'angry' . . . You can only make certain comments, give certain advice. I can only say 'Yes, thank you' or 'No, thank you'. Either of us may be right, or wrong. And beyond that there's love and strength and one or two things, one can get.

On the 27th he arrived at his Club in Whitehall Place, and in a further letter to Mrs. Cornford, written that evening, he gave expression for the first time to an idea that was to prove important and fruitful in his imagination—the identification of a place with the people who live in it.

Oh Lord, this England place you all talk so much about, turns out to be grey with rain and drizzle.

I've been so thirsting for England (not that I've really got much feeling for the place—but England = places + atmosphere + people I know). I've an idea I may work in Grantchester. Do you know the feeling when one's looked forward to a thing very much a long time, and pictured it vividly, and then, when it comes (a party it used to be perhaps) you're a little tired possibly, and you've thought about it too much—and it doesn't come off. Everything's *there*, just as it ought to be, only—the emotions don't come.

There's the ices, and the games, and the lights, and the decoration, and the laughter, and the supper-table, only—where's that happiness business? It's really a state of tiredness. It generally passes in a minute. I've now got it. I expected England and my friends to be—so wonderfully fresh and beautiful and invigorating . . . and now I'm here, and there's only the Strand, and the National Liberal, and X. and Y. and Z.—trotting their round . . .

While in London he screwed himself up to the point of broaching to his mother the idea of breaking away for several months. 'I feel it is so probable that I shall only get iller and iller whatever I do in England. Many of my friends are very eager I should go off to some place like California where the climate is good and I could find some physical work of a steady kind to do.' The Cornfords were urging it; Lowes Dickinson had actually offered to help him with the expenses. There was small hope that Mrs. Brooke would approve. At the same time he wrote to Dudley in Berlin:

Frances Cornford, who is the only decent person in this country who knows about it all, and understands, and is good, is a great blessing. She turns out to be a fine person. The only emotion I have nowadays is thankfulness for what good people there are.

Frances wants me to go to America or somewhere for a year for Ka's sake, for mine, and for everybody's. America means, if possible, some physical work and little or no mental. California . . .

and then his forlorn hope, slender enough, that some day things might turn out well for him and Noel.

I daresay I could work it. There's a good deal of love for me to go on . . . Supposing, they say, I came back in a year *well*; all would be clear, and might turn out successfully—and anyhow I'm too weak and exhausted to bear reverses now . . .

Then comes my crux: that my nerve has gone.

It's that. Do you see how I'm racked? There's poison round.

On September 17 he arrived at Gray's Inn to stay for a week. Not long before he had written his name on an envelope and pinned it to the front door at the top of the winding stone stair. He had been invited to make this his London *pied à terre*. In the flat on two floors, now packed with modern paintings, there was a small spare room overlooking the front entrance, with a view of roof-tops towards Holborn. Here he was looked after by Marsh's bed-maker, as he called her in Cambridge fashion, a comfortable body from Derbyshire with a sharp eye for economy, and a cacophonous laugh. Marsh himself, away at the Admiralty during the day, lived in a regulated whirl of social engagements, so for much of the time Brooke was able to have the place to himself. In its bachelor serenity the atmosphere at Raymond Buildings was reminiscent of Lowes Dickinson's room in Gibbs's Building, though one got the impression that much too much in the way of books and pictures was being crammed into a small space; and here there was an alcove under the stairs, like a cupboard without a door, furnished with the convenience of a telephone jutting out from a wall-bracket on a stem of ornamental iron, down which one could shout arrangements to the Ranee at Rugby; and there was Mrs. Elgy to bring in plain but wholesome food on a tray, and lay it, as requested, on the floor by the fire; and then there was Marsh himself, anecdotal at breakfast, ready with the apt quotation even before he was dressed, in whose presence sweet reasonableness reigned unchallenged; spiritual or mental confusion was so foreign to his neighbourhood, that Brooke must often have felt able to delude himself for hours on end, that Cannes, Starnberg, the doleful woods near Bibury, and even the 'estranging sea' itself, were all the figments of a dream.

Chapter X

ENTER PERDITA

(*September 1912–May 1913*)

On arrival at Raymond Buildings he found Marsh wanting to take him out again. The wood-yard at King's Cross was ablaze. They ran out and hailed a cab, and on the way picked up Wilfrid Gibson, the young poet from the north on a first visit to London. An immense throng had gathered at the fire, and so as to prevent themselves from being jostled apart in the crush, the three of them linked hands, swaying in the press of people with a great light wagging across their faces. It was Brooke's first meeting with one of the three poets who became his heirs.

At about midnight of the next day the conversation at Gray's Inn was of some consequence. Brooke and Marsh were alone, discussing how the British public might be provoked into taking more interest in contemporary verse. Brooke—consciously or no—came out with a variation of a pleasantry of his in a letter to Lucas written in 1907. He was then engaged in writing an article on what he called 'great slabs of minor verse' for the *Cambridge Review*. It was his first public essay in criticism, and he had before him seven volumes, 'all the same,' he told Lucas, 'and all exactly the stuff I write. I frequently wonder whether I have not written them all myself under a pseudonym and forgotten about it.' On the present occasion, he facetiously proposed writing the entire contents of an anthology of 'new' writers, adopting a dozen pseudonyms, equally divided between male and female, and then, while the striking individuality and merit of all twelve was being acclaimed by the critics, he would spring his surprise in, say, the correspondence column of *The Times*, using that platform to expose the general gullibility and inertia. To this, as is now well known, Marsh replied that Brooke might as well spare his pains. He could probably name twelve actual poets whose work if grouped together would show clearly enough that English poetry still flourished.

Next day, Gibson, Drinkwater, Harold Monro, and Arundel del Re, his assistant on the *Poetry Review*, were all invited to luncheon at short notice. They met at Gray's Inn, and a new enterprise that Marsh wanted to call *Georgian Poetry*—no one really liked the name, but no better suggestion was forthcoming—came into being, with Marsh as editor, and Monro's Poetry Bookshop as the publishing house. This shop did not as yet officially exist, though Monro had recently found suitable premises at 35 Devonshire Street, off Theobald's Road. It stood conveniently near Gray's Inn, and when the inaugural meal was over the party walked round to inspect what was then known among them as 'the future Poetry Review House'. Drinkwater, brought along by Monro, was a newcomer to both Marsh and Brooke, and that evening Brooke called in his old Rugby friend, Denis Browne (now organist at Guy's Hospital) to meet Gibson and his host. A new circle of friends was coming into being round the Georgian idea, with Marsh's rooms as their meeting ground.

What interested Brooke most was the organization of the publicity. It appealed to his practical sense. As for the selection, his chief concern, according to Monro, was that the anthology should startle its readers out of their apathy. Marsh, on the other hand, did not believe that 'shock' was the best method of achieving their end, nor that violence was necessarily an aspect of literary merit. He favoured an appeal to the sensibilities of the general reader, not agitating the social waters, but winning by wooing public interest. For him the social values and those of art were not necessarily antithetical. They were complementary and of mutual service. He had no policy as an anthologist, trusting that an orderly exposition of his own taste would be enough to make his point. In this he was to succeed beyond his dreams, and no one could complain, but it was rather a different kind of achievement from what Brooke himself envisaged. Leaving the editor to make his selection, he went home to Rugby.

'I've been meeting a lot of poets in London,' he wrote to Mrs. Cornford, 'they *were* so nice: very simple, and very goodhearted. I felt I'd like, almost, to live with them always (and protect them).— But London won't do.' He was refreshed—'I do believe, just now, that God's giving me a kind of respite. He seems to have ceased to fiddle with me for the last week or seven days'—but he was restless.

For the moment. One can't—I can't—be properly and permanently all right till I'm married. Marriage is the only thing. But, oh dear! one's very reluctant to go into it without love—the full business. Love, love—I feel so awfully hungry for it, sometimes. To have had it once—the complete thing—does seem so much more important in life than anything else. And life's very short. Marrying without love seems like shutting such an irrevocable door on all that matters. So that even peace and freedom to work scarcely count. I think, you know, love's more important for men than for women. You, if you miss that in its fullness, have probably, children: and half your life's fulfilled. But we've only the one thing to pray for: and, if we miss it—work and so on.

It comes on me that it's rather a truism that Love's an Important Thing. I'm sorry. It's a remark I found I *couldn't* make to Mother at dinner: and one must work off one's loneliness somehow! But, as Bryn disgustedly observed to a sister, after a long general conversation with me some weeks ago, 'Rupert holds such dreadfully conventional views nowadays!' So again, I'm sorry.

The only disturbing piece of news was that the Ranee was opposed to California. 'She was frightfully upset. I shall have it out with her some time. She thinks any kind of physical work would be very bad.' To this Mrs. Cornford replied, 'I'm sorry about your mother. I do believe mothers matter more than this generation is inclined to give them credit for.' This, she admitted, was perhaps another truism in return for his about love. She saw no objection to such things. 'At the age of ninety one will have waded through blood and tears to the morality of the Latin Grammar—at least *my* Latin Grammar was very profound. The other truism I believe *passionately* in, as you know, is "regular occupation", if you really can begin something of that sort straight away. You seemed too shattered and ill when you were here, I thought you couldn't possibly mend without making a break and starting clean.' She had just seen Ka off at Victoria. 'I do enjoy every day with her so much, all the little things like cheese and yellow leaves and fires, they matter to her and they matter to me. Perhaps they do to all women. I wish she was my sister.'

To Marsh he wrote, 'Do you want it called *The Sentimental Exile* or *Grantchester*?' He couldn't revise it. 'I fear it'll have to remain its misshapen self. I get so excited, wanting to scrap those poems, and write you much better ones, that'd fairly boom the book and obliterate poor Jan [Masefield]—but I shan't.' He endorsed the dedication, but with reluctance. 'You know, I don't rate Bridges so highly. I think Yeats worth a hundred of him. But he's a fine figure; so perhaps it'd be all right'; then a few days later, 'I find myself believing

I can make a rival better selection from the same poets! Of course, I can't set up to advise you, but I can taunt.'

Early in October he went to stay with Middleton Murry, editor of *Rhythm*, and his wife, Katherine Mansfield, at Runcton Cottage, near Chichester. It was they who had found lodgings for Gibson when first he came adventuring south from Hexham, and of him they talked, and of the Georgian experiment, and Brooke in macabre mood, astonished his hostess with a tale he had picked up somewhere about an old woman who sat at her open window for so long that at length the neighbours broke in, only to discover that the lower part of the body had been devoured by her own cats.

On October 8 he brought his bag to Raymond Buildings, and Marsh took him to the Moulin d'Or to meet Walter de la Mare and, as was becoming the custom after a meal out, all three went back to continue the talk in Marsh's rooms. This was his first meeting with the second of his three heirs. Another day Gibson, Marsh, and Brooke spent the evening with T. E. Hulme, in the decaying grandeur of his apartments in Frith Street, once a saloon of the Venetian embassy. Hulme, the philosopher-poet, translator of Bergson, whose ideas adapted from the French Symboliste poets prompted Ezra Pound to formulate the conception of poetry known as Imagism, was the young figure-head of an obscure movement in literature that was to enjoy none of the popular success of the Georgians until it emerged as the forerunner of a style characteristic of the modern poetic mind. It was the poetical underground movement, at present drawing its nourishment from France, soon to absorb the principles of psycho-analysis, and found a new tradition, reopening and widening that breach between the artist and the general reader which the success of the Georgians had partially closed. It was to demonstrate in fact, that the gulf *cannot* be closed. Along with everything else in the modern society poetry was becoming the concern of specialists. The social values of the Georgians (a group particularly conscious of its audience, which accounts for their efforts to revive the verse drama) did not come into it at all; there was no question of attracting the public closer to the poets, for the poets were busy, talking brilliantly among themselves and sometimes even *to* themselves. Only they could understand their own language, and it was as if the ministers of a once popular faith were conducting a ritual not only among members of their own order, but exclusively for their own benefit, regardless of their dwindling congregation. This was the antithesis of Georgian-

ism; and here were Marsh, Gibson, Brooke, Hulme, F. S. Flint, and
Ezra Pound, blandly consorting, unaware of the division of principle
among them, so that Pound himself, recommended by Brooke, was
invited to contribute to the first Georgian anthology, as if there were
nothing incongruous in the idea. But neither movement had as yet
developed its own identity, and the anti-Romantics led by Hulme were
lacking the cohesion enjoyed by Marsh's companions. There was no
love lost, for instance, between Hulme himself and Pound, the former
(a young man of formidable physique) having made up his mind
exactly at what point his patience was going to give out altogether
and he would be impelled to kick the latter downstairs.

Next morning Brooke went to the Old Vicarage and read a short
paper in Cambridge, probably to the Society, since it was Saturday
evening; and he had agreed to address the 'Heretics,' a few weeks
later. He called it 'In Xanadu', and his listeners, those who had never
heard the speaker before, must have been puzzled. He said he had
recently experienced two symptoms of advancing life; he woke up in
the middle of the night and thought about his friends, and he constantly found himself meditating on what he could only call 'goodness'. In the past he had been content with an intellectual understanding of ethics, but now, 'out of the corner of his mind's eye', he
perceived something more. Moral taste, like an instinct for Beauty,
was an element of character that could be cultivated. 'It is the most
important thing in a man—its possession the only thing I care for—
or should caré for—in a man. Its absence almost the only thing I
hate.' He contended that 'love of goodness' produced as distinctive a
brand of character as the acquisitive instinct or the love of Beauty.
'And I also think, now, that this passion for goodness and loathing of
evil is the most valuable and important thing in us. And that it must
not in any way be stifled nor compelled to wait upon exact judgement.'
He ended by saying that if ever in life one detects evil 'one should
count five, perhaps, but then certainly hit out . . . It's the only battle
that counts'.

There was no mention of his 'states of mind', no reference to Moore
although he said nothing directly opposed to that chapter on ethics in
Principia Ethica which, however, his undergraduate contemporaries
had ignored. It was partly this talk, no doubt, which led E. J. Dent
to remark that for some reason there had been 'a shift in the core of
his being' since Brooke's recent visits to Germany. Earlier that same
evening, before giving his talk, he had dined at Magdalene with

A. C. Benson. 'I felt him to be oppressed by a great weariness of the life he had been living,' Benson recalled. Brooke was deciding to travel, but asked for no companion. Benson was puzzled to notice that his guest seemed anxious to 'obliterate by all possible means something which seemed almost like an obsession; for he spoke of his trouble very seriously, and even with a sort of terror, as if he had for the first time realized that there might be onsets which he could not resist, and wounds which he could not cure.'[1]

The wounds were still open, but now there was a new element in Ka's life, and to Brooke, so fearfully concerned for her well-being, it represented a distinct sign of hope. He welcomed her growing friendship with Keynes, but even there, it seemed, the waters were far from placid. After talking with Gwen Raverat, Brooke must have thought it would help Ka to have his comment on the new situation. He wrote from Grantchester.

Geoffrey popped in on Sunday and lunched. I thought him extraordinarily nice. Today Gwen told me (don't be angry with her) of your fuss with *him*. It was that, I suppose, you nearly wrote about. It doesn't distress me to know about it. I'm concerned lest in any way it should end in him not seeing you. He's a good person—and so unique in London—the London you and I know.

When I've thought of you, what you could be doing, I've sometimes suddenly thought 'She may be with Geoffrey', and glowed content. I don't see the point in him not 'knowing'—unless you fell in love with him. I wish you would. His devotion to you makes me rather happy. When I feel desperately helpless to aid or sustain you it's the one thing I can fly to, the thought of the immense love and reverence people have for you—Gwen, Frances and the rest.

It also rather sends him up in my estimation.

There's a thousand tiny things. I'll write again, for it's late now. Frances is superber than ever. And oh! Dudley . . . !

When I meet Jacques and Gwen I love them very much. And then suddenly they throw an arm around each other's neck, or touch hands: and I go sick with envy, and blind—and generally say something to hurt them.

He remained at the Old Vicarage for the rest of October, visited only by Gibson, who was amazed by his industry. Brooke was hurriedly finishing a few pieces for the next issue of *The Poetry Review*. 'I rather marvelled that poems could be written because Monro wanted them,' Gibson wrote to Marsh from Grantchester, 'and to catch posts, and telegrams about them being sent off between the verses. It seemed queer . . . anyhow from the spectacular point of

[1] *Men and Memories*, A. C. Benson, John Murray, 1924.

view it was superb.' Later he sent a post card. 'I have so often wondered how it was done. I'd have written you a letter, but we haven't a penny stamp between us.' A telegram of Brooke's to Monro ran 'Have written four poems, do you want more'.[1]

About a fortnight later Monro himself was in Cambridge, lecturing on the Contemporary Poet, by which he meant 'the poet that had caught the spirit of Darwin, that spirit which had so altered our attitude, and rendered obsolete so many ways of talking about life'. He called them (not Georgians) but 'Impressionists'. Chief of them he said was Ezra Pound, but he also gave high praise to Flecker, Gibson, and Brooke, and he told Cambridge of the Poetry Bookshop where there would be a lounge and bedrooms 'for such as present a sonnet and a shilling at the door'.

On November 1 Brooke was at Gray's Inn, looking at Marsh's spare typescript of *Georgian Poetry* (the top copy had been sent off to Monro on October 16 for printing); on the 5th he paid a second visit to the exhibition of Post Impressionist artists at the Grafton Galleries and made notes for two articles on modern painting.[2] He preferred the term 'expressionism', which the Germans used to describe the same thing. 'It recognizes what is, roughly, the main reason of this modern art—a very sensible one—namely, that the *chief* object of a good picture is to convey the expression of an emotion of the artist, and *not*, as most people have been supposing, his impression of something he sees.' He accorded the highest praise to Matisse; and among the sculptors, none of them, not even Matisse, whom he thought commonplace by comparison, could touch Eric Gill. (A few months after this Brooke wrote to Gill, having met him with the Cornfords. 'I hasten to send you £10 before my conscience can awake a storm against my giving so little for so much.' He was giving Ka Cox a Madonna and Child as a memento.) Brooke's old acquaintance, Duncan Grant, was also exhibiting. There was a 'grave loveliness in *The Dancers*. His genius is an elusive and faithless sprite. He may do anything or nothing,' Brooke wrote. 'What an eye for beauty! Why aren't his pictures better?' He also remarked of Grant 'One always feels there ought to be more body in his work, somehow. Even his best pictures here are rather thin. But there is beauty in *The Seated Woman*.' This was a coincidence. The model for the draped figure was Ka.

[1] Three of them were *Mary and Gabriel*, *Beauty and Beauty*, and *Unfortunate*.
[2] *The Cambridge Magazine*, Nov. 23 and 30, 1912.

Wearing the green and purple striped shirt he had demanded from Rugby, he left for Berlin. He still thought of translating Wedekind, and wanted to sort out the copyright. He stayed with Dudley Ward and his wife.

It's nice with these two little people—save for those moments that occasionally come to us celibates·when we stay with married people—when they talk together—or something—and one suddenly finds oneself four million miles away from any human companionship, on the top of a frozen mountain, among stars and icicles. Oh, well. I shall work.

Although one of the attractions of Ward's refuge in Berlin was its distance from the country in which Ka was living (she had agreed to leave England, but was dallying) they were still corresponding about twice a week and achieving nothing. She had finally broken from the 'other man', and sent his last letter to Berlin, as written evidence. He posted it back. 'It's not for me to destroy it . . . You are far better to me than I deserve.' She even offered to contribute towards the cost of his trip to California, if ever he made up his mind to go. He could not accept, he said, for he had hurt her too much. She argued that it would be spending the money where it was most useful. 'It'd be more useful in almost anything else,' he replied. '. . . Oh, child, oh my dear. I can't take money. I know you don't want to hurt, my dear. You don't hurt, yet you do. Or rather I do. Don't waste yourself or anything of yours on me . . . It would be wonderful, if you could be your lovely self again. It would give me a sort of peace, to know it.'

He worked hard, enlarging his old dissertation for King's, made no headway with the Wedekind affair, worked out in detail a high-powered and elaborate advertising campaign for *Georgian Poetry* which he sent to Marsh—'You'll be able to found a Hostel for poor Georgians on the proceeds'; and one day met Hulme off the train. 'I show him round and talk to him,' Marsh was told. 'He's an amiable creature, and a good talker; though I don't think much of him as a philosophic thinker. But he has an extraordinary power of observation, and a good memory.'

A belated review of me, commendably short, has just appeared in the Oxford Magazine. I give myself the pleasure of copying it exactly for you.
'Mr. Rupert Brooke's *Poems* show a good ear for metre, but otherwise have little merit. The language, though forcible, is not only vulgar, but often positively savours of the gutter. The book is full of bad taste, and is at times positively revolting. Especially disgusting is "Dead Men's Love", a

matter which, if treated at all, should be treated with reverence, not with ribaldry.'

The last sentence is mysterious.

Hulme was in Berlin for an international Convention. He did not like Brooke, we learn from his biographer, so he must have been starved of more congenial acquaintance, since he spent a fair proportion of ten days in Brooke's company. They went the rounds of concerts and galleries, or sat in the Café des Westens. 'He was always carrying his Webster about with him reading it casually in cafés.' During a suburban train journey one day, Brooke asked for his opinion on the nature of tragedy, saying he was trying to deal with the problem in his essay on Webster. Hulme put forward a theory which, he said, was a legacy from the romantic artists and known among the German philosophers of art as *Einfühlungsästhetik*, 'feeling oneself into the subject,' along the lines of a poem, that is, or into the design of a painting, so as to judge of its value by the impression on one's sensibilities. Brooke was sceptical, seeing a danger in lumping together under one heading things that were in fact diverse, and the theory propounded by Hulme, he thought, was a case in point. It was valid for the visual arts, but 'when it is contorted to cover the other arts' (he wrote in his essay after this conversation) 'the result is ludicrous'. Neither would Hulme himself have defended it. His biographer accounts for his bringing it up by saying he was probably trying to help Brooke to understand his own romanticism.[1] In that case it's a pity Hulme did not admit what he was trying to do. They might have reached a better understanding of one another.

Another night they were strolling together near the overhead railway which crossed the road by Ward's flat before coming to a halt at the station for the Zoo. Every so often the trains rumbled over the bridge, trailing their smoke, and the two men were discussing the process whereby a work of art was first engendered in the mind when another train came thundering over, and Brooke declared he had been thinking about these trains; they had suggested to him a poetic image. He said that, with him, the first direct step in composition was to arrive at an isolated yet finished line with its own movement and measure. This served as a pattern for the rest. We do not know which line set the pattern, but the poem he had begun was *The Night Journey*. The train roaring into the unknown darkness is used as an image of those forces within a man which drive him, 'borne by a will not his,'

[1] *The Life and Opinions of T. E. Hulme*, A. R. Jones, Gollancz, 1960.

always onward to some predestined end. The verse, a single sentence being sustained through more than four stanzas, suggests the forward movement it describes. Its companion among Brooke's poems is *Town and Country*, the poem of a little more than a year earlier, written while Virginia Stephen was staying at the Old Vicarage. Both poems of the same technical pattern share the same dream-like quality verging on nightmare. In the later piece, although the soul's objective at the start of the journey is 'to meet the light or find his love', the final words are 'We are alone'; nothing has happened beyond the soul's surrender to an overwhelming impulse 'unstumbling, unreluctant, strong, unknowing', and the only outcome is an eternity of the same unflagging momentum in some ampler sphere beyond sublunary things. It is a curious poem, developing the image of the rushing train and stopping at that. The early poem embroiders a fancy; the later one suggests a belief concerning our human condition for which the non-stop trains at Charlottenburg provided the image. A great deal of Brooke's work is autobiographical (romantic in the sense that Hulme would deplore) and it is possible that the train became associated in Brooke's mind with a recent conversation at Conduit Head. Talking things over with Mrs. Cornford, he had begun to think that the events of the past months could only be explained by his having been driven by some inexplicable force far stronger than his will, even outside his own passions, which were only the instruments it had used—

> *As a man, caught by some great hour, will rise,*
> *Slow-limbed, to meet the light or find his love;*
> *And, breathing long, with staring sightless eyes,*
> *Hands out, head back, agape and silent, move*
>
> *Sure as a flood, smooth as a vast wind blowing;*
> *And, gathering power and purpose as he goes,*
> *Unstumbling, unreluctant, strong, unknowing,*
> *Borne by a will not his, that lifts, that grows,*
>
> *Sweep out to darkness . . .*

'I have not been able to show,' wrote Mrs. Cornford in her notes, 'the way the great forces of life got hold of them and thrust them about: the way she at first was so blandly unconscious of this and just gave little self-complacent reasons for what they made her do; the way he realized it too much . . . his male first conceptions about life were bleeding and broken; he was always re-thinking and always constructing a new universe in the light of his new experiences. Often he was like a man trying lightly to mock at an earthquake which had knocked his house flat.' As for the lightly mocking vein, to this period belongs a morsel of light verse in sonnet form marked 'Poor, but to be published,' though it has never featured among his poems.

> Hate you? Ah, no! I've much to thank you for,
>   —New passion in my latest love-sonnets
>   A fresh store of exotic epithets,
> A novel pose . . . yes, Lilith-Eve, and more—
>   —You've stayed me with apples—from the
>   Knowledge Tree!
> I dreamt. You taught me what the dream was worth.
> I played my part (not clumsily!) Henceforth
> I'll sit in the stall and watch the comedy.
>
> Ha! now that hero rants (as I, ere while!)
> I like the lad: his soul's one scarlet flame
> Lit by Her lips (where lurks your subtle smile!)
> In the end they fade and shrivel up and die . . .
> We laugh at their brave antics, God and I.

Before Hulme left Berlin, Brooke asked him what he would do if there was a war, for the situation between Germany and Russia was growing more critical. After saying he would try for a job as a war correspondent, Hulme was surprised to hear that Brooke had already asked Masefield to recommend him. 'I've made vague arrangements to chuck the dissertation,' Brooke wrote to Ka, 'and go off as a correspondent, if Russia and the rest get fighting. It would be fun. In that case England wouldn't see me for a bit—for ever, if a bullet or the cholera were kindly.' It was another of his jaded and censorious communications, but it ended 'Be proud of the fineness we have done together. And think in years.'

He arrived in London December 12, 1912, spent the night at Gray's Inn, and went on to Cambridge for three days. 'My dissertation's in an awful state,' he had told Marsh in his last note from Germany. He was now pulling it into shape. So much depended on it, and by now it must have seemed as if he had written the first draft in a previous existence. The talks with Hulme in Berlin had led to revisions in the opening pages on the nature of Tragedy, and having got these retyped, he at last submitted the work at King's.

ENTER PERDITA

The Winter's Tale was on at the Savoy. Marsh's custom of going back stage after the performance to see his friends in the cast, now led to the beginning of a new phase in Brooke's private life. Henry Ainley introduced Marsh to Perdita, the character being portrayed by Cathleen Nesbitt, and both players were invited to supper at Gray's Inn a week later. Brooke had been present at the first night, and seen the play for a second time before leaving for Charlottenburg. On December 20 Ainley brought Miss Nesbitt to supper when the other guests were Gilbert Cannan, Elliot Seabrooke the painter, and Brooke, for whose benefit the occasion was devised. He had been moved by the spectacle of Leontes, charmed by Perdita. Now he was sickening for his Christmas influenza, and a few days after the supper party Miss Nesbitt received a diffident invitation to call on the patient at Gray's Inn, or not to call, according to the degree of her fear of infection. She also received the unexpected gift of two books of poems.

I've been so shocked at your opinion of Hardy's poetry, that I send you some to read between the acts when you're done with Morgan Forster. Will you look at it? I enclose also (to gratify myself rather than you) an even newer and even drearier work. Don't bother to read it. I just found I'd like to give it to you. The scratches in it are corrections of the imbecility of compositors and the prudery of publishers.[1]

Cathleen Nesbitt was three years younger than Brooke. Although born in Cheshire, she was of Irish extraction, and had been educated in Belfast and France. A pupil of Rosina Filippi, she had made her first appearance at the Court Theatre in 1910. In the following year she was touring with the Irish Players in the United States, and earlier in this year (1912) she had played a season at the Abbey Theatre, Dublin. The Irish Players, America (which Brooke was planning to visit) and contemporary literature, all went to provide a common basis of interest at the promising start of a new friendship. Cathleen Nesbitt, who looked even younger than her years, was well cast as Perdita, with dark hair and the delicately proportioned features which characterize beauty rather than prettiness. Unawares, and through no virtue of her own, she enjoyed a special advantage over every other woman of Brooke's acquaintance. She was 'the perfect

[1] It was his custom to substitute the original title *Lust* for *Libido* in the copies he gave away.

stranger', in no way associated with his past existence, and totally ignorant of it. He was innocent and unoffending in her eyes, and she in his, and unwittingly she brought into his life something of the freshness and ideal 'innocence' from her own sheep-shearing scene in *The Winter's Tale*. As Perdita he had first set eyes on her, and so she remained. It was as if he had been a Leontes all these months—'Stars, stars! and all eyes else dead coals'—and had suddenly discovered a means of escape from himself by assuming the role of a workaday Florizel. And so it was, but nothing could affect the load of his responsibility for Ka, nor ever finally detach his imagination from Noel; too much of regret and poignant recollection were there involved on that deeper plane where the past, although obscured, is always present.

In this month of December a show opened at the London Hippodrome which nightly delivered an overwhelming assault of delightful and invigorating vulgarity, noisy with brash splendours, magnificently unashamed, in perfect accord with that element of animal violence which had been quietly stirring under the elegance of late Edwardian society, even in such unlikely places as the poems of Masefield and Abercrombie and Brooke himself. The agitation for women's suffrage and social reform, *The Everlasting Mercy*, Georgian Poetry itself at this initial stage, here it was, or here it seemed to be, cooked up into a spectacle, set all abounce with unfamiliar and broken rhythms, and roared across the footlights under the title *Hullo Ragtime*. If ever the anti-Victorian intellectual had made a principle of irreverence, here it was in a popular cascade, not sung exactly, but 'coon-shouted', as the term was, by Ethel Levey, a woman of barbarous vigour with cropped hair under a wagging osprey, hobble skirt, and a bracelet on her ankle, while conventional musical comedy, whether English or Viennese, succumbed politely in waltz-time, or lingered on as a relatively demure refuge for the middle-aged. Cathleen was rehearsing at the Haymarket, but there was plenty of opportunity for Brooke to escort her to the Hippodrome or, when she was not free, anyone else at hand as much for the pleasure of watching his companion's amazement as for the bracing shindy of the show. The American invasion of rag-time was a social event which Brooke welcomed as a sign of the times. Morris, Wilde, Shaw, Wells, G. E. Moore, and the Fabians, they were all like intellectual sappers who had undermined the drawing-room and the conservatory on the mezzanine floor, and now it only wanted *Alexander's Ragtime Band*, played by the American Ragtime Octet, and coon-shouted by an Amazon, to push over the whole caboodle. During the next few months Brooke saw it ten times.

He spent Christmas at Bilton Road. 'Even Rugby is full of Georgian Poetry!' he reported to its editor at Gray's Inn. Ka had at last decided to go abroad. 'I'll sleep a fortnight without a care in the world,' Brooke wrote, 'if I can think you're out of England at last and fairly well.' She was hoping to stay with the Wards in Berlin, and then, perhaps, cross over into Poland. She could meet him again, he said, if she really thought it would serve a good purpose, but 'not from any silly emotional craving . . . Only, don't stay longer in England and then only loiter helplessly, round London. Better die *en route*.' On the last day of the year he travelled back to London, took Marsh to the Hippodrome, and after supper at Raymond Buildings, they sallied out again and walked to the steps of St. Paul's where the usual multitude was gathering to celebrate the New Year. A long and terrible year for him was drawing to an end at last in a clamour of bells, cheers, tears, catcalls, Auld Lang Syne, and ragtime.

Next day, January 1, 1913, he took the train for the Lizard in Cornwall where he stayed in lodgings with the Cornfords and wrote two articles on H. J. C. Grierson's new edition of Donne's poems published by the Clarendon Press. Stanley Spencer's painting *John Donne arriving in Heaven*[1] provided him with a starting point. ' "I don't know who John Donne is," a sturdy member of the public was lately heard to remark in front of it, "but he seems to be getting there." Unconsciously, he summed up Donne's recent history. Of all the great English poets, his name is least known beyond "literary" circles; but he is certainly getting there.' Brooke was in the forefront of the Donne revival. 'He was the one English love poet,' he wrote, 'who was not afraid to acknowledge that he was composed of body, soul, and mind; and who faithfully recorded all the pitched battles, alarms, treaties, sieges, and fanfares of that extraordinary triangular warfare,' and as an avowed follower of Donne, he picked on a quality he shared with his great predecessor. 'Donne feels only the idea. He does not try to visualize it . . . His poems might all have been written by a blind man in a world of blind men . . . And as Donne saw everything through his intellect, it follows, in some degree, that he could see everything humorously . . . it was part of his realism.' Brooke tried to define metaphysical wit, managed to bring in Ethel Levey

[1] On exhibition in London among the Post Impressionists.

twice, and asserted, a revolutionary judgement for those days, that Donne is 'by far the greatest of our love poets'. Geoffrey Keynes was starting his bibliographical interest in the poet, so of course he was consulted 'to know if you've anything of interest to point out about it', and regaled with a rhyme about a picnic on Ditchling Beacon. They were going to call on Eric Gill.

> The view is very sweet, and very
> Pretty, from there to Chanctonbury . . .
> Chicken and sausage-roll laid out,
> Pudding and stout, Oh Jesus, stout!
> My mouth is covered with stout froth—
> The green grass is my table-cloth.

In more elevated mood he was writing his poem *Funeral of Youth*, undeterred, Mrs. Cornford noticed, while people chatted and banged about the room. The news came that Ka had actually left the country. 'I'm afraid you'll find Berlin rather bad for a few days,' Brooke wrote. 'Places are so reminiscence-ful . . . Eat plenty.' It was now Mrs. Cornford's aim not only to hurry the other one also out of the country, but set him travelling in the opposite direction. Mrs. Brooke, rather naturally, still could not see any adequate reason for going so far afield; Masefield was against the idea of 'fruit-picking'; Gilbert Murray and his daughter Rosalind were opposed to his globe-trotting when he should be starting a career. Brooke himself, however, made desultory inquiries about sailings to New York, and wanting more time to write articles which could come out in his absence (so that he might not be entirely forgotten while he was away), wrote to Marsh, asking if he could come to Gray's Inn for a while, and forget himself in the distractions of a London season.

He took over Marsh's spare room again on January 15, and the following weeks were a round of social encounters and visits: to Middleton Murry and Katherine Mansfield in Chancery Lane; to Ditchling to see Eric Gill; to Sevenoaks to call on W. H. Davies; to spend an evening at Gray's Inn with Hugh Walpole; to the Poetry Bookshop (it had been officially opened on the 8th); to the Post-Impressionists; to see Marie Lloyd at the Tivoli; luncheon on January 22 at the Moulin d'Or with de la Mare, W. H. Davies, and Marsh, and after dinner to Woburn Place for coffee with Yeats and Pound. St. John Ervine, a new acquaintance, wrote to Brooke after this occasion: 'Yeats talked about you the other night. He thinks you are likely to be a considerable person if you can get rid of what he calls "languid sensuality" and get in its place "robust sensuality". I suppose you will understand this.' Yeats also remarked: 'He is the handsomest man in England, and he wears the most beautiful shirts.' Brooke's shirt on that occasion had been specially made for him by Ka. She was now asked to advise Yeats.

O, a message to you from Mr. Yeats. He drew me aside, as I, with others was leaving, Monday night, and asked where I got my shirt from—'A present' said I. He so wanted to know where he could get such stuff—he needs a dark flannel semi-pyjama garb to wear in the mornings about his house—I promised to find out where he could get the *stuff*—'You'll never get anyone who can make it as this is made' I flung at him, as I vanished.

'I think of you continually; almost every hour. But I aim at filling my life so chock-full that I don't have time to worry.' In this he was partially successful, but the policy of keeping his life in separate compartments met with a new complication.

Eddie brought my letters in one morning, and complained that they were —as usual—from myself—from Germany. You, of course! It was far more like my handwriting than my own is, he complained. For he often gets letters from me that—from the envelope—he can't make out who the devil it is. But your handwriting he always knows for mine instantly.

On the 24th he went to stay with the Raverats at Manor Farm, near Royston, where he wrote to Marsh, very tentatively seeking his aid in the developing friendship with Miss Nesbitt.

It *had* just occurred to me, that, as Mrs. Ervine has to go on from us to the theatre, and we shall probably pick her up there afterwards, and as they know her, and as it's so ridiculously convenient, we might include in the party, on one or other occasion, quite incidentally—oh dear me!—Cathleen. But no doubt it's quite impossible—I suppose she dines with Millionaires every night—I can see a thousand insuperable difficulties—it was scarcely worth while mentioning it . . .

Ever

R.

Back at Gray's Inn for the end of the month, he dines with Marsh, Mr. and Mrs. St. John Ervine, and Miss Nesbitt; attends the Shaw-Belloc debate with Ervine; afterwards to Raymond Buildings where he reads aloud his play *Lithuania* to Marsh, the Ervines, and Miss Nesbitt, who had rejoined them after her show. And so it goes on. For the early days of February he was in Rugby, feeling a little riled that Gwen Raverat, who was becoming a distinguished wood-engraver, had hesitated to send any drawings to Middleton Murry's *Rhythm* because of its evident support of the 'modernist' tendencies in art. Albert Rothenstein was its art editor, but Brooke was now on the committee with Middleton Murry. Mrs. Raverat being an old friend, it fell to him to protest. 'I hope the things you hate in it,' he affirmed, 'the "modernness and desire to shock" will continue. Of course, it's modern. It's all by people who do good work and are under thirty-five. It shows there *are* such, and that they're different from and better than the *Yellow Book* or the *Pre-Raphaelites* or any other body. Do you think it ought to look as if it was written by Gosse and Tennyson and illustrated by Whistler and Madox Brown? . . . As for "shocking", it's impossible to do much good or true work without shocking all the bloody people more or less.' He won his point, and also enlisted Dent and Denis Browne as music critics, then in February the social round begins again. On the 8th he goes to Cambridge to stay with Marsh's father, Professor of Surgery and Master of Downing College. In the evening they attend a dinner in honour of Charles Lamb, and Brooke meets Henry Newbolt. On the following evening at Downing A. E. Housman dines with the Master, then watches Professor Marsh and Brooke playing billiards. Rupert was not on form, for on the way back to Downing after the Lamb dinner he had looked in at King's to see if there was any mail and picked up two letters.

He had at last broken to the Ranee his final resolve to visit the United States, and now her reply was to hand. 'Why are you so unsatisfactory?' she ended. 'Is it my fault?' It was nearly three in the morning when he gave up trying to answer his mother and turned to deal with the other letter, which was from Ka. By now they were separated by many hundreds of miles, but they would not leave each other in peace. They could not agree to differ. 'I can't unlearn what I've learnt,' he had recently assured her. 'It's no good basis for an understanding to pretend that last year never happened.' And he was maintaining that he had found wisdom: 'Also, I know about love. It's all right if one can be taken in, enough, and all happens to go happily. But one can't *keep* it at that. Love *is* being at a person's mercy,' and then, with an apology for his parsonical tone, he launched into a homily on the nature of a promise. Some days passed and then she was fearing he must be ill because he hadn't written again. 'Don't fuss about me. I'm not ill, and never shall be again. I'm permanently as I am . . . If ever we meet again, it's got to be from strength—not weakness.' And now came the crisis of this new unhappy phase. During the Lamb dinner Raverat had passed on the news that Annemarie Ward had given birth to a son, which had the unforeseen effect of making Brooke feel as if he had missed his only chance. With this weighing on his mind, as well as his mother's distress, he tried to do what he could in answer to Ka's cry of loneliness from Berlin. His starting-point was the 'good' news which for both of them had only revived the old regrets. 'It was, quite unexpectedly, an awful blow for me—the news. Queer. A sort of jealousy, I suppose. It has fairly hurried up my departure.' He feared that Ka herself might be feeling much the same, but more poignantly, since she was on the spot. 'You don't know how I want to help you, child. I've loved you so and we're so closely entangled: I can't grow whole unless you do.'

You're lonely. I can't bear it. I wish I could give anything. I'd cut and tear myself all day, if it'd do anything. I'd cut my hand off. Oh my God, I can't have you going on like this. Dear child, we must build up. You see, we, or good, or something, *did* conquer. Things were retrieved from the worst. But if we don't build up—if we suffer and suffer and go to pieces now—evil wins, after all . . . Let's both do it. We must. The Cause is at stake.

One thing had touched him deeply. ' *"Courage, le diable est mort!"*—who do you think wrote that to me?—poor old Goldie [Lowes Dickinson] just before he set out for India.' They must both reconstruct their separate lives, only in this way will the devil which has dogged them all this while be finally overcome. He finished his letter next day, exhausted with nagging trouble and lack of sleep, and at dinner could hardly focus his attention on Housman, the one man whom he had longed for so many years to meet. Numb, stupid with heartache, he listened to Housman's gentle encouragement of his verses, and for a moment, if for a moment only, he may have forgotten that he was helpless to give Ka the love she needed. And in that spirit he returned to London, more than ever glad of the petty distractions; meals at Treviglio's; and Gosse and *Hullo Ragtime* in strange conjunction.

After a few days of dining out, without a moment to himself, which at any other time would have been an affliction, he was back again in Cambridge, addressing the 'Heretics' Society in Petty Cury. His subject was the contemporary Theatre, and his remarks, on Strindberg in particular, reveal much more of him at this stage than do his published literary opinions. He spoke in a soft voice, we are told by

John Harris, a friend who recalled the occasion long afterwards, and sometimes inaudibly, and he had a way of uttering 'a literary effrontery without the slightest change in tone'. He read from a desk, ran his fingers through his hair, spoke with 'a curious mixture of nervous enthusiasm and aloofness, and, as he came to the end of a sheet, tossed it away with a brusque flick of the wrist.' He began with a resounding tribute to Gordon Craig, as against 'that energetic fraud, Max Reinhardt'. Then he turned to the Diaghilev ballet, which was 'handicapped by the extremely tawdry and inharmonious scenery and dresses of a Russian jew called Bakst', nor were there enough good dancers for all the leading parts. Coming to the drama, plays were interesting out of all proportion to their merit as art, probably because they were more in touch with the ordinary business of life. 'Painting's a dull business; and a little poet goes off into a corner and writes, his back to the world, about his own little affairs. Very dreary. But plays are in some sort blood relations to what's in the hearts of men.'

Let no one suppose he was going to confine his praise to foreigners, Dostoevsky and Strindberg were influenced by 'that astounding incomprehensible foreign novelist they picked up, a passionate figure swathed in the queer mists of his western fatherland—Charles Dickens.' But one must be wary in judging writers in a foreign tongue, since few could have any real knowledge of the background of their work. The Germans can make sense of *Arms and the Man* and understand *Caesar and Cleopatra* almost better than an audience in England, but *Candida* leaves them utterly bewildered. 'Dramatists put up their plays against a certain background: a foreigner is apt to see them in the void.' How often do we find literature being misunderstood. What about the Elizabethans and their ridiculous admiration for 'that third-rate Latin tragedian Seneca'—they imagined he stood for classic drama! 'English literature has been built up on a reverent misunderstanding of the classics.'

Ibsen (whom the lecturer, we recall, so much admired in 1911) is described as 'rather unhealthy', though he had performed one useful service: he had demonstrated that the human soul subsisted on lies. 'Take away self-fostered illusions and you take life. There's your dilemma and your tragedy—truth or life? And how empty each is without the other!' He thought Ibsen's construction mechanical. His realistic avoidance of the soliloquy and all improbabilities were 'examples of that ghastly and misapplied ingenuity of technique which a generation had patiently worshipped'. Brooke grew more and more exasperated. 'Everything leads to something else nowadays!' and then he must have been having a private joke with someone in the audience who had read his own *Lithuania*—perhaps the Cornfords were there—when he added 'You would bet your entire fortune that, after they've killed the stranger for his money, he turns out to be the long-lost son.' But chiefly Ibsen was deplorable for his support of Feminism. Brooke's passionate loathing of this, and all that the term implied, made him rate Strindberg (whom he first discovered in 1911 through talks with Estrid Linder) very much higher than any other dramatist of his time. Strindberg, too, had a thesis, he said, but a far healthier one than Ibsen. 'He is out to declare that men are men and women women. It sounds an easy thing to say, but it's not. The pain of the statement nearly drove him mad.' He read aloud passages from *The Dance of Death* and *The Father*. The brutality, he said, 'and the strength of that bitterness, are wholesome.' He also quoted from *The Dream Play*, explaining that of all the dramatic unities it observed the only one that mattered, the unity of feeling. It was Strindberg, more-over, who had taught us that human beings are driven, unconsciously, helplessly, by a power infinitely greater than themselves. 'When lovers first kiss—I am *told*—they feel as if, almost physically, two gigantic invisible hands were softly, irresistibly, pressing their heads together. By such vast and uncomprehended compulsion are Strindberg's people in part moved; as people are in real life, as we are driven, with or against each other, to life or death, to pleasure and pain, but mostly pain, by forces we never quite understand'—which makes it clear that Strindberg, no less than personal experience, made his contribution to the poem *The Night Journey*. At this point we must break away from the lecture, leaving Brooke to wind up with a tribute to Frank Wedekind, who was still to be met with 'any day, in the café Odeon at Munich, in the further right-hand corner by the big coat-rack, you know,'—so as to examine a little more closely his views on Strindberg, for there, and there alone, he gave away some-thing of his new attitude to life.

Having decided to put 'the thick of the world', as he called it, be-tween himself and his old life, he felt he should be in no haste to go. He wanted to polish off certain articles. Among these there was one adapted from his remarks on Strindberg. It appeared in *The Cambridge Magazine* during October, 1913. The occasion for it was the publication by Messrs. Duckworth of the plays translated by E.

Björkman, and the article reproduced part of the Cambridge Lecture word for word, but much was added. We get the impression that Brooke considered the social circumstances in which Strindberg had worked were something like his own.

The trouble with Strindberg seems to have been that he was a passionate lover; and he was born into an age and a community tragically unfit for passionate lovers. His generation—or rather the vocal part of it, the intellectuals among the upper middle classes—in justifiable reaction against the erotic sentimentalism of their fathers, turned towards lovelessness. The morbid symptom of lovelessness is that denial of sex called feminism, with its resultant shallowness of woman and degradation of man. Feminism disgusted Strindberg, who was born with a curiously high standard of emotional and intellectual morality; its accompaniments of natural and unnatural vice shocked him. We know what Shakespeare suffered through one light woman. Strindberg was plunged into a generation of light women.

Himself by now in active revolt against at least one clause of the Fabian Basis, one feature of the influence of Bedales, one trait of the enlightened 'Bloomsbury' character as he conceived of it, Brooke went on to point out—in terms which, read with our after knowledge, cannot conceal the warmth of fellow feeling—that Strindberg 'a congenital monogamist, was born into a community suffering from a "woman's movement".' He not only stood for the tragedy of Feminism, but also for the revolt against it, and especially against its apostle, 'a great and dirty playwright, Ibsen'. The venomous dismissal of the author of *A Doll's House* came from the same distempered source as the complaints levelled against his own friends (equally enlightened, unaware of guilt, and rejected out of hand) the brothers Strachey, for instance; the daughters of Sir Leslie Stephen and the rest, people 'remarkable as individuals' as he was obliged to admit, but whose 'collective atmosphere', he believed, was responsible for Ka being able in all honesty to remark 'There's no need to love' while incidentally making men fall in love with her. He had come to think that the revolt against Victorian hypocrisy was doing harm as well as good. It had so far broken down the artificial barrier between the sexes as actually to blur their essential difference. He saw himself, and Ka as well, as the victim of Feminism. If some false conventions had been overthrown, a pernicious intellectualism, he felt, was being set up in their place. At the Heretics there was a mixed audience. The presence of young women from Newnham and Girton no doubt gave the lecturer an opportunity for spreading the gospel of Strindberg with more zeal than if he had been in the monastic circle of the Apostles. Having said his say, he travelled to London and to Raymond Buildings, that oasis of sweet reason, as it must have seemed to him, where Ibsen and Strindberg were merely two notable dramatists, the one rather more technically proficient than the other, and neither of them anything to fly into a rage about. And there he adapted his lecture for the *Cambridge Magazine*.

The month of February continued sociably with the Russian Ballet, an evening at Well Walk with Masefield who had read *Lithuania* (he thought that its best chance was on the bill of a music-hall, since the playing time was barely half an hour) and jaunts to Hampton Court and Kew with Cathleen Nesbitt. On March 1 Marsh came home from the Lakes to find a note on the hall table. 'Don't be surprised to find me giving a tea party. Come in and join us.' Brooke was there, addressing Miss Nesbitt by her Christian name. Next day Brooke again read aloud his play. Gibson and Denis Browne were there, Duncan Grant and Geoffrey Keynes; and in the evening, after supper with the Ervines at Hendon, Brooke and Marsh left the house with Yeats and the three of them walked home; on the 5th Edward Thomas came to breakfast. This was not the success it should have been. Thomas seemed ill at ease, a condition not uncommon among people meeting Marsh for the first time. Marsh consoled himself by putting it down to dyspepsia. On the 7th Brooke attended the last night of the Ballet season at Covent Garden, and next morning the news reached him at Gray's Inn that he had been elected a Fellow of King's.

He had tied fifteen votes with Noel Compton-Burnett, who had submitted a dissertation on Lord Palmerston.[1] Three days later Marsh gave a dinner party in his rooms. It became a celebration of the Fellowship. Yeats sat at the end of the table opposite his host, and the ladies, whom Brooke was meeting for the first time, were Miss Violet Asquith, the Prime Minister's daughter, Lady Cynthia Asquith, and the wife of Marsh's chief at the Admiralty, Mrs. Winston Churchill. To Compton-Burnett it was no doubt gratifying news; but to Brooke his Fellowship was an event of especial significance, a turning point, affecting him beyond the region of his academic life. He had justified himself in the eyes of the Ranee. She need no longer be at a loss to know how he would ever find a niche and a

---

[1] The specialist judge of Brooke's work was C. E. Vaughan, Professor of English at Leeds, who had published an edition of *The Duchess of Malfi* in 1896.

purpose in the scheme of things. At once her relationship with him became easier, although she still could not, in all conscience, approve of this preposterous idea of grading oranges in California. No doubt, however, she thought the Fellowship would give him a more responsible attitude to his future. She seemed to withdraw her objections, confident that more sober counsels would prevail without her aid. Brooke sent two telegrams, one to Rugby, and another to the Provost, signifying his proud acceptance, which for some odd reason was put into his hand in the course of a service in the Chapel. 'The first,' M. R. James observed, 'the first I remember to have received there.'

On the 18th he handed over his latch-key of Marsh's flat to Middleton Murry, and was admitted at King's the following day. There he picked up a letter from Ka, which was a little more reassuring than usual, and went home to Rugby. 'Your letter,' he wrote to Ka, 'reached me at King's during the last five minutes of my life as a non-fellow (you know how nervous I am!) . . . But my poor little ignorant Ka, it's very hard stooping to converse with such as you.' It was now impossible for him to leave the country at once. 'I've got anyhow to wait till April 25 in England to take my M.A. degree (higher and higher from you, my dear!)' She seemed happier, more reconciled. The relief to him was boundless. 'You build; and turn from me, as much as you can.' And three days later he wrote again. Marsh had come up to Rugby. They had gone for a long walk. 'There's even in England a sort of perfunctory ritual of green shoots, blue skies, showers, etc. . . . The queer thing is, that now I've hardened myself a good deal, and cut off other emotions, fairly short, ambition grows and grows in me. It's inordinate, gigantic. It's no use; it doesn't even make me work. I just sit and think ambitious thoughts.' A thought of another kind was that with Ka recovering in mind and body, and rebuilding a life of her own, he was at last more free to pitch his affections in another key. He began his letter to Cathleen with a quotation in Greek from Sappho, a few lines in German, and the comment 'that's for *you*. Just to teach you a befitting humility in the presence of the learned.' He was just back from Cambridge. 'I dined solemnly with very old white-haired men at one end of a vast dimly-lit hall, and afterwards drank port somnolently in the common room, with the College silver and seventeenth-century portraits and a sixteenth-century fireplace and fifteenth-century ideas. The perfect don, I.'

He was anxious not to make the same mistake again. He had let Ka realize his need for her, yet how else does one convey the sentiments of affection? 'If you don't know that you're the most beautiful thing in the world,' he wrote to Cathleen, 'either you're imbecile, or else, something's wrong with your mirror . . . But there aren't any words, most radiant: I can only measure it by its result—as one records the light of the sun on photographic paper, or the rain of all the heavens in a little water-gauge.' He sent her a copy of Belloc's *The Four Men*, and wrote again before she could reply:

It is very likely that one day I shall kidnap you into a motor as you're leaving the theatre, whirl you off to some very distant village on a high cliff over the sea, and immure you there in a cottage, feeding you on cream and beer and ambrosia and chops, but never permitting you to return to use up your transient and divine self in that bloody London. No one will know whither you've vanished. And I shall surround the cottage with a ring of cows; so you will not be able to escape. I shall wait upon you: and in the intervals look at you.

He thought it safe to spin hyperboles of admiration without in any way making his pride a hostage, or running the risk of her taking him too seriously.

I am infinitely thankful that you exist.

Your eyes are well set in, and very lovely. They change a great deal, from the beauty of softness to the beauty of light; so that I don't even know what colour they are (I do, in a way): but they're always lovely.

It was well thought of that your nose should have that ripple in the middle. If you had had a straight unindividual nose, you might merely have been a goddess. You're something so far more wonderful and beautiful.

The lines of your cheek and jaw—the Greeks may have *dreamt* of that, I think. They tried to get something of that effect in stone, once or twice—poor bunglers!

It was a long time since he had been able to indulge his high spirits.

Tell me, assure me, that you look just like you did; but better (and less white). Beer and early sleeping and country-walks, and the Cheshire Cheese —you've probably become entirely a country maiden. Shall I meet a bouncing red-faced plump hearty rustic wench in a print frock and a sunbonnet, who'll dip a curtsey and grip my hand and shout 'Whoi, 'ow's 'ee, laad?'— and it'll be you? I drivel.

This was the fourth letter in four days. As always, when life was going either very well or ill, it affected him physically, and he was now in bed with a fever. Was he perhaps being a nuisance? Awful thought. 'I'd hate that you felt I desired (but I *do* desire)—aimed at, I mean, or claimed, replies. Oh damn it, I get tied up. You *do* see what I'm driving at, *don't* you?' He could but wait and see. The Spring was as much to blame as anything else for his condition.

But, oh my dear there are things to be done! I want to walk a thousand miles, and write a thousand plays, and sing a thousand poems, and drink a thousand pots of beer, and kiss a thousand girls, and—oh, a million things: I daren't enumerate them all, for fear this white paper'ld blush. I wish I could get you from the theatre for a week, and we'd tramp over England together, and wake the old place up. By God, it makes one's heart sing that such a person as you should exist in the world.

Cathleen was not taking him too seriously, as he had intended, but it was a little galling that she should say as much. The only answer was not to be put out and to carry his extravagances a stage further.

I am, by the way, insulted (I remember). You say that I get drunk on my own words. It is a thing no lady should say to a gentleman. I daresay Irish girls are very badly brought up. I had a good mind to reply with a lot of dirty insults in German. I'll have you know that I am entirely, deplorably, cynically, sober. Nor do I hang anything on pegs (not even my clothes). I've tried that game before—and the pegs give. These plaster walls! (and wooden pegs!). I refuse to be bullied by your knowledge of mankind. I have written no sonnets to you, yet (and when I *do*, they'll be a dam sight better than what you quote). I merely state the fact that you are incomparably beautiful. It would be absurd to be intoxicated by phrases. I admit that, being human, I get drunk when I drink a lot of champagne, and I get tipsy—blind—when I see you, sometimes (it takes me in much the same way; once I couldn't walk). But, in my sober moments, I say, quite justifiably, 'that is good champagne'. Damn it, one must be allowed to comment on the facts of existence. I merely, offhandedly throw out a few facts. 'This Book is Red'. 'It is raining'. 'That tree is tall.' 'Consols are at $73\frac{5}{8}$.' 'There is no God.' 'Cathleen is incredibly, inordinately, devastatingly, immortally, calamitously, hearteningly, adorably, beautiful.' I will expand this, some time. At present I am heated. I always get so excited when I argue. I'm afraid it's a sign of lunacy.

By the end of March he was fit again, and Marsh was planning to include him in the forthcoming events of the London season—a *soirée* at Lady Plymouth's; Forbes Robertson in *Hamlet*; Violet Asquith's birthday dinner at 10 Downing Street; and Brooke himself was making arrangements to see the Raverats, Denis Browne, and have tea back-stage at the Haymarket with Cathleen. 'Isn't that too romantic! I've never been into an actress's dressing-room in my life before.' To Cathleen it was 'At $27\frac{1}{2}$ minutes past four I shall walk in and demand of that "two-handed engine at the door" to be conducted to your room. Will he do it? I'm terrified.'

He was soon to sit for the photographer who would one day make his appearance more familiar than his poems. He wrote to Cathleen from Rugby.

If your photograph looks *too* ridiculous, I may go mad and break it. So beware! How many photographs do you have taken a month, I wonder. What a life! Even we literary men, though, have our little moments. My celebrated amateur photographer who took me for his collection of Eminent Poets has just sent me two gigantic works of Art, on eternal paper—a new process—depicting a tortured elderly man reflecting in prison on the earlier plays of M. Strindberg—me, he says. I shall present them to the nation. Now I'm bombarded by an American photographer called Sherrill Schell (!). You know all about America—does he exist? He says he's in London for a month—I suspect him of being a fraud.

Astonishing and alarming woman, to prefer Strindberg to Ibsen. I do. I do. But how the Hell do *you* know that he's preferable?

He had been reading Tchekov. Another author new to English readers whom she would enjoy, especially the end of *Uncle Vanya*.

There's a lovely old nurse who comforts the love-sick girl, when all's at worst, and everyone's at odds with everyone, and they've all messed their affairs, and everybody's talking and worrying——

'It's all right, my baby. When the geese have cackled they will be still again. First they cackle and then they stop.'

Isn't that divinely lovely? I weep at it.

I've so much to say, like you. What shall we do, when we meet? Shall we both talk at once, for an hour. Or shall we have to lay down rules, like the Shaw-Belloc debate?——

His lines on Grantchester had won him the prize[1] for the best poem of last year in the *Poetry Review*. 'A double satisfaction: in defeating Sturge Moore and James Stephens and Gibson and Abercrombie and several others who are *really* better than I, and in receiving £30!' There was no end to the things he wanted to say. 'I see we shall scarcely know *Hullo Ragtime* when we see it again: for Ethel Levey has introduced *Waiting for the Robert E. Lee* in her own version, and some new performers have appeared . . .'

Life is superb. The spring makes me almost ill with excitement. I go round corners on the road shivering and almost crying with suspense—as one did as a child fearing some playmate is waiting to jump out and frighten one—I fear green——

Next morning, still in Rugby, he again tried to do justice to the

[1] The judges were T. E. Hulme, Edward Thomas, Harold Monro, Henry Newbolt, Edward Marsh, and Ernest Rhys.

genial season which he had sampled in the company of old Robert Whitelaw.

But oh, but oh, *such* a day, Cathleen! 'Spring come complete, with a leap, in a day', said the wisest and nicest man in Warwickshire, my godfather, an aged scholar—seventy—infinitely learned in Greek, Latin, English and Life. He said it was a quotation from Browning. It certainly fitted. I took him a walk. The air had changed all in a night and had that soft caressing-ness, and yet made you want to jump and gambol. *Alacer* and not *acer*[1] was, we agreed, the epithet for the air. (Latin *is* one of your accomplishments?) And all the evening from tea to dinner I wandered up and down the road glorying, and grieving that you were shut up in a town, far from this. Oh, it's *mad* to be in London, with the world like this! I can't tell you of it. The excitement and music of the birds, the delicious madness of the air, the blue haze in the distance, the straining of the hedges, the green mist of shoots about trees—oh, it *wasn't* in these details. It was beyond and round them, something that included them. It shall be like that on Sunday week, and I'll take food in a rucksack and we'll eat it under a hawthorn-bush. It's the sort of day that brought back to me what I've had so rarely for the last two years, that tearing hunger to do and do and do things. I want to write ten pages to you: to finish a play of Tchekoff's: to write several poems: to start a play I've thought of: right through the night: tasting it all: anything so long as I'm *working* at it. And at dawn to run three miles and bathe. You wrote the other day that you were going to LIVE. I understand now. By God, there are such things to do! . . .

Cathleen had received so much extravagant admiration of her appearance that she was inclined to protest. It was only one of the attributes he *claimed* for her, not herself, that he was complimenting. 'I'll even grant your elderly wisdom that it's not to you but to your beauty that we kneel,' he says, then pulls himself up. 'Perhaps this is that alcoholic writing I was to avoid'—and, taking her point on the theme of Beauty, makes another of his own, 'How's a poor mortal man always to distinguish between it and you?' He posted his letter on the way to Birmingham where he arrived at the Repertory Theatre in time for the curtain to rise on a double bill of Shaw and Yeats. He had hopes of *Lithuania*, but they were dwindling. Gilbert Cannan had given an adverse opinion; Miss Horniman of the Gaiety Theatre, Manchester said she had known six other melodramas on the same theme; Granville-Barker was so far silent; Drinkwater declared it showed promise of a dramatist, but Brooke himself was more concerned to talk him into reviving one of the tragedies of John Webster. His was the company to do it. Perhaps Drinkwater argued that he was losing

[1] i.e. *brisk* and not *stinging*.

enough money over Yeats. At any rate, while Webster provides the topic we may look at the Fellowship dissertation on his plays. It was Brooke's most interesting achievement in prose.

III

Although *John Webster and the Elizabethan Drama* is one of the necessary books for a serious student, it is nevertheless what has been called a 'Hussar-ride' of criticism. Had we not grown accustomed to Brooke's papers meant for private consumption by the Apostles, we might suspect that in these opening pages one of his principal aims was to weed out his readers by discouraging those of limited patience from reading any further. Here are the states of mind again and the effronteries delivered, as Scott said of Byron, with 'the negligent ease of a man of quality', and we can almost hear the apostolic chuckles of amusement, and smell the anchovy toast that Henry Sidgwick's biographer regarded as 'an indispensable and perhaps symbolic adjunct' at such gatherings. In the first few pages Brooke decides there is probably no such thing as Art, condemns all chronicle plays, brushes aside the comedies of Shakespeare with the phrase 'pink magic', and expects us to share his relief when he remarks 'We are luckily spared the exact dates of Webster's uninteresting birth and death'—'which,' said a reviewer of the published book, 'means nothing, for there is no "luck" in an absence of material.'

If we wonder why Bilton Road should seem to be glanced at so un-filially with 'the filthy and degraded standards of the modern middle-class drawing-room', we read on to learn that it's because the Elizabethans 'liked obscenity; and the primness and the wickedness that do not like it have no business with them'. We then come to the medieval drama. It cannot be properly understood and is hardly worth the effort, since it came into being when 'the double night of barbarism and Christianity settled down over Europe', which brings the author to assert that 'for eighteen hundred years, religion, when it has been strong enough, has persecuted or starved the arts'. That the electors at King's were able to take such absurdities in their stride is the measure of the change of climate in the universities since the Victorian day, not long before, when Jowett was reported as having thundered at a free-thinking undergraduate: 'Find a God by the end of the week, or go down.' But this whole introduction is provoking.

Clearly the author wants us to argue. So we do. 'Filth, horror, and wit were his legacy,' we read of Marston, 'it was a splendid one.' If they were splendid in Marston, why do they not redeem Middleton who is casually dismissed and is the coarser of the two? And why, having over-estimated Marston, does he qualify the praise by saying he couldn't write a comedy? What else is *The Malcontent*? and it's all very well to say 'a play of Webster's is full of the feverish and ghastly turmoil of a nest of maggots', and leave hanging in the air the implication that he relished corruption for its own sake. But was not a motive behind those horrors his need to extract almost superhuman passion from his characters, to induce, in fact, 'passionate states of mind'? and was not the aim and end of it all to lift us at length out of the squalor and make us marvel at the grandeur of human endurance? 'Of course, *of course*!' one imagines Brooke replying. Then why doesn't he say so? He wants to shock the reader into seeing through the ugliness for himself. Just in case we have nothing more than a mild liking for polite letters, and are content, he holds up Webster as a reproach. He wants to discredit the literature of elegant detachment, and badger us into making a distinction between real feeling and conventional decorum. But what *is* all this about Elizabethan obscenity? It isn't that the Elizabethans were so much obscene as unselfconscious. Surely it's thinking that determines coarseness as either clean or unclean? To any normal mind it is no worse, and certainly no better, than an aspect of essential truth. What to another seems vicious might to Brooke be only 'a tang of delightful coarse gaiety like a country smell in March'. And so we go on, protesting from page to page, and gradually Brooke builds up a picture of an Elizabethan dramatist which is vivid and convincing.

The great age of tragedy that ended with Webster petered out in a vogue for romantic dramas typified by the work of Beaumont and Fletcher. Brooke is at pains to point the contrast, making out that those later plays suffered from an enfeebling malaise of 'sweetness', a falsification of the truth, from which our literature has never fully recovered. 'As the edge of a cliff seems higher than the rest for the sheer descent in front of it,' he writes, 'the Webster of these two plays appears even mistier and grander than he really is, because he is the last of earth, looking out over a sea of saccharine.'

It was original at that time to be stressing the influence of an audience in determining the character of its drama, and he was making a discovery when he illustrated Webster's borrowings from Donne,

Sidney, and Florio's Montaigne—'Originality is only plagiarizing from a great many'; he was at his best when, describing the arrival of Elizabethan tragedy—through Marlowe and Kyd—out of native forms that were dead and Latin models that were dull, he wrote, 'To say that they grafted the energy of popular tragedy on the form of classical would be to wrong, by a soft metaphor, their bloody and vital violence. It was rather as if a man should dash two dead babies together into one strident being'. And another image of no less imaginative power describes the poetic process itself as Brooke saw it. 'The poet thinks only half in words, and half in ideas. Or, rather, with ordinary people ideas lead to one another, suggest one another, through ideas. With poets they do it through words quite illogically. The paths of association in the brain are different in the two cases. A word is an idea with an atmosphere, a hard core with a fringe round it like an oyster with a beard. Poets think of the fringes, other people of the core only.'

The actual study of Webster's work is a brilliant but relatively thin slice of analysis sandwiched between three introductory chapters dealing with the nature of art and the drama, and layer upon layer of appendices that fill half the book. It is as if his plan were to unburden his feelings in the principal section and reserve his facts and arguments for an enormous footnote. His theory that Heywood, not Webster, wrote *Appius and Virginia* is developed with minute scholarship, and although it is only the first of no less than ten appendices, it was thought sufficiently important to warrant separate publication.[1] As a whole this learned but wonderfully un-stuffy treatise throws the light of a rare sensibility on a dramatist whose greatness was neglected in those days no less than the true stature of the poet Donne. In the revival of those two major writers Brooke was not alone, but he was among the first. He was certainly the liveliest. In April, 1913, talking with the actors in Birmingham, Brooke in himself, one feels, had reached that point described in his book when the Elizabethan drama was at last free of its 'boyhood', a moment, he said, when 'the nature of man became suddenly complex, and grew bitter at its own complexity'.

---

[1] *The Modern Language Review*, Vol. VIII, No. 4, October 1913. Brooke won several supporters for his theory, but in the definitive edition of Webster's plays, published in 1927, the editor, F. L. Lucas, does not accept it without reservation, allowing only that 'part of *Appius* probably *is* Heywood's, though less than has been supposed'.

From Gray's Inn he wrote to Cathleen, but since he would be meeting her for tea in the Theatre before the letter could arrive, his account of the morning just gone by in Birmingham could afford to be lacking in substance.

> I sat watching a rehearsal of *The Silver Box* this morning. A young man behind and near me looked superciliously at me for some time. Then he caught my name (which is Brooke). He leant forward and seized me by my hair and said 'Is your Christian name *Rupert*?' I answered cautiously but on the whole in the affirmative. 'Then' he said 'I've heard your name on Cathleen Nesbitt's lips.' 'Lips—?' I said, and broke off abruptly. And after a pause, I very wittily remarked '. . . oh?' a little dimly. His eyes put an aureole round my head (very rightly): I adjusted it, and found him saying 'Oh, I know her!—a Very Remarkable Personality.' So I answered, wagging my head 'You should see her doing multiplication!' He looked suspicious, but was called away . . . He seemed to worship you. (So do I) But see how you sprinkle aureoles among your friends! I dreamt last night you were playing in a sketch at the *Palace*. What does it portend?
>
> As for those photographs—my dear, they're as large as the side of a house: one can't get them through an ordinary doorway. And they're absurd. Bloody bad. I'll bring them to London for you to laugh at.

A few days later he sat again for his portrait. This time the results were of a very different order. The American photographer Sherril Schell, who had been recommended by Francis Meynell, was living in a flat in St. George's Square, Pimlico, near the Thames embankment. There was a fog on the day Brooke called and was asked to hold each posture for one minute. The photographer was using no artificial light, and there were to be twelve exposures. Schell had been warned to expect a youth in a black shirt and a red tie. The young man who turned up at the appointed hour wore a blue shirt and necktie of the same colour 'a long piece of silk wide enough for a muffler, tied like the ordinary four-in-hand'. He gave Schell the impression of being about five feet ten inches in height, inclined to stoop when standing; and when he sat he lounged or bent forward, chin in hand. The movements were not graceful, the hands on the large side and strong. His face was 'more remarkable for its expression and colouring than its modelling'. The complexion was ruddy and tanned—not pink and white, as Schell had been led to expect—the eyes deep set, the mouth more expressive than strong 'and the lines of his chin could have been more firmly drawn'. After remarking a face well shaped, and wearing a 'spasmodic wistful expression', Schell added 'but he narrowly escaped being snubnosed'. His hair was 'golden brown with sprinklings of red', his voice rather husky. There was, Schell noted, an extraordinary candour in his glance, and his presence suggested 'vitality'. He talked of the Russian Ballet, of Ethel Levey and *Hullo Ragtime*; he was keen to go abroad, and get work, and he asked about the animals and trees, especially the fabled giant trees, of America. Of all the positions in which Brooke sat for his portrait, the twelfth and last became the most familiar, furnishing the poems with a frontispiece, a memorial plaque in Rugby Chapel with a model, and a legend with a visual image that met the needs of a nation at a time of crisis.

It was the face of a Known Soldier whose comrade lay anonymous under a slab in the Abbey. It was Brooke as Youth, perhaps, not Brooke. Mr. Schell writes of this last portrait as 'a pose that he himself suggested, his face in profile showing his bare neck and shoulders. For this he stripped to the waist, revealing a torso that recalled the young Hermes'. When the plates were developed and the pictures reached Cambridge, Raverat was so disconcerted he didn't know whether to laugh or cry. 'It's positively obscene about Rupert,' he exclaimed in a letter to Keynes. 'Let us write him a very insulting letter, suggesting that a photo of him completely in the nude would doubtless find a large sale.' No one could deny that the pictures were the work of a master in photography, but this one seemed a travesty of the true man whose beauty, if that must be the word, was lovely in that it was unconscious. The picture became known among his Cambridge acquaintances as 'Your favourite actress'. Brooke was a week-end guest of George Wyndham at Clouds near Salisbury when he sent his own opinion to Cathleen.

> Nothing's happened: except that my American photographer has sent me a photograph of me—very shadowy and ethereal and poetic, of me in profile, and naked-shouldered. Eddie says it's very good. I think it's rather silly. But anyhow, I don't look like an amateur popular preacher—as in those others.
>
> And no one will ever be able to put it into an interview, with the words 'We want great serious drama' underneath.

Indeed they could not. But must one always be giving an impersonation of a Nonconformist minister or Strindberg or Youth at the Helm in one's photographs? he must have reflected. His gift of nature had its humorous side, but his friends searched his portrait in vain for that 'candour in his glance' which Schell observed and through which alone, in their eyes of long acquaintance, the genuine man looked out.

Meanwhile the meals at the Cheshire Cheese with Middleton Murry and the staff of *Rhythm*; the Max Beerbohm private view; the footling play at the Queen's and the 'jolly' one at the Court; the Pavlova matinee; dinner at the Ritz and the whole party in three boxes at the Hippodrome; another late supper at Raymond Buildings (Violet Asquith, Diana Manners, Cathleen Nesbitt, Basil Blackwood, Gilbert Cannan, Henry Ainley); talks at Treviglio's, the Chantecler, and the Moulin d'Or, continued throughout April and the early days of May. The centrepiece of these Edwardian occasions was the birthday dinner at 10 Downing Street on April 15, when Marsh and Brooke were the guests of Violet Asquith, and Brooke sat at dinner between Mrs. Bernard Shaw and Felicity Tree. Among his fellow guests ('a most extraordinary conglomeration' he told his mother), were Shaw, Gosse, Barrie, Masefield, Augustine Birrell, Walter Raleigh, Haldane, Lady Crewe, and the Raymond Asquiths, and the flow of soul went on until just before 1 a.m. Then (although Brooke had taken over Albert Rothenstein's flat at Thurloe Square, Kensington, so as to give another and more needy poet a chance of Marsh's spare room) he went back to Gray's Inn for the night, because he could not stop reconstructing the night in talk and by morning so many of those good but ephemeral remarks might otherwise be lost for ever.

Apart from a walk, cooking sausages at the roadside, with Raverat in the Chilterns, and a trip to the *Pink and Lily* near Princes Risborough with Cathleen, the social round in the metropolis continued unremittingly until May 9, when Marsh, a kind of master of ceremonies, left home to tour the Mediterranean with the Asquiths and the Churchills, and as a parting gift gave Brooke a set of Jane Austen's novels to read on his travels. Reginald Pole, the Kingsman who played Richard II for the Marlowe Dramatic Society, had written in praise of life in the South Seas; Justin Brooke had given an intriguing report of Canada; and now Naomi Royde Smith, literary editor of the *Westminster Gazette*, hearing of Brooke's willingness to travel, was suggesting that he should visit the United States and Canada with all expenses paid and the fee of four guineas for each of a series of articles giving his impressions. There was something of a risk, for he had as yet published no prose beyond his entries on her competition page: in fact she only had his last year's article on Compton Mackenzie's *Carnival*[1], which had won him a second prize for the review of a novel, to show her editor J. A. Spender as evidence that the funds would not be wasted. This proposal eased the financial problem. He asked the Grand Trunk Pacific Railway for a 'round-trip' ticket. He was now impatient, for what Strachey called his 'horrors' were again afflicting him.

On the day of his return from Birmingham he visited Cathleen for tea after her matinee, saw Forbes Robertson in *Hamlet*, and afterwards accompanied Eddie Marsh to a party at the Goupil Gallery given by Lady Plymouth for the Contemporary Art Society. There Lady Ottoline Morrell, hostess of those friends from whom Brooke had estranged himself, drew Marsh aside, told him it had come to her ears that Rupert was thinking her 'wicked', so wouldn't this be a suitable moment to put herself right with him? for she had not taken offence. Naturally getting every encouragement (for Marsh was ignorant of Brooke's personal affairs) she went over to make peace, declaring she was only anxious to be friends. The gesture was magnanimous, and, fortunately, such was Brooke's presence of mind that she was given no cause to suspect it was made in vain. But it was. 'I'm not entirely sane yet,' Brooke explained to Mrs. Cornford, and to Ka abroad. 'It's difficult to refuse publicly to shake hands.' The obsessions of the previous year were aroused, the ensuing month of going the social round between The Cheshire Cheese and the Ritz was only a shallow surface of distraction over the old regrets, revulsions, fears amounting to terrors, which he poured out almost daily in his letters to Ka. 'You see, there are moments when I'm overwhelmed by the horror of your incapacity, and the pain's so great that I want to tell the people that *do* care for you, that if anything goes wrong with you while I'm away I'll kill them (and you) when I come back . . . oh, I can't go on.' Nor was he any less concerned for Noel though 'she, I think, neither knows nor cares where or what I am'. Then every so often the asides thrown in about the normal world—'It's funny to think that rag-time means, perhaps, nothing to you . . . *Rhythm* is coming out as *The Blue Review*,' or the momentary harking back: 'Salzburg. It's funny how one can take three days out of the middle of

---

[1] He ended his article by saying a book needs thinking out 'in half-painful ecstasy, not with pleasant quiet. The Devil of Sentimentality must be cast out, and the true God, terrible, austere, and clean, must be obeyed and served—a high and difficult service.'

Hell, and they can be clear and beautiful, almost as if nothing had ever happened. How wonderful you were.'

After a few weeks, early in May, Ward came to London from Berlin, and stayed with Brooke in the 'spare cupboard' at Thurloe Square. 'At 5 a.m. he will discover that it opens on the railway,' Ka was told in a relaxed interlude, but Ward had no very reassuring news to give of Ka, who had recently been his guest. She was now on her way through Poland to stay with a friend somewhere in Russia. She was a depressed invalid, unable to sleep. Brooke laid his anxieties before Mrs. Cornford:

'Most young women have husbands to look after them, or fathers and families. Ka has no one—her family know nothing of her real life, and she won't see much of them. So her friends have to look after her . . . I can't ever marry her, because of the great evil she did me. So I must get apart from her, even to the extent of not writing, to be fair to her. So I (not willingly) shovel the entire responsibility of Ka on to the shoulders of all of you, her friends. I don't mean that they all ought to go and live with her! But she's the sort of person who is blind and helpless and lovely as a vegetable . . . Don't be misled by the fact that she gives you more than you give her. She's helpless for all that . . . She needs direction and patient love, so. Oh God she's in such a bad way, just now.

I only mean in that she's lonely and miserable. Do often write to her and help her and look after her. And make other people do it.

And I hope she'll come to you two for advice, if she needs it ever. I shall try to make her.

Don't tell her I told you all this.

I don't really feel going off to be nearly as 'Hellish' as you imagine. I've really got quite callous in my feelings by now. I'm not excited by travelling. But I've the feeling of shaking the dust of a pretty dirty period of my life off my feet. And that makes up for any tear there may be.

Mrs. Cornford was already only too aware that her idea of planting the ocean between them was being nullified by the post, so she begged him to follow his own good counsel, and she succeeded in extracting a promise that he would write only once again. Ka, for her part, still believed that he only had to recover from an illness of the mind and he would be as glad as ever of her love. Therein lay the tragedy for them both. And now his task was to send her the most gentle, yet most conclusive, of good-byes. 'Good luck, and enjoy Poland,' he scribbled, but that didn't count. He kept his promise, but it took him over three weeks to compose the healing sort of letter that his duty to her demanded, and she deserved, and he did not post it until he had grown accustomed to living as a stranger in New York.

Declining an invitation to a ball, he wrote to Cathleen, 'I gave up dancing when I reached the Byronic, sick-o'-the-world, old, old, stage, at nineteen'. He must now break it to her that he is going abroad and give her as much good reason as his loyalties elsewhere will allow. There had been someone else. 'I've got to go for a bit, because I promised . . . Do you know how human beings tear each other? I've been so torn, and torn so. But everything's very complicated, and one day I'll explain. Maybe. Anyhow, there's my promise: I've got to wander for a bit. You chain one to England horribly.'

'I shall write to Ka once before I go,' he told Raverat, 'and then distance and time will work the break, gradually. It's a bloody world.' He'll be back in a few months, to go for another walk in the Chilterns, if not, there's always the next world—

> Shall we go walks along the hills of Heaven
> —Rucksack on back and aureole in pocket—
> And stay in Paradisal pubs, and drink
> Immortal toasts in old Ambrosia,
> Fry wings in nectar on the glassy sea,
> And build the fire with twigs of amaranth?

'The Granite Woman is resigned to my departure,' he told Gwen, but begged Jacques to assure the Ranee that this expedition was for the salvation of his soul and no idle whim. He was now like the vagabond in his talk at Rugby long since, feeling 'the quicksilver in the heart'. He asked Edward Thomas to meet him in town, for then he could 'leave the Muses of England in your keeping—I do that anyhow'. On his last evening there was a farewell party in a dive off Regent Street. Gibson, Geoffrey Keynes, and Middleton Murry were there. He missed James Strachey, although he hadn't been invited. They had met once or twice of late, but Brooke was inhibited by a kind of barrier of pride which he could neither surmount nor throw down, even although it was all of his own making. What with Geoffrey's growing affection for Ka—things might yet come right, with a rightness of sorts, in the end, even if he were still the odd man out.

Two days before sailing he met J. A. Spender, and was officially engaged as a correspondent of the *Westminster Gazette*, the only professional post he ever held. Then he dropped a line to Marsh in the Mediterranean. 'I told the Ranee to write to you if she wanted to know about my literary affairs . . .

ENTER PERDITA

I commend into your keeping all England, especially
       Wilfrid
       Cathleen
       The Nine Muses
       and the Spirit of Wisdom and Goodness
—some others, but I forget for the moment.

On May 22 he was seen off at Euston by Geoffrey Fry, the faithful St. John Lucas, and Denis Browne, who at the last moment bought him a box of station writing-paper as a parting gift. Only when the train was moving out did it dawn on him that he had left behind all his introductions to various worthies on the other side of the Atlantic. Then he wrote a line to Ka 'Be well, and return to England when you like. Soon, I hope. Love. Rupert'.

At Liverpool he gave sixpence to an urchin who answered to the name of William and gave him instructions to wave from the quay and look sorry. He boarded the *Cedric* and dumped his bag in Cabin 50, which he had chosen for the whimsical reason that it was the same number as the Ranee's telephone at Bilton Road. He was desperately tired. Perhaps he recalled Frances Cornford's remark when she started all this nearly a year ago. 'I believe the point of going so far is to forget us all, like a deep sleep.'

The gangway was pulled ashore. William waved.

Chapter XI

A DEEP SLEEP

(*May 1913– June 1914*)

The first thing was not only to thank Denis for 'the most taste-ful notepaper Euston could produce' but to explain that his letters of introduction would be found in two piles on top of the cabinet of drawings at Thurloe Square. They should be sent express to the Broadway Central Hotel. One day Denis must collaborate with him on a musical show, he suggested, some revolutionary form in which 'satire and suffering and dirty jokes and triumphal processions shall be so mixed together that the public won't know whether it's on its head or its heels for joy. We might do a Georgian Pantomime. Oh we're all going to wake up England when I return from the West.' Then a desultory stroll to the Purser's office led to his using the next page of Euston paper on Cathleen.

You'll not take it in a bad sense if I tell you that there was never anybody so nice to go away from as you! *Really*, my dear! I arrived solitary on the boat. After it had started I asked at the office—more to show that I existed than in the dimmest hope of getting anything—were there any letters for Rupert Brooke. And out, astonishingly, came a letter and a telegram; and both from divine *you*. And the letter you'd been writing all those last good days, secretly! Was there ever so nice a person? The *fact* you'd written it upset me more than I can say. And then the letter itself! I sat on my bed and laughed and cried over it. And two hours later I went past again and there was, stuck up, a list called 'Unclaimed Mail'. (I thought it sounded as if a lot of knights who had promised to equip themselves for the quest of the Holy Grail, had missed the train, or married a wife, or overslept, or some-thing)—and at the top of the list 'Mr. Rupert Brooke'. 'Good God!' I thought, 'there *is* somebody else who has remembered my existence!' But there wasn't! There was only that absurd Cathleen again, sending a silver boot, of all mad things in the world! You can't think how it cheered me up, this string of communication with you. I felt as if your love was so strong it reached with me all the way.

More pressing was the need to begin his letter to Ka. 'Oh it's bitter destroying and breaking things two have built together—intimacies and trusts and friendliness,' he confided in Cathleen rather cryptically. 'It's like cutting something out of oneself.' He was making no headway, the effort had left him 'sore and angry', so he was now telling Cathleen of his fellow passengers.

There's the American youth who came up to me the first day and said 'Say, are you a Peer?'

I said I wasn't.

He said 'I guess you'll find Amurrica vurry different from England. In Amurrica we reckon one man's every bit as good as another.'

I was very kind, and didn't remind him of the cars which are half for white and half for coloured persons. I just said 'Oh! . . .'

Then he said 'Would you like to hear me re-cite the American Constitution?' 'Yes!' I said. Cathleen, he recited it!—or a lot of it. It begins. 'All men are born free equal and happy.'

And Geoffrey Keynes was given news of his first taste of clam chowder.

> *In England oh the cauliflowers*
> *They blow through all the English hours,*
> *And all New York's clam chowder is*
> *Less dear than Rugby strawberries.*

I can keep it up for days.

They docked an hour after sunrise. The luminous trains crossing Brooklyn Suspension Bridge seemed like shuttles of fire. New York, a 'piled promontory' between the East and Hudson Rivers, 'still lay asleep in a queer, pearly, hourless light,' and the distant outlines of the Singer and Woolworth buildings seemed to him classical in feeling, yet not of Europe, the temples of some unfamiliar faith. 'Wal, I should smile,' said an American voice beside him. 'I guess this is the Land of Freedom.' 'Anyway,' exclaimed another, 'it's some country.'

He was lost. *Terra firma* reeled beneath him, and three times he nearly fainted. People in the hotel seemed to be always telephoning or sending telegrams. On his second evening he took a tram. 'A wary eavesdropper can always surprise the secret of a city,' he thought, but found himself mistaken. He was puzzled. Men took off their jackets and went on talking in shirt-sleeves; they wore loose-cut trousers and belts, everywhere great 'freedom of movement', many of either sex were handsome, few beautiful or pretty. 'Why do American faces never wrinkle? Is it absence of a soul?' Everywhere there was evidence of an implicit faith in advertising. 'This underwear does not impede the body in any direction,' seemed somehow symbolic, and among the services offered he remarked on 'funeral ingenuities that would have overwhelmed Mausolus and make death impossible for a refined man'. After a day or two he thought the United States superior to England in architecture, jokes, drinks, fish, and children's clothes, and an American walked better, 'more freely, with a taking swing'. Fifth Avenue was what 'the streets of German cities try to be . . . One feels rich and safe as one walks'; and now the elevated train clanged and swerved perilously overhead, or newsboys called the baseball news; wits cried their obscure challenges to one another, 'I should worry!' or 'She's some Daisy', and at night the vast illuminated sky-sign of a woman's head reminded him of Pater's Mona Lisa—'She is older than the sky-scrapers amongst which she sits'—and every so often she winked portentously, 'obliterating a great tract of the sky'. After a day or two he sent his first report to the Ranee. 'America is much more like England than I'd expected,' he said, not wishing to go into all the differences which he had already described for readers of the *Westminster Gazette*. 'I'm getting not to notice the American accent. So perhaps I'm developing one.'

On June 5, bearing an introduction from Lowes Dickinson, he went by train and ferry to Staten Island and met Russell H. Loines. Some years before, on Dickinson's first visit to New York, Loines had proved something more than a host. 'He helped to make the continent less like Niagara,' wrote Dickinson's biographer, E. M. Forster, and this performance he now proceeded to repeat for Brooke; he introduced him to the manageress of advertising at Wanamakers store, who demonstrated a bewildering range of wares, from a genuine Holbein, as it seemed, to a packet of pins; then Loines took him canoeing, shooting rapids, up the Delaware River. From somewhere on the bank, after a night out, sleeping under his greatcoat, Brooke wrote to Cathleen.

O little I slept tonight; and it wasn't the thought of you kept me awake, bad luck to you (though I'm equal to saying it was); but a bloody little Mosquito. Now the little white wisps of mist are creeping and curling along the face of the great wide river to my right, and the hills and woods over to the left are solemn and new and mysterious in the inhuman morning light. They look as if they'd just come back—where from?—and were lining up to perform their dull daily task of background, a little perfunctorily. They're like supers who despise both play and principals, yet have to stand there performance after performance. Where do they go to at night?

Yesterday morning I escaped with an American lawyer to this river.

Seventy miles from New York City. We found a canoe of his and paddled down, and bathed (Oh, my dear!) and paddled on—nearly four hours. We fetched up by a pub and ate there. Such eggs. The kindly woman said 'Come *right* in, boys!' and, later, 'If you two boys would like . . .' And the lawyer is middle-aged, and I, as you know very well, am not *at all* young. So we were very pleased.

They paddled another twenty miles or so to a farmhouse where lived an artist friend of Loines' among fireflies and the shindy of many frogs. At first (writing on his knee in an interval at the Fulton Theatre) he had reported to Cathleen that life in America was having no effect on him beyond making the hair on his arms grow, but now, from paddling for five hours in the sun, there was nothing but 'a swollen redness'.

But it was great. And a million things happened. Once, we came round a wild turn of the river, and there was a voice singing wonderfully, and when we got round, we saw a little house, high on the bank, with an orchard, and a verandah, and wooden steps down to the great river, and at the top of them was a tall girl, very beautiful, standing like a goddess, with wonderful red hair, her head thrown back, singing, singing.

Later in the month he stayed in Beacon Street, Boston, a place eminently hospitable, he considered, and 'a delicious ancient Toryism is to be found here . . . Yet Boston is alive. It sits in comfortable middle-age, on the ruins of its glory. But it is not buried beneath them,' and what with the relative quiet and the traces of eighteenth-century elegance it was not only hospitable but made you feel at home without meaning to. He called on Amy Lowell and, again introduced by Dickinson, on Ellery Sedgwick, at his editorial office of the *Atlantic Monthly*. Moved to record the impression made by his visitor, Sedgwick described 'a face pagan, Praxitelian, shaped before the "pale Galilean" had made the world grow gray at His breath . . . A young man more beautiful than he I had never seen. Tall beyond the common, his loose tweeds accentuated his height and the athletic grace of his walk. His complexion was as ruddy as a young David's. His auburn hair rippled back from the central parting, careless but perfect . . . Man's beauty is much more rare·than woman's. I went home under the spell of it and·at the foot of the stairs cried aloud to my wife, "I have seen Shelley plain!" '[1]

He could not linger for more than two days, for he was 'lured across the river to a place called Cambridge', to attend 'the equivalent

[1] *The Happy Profession*, Ellery Sedgwick, Little, Brown & Coy and the Atlantic Monthly Press, 1946. (London, 1948).

of May Week' at Harvard. Here he witnessed the Harvard-Yale baseball match. 'A cricketer is fascinated by their rapidity and skill in catching and throwing. There is excitement in the game, but little beauty except in the long-limbed "pitcher" whose duty it is to hurl the ball rather further than the length of a cricket-pitch as bewilderingly as possible.' Brooke reflected that in his efforts to combine speed, mystery, and curve, the 'pitcher' might be a valuable object of study for Nijinsky. But more impressive than anything was the 'cheer-leader', passionate, possessed by a demon, bounding in the frenzy of his inspiration from side to side, contorted, rhythmic, ecstatic. 'It seemed so wonderfully American, in its combination of entire wildness and entire regulation, with the whole just a trifle fantastic.' And then there was the Commencement parade of veterans from the eighteen-fifties down to the youths of 1912, but showing a poignant gap where the men of late middle-age would be parading had they not fallen in the Civil War. 'I wonder if English nerves could stand it. It seems to bring the passage of time so very presently and vividly to the mind . . . Perhaps it is nobler, this deliberate viewing of oneself as part of the stream. To the spectator, certainly, the flow and transiency became apparent . . . In five minutes fifty years of America, so much of America, go past one.' During his visit he tabled one criticism: 'The American universities appear still to dream of the things of this world. They keep putting up the most wonderful and expensive buildings. But they do not pay their teachers well. Yet Harvard is a spirit, a way of looking at things, austerely refined, gently moral, kindly. The perception of it grows on the foreigner. Its charm is so deliciously old in this land, so deliciously young compared with the lovely frowst of Oxford and Cambridge.' Among the seniors Carlyle and Emerson were the principal heroes, and Victorian England the especial subject of their scholarship. Many had attended the lectures of Dickens and Thackeray. 'One of them bent the kindliness and alert interest of his eighty years upon me. "So you come from Rugby," he said. "Tell me, do you know that curious creature Matthew Arnold?" I couldn't bring myself to tell him that, even in Rugby we had forgiven that brilliant youth his iconoclastic tendencies some time since, and that, as a matter of fact, he had died when I was eight months old.' But it was the undergraduates who were the making of his visit. 'They turn out to be an infinitely charming set of people who welcomed me with the openest of hearts and arms,' he told Cathleen. 'And so young!'

A DEEP SLEEP

On the way back he called at Yale (attracted, at both universities, by the interest in the experimental theatre) and having reported his adventures to Loines, resumed the page he had put aside on the *Cedric*. It was weighing on him more heavily every day—his farewell to Ka.

I've kept thinking how to write in such a way as would be best for you. But I won't try to. There are disadvantages in telling the truth. But between us it is still the best.

My dear, I've been worrying so about writing. And almost every night as I crossed I dreamt about you. And you always seemed in pain. I hope to God nothing extra is wrong.

He realizes that however they manage to buy peace, she must pay the most. Nothing has been gained by their letters of the past months, for he is powerless to help her towards self-fulfilment. 'It remains that we know each other better than anybody else'; their best hope lies in making a complete break with the past.

You *must* get right clear of me, cease to love me, love and marry somebody—and somebody worthy of you.

Oh my dear, let's try together to put things right. It's so hard to know what to do—one's so stupid and blind and blundering.

What I feel about you is this—I'm not arguing if it's true, I just state it as it comes to my heart—'Ka is more precious than anything. She has marvellous goodness and greatness in her. She has things so lovely it hurts to name them. She is greater and better, potentially, than any woman I know: and more woman. She is very blind, and infinitely easy to lead astray. Her goodness makes her a prey. She needs looking after more than anybody else in the world. She's a lovely child.'

And with that in my heart I have to leave you. It's very difficult. Oh Ka, you don't know how difficult it is! So have pity on me. And forgive my breaking out like this.

He has felt cowardly. 'I funk writing to you. Because it makes me concentrate on thinking about you . . . I haven't touched this letter for days and days.' He only does her harm by keeping himself alive in her heart. But she is blessed in the possession of staunch friends, and she must look to them for support.

Dear child, dearest Ka, whom I've loved and known, you must get well and happy, and live the great life you can. It's the only thing I care for. Oh, child, I know I've done you great wrong. What could I do? It was so difficult. You had driven me mad.

I'm sorry for the wrong. It's the one thing in the world I'm sorry for: though I've done a lot of evil things.

I can't bear it that it is I have hurt you.

But you'll grow, and be the fine Ka. —In the end I know you, that you can't be broken or spoilt, I do know you.

He won't be writing again. 'In a few years we'll meet. Till then we can dodge each other. If we meet we're big enough to manage that. The creatures who watch won't get much change out of us.' He will always think and speak of her with honour.

There's one thing. Do you mind? I want to break the rule and give you a thing. A statuette of a mother and a child. It's now kept for me by Eddie. A tiny thing. He knows you're going to send him an address to send it you at. So when you're in England, will you send him the address?

I give it you; because you'll be the greatest mother in the world. And I'll not be anything but sad, till I've heard you're happy, and with a child of your own.

Let it stand: not for what we did: but for what we learnt.

I thought at one time I'd only learnt bad from you: now I know that before and after and over it all I learnt good—all that I have.

I've got to leave you. But if ever it happens you're in ultimate need of help—it may—you know I'll come, at any time and from any place, if you want it.

I'm very happy and well, travelling. And in the end I'll get back and work. Don't think of me.

Please, Ka, be good and happy: and stick to and be helped by your friends. That's the last thing I ask.

This is so bad a letter: and I wanted to make everything clear. Do believe. See what I've tried to write.

Preaching and everything aside, let's just be Ka and Rupert for a minute: and say good-bye. I'll be loyal to the things we've learnt together: and you be loyal. And life'll be good.

Dear love, good bye

RUPERT

He posted this on June 25, and as he walked down Third Street to his hotel he was overcome with the old anguish, and as usual he became physically ill with the strain. Russell Loines called and took him home to Staten Island. After two days he pulled himself together enough to try and get *Georgian Poetry* published in New York, failed owing to difficulties of copyright, wrote to Monro of his lack of success and his excitement in the discovery of a new poet of genius, Edward Arlington Robinson, then boarded the Montreal Express. By the time he was looking at Canada from the carriage window, he was conscious of being free of a very heavy load. There was absolutely nothing more he could do for Ka. 'You and I are situated queerly alike,' he wrote to Cathleen. 'We both of us have to hurt another person, and therein ourselves too. A bloody job. Let's be the kinder

to each other . . . We will deal honourably in the old high way of love
—(is that a quotation? or have I invented it?).'

II

He was on the Montreal Express, writing to Marsh. 'I've been diving
into many sides of New York lately. The low foreign part is rather
fascinating. Bohemia in New York rather cheap—even worse than in
London. Theatres are not very good: *revues* the best thing they do.
I've found one poet and some poetesses.' The Laureateship was the
burning literary topic. 'They think Le Gallienne is in the running,
otherwise they're fairly sane. Except that everybody here thinks
Noyes a *big* poet, bigger than Yeats or Bridges, for instance. I can
only gape . . . I say, do just see that the Laureateship is kept. It
would be a frightful scandal if it were abolished. Why not Bridges?'
He did not know that Marsh, still aboard the *Enchantress* with the
Asquiths, was already recommending Bridges to the Prime Minister.

He glimpsed Montreal briefly from a motor-wagonette, and the
whole place, judging by the guide's remarks, seemed to consist of
banks and churches, the population busily engaged in 'laying up
riches in this world or the next'; went on to Quebec the same day,
made friends with an American business man with whom he toured
the streets in a *calèche*, who burst into a refrain of the Star Spangled
Banner as they passed the American Consulate. 'His mind was even
more childlike and transparent than is usual with businessmen,'
Brooke told his readers of the *Westminster*. 'The observer could see
thoughts floating into it, like carp in a pond. When they got near the
surface, by a purely automatic process they found utterance.' Together they strolled about the Citadel, which seemed imbued with
'the radiance and repose of an immortal'; then Brooke sat on Dufferin
Terrace overlooking the Lower Town, by turns reading *Lycidas* or
watching the play of shine and shadow on 'the most glorious river in
the world'. By the evening he was aboard a boat going down the
St. Lawrence and up a northern tributary, the Saguenay, as far as the
village of Tadousac. 'My dear, it's not a river,' he exclaimed to
Cathleen, 'it's a part of Hell, got loose. It's very narrow by Canadian
standards—'

varying from ¾ mile to 300 yards across (the St. Lawrence is eighteen miles
wide where we leave it). And it's just the same depth—varying between

200 yards and a mile. Each side there are terrific cliffs, sometimes two thousand feet straight out of the water, of black granite. Pines occasionally, but mostly bare. The water in the river is jet black and absolutely smooth. This goes on for fifty miles. It's like some ghastly dream of Dante's. 'Fair gives me cold feet.' As evening came on and everything got blacker and stranger, and the mountains grew wilder and the river more sinister, I got restless and started prowling round the ship. Then I noticed the face of the river was queer, and as I watched it, I began to think I could see things coming out of it—large black things you know—I don't know what—turning and looking at you and bellying—so I came and shut myself in here, in my cabin, and read Jane Austen, and started this letter to you. Now I'm going to sleep. God guard you—and me in this place. I don't like these foreign lands—not wholesome. Pray for me.

At Tadousac, he bathed in the Saguenay, dried himself on his hand-kerchief, and ran back to the hotel after the coldest experience of his life. By July 9 he was again at Montreal, on the way to Ottawa where, before presenting his two introductions, he wrote to Marsh from the Hotel Windsor.

Lord—I've not really given the Canadians much chance yet. But my impression is that they have all the faults of the Americans, and not their one lovely and redeeming virtue, 'hospitality'. That 'hospitality' is often sneered at in the Americans: but it merely means that with the nice ones, you can be at once on happy and intimate terms. Oh dear, the tears quite literally well up into my eyes when I think of a group of young Harvard people I tumbled into—at Harvard—they were connected with the theatrical movement there, and they had the charm and freshness and capacity for instantly creating a relation of happy and warm friendliness that, for instance, Denis has. It's a nice thing.

Masefield had given him an introduction to the poet Duncan Campbell Scott, a civil servant in charge of Indian Affairs, whose poem *The Piper of Arll* had influenced Masefield before he started his literary career. He proved as good a friend as Loines of Staten Island, enjoyed hearing of the Georgian brotherhood, and for most of his eight-day visit, Brooke lived under his roof. He began to enjoy Canada, and think of England with mild nostalgia. He wrote to Marsh from the Royal Ottawa Golf Club where he generally ate the midday meal:

You, at home, have no conception how you're all getting a sanctity and halo about you in my mind. I dwell so much and so sentimentally on all the dear dead days, that I'm beginning to see no faults and all virtues in all of you. *You*, my dear, appear perfection in every part. Your passion for anagrams is a lovable and intellectual taste. Your acquaintance with Ottoline Morrell a beautiful thing. Your lack of sympathy with the Labour

Party turns to a noble and picturesque Toryism. Even your preference for gilded over comfortable chairs loses something of its ugliness in my heart. Of you and Wilfrid and Norton and the Society and Duncan and Cathleen and even Alfred I think incessantly devotedly and tearfully. Even of figures which, to be frank, have hovered but dimly on the outskirts of my consciousness, I am continually and fragrantly memorial.

Recalling Violet Asquith's birthday party, he grew lyrical.

> *Would God I were eating plovers' eggs,*
> *And drinking dry champagne,*
> *With the Bernard Shaws, Mr. and Mrs. Masefield,*
> *Lady Horner, Neil Primrose, Raleigh, the Right*
> *Honourable Augustine Birrell, Eddie, six or*
> *seven Asquiths, and Felicity Tree,*
> *In Downing Street again.*

His other introduction in Ottawa was a letter from Hugh Dalton's father to the Premier, Sir Wilfrid Laurier. 'I am an English Socialist and a writer' ran the note enclosed with Dalton's letter. Brooke found himself lunching *à deux* with the distinguished elder statesman, and greatly admiring his host, although he seemed 'very French in his sympathies. I don't trust his policy,' Brooke wrote to his mother, 'because I don't believe he *really* wants to pay anything in any form towards the Navy.' However, all in all, 'Laurier was a nice old man.' Ottawa was a place of quiet streets bordered with trees, and the evenings spent reading aloud to Scott, or the trips on the dusty roads leading out of town to Meach's Lake and Kingsmere, gave him an altogether more favourable impression of the Dominion. In those outlying regions, where only a few villages lay between him and the North Pole, as he was told, he noted the aromatic thimbleberry blossom, and the purple fireweed, which is the first vegetation to spring up in the prairie after a fire and so 'might be adopted', he thought, 'as the emblematic flower of a sense of humour'.

He boarded a boat at Prestcott, sailed up the St. Lawrence and across Lake Ontario, arriving at Toronto on July 21. He at once called on Scott's friend Edmund Morris, the painter. There was a meeting that evening in the Old County Buildings in Adelaide Street East, and Morris took him along. Since the members of Toronto's Arts and Letters Club were well up to date with news of the Georgians they took a special interest in their visitor. In his shabby dark grey suit and wide brimmed hat 'he looked the veritable picture of a young

Greek God—of Apollo himself', wrote R. H. Hathaway, who observed that his guest was quiet and undemonstrative, and free of mannerisms, though he tossed his head and ran his fingers through his hair. It was odd, he thought, that he should at once be so obviously virile yet have 'the colouring of a girl'. Of the Canadian poets Brooke admitted he had read only Bliss Carman; Yeats was his particular hero; but on the subject of Kipling or Noyes he was unwilling to be drawn. At the King Edward Hotel he wrote *Doubts* ('When she sleeps, her soul, I know, Goes a wanderer on the air'), first called *To Cathleen*, and posted it off to her as a reminder of his existence; talked politics with Sir John Willison, Canadian correspondent of *The Times*, entertained Edmund Morris and his friends from the Club and wrote to Marsh:

I've found here an Arts and Letters Club of poets painters journalists etc., where they'd heard of me, and read G.P., and, oh Eddie, one fellow actually possessed my 'Poems'. Awful Triumph. Every now and then one comes up and presses my hand and says 'Wal, Sir, you cannot know how memorable a Day in my life this is.' Then I do my pet boyish-modesty-stunt and go pink all over: and everyone thinks it too delightful. One man said to me 'Mr. Brooks (my Canadian name), Sir, I may tell you that in my opinion you have Mr. Noyes skinned.' That means I'm better than him: I gathered a great compliment, here. But they're really quite an up-to-date lot: and very cheery and pleasant. I go on, tomorrow, to the desert and the wilds.

Another topic of Brooke's at the Club was a new venture which he had first heard of in Ottawa where a letter from Wilfrid Gibson had overtaken him.

'You are, of course, too young to remember "The Shilling Garland",' wrote Gibson. It was a series of ten little books of verse edited by Laurence Binyon. There was now a scheme to start a 'New Shilling Garland'. Gibson had got the idea while talking with Lascelles Abercrombie in his cottage called The Gallows at Dymock in Gloucestershire. If three or four of them stood together, his argument ran, they might fare better on the market. The Georgian anthology had already shown this to be a sound principle. Meanwhile Brooke must keep it to himself. 'I don't want the rotters to hear of it,' wrote Gibson, 'until it's too late to include them.' Brooke regarded this proposal as a great compliment. Whether with Sedgwick in Boston, or Campbell Scott in Ottawa, it was Gibson, he found, who was the most highly esteemed of all his circle. The name was altered to the *Gallows Garland* and finally to *New Numbers*. Printed in Gloucester and issued by Abercrombie and his wife from The

Gallows cottage, it was going to prove even more important to Brooke than his association with Marsh and the Georgians. From his hotel in Toronto he wrote to the Ranee, telling how it was 'rather a score for me, as my "public" is smaller than any of theirs!' and to Gibson he declared he was 'all for amalgamating our four publics [Drinkwater was the fourth] the more that mine is far the smallest! I'm afraid I shall be outwritten by you fluent giants . . . I foresee the average number will read as follows—'. There was gentle and nicely aimed satire in his imaginary Table of Contents:

1. Lascelles Abercrombie: *Haman and Mordecai.*
2. John Drinkwater: *The Sonority of God: An Ode.*
3. W. W. Gibson: *Poor Bloody Bill: A Tale.*
4. Rupert Brooke: *Oh Dear! oh, Dear! A Sonnet.*
5. Lascelles Abercrombie: *Asshur-Bani-Pal and Og King of Bashan.*
6. John Drinkwater: *William Morris: an Appreciation in verse.*
7. W. W. Gibson: *Gas-Stoves: No. 1. A Brave Poor Thing.*

From Toronto he made his way to Niagara Falls. Inevitably they moved him to reflections on the destiny of man and nations—'And as incessant, as inevitable, and as unavailing as the spray that hangs over the Falls, is the white cloud of human crying.' It occasioned the best of his descriptive letters to the *Gazette*, but having sorted his notes he sat beside the thundering waters and with blown spray settling on his paper, wrote to Scholfield of the remote A.D.C. days in Cambridge.

> *My heart is sick for several things*
> *Only to be found in King's . . .*
>
> *I do recall those haunts with tears,*
> *The Backs, the Chapel, and the Rears . . .*
>
> *O spots my memory yet is gilding,*
> *O Jumbo Arch! O Wilkins Building!*
>
> *There we pursued the Truth amain,*
> *With Dialectic and Champagne,*
> *And through the young and purple night,*
> *Still holla'd after 'What is Right',*
> *And played the young philosopher*
> *From Hesperus till Lucifer,*
> *And stalked and startled from her nest*
> *The subtle bird,* quod verum est,

A DEEP SLEEP

And linked with the new risen sun,
τὸ καλόν with τὸ ἀγαθόν,
Dear spot where I was taken short,
O Bodley's Court! O Bodley's Court!

'I'm so impressed by Niagara,' he went on, lapsing into prose. 'I hoped not to be. But I horribly am.' He felt bound to admit he was, most regrettably—

a Victorian at heart, after all. Please don't breath a word of it: I want to keep such shreds of reputation as I have left. Yet it's true. For I sit and stare at the thing and have the purest Nineteenth Century grandiose thoughts, about the Destiny of Man, the Irresistibility of Fate, the Doom of Nations, the fact that Death awaits us All, and so forth. Wordsworth Redivivus. Oh dear! oh dear!

At Sarnia, after two days, he took the boat and crossed Lakes Huron and Superior. 'We seemed to be ploughing aimlessly through the phantasmal sand-dunes of another world.' Beside him on deck sat a little old woman in black who was so devoted to humanity that she waved a minute handkerchief whenever she distinguished a sign of life on the distant shore. The youth in the next chair to her was writing to Edmund Gosse, recommending the poems of Edward Arlington Robinson. 'He has a queer kind of intimacy with the small objects and affairs of life, very like de la Mare's; and a similar, but less subtle, musical power over common words and phrases.' Then he glanced up at his elderly companion, who waved again, at the vaguely human shapes on a passing boat, and he turned back to his letter, bringing Gosse into the scene.

I'm writing on Lake Superior. We're steaming along in a little low fog, which just doesn't come up to the top deck, but completely hides the surface of the sea. Occasionally little cones and peaks of the mist float by, and the sun catches them. It is slightly uncanny; like everything in these lakes. I have a perpetual feeling that a lake ought not to be this size. A river and a little lake and an ocean are natural; but not these creatures. They are too big, and too smooth, and too sunny; like an American business man.

The last stage of the journey, starting from Port Arthur, was by train. In the early morning, lifting the blind a few inches, he saw no sign of life—only rocks, pine woods 'and the occasional strange gleam of water'. He reached Winnipeg on July 30, dumped his luggage in Medwin Street and next day started out with his host, Howard Falk, to a hunting lodge near Lake George, and in case he should feel sated with spectacular scenery he took with him the works of Ben

Jonson and Jane Austen. 'No one is *thinking* of the lakes and hills you see before you,' he pondered. No names, no tradition. Only pools of water and lumps of earth 'dumbly awaiting their Wordsworth or their Acropolis to give them a soul'. In Europe there is always serenity and the spirit of a purpose at rest. Here the land is virginal, every lake new born, and each day is as the first day. Amazed by the grandeur of the prospect on all sides, he was yet aware of a stirring discontent. 'For it is possible, at a pinch, to do without gods. But one misses the dead.'

They arrived at a log cabin overlooking the lake, about seventy miles from Winnipeg, and on August 3 Brooke wrote to the Ranee, 'I never expected to pass my twenty-sixth birthday with a gun and fishing tackle, without any clothes on, by a lake, in a wood infested by bears, in a country where there aren't ten people within five miles and half of those are Indians.' Two days before he described an adventure for Cathleen. Bryan, the trapper, came back after dark, calling across the water. Brooke, Falk and the wife, ran down to the edge as—

the canoe came right up, and we distinguished an immense deer, the size of a small pony, dead, strapped into the bottom of the canoe. It weighed 500 lbs.: and they had paddled the canoe six miles, all round by the shore, the water up within half an inch of the gunwales, from the place where they'd shot him. They emptied him out into the muddy edge of the water; we lit a great fire of birch, spruce, and tamarack wood to see what was going on; and we all set to work to string him up for the night (he had been disembowelled). For two hours we pulled and hauled at this creature, tugging at a rope over the branch of a birch. Then the trapper got an axe and hacked the beast's head off: with the great antlers it weighs some hundred pounds. At length we got the carcass hanging up and supported it with sticks. I got cut and scratched and smeared with the creature's inside. It was a queer sight, lit up by the leaping flames of the fire, which the woman fed—the black water of the lake, muddy with trampling at the edge, and streaked with blood, the trapper in the tree, this great carcass hanging at one end of the rope, my friend and an Indian and I pulling our arms out at the other, the head gazing reproachfully at us from the ground, everybody using the most frightful language, and the rather ironical and very dispassionate stars above. Rather savage. Bryan said, once 'Brought it all the way home so as you could see it, kid', to his wife; so she was in an ecstasy of delight all evening.

August 3.

Today, O my heart, I am twenty-six years old. And I've done so little. I'm very much ashamed. By God, I'm going to make things hum, though.

But that's all so far away. I'm lying quite naked on a beach of golden sand, six miles away from the hunting-lodge, the other man near by, a gun between us in case bears appear, the boat pulled up on the shore, the lake very blue and ripply, and the sun rather strong. We 'trolled' for fish coming, which means, you may know, putting out a piece of bright twisting metal with hooks and letting it drag after the boat. It rotates, and flashes, and large fish think it a little one, and swallow it. So! we caught two pike on the way out, which lie picturesquely in the bows of the boat. Along the red-gold beach are the tracks of various wild animals, mostly jumping deer and caribou. One red deer we saw as we came round the corner, lolloping along the beach, stopping and snuffing the wind, and going on again. Very lovely. And the meat wasn't needed, so we didn't shoot at it (I'm glad—I'm no 'sportsman'). We bathed off the beach, and then lit a fire of birch and spruce, and fried eggs and ate cold caribou-heart, and made tea, and had (oh!) blueberry pie. Cooking and eating a meal naked is the most solemnly primitive thing one can do.

And—and this is the one thing which will make you realize, that I'm living far the most wonderfully, and incredibly romantic life you ever heard of, and *infinitely* superior to your miserable crawling London existence— the place we landed at is an Indian Camp. Indians when they go away from a camping-ground take the strips of birch-bark which answer to canvas in our tents, but leave the poles standing for the next visit——

He left Winnipeg on August 4, called at Regina, and reappeared next at the King Edward Hotel, Edmonton. He was interviewed by the press. 'I just put my cigar in the corner of my mouth, and undid my coat and put my thumbs under my arm-pits, and spat, and said, "Say, kid, this is some town!" He asked me a lot of questions, of which I did not know the answer. So I lied. I gave the poor old *Westminster*, for instance, a circulation of a million and a reputation that would make Spender's few prim grey hairs stand horrid to the heavens, if he knew.' He was also claiming to have acquired the knack of blowing into newspaper buildings and, without batting an eyelid, declaring, 'I want to talk for an hour to the Chief Editor.' He could also, as he informed Cathleen, 'lean across the counter with a cigarette and discuss the Heart with the young lady who sells cigars.' He was regarded chiefly as a political observer. 'When I come back,' he wrote to Marsh, 'I shall demand a knighthood from Winston. I've been delivering immense speeches in favour of his naval policy.' He was also suffering mild attacks of home sickness before meals.

England—I dreamt, last night, that at Vancouver I got sick of the trip and came back to England, and landed at Grantchester (you should have seen how we drew up at the Boat-house), and wired to you that I was going to stay a night with you in London, and caught the 4.55—and, oh, woke. Would you have been there? I've a sort of idea you'll go to Venice or some lovely place in September. I envy you. You can't think how sick one's heart

gets for something *old*. For weeks I have not seen or touched a town so old as myself. Horrible! Horrible! They gather round me and say, 'In 1901 Calgary had 139 inhabitants, now it has 75,000': and so forth. I reply, 'My village is also growing. At the time of Julius Caesar it was a bare 300. Domesday Book gives 347 and it is now close on 390.' Which is ill-mannered of me.

Oh, but I have adventures—had I only anybody to tell them to! For a day I travelled with a Scotch Whisky manufacturer, a Radical. At Euston he had got into the carriage with a woman who had turned out to have nursed the late Duke of Sutherland up to the last. 'And she gave me most interesting particulars about the Duke's passing away.' Isn't it extraordinary what things complete strangers will say to each other?

I suppose you won't be sailing the Admiralty Yacht, near 'Frisco this September? Can't you persuade Winston to inspect the Panama Canal? and I'd come down and join you. It's frightfully important.

The *Calgary News Telegram* carried a headline 'General European War is opinion of Political Writer from Great Britain'. Brooke was reported as saying that Canadians did not appreciate the threatened crisis, and that 'conditions cannot be righted without a struggle in which practically every country will participate'. In Calgary he dined with the 'old timers', the last of the original settlers who knew the town when its population was a little over forty, then he visited the Indian Reserve, the 'Stonies', where he stood in the Agent's office, watching the Indians come in for tobacco or a dose of Epsom salts. 'An Indian in a blanket and fur and gaudy trimmings would sidle into the room. Then for ten minutes he would stand silent. You must never hurry an Indian. Then he takes the pipe out of his mouth, says "Um" and puts it back again. Five minutes pass. Then he looks at the ceiling, and says ". . . Um . . . Salt". '

From Calgary to Laggan, the Rockies and the Selkirks; Banff and four days in Chateau Lake Louise; then Vancouver, British Columbia, (In the train a lady from Chicago gave him some peanuts and said she supposed he would have to be getting back in time for the school term in England. 'So I blessed her for thinking me under twenty, and wept'); then two days in Victoria on Vancouver Island, where he was shocked to read that Edmund Morris, his friend at Toronto, had been drowned while bathing. But all this while he had felt no inclination to write. 'As for my poems,' he wrote to Marsh, 'I know I've only sent three . . . But damn it, what's the good of a friend if he can't sit down and write off a few poems for one at a pinch? That's what I count on your doing, if the editors press.' Marsh was to ask two guineas for any poem he managed to dispose of to a magazine. This letter from Vancouver had opened with downright abuse. 'Why the Devil weren't you taught American as well as Latin and Greek?' Confronted with the proofs of a *Westminster* article containing the slang phrase 'You bet your,' Marsh had taken it upon himself to add 'boots', supposing Brooke had omitted the word. He had not, and he was furious, and having vented his spleen in unprintable terms, made the transition with 'Lights up. Public may come in. This is the sort of letter that doesn't look well in a Biography.'

At Victoria he heard from Russell Loines for whom he had ordered a copy of his *Poems*. Loines was preferring *The Fish* to the love poems.

I'm sorry you think my Muse less at home with women than with fish. For I write more about the former. And now that I've got on to plays, I'm advised that women characters present less difficulty in the staging than fish. But perhaps the reason is that I've met nicer fish than women, on the whole.

He left for Seattle by water, then travelled on the train to San Francisco through the American Rockies.

He arrived at the Hotel San Francisco on September 15, and soon made the acquaintance, through Loines, of Professor Chauncey Wells of the University of California. He turned up late for dinner at Piedmont Avenue, was pressed to stay the night, and so appeared at breakfast next day in his evening clothes. It was the beginning of a real friendship, and soon he was happier than he had been for weeks, but he was suffering from the heat. September 21 was the hottest day since 1871. On 28th he telegraphed Loines to send him 250 dollars, for he was being tempted to go still further afield, to the South Seas. By the end of the month he was at Stanford University, reading aloud from the Georgian anthology, and discovering more kindred spirits. He was now staying with Professor Wells, making the acquaintance of the novelist Isobel Mackay, and Leonard Bacon, and writing to Marsh:

California is nice, and the Californians a friendly bunch. There's a sort of goldenness about 'Frisco and the neighbourhood. It hangs in the air, and about the people. Everyone is very cheery and cordial and simple. They are rather a nation apart, different from the rest of the States. Much more like the English. As everywhere in this extraordinary country, I am welcomed with open arms when I say I know Masefield and Goldie! It's very queer. I can't for the life of me help moving about like a metropolitan among rustics, or an Athenian in Thrace. Their wide-mouthed awe at England is so touching—they really are merely a colony of ours still. That they should be speaking to a man who knows Lowes Dickinson, who has met Galsworthy, who once saw Belloc plain! . . . What should we feel if we could speak with an *habitué* of the theatre at Athens, Fifth Century, or with Mine Host of the Mermaid? All that they have with me, the dears! Yet I don't know why I write this from California: the one place that *has* a literature and tradition of its own, to some extent.

He booked a place on the S.S. *Sierra* which was due to sail on October 7, and told Marsh of his plans.

I leave for Honolulu on Tuesday. Then Samoa, Fiji, Tahiti, and a resting-place at the bottom of the Pacific, all among the gay fish and lovely sub-marine flowers. Will you all come, like the Titanic widows, and drop some wax flowers, a Bible, and a tear or two, on the spot where I'm reputed to have gone down? I hope so.

You may continue writing to me. Letters will reach me occasionally, I suppose. And you may figure me in the centre of a Gauguin picture, nakedly riding a squat horse into white surf.

He was sad at leaving Piedmont Avenue, but the money from Loines was now to hand, the last of his Westminster letters was despatched —in spite of having lost all his notes and several rough drafts of poems somewhere in British Columbia—and he was obeying a true instinct.

III

The sea was calm for his passage to the islands where his gifts were to come as near to being fulfilled as they would ever be. In the evening a gang of youths, mostly half-castes on the way home to Honolulu, strummed on diminutive mandolins, and sang 'their sad Hawaiian songs which are all vowels', and a moon, almost too clear and bright to be entirely true to unaccustomed eyes, shone down on 'the queer Pacific waters, and there are banks and banks of strangely coloured clouds, and flying-fish flicker along the waves, and the stars are very near'. His companions were a Bavarian priest, an elderly Russian Jew from New York, and a youth who explained that he was Danish, Chinese, and Hawaiian in origin, 'rather a good mixture for looks.' When not composing *Clouds*, a simple fancy in which the clouds at night are imagined as the spirits of the dead passing over the world of men and watching them come and go, a sonnet worked out and sustained with mastery of the form, he was drafting another sonnet described as 'suggested by some of the proceedings of the Society for Psychical Research'. He was recalling a talk once given by A. C. Pigou to The Dickinson Society at King's which in turn must now have reminded him of a passage in Marvell's *Dialogue between Soul and Body*.

> *O, who shall from this dungeon raise*
> *A soul enslaved so many ways?*
> *With bolts of bones, that fettered stands*
> *In feet, and manacled in hands;*
> *Here blinded with an eye, and there*
> *Deaf with the drumming of an ear.*

In *Psychical Research*, which continues the theme of *Clouds*, the dead are no longer 'rounds of snow' or shapes of vapour, but unsubstantial spirits who can 'turn and run Down some close-covered byway of the air', and ardent in their timeless plane—

> *Learn all we lacked before; hear, know, and say*
> *What this tumultuous body now denies;*
> *And feel, who have laid our groping hands away;*
> *And see, no longer blinded by our eyes.*

The variation on Marvell resulted in a poem worthy to stand with *Clouds*. Less satisfactory, because it was clearly intended as only part of a narrative sequence of which the rest, or most of it, was never written (he was planning a series on the lines of Meredith's *Modern Love*) was the third sonnet begun on this voyage and entitled *A Memory*;[1] but the poem is of special interest to any student of Brooke's method, for the experience he wanted to confine within the given form was described in a letter to Cathleen while the poem was still in the rough and he was still on board.

And yet, oh loveliest fool in the world, you're wise. And you wrote wise things to me. For it is true, what you said about the evil of a woman gratifying her instinct of kindness by ways that may wake other things in the man—the danger of it, anyway. But how's she to know, poor lady, till she gets wise in the ways of the world? It's a bad business. I told you I was in love with a girl for three or four years, and then she got tired of it—of the little she'd ever found in it? Once, towards the grey end of that—I'd sort of put my love away, numbed it, for I saw things were going ill. But I was desolate and rather hungry. And one day—we were staying in the same house—we'd arranged to get up *very* early, and go out and pick mushrooms together in the summer dew, for breakfast (oh youth! youth!)—I crept along, having woken and being unable to sleep another hour, to her room, some little while before dawn. She was sleeping. I knelt down by her and kissed her forehead to wake her, and put my head on her hand; and she

[1] G.K., p. 39.

woke, and felt fond of me I suppose, and pulled my head against her heart and held me a minute. And I thought I had found heaven. And all my love woke worse than ever. But she didn't mean anything, you know. Only she felt fond of me. But it made the breaking about nine hundred times harder; we both paid a lot for it, I most. Luckily, that was all we had to break. For she was too wise, and something in her heart too strong, for her to give herself to me, because she loved and pitied me in that way; nor did I love her little enough to want it given—in that way. Else it would have been a thousand times worse: as I know from later things.

But I put it—the episode—into a sonnet, in a series about imaginary people . . . At least, the sonnet's not done yet. But it ends with this—only it'll be changed and better (I hope)

> 'Child, you should not have done't! for the poor gain
> Of that short moment's soon forgot delight
> And sleepy mother-comfort. Could you know
> How easily Love comes laughing from the night
> With eyes of hope! And love that's wakened so,
> Takes all too long to lay asleep again.'[1]

(Clumsy, clumsy!) But it *does* take all too long, my dear. It's not worth it. Yet there was another time when I was in trouble, and she gave me strength and calm. One *can* help. I suppose a woman has to judge by the particular case. But I think she ought always to go a little less far than she thinks she can, unless she knows men *very* well. For men catch fire quicker than women, though they may not burn so long. Lady, is it not true?

He goes on to contend that all men and women alike are basically children, or rather he implies that all human creatures are children *to one another*. 'That is the final rule of life, the best one ever made. "Whoso shall offend one of these little ones" . . . remembering that all of the eight hundred millions on earth, except oneself, are the little ones . . . My heart and my belief were so deadened, before I found you . . . You give me great riches . . . I pray you, love good and keep away from the evil things of the world, for my sake and for your sake and for our sake.'

S.S. *Sierra* arrived at Honolulu on the 15th, and Brooke made his way to the Moana Hotel on Waikiki Beach about five miles along the shore from the town. The hotel was tucked away in an arcade of

---

[1] This sestet became (G.K., p. 39):

> It was great wrong you did me; and for gain
> Of that poor moment's kindliness, and ease,
> And sleepy mother-comfort!
>   Child, you know
> How easily love leaps out to dreams like these,
> Who has seen them true. And love that's wakened so
> Takes all too long to lay asleep again.

shops, and the custom was for the guests to sit outside in wicker chairs, drinking, watching the folk go by. He was not very taken with the place. 'It really *is* tropical in character,' he wrote to the Ranee, 'like some of the gardens and places at Cannes, on an immense scale,' but the tourist trade was too much in evidence; the exotic strangeness of giant ferns, plentiful hibiscus and tapering coco-nut trees, too quickly grew familiar, and while seated under a Hau-tree, watching the Hawaiian women wading and swimming for sea-weed, he was moved to devise for Cathleen's entertainment what he called a 'litany' of memories, the cherished things he was parted from and longed to find again—'The Chilterns, Hampton Court, *Hullo Ragtime*, Raymond Buildings . . .

Those are the things that hold one. For those reasons I can't ever accept smaller things. Isn't it so? Aren't we bound to be faithful to each other, whatever happens? I mean, 'though I marry elsewhere, and marry often', as they say in *The Importance of Being Earnest*, I shall be true to you, because I can't, now, do less than the fine things. Do you think this all nonsense, dear child? Be forgiving to my awkward attempts to express myself. I demand forgiveness, as one human from another. We're all in the same difficulty, this inability to express oneself decently without sham or awkwardness or sentimentality.

The memories were not all of Cathleen. He was feeling at a blessedly safe remove in time and space from that other Cannes, and in *One Day*,[1] the sonnet beginning 'Today I have been happy,' where for the first time he succeeded in recollecting Ka without disquiet, and discovering 'Stray buds from that old dust of misery', he happened upon a poetic symbol for this novel experience (recalling the events of 1912 without anguish) which resulted in the best contribution so far to his 'Modern Love' series. The thought of Ka was like a harmless stone held in the hand—

> *So lightly I played with those dark memories,*
> *Just as a child, beneath the summer skies,*
> *Plays hour by hour with a strange shining stone,*
> *For which (he knows not) towns were fire of old,*
> *And love has been betrayed, and murder done,*
> *And great kings turned to a little bitter mould.*

Evidently not quite satisfied, he tried to convey the same idea another way. *Waikiki*,[2] the other sonnet begun at this time, recalls

[1] G.K., p. 38.
[2] G.K., p. 37.

Seaside, his first satisfactory essay in the form, written in 1908, having taken the plunge and signed the Fabian Basis. There, at Torquay, it was 'the friendly lilt of the band' on the decorous promenade, heard from a distance on the shore. Here again it is night, and 'Somewhere an *eukaleli* thrills and cries And stabs with pain the night's brown savagery'. He is once more at the water's edge, 'and dim waves creep to me, Gleam like a woman's hair, stretch out, and rise'. Behind the poem is the remembrance of that distressful Sunday in February, 1912, when he was staying by the Starnberger See. Now it's the Pacific, the ripples are suggesting an erotic image, 'And new stars burn into the ancient skies . . .'

> *And I recall, lose, grasp, forget again,*
> *And still remember, a tale I have heard, or known,*
> *An empty tale, of idleness and pain,*
> *Of Two that loved—or did not love—and one*
> *Whose perplexed heart did evil, foolishly,*
> *A long while since, and by some other sea.*

After a few days he took a boat to Kanai, a small island of the group about seventy miles away, having picked up in San Francisco an introduction to a landowner there. He stayed four days. The main event was an excursion on horseback to a waterfall. It was a rough trail through scrub and they crossed a river that washed against the horses' bellies. 'English horses couldn't stand it,' he told the Ranee, 'they'd have broken their legs'; the fall itself was 'not very voluminous' in the eyes of a recent visitor to Niagara, but it cascaded from two hundred feet up, and the basin at its foot provided a cool and deliciously hazardous bathe. He was back, smarting with sunburn, at Moana arcade, Honolulu, by October 20, and on the 27th he boarded the S.S. *Ventura*. She crossed the Equator on the 31st. A horse-play Neptune duly appeared, and several passengers, Brooke among them, were ignominiously thrown into a canvas bath. He wrote to Cathleen.

Having lain in my bunk writing sonnets an hour or two, I just wandered up, and in the saloon I found a man and woman playing duets, hard—members of your profession I fancy, a touring company, she with a back as broad as it's long. And *that's* what you'll come to, my dear, second lady in a company wandering the Pacific, as broad as you're long, and crowned with bright yellow hair. And what were they playing? Why *Hullo Ragtime*, in a piano score, right through! I retired to my bunk here again, in confusion and tears.

How those foolish melodies—for we had them all, from *Military Mary*

Ann, up—or down—to *Dixie*—bite at one's heart! What does it all mean? There's such a glow over it—over such an immediate past.

On November 2 the *Ventura* put into the harbour of Pango, Samoa. Later that same night Brooke went aboard a schooner going to Apia, eighty miles off, and after sleeping the night on deck, curled up among some sugar-casks, described for Cathleen an adventure of the night before. First, he 'went a walk under the coco-nut palms with a naked baby of five or six holding each hand (one said his name was Fred)' then, after a coco-nut supper, the Dancers appeared.

In the evening, the wharf was covered with torches, lamps, and a mass of Samoans, all with some 'curios' or other on little stalls. The sailors and passengers from the ship wandered among them buying or bartering. The Samoans were rather indifferent about money but would give anything they had for old clothes. Great bronze men, with gilded hair, and godlike limbs lay about on the grass, while their women held up pieces of 'kapa'—which is bark beaten into a stiff cloth, and covered with a brown pattern—and grinned and beckoned and gesticulated. And the whole was lit up by these flaring lights against the tropical nights and the palms and stars, so that it looked like a Rembrandt picture—you know those things where there's a light on the immediate figures and faces, and the rest are in inky darkness? After dinner six girls and six men came on board and performed a *siva-siva* on deck, before the astonished eyes of the American and Australian passengers. A *siva-siva*, my dear, is a Dance. But not what you (poor stepper of hideous American stuff) or I or M. Nijinsky mean by dancing. Nearer M. Nijinsky's, but far even from him. Much of it I could not understand; some I felt it my duty, as an English gentleman, not to. Both girls and men were naked to the waist, and glistening with coco-nut palm oil. The dancing was on a background of high nasal wailing—which seemed to be telling a story—hand-clapping, and convulsive rhythmic movements of the body. This was carried on sitting, to begin with; but at the exciting moments they leapt to their feet and careered jerkily around. Their eyeballs stared and they indulged in strange pantomime. The men frequently pretended to be animals, leaping about on all fours. One of them took it into his head to be a dog, at one moment. Approaching the chief woman performer with howls and barking, he threw up his hind leg and went through the motions of a dog who throws up his leg against a wall, she being the wall. That was a humorous episode. Most of it consisted of the women facing each other, in a crouching position, wailing rhythmically, and making very slight rhythmic motions with their hands feet and thighs. As the crisis approached, the movement grew slighter, and in proportion, more exciting. Which is queer. It was all very thrilling and tropical and savage. I felt strange ancient raucous jungle cries awaking within me . . . The dancers vanished, after half an hour, precipitately into the darkness.

Meanwhile the *Ventura* was heading for Sydney, bringing the sonnet *Clouds* addressed to Harold Monro—'I *cannot* write when I'm travelling'—and several other pieces on their way to Gray's Inn for Marsh to pass on to the editor of *New Numbers*. 'These go to Wilfrid immediately. A few more are half out and shall follow somewhen. I am becoming indistinguishable from R.L.S:, both in thinness, in literary style, and in dissociation from England. God have mercy on my soul! I have crossed the Equator, and so am a Man at last.' From Apia he returned to Pango, and on about the 13th boarded the S.S. *Torfua* for Fiji. On deck he wrote to Marsh, imagining his letter coming to hand and coinciding with a drizzle over Raymond Buildings—

a chilly dampness in the air, and the theatres glaring in the Strand, and crowds of white faces. But I can't help *thinking* of you trotting through crisp snow to a country church, holly-decorated, with little robins pecking crumbs all around, and the church-bells playing our brother Tennyson's *In Memoriam* brightly through the clear air. It may not be: it never has been—the picture-postcard Christmas. But I shall think of you so. You think of me in a loin-cloth, brown and wild, in the fair chocolate arms of a Tahitian beauty, reclining beneath a bread-fruit tree, on white sand, with the breakers roaring against the reefs a mile out, and strange brilliant fish darting through the pellucid hyaline of the sun-saturated sea. Oh, Eddie, it's all true about the South Seas! I get a little tired of it at moments, because I am just too old for Romance, and my soul is seared. But there it is: there it wonderfully is: heaven on earth, the ideal life, little work, dancing, singing and eating, naked people of incredible loveliness, perfect manners, and immense kindliness, a divine tropic climate, and intoxicating beauty of scenery. I came aboard and left Samoa two days ago. Before that, I had been wandering, with an 'interpreter'—entirely genial and quite incapable of English—through Samoan villages. The last few days I stopped in one, where a big marriage feast was going on. I lived in a Samoan house (the coolest in the world) with a man and his wife, nine children, ranging from a proud beauty of 18 to a round object of 1 year, a dog, a cat, a proud hysterical hen, and a gaudy scarlet and green parrot, who roved the roof and beams with a wicked eye, choosing a place whence to — twice a day, with humorous precision, on my hat and clothes . . .

And Eddie, it's all true about, for instance, coco-nuts. You tramp through a strange vast dripping tropical forest for hours, listening to weird liquid hootings from birds and demons in the branches above. Then you feel thirsty. So you send your boy—or call a native—up a great perpendicular palm. He runs up with utter ease and grace, cuts off a couple of vast nuts and comes down and makes holes in them. And they're chock-full of the best drink in the world. Romance! Romance! I walked 15 miles through mud and up and down mountains, and swam three rivers, to get this boat. But if ever you miss me, suddenly, one day, from lecture-room B in King's, or from the Moulin d'Or at lunch, you'll know that I've got sick for the full moon on these little thatched roofs, and the palms against the morning, and the Samoan boys and girls diving thirty feet into a green sea or a deep mountain pool under a waterfall—and that I've gone back.

Romance. That's half my time. The rest is Life—Life, Eddie, is what you get in the bars of the hotels in 'Frisco, or Honolulu, or Suva, or Apia, and in the smoking-rooms on these steamers. It is incredibly like a Kipling story, and all the people are very self-consciously Kiplingesque. Yesterday, for instance, I sat in the Chief Engineer's cabin, with the First Officer and a successful beach-comber lawyer from the white man's town in Samoa, drinking Australian champagne from breakfast to lunch. 'Today I am not well.'

He was planning the future—'I have a growing vision of next summer term spent between King's and Raymond Buildings'—giving up the National Liberal Club 'because I hate the Liberal party and the Marconi affair and the whole mess and Rufus Isaacs as Lord Chief Justice', and feeling drawn to the Savile Club, except for the risk of bumping into Lytton Strachey there.

There's nothing else in the way of my European existence, I think. That part of it which is left, out here, reads Ben Jonson. Kindly turn up his *New Inn* (which is sheer Meredith) and read Lovel's song in Act IV. The second verse will dispel the impression of the first, that it is by Robert Browning. The whole thing is pure beauty.

He arrived at Suva, Fiji, on November 19, and found a room at McDonald's Hotel. The letter he posted to Dudley Ward spoke well of the German administration of Samoa, and told how the plantations were worked by indentured Chinese coolies 'because the Samoan can, and will, live without working. He puts an hibiscus in his hair, twines a gaudy loin cloth round him, takes a few bananas and a coco-nut and goes off bathing with the girls, singing as he goes. That is the end of life. Tra, la!' Surely an ideal existence!

On the whole, my dear, I'm agreeably surprised at the excellence of German control here. I daresay you knew of it. I'd drunk in that 'Only We can Colonize' dope (Excuse my Americanisms). I suppose they can afford to take trouble and give time to what they *have* got. The only thing is, they may not be able to keep it, as we could. The Germans don't seem adventurous. They come out here, do their bit, and get home again. But, even here, the English stay, some of them. If the German *does* stay, he gets denationalized—I met several such. (They say there's a brother of von Bülow on the beach, but I didn't strike him.) But the Englishman strikes roots, imagines he's in a story by Kipling, and elects himself perpetual vice-consul. There are lots about here, mostly married to natives. One was sent down from Wadham in '83, ordered out of England, cut off by his father (of the Landed Gentry). He still dresses for dinner, among his chocolate brood. My Country! my country!

'The South Seas are heaven,' he ended, 'but I no angel.' Having already paid his tribute to the grave of R. L. Stevenson at Samoa, Brooke was naturally put in mind of Edmund Gosse to whom an account of his peregrinations was long overdue. Eddie Marsh must address it with the correct titles, 'lest he fly into a rage', and, if he wished, read and approve before sealing the envelope.

Forgive this gaudy tropical notepaper. It's all I can find. I've just got into this place, from Samoa. I said to myself 'Fiji is obviously the wildest place I can get to round here. The name, and pictures of the inhabitants, prove it.' And lo! a large English town, with two banks, several churches, dental surgeons, a large gaol, auctioneers, bookmakers, two newspapers, and all the other appurtenances of civilization! But I fancy I'll be able to get some little boat and go off to some smaller wilder islands. This place and the country round have been stocked with Hindus, to work the plantations. Fifty thousand of them. For the Fijian has that curious quality, inexplicable and abhorrent to the white man, that he will not work for other men, as long as he has enough to live on without. And in this magic part of the world, so long as he is left a few patches of land of his own, he can do this. He has only to shin up a coco-nut tree, and pull out a root, and there's food for the next week. Perplexing country! At home everything is so simple, and choice is swift, for the sensible man. There is only the choice between writing a good sonnet and making a million pounds. Who could hesitate? But *here* the choice is between writing a sonnet and climbing a straight hundred-foot coco-nut palm, or diving forty feet from a rock into pellucid blue-green water. Which is the better, there? One's European literary soul begins to be haunted by strange doubts and shaken with fundamental fantastic misgivings. I think I shall return home.

But if I *do* return, I know I shall be wanting, every now and then, to slip away to the South Seas once more. The attraction's queer. It's not really Romance. At least, I associate with Romance, something of veiled ladies, and moonlit serenades, and narrow Venetian or Oriental streets. Something just perceptibly feverish. But this is quite another world. It's getting back to one's childhood somehow: but not to the real childhood, rather to the childhood that never was, but is portrayed by a kindly sentimental memory; a time of infinite freedom, no responsibility, perpetual play in the open air, unceasing sunshine, never-tiring limbs, and a place where time is not, and supper takes place at breakfast-time and breakfast in the afternoon, and life consists of expeditions by moonlight and diving naked into waterfalls and racing over white sands beneath feathery brooding palm-trees.

Oh, it's horribly true, what you wrote, that one only finds in the South Seas what one brings there. Perhaps I could have found Romance if I'd brought it. Yet I do not think one could help but find *less* trouble than one brings. The idea of the South Seas as a place of passion and a Mohammedan's paradise is but a sailor's yarn. It is nothing near so disturbing. It is rather the opposite to alcohol, according to the Porter's definition,[1] for it promotes performance but takes away desire. Yet I can even understand Stevenson finding—as you put it—the Shorter Catechism there. One keeps realizing, however unwillingly, responsibility. I noticed in myself and in the other white people in Samoa, a trait I have remarked in schoolmasters and in the 'agents' who are appointed in Canada to live with and look after the Indians. You know that sort of slightly irritated tolerance, a lack of irresponsibility that marks the pedagogue? One feels that one's a White Man—ludicrously. I kept thinking I was in the Sixth at Rugby, again. These dear good people, with their laughter and friendliness and crowns of flowers—one feels that one must protect them. If one was having an evening out with Falstaff and Bardolph themselves, and a small delightful child came up with 'Please I'm lost and want to get home', wouldn't one have to leave good fellowship and spend the evening in mean streets tracking its abode? That's, I fancy, how the white man feels in these forgotten—and dissolving—pieces of heaven, the South Seas. And that perhaps is what Stevenson felt. I don't know enough about him. His memory is sweet there, in Samoa; especially among the natives. The white men—mostly traders—who remain from his time—have—for such people—very warm recollections of his personality, but—with a touch of pathos—avow themselves unable to see any merit in his work. Such stuff as the *Wrong Box* they frankly can't understand a grown man writing. I went up the steep hill above Vailima, where the grave is. It's a high and lovely spot. I took a Samoan of about 20 to guide me. He was much impressed by Stevenson's fame. 'That fellow' he said 'I think every fellow in the world know him'. Then he looked puzzled. 'But my father say,' he went on, 'Stevenson no big man—small man.' That a slight man of medium height should be so famous, puzzled him altogether. If he had been seven feet high, now! Fame is a curious thing.

On the 22nd, the day he set out on his next excursion over the water, he posted a curious request to the Ranee. She must write to all his relations on the attached list, asking them to fill in a form (a typed specimen was enclosed—*Width of foot*—*Length of big toe*, etc.) for he suspected the bone formation that was enabling him to entertain the Fijian natives by using his right foot with the dexterity of a third hand was an inheritance from the Cotterill side of the family. One can imagine the Ranee preferring to regard this accomplishment as a peculiarity of the Brookes, and finding an excuse for not writing round to all her relatives including Aunt Fanny, asking them to be so good as to send her at their convenience the measurements of their toes. Anyway, we hear no more of the inquiry, and the natives went on grinning while their visitor drew faces for them with his prehensile toes.

[1] 'It provokes the desire, but it takes away the performance.' See *Macbeth*, Act II, Scene 3.

A DEEP SLEEP

Accompanied by a land commissioner called Armstrong, he embarked for the island of Kandarva, in a small cutter, sleeping on deck because the cabin was infested with cockroaches. They were put up in the chief's hut, lived on yam and turtle, and played Fijian cricket, a violent form of the game which disregarded most of the rules. After five days they were back at Suva, where news of Cathleen's conversation on *Antony and Cleopatra* with Granville Barker provided a lively digression.

I say, if your Mr. Barker says such damn silly things about Shakespeare, I shall cut the last link with intellectualism, and become a Tariff Reformer, an Anti-Socialist, and an admirer of Mr. Lewis Waller. 'O withered is the garland of the war!' etc.—not meaning anything indeed! The cad! The green-eyed cad! How the devil *dare* he talk like that. Not 'mean' anything. I could take you—even you, a mere woman, and Irish at that—through the whole speech, word by word, and explain *exactly* what it means, each phrase, line, and sentence. And by God that a man who wrote *The Marrying of Ann Leete* and some of the darker portions of *Waste* should complain that A and C doesn't mean anything. The swine! the goat! the actor-manager! the stay-at-home, puking, God-forgotten, grease-paint-stinking, clod-pole! Were I by him, I should say 'Brother-in-law!'—or the Hindu word for it—which is a very severe and compendious Indian insult; it implies 1. that the person you're speaking to possesses a sister, 2. that the sister is of light virtue, 3. that you, the speaker, have had personal proof of it. Ingenious, isn't it? Reminds me of another compendious insult I heard the other day.

A. (to B. a drunken-looking, grey-eyed lout). 'I suppose you're Irish, aren't you?'
B. 'Irish, is ut? No, bedad!'
A. 'Then there must have been an Irishman on tour with your mother.'
Again the triple insult, you see, 1. You're Irish, 2. Your mother was an actress, 3. Her virtue, as we say in Canada, wanted sandpapering.

As so often these days, when the mail to Europe was in his mind, he toyed with schemes for the days to come.

Child, I see that I'm going to have the Hell of an uncomfortable life. I want too many different things. I keep, now, pining after London and all the things you've been seeing and doing. I want to talk, talk, talk. Is there anything better in the world than sitting at a table and eating good food and drinking great drink and discussing everything under the sun with wise and brilliant people? I want to sit at the table at Eddie's, with you there and Violet Asquith's brilliance, and Gilbert's wise silences, and Eddie's monocular stories—and TALK. Oh, but I'm going to have the loveliest rooms in King's. And I'm going to spend 5 days a week there, and three in London (that's 8 stoopid) and in King's I'm going to entertain all the mad and lovely people in the world. And I'm never going to sit down to dinner without a philosopher, a poet, a musician, an actress, a dancer, and a bishop, at table with me. I'm going to get up such performances, that'll turn old Cambridge upside-down. I'm going to have Yeats and Cannan and Craig and Barker to give a lecture each on modern drama. I'm going to have my great play in the Grantchester Garden, with Clotilde dancing in it. I'm going—oh, Hell, I don't know what I'm going to do. But every morning I shall drift up and down the Backs in a punt, discussing everything in the world, with anybody who desires.

To Denis Browne he confessed that he had lost his knowledge of art and literature, his 'fragmentary manners', and much else that pertained to civilization, 'but I have gained other things, a rich red-brown for my skin, a knowledge of mixed drinks, an ability to talk or drink with any kind of man, and a large repertoire of dirty stories. Am I richer or poorer? I don't know.' And then there was Raverat, who must be wanting to know whether this break with the past was having the effect that Mrs. Cornford and all his friends were hoping for. 'I wander, seeking peace, and ensuing it,' Brooke told him. 'Several times I've nearly found it: once, lately, in a Samoan village. But I had to come away from there in a hurry, in a boat, and forgot to pack it. But I'll have it yet. Fragments I have found, on various hills or by certain seas. It would be wonderful to find it.' He went on:

Oh, I shall return. The South Seas are Paradise. But I prefer England. I shall return when I'm certain. I'm nearly certain now. I'd once thought it necessary to marry. I *approve* of marriage for the world. I think you're all quite right. So don't be alarmed. But not for me. I'm too old. The Point of marriage is Peace—to work in. But can't one get it otherwise? Why, certainly, when one's old. And so I will. I know what things are good: friendship and work and conversation. These I shall have. How one can fill life, if one's energetic, and knows how to dig! I have thought of a thousand things to do, in books and poems and plays and theatres and societies and house-building and dinner-parties when I get Home. Ho, but we shall have fun. Now we have so painfully achieved middle-age, shall we not reap the fruits of that achievement, my dyspeptic friend?

He would like his friends to come together in good fellowship, so that he might be amongst them all at once. Jacques and Gwen, for instance, should call on Marsh in London, and try to get over their dislike of him. 'It's eccentric, I admit, to conceal a good heart beneath good manners, but forgivable, surely. And he'd love to see you. He's really so nice, and deserves well.' On balance, Brooke reflected, he had been blessed in many ways.

And there is no man who has had such friends as I, so many, so fine, so various, so multiform, so prone to laughter, so strong in affection and so permanent, so trustworthy, so courteous, so stern with vices, and so blind to faults or folly, of such swiftness of mind and strength of body, so polypist[1] and yet benevolent, and so apt both to make jokes and to understand them. Also, their faces are beautiful, and I love them. I repeat a very long list of their names, every night before I sleep. Friendship is always exciting and yet always safe. There is no lust in it, and therefore no poison. It is cleaner than love, and older; for children and very old people have friends, but they do not love. It gives more and takes less, it is fine in the enjoying, and without pain when absent, and it leaves only good memories. In love all laughter ends with an ache, but laughter is the very garland on the head of friendship. I will not love, and I will not be loved. But I will have friends round me continually, all the days of my life, and in whatever lands I may be. So we shall laugh and eat and sing and go great journeys in boats and on foot and write plays and perform them and pass innumerable laws taking their money from the rich.

I Err. I praise too extravagantly, conveying an impression that friendship always gives peace. And even at the moment I have a hunger too rending for complete peace, to see all your faces again, and to eat food with you.

And he ended, 'Won't 1914 be fun!'

Early in December he sailed to the island of Taviuni for the funeral of a young Fijian princess who had died of pneumonia and whose body was on board. On arrival he sent a postcard to Cathleen. 'Tonight I travelled 70 miles in an auxiliary cutter with the corpse of a Princess. Have you ever done that?' After three days of feasting and ceremonial he was back in Suva, and setting out on a long walking expedition with two native companions, 'to carry my bag and rug and guide me'. They covered about fourteen miles a day, staying the night in native villages, and both his attendants begged him to let them live and die for him and wait upon him at Grantchester. While on the trail he wrote to Violet Asquith.

Forgive this paper. It's limpness is because it has been in terrific thunder-storms, and through most of the rivers in Fiji, in the last few days. Its marks of dirt are because small naked brown babies *will* crawl up and handle it. And any blood-stains will be mine. The point is, will they . . . It's absurd, I know. It's twenty years since they've eaten anybody, in this part of Fiji, and far more since they've done what I particularly and unreasonably detest —fastened the victim down, cut pieces off him one by one, and cooked and eaten them before his eyes. To witness one's own transubstantiation into naked black man, that seems the last indignity. Consideration of the thoughts that pour through the mind of the ever-diminishing remnant of a man, as it sees its last limbs cooking, moves me deeply. I have been meditating a sonnet, as I sit here, surrounded by dusky faces and gleaming eyes: 'Dear, they have poached the eyes you loved so well.' It'd do well for No. 101 and last, in a modern sonnet-sequence, wouldn't it? I don't know how it would

[1] [Note by R.B.] = of many faiths, *not* bespattered by a parrot, O Greekless!

go on. The fourth line would have to be 'And all my turbulent lips are *maître-d'hôtel'*—I don't know how to scan French, I fancy that limps. But *all* is very strong in the modern style.

The idea comes out in a slighter thing.

> *'The limbs that erstwhile charmed your sight,*
> *Are now a savage's delight;*
> *The ear that heard your whispered vow*
> *Is one of many* entrées *now;*
> *Broiled are the arms in which you clung*
> *And devilled is the angelic tongue;* ...
> *And oh! my anguish as I see*
> *A Black Man gnaw your favourite knee!*
> *Of the two eyes that were your ruin,*
> *One now observes the other stewing.*
> *My lips (the inconstancy of man!)*
> *Are yours no more. The legs that ran*
> *Each dewy morn their love to wake,*
> *Are now a steak, are now a steak!* ...'

Oh, Dear! I suppose it ought to end on the Higher Note, the Wider Outlook. Poetry has to, they tell me. You may caress details all the main part of the poem, but at last you have to open the window—turn to God, or Earth, or Eternity, or any of the Grand Old Endings. It gives Uplift, as we Americans say. And that's so essential. (Did you ever notice how the Browning Family's poems *all* refer suddenly To God in the last line. It's laughable if you read through them in that way. 'What if that friend happened to be— God?' 'What comes next—Is it God?' 'And with God be the rest', 'And if God choose, I shall but love thee better after Death'—etc. etc. I forget them all, now. It shows what the Victorians were.) So must I soar—

> *'O love, o loveliest and best*
> *Natives this body may digest,*
> *Whole, and still yours, my soul shall dwell,*
> *Uneaten, safe, incoctible.'*

It's too dull. I shall go out and wander through the forest paths by the grey moonlight. Fiji in moonlight is like nothing else in this life or the next. It is all dim colours and all scents. And here, where it's high up, the most fantastically shaped mountains in the world tower up all around, and little silver clouds and wisps of mist run bleating up and down the valleys and hill-sides like lambs looking for their mother. There's only one thing on earth as beautiful: and that's Samoa by night. That's utterly different, merely Heaven, sheer loveliness. You lie on a mat in a cool Samoan hut and look out on the white sand under the high palms, and a gentle sea, and the black line of the reef a mile out and moonlight over everything, floods and floods of it, not sticky, like Honolulu moonlight, not to be eaten with a spoon, but flat and abundant, such that you could slice thin golden-white shavings off it, as off cheese ... and among it all are the loveliest people in the world, moving and running and dancing like gods and goddesses, very quietly and mysteriously, and utterly content. It is sheer beauty, so pure that it's difficult to breathe in it—like living in a Keats world, only it's less syrupy. Endymion without sugar. Completely unconnected with this world.

There is a poem—

> *'I know an Island,*
> *Where the long scented nights pass slow,*
> *And there, twixt lowland and highland,*
> *The white stream falls into a pool I know,*
> *Deep, hidden with ferns and flowers, soft as dreaming,*
> *Where the brown laughing dancing bathers go.'*

It ends, after many pages,

> *'I know an Island,*
> *Where the slow fragrant-breathing nights creep past,*
> *And then, twixt lowland and highland,*
> *A deep, fern-shrouded murmurous water glimmers;*
> *There I'll come back at last,*
> *And find my friends, the flower-crowned laughing swimmers,*
> *And . . .'*

I forget. And I've not written the middle part. And it's very bad, like all true poems. I love England; and all the people in it; but oh, how can one know of heaven on earth and not come back to it? I'm afraid I shall slip away from that slithery murky place you're (I suppose) in now, and return. Ridiculous.

I continue in a hot noon, under an orange tree. We rose at dawn and walked many miles and swam seven large rivers and picked and ate many oranges and pine-apples and drank coco-nuts. Now the two 'boys' who carry my luggage are asleep in the shade. They're Fijians of twenty-three or so who know a few words of English. One of them is the finest made man I've ever seen: like a Greek statue come to life: strong as ten horses. To see him strip and swim a half-flooded river is an immortal sight. Last night we stayed in the house of a mountain chief who has spasmodic fierce yearnings after civilization. When these grow strong he sends a runner down to the coast to buy any illustrated papers he can find. He knows no English, but he pastes his favourite pictures up round the wall and muses over them. I lectured on them—fragments of the *Sketch* and *Sphere* for several years— to a half-naked reverent audience last night (through my interpreters of course). The Prince of Wales, looking like an Oxford Undergraduate, elbows two ladies who display 1911 spring fashions. A golf champion in a most contorted position, occupies a central place. He is regarded, I fancy, as a rather potent and violent deity. To his left is 'Miss Viola Tree, as Eurydice', to his right Mrs. Granville Barker as Jocasta (or whatever the lady was called), looking infinitely Mycenaean. I explained about incest, shortly, and Mrs. B. rose tremendously in Fijian estimation. Why do people like their gods to be so eccentric, always? . . . It is so hard to explain our civilization to simple people. Anyhow, I disturbed their theogony, and elevated Lillah [McCarthy] to the top place. How Eurydice came in puzzled them and me. I fancy they regard her as a holy ghostess, in some sort.

It's very perplexing. These people—Samoans and Fijians—are so much nicer, and so *much* better-mannered than oneself. They are stronger, beautifuller, kindlier, more hospitable and courteous, greater lovers of beauty, and even wittier, than average Europeans. And they are—under our influence— a dying race. We gradually fill their lands with plantations and Indian coolies. The Hawaians, up in the 'Sandwich Islands', have almost altogether gone, and their arts and music with them, and their islands are a replica of America. A cheerful thought, that all these places are to become indistinguishable from Denver and Birmingham and Stuttgart, and the people in dress and behaviour precisely like Herr Schmidt, and Mr. Robinson and Hiram O. Guggenheim. And now they're so . . . it's impossible to describe how far nearer the Kingdom of Heaven—or the Garden of Eden—these good naked laughing people are than oneself or one's friends. But I forgot. You are an anti-socialist, and I mustn't say a word against our modern industrial system. I beg your pardon. . .

I suppose you're rushing from lunch party to lunch party, and dance to dance, and opera to political platform. Won't you come and learn how to make a hibiscus wreath for your hair, and sail a canoe, and swim two minutes under water catching turtles, and dive forty feet into a waterfall, and climb a coco-nut palm? It's more worth while.

He returned to Suva, limping with a septic foot, and on December 14 left Fiji aboard R.M.S. *Niagara*. The plan was to make for Tahiti via Auckland, but he missed the connexion in New Zealand and, moreover, had run short of funds. However they took him in at the Grand Hotel, Auckland, and first he kept a promise, setting down for Reginald Berkeley, a young Englishman he had gone around with in Suva, a few points on life and literature. In drafting a play the *obvious* must be avoided, 'for it's generally sentimental and it's rarely precise—the remedy for sentimentality . . . I beseech you, attempt reticence in situation, compression in the writing.' One should follow Stevenson's example, and for exercise write a page of deliberate imitation. 'It seemed to me that one of the things you needed to do soon, is to develop more individuality and depth of style. You've ideas enough, but they lose atmosphere in transition from your mind to your paper. It always happens, a little.' Then he came to the most important point of all.

Finally, I charge you, be kind to life: and do not bruise her with the bludgeon of the *a priori*. Poor dirty woman, she responds to sympathy. Sympathetic imagination with everybody and everything is the artist's one duty. He should be one with every little clergyman, and the stockbroker's most secret hopes should be his hope. In the end, the words of Strindberg's heroine are the only motto 'The race of man is greatly to be pitied.' Isn't that true? Hatred should be given out sparingly. It is too valuable to use carelessly. And, misused, it prevents understanding. And it is our duty to understand. For if we don't, no one else will.

Writing to Cathleen of his great walk on Fiji, he told of Abel, his giant guide, who carried him across rivers when he was tired of swimming them.

I think of bringing him back with me as a servant and bodyguard to England. He loved me because though I was far weaker than he, I was far braver. The Fijians are rather cowards. And on precipices I am peculiarly reckless. The boys saved me from rolling off to perdition about thirty times, and respected me for it—though thinking me insane. Would you marry me if I turned up with two vast cannibal servants, black-skinned and perpetually laughing—all of us attired only in loincloths and red flowers in our hair? I think I should be irresistible.

For Christmas he moved to Wairaki of the hot springs, having telegraphed to Chauncey Wells, asking for a loan of fifty pounds. His foot was now badly infected, and he had caught a chill. He was on relatively familiar ground, among English faces and snuffling with an English rheum. Another stage of his expedition was at an end. He needed a doctor, and a rest.

I'll describe New Zealand another day. It's a sort of Fabian England, very upper middle class and gentle and happy (after Canada), no poor and the Government owning hotels and running charabancs. All the women smoke, and dress badly, and nobody drinks. Everybody seems rather ugly—but perhaps that's compared with the South Seas.

He followed up his marconigram to Wells with a letter written on Christmas Day.

New Zealand is a queer place. If you go a walk along the road, and happen to look down at the puddles, you will notice they keep bubbling. Stoop down and put your finger in them and you know why. They're boiling. You turn to examine what looks like a rabbit hole in the wayside. Suddenly a strange rumbling proceeds from it. You stand back frightened. An enormous geyser of steam and boiling water bursts from it, plays a minute or two, and lapses again: to recur at a regular interval of 10 seconds, two minutes, an hour and a half, or whatever it may be. The whole country is built on a thin crust of rock and deposit, over thousands of feet of boiling mud and water. Occasionally one can thrust one's walking stick through. A terrifying place. I expect it will give soon. The people are pleasant, quiet, and affectionate. Very English, in accent clothes mind and everything.

'There are the same troubles between unions and employers, and between rich and poor,' he told the Ranee. 'I suppose there'll be no peace anywhere till the rich are curbed altogether.' He was angry about the strike in Dublin. 'I always feel in strikes that "the men are always right," as a man says in *Clayhanger*.' There was a fund, so he had seen in a newspaper, with Erskine Childers as treasurer. 'Could you send two guineas in my name? I'll settle when I get back. But I'd like it done immediately.' The newspaper also informed him that Cathleen was giving a good performance in *Quality Street*, and there too were several of his *Westminster* articles at last in print—'painstaking dreariness,' he thought, being still under the weather.

He was staying on a sheep-farm at Ruani, in the centre of North Island, a guest of the Studholme family whom he had met on the boat from Suva. He lingered for a week, watching the sheep-shearing, and trying not to argue too acrimoniously with his host, whose views on labour problems in Ireland and elsewhere were far from Fabian in character. On January 5 he was at Wellington, consulting a specialist about his poisoned foot, and two days later he sailed for Tahiti.

IV

Clara Butt and her husband were on board. The first evening ashore at Papeete, the principal town of Tahiti, was given over to a good-bye dinner. 'She's over six feet high,' Brooke wrote to the Ranee, somewhat intimidated, 'and must weigh sixteen stone and has a bass voice like a man's.' After a day or two he found a *pension* in a native village called Mataia, some thirty miles from Papeete. There was a verandah overlooking the sea, and thirty yards from the house there stood a small wooden pier for the fishing boats from which one could dive into deep water. Bed and board, with all meals, including cheap French wine, came to 6s. 3d. a day, and the household consisted of a half-caste and his wife, who ran the place, and two other Englishmen from a ranch in Canada—good company for bathes and expeditions into the hills with the natives. At Mataia there was a fairly regular routine. They rose at 6 a.m. and bathed; at 6.45 there was coffee and fruit, then Brooke worked until 10.30. After the main meal at 11 he slept from noon till 1.30, and worked again or explored the hills until 6.30, and the evening meal. When there was no night fishing everyone retired to bed shortly after 10. 'We find every kind of fish about here,' Brooke wrote to his mother, 'fresh water and salt, from sharks to eels and prawns, and we catch them in every conceivable kind of way, netting, spearing, and line. It's an ideal life. The half-caste and his Australian wife are very decent simple people. And the natives, though more civilized and more spoilt than in Fiji or Samoa, are many of them extraordinarily good companions.' Growing more agitated about his depleted funds, he wrote again to Chauncey Wells. 'Life in the country is like Greece without the intellect. A serious omission, I confess, but the whole is refreshing to people like you and me who are used to parts of the world which, at their highest, don't aim at much more than the Intellect without Greece.' He was surprised to find Tahiti so unspoiled, 'and Gauguin grossly maligned the ladies,' he told Eddie Marsh. 'Oh I know all that about expressing their primitive souls by making their bodies squat and square. But it's blasphemy.'

Three weeks passed, Wells sent the cash, but Brooke still did not have enough to pay his passage to San Francisco. By this time, however, he was only too glad to be stranded. For once there was nothing he was hankering for. He was at peace. The boats came and went at Papeete, and he wrote to Cathleen:

Europe slides from me, terrifyingly. There are but one or two things that prevent me letting time flow over me here till I turn to white sand and scented dust and little bright fish: a friend or two, a certain worthless Irish lady, the thought of some enemies I want to smash, the ever-rarer memory of primroses and English hedges, a thought of running a theatre . . .

Will it come to you having to come and fetch me?

The boat's ready to start. The brown lovely people in their bright clothes are gathered on the old wharf to wave her away. Everyone has a white flower behind their ear. Taatamata had given me one.

Taatamata, brought in so casually, was no name picked at random for sake of a touch of local colour. She was a girl at Mataia. According to one report she was a daughter of the chief of that village. Brooke and she conversed in pidgin French with a smattering of English thrown in here and there. She was the Mamua to whom the poem *Tiare Tahiti*, possibly the best of Brooke's poems, was addressed, a native girl of rare grace and intelligence, and by the first week of February the two of them were intimate friends. Nothing more is known of her, although a crumpled snapshot of a native girl in an enormous straw hat, and naked to the waist, leaning against a wattle fence and smiling, may be the Mamua who was regaled with a lyric exercise in the Platonic Ideas, and addressed in smoothly accomplished octosyllabics:

A DEEP SLEEP

Mamua, when our laughter ends,
And hearts and bodies, brown as white,
Are dust about the doors of friends,
Or scent a-blowing down the night,
Then, oh! then, the wise agree,
Comes our immortality.
Mamua, there waits a land
Hard for us to understand.
Out of time, beyond the sun,
All are one in Paradise,
You and Pupure are one,
And Taü, and the ungainly wise.
There the Eternals are, and there
The Good, the Lovely, and the True,
And Types, whose earthly copies were
The foolish broken things we knew . . .[1]

Pupure, meaning 'fair', was Taatamata's name for him. Among his new companions he was no longer remarkable for his physique, and even his one conspicuous feature, his colouring, was not thought beautiful so much as odd. It must have been a refreshing change to feel relatively commonplace. The poem proceeds, very skilfully separating Mamua herself from the gentle mockery of Plato, although she is of course involved in it, imagined walking with her lover in a Platonic paradise 'Where feet to Ambulation fade,' until the intellectual joke is pressed home to the absurdity of:

And there's an end, I think, of kissing,
When our mouths are one with Mouth.

and the manner in which all thought of the bodiless Ideal is then brushed aside and the passing earthly moment finally preferred, with all its human relish of 'faces individual, Well this side of Paradise!', is characteristic of Brooke at his best.

Hasten, hand in human hand,
Down the dark, the flowered way,
Along the whiteness of the sand,
And in the water's soft caress,
Wash the mind of foolishness,
Mamua, until the day . . .

[1] G.K., p. 25.

The simple lyric grace is sustained, and the private joke, although so closely interwoven with the tender sentiment, never falsifies it. Marvell was able to share his sophisticated wit with his coy mistress, and even woo her with his conceits. Brooke, perforce, must smile to himself, and yet from the heart of the poem, which is the cherishing love in it, Mamua is never excluded.

At the same time, on the verandah at Mataia, he was writing *The Great Lover*. 'I hope you are writing something *objective*,' ran the advice from Marsh which came to Tahiti. 'I think each of the poems you have sent home is lovely in itself, but when one looks back at them as a group they have all "Dear" and "Love" in them, nothing like the variety in your first book.' Later, he explained, 'By the way, when I made my impertinent remark about your running Love to death, or whatever I said, I didn't mean love as a subject but Love as an abstraction—it seemed to be becoming a mannerism of style.' *The Great Lover* is scrupulously, almost defiantly objective, and the opening paragraph is deliberately misleading, inflated into the utmost pomposity of style, rather in the manner of Francis Thompson ('The inenarrable godhead of delight,' and so forth) so that one is led to expect some tremendous climax of rhetoric, piling the Pelion of Thompson on the Ossa of Patmore, for nothing short of some magniloquent display of religious eroticism, one feels, could warrant such a preamble. But then with deftly contrived bathos the reader drops into a catalogue of trifles, such as holes in the ground and 'the comfortable smell of friendly fingers' (a reminiscence, he declared, of his childhood's cook at School Field), little things which are all the more telling and distinct on their miniature scale for the vague and grandiose bow-wow which has gone before; then again, as at the close of *Tiare Tahiti*, the graver note, as if to show it was something more than a joke, that meant what he said. Once more the gravity has made fun of itself, as was remarked in the case of *The Old Vicarage, Grantchester*, and the levity has taken itself seriously.

The first of his more extended South Sea poems had been written at Fiji and sent to Marsh from Auckland. 'I fire this off as I've finished it,' he wrote before Christmas. 'Store it away with the rest. It's even worse. I'll send something real soon,' and he added, 'How shall I ever stand England? You'll all have to pretend you're very savage, and gnaw your food, growling, on the floor, and dance strangely for me by night, and moan rhythmic chants: or else I shall return to the South Seas again.' Marsh, not fitted by nature to turn savage, was yet enthusiastic, 'I'm enraptured by the Fish's heaven, it is brilliantly amusing, and also beautiful. It certainly mustn't come out in *New Numbers* as all the clergymen would at once withdraw their subscriptions! so I've sent it to Jack Squire.' *Heaven*,[1] a satire on orthodox religion so gentle and oblique that it could only offend the most bigoted reader devoid of humour, deserves its place beside the poems that followed in Tahiti. This excellent piece is supposed to have been suggested by a postcard at Honolulu, and there is some evidence for this. Writing to Loines from the Moana arcade, thanking him for sending a supply of cash, Brooke confessed, 'I spend it riotously on picture postcards of highly coloured fish, with which the water is full, and on pineapples, which can be got for ten cents each, perfect ones'.

Probably the first of the Mataia poems (dated January) was *Retrospect*,[2] which is in effect an elegy to the memory of the 'mother-quiet' of Ka. He is once again able to recollect her in passionless tranquillity, granted she is held at the aesthetic distance of a work of art, and having long since fallen out of love, he achieves, in retrospect, as though at the last moment, a grave love poem worthy of its theme, resolving all that 'loud confusion of the heart' with a kind of benediction and a dying fall. At the Hotel Lavinia, Papeete, he wrote to Marsh, 'I'm sending a registered package of stuff. There seems to be too much of it for the world to run the risk of losing.' *Retrospect*, *Tiare Tahiti*, *The Great Lover*—add to them *Heaven*, and of the five sonnets from Honolulu and Fiji two—*Clouds* and *Psychical Research*—these, though there were other things to come, are the poems which best reflect Brooke's character. An Edwardian Marvell in miniature had come to maturity.

Normally there would have been no need to travel the thirty miles to Papeete if he wanted to register a package, but in mid-February he sustained an injury which rendered him inactive, providentially obliging him to work on the poems while there was leisure. It did more than temporary damage to his system. It was at Mataia, swimming under water near the pier opposite the pension, he espied a turtle, gave chase and, coming up to it from beneath, grazed his left leg on a jag of coral. The sores brought about by coral poisoning are quick to suppurate and slow to heal, and the leg was infected in five places. Dabbing with iodine only made them worse, as also did mere bathing,

[1] G.K., p. 35.
[2] G.K., p. 28.

and by early March he was advised to consult a doctor in Papeete. He was sent to bed in a downstairs room at the back of the hotel, and there, while he touched up the poems, he was nursed by 'Mamua', who had come with him to town. In the letter to Marsh announcing the registered package, he told how he had been lying on his back for the last nine days 'suffering intensely while I swob my skinless flesh with boiling disinfectant'. It was the first week of March, 1914. For a while he was running a high temperature, but there were compensations.

I lie in a hovel at the back of the hotel and contemplate the yard. The extraordinary life of the place flows round and through my room—for here no one, man or woman, scruples to come through one's room at any moment, if it happens to be a short cut. By day nothing much happens in the yard—except when a horse tried to eat a hen the other afternoon. But by night, after ten, it is filled with flitting figures of girls, with wreaths of white flowers, keeping assignations. Occasionally two rivals meet, and fill the darker corners with cursings and scratching. Or occasionally a youth intercepts a faithless lady and has a pretty operatic scene under my window. It is all—all Papeete—like a Renaissance Italy, with the venom taken out. They're three-quarters savage, but without savagery. No, simpler, light-come and light-go, passionate and forgetful, like children, but all the time Southern Pacific—that is to say, unmalicious and good-tempered. I have been nursed and waited on by a girl with wonderful eyes, the walk of a goddess, and the heart of an angel, who is, luckily, devoted to me. She gives her time to ministering to me, I mine to probing her queer mind. I think I shall write a book about her—only I fear I'm too fond of her.

The month of March came to an end, and he was limping on the verandah at Mataia, with no inclination to make the effort of starting home. He wrote to Phyllis Gardner, a friend of the Fabian days, warning her not to wander abroad, or not for long. 'It becomes a habit—landing in a fresh port with a light heart, a full bag, and an empty stomach, you stay there a few days or weeks or months, make some friends, see some queer things; and then, one gay morning, a boat blows in, and the rumour goes round that she's bound for the Isles of the Blest. And in you jump, with your bag, heavier by a few memories, and the anchor's up . . . and out and on you go again . . . The South Seas have got into my blood.' The mail boats were erratic, and he felt sure a lot of letters from Eddie Marsh *must* be held up somewhere.

Your letter of November announcing your marriage with Cathleen: your kindly Christmas information about the disastrous fire in Bilton Road and the disposal of the Ranee's and Alfred's cinders; Your New Year's epistle announcing your, Wilfrid's, and Albert's Knighthoods; the later letter that recounted your series of conversations with Shaw, the Earthquake, the war with Germany, Mrs. Elgy's illegitimate twins, Gilbert's trial, Masefield's latest knock-about farce, Arthur Benson's duel . . . all these I have not yet had. They await me in 'Frisco. So I take up the thread at the 25th of January —now itself some way down in the heap of yesterday's seven thousand years. I study them rather confusedly. Flecker—Wilfrid—poetry—plays— Moulin d'Or—the Saville—*Hullo, Tango!*—they all stir, these names, some dusty memories away in the back of my subconsciousness. Some-when, they must have meant something to me, in another life. A vision of taxis across the orange and green of the sunset. For a moment the palms dwindle to lamp-posts.

> *'So a poor ghost, beside his misty streams,*
> *Is haunted by strange doubts and fugitive dreams,*
> *Hints of a pre-Lethean life, of men,*
> *Rocks, stars, and skin, things unintelligible,*
> *And the sun on waving grass, he knows not when,*
> *And feet that ran, but where he cannot tell.'*

(You recognize the master-hand?)

The scrap of verse became part of his last South Sea poem, the sonnet *Hauntings*, an overflow, as it were, from *Retrospect*, recalling 'the ecstasy of your quietude', but the long screed continues. He will make it a custom in future to spend half the week at Raymond Buildings.

But, my dear, I doubt if you'll have me. The Game is Up, Eddie. If I've gained facts by knocking about with Conrad characters in a Gauguin entourage—I've lost a dream or two. I tried to be a poet. And because I'm a clever writer, and because I was forty times as sensitive as anybody else— I succeeded a little. *Es ist vorüber: es ist unwiederruflich zu Ende.* I am what I came out here to be—Hard. Quite, quite hard. I have become merely a minor character in a Kipling story. I'll never be able to write anything more, I think. Or perhaps I can do plays of a sort—I think I'll have to manage a theatre. I feel very energetic: and very capable. Is that a great come-down? I think that what I really feel like, is living. I want to talk and talk and talk . . . and in the intervals, have extraordinary adventures. Perhaps this too, is a come-down. But haven't I, at 26 reached the age when one should begin to learn? An energy that has rushed upon me with the cessation of my leprous skin-disease and the approaching end of six months' peace of soul, is driving me furiously on. This afternoon I go fishing in a canoe with a native girl on a green and purple reef. Tonight from ten to two, spearing fish in the same lagoon by torch light. Tomorrow up into the mountains at dawn on foot with a mad Englishman, four natives, and a half-caste, to a volcanic lake in the interior. There we build a house and stay for two days. The natives return, and the M.E. and myself swim the lake and push on for a pass down to the other coast. Perhaps we get it. Perhaps not. In any case we hope to see some ghosts—they abound in the interior. They come to you by night, and as you watch them their bellies burst and their entrails fall to the ground, and their eyes—unpupiled balls of white—fall out too, and they stink and shine.

'I hope my last lot of verse struck you as more "objective",' he ended. 'It's funny, I'd intended to confine myself more to "love" than I have. I meant to do a series—sequence—on a more or less imagined and eventless love-story. But I've not had the peace of mind and repose to think it out.' Having got this far, more money came from the trusting Professor Chauncey Wells of Berkeley, more than enough to pay his passage, and a boat was in, and it seemed rather safer after all to post his registered package in San Francisco, and there were sudden and sad good-byes at Mataia. He went aboard at Papeete.

It was about April 5 when the *Tahiti* weighed anchor. What Taatamata felt was known long after. On the third night, writing to Cathleen, Brooke watched out for the Southern Cross. It never appeared, but he knew it was still there for 'those good brown people in the Islands . . .'

And they're laughing and kissing and swimming and dancing beneath it. But for me it is set. And I do not know that I shall ever see it again. It's queer—I was sad at heart to leave Tahiti, but I resigned myself to the vessel, and watched the green shores and rocky peaks fade with hardly a pang. I'd told so many of those that loved me, so often, 'Oh yes, I'll come back . . . next year perhaps: or the year after . . .' that I suppose I'd begun to believe it myself. It was only yesterday, when I knew that the Southern Cross had left me, that I suddenly realized that I'd left behind those lovely places and lovely people, perhaps for ever. I reflected that there was surely nothing else like them in this world, and very probably nothing in the next: and that I was going far away from gentleness and beauty and kindliness and the smell of the lagoon and the thrill of that dancing and the scarlet of the *flamboyants* and the white and gold of other flowers . . .

Mia cara, or rather *tau* here, I greatly desire to see you. Your image in my heart breaks like a flower (*Masefield: adapted*). Do flowers break? Anyhow, what your image does is to dwell in some innermost corner of my heart and bloom there all the time and fill it with perfume. And that drowns—out-sings, out-perfumes, out-sweets—(*damn* the English language) certain other reprehensible corners of my heart, that whisper to me 'There's a village in Samoa, with the moonlight on the beach' or 'I've heard of a hill in Japan' or 'One said, there's an inn in Tibet, over a sheer precipice' or 'The Victoria Nyanza is an attractive Lake' or 'That trail in the North West, up the Mackenzie—Morris *said* he'd go, whenever I wanted' or 'I wonder if it's true, about that flower in the Andes, that smells like no other flower upon earth, and when once a man has smelt it, he can't but return there to live in those hills in the end, though he come back from the ends of the earth' and——

There are too many vagabond winds blowing through this evil and idle heart of mine, child. Do not let me wander. You are better than wandering. Or rather, wander a little with me. For that won't be wandering: I'll be Wordsworth's lark

> 'that soars, but does not roam,
> True to the kindred points of heaven and home.'

For I'll lie between your face and your heart, then; and your face is heaven and your heart is home.

La! La! these scraps of English poetry start whispering within me. That means I'm north of the Equator, doesn't it? It's a good sign, perhaps. English thoughts are waking in me. They'll fetch me back.

He conveyed his news to Frances Cornford by addressing himself to her daughter Helena, who was not yet a year old. Perhaps it would reach her at Conduit Head in May. 'But you won't have gone dabbling in the dew, in Justin's car, at Overcote. No, indeed. You young folks don't do these things. There *were* days . . .' English thoughts were faintly stirring within him—'grey, quiet, misty, rather mad, slightly moral, shy, and lovely thoughts. But very faintly so. England is too vague and hidden and fragmentary and forgotten a thing. One'll not be able to have really, such things as English thoughts while England's under that irresponsible and ignorant plutocracy which your aged parents support and obey'. In fact the thought of London appalled him, leading him to use language unsuited to the ears of an infant of six months, saying its ways were thronged with 'lean and vicious people, dirty hermaphrodites and eunuchs, moral vagabonds, pitiable scum'. Troubled with a brief recurrence of the old bitterness, he even vented the spleen of his anti-Semitism—which at times could be virulent (a disagreeable result of his admiration for Belloc) though generally reserved for Raverat alone—so grim was the prospect of a return to the modern world.

Helena, do not go beyond civilization. It is unsettling. Inside civilization one can realize the beastliness of it, and labour—if one's honest, as I hope you'll be—to smash it. But when you get *outside*, you realize the advantages of not being in it *too* acutely . . . Helen, do not, as you grow older, become a feminist: become, I pray you, a woman.

As he drew near to San Francisco the old angers returned.

V

He was fond of Chauncey Wells and his wife, and well he might be, for the gentle professor at Piedmont Avenue, together with Loines on Staten Island, had been acting as a far-flung branch of the bank at Rugby, stored the luggage that Brooke abandoned before leaving for Honolulu, and provided an address for the accumulation of mail. For a moment Brooke's heart stopped as he turned the letters over and noticed that for some reason or other Ka was soliciting his attention. 'I was frightened to see your handwriting,' he replied, adding wanly, 'Yes, we'll carry off chance meetings. I think we'd better even enjoy them.' There was an old message from Marsh about *New Numbers*. 'England expects of you more than one sonnet,' but most of these things he put aside to deal with on the train to Arizona, and in a discussion on Socialism in the garden at Piedmont Avenue he seemed to his host unduly despondent. 'We shall never,' he said, 'never learn to live decently together until it's too late.'

On April 23 he took the train to Arizona, and wrote to the Rānee, sitting on the edge of the Grand Canyon. The opposite rim, he said, was thirteen miles away. 'It is filled with what would be respectable mountains—at least Snowdon's size—on the level, but here don't come up to the edge of the chasm.' (To a friend he described it as 'very large and very untidy, like my soul. But unlike my soul, it has peace in it.') The newspapers were giving grave news. 'But there's nothing like the popular excitement a war generally causes. It'll be a "sort of war"—dragging on and on.' Marsh was sent a page of ill humour, only relieved by a tribute to the roses and hyacinths at Piedmont Avenue, beginning 'How I hate civilization and houses and trams and collars . . . One must remember one has trousers on again.' And Hilton Young (Lord Kennet), a friend of early Cambridge days, fared little better.

Can you dive for turtles? I will teach you. Can you climb a coco-nut tree with bare feet? I will show you how. Can you spear fish? eat octopus? dance obscene primitive dances, and chant in 7/11 rhythm? All these things shall be yours, if you will but buy a 2000 ton yacht and fit her out and take me as sailing-master. For myself, I shall return there for ever. I'm only coming back to put a bullet in Sir Edward Carson, and another in Mr. Murphy, who smashed the Dublin strike. Then I shall bid farewell to plutocratic dirty England: and back to the lagoons.

Your last chance of escape. Mark it.

Cathleen was given to anticipate all sorts of 'profound probings, and questions, and joint investigations into the soul—peering hand in hand like timid children round the corner of a gigantic doorway, into a dark room, in which are faintly discernible—shapes—moving, perhaps? *are* they monsters, or gods?' For all his ambition to manage a theatre or write plays, he harboured an attitude to the theatrical profession which was rather more than slightly mid-Victorian, and he was constantly amazed, as now, 'that you should move in those ghastly places and in that ghastly profession, and yet remain so lovely'. He was darkly suspicious of London's influence. 'It's good to resolve to be at peace with all the world!' he had written from California, 'but don't make peace with evil. One mustn't. I have seen it lead to such pain and disgrace.' But now, having told her the probable date of his return to England, his main injunction was of another sort.

My dear, one thing I would implore of you. It's very silly. But don't tell anybody the exact date I'm coming back. It's my fancy to blow in on them unexpected. Just to wander into Raymond Buildings, and hear Eddie squeak 'Oh, my *dear*! I thought you were in Tahiti.' It's awfully silly and romantic. But the thought does give me the keenest and most exquisite pleasure. Dear child, don't give away one of the first poets in England, but there is in him, still, a very very small portion that's just a little childish.

Back in the train, now steaming for Chicago, a diatribe against civilization was devised for Raverat, beginning mildly enough—'I went without letters for many months (it *was* so nice). But when I got back to civilization (screams of laughter) I found a million'—and developing into an attack on industrial employers that quell strikes by force—'I sometimes wish I was a Christian, or of some known religion, to be able to *curse* these people'—culminating in a revised version of the Beatitudes, of which the last is 'Blessed are you, when men do curse you and despitefully use you, for ye shall go back with a few friends and a big stick and knock hell out of them'—through a digression on his reading of Boswell—'I've discovered that Dr. Johnson's the only man I love. An Englishman, by God'—and concluding with a flat denial: 'No, I don't think of Ka with pleasure. It hurts to think of her—I often do it—because I feel so anxious about her. I don't want to think of her. I should pray: were there anything to pray to!'—and every now and then an aside such as 'Thank God the train has run into a buffalo, and, for the moment, stopped.' Something about Raverat always made him rampage.

On April 29 he arrived at the Auditorium Hotel, Chicago, left a note at the Fine Arts Building next door (where the Chicago Little Theatre then had premises) and after the evening performance of *Hedda Gabler* presented himself to the director, Maurice Browne, and his wife, the actress Ellen Von Volkenburg. The introduction from Harold Monro proved very fruitful. On three successive nights they were up almost till dawn, 'surging across the tiny room,' according to Browne's report, reading aloud, singing folk-songs, arguing; and Browne fetched over Arthur Ficke, the poet of Iowa, editor of the *Chicago Evening Post*, from Davenport, and Llewellyn Jones, a patron of letters, and they all listened to *Lithuania* (Browne was the first producer of the play a little over a year later), the South Sea poems, admired the sea-shells and other souvenirs of Tahiti, heard tell of an alleged Gauguin find—a painting on a glass door which somehow got lost on the journey—Brooke himself the while sitting on the floor with his back against a wardrobe. He could read well, according to Browne, 'quietly and shyly, with little tone-variation, dwelling slightly on significant vowel-sounds each empha-sizing rhyme and rhythm . . . taking care of the sound and letting the sense take care of itself.'[1] And he was observed on Michigan Avenue, 'his right hand swinging his hat—some broad-brimmed high-crowned ridiculous featherweight, plaited from South Sea straw, of which he was inordinately vain—his long legs striding carelessly and freely, his eyes fixed straight ahead, utterly unconscious of people and things, for he's talking.' His hair, by now a sort of bleached gold, was the colour of his skin, and his suit apparently matched both. 'Every woman who passes—and every other man—stops, turns round, to look at that lithe and radiant figure.' Having come from the islands where his physique was nothing remarkable, he was once again the cynosure of all eyes. 'It seems as if the youth of all the world . . .' The amazed hyperboles begin all over again.

Eugene Hutchinson, however, whose studio was near by, being a skilled photographer and observer of man, recorded his sitter with no less careful admiration than his compatriot Schell in London a year before. He too had listened to the readings, but was rather more taken with the personality than the poetry—'For I had found myself confronted by an unbelievably beautiful young man. There was nothing effeminate about that beauty. He was man-size and masculine, from his rough tweeds to his thick-soled English boots. He gave me the impression of being water-loving and well-washed. Perhaps this

[1] *Recollections of Rupert Brooke*, Maurice Browne, Alexander Greene, Chicago, 1927.

was due to the freshness of his sun-tanned face and the odd smooth-ness of his skin, a smoothness you see more in women than in men . . . He seemed like a Norse myth in modern clothes. Yet there was no vanity in the man . . .' Hutchinson happened to be present when there was a discussion on the stage of the empty theatre: the artistic tem-perament, why, in the male, was it so often compounded of feminine attributes? Brooke leaning against a property column, contributed nothing until the end. 'Then he startled us by the vigour and decision with which he stated that, notwithstanding Havelock Ellis and Kraft-Ebbing, this mixture of the sexes was all wrong, that male was male and female was female, and any intermingling of the two was calamitous. In other words, this Shelley-like youth with his hyper-sensitive face and his girlish smoothness of skin and his emotional blue eyes was trying to tell us that manliness in men was the one hope of the world.'[1] The reader of a previous chapter will realize that it was rather the womanliness of woman which must have lain behind the large hope Brooke had in mind. It was another of his anti-feminist outbursts. In such company, he might well have gone on to talk of Strindberg, but he did not. *The Little Review*, a month or so later, quoted Yeats declaring that he was ' "the most beautiful young man in England" . . . but it was rather silly of Mr. Yeats to add that he is also the wearer of the most gorgeous shirts.' Ka's handiwork was not in evidence on Michigan Avenue.

After a night at Fort Pitt in Pittsburgh, he arrived at the New Willard Hotel, Washington, on May 5, and was shown the sights by the Marchesa Mannucci Capponi, a young widow of American birth whose companionship he had enjoyed, to the point of a fleeting romance, at Lake Louise in Canada, some while before. In the inter-val she had visited England and actually made her way to Rugby, charmed the Ranee into receiving her with cordiality, and delivered a reassuring account of her son. Among the private jokes the Mar-chesa shared with Brooke was the notion that he was un-gallant on principle, which explains the story he sent her from Lake Louise, she having had to leave the place some while before him. He was out on a long walk in the hills alone, when seven females rushed up to him in alarm. 'We have seen a bear. Will you protect us back to the hotel?' and the reply he claimed to his credit was 'I want to be alone. There are already too many females in the world. Go. And I hope you meet the bear.' He did not see them in the hotel that evening.

[1] *Red Wine of Youth*, Arthur Stringer, The Bobbs-Merrill Company, New York, 1948.

A DEEP SLEEP

He dined with the British Ambassador, having no dress-clothes, nor even any pyjamas to return to at the hotel, an awkward vicissitude accounted for in a letter to Browne.

Isn't it typical of America that the *Auditorium* porter checked all my luggage to Washington, Pennsylvania? Now if I'd been in England, my luggage wouldn't have gone a thousand miles in the opposite direction. But if it *had*, I should never have seen it again. Whereas, this being America, it has been located and is to arrive here tomorrow. A nation of kindly dreamers.

His fellow guest at the Embassy was O'Shaugnessy, the U.S. Consul in Mexico, who had much to tell of the serious troubles there, and Brooke dined well, unaccustomed as he was to champagne, 'and got so excited that on returning here I had to have a bath and dance many obscene dances, in lonely nakedness, up and down my room, to get sober'. He was writing to Cathleen, too excited to sleep, for he had booked his passage home on the *Philadelphia*, so as to be with Browne and his wife on the same boat; and last night he had dreamed a dream of happy omen. 'Friends I had known long ago, between whom and myself evil and pain has come, greeted me in the old first way,' and all the others were 'wonderfully the same'. He woke laughing and crying.

I felt I *must* get back—I telegraphed to Browne, flew to some agents, and in consequence—I sail from New York on May 29: and reach Plymouth (o blessed name o loveliness! Plymouth—was there ever so sweet and droll a sound? Drake's Plymouth! English, western Plymouth! city where men speak softly and things are sold for shillings, not for dollars, and there is love and beauty and old houses, and beyond which are little fields, very green, bounded by small piled walls of stone—and behind them—I know it, the brown and black, splintered, haunted moor. By that the train shall go up—by Dartmouth, where my brother was—I will make a Litany—by Torquay, where Verrall stayed, and by Paignton, where I have walked in the rain: past Ilsham, where John Ford was born, and Appledore, in the inn of which I wrote a poem against a Commercial Traveller; by Dawlish, of which John Keats sang; within sight of Widdicombe, where old Uncle Tom Cobbley rode a mare; not a dozen miles from Galsworthy at Manaton; within sight, almost, of that hill by Drewsteignton on which I lay out all one September night, crying. And to Exeter. And to Ottery St. Mary, where Coleridge sojourned; And across Wiltshire, where men built and sang many centuries before the *aquila* . . . Oh, noble train, oh glorious and forthright and English train, I will look round me at the English faces and out at the English fields—and I will pray . . .)—reach Plymouth, as I was saying when I was interrupted, on Friday June 5.

By May 18 he was at the Hotel Bellevue, Boston, bidding his

friends good-bye, the Humes and others; he stayed a night at Yale, and a few days later turned up on Staten Island to describe his adventures and repay his debts to Russell Loines. Here more mail had accumulated. Marsh was answering the letter from Tahiti in which Brooke had threatened to throw in his poetical hand ('The game is up, Eddie . . . I am what I came out here to be—hard, quite hard.') Marsh took it only half seriously, but, on the other hand, he was careful not to be flippant in reply, just in case. 'You have achieved your instrument, and I expect a time will come when you will want to play on it again. It will be the bitterest disappointment of my life if you aren't "among the English poets when you die" as Keats said.' By this time the South Sea poems were at Gray's Inn—'Plato would have been much flattered by your not being able to get away from the Ideas,' was the comment in a letter of a later date among these others —but nevertheless, Brooke *was*, perhaps, by now a little hard. Having cultivated a defence against the thoughts and associations of one kind, he was lucky still to have his delicate sensibilities as alert as ever and wide open to the world. Many an older man, confronted with the same necessity, and likewise toughening his resistance to the onset of some particular recurring pain, has found it impossible to confine his armour to a single spot, the subconscious mind as it were demanding all or nothing by way of a shield; and after a while, with no apparent change, he walks abroad encased in the hide of a plated dinosaur, impervious to feeling of any kind whatever (saving only the most crude) and sorrowfully endorsing Coleridge's lament, 'I see not feel how beautiful they are'. But Brooke was twenty-six, and a young man of strong character.

The news from Cathleen was nothing exceptional from a young woman in the professional theatre who could not always afford to pick and choose her play, but to Brooke, not only ignorant of the profession but of that sense of iron necessity which from time to time obliges any artist to compromise, the signs were rather disquieting. '*General John Regan, Quality Street*, a London season, and a rumoured farce with Hawtrey—*what* a year! Oh you devil, you devil!' To anyone else this would only suggest a varied and promising career, with good parts and fairly regular employment, but Brooke was incapable of seeing it in that light, for in his heart of hearts he deplored her being a professional woman of any sort. 'You, the one lovely and wise person among all those painted shades . . . *Why* did I go away and leave you a year?' Why must she be at once a goddess and 'the bloodiest fool that ever plagued mortal poet? . . . Forgive my anxiousness about you. It's partly because I'm lonely . . . I have staked very much on you, Cathleen.' It's as if he were on the point of losing his nerve. 'By God, London's a bad place. I know it. It's full of lust, and of hard mouths, and empty, empty eyes, and of din and glare that are gay for a time . . . So little of beauty is left clean and standing by this ruinous age, and I have seen so many things crumble. One must "set up one's rest" somewhere. I *will* not let you fade. If ever you wish to "bedim the lovely flame in you" I will kill you, and myself too, before it can happen. What do I care for *you*, when there's Beauty to fight for?'

'That's rant,' he goes on to admit, but the impulse beneath it was genuine enough. 'Worship and love are very hard to shake off: impossible. They pursue you more unescapably than the Furies Orestes. You may take the wings of the morning, and flee to the uttermost parts of the sea. But you will not evade my love. If ever you denied Beauty and Goodness, you would suffer pain, and I should suffer pain, unceasingly and infinitely. But you could not escape me.' Knowing nothing of the root of his unsureness, she must have been given seriously to wonder what on earth these sudden and frantic threats and protestations were in aid of. How could the prospect of a farce with the admirable Hawtrey, for instance, have touched off such a passionate fusillade? But to him, with the exception of a handful of friends and a few places, which seemed like so many deities and their shrines, London was corrupt—no fit place for a non-Christian—and drawing nearer as he was to what he had called 'civilization (screams of laughter)' he was more and more coming to realize that he had indeed 'staked very much' on one individual. The only real danger to this relationship was something in himself; he might find it impossible ever again wholly to entrust his future to an 'emancipated' woman, no matter how blameless she might be. His detestation of feminism was making things very difficult, for by 1914 what other sort of young woman was there to be found? and there was a part of him already sullenly resigned to bachelorhood, the part which felt itself committed for life, in sickness and in health, and in perpetual absence, to Ka.

By now he had abandoned the idea of walking into Gray's Inn out of the blue. There was some advantage in a welcome that was properly organized. 'If you see Eddie, you can make him arrange a meal that day (provisionally) for all of us. What's Eddie for except to arrange meals for all of us?' This because Marsh was almost the only one of his close acquaintance (except perhaps Geoffrey Keynes) who was not the sort of person to let his luggage go on by itself to Pennsylvania, and could be relied on never to muddle a date. He was, in fact, a great convenience.

The *Philadelphia* was due to sail on the 29th, and the last five days were spent at the McAlpin Hotel in Greeley Square, New York. 'I can't sleep for thinking of England,' he wrote to Marsh, and followed it with a marconigram 'Will you be in London Friday night June fifth I shall'. He was surprised to receive a portrait of a total stranger (they had sent the wrong photographs) recognizing only the name of the photographer he had sat for in Chicago. 'Hutchinson,' he wrote to Browne, 'who has a distressingly modern mania for photographing the soul instead of the body, has sent me a lovely reproduction of a beautiful middle-aged woman playing a piano, thinking of the *Ewigkeit*, in profile, facing the dawn. "Is *that* the mouth that touched Tahitian lips and drained the topless tankards of Berlin?" No, no! I have not changed so much,' and to Hutchinson himself, recalling the discussion on the stage, 'The soul of persons who write verse is said to be hermaphroditic, but not, I protest, so feminine.'

Carrying his enormous straw hat, a folder of the correct photographs (only a little smaller than those of the year before, described for Cathleen as 'my dear, they're as large as the side of a house; one can't get them through an ordinary doorway', magazines, books (Marsh had sent him the six best newly out, including Lawrence's *Sons and Lovers*—'It's so extraordinarily vivid in conception of scenes,' wrote Brooke. 'He's always *hectic*, isn't he, a little? But I must proceed. He's a big man.') and a writing-case, he mounted the gangway, and was at sea. Of an evening there was three-handed bridge with the Brownes to the strains of a Glee Club that was on board and liable to burst into 'You are my sun, won't you adore me?' in unexpected places; or he would sit with Ellen Von Volkenburg, exchanging anecdotes. 'When he finished a story,' she entered in her journal, 'he would set his eyes ahead until the queer little cast came in one of them, run his fingers through his hair with ferocious energy, pause, grasp his nose between his thumb and forefinger, tweak it gently two or three times . . . stop, pull his Jaeger blanket high around his head (leaving none of it to protect his legs) and start on some fresh recollection.'

He competed with Browne and Ronald Hargreave, the painter,

writing a sonnet to a given rhyme scheme,[1] and on getting a note from Hargreave which said he was so ashamed of his effort that he had jumped overboard, Brooke inscribed a 'threnody' in Miss Von Volkenburg's journal (Fifi was the nickname of a girl on board)—

> *The world's great painter soul, whom we deplore,*
> *Loved California much, but music more.*
> *His verse—but hush! the poor man's dead and gone*
> *What Fifi lost the mermaidens have won.*[2]

Coming into Plymouth, the smell of new-mown hay was noticeable quite far out at sea. On land they heard of the *Empress of Ireland* sunk in the St. Lawrence with severe loss of life. When Brooke a year later again gave thought to this disaster, his circumstances were of another kind. For the present nothing could mar the joyous anticipation. Cathleen, Marsh, and Denis Browne, were at Euston at 2.45 a.m. when the train came in very late. He was waking from a deep sleep, but never so deep as to have been altogether free of memorable dreams.

[1] G.K., p. 60.
[2] *Recollections of Rupert Brooke*, Maurice Browne, Alexander Greene, Chicago, 1927.

Chapter XII

ONE OF A NUMBER

(*June 1914–February 1915*)

After his first night in England, he took the train to Rugby. 'I've such a warmth for the Ranee,' he had written from America, and the sight of her at home again in Bilton Road, as if he had only been away for a long week-end, evoked a genuine glow of filial affection. In the next five days he exchanged with Marsh no less than eight notes or second-thought postcards about a party at Raymond Buildings. 'Don't overweight it with mimes, though. In a majority they're tiresome,' he warned, then, oddly for a Socialist, 'You can't think of another gentleman to balance the actors and artists?' He was at last beginning to calm down, he said. 'England is *too* wonderful.' After three days he went to meet André Gide, who was staying with the Raverats near Royston, and found Marsh had written, 'I'm sorry the party is going to be so horrible,' but the male gentry, he regretted to say, were too stupid and the female too clever, for the occasion. On the 11th Brooke returned to Raymond Buildings, saw *Les Papillons* and *Petrouchka* (not to mention Queen Alexandra, Shaw, George Moore, and other figures held in legendary awe in Tahiti) at Drury Lane, and the homecoming party took place at Gray's Inn. Hugh Walpole and Desmond MacCarthy were among those who stayed on late and watched Brooke demonstrating a Samoan *Siva-siva* dance under the sober plane-trees as dawn broke over Holborn.

Meanwhile Mrs. Cornford, ill and being nursed by Ka, was moved gently to remonstrate, standing up for her sex which Brooke had maligned in a letter from the Pacific. 'Do not be muddled, Frances,' he wrote in explanation, 'I am not insulting women. There *was* a time when I despised them a little, perceiving what fourthrate men they made. But lately I've cheered up, noticing what supreme women they make. Have you ever noticed? Think of Gwen. Think of Ka (all her glory woman-ish, and what weakness she had feminist)'. He offered to seek out Mrs. Cornford and tell her traveller's tales about the South Seas. 'You are the only person, Frances, who ever believed all my lies!' In reply she accounted for her credulity by saying it must be a family trait. Her grandfather, Charles Darwin, when a small boy, was told that if you entered a sweet-shop wearing your hat in a certain way, tilted over an eye, you could help yourself to any cake you liked without paying. 'He was so surprised when it didn't work.'

At dinner the day after the homecoming party, Brooke met what Maurice Browne, another of the party, described as 'a small, dark, shy man, with spectacles and straight, slightly greasy-looking hair' and 'a queer little green hat which tipped up preposterously in front'. One day Brooke would make him the third of his three heirs, but now he took him back to Raymond Buildings for the night. It was curious that he had never before met the founder of *New Numbers*, Lascelles Abercrombie. 'I think he's very remarkable,' Brooke wrote to Ka next morning. 'He laughs very well.'

Ka had suggested a meeting. How did she know he was back? he wondered. 'Was it in the *Morning Post*?' No, he wouldn't be intolerably 'fussed' at the sight of her again.

Only, I'm not certain about you. I can't be of course, because I don't know what you're like now. It seems to me very probable that either you will dislike me, and be annoyed after seeing me, or you will like me, and be disturbed and uncomfortably reminded. I know you're very sensible and all that, but I fear the feeling that the friendlier we got the more disturbing it'd be. It would put such a constraint, a bloody constraint on us.

He placed on her the full responsibility. 'Do realize it, and, if you are likely to be upset by me, honestly don't arrange a meeting. There's trouble enough in the world.' So they met in a tea shop, and afterwards each wrote to the other, anxious lest the strain had proved too much. 'You looked tired as you leant over the back of a chair,' wrote Brooke. 'I was frightened.'

On the 18th he attended the first performance of Stravinsky's *Le Rossignol*, and again brought Abercrombie back for the night; on the 20th he was at *The Pink and Lily*, near Princes Risborough, with Marsh, Ben Keeling and Dudley Ward, and Cathleen joined them for the day, and afterwards Brooke wrote to her of the planning of a second volume of *Georgian Poetry*.

Eddie and I had a perfectly glorious day yesterday; we dissected and discussed and adjudged all the poets with infinite perspicacity and responsibility, and then we walked by those glorious woods to Wendover (you know the walk from Wendover, my dear) and drank much beer there, and ate, and started back, and slept in the heather, and walked on through arcades of mysterious beechen gloom and picked flowers and told stories and got back to roast beef and more beer and poems. I wish you had been there.

She was going to play Synge's Deirdre. 'You must burn into it, as you learn it. Live for it, wonderfully *be* it.' And then he went to stay with Gibson and his wife at Greenway, only a few minutes' walk from The Gallows, the home of *New Numbers*.

Lord Beauchamp, the landlord, converted two timbered cottages into one, with a small courtyard, and a garden sloping upward to a row of seven great elms, and it was named *The Gallows* because a highwayman had been hanged at the front door. While Brooke was in Toronto Lascelles and Catherine Abercrombie called on a printer in Gloucester, chose the format and arranged for all the copies of each edition of their quarterly, *The Gallows Garland*, as it then was, to be sent to their cottage. A business-like writing desk was presented to Catherine for her keeping of the accounts, and by now the inaugural number had been posted to the two hundred subscribers, Catherine jogging the cradle with her foot while she copied out the addresses, and Gibson, suddenly turning a ghastly white from licking so many stamps. From here the South Sea poems were first given to the public, as also the sonnets that were yet to come.

'I've written to Lawrence at three addresses,' Marsh wrote to Brooke at Greenway, 'all of which appear to be bogus.' Both Dudley Ward and Brooke were agitating to meet the author of *Sons and Lovers*. Meanwhile there was a reunion of the Apostles in London, and for the last time many of the characters in Brooke's past life came together in the Connaught Rooms: Moore, Shove, Norton, James Strachey and Maynard Keynes, and this time it was John Sheppard, Brooke's tutor at King's, who was brought back to stay at Gray's Inn. Next day D. H. Lawrence and his wife Frieda, traced at last, turned up to lunch at the Moulin d'Or, and Marsh took them and Brooke along to the Allied Artists exhibition at Holland Park. Brooke and Lawrence were observed in lively talk and roaring with laughter. It was the start of another London season for Brooke, and the only events of his life were conversational meals and brief encounters. He is at 10 Downing Street, where Ruth Draper recites and Steuart Wilson sings; meeting Gaudier Brzeska at the Moulin d'Or, Denis Browne at the Russian Ballet; supping with J. M. Barrie at the Savoy, and a man with a biograph apparatus comes in, takes a moving photograph of the table, and gets into his lens—Barrie, Shaw, Yeats, Chesterton, Granville-Barker, Mr. Asquith, Mrs. Patrick Campbell, Ricketts, Marsh and Brooke, the latter seated between Marie Tempest and Gerald du Maurier; on July 9, Paul Nash, Siegfried Sassoon, and W. H. Davies, are at breakfast with him at Gray's Inn. After a while Brooke is left alone with Sassoon. 'What were the white people like in the places you stayed at in the tropics?' asks Sassoon. 'Some of them,' Brooke says, 'were rather like composite characters out of Conrad and Kipling,' Sassoon then passes a rather disparaging remark about Kipling's verse being 'tub-thumping stuff', 'But not always, surely,' says Brooke. 'I used to think rather the same myself until Eddie made me read *Cities and Thrones and Powers*. There aren't many better modern poems than that, you know.'

Sassoon took note of 'the almost meditative deliberation of his voice. His movements, too, so restful, so controlled, and so unaffected. But beyond that was my assured perception that I was in the presence of one on whom had been conferred all the invisible attributes of a poet. To this his radiant good looks seemed subsidiary. Here, I might well have thought—had my divinations been expressible—was a being singled out for some transplendent performance, some enshrined achievement.'[1] When Sassoon left, after about half an hour, and Brooke, closing the door, turned back, in Sassoon's phrase, 'to being his unimpeded self,' it is probable that he took pencil and paper and carefully reconstructed from memory a short monologue just delivered by W. H. Davies at the breakfast table. The entry in his notebook is not dated, but the subject of painting was more likely to have been suggested within Marsh's crowded walls (transformed since Brooke's departure for America with the newest works of the Spencer brothers, Gertler, and others) than on the previous occasion when the poets met. There was a Boswell in Brooke, too seldom given exercise. One imagines him catching the expression on Paul Nash's face—the host has left for his office at Whitehall. Brooke, Sassoon, Davies, and Paul Nash are still at the table. Davies speaks.

I've got very fond of pictures in the last two years. I've got one lovely one. It's an early Victorian landscape, oh, a very beautiful one. A friend of mine saw it in an old shop. He couldn't afford it. But he told me and I bought it. Only two pounds. The frame alone is worth two pounds; it's an

[1] *The Weald of Youth*, Siegfried Sassoon, Faber and Faber, 1942.

awfully good frame, my friend says it's worth quite two pounds, and he's an artist, so it must be. And the picture's a good one. He says it's a good one, and he's an artist, so of course he knows. And every one who has been in my room has admired it very much. So it must be good. But I've got two other pictures. I used to like them very much, but I don't now. Oh, I can't bear them. I'd break them up; only, you know, they've been in the family a long time. I've put them in a dark corner with a screen in front of them. But I tell you, if a man came in and said 'Look here, I'll give you a pint of beer for those two pictures,' I'd take it. Yes, and I'd share the beer with him, too.

Next day Brooke lunches with Henry James and Mrs. Belloc-Lowndes. Then he goes to Cambridge and, dining with A. C. Benson, hears that Quiller-Couch, Professor of Literature, will be glad of his assistance next term. 'At last I shall have to read *The Faerie Queene*!' he comments, and Benson remarks in his diary, 'He is more mature since his travels'. On the 15th, again with the Asquiths at 10 Downing Street, Denis Browne plays and Steuart Wilson sings; then Ronald Storrs and Stanley Spencer come to breakfast at Gray's Inn. July 24 was the next important day: Marsh took him to dine with the Duchess of Leeds, and he sat at table between Lady Gwendoline Osborne and a new acquaintance, the young Lady Eileen Wellesley, daughter of the Duke of Wellington. After the meal several of them went on to Sir Ian Hamilton's at Hyde Park Gardens to see Marjorie Hamilton dance, and for the first time Brooke met the man who was to be his Commander-in-Chief. Denis Browne, Marsh, Brooke, left together with Lady Eileen, and they all escorted her home to Apsley House in a fourwheeler. A new friendship began.

He was planning to see the Raverats again, assuring them that the influence of London was still as corrupt as ever. 'I think most human beings are all right, if they're let grow,' he told them. 'It's only that the atmosphere is so *bloody* nowadays that only the stupid are fairly untouched, the sensitive wither like a bug-befouled leaf.' No, he would rather *not* meet them in their favourite restaurant in town. 'Soho makes me sick. So does Mongolian music. I *do* think you're degraded.' As in the early months of 1913, his light-hearted sociability had become a façade behind which he smouldered, and when, on introducing Cathleen to the Cornfords at Cambridge, he heard her speak of a possible tour of the United States in what he considered to be a play of only commercial appeal, he was more than ever perturbed and pursued the matter by post. 'You not only trust and believe in *people*—which is mad enough—but you trust and believe in

the world, which is madder. You take, so much, what's offered you
. . . My dear, if you put cut flowers in red ink for water, the blossom
goes red, and men are even more coloured and made by their surroundings than flowers, and women even more than men . . . You
don't know how I ache that you should be fed with the most beautiful
and radiant things in the world—like the children in Plato's Republic.'
She must learn to take a longer view. 'Taking the most lucrative
affair at the moment is the most hopeless way of proceeding,' then
having dealt with the professional aspect—'I think you're probably
not very clever at working a "career" '—he turned to his private
concerns. There he felt bound to admit he was losing his nerve.

I tried to explain a little. But if you could see sometimes in my mind,
you'd understand how desperately frightened and miserable I become at the
thought of you going away. Dear love, I've been through evil places, and
I cling all the more graspingly to the peace and comfort I find more and
more in loving you and being with you. It grows as I see love in you for me
grow. Love in me grows slowly, and differently from the old ways—I
thought the root was gone. But it's there. It's the one thing I've got, to love
you, and feel love growing, and the strength and peace growing, and to
learn to worship you, and to want to protect you, to desire both to possess
every atom of your body and soul, and yet to lose myself in your kindliness,
like a child. It might be that, in the end, it wouldn't do, and we'd find that
I didn't love you enough, or you me. But there's the hope and the great
chance. We're so far towards it. The more I know you, the more I love. And
the more I know and love, the more I find you have to give me, and I to
give you. How can I let this growing glory and hope be broken, and let
myself go adrift again? Dear love, I *daren't* go wandering. You don't know
what a helpless poor fool I am. It's only in love and marriage I can find
peace. The rest is Hell. I want to love and to work. I don't want to be washed
about on these doubtful currents and black waves or drift into some dingy
corner of the tide.

It overwhelmed him afresh to recall how easily the sensitive nature
can be deflected from its straight and proper course. The old troubles
were by no means resolved. He had been utterly dismayed to discover
that Ka was still patiently waiting for him to come to his senses and
recapture the gladness of that summer in 1911, for he was powerless
to do anything whatever about it. Sooner or later, he reflected, everything fell so far short of perfection. If he had not endowed Ka with such
superhuman qualities, perhaps he might never have been so outraged
when she conducted herself like the normal and mortal-sized young
woman that she was. And now, as for Cathleen, who evidently
thought herself better fitted to be a life-sized actress of promise,

earning a livelihood, than a 'goddess', he could not see that she was only being drawn to do what any young woman in her position might consider the sensible thing. He broke off his argument near the start, candidly giving himself away. 'I'd better state, before going further, that as a matter of fact I loathe women acting in public.'

Soon followed the only occasion when a sudden impulse proved stronger than his prudence. The foyer at Drury Lane was crowded. Unexpectedly confronted after this long while by Lytton Strachey, he turned on his heel, refusing the proffered hand; and as several of his acquaintance were standing by, among them Ottoline Morrell, there was consternation, a puzzled silence and an exchange of glances, only cut short by the rescuing bell for the next Act. Brooke touched on this obliquely in a note to Cathleen. 'The number of beastly people at Drury Lane is the only good reason for going there. One can be offensive to them. I'm in a dam' bad temper.' It may have been of this occasion that Lytton Strachey remarked, 'Everyone was there, including Rupert *en beauté* in the stalls'.

On his return from a visit to the Raverats near Royston the newspaper headlines were saying that Austria had declared war on Serbia, but for a few hours more the ordinary run of things continued, as Marsh's diary shows.

An American poet called Conrad Aiken came to see Rupert at Breakfast time. Rupert and I lunched with Victor and Pamela Lytton and the four children. Rupert and I dined with Denis at *The Good Intent*, tried to get into the Victoria Music Hall but there were no seats. Went to see the Spanish dancers at Earl's Court instead, went on to Denis' rooms at Shawfield Street. He hadn't got a latchkey, and Rupert performed gymnastics and climbed in at the window off my shoulder. Clive Carey came in, Denis and he played and sang.

On the following day D. H. Lawrence and Frieda were sitting with Brooke at the Ship restaurant, awaiting their host. At length Marsh ran in, 'I believe Sir Edward Grey has just prevented war with Germany!' he cried. That evening Marsh and Brooke dined at 10 Downing Street, and Brooke sat between the Prime Minister and his daughter Violet. Opposite was Winston Churchill, First Lord of the Admiralty, whom he had not met before. Mr. Churchill offered to help him to a commission, if it should come to that. Next morning Brooke left for a long week-end with the Ranee. She awoke him next day with a newspaper in her hand. Germany had declared war on Russia. He wrote to Raverat.

Everyone in the governing classes seems to think we shall all be at war. Everything's just the wrong way round. *I* want Germany to smash Russia to fragments, and then France to break Germany. Instead of which I'm afraid Germany will badly smash France, and then be wiped out by Russia. France and England are the only countries that ought to have any power. Prussia is a devil. And Russia means the end of Europe and any decency.

I suppose the future is a Slav Empire, world-wide, despotic, and insane.

Stanley Spencer had failed a rendezvous at Marble Arch. 'I spent my time leaning against that large dust-bin,' Brooke wrote to him on the same day, 'and composing a long poem against all artists and all faithless people who defile God's fair world by parodying it with dirty smears of paint on little bits of wood.' It was no longer possible to give more than a passing thought to merely private affairs. 'If fighting starts I shall have to enlist, or go as a Correspondent. I don't know. It will be Hell to be in it, and Hell to be out of it. At present I'm so depressed about the war, that I can't talk, think, or write coherently.' To Lady Eileen he complained that as opposed to the Celt who, when dejected, can brood on 'the moth-hour and the pale oval veils of dawn', an Englishman's melancholy was 'an uninspiring thing, a conglomeration of swear-words and uncharitable thoughts and awkward limbs. That am I.' He was in no mood to write a proper letter, but since his new friend was a most charming young woman, he made the effort.

It is raining. Every now and then one goes out and buys an evening paper to find the news. And the news is always a little worse. Half the day I have been trying to read Maurice Baring on Russia; and the rest of the time I have sat staring at an unfinished long poem on the fact that mountains, and mules, and other people's ideas, really exist only inside one's own mind. A comfortable thought—perhaps. But the poem, like the reading M. B., doesn't progress. I grow irritated with Russia, and more than irritated with myself and my poem. What a state of mind for the 1st of August! If war comes, should one enlist? or turn war correspondent? or what? I can't sit still. I wish I could fly. One feels as depressedly restless as in those dreadful pauses of a day or two after one's sent off a proposal of marriage, and before the reply comes. What *will* happen tomorrow? and whatever it is, won't it be dreadful?

He had gone to Rugby at the end of July, so as to be with the Ranee and Alfred for his twenty-seventh birthday. The round of London gaiety was over, and after his long spell at Gray's Inn he wrote to Marsh, 'Mrs. Elgy, in a flood of affection for me at my departure, put any little gifts she could find into my bag. Frances Cornford's

Poems, and *Les Caves du Vatican*, are the only ones I've yet found. Maurice Baring on Russia I took myself . . . Also, I have your green trunk. Now the thing has really come,' the letter went on, 'I feel as if I *can't* sit still . . . Do you have a Brussels-before-Waterloo feeling? that we'll all—or some—meet with other eyes in 1915? . . . and I'm vaguely frightened. I feel hurt to think that France may suffer. And it hurts, too, to think that Germany may be harmed by Russia. And I'm anxious that England may act rightly. I can't bear it if she does wrong.' Marsh must please use his influence to keep Cathleen in the country. 'Will you have to start a series of Georgian Actresses?'

On August 2, the last Sunday of the old world at peace, the brothers thought they would go for a spree in Mrs. Brooke's motor car, and that evening Brooke described the outing for Eileen Wellesley.

We looked at all the places thirty miles away. We'd decided we wanted to go thirty miles away. Finally I chose Hampden-in-Arden. I remembered once passing through a station of that name. And I've always wanted to see the forest of Arden. Hampden-in-Arden. What a name to dream about! Perhaps one shouldn't have *gone* there. Arden—it's ten miles north of Stratford—is a little tamed nowadays. No holly and horns and shepherds and dukes. We caught one glimpse of a hart weeping large-eyed on the brink of the Stratford-Birmingham canal. Neither Rosalind nor Audrey. And Orlando's in an O.T.C. on Salisbury Plain. Everyone else was Jaques: I a shadowy Touchstone.

But it *is* lovely. It's the sort of country I adore. I'm a Warwickshire man. Don't talk to me of Dartmoor or Snowdon or the Thames or the lakes. I know the *heart* of England. It has a hedgy, warm bountiful dimpled air. Baby fields run up and down the little hills, and all the roads wriggle with pleasure. There's a spirit of rare homeliness about the houses and the countryside, earthy, uneccentric yet elusive, fresh, meadowy, gaily gentle. It is perpetually June in Warwickshire, and always six o'clock of a warm afternoon. Of California the other States in America have this proverb: 'Flowers without scent, birds without song, men without honour, and women without virtue'—and at least three of the four sections of this proverb I know very well to be true. But Warwickshire is the exact opposite of that. Here the flowers smell of heaven; there are no such larks as ours, and no such nightingales; the men pay more than they owe; and the women have very great and wonderful virtue, and that, mind you, by no means through the mere absence of trial. In Warwickshire there are butterflies all the year round and a full moon every night . . . and every man can sing 'John Peel'. Shakespeare and I are Warwickshire yokels. What a county!

This is nonsense; and I will grant to you that Richmond Park is lovelier than all the Midlands, and certainly better inhabited. For Hampden was just too full of the plutocracy of Birmingham, short, crafty, proudly vulgar men, for all the world like heroes of Arnold Bennett's novels. They were extraordinarily dressed, for the most part in very expensive clothes, but without collars. I think they'd *started* in collars, but removed them by the way. They rolled out of their cars, and along the street, none so much as five foot high, all hot, and canny to the point of unintelligibility, emitting the words 'Eh . . .' or 'Ah, lad . . .' at intervals. They were profound, terrifying, and of the essence of Life: but unlovely. But in Richmond Park there's you.

Next morning there were all the genial commonplaces of a birth-day, and—essential emblem of continuity in a crumbling universe—a parcel from Aunt Fanny. Early next day he left for Norfolk. The Cornfords were on holiday in what they called 'a bulgey-windowed house built by a sea-captain' near the shore at Cley-next-the-Sea, Norfolk, and there Brooke joined them on the day of the ultimatum to Germany, having been enjoined to bring with him an armful of news-papers and five yards of mosquito netting. That night at Cley he had a nightmare 'because I felt badly about the war', he told Cathleen next morning. 'Let my love wind round you and comfort you and be a guard over you and a sweetness and a glory for you.' He woke up to learn that England was at war. Neither he nor his host, F. M. Corn-ford, uttered a word all day, but that evening, alone with Frances, he started talking of Ka. 'The best possible thing that could happen for her,' he said, 'is that I should be blown to bits by a shell. Then she would marry someone else and be happy.' It had never occurred to Frances that anyone but 'soldiers' fought battles, so she came out with 'But Rupert, *you* won't have to fight?' He looked at her gravely, and said: 'We shall *all* have to fight.'

Next day he bathed, but felt unaccountably cold, then rallied his spirits, stuck a poppy behind his ear, and said, 'This is what we did in the South Seas!' explaining that if the flower was behind the *left* ear it denoted a heart fancy-free and waiting for romance, if behind the *right* ear the wearer was off the market, having found a sweetheart, nevertheless the custom was for the young men to wear a flower over *both* ears at once; and he fooled around, shaking his hair loose to amuse the infant Helena, and said he hoped she wasn't going to turn Polynesian after she had swallowed one of his souvenir beads. When the talk was of *Mrs. Gill*, the poem of macabre fantasy in de la Mare's *Peacock Pie*, Frances remarked in awe, 'How does he *do* it?' 'He does it too much,' cried Brooke, chipping in, but went on to say that, even so, de la Mare was probably the best of his con-temporaries.

But of course the gaiety was shallow. 'I feel dazed and troubled these days,' he wrote again to Cathleen. 'The general uneasiness and tension of mind seems to take all the strength out of me,' and he appealed to Marsh, 'I feel you're the one link I have with the heart of things in these bloody times . . . I want to know if I can find something to do. I can't work.' But the post was not enough. He turned up in person at Gray's Inn, and next morning sent a report to Cathleen who was on tour.

I've just been to a music-hall. I feed with Eddie every night from 9 to 10. Then he goes back to the Admiralty. Tonight I turned into the Coliseum. It was pretty full. Miss Cecilia Loftus was imitating somebody I saw infinite years ago—Elsie Janis—in her imitation of a prehistoric figure called Frank Tinney. God! how far away it all seemed. Then Alfred Lester. Then a dreadful cinematograph reproduction of a hand drawing patriotic things—Harry Furniss it was—funny pictures of a soldier and a sailor (at the time, I suppose, dying in Belgium); a caricature of the Kaiser, greeted with a few perfunctory faint hisses. Nearly everyone sat silent. Then a scribbled message was thrown; 'War declared with Austria 11.9.' There was a volley of quick low handclapping—more a signal of recognition than anything else. Then we dispersed into Trafalgar Square, and bought midnight war editions, special. All these days I have not been so near tears. There was such tragedy, and such dignity, in the people.

He explained to Raverat that 'one can't "go and fight" in England'. Volunteers were not being admitted to the forces, and joining the Territorials would only lead to six months' training and then at best a dull job with the garrison of a seaport, or, at worst, guarding a footbridge in Glamorgan. 'Unless any country gets smashed, it'll probably be the people that hold out longest who win.'

Mrs. Cornford wrote to say she couldn't believe the war was a reality—'the sea and the pebbles are so exactly the same,' and he replied with the assurance that everyone in town seemed serene and confident; food prices had actually dropped; there was less unemployment; the Expeditionary Force was in Belgium, 'probably fighting by now'. The war had even penetrated to Cley, Frances told him. It consisted of five polite, tired ladies in a Red Cross class, trying to make one bed and arguing about the correct way of turning down the top blanket. He *must* try to put Ka from his mind, and for her sake, not try to see her, for 'one's body and nerves remember longer and more acutely than one's conscious mind which one can manage'.

His first idea, to go over and help the French garner their crops, was now dropped, as also was the idea of reporting for a newspaper.

But it wasn't easy to enlist. He was amazed by Harold Monro's experience, who turned up on a motor-bicycle to volunteer, was rejected because his engine was of the wrong kind, reappeared next day with another engine, and was told there was no room. Meeting J. C. Squire in the street, 'Well, if Armageddon is *on*,' Brooke said, 'I suppose one should be there.' But how does one do it? To Eileen Wellesley he expressed his feelings in more detail.

It's not so easy as you think—for a person who has no military training or knowledge, save the faint, almost prenatal, remembrance of some khaki drilling at Rugby—to get to the 'front'. I'm one of a band who've been offering themselves, with vague persistence, to their country, in various quarters of London for some days, and being continually refused. In time, one of the various doors we tap at will be opened. Meanwhile, I wander.

One grows introspective. I find in myself two natures—not necessarily conflicting, but—different. There's half my heart which is normal and English—what's the word, not quite 'good' or 'Honourable'—'*straight*', I think. But the other half is a wanderer and a solitary, selfish, unbound, and doubtful. Half my heart is of England, the rest is looking for some home I haven't yet found. So, when this war broke, there was part of my nature and desires that said 'Let me alone. What's all this bother? I want to work. I've got ends I desire to reach. If I'd wanted to be a soldier I should have been one. But I've found myself other dreams.' It was that part, I suppose, which, when the tumult and unrest in me became too strong, sent me seeking for a correspondentship. At least, it was some individualist part in me which said 'It's the biggest thing in your seventy years. You'd better see as much of it as you can. Go, for some paper, immediately.' Base thoughts, those: when decent people are offering their lives for their country, not for their curiosity. You're quite right. It's a rotten trade, war-correspondent.

I came to see that. I came to London a few days ago to see what I could do that would be most use. I had a resentment—or the individualist part in me had—against becoming a mere part of a machine. I wanted to use my intelligence. I can't help feeling I've got a brain. I thought there *must* be some organizing work that demanded intelligence. But, on investigation, there isn't. At least, not for ages.

I feel so damnably incapable. I can't fly or drive a car or ride a horse sufficiently well . . .

He gave a reading of his poems at The Poetry Bookshop (to about seventy people this time, as against the six of the former occasion); accompanied Ben Keeling for a few days of drilling with an O.T.C. Unit, the Inns of Court, then he changed his mind, wrote to Andrew Gow who was at Cambridge dealing with applications for commissions, and on August 22 took the train to Rugby, where he finally broke it to his mother that he must go and fight. 'I've filled up some of the less impudent questions you asked me,' he wrote to Gow from

Bilton Road. 'Can't I put on it that I talk German like a bird and French like an Englishman?' He wasn't going to put up with a staff appointment. 'I'm volunteering for active service, if you've any way of noting that.' Item three of his numbered points required no action on Gow's part. It was simply 'To Hell with the Prooshians'.

The allies were falling back past Cambrai and Douai, the New Zealanders took Samoa, and in an article praising its people Brooke touched on an idea that was curiously Lawrencian in character, saying that while the Samoans 'are not so foolish as to "think", their intelligence is incredibly lively and subtle'; even a European living among them, 'soon learns to *be* his body (and so his true mind) instead of using it as a stupid convenience for his personality, a moment's umbrella against the world.' At the same time he sent Marsh a new poem marked 'in the rough', entitled 'Unpacking or Contemplation or The Store, or whatever', and beginning, 'When colour goes home into the eyes'.

He came back from Rugby and attended the first night of *Outcasts* at Wyndham's Theatre. 'Gerald du Maurier took to drugs and was nervous and irritable and bit his fingers, all in the approved stage way. And of course he did it very well . . . I could have written a better play with my foot,' but the climax (not shared by the rest of the audience) occurred when du Maurier on stage held up the magazine he was reading, 'a French obscene journal', according to the situation in the play, and revealed that it was a copy of *New Numbers*. 'Murmurs of subdued applause from me,' Brooke added in his account to Cathleen, and there were sounds of muffled amusement from Marsh, who had evidently been in collusion with the star player. 'No other tidings,' he concluded. 'One of the less creditable periods of my life enmeshed me with the intellectuals. I hover on their fringes yet: dehumanized, disgusting people. They are mostly pacifists and pro-Germans. I quarrel with them twice a day.' Then, following Mrs. Cornford's advice, he tried to make Ka understand that it was largely so as to avoid subjecting her to further strain that he was again declining one of her invitations.

And then, the thought of you—at least, if it's made vivid by your presence —makes me deeply and bitterly ashamed of myself. I don't know *why*—I mean, it's not that my mind condemns me, especially, in any way. I only know that—inevitably or not—through me you have been greatly hurt, and two or three years of your life—which can be so wonderful—have been changed and damaged. And I'm terribly ashamed before you.

And there's just the general case of old wounds: that everybody has a better chance, if they're given the best opportunities to close and stay closed.

It's for these reasons, and only these, that I want not to see you too frequently or too much . . .

I don't seem to myself to do very much with my existence. And I don't know of anything I very much want to do with it. I think I find the world fairly good, on the whole, because that handful of existences I know about and care for—Dudley's and the rest—are, on the whole, happy and good. But of them all yours has to be the one which seems to me most important. Till I think you're complete, I shan't be happy. When you're married and happy, I shall believe that the world *is* good. Till then, I shall be conscious of —general—failure. It's the one thing I hope for, in a confused world.

In the street he met Geoffrey Keynes wearing the uniform of an officer in the R.A.M.C. Envious that Geoffrey should have got into khaki before him, he was now more than ever impatient. Fortunately a door of sorts already stood open for him. A few days ago, Marsh had been able to tell him of a new unit that was being formed, a land force under the command of Major-General Paris and administered by the Admiralty. The Royal Naval Division would consist of men from the Royal Marines, the naval reserve, and others who had already served at sea. Brooke was going to apply for a place in it together with Denis Browne. They would be enrolled as Sub-Lieutenants of the Royal Naval Volunteer Reserve attached to His Majesty's ship *Victory*.

The gift of a sleeping-bag arrived from the Cornfords. On his application form for a commission, dated September 15, he gave King's as his permanent address, and the Provost, M. R. James, signed as sponsor of his good character. He was back with the Ranee at Rugby when he heard that Marsh was going to recommend Denis and himself 'for all I'm worth. I can make play with Winston having promised you an appointment,' and a day or so later news came that no official form or interview would be needed. 'I'm glad I could do it for you, since you wanted it,' Marsh wrote, 'but I feel I'm "giving of my dearest", as the newspapers say. Don't tell a soul that I did it all on my own or I shall be plagued to death.'

He lingered a day or two, 'bidding a modified farewell to my mother,' as he put it in the course of a confessional letter to Eileen Wellesley, who seemed to be taking such a favourable view of his character that, out of friendship, he felt she ought to be disabused. He was really rather horrible, if the truth were known, not especially fickle-hearted, but 'I *am* rather hard-hearted. I usen't to be. I think one of the things that appals me is my extraordinary selfishness: which isn't quite the same as hardness of heart, though it helps. I mean, I just enjoy things as they come, and don't think or care how they affect other people.' So she must be a little more realistic, for he was grieved to admit he had done harm in his day. 'I expect it will be the best thing for everyone if a stray bullet finds me next year . . .'

And another thing is (this sounds like a catalogue of German atrocities) I'm really a wolf and a tiger and a goat. I am—how shall I put it—carried along on the tides of my body, rather helplessly. At intervals I realize this, and feel rather aghast.

Oh, it's all right if you don't *trust* me, my dear. *I* don't. Never trust me an inch.

Oh, I'm rather a horror. A vagabond, drifting from one imbecility to another. You don't know how pointless and undependable and rotten a thing you've got hold of.

Don't laugh. I know it's funny. But it's all true.

He was being measured for his uniform. 'It's terrible,' he wrote to the Marchesa Capponi. 'But it will end all right, and lead to better things. A lot of people die, and others mourn them. But they'll do that anyhow. Death doesn't matter.' It was about September 23 when he lunched with the First Lord and Marsh at the Admiralty, and later that day took Cathleen into his confidence, asking her forbearance.

Winston was very cheerful at lunch, and said one thing which is exciting, but a *dead* secret. You mustn't *breathe* it. That is, that it's his game to hold the Northern ports—Dunkirk to Havre—at all costs. So if there's a raid on any of them, at *any* moment, we shall be flung across to help the French reservists. So we may go to Camp on Saturday, and be under fire in France on Monday! I'm afraid the odds are against it, though.

Your letter was a great comfort to me. I read it twice a day.

Queer things are happening to me, and I'm frightened. Oh, I've loved you a long time, child: but not in the complete way of love. I mean, there was something rooted out of my heart by things that went before. I thought I couldn't love wholly, again. I couldn't worship—I could see intellectually that some women were worshipful, perhaps. But I couldn't find the flame of worship in me. I was unhappy. Oh, God, I *knew* how glorious and noble your heart was. But, I couldn't burn to it. I mean, I loved you with all there was of me. But I was a cripple, incomplete.

From time to time he was at the Crystal Palace training depot, sorting equipment for camp, and earning the nickname of the Handy Man. He wrote explaining to Raverat that he hadn't precisely joined the Army 'but I've joined the Navy—a more English thing to do, I think'. It looked as if it were going to be a pretty serious business,

'and I felt that if we were going to turn into a military nation and all
the young men go in, I should be among them. Also, I had curiosity.'
On the 25th he lunched with Marsh and Robert Bridges, and then had
one more day of civilian life. On Sunday, September 27, Denis
Browne called at Raymond Buildings. He was in uniform. Marsh saw
them off at Charing Cross. They were joining the Anson Battalion,
2nd Naval Brigade, which was encamped on Lord Northbourne's
estate at Betteshanger Park, near Eastry, on the coast of Kent. There
were five Battalions in the Brigade—Drake, Howe, Hood, Nelson,
and Anson—and Brooke was the Sub-Lieutenant in command of the
15th Platoon, D Company, a unit of thirty men. Halted on the Marne,
the Germans were advancing on the Scheldt and bombarding the
outer defences of Antwerp.

II

Most of the men, destined to wear khaki, were still in naval uniform,
stokers from Northumberland, northern Scotland, and Ireland. The
first few whose names Brooke asked replied in what seemed like
unintelligible Celtic. He inspected their kit and their rifles, led them
in a night 'attack', and marched for hours under a full moon. This
sort of thing, he thought, was all very well for Alfred, now an
officer in the Post Office Rifles; his men 'the pick of English postmen',
could walk miles without turning a hair, but the Ansons, forbidden to sing lest they give away their position to the 'enemy',
grumbled. On October 1 they were roused at five and ordered to pack
their kit. Nothing more happened. 'I think of nothing at all, hour
after hour,' he wrote to Eileen Wellesley. 'Occasionally I'm faintly
shaken by a suspicion that I might find incredible beauty in the
washing place, with rows of naked, superb men, bathing in a September sun or in the Camp at night under a full moon, faint lights
burning through the ghostly tents, and a distant bugler blowing
Lights Out—if only I were sensitive. But I'm not. I'm a warrior. So
I think of nothing, and go to bed.' Three more days passed with
boxing, football, drill, and a polite bath at the Rectory. Then there
was news.

At five on Sunday, October 4, the bugle sounded, and the Brigade
Major ran in to say they were off to France. There was cheering
among the tents. They marched to Dover behind a band playing
music-hall tunes. At Dover the people waved, thrust apples into

their hands, ran into the ranks, kissed them and wept. 'I felt very elderly and sombre and full of thoughts of how human life was like a flash between darknesses.' The theme song of his Platoon was 'Hullo, who's your lady friend?' and they roared it on the quay. When they got on board there was no food for the officers, So Brooke and a few others went ashore again and came back loaded with provisions from the Lord Warden Hotel. Two escorting destroyers met them at sea. A letter to Cathleen gives the sequel.

We sailed that night, and lay off Dunkirk next morning, waiting for the tide: spent the afternoon unloading; and then sat in a great empty shed, a quarter of a mile long, waiting for orders. After dark the senior officers rushed round and informed us that we were going to Antwerp, that our train was sure to be attacked, and that if we got through we'd have to sit in trenches till we were wiped out. So we all sat under lights writing last letters: a very tragic and amusing affair. My dear, it *did* bring home to me how very futile and unfinished life was. I felt so angry. I had to imagine, supposing I *was* killed. There was nothing but a vague gesture of goodbye to you and my mother and a friend or two. I seemed so remote and barren and stupid. I seemed to have missed everything. Knowing you shone out as the only thing worth having . . . Men kept coming up and asking things. One said 'Please, Sir, I've a bit o' money on me. It's not much to me: but it'd be a lot to my wife: we've got fourteen children: and supposing anything happened to me. I wouldn't like them bloody Germans to get hold of it.' What should he do? We arranged he should give it for the time to the parson . . . We *weren't* attacked that night in the train. So we got out at Antwerp, and marched through the streets, and everyone cheered and flung themselves on us and gave us apples and chocolate and flags and kisses, and cried *Vivent les Anglais* and 'Heep! Heep! Heep!'

The Belgians were falling back across the Nethe, but it was already too late by about twelve hours for the new reserves to hold the enemy from Lille and give the Belgians time to retire behind Ghent towards the main allied forces. The best part of a day had been wasted unloading equipment at Dunkirk, and the men had stayed on board in the harbour, playing cards for nearly eight hours before the order came to land. Meanwhile the German howitzers were pounding the outskirts of Antwerp to rubble. The Brigade marched to Vieux-Dieu, meeting wagons of dead, and the wounded, supporting one another, and orderlies on horses, and mobile guns, retreating from the bombardment. Then suddenly turning a corner, the Battalion was led through an armorial gateway into the grounds of a deserted château. It was night.

Little pools glimmered through the trees, and deserted fountains: and round corners one saw, faintly, occasional Cupids and Venuses—a scattered company of rather bad statues—gleaming quietly. The sailors dug their latrines in the various rose-gardens and lay down to sleep—but it was bitter cold—under the shrubs. It seemed infinitely peaceful and remote. I was officer on guard till the middle of the night. Then I lay down on the floor of a bedroom for a decent night's sleep. But by 2 the shells had got unpleasantly near. A big one (I'm told) burst above the garden; but too high to do damage. And some message came. So up we got—frozen and sleepy—and toiled off through the night.

In the château were Denis Browne, Arthur (who was called 'Oc') Asquith, Violet's brother, Brooke, the Padre, and the officer commanding the Ansons, whom we shall call, simply, the C.O.—an officer recently transferred from a crack Regiment of the Army, and evidently no more devoted to the Navy than it was to him. He was already unpopular. (Addressing his men at Dunkirk, perhaps it was a little ill-judged to declare that if they weren't wiped out in an attack on their train to Antwerp they would almost certainly catch it when they arrived.) At a baronial table lit by one candle in a bottle that flickered against the tapestries, the Anson officers sat in scowling silence, and ate with their fingers.

At dawn they were ordered to relieve the Belgians in trenches at a point called Fort 7, an antiquated strongpoint built in 1860. Along this line the 2nd Belgian Division and three Brigades of the British R.N.D. were trying desperately to hold the enemy advance. 'It's queer to see the people who *do* break under the strain of danger and responsibility,' Brooke commented in his letter. 'It's always the rotten ones. Highly sensitive people don't, queerly enough . . . I don't know how I should behave if shrapnel was bursting on me and knocking the men round me to pieces. But for risks and nerves and fatigue I was all right. That's cheering.' They repaired collapsing trenches, and waited at the alert. 'Once or twice a lovely glittering aeroplane, very high up, would go over us; and then the shrapnel would be turned on it, and a dozen quiet little curls of white smoke would appear round the creature—the whole thing like a German wood-cut, very quaint and graceful and unreal.' By the evening Wylrick Station was destroyed, and with it most of the Brigade's luggage, including Brooke's clothes and a number of unfinished manuscripts; the château where they spent the night had received a direct hit, and the oil-tanks at Hoboken were flooding the meadows with blazing petrol.

Since the forts on the left were now rubble, the order came to withdraw, and the Ansons (some of them had to be pulled bodily from the trenches) began the twenty-five mile march to Saint-Gilles. Flames from the Hoboken tanks licked across the road, the smoke was blinding; the carcases of horses and cattle were sizzling in the heat. At last they reached a pontoon bridge over the Scheldt, and as D Company began to cross, two German spies were caught in the act of blowing the bridge, and were shot. Once over the other side (it was the night of October 8) Brooke marched wearily into one of the major events of his life. He discovered a Cause that never while he lived grew dim or faltered from perfection. Some days later he was writing to Leonard Bacon in California. He told how on the march the heavens and the earth were lit up by the glare from the lakes and rivers of burning petrol—'hills and spires of flame. That was like Hell, a Dantesque Hell, terrible.' But later, he said, having crossed the pontoon bridge, 'I saw what was a truer Hell.'

Thousands of refugees, their goods on barrows and hand-carts and perambulators and waggons, moving with infinite slowness out into the night, two unending lines of them, the old men mostly weeping, the women with hard drawn faces, the children playing or crying or sleeping. That's what Belgium is now: the country where three civilians have been killed to every one soldier. That damnable policy of 'frightfulness' succeeded for a time. When it was decided to evacuate Antwerp, all of that population of half a million, save a few thousands, fled. I don't think they really had any need to. The Germans have behaved fairly well in the big cities. But the policy of bullying had been carried out well. And half a million people preferred homelessness and the chance of starvation, to the certainty of German rule. It's queer to think one has been a witness of one of the greatest crimes of history. Has ever a nation been treated like that? And how can such a stain be wiped out?

'The eye grows clearer,' he said, 'and the heart. But it's a bloody thing, half the youth of Europe, blown through pain to nothingness, in the incessant mechanical slaughter of these modern battles. I can only marvel at human endurance.' He had volunteered from a sense of duty, anger, even curiosity. Now it was another thing. This was something bigger than the struggle for social reform; an issue even clearer than the Fabian Minority Report which had waved a splendid banner and petered out; a cause loftier and more demanding than man's love of woman, and there was now no shred of doubt left in his mind that what Britain was fighting for was something infinitely greater than herself. Everything he was once so passionately concerned about had dwindled in significance—the 'sick hearts that honour could not move' . . . 'And all the little emptiness of love'. It was a sensation as of 'swimmers into cleanness leaping'; the forlorn tangle of his private existence, his obsessive disgust, the sense of futility and failure, were all resolved in the realization of one purpose, as if for years he had been restlessly tossing in his sleep and had suddenly been shocked awake. By coincidence, venting the wonder of his private relief, he expressed a public sentiment. 'Now, God be thanked Who has matched us with His hour, And caught our youth, and wakened us from sleeping.' And in the sestet of this sonnet (the first of a new order) he summed up in plain terms—which have all the look of a public utterance—a world of personal feeling. 'Oh we, who have known shame, we have found release there . . .'

Still marching to Saint-Gilles through the bedraggled men and women ('the old men mostly weeping, the women with hard drawn faces') the cattle, overloaded prams, wagons—'Often the carts had no horses and they just stayed there in the street waiting for a miracle'— and even London omnibuses which informed the pedestrian that he could be taken to Hammersmith and at a price could witness a performance entitled *Potash and Perlmutter*, many of the Ansons dropped out by the way; Denis Browne developed blisters on his feet, but Brooke managed to keep in the ranks, and coming to a church in a village square, the column halted and he pushed open the door, thinking to find a nook to sleep in, but the place was full of stertorous darkness; not an inch of the floor up to the altar steps was free of human shapes, exhausted, motionless, asleep.

At dawn they reached the troop trains, which carried them to Bruges. There they could eat at last and sleep the night, and next morning they moved on to Ostend. Early in the morning of October 9, once more aboard a transport, there was a thick mist, but they knew where they were. It was Dover Pier.

Dinner was over at the Admiralty when Oc Asquith and Brooke walked into the lobby of the First Lord's office, and Marsh took them straight in to Mr. Churchill. There by turns they pieced together their story of the Expedition. Antwerp had fallen.

III

When Marsh got back to Raymond Buildings that night, Brooke was in the bath, ready with another instalment of the saga, having discovered that he was a casualty of sorts. But the sack of Antwerp had done him no worse injury than the dust in the passages at Rugby. He could hardly see for the smarting attack of conjunctivitis. The next four days were spent with the Ranee. She called in the neighbours, so as to watch them registering amazement over the teacups, such tales there were to be told, and the aged Whitelaw listened and was grieved by man's inhumanity to man. At leisure, Brooke reckoned his losses—Mrs. Cornford's sleeping-bag, the field glasses given him by E. M. Forster, and most of his clothes, all were blown up in Belgium. He had to start fitting himself out afresh.

In London again by the 16th, he saw Laurette Taylor in *Peg o' my Heart* at the Comedy, turned up at a play-reading at the house where Brynhild Olivier (now Mrs. Popham) was living, and surprised several of his old acquaintance with the spectacle of his cropped hair, now rather lustreless, and his manner curiously subdued—not the least of the surprises being that he happened to walk in accompanied by Noel, an adult young woman of twenty-two now advanced in her studies of medicine. He also looked in at the Poetry Bookshop, caught Monro at home, and sat on the edge of the table, haggard in face, his eyes blood-shot, and talking of nothing but the war.

For a few hours he was at Lowestoft with Cathleen. He was on the shore, reading aloud Donne's *The Anniversarie*.

> *Who is so safe as we? where none can do*
> *Treason to us, except one of us two*

and must then have got the idea of quoting that first phrase as a theme on which the rest of his sonnet would be a variation. 'I feel so happy in this new safety and brightness,' he wrote to her soon afterwards, probably while he was still at work on the sonnet which celebrates 'our hid security', and ends:

> *War knows no power. Safe shall be my going,*
> *Secretly armed against all death's endeavour;*
> *Safe though all safety's lost; safe where men fall;*
> *And if these poor limbs die, safest of all.*

The second of the war sonnets was a love poem. The others were going to be pitched in a very different key, but already it was growing clearer to him every day that a country was its people, and the essence of the people one's especial friends, so that he saw Patriotism as a kind of personal loyalty. 'Do you know what a trust you hold for the world?' he wrote to Cathleen a few days after war was declared. 'All those people at the front who are fighting—muddledly enough— for some idea called England—it's some faint shadowing of the things *you* can give that they have in their heart to die for.'

Rejoining his unit at Betteshanger on October 18, he picked up a disturbing report from Denis Browne. 'Awful rumour prevails here that the Old Vicarage is to be destroyed,' he wrote to Mrs. Cornford, and he asked Gwen Raverat to go and make a painting of it, 'quietly and sadly, as befits the end of an epoch.' Then he sent Ka a cool little list of requirements—a tin mug, toilet paper, a bit of sweet-scented soap, etc. She would know where to get things quickly and cheap.

The unit was being moved from camp. On the 25th Brooke was in charge of the baggage-loading party on Sandwich station, and three days later the Ansons were installed in barracks at Chatham. Their relatively few trained men were being posted away: raw recruits from the depot at Crystal Palace took their place. 'It's rather like trying to build a statue out of sand,' Brooke bitterly complained to Marsh, though the root of the trouble was the disaffection among the men because of the C.O. 'All the other officers are rebelling too.' It was an uncomfortable situation, and the friends (Asquith, Brooke, Browne) dared not apply for a transfer lest they should be separated. Suddenly, however, there was a thrilling diversion, for the German Fleet was reported at sea. An enemy warship had been sighted off Yarmouth. Leave was cancelled. The general flurry of a false alarm prompted Brooke to remark 'Elderly men rushed about pulling down swords from messroom walls and fastened them on with safety pins'. Striking a graver note, he dashed off an invasion postcard to the Ranee. 'If it's in Kent, we may get to the front, I hope so.'

Then there was an easing of tension. Everything in the barracks sank back into its former state of simmering unrest. How could the officers apply for a transfer when it meant leaving their men 'to flounder in this morass of incompetence'? Perhaps the best thing in the long run would be if the whole affair should come to 'a ghastly head', and the entire unit apply to be shifted into some other branch of the service. This would be something like mutiny. While Marsh was trying to sort this out at the Admiralty, certain minor problems began to resolve themselves: the Old Vicarage was spared, 'It shall yet be left for that slow Prussian, Time, to reduce it,' Brooke told Dent, saying he intended to buy the freehold with his prize money after the war; and Mrs. Churchill, whom he called on in London, gave him assurance of £40 kit allowance in compensation for the property lost in Belgium.

By the middle of November he heard that the sub-lieutenants of D Company were going to be cross-posted to the Hood Battalion. That was all very well, but the first development was that Denis Browne found himself at Sheerness with the Howe Battalion; Asquith turned up with the Hood; and for another week Brooke remained at Chatham, feeling stranded, but catching up with his mail. His men were still being re-equipped after Antwerp. This meant kit inspections. He wrote to Cathleen, telling how his job was—

to make a list the other day, of all their 'kit'—to compare with what they should have. I soon found that questions about some of the articles on the lists were purely academic. 'How many handkerchiefs have you?' The first two men were prompted to say, none. The third man was called Cassidy, 'How many phwat, sorr?'
'Handkerchiefs?'
'?'
'Handkerchiefs, man, handkerchiefs!'
(*In a hoarse whisper to the Petty Officer*) 'Phwat does he *mane*?'
(*P.O. in a stage whisper*) 'To blow yer nose with, yer bloody fool!'
Cassidy (*rather indignant*) 'None, sorr.'

The serious problem was his altered relationship with certain of his male friends. Not all of them shared his views of the war. He was relieved when Cathleen grew impatient with her routine in the theatre. 'If you were a man,' Brooke wrote, 'there'd be no excuse for you to go on acting. You'd be despicable.' The nation seemed half asleep.

I'm rather disturbed, my dear one, about the way people in general don't realize we're at war. It's—even yet—such a picnic for us—for the nation—and so different for France and Belgium. The millions France is sacrificing to our thousands. I think—I *know*—that *everyone* ought to go in.

It was then that E. J. Dent wrote asking him if he would contribute to a fund for sending one of his former Cambridge friends to a distant country where the climate would ease the trouble in his lungs. Brooke's reply was that if anyone had a spare penny it should go to the Belgian refugees. 'I've seen those widows and children. I can't help feeling, I mean, that there's bigger things than bronchitis abroad. I know a girl who is consumptive. Her doctor said she'd probably die if she didn't spend this winter in a sanatorium. She's doing Belgian refugee organization and clothing in London, and is going to stay at it.' If his advice were asked he'd say, 'There's nothing like disregarding weakness,' and he went on:

In the room where I write are some twenty men. All but one or two have risked their lives a dozen times in the last month. More than half have gone down in torpedoed ships and been saved *sans* their best friends. They're waiting for another ship. I feel very small among them. But that, and the sight of Belgium, and one or two other things make me realize more keenly than most people in England do—to judge from the papers—what we're in for, and what great sacrifices—active or passive—everyone must make. I couldn't bear it if England daren't face or bear what Germany is facing and bearing.

He ended: 'Geoffroi has had a leg blown off. Peguy, the poet is killed . . . I am envious of our good name!' He was conscious of a widening gulf that had opened between himself and non-combatants. 'Yet it's not that,' he tried to make Cathleen understand. 'It's the withdrawal of combatants into a special seclusion and reserve.' It was as if they were under a curse or a blessing or a vow. 'The central purpose of my life, the aim and end of it, now, the thing God wants of me, is to get good at beating Germans. That's sure. But that isn't what it was. What it was I never knew, and God knows I never found it. But it reached out deeply for other things than my present need. There was some beauty and holiness it should have taken hold of.' And yet, as he wrote in the third sonnet, which by now he had begun, the thought of those already killed had brought him a sense of Holiness, lacked so long, and Love, and Pain. More difficult for him and saddening, was the sense of separation from such an especial friend, benefactor, and ornament of King's, as Lowes Dickinson. While on leave after Antwerp, Brooke called on him, found him out, and wrote, 'I hope you don't think me very reactionary and callous for taking up this function of England. There shouldn't be war—but what's to be done but fight Prussia? I've seen the half million refugees in the night . . .' Dickinson would not have sympathized with his notion of the anthropomorphic State, and perhaps it was a good thing that the philosopher was not at home. Brooke had found his own purpose and his peace. Argument was a thing of the past: even the gentlest kind of civilized dispute such as prevailed at Gibbs's Building with Dickinson standing before the fire, never gainsaying, but tactfully inclining toward dissent with 'Well now, that is a very interesting point of view, but . . .'

Brooke never glorified war, as some have supposed, but he celebrated in exultation the discovery of a moral purpose. 'Honour has come back, as a king, to earth.' The third sonnet ('Blow out, you bugles') was begun as news came in of his school-friends, one after another, killed or missing. Fittingly it borrows its tone and manner from the poem by Henley, which it transcends, and which he read aloud in the course of his talk at Rugby, on that last Sunday evening of his school days. In a note-book of early 1912 appears the isolated line, 'And I am come into my heritage'—possibly some love poem for Ka was started and laid aside. Now the larger theme is Love, and the line, fetched out again from memory, becomes 'And we have come into our heritage', the concluding line of a sonnet, a sort of plinth on which he builds the rest; a poem about his new discovery, naming the human qualities of which his generation at School Field are turning out to be the heirs. He calls them Holiness, Honour, and Nobleness; those qualities of spiritual richness he had only just been telling Cathleen that his life had somehow lacked—'There was some beauty and holiness it should have taken hold of.' But the poem is more personal than that. Writing this month to Rosalind Murray (Mrs. Arnold Toynbee) congratulating her on the birth of a son, he tried to give her some idea of his thoughts at Dunkirk, when the C.O. addressed the unit and told them they were 'all going to be killed at Antwerp'. Now he was miserable, he said, because most of his school friends were wounded or missing. 'Perhaps our sons will live the better for it all.' Then at Dunkirk, 'I didn't think much (as I'd expected) what a damned fool I was not to have written more and done various things better and been less selfish. I merely thought, "What *Hell* it is that I shan't have any children—any sons." I thought it over and over, quite furious, for some hours.' And so, at the central place of his new sonnet, the climax of the octave, ending a list of treasures, 'rarer gifts than gold', which the dead bequeath to their survivors, he placed, 'those who would have been, Their sons, they gave, their immortality',—which, Mrs. Cornford, knowing the background, once remarked, 'is what you might call a very *expensive* line.'

These were among his thoughts at Chatham, when on coming back from a visit to de la Mare, a patient in Guy's Hospital, he found the long awaited posting order. The immediate result was exasperating. Following the instructions, he found himself at Portsmouth with the Nelson Battalion. 'I can only wish things may get bad enough for the affair to disintegrate and we'll all get shifted into the army,' he

fulminated at Marsh. For a few days he practised on the range with a
Maxim gun, and 'stood by' for another invasion scare. 'I rather hope
they will try it,' he wrote to the Ranee. 'I'm sure it will fail of its
purpose (to terrify us) and it will wake people up a bit.' In the same
vein he wrote to Raverat, saying that he was dissatisfied with the
English. 'The good ones are all right . . . But there's a ghastly sort of
apathy over half the country. And I really think large numbers of male
people don't want to die. Which is odd. I've been praying for a
German raid . . . A Frenchman is the one person with something to be
proud of!'

He now heard from Oc Asquith that there was a vacancy in A
Platoon of a Company commanded by Bernard Freyberg of the Hood
Battalion, so Brooke wrote off at once, his letter crossing with a telegram from Marsh, 'All is changed again, and you are all to go to
Hood, which is splendid, it will be done a little gradually, but all will
come right in the end.' Brooke's reply was cautious, 'I'm too cynically bitten by the world to count on anything till I *see* it.' The Hoods
were commanded by Colonel Quilter, so the aim now was to be
vouchsafed a place in 'Abraham Quilter's bosom'. He was acting-
Adjutant at Portsmouth, and feeling slightly grand, when a huge con-
signment of woollies arrived from the indefatigable Aunt Fanny 'on
behalf of the Mayor and Corporation of 'Bournemouth', just in time
to double the weight of his baggage, for he was disinclined to
squander them on the Nelsons. He must arrive at the Hood laden
with winter comforts! At that point one of his best friends at Rugby
was reported missing. A hundred years hence, he reflected, they'll
say, ' "What an age that must have been!"—What'll *we* care? Fools!'
He was deeply grieved.

On the last day of November he reported to Quilter in the encampment about four miles from Blandford, Dorset. This was satisfactory,
except that Denis Browne was now in Portland, still with the Howe,
and growing rather fond of his Battalion. 'The Howe is not a
Battalion,' Brooke wrote to him. 'It is a query.' On the way through
Bournemouth he caught sight of a play-bill advertising *Butterfly on a
Wheel* with Cathleen Nesbitt as the principal attraction. 'I hope you'll
be giving up this beastly stage business soon,' he wrote, then turned
to examine his new circumstances. He was now sub-lieutenant in
charge of No. 3 Platoon, A Company, Hood Battalion. Arnold
Quilter was a fine soldier and well liked, and there was Freyberg, the
Company commander, destined for high distinction; a Cambridge

man, formerly the biologist on Scott's South Pole Expedition; also 'a very charming and beautiful American youth, infinitely industrious', Johnny Dodge. It seemed as if the men of sensibility were the first to awaken. For Russell Loines in New York he tried to convey something of the spirit of the times.

There are a few people who've been so anti-war before, or so suspicious of diplomacy, that they feel rather out of the national feeling. But it's astonishing to see how the 'intellectuals' have taken on new jobs. Masefield drills hard in Hampstead and told me with some pride, a month ago, that he was a Corporal and *thought* he was going to be promoted to Sergeant soon. Cornford is no longer the best Greek Scholar in Cambridge. He recalled that he was a very good shot in his youth and is a Sergeant-Instructor of Musketry. I'm here. My brother is a 2nd Lieutenant in the Post Office Rifles. He was one of three great friends at King's. The second is Intelligence Officer on H.M.S. *Vengeance*, Channel Patrol. The third is buried near Cambrai. Gilbert Murray and Walter Raleigh rise at six every day to line hedgerows in the dark and 'advance in rushes' across the Oxford meadows. Among the other officers in this Division are two young Asquiths, an Australian professional pianist who twice won the Diamond Sculls, a New Zealander who was fighting in Mexico and walked three hundred miles to the coast to get a boat when he heard of the war, a friend of mine Denis Browne—Cambridge—who is one of the best young English musicians and an extremely brilliant critic; a youth lately through Eton and Balliol who is the most brilliant man they've had in Oxford for ten years; a young and very charming American John Bigelow Dodge who turned up to fight 'for the right'—I could extend the list. It's all a terrible thing. And yet, in its details, it's great fun. And—apart from the tragedy—I've never felt happier or better in my life than in those days in Belgium. And now I've the feeling of anger at a seen wrong—Belgium—to make me happier and more resolved in my work. I know that whatever happens I'll be doing some good, fighting to prevent *that*.

The officers at Blandford lived in wooden huts, each holding accommodation for eight men, with just enough space for each officer to exercise his taste for interior decoration. Here at last Ka the resourceful came into her own, for naturally Brooke turned to her. He apologized for the intrusion, but 'one must look nice to soothe one's nerves after marching'. What was the cheapest stuff for curtains? The following were the window measurements. How does one distemper a wall? He was having a table made, but could she *make* someone send him a deck-chair? Margery or Noel might help, 'That's what all you civilians are for, isn't it?' He was in bed and feverish, having been inoculated for typhoid. It must be horrible to be sick with *deliberate* typhoid, Marsh commiserated, having received a note.

'I hear Winston's expected,' Brooke wrote. '*Insist* on coming with him!' Couldn't Abercrombie be made assistant clerk to the Admiralty so that he could come too and discuss the next issue of *New Numbers*? 'I hope it'll be one of our good muddy days, to let Winston see what life's like.' And by the way, had he forgotten that Browne was still stranded in Portland?

The First Lord's visit was still being anticipated when Brooke wrote to thank Ka for a parcel of wall maps and little flags to indicate the line of enemy advance. 'My God, this mud! We hope to get Winston down *into* it. Then we may obtain alleviation.' Then followed exactly the kind of inquiry that Ka, alone of all Brooke's acquaintance, could be relied on to answer. 'I've got to amuse two hundred and fifty stokers at Christmas. I think of buying them all Turkeys. Can you tell me how much a Turkey costs, and how many men (stokers) it feeds (*with* sausages)?'

His room was just under fifteen feet long and eight feet wide. There was a stove in one corner and in the opposite corner a bed. He favoured scarlet for the curtains. The Ranee supplied a chest of drawers. Furnished at last, he settled into the new routine. A ship's bell sounded the watches; shopping in Blandford was 'going ashore'. Denis Browne turned up, and now the four other officers in his Company were Oc Asquith, Browne, Dodge the American, and Patrick Shaw-Stewart, the brilliant scholar of Eton and Balliol, who had given up a post in Baring's Bank, and was often in and out of Raymond Buildings in the old days. Brooke had last caught sight of him as embarkation officer on the jetty at Dunkirk.

By mid-December Asquith had influenza; many of the men were affected by the fumes from the coke stoves, and Brooke himself was in poor shape. The loss of more than one friend of the Rugby days was weighing on his mind, and he began a fourth sonnet, *The Dead*, with the line, 'These hearts were woven of human joys and cares,' perhaps the best poem of this growing series. A slight ambiguity in the sestet contributes a sort of 'magic' that Brooke never achieved elsewhere. The dead at the opening are unnumbered, they suggest 'waters blown by changing winds'. At length 'Frost, with a gesture, stays the waves that dance', then 'He' quietly intrudes, who by the grammar must be the Frost, and by analogy Death, but by the feeling of the whole is some individual casualty singled out from the multitude to stand for those others who had 'gone proudly friended'—

ONE OF A NUMBER

He leaves a white
Unbroken glory, a gathered radiance,
A width, a shining peace, under the night.

Then a disturbing dream left him more than ever dejected. He confided in Dudley Ward.

Last night I rolled about in this so-called bed. I've been bad lately with inoculation, a cough and things. And I dreamt I landed at Papeete, and went up between the houses, and the air was heavy with sunshine. I went into the house of a half-caste woman I know and she gave me tea, and talked. And she told me about everyone. And at last I said 'And how and where's Taata-mata?' And she said 'Oh—didn't you know?' And I said 'No.' She said 'She's dead.' I asked (knowing the answer) 'When did she die?' 'Months ago, just after you left.' She kept evading my eye. After a long silence I asked (feeling very sick) 'Did she kill herself?' The half-caste nodded. I went out of the house and out to the lagoon, feeling that a great friendliness—all the place—had gone against me. Then I woke with a dry throat, and found a frosty full moon blazing in at the window, and the bugle hammering away at the 6.30 *Reveille*. Perhaps it was the full moon made me dream, because of the last full moon at Mataia (about which there is an unfinished poem: now in German possession). Perhaps it was my evil heart. I think the dream was true. 'There is no health in me' as we used to say in some Confession in Chapel. And now I'm not only sicker with myself than ever: but also I've got another bad attack of *Heimweh* for the South Seas.

It brought up again the old, insoluble problem. If there had been no war he would have been content to sink into a celibate middle-age, and become 'a less distinguished Eddie', but the thought of his surviving the hostilities makes him think again.

I agonize every night. At times I want to wire to almost anybody 'Will you be my widow?' And later, I sigh that I'll be free and the world before me, after the war.

It's partly dependent on my premonition. If I think I'll survive, I plump for freedom. When I feel I'll be killed (which is my general feeling and deepest), I have a revulsion towards marriage.

A perplexing world.

Putting the same case to Raverat, 'There's the question,' he wrote, 'to ponder in my sleeping-bag, between the thoughts on the attack and calculations about the boots of the platoon. Insoluble, and the weeks slip on. It'll end in my muddling that, as I've muddled everything else. Wow!' However, he admitted that he was really rather happy. 'I've a restful feeling that all's going well, and I'm not harming anyone, and probably even doing good.' So one day passed

476

drizzling into the next, and he awoke to ' "Six-thirty, and you're Orderly Officer today, Sir," and the corpse-like light that precedes those queer green chalky dawns.'

The First Lord's visit was postponed. Violet Asquith called on her brother, found him in poor condition and Brooke in hardly better case, so she took them both to Lady Wimborne's house at Canford. There Asquith again developed influenza, but Brooke soon recovered enough to make Oc's sister the first to see his four sonnets in rough draft before getting back to camp without having to apply for sick leave. Then the Christmas preparations began: the Ranee must please send three bottles of his 1887 vintage port and—an item she gibbed at—mince pies for a hundred and fifty men. Uncle Alan at King's sent a pound, which provided Halma, Draughts, and playing cards. Many of the stokers, having originally joined for naval service, and finding themselves in what they regarded as more or less the army, lived in a perpetual state of grouse, and there were several who could not resist the opportunity of getting drunk whenever they 'went ashore' into Blandford. Such sober pastimes as throwing hoops on to pegs, for which Uncle Alan also supplied the wherewithal, were a most useful resource for providing a diversion. The scheme was that the Ranee should supply the provisions for tea, while Ka, now living in a hut on Salisbury Plain, saw to the midday meal; but there was a hitch with the commissariat at Bilton Road, and on Christmas Eve Ka was suddenly galvanized into activity. While shopping with Denis Browne in Bournemouth, and paying his last call on Aunt Fanny at Grantchester Dene, Brooke launched a telegram.

Send mince-pies for sixty men and a few cakes to me Blandford station immediately get someone to help you.

'The stokers *woke* drunk on Christmas morning,' he was writing to Cathleen after supper. 'One of them has been drunk since seven. He neither eats nor drinks, but dances a complicated step up and down his hut, half-dressed, singing "How happy I am! How happy I am!" A short fat inelegant man, in stockinged feet. What wonders we are!' Brooke himself, infected by an atmosphere conducive to feeble jokes, went on to make rather a good one about the new novel by Gilbert Cannan which Cathleen had sent him. 'Gilbert on Love seems rather crabbed. I'll look into it more: seeking the truth e'en at the Cannan's mouth, like the good soldier I am.' On a higher plane he told of a letter from Masefield 'saying he was proud to know me, because I'd done a fine thing. It gave me a queer thrill. But it seems an odd way of looking at it.' The important information in the letter was concealed in the passage: 'There's no news. Occasional scares. On Wednesday I (don't tell a soul) started a sonnet. If it gets finished, you shall see it. What a fall!' That Wednesday was the 23rd. He was probably at Canford. In a note-book blank except for 'German shells carry further back than forward' and 'Thompson, Officers' Mess, doesn't make his bed up', he began this fifth sonnet with the words 'If I should die, think only this of me'. He must have worked on it after the revels on Christmas Day, for late that night, apologizing for a hasty scribble, he wrote to Eileen Wellesley: 'I've spent the day shepherding drunken stokers. And when they had all drunk themselves to sleep, and I had an hour free, I was traitorous and wrote a sonnet. Will you forgive me? And now I'm reduced to writing in bed.' He was due to have leave of absence from the 30th to January 5. On the evening of Boxing Day he wrote to Violet Asquith who was inviting him to stay at Walmer Castle. 'Can you really find room for me among all those Field Marshals? And may I wear my oldest khaki and finish a sonnet?' and in another note of the same day 'I must retire to my cabin to write the remainder of my promised sonnets. One more is turning out *fairly* good. It's rather like developing photographs.' Just audible in the distance, Denis Browne was playing *Petrouchka* on the mess-room piano.

IV

While seeing in the New Year at Rugby he planned an evening out at the Theatre. Marsh will please consider candidates for the party under three heads; people one *likes* to be with, amusing people '(very important after Camp). If you knew how really desirable a good joke becomes to one after the mud—like a good liqueur or a divine sweet. If for instance Maurice Baring were back from the front . . .' and, thirdly, 'WOMEN . . . Is there still any place one can drink alcohol out of tea-cups?' At the same time he answered Eileen Wellesley's inquiry as to his views on Immortality.

You asked about Life after Death; so, like a good sailor, I referred the question to Divisional Headquarters. They said there was no *definite* information: but that the Admiralty Regulations (para. 412a. (2)) lay down that it is only for the Church of England. So I'm all right. Are you? Appar-

ently one can choose between huts and billeting. I think I shall try to be
billeted. Of course, it's a risk.

To his Uncle Alan he was distinctly sanguine about the duration of
hostilities:

A Happy New Year to you all. I'm feeling very confident about the war.
Not so confident as the Staff at the Front, who predict a sudden cracking on
the part of the Germans, peace in April. But I think we should do it by
August.

On January 2 he arrived at Walmer Castle to stay two nights, and
was back in London on the 4th in time to join Denis Browne for
luncheon at the Admiralty with the Churchills and Mr. Asquith. In
the evening the theatre party was Marsh, Browne, Oc and Violet
Asquith. Feeling affluent he gave them all dinner at the Carlton Grill-
room, for he had received the first instalment of his compensation
money from the Admiralty. Then they all went to the Revue at the
Ambassador's. Next morning at Gray's Inn, Brooke heard that
Flecker had died in Switzerland. He had to cut short a meeting with
Cathleen so as to write his friend's obituary for *The Times*. From
Blandford he wrote to Marsh.

I jotted notes, and the *Times* interwove their gems. 'Educated at Balliol,
(then me) his muse was stertorous with the lush slumbers of the east. His
father is the Rev. W. Flecker. Apollo yielded to Marsyas, and fled crying
strangely . . .' What a bloody jest: and a bloody world.

He recalled the last time he saw Flecker, sitting at that same table in
Raymond Buildings where the obituary had just been composed, and
copying out the serenade from *Hassan* in Marsh's album of poems in
manuscript.

The article appeared next day. 'His conversation was variegated,
amusing, and enriched with booty from the byways of knowledge . . .
He sought beauty everywhere, but preferred, for most of his life, to
find her decoratively clad.' His scholarship was 'qualified by a
picaresque romanticism'. The melancholy task accomplished, he sent
a note to Lady Eileen. 'He was my friend. Who'll do the *Times* for
me, I wonder? Damn them.' He returned to Blandford and found a
letter waiting for him. It was dated 'Le 2 Mai 1914'.

'. . . I just wrote you some lines to let you know about Tahiti today
we have plainty Argentin Espagniole . . . that time you left me I been
sorry for long time' . . . It ended 'excuse me to wrrite you shot letter
Hope you good health and good time.' A month ago, almost to the

day, Brooke had told Dudley of his bad dream. He now wrote to him again.

We started out at 8.30 this morning; and got home at three, after hard 'fighting' and marching. And waiting for me in the ante-room was a letter forwarded by the Dead Letter Office from Ottawa, 'recovered' by divers from the wreck of the *Empress of Ireland*. Rather frayed at the edges, and the ink much washed out. But it was a letter from Taatamata, which she gave to a man to post, who was going up to 'Frisco in a boat. And he posted it in Vancouver. And it went by the E. of I. down the St. Lawrence, beyond the Sagonsac, where I bathed; and sank with Laurence Irving: and lay at the bottom from June to December. And this evening I puzzled out the French and English misspellings, and, being very tired and slightly drunk, gulped a good deal.

I think Life's FAR more romantic than any books.

Harsh realities of the hour reasserted themselves in the form of rifles with telescopic sights. They cost eight guineas each. Would the Ranee go halves with him in the purchase of such a weapon for his Platoon? All the officers were buying them. As for his recent luncheon at the Admiralty, 'I didn't get *much* out of Winston,' he said, 'But I gathered we *might* be going out within six weeks or so.' History knows what the First Lord could not divulge. The Grand Duke Nicholas of Russia was hard pressed. If the British were to force the straits of the Dardanelles, munitions could be got through to the Czar, Russian wheat be released to the Allies, and the Turks attacked from the peninsula of Gallipoli. The Royal Naval Division was already earmarked. On January 15 General Paris addressed the officers at Blandford. All he could tell them definitely was that a campaign was in preparation, but it would mean another six weeks' training. 'God knows how I shall live through the interval, till we can blessedly get out,' Brooke wrote to Ka, but he had recovered something of his first enthusiasm, and was hoping to infect Drinkwater. 'I'd not be able to exist for torment if I weren't doing it . . . Better than coughing out a civilian soul amid bed-clothes and disinfectant and gulping nieces in 1950 . . . I had hopes that England'ld get on her legs again, achieve youth and merriment, and slough the things I loathe—capitalism and feminism and hermaphroditism and the rest. But on maturer consideration, pursued over muddy Dorset, I think there'll not be much change.' But that little, he thought, would be for the better. 'Certain sleepers have awoken in the heart.'

Come and die. It'll be great fun. And there's great health in the preparation. The theatre's no place now. If you stay there you'll not be able to start afresh with us all when we come back. Peguy and Duhamel; and I don't know what others. I want to mix a few sacred and Apollonian English ashes with theirs, lest England be shamed.

Lost to sight among days of rain and war-time routine, he reappears for a moment, clattering over Stourpaine House, an empty shell that Raverat had seen advertised for sale. Asquith and Denis Browne are trampling upstairs while Brooke goes down to find a foot of water in the cellar. 'Slightly deliquescent,' is his verdict. Resisting the temptation of a hut-dweller to regard all brick structures as paradise, and although it is indeed 'ugly enough to please you'—he feels Raverat should see it for himself. 'There are not enough flies for you to catch.' It was evidently *not* a bargain. His next concern was financial. He was trying to induce the Admiralty to make a revision in the rate of pay for the stokers. A man of the lowest rank who became 'rated up' one step to the rank of 'leading hand' received no corresponding adjustment in his earnings. The point was not that he deserved more, but that to be effective he needed the respect of those beneath him, and this he could not command from men who knew his pay was no better than theirs. Shaw-Stewart called on Marsh at the Admiralty, and put forward the details of Brooke's scheme. In the meantime, on leave again in Lady Wimborne's house at Canford, Brooke was correcting the proofs of *New Numbers*. Gibson acknowledged the manuscripts of the sonnets on January 13. 'This is fine! It's good to have your poems at last—and they're well worth waiting for.' Brooke made his own comment, sending a spare copy of the proofs to Cathleen. 'My Muse panting all autumn under halberd and cuirass could but falter these syllables through her vizor. God they're in the rough, these five camp children. 4 and 5[1] are good though, and there are phrases in the rest.' He was sitting, he said, by a log fire in a house built by Vanbrugh, with a Scuola di Bellini on the wall above him, smoking, reading, touching up the poems, mindful of bygone days and wars.

Where our huts are was an Iberian fort against the Celts—and Celtish against Romans—and Romans against Saxons . . . Just over the hills is that tower where a young Astronomer watched the stars, and a Lady watched the Astronomer.[2] By Tarrant Hinton, two miles North, George Bubb Dodington lived and reigned and had his salon. In Tarrant Crawford, two miles South, a Queen[3] lies buried. Last week we attacked some of the New Army in

[1] *The Dead* and *The Soldier*.
[2] *Two on a Tower*, Thomas Hardy.
[3] Queen Joan of Scotland, daughter of King John of England.

Badbury Rings—an ancient fort where Arthur defeated the Saxons in—what year? Where I lay on my belly cursing the stokers for their slowness, Guinevere sat, and wondered if she'd see Arthur or Lancelot return from the fight, or both, or neither, and pictured how they'd look; and then fell a-wondering which, if it came to the point, she'd prefer to see.

He seems to have kept the sonnets by him until after his new year leave. At Walmer Castle he copied out *The Dead* for Violet Asquith. Telling her now of the others, he said there were 'none as good—one nearly as good—as the one I gave you', and few readers would cavil with his opinion that *The Dead* was not only a better poem than *The Soldier* but the best of the five. The latter is more well known, however, and more of his private history lies behind it.

The Old Vicarage, Grantchester is a serio-comic poem of local patriotism. Soon after it was written in 1912, James Strachey, it will be recalled, went out to Cologne, having been asked to bring with him the new book by Belloc. Not only did it turn out to be exactly suited to Brooke's mood, but ever afterwards it held a special place in his affections, so that when he gave a copy to Ellen Van Volkenburg in Chicago she discovered he almost knew it by heart. *The Four Men*, a fantasy on the same theme as 'The Sentimental Exile' (*The Old Vicarage*), describes an imaginary event in October 1902, when the author decides to find his way back to his native place in the Sussex valley of the Arun. Three others go along with him, one of them a local deity disguised as an old man of Sussex called Grizzlebeard. Aware that the open countryside which he has known so long is doomed to change and finally vanish with the years, Belloc sets out to make his four-day pilgrimage a chronicle of the cherished sights and sounds that soon must pass away. 'He would, if he could, preserve his land in the flesh, and keep it there as it is, for ever.' But since he knows he cannot do that, 'At least,' he says, 'I will keep her image, and that shall remain.' Arrived at Lavington, the long walk near an end, the sound of bells reminds the pilgrims that the day is November 2, 'the Day of the Dead'; the narrator's companions dissolve in air; the Arun valley lies spread out before him, and trying to preserve his feeling in verse, a single line occurs to him—'One with our random fields we grow'. He reflects 'The way in which our land and we mix up together, and are part of the same thing, sustained me'; if a man's being is rooted in one steadfast piece of earth which has nourished him 'and if he can on his side lend it glory and do it service, it will be a friend to him for ever, and he has out-flanked Death in a way'.

Having become a part of what he loves, he will share its continuance.
' "No, certainly," I answered to myself aloud, "he does not die." '
There follow four stanzas. This is the first:

> *He does not die that can bequeath*
> *Some influence to the land he knows,*
> *Or dares, persistent, interwreath*
> *Love permanent with the wild hedgerows;*
>   *He does not die, but still remains*
>   *Substantiate with his darling plains.*

But the sonnet about 'some corner of a foreign field That is for ever
England' had more complex roots. Following the catalogue of simple
things held in honoured remembrance (*The Great Lover*) came *The
Treasure* (which he considered calling *Unpacking* or *The Store*), the
first poem written after August 1914, and eventually placed as a sort
of preface to these five war sonnets, being itself a sonnet upside
down, beginning with a sestet, and in shortened lines. Its theme is
much the same as both *The Great Lover* and the fifth sonnet, where we
read of 'the thoughts by England given; Her sights and sounds . . .'
and of much else that is stored 'behind the gateways of the brain', as
he had explained in *The Treasure*. It is as if *The Great Lover* and its
overflow had flowed on yet again and come to rest in the sestet of
this last sonnet where the poet 'unpacks', in a special sense, 'Gives
somewhere back the thoughts by England given'.

About the same time as *The Treasure* he wrote an article for the
New Statesman called *An Unusual Young Man*. It was an unusual performance. In the guise of 'my friend', whose reflections were being
set down, this was the nearest Brooke ever got to writing a passage
of autobiography. He must have started it early in August, while still
with the Cornfords at Cley. It offers an impression of his feelings on
hearing of the outbreak of war. Getting the news while at Brooke's
favourite spot in Cornwall, the 'friend' recalls those places and people
he had known round Munich and Berlin, including 'the quiet length
of evening over the Starnberger See'. He is aware now of that same
duality in his mind that he had experienced at the time of 'his first
deep estrangement from one he loved', the upper part dashing aimlessly to and fro from one half-relevant thought to another, 'the
lower, unconscious half labouring with some profound and unknow-
able change'. The memories range over his life among the two
peoples who are now at strife. 'But as he thought "England and

Germany" the word England seemed to flash like a line of foam.'

It is not until the end that he gives a clue to the reason why the young man of the title is particularly unusual. He evades none of the horror, picturing himself engaged in an effort to repulse an enemy raid on the coast, recognizing old friends, and 'slashing at them in a stagey, dimly imagined battle', and then 'To his disgust the most commonplace sentiments found utterance in him'. Finally comes the admission 'At the same time he was extraordinarily happy'. Brooke had to unburden his feelings somehow, but such was his happiness at a time of general disaster, a sensation so peculiar to himself, that he could only offer them to the public as the thoughts of an admittedly unusual young friend.

In Belgium, a month or two afterwards, this private happiness in the resolution of his problems was given a new dimension. After so many disenchantments, it was absorbed in an exaltation of spirit, the discovery of a cause too great to be merely personal, and one that could never let him down, even if it ended in defeat. If there was no other way out of the 'muddle', as he called it, here was the chance not only of going blameless but with honour. His first happiness was endorsed, and now it was enlarged into a sense of vocation, because, as Grizzlebeard said, 'A man is more himself if he is one of a number; so let us take that road together, and, as we go, gather what company we can find.'

Accustomed to making play with the Platonic Ideas, and already prone to the sentiment of local patriotism, Brooke substituted the word that 'flashed like a line of foam' for Sussex, saw England as an idea whose reality was rather in the mind than on the map, carrying Belloc's idea to a point where it became something new and all his own. Instead of the patriot being 'substantiate with his darling plains', Brooke made them substantiate with *him*, a part of his mind which, if needs must, is buried with him in the corner of some foreign field. 'He does not die, but still remains,' said Belloc. 'If I should die,' says Brooke, it is England which remains, even on foreign soil. The original idea is transformed. Brooke's title was *The Recruit*, as an early manuscript shows. Possibly the editors of *New Numbers* asked for the alteration. The 'soldier' was meant by Brooke to be still a civilian, someone who had discovered a way of bequeathing his possessions; his country to the earth (which in a way would *become* his country) and the rest, the sights and sounds, would somehow be returned whence they came, for others to enjoy; he would, in fact, 'unpack' the good things on the inventory of the great lover, or the store of memories belonging to the unusual young man, or the sights and sounds of the recruit, however you choose to think of them or him. The poetical manner is candid like the author's face. Not only has the Anglo-American tradition that was to follow in English verse, made the simple rhetoric outmoded, but the attitude of mind itself, the unquestioning acceptance of a state of affairs, has become suspect. To many it must seem as naïve as saying the Apostles' Creed and meaning what one says. Brooke wrote straight from the shoulder, as it were, without what the fashionable modern would regard as the saving grace of a qualifying remark. And yet therein lies the strength. For him, as for any other kind of martyr, there were no two ways about it. He had not only arrived at a faith but at mastery of the traditional style.

> . . . *And think, this heart, all evil shed away,*
> *A pulse in the eternal mind, no less*
> *Gives somewhere back the thoughts by England given;*
> *Her sights and sounds; dreams happy as her day;*
> *And laughter, learnt of friends; and gentleness,*
> *In hearts at peace, under an English heaven.*

v

By the beginning of February he was on sick-leave with a bad cold. For several weeks past he had barely spoken above a whisper. 'I can only communicate with the outside world by Morse or Semaphore. Which do you prefer?' a friend was asked. After a day in bed at Gray's Inn, he got up to dine with Sir John and Hazel Lavery and watch the painter begin his portrait of Lady Diana Manners posing in a red gown and a diadem of poinsettias. The next night he was at Admiralty House again for dinner, and in the morning was so ill that Marsh's housekeeper declared herself unable to give him proper attention, so he was moved into the care of the Asquiths at 10 Downing Street. There he remained nine days, although he was up after a week and downstairs when Lowes Dickinson came to dine. But that was not the main event of his convalescence. At the invitation of Violet Asquith, Henry James came over and sat and talked at his bedside. It was probably the closer friendship reached on this occasion that moved James to write the Preface to Brooke's reprinted articles for the *Westminster Gazette*, the last work of his life. The so-called December issue of *New Numbers* was not yet out. Henry James had not seen the sonnets. On a page of Downing Street writing-paper Brooke had begun the ambitious 'threnody' that might grow into a sequel to the fifth sonnet. So far there was only a small fragment.

> *All things are written in the mind.*
> *There the sure hills have station, and the wind*
> *Blows . . . in that placeless air.*

From Whitehall he went for two days to Walmer Castle, then, back in town on February 14 and dining again at the Admiralty, enjoyed another memorable *tête-à-tête*. Marsh and Brooke were alone with Mr. Churchill—at dinner Brooke asked his fellow guest to be his literary executor—then after a while Brooke was left on his own with the First Lord who happened to be at leisure after preparing a speech· and in expansive mood. All that we know of the talk—beyond our assuming that it must have been now that Mr. Churchill heard of Brooke's presentiment of death—was given in a note to the Ranee.

Eddie had to go off after dinner to work, so I spent an amusing evening with Winston, who was too tired for work, after preparing his speech (a good speech). He was rather sad about Russia, who he thinks is going to get her 'paws burned', and disposed to think the war *might* last two years, if Russia got at all badly smashed. But he was very confident about the Navy and our side of Europe.

At heart Brooke was depressed, chiefly because the number of Rugby and Cambridge casualties was daily increasing. 'It forestalls Time too much,' he wrote to Gosse, 'in stripping the world away from one'; and then a small oversight grew out of all proportion in his conscience, and he experienced a sharp recurrence of the old self-reproach. During his convalescence at Downing Street he had gone out one evening to meet Ka, but only afterwards did he learn that it was her birthday. 'I feel so angry and ashamed,' he wrote to her. 'I've grown older and evil and selfish, but the only thing I do want in the world is that I should do you as little harm or hurt as possible, to give ʃou what little good I may . . . You live finely.' The prolonged hiatus in his active campaigning was renewing his dissatisfaction with his unmarried state. 'How divine,' he wrote to Raverat, 'to have even a few hours of what the rest of life is a grey pre-existence to— marriage: with, oh! *anybody*.'

On February 17 the First Lord with Marsh in attendance inspected the Royal Naval Division at Blandford. It poured with rain. He arrived after the men had been dismissed and asked for the parade to be recalled, 'but that was after we'd stood out, a battalion of Lears, in the pitiless storm for half an hour'. They marched through slush, but their spirits were soaring. 'At one point I emerged from the mud with my platoon,' Brooke wrote to Violet Asquith, 'under the wheels of a car, in the midst of a waste. And in the car were what I thought were two children, jumping about, clapping their hands, whistling and pointing. It was Eddie and Clemmie [Mrs. Churchill].' Marsh lunched with him and Freyberg in the Hood Mess. 'He told us all the jokes from *The Times*, and all the atrocity stories: things we never hear. The wardroom was fascinated by him, and said in chorus, when he left, "What odd eyebrows!"' Shaw-Stewart had lost seven pounds at poker. Oc was well, Quilter roaring-well—'There's a fine sun and a clean wind.' He was exulting, a stream of many tributaries all at last, as he had said, 'flowing to one end.'

On February 20 Quilter again addressed his officers at Blandford. The effect on the whole unit was electrifying. 'It's too wonderful,' Brooke wrote to Dudley. 'And the best expedition of the war. Figure me celebrating the first Holy Mass in St. Sophia since 1453.' He asked for a medicine chest, including morphia. The Ranee was told that he was going to be part of a landing force to help break through the Hellespont and the Bosphorus, take Constantinople, and open up the Black Sea. The fighting would last six weeks at most; they would be back in May. They were only taking provisions for a fortnight after landing, so nothing prolonged was anticipated. 'At any rate, it will be much more glorious and less dangerous than France.' He made no mention of the rumour that had come his way, that the Hood was being thought of as a spearhead of the landing and 75 per cent casualties must be expected.

With his platoon sergeant; Saunders by name, he carried out an intensive kit inspection. There were four sections in his Platoon, each of eleven men. Robson, Martindale, Warren, and Heslop, are noted as having either lost this or been found short of that, and from an old note-book containing scraps of Greek he talks to the men on maintenance of the rifle, the Maxim gun, and characteristics of fighting in support of cavalry. When the German cavalry attacks, it at once falls back to expose the infantry, etc. Any questions? Exulting, he writes to Violet Asquith.

Oh Violet it's too wonderful for belief. I had not imagined Fate could be so benign. I almost suspect her. Perhaps we shall be held in reserve, out of sight, on a choppy sea for two months . . . yet even that—But I'm filled with confident and glorious hopes. I've been looking at the maps. Do you think *perhaps* the fort on the Asiatic corner will want *quelling*, and we'll land and come at it from behind and they'll make a sortie and meet us on the plains of Troy? It seems to me strategically so possible. Shall we have a Hospital Base (and won't you manage it?) at Lesbos? Will Hero's Tower crumble under the 15in. Guns? Will the sea be polyphloisbic and wine dark and unvintageable (you, of course, know if it is)? Shall I loot Mosaics from St Sophies (yes, I understood your telegram)? and Turkish Delight? and Carpets? Shall we be a Turning Point in History? Oh, God!

I've never been quite so happy in my life, I think. Not quite so *pervasively* happy; like a stream flowing entirely to one end. I suddenly realize that the ambition of my life has been—since I was two—to go on a military expedition against Constantinople. And when I *thought* I was hungry, or sleepy, or falling in love, or aching to write a poem—*that* was what I really, blindly, wanted. This is nonsense. Good night.

A few days passed with more kit inspections and dismantling the huts, then on 24th, the people began arriving from London for the King's visit next day. Telegrams were exchanged between Blandford and Gray's Inn. Could the Hood put Marsh up for the night? *Yes rather will stow you somewhere* came the reply. Could Mrs. Churchill and two of her friends be given luncheon in the Mess? *Yes rather what fun Quilter says prepare ladies for hardships will you bring Elliott's Turkey in Europe and any thinkable useful books for voyage.* That evening was Brooke's last social occasion in England. Dining with Mrs. Henry Guest, he sat between Violet Asquith and Lady Gwendolen Churchill; among the other guests were Mrs. Asquith, Mrs. Winston Churchill, and old Lady Wimborne. Marsh, meanwhile, was in the Hood Mess with Denis Browne, and at midnight Brooke looked into his cabin to give an account of his dinner. Next morning he breakfasted with Marsh at seven. Later in the morning the band played for the march past, and to His Majesty in person the Royal Naval Division sang 'God Save the King', and cheered, then the younger ladies of the night before were guests of Bernard Freyberg in the Hood Mess. Shortly before four in the afternoon, standing alone at the roadside, Brooke caught sight of Marsh driving alone up to London, and saw him turn and wave.

At 7.15 p.m. on the 27th, the Battalion, wearing their web equipment and pith helmets, marched the ten miles to Shillingstone. From there they travelled by train to Avonmouth Docks and boarded the

ONE OF A NUMBER

Grantully Castle, a Union Castle liner of 7,612 tons, converted into a troop transport. Among the despatches from the Admiralty that were brought aboard was a package for Brooke containing an amulet and an explanatory note from Marsh. 'My dear, this is from a very beautiful lady who wants you to come back safe—her name is not to be divulged. I have promised that you shall wear it—and I beseech you to make my word good. It's a very potent charm . . .'

The Ansons were sailing on the same ship, also the 2nd Brigade Staff, a considerable number of mules, and immense piles of equipment were made fast with ropes on the upper deck. By 5.50 on the morning of February 28 Brooke had organized his men and their baggage and retired to his cabin to get a few hours' sleep. He wrote one letter before turning in, not yet having told Ka of the expedition. 'Isn't it luck?' he exclaimed, after telling her the objective was Constantinople. 'I've never been so happy. 80 or 100 thousand of us altogether . . . Goodbye. Please keep well.' On waking, he sent ashore a kit-bag full of dirty clothes for the Ranee to cope with at Rugby, having discovered too late that he was bound on a Crusade with only one pair of pyjamas.

They sailed that day. The only person he knew on the quay was Violet Asquith, by turns waving to her brother and himself. Two destroyers escorted the *Grantully Castle* as far as the mouth of the Channel. By March 1 they were in the Bay of Biscay, and she had begun to roll.

Chapter XIII

SAILING TO BYZANTIUM

(*February–April 1915*)

On the lower deck they were playing a melodeon. Elsewhere Denis Browne had got hold of a piano and was trying to induce a grumbling semi-circle of stokers to sing folk-songs. Most of the men had been trying to stave off the moment of vaccination by every conceivable means; Brooke's platoon had had to be cajoled and bullied, even implored, into submission. In his efforts to boost the morale Browne was assisted by the other musician of the Hood, F. S. 'Cleg' Kelly, a versatile young man, now turned chorus master, who had rowed in the Oxford Eight and three times won the Diamond Sculls. By day there were Company parades and classes in Semaphore on deck, the groups packed so close to one another that it was all an instructor could do not to be distracted by the eloquence of his neighbour. Shaw-Stewart, for instance, sandwiched between Dodge and a group under instruction from Brooke, only succeeded in stopping his ears to the racy Americanisms of the one to fall next moment under the spell of the polished phrases overheard from the other side.

After the first day, when he was sick, Brooke began taking part in the life of the ship, and soon the hour came when, stirred by the smell of land, he scanned the horizon, and wrote to Violet Asquith.

All day we've been just out of sight of land, thirty or forty miles away—out of sight, but in smell. There was something earthy in the air, and warm —like the consciousness of a presence in the dark—the wind had something Andalusian in it. It wasn't that wall of scent and invisible blossom that knocks you flat, quite suddenly, as you've come round some unseen corner in the atmosphere, fifty miles out from a South Sea Island. But it *was* the good smell of land—and of Spain, too! And Spain I've never seen, and never shall see, maybe. All day I sat and strained my eyes to see, over the horizon, orange groves and Moorish buildings and dark-eyed beauties and guitars and fountains and a golden darkness. But the curve of the world lay between us. Do you know Jan's [Masefield] favourite story—told very melodiously with deep voice reverence—about Columbus. Columbus wrote a diary (which Jan reads) and describes the coast of America (before Johnny Dodge's day) as he found it—*the* divinest place in the world. 'It was only like the Paradise of the Saints of God'—and then he remembered there was *one* place equal to it, the place where he was born, and goes on—'or like the gardens of Andalusia in the spring'.

He said they were all living in 'the most trustful ignorance of what's to come'. Some people actually thought the show would be over before they arrived. He feared the opposite. 'I rather figure us scrapping forlornly in some corner of the Troad for years and years. Everyone will forget all about us. We shan't even be told when peace is declared.' As for writing anything, he hadn't the strength of mind to withdraw himself from the current of the day's routine and think. 'Perhaps I never have, even in peace. I'm a hand-to-mouth liver, God help me.' Just in case he might not be writing again, he ended in a way that, if the need arose, could be taken as good-bye.

Do not care much what happens to me or what I do. When I give thought to it at all, I hate people—people I like—to care for me. I'm selfish. And nothing but harm ever seems to have come of it, in the past.

I don't know. In some moods that thought seems wrong. Generally right. I don't know the truth about that—or about anything. But somewhere, I think, there's bad luck about me.

There's a very bright sun, and a lot of comedy in the world; so perhaps there's some point in my not getting shot. But also there's point in my getting shot. Anyway, you're very good to me.

In the small hours of March 8 they put into Malta, anchored off the Fish Quay, and the men were to be granted leave ashore until midnight. This was an opportunity for catching the mail, so Brooke was writing until 5 p.m., the hour when shore leave began. Marsh must be sent a message for the mysterious donor of the amulet. So far it was all so peaceful, he said, that it was hard to believe they were anything but a rather odd assortment of tourists. 'War seems infinitely remote, and even the reason, foreseeing Gallipoli, yet admits that there are many blue days to come, and the Cyclades.' He was wearing the five-pointed jewel round his neck with the identification disc.

Please thank Anonyma and say I'm quite sure it'll bring me luck. But what 'Luck' *is*, we'll all wait and see. At least, we'll all wait, and you'll see, perhaps. I can well see that life might be great fun: and I can well see death might be an admirable solution. At that, quote to her something appropriate from the *Apology*, and leave her to her prayers.

If anything should happen to him, he added, Marsh must first inform the Ranee, then Dudley Ward, who would know how to get in touch with the wider circle of friends. To Dudley himself he wrote thanking his wife for a gift of handkerchiefs, 'I shall tie them round my scimitar-lopped stumps,' and described his situation. It was the night before Malta.

It is my watch. I have just picked my way over forms recumbent on the deck, and under hammocks, visited twenty sentries, smelt the stale smell of sleeping stokers, and noticed the beginnings of the dawn over Africa. The sky is a grim silver, and beyond Carthage there's a muffled half-moon whirling faintly round in clouds.

He reckoned there were a quarter of a million Turks ahead. 'We are ten thousand. This is some expedition.' Ka was repaid the nine pounds or so she had spent on sausages and turkeys. He talked of 'Polynesian sunsets' and Spring 'a warmth you northerners have forgotten'. This campaign may turn out to be a picnic. 'It all depends on what the fleet have done by the time we get there . . . I'm not always so "hard" as I seem . . . Don't worry about it.' For Raverat, as was his custom, he adopted a boisterous pose.

This is probably the first letter you ever got from a Crusader. You expect to hear that we saw the sea-serpent off Algiers, that the Patriarch of Alexandria has blessed us, and that an outbreak of scurvy was healed by a prompt application of the thigh-bones and pelvis of S.S. John the Divine, Mary Magdalene, and Chrysostom. Not a bit. But the early Crusaders were very jolly people. I've been reading about them. They set out to slay the Turks—and very finely they did it, when they met them. But when they got East, to the Levant and Constantinople, were they kind to their brother Christians they found there? No. They very properly thwacked and trounced them, and took their money, and cut their throats, and ravished their daughters and so left them: for that they were Greeks, Jews, Slavs, Vlachs, Magyars, Czechs, and Levantines, and not gentlemen.

So shall we do, I hope. But, for the present, we've been gliding through a sapphire sea, swept by ghosts of triremes and quinquiremes, Hannibal on poop, or Hanno. Oh, and we came down by Spain, and saw Algiers, and thought of the tribes of dancing girls, and wept for Andalusia. And now we've left Trinacria behind (you would call it Sicily) and soon—after Malta—we'll be among the Cyclades. There I shall recite Sappho and Homer. And the winds of history will follow us all the way.

Stepping ashore in the late afternoon, he shared a *caroche* with Oc and Denis, toured the streets—they reminded him of Verona—dined at the Union Club, and bought tickets for *Tosca* at the Opera House. During the meal Charles Lister walked in and hailed Shaw-Stewart, an old friend of his at Eton and Balliol. The only surviving son of Lord Ribblesdale, Lister held an appointment on the Divisional Staff on the strength of his knowledge of Turkish, but he was easily persuaded to apply for a transfer to the Hood. So with the good prospect of his joining their band of Argonauts, they all went off to the Opera. The boxes were crammed with men from the boats, beckoning, whistling to each other, throwing things to attract attention—'How the Hell did *you* get here?' would be shouted down into the stalls, and throughout the interval there was a babble of recognition and unexpected encounter. Valetta, thought Brooke, was like an Italian town drawn in silver-point, 'livable and serene, with a sea and sky of opal and pearl and faint gold around', and it seemed nearer than any place he had come upon to what an ancient Greek must have witnessed when he sailed into an anchorage on the coast of classical Greece.

As they weighed anchor at 11.30 a.m. next morning, a French vessel came in, and Denis Browne hurriedly mustered his little band on deck and played the Marseillaise, and the Frenchmen were heard cheering as the *Grantully Castle* moved out into the open waters. It was the evening of March 11 when they sighted Lemnos and sailed into the harbour of Mudros Bay, passing the new battleship *Queen Elizabeth*, the *Agamemnon*, and the *Nelson*. The anchorage was crowded. Next morning a Russian battleship with five slim funnels rode at anchor close by, and someone in the Hood christened her 'The Packet of Woodbines'.

For a week there were days ashore, strolling around the capital town of Kastro or out into the orchards where the almond trees were opening their blossom. In the evening the hills in the distance changed colour, and the immense anchorage was speckled all over with lights. 'We saw—they *said* we saw—very far away, Olympus,' Cathleen was told. 'But with strong field-glasses I could not certainly see the gods. However, its head was shrouded in mist. Also, there was—I think— Parnassus; even farther away than usual, with Wilfrid and Shakespeare and the rest on it. And my eyes fell on the holy land of Attica. So I can die.' He knew of no plans, and there wasn't even any news from the Dardanelles. 'At any moment we may be fetched along to kill the Paynim.' Even training was at a standstill.

On March 18 they were ordered to sail for Turkish waters. Next morning *reveille* was at 4 a.m. At 5 all ranks fell in on deck in marching kit, and soon they were entering the straits of the Dardanelles. After the anticlimax, Brooke wrote to Ka.

My own lot have seen no fighting yet, and very likely won't for months. The only thing that seems almost certain is that one doesn't know from day to day what's to happen. The other day we—some of us—were told that we sailed next day to make a landing. A few thousand of us. Off we stole that night through the phosphorescent Aegean, scribbling farewell letters, and snatching periods of dream-broken excited sleep. At four we rose, buckled on our panoply, hung ourselves with glasses compasses periscopes revolvers food and the rest, and had a stealthy large breakfast. *That* was a mistake. It is ruinous to load up one's belly four or five hours before it expects it: it throws the machinery out of gear for a week. I felt extremely ill the rest of that day.

We paraded in silence, under paling stars, along the sides of the ship. The darkness on the sea was full of scattered flashing lights, hinting at our fellow-transports and the rest. Slowly the sky became wan and green and the sea opal. Everyone's face looked drawn and ghastly. *If* we landed, my company was to be the first to land . . . We made out that we were only a mile or two from a dim shore. I was seized with an agony of remorse that I hadn't taught my platoon a thousand things more energetically and competently. The light grew. The shore looked to be crammed with Fate, and most ominously silent. One man thought he saw a camel through his glasses . . .

There were some hours of silence.

About seven someone said 'We're going home'. We dismissed the stokers, who said, quietly, 'When's the next battle?'; and disempanoplied, and had another breakfast. If we were a 'feint', or if it was too rough to land, or, in general, what little part we blindly played, we never knew, and shall not. Still, we did our bit: not ignobly I trust. We did not see the enemy. We did not fire at them; nor they at us. It seemed improbable they saw us. One of B Company—she was rolling slightly—was sick on parade. Otherwise, no casualties. A notable battle.

Possibly the severe naval losses from mines during the heavy bombardment of the coastal defences on the 18th had made a landing impracticable. Anyway, as the Hoods and the Ansons sailed back to Lemnos they were given to understand they had taken part in a 'feint' attack. It was now rumoured that the ship's freight would have to be reorganized; guns, troops, ammunitions, stores, mules, all must be rearranged. In that case perhaps it was a good thing they had done no more than 'demonstrate'. Morale was no longer at the flood, but they did not have long to wait before the next signal to move. At Lemnos on the 24th they again weighed anchor; sighted Patmos ahead, and Rhodes; then a man died on board. He was buried on shore when they reached Port Said. Some thought this a bad omen. But nothing could for long affect the general enthusiasm for this enterprise, not even the dire conditions where they were soon encamped.

They disembarked on March 28, and the tents were pitched out-side the docks on a waste of dirty sand about three minutes' walk from the Arab quarter of the town. Standing with one's back to the ships and the town there was nothing in sight but sand. Nearby, but on a lower level, and so not visible, were the salt lagoons of the delta and the Suez Canal. The sand was adrift on the wind practically all the time and it penetrated everything. At first Brooke shared a tent with Commander Freyberg, Dodge, and a lieutenant Nelson, but he was with them only two nights, for his name was the first among those drawn for short leave. The officers were being sent off to Cairo in batches of three every forty-eight hours.

He took the train with Shaw-Stewart and Asquith, and stayed at Shepheard's Hotel. That day (March 30) they called on some friends of Asquith's, Lord and Lady Howard de Walden, and Aubrey and Mary Herbert, among others, and motored out to the Pyramids, rode around on camels for an hour, looked at the Sphinx, drove back, and went a donkey-ride through the streets by moonlight. Although the heat was moderate, all three officers had taken the precaution of wearing their pith helmets. They spent the next morning in the Bazaar. Brooke bought a small glass tear-bottle for his mother, an amber necklace, and he fingered Ptolemaic coins and semi-precious stones. After luncheon they paid a visit to the Citadel where, sitting in the shade, Brooke read aloud to Asquith the passage in *Antony and Cleopatra* describing the queen's barge on the River Cydnus. That night they got back to camp. A fragment of diary containing only two entries reads: 'An odd day yesterday. In the afternoon an expedition to the Pyramids and the Sphinx with the Herberts. The usual vague upper-class expedition, ways and means of locomotion improvized and snatched.' No more. He was feeling out of sorts.

Next morning there was a route march, and by the time Shaw-Stewart dismissed his men at noon, he was feeling as if he had caught a touch of the sun. Lister, now an officer of the Hood, looked in on him in the afternoon, found him sick and starting an attack of dysentery, hired a cab from the town, and took him to a room in the Casino Palace Hotel overlooking the sea. All that morning until one o'clock Brooke was busy with his platoon in a field-firing exercise, running to and fro across the sand to judge their marksmanship. It was cer-tainly hot, but he wore his helmet, and was still active at sundown, if a little subdued in spirits, when he went with Denis to dine and call on the afflicted Shaw-Stewart at his hotel. Next morning he told

Denis he had twice been sick in the night. Since the Cairo leave there had been a general reshuffle, including the allotment of tents. Denis and Oc Asquith were now his tent companions, and the four platoons of A Company were under the command of 1, Sub-lieutenant Dodge, 2, Shaw-Stewart, 3, Lister, 4, Brooke.

It was now April 2, and the Division was going to be reviewed before midday by Sir Ian Hamilton, the C-in-C. Racked with headache, Brooke pulled his camp-bed out of the tent, and set it up under a green canvas awning, for it was a little cooler there; the day grew close and sultry, there was a singing in his ears, his head throbbed. Not far away he heard the commands of the officers at the Review; the columns marched past, and a baleful mist of dust kicked up by the men on parade drifted towards the sea. After a while he was disturbed by the sound of unfamiliar voices, and then Sir Ian Hamilton was sitting on the edge of his bed, offering him an appointment on the Staff at Headquarters aboard the *Queen Elizabeth*. Word went round that the Commander-in-Chief had sat with the sub-lieutenant 'talking poetry', and Brooke never disabused his companions, not even Denis Browne. It seems he did not want anyone to think he had considered the proposition even for a moment, and indeed he had not, but it was simpler and less embarrassing to make no mention of it. Parting from Colonel Quilter at noon, Sir Ian said, 'Mind you take care of him. His loss would be a national loss,' and in a letter to Marsh, dictated on the way back to Cairo, he reported that he had found Brooke 'rather off colour for the day, poor boy', but there was nothing to worry about. 'Rupert Brooke very naturally would like to see this first adventure through with his own men. After that I think he would like to come to me. It was very natural and I quite understand it—I should have answered the same in his case had I been offered a Staff billet.' Sir Ian also recorded the interview in his diary, but added 'He looked extraordinarily handsome, quite a knightly presence, stretched out there on the sand with the only world that counts at his feet.' Probably Brooke had been ready with his answer, having heard from Marsh: 'It was entirely his own idea to ask you, so don't think that I put it into his head. Winston was all for it.' Meanwhile the Ranee was writing to Gray's Inn, 'I do hope he won't be foolish enough to refuse, but surely he daren't.' It is immaterial whether Marsh was telling nothing but the truth. Doubtless in his view the end justified the means, and so he would have considered it worth trying, but it's inconceivable that anyone who knew Brooke at all well could have anticipated any other result. There was indeed the faint possibility, entertained by the Ranee, that he might have regarded the proposal as an order from his superior officer, but very properly it was put to him as an invitation. There was no need for him to recall the words of Grizzlebeard. 'A man is more himself when he is one of a number . . .' for by this time the solitary release of writing a poem was no longer sufficient justification for his existence. He was glad of his companions, and proud of them, and his whole being was a stream flowing to one end.

In the early afternoon he got up, dressed, his head swimming and sweating, sent a stoker to fetch a cab, and drove to the Casino Palace Hotel. He could barely mount the stairs to Shaw-Stewart's room, Number 17, where the manager said he would have another bed put up on the opposite side of the room. His temperature was 103. Kelly had looked in earlier, so Patrick already knew of the march past and that the C-in-C had found a spare moment to 'talk about poetry' in the Hood lines, but he was very surprised when Brooke himself staggered in. He looked exhausted and was obviously in a high fever. A civilian doctor was alarmed and said he should go to hospital. But next morning he seemed rather better, or at least he made out that he was, knowing that if he got stuck in some hospital he would be left behind when his Battalion moved on; besides, as he said to Patrick, he refused to be immured in a 'crowded ward with tiresome brother officers'. So the doctor retired from the scene, and the Regimental M.O. took over. He ordered a diet of arrowroot for both patients, nothing else to eat or drink; for they were both suffering from a sharp attack of dysentery, sharing Brooke's overcoat for their excursions down the passage, exchanging weak jokes and, as the days passed, growing their beards—the one red, the other golden brown—lying under tents of mosquito netting in a state of complete vacuity of mind. In the note-book where at the same time he wrote the lyric 'As the Wind, and as the Wind' (because Denis Browne wanted something to set to music) we find the following memorial ballade of the forty-eight hours when they were confined to arrowroot.

> *My first was in the night, at 1,*
> *At half-past 5 I had to run,*
> *At 8.15 I fairly flew;*
> *At noon a swift compulsion grew,*
> *I ran a dead-heat all the way.*

SAILING TO BYZANTIUM

I lost by yards at ten to 2.
  This is the seventh time today.

Prince, did the brandy fail you, too?
  You dreamt that arrowroot would stay?
My opium fairly galloped through.
  This is the seventh time today.

After a few days they were promoted to the consumption of small
Mediterranean soles, which did little more than whet the appetite, and
the Italian waiter who looked after them seemed wantonly uncomprehending. 'Rupert did better with gesticulating English than I with
Italian,' said Patrick, 'which made me furious.' From the second day in
the hotel Brooke was bothered by a small sore on the left side of his
upper lip, and for two days it swelled a little and throbbed, then as his
general state improved, seemed to right itself. The M.O. attached no
importance to it. The sequel showed he was mistaken. Under cover
of what was obviously sunstroke, a secondary, and in Brooke's case
more dangerous, trouble had given a warning sign that passed
unheeded.

Lister called one evening and parodied the Divisional instructions,
and Browne remarked that the two patients under their gauzy tents
made him feel as if he were visiting a harem. He handed round a letter
he had just got from Marsh, giving a lively description of a visit to
the front in France with Mr. Churchill. 'Rupert and Patrick, both
suffering from acute diarrhoea,' Denis reported to Gray's Inn, 'read it
with gurgles and fled to the rear.' After four days Brooke tried to
while away the time finishing some letters. No mail from England
had come to hand until they got back to Lemnos after the *feint* attack,
and then there was only a postcard from Aunt Fanny and a note from
Ka, but rumour had it that eighty mail-bags had either fallen overboard, or were held up at headquarters. He now told the Ranee of his
illness—'The glare is awful here'—and of Sir Ian's offer, 'but I
shan't take it. Anyhow, not now, not till this present job's over.' He
was sending the tear-bottle, said to have been found in a tomb. 'But I
imagine it's really very recently manufactured. Still it's amusing; and
if you clean out the inside with a little warm water, it might look
nice, and hold scent.' The amber necklace went off to Cathleen, with
an account of the torrid sun and the sand which had pulled him down.
'We ate sand and drank it, and breathed and thought and dreamed it
. . . I think I'll be well for the fighting.'

By April 8 a week of acute but hilarious discomfort had passed in Room 17. Shaw-Stewart was more or less restored, but Brooke, whose trouble had begun later, was thin and drawn in the face and unsteady on his feet. Colonel Quilter looked in and said they were to sail for Lemnos at dawn the day after tomorrow. Observing Brooke's condition, he strongly recommended that he should stay behind for a spell of convalescence at the military hospital. Brooke thought otherwise. 'It would look pretty silly,' he said to his companion when the Colonel was gone, 'if the *Grantully Castle* proceeded to hang around Lemnos for three weeks in blazing sunshine!'

So next morning they shaved off their beards, and Brooke spent the day finishing off some letters. To Eileen Wellesley he sent a package containing two semi-precious stones. 'I believe they contain flaws, which seemed to my inexpert eye to add to their attractiveness. Poor things, yet not as ugly as most stones.' For Violet Asquith he managed to write a fairly full account of his experiences, including the day of the march past. 'Afterwards Sir Ian came to see me a moment. A notable meeting, it was generally felt: our greatest poet-soldier and our greatest soldier-poet. We talked blank verse. He looked very worn and white-haired. I thought him a little fearful—not *fearful*, but less than cocksure—about the job.' He was taking a brighter view of his leave in Cairo and the donkey-ride under a full moon. 'A *most* odd dream. My attention was divided between a perishable donkey and Immortal Beauty. Both seemed just to evade me. We seemed more than usually incidental.' Then he explained the object of a parcel.

I poked about in a bazaar. And there I found a foolish little bluish stone, like London milk or the white of an uncooked egg. It reminded me of a worser lyric by Keats. I had it sent you—or perhaps the Egyptians, in packing, stole it—in the slight hope that *something* might reach you from me on your birthday (but it won't): and that it might at least say that there I *was*, more tourist still than soldier, and, in my watery amorphous aimlessness, my solitude, my (I thought) almost charming moony pathos, not unlike that blear little stone.

We're a gay enough little party in the Hood. A softened Colonel is well and patient. Charles I like more as I see him more. I didn't realize what awareness and subtlety he concealed under that equine madness. Imagine what an extraordinary, an unprecedented, conglomeration of sound Oc and I and Denis Browne put up with, when you learn that Patrick and his loud titter, Cleg Kelly with his whinny, and Charles with his great neigh, are all in the same tent. The sound from it frights the Egyptian night, and sends the ghosts of Antony and the gypsy scudding away across the sand.

The two invalids disposed of their mail on land, found their cabins aboard, and retired to bed. There was no night watch for either of them; they were on sick leave. At 6 a.m. the following morning, April 10, the *Grantully Castle*, this time without the Ansons on board, and consequently a more habitable craft, again put out to sea.

II

They steamed very slowly, for they were towing a lighter for disembarking the troops; then a wind got up off the island of Kos and it broke loose, and a day was wasted while they cruised in vague circles, hoping to locate it. Brooke remained in bed for three days. During the first day at sea he wrote the second of the two entries in his journal:

There are moments—there have been several, especially in the Aegean— when, through some beauty of sky and air and earth, and some harmony with the mind, peace is complete and completely satisfying. One is at rest from the world, and with it, entirely content, drinking to the full of the placidity of the loveliness. Every second seems divine and sufficient. And there are men and women who seem to do what one so terribly can't, and so terribly, at these moments, *aches* to do—store up reservoirs of this calm and content, fill and seal great jars or pitchers during these half-hours, and draw on them at later moments, when the source isn't there, but the need is very great. I wish there were more people of that character about on this expedition. Oc has a touch of it: he has a phial or two; he hasn't forgotten his water-bottle. And perhaps Shadbolt—if he can't throw you a *bucketful*, sprays himself as he dresses every morning. He seems pleasantly damp. Perhaps married people—if only they've got receptacles—get a good deal more often within reach of the wells than the rest of us.

For some days he remained in his cabin until after midday. He seemed to grow fit again, and he was happy enough, feeling in the vein to write while the leisure served. He picked up an unfinished letter to Abercrombie. 'Sunstroke is a bloody affair. It breaks very suddenly the fair harmonies of the body and soul. My head was shattered in three parts, and my diarrhoea was part of the cosmic process.' Then after this interval he went on:

(Later, at sea) I know now—more certainly every day what a campaign is. I had a suspicion from Antwerp. It is continual crossing from one place to another and back, over dreamlike seas: anchoring, or halting, in the oddest places, for nobody knows or cares how long; drifting on, at last, to some other, equally unexpected, equally out of the way, equally odd spot:

for all the world like a bottle in some corner of the bay at a seaside resort. Somewhere, sometimes, there is fighting. Not for us. In the end, no doubt, our apparently aimless course will drift us through, or anchor us in, a blaze of war, quite suddenly; and as suddenly swirl us out again. Meanwhile— the laziest loitering lotus-day I idled away as a wanderer in the South Seas was a bustle of decision and purpose compared to a campaign.

One just hasn't, though, the time and detachment to write: I find. But I've been collecting a few words, detaching lines from the ambient air, collaring one or two of the golden phrases that a certain wind blows from (will the Censor let me say?) Olympus, across these purple seas. In time, if I'm spared, they'll bloom into a sort of threnody—really a discussion of England—which I have in my head, which has signs of merit.

He had seen, he said, a review in *The Times* of the last *New Numbers*. The critic was laudatory of the sonnets, and yet unperceptive. 'He didn't seem to realize that it was "goodbye". Perhaps we should have put in a slip to say so; and extracted, even in these times, a few tears, a few shillings.'

On the fourth day he began light duties, and found they were coming into port. It was Lemnos again, but now the anchorage of Mudros Bay was congested with every conceivable variety of craft from gaunt battleships to craft which looked like, and probably were, Thames barges and tugs from Merseyside. There was no room. The R.N.D. transports received a signal to make for the harbour of Trebuki Bay on the southern tip of the island of Skyros. So the slow *Grantully Castle* continued her voyage.

On deck the men passed the time with Swedish exercises and machine-gun drill, or groups were sending messages to one another in semaphore; the sub-lieutenants supervised, and as evening came diced for the night watches. At one table in the dining saloon sat Lister, Asquith, Kelly, Dodge, Browne, Shaw-Stewart, and Brooke, who were given the name of the Latin Club. Learned in classic lore they certainly were, but it was Greek history and legend that more often spiced their conversation. The parallel with the wars of Agamemnon was irresistible. Shaw-Stewart was using his Herodotus as a guide-book, and in their correspondence they were evading the Censor by means of Homeric allusions. The *Grantully Castle*, they said, was on her way to call at the island where Philoctetes, the archer, was bitten by a snake, and then pass along the edge of the tyranny of Miltiades, and their friends at home would understand where they were. Another declared he was now bound for a small island 'not unconnected with the education of Neoptolemus'. Moreover, aware

that Constantinople was their objective, Byzantium was often their
theme. 'I shall take Constantinople,' exclaimed Shaw-Stewart, 'and
avenge the Byzantine Empire.' Their campaign would be over in a
month or so, and they would have added a new episode to the legends
of windy Ilios. 'The future's an absolute blank,' Brooke wrote to the
Ranee. 'But certainly, if anyone in this war is lucky, we who are on
this job are.' He admitted to having had an internal upset—'unless it
was some poison in the food'.

The Hood was in better spirits without the Anson on top of it, and
on April 15, still at sea, there was a fancy dress ball. Kelly and
Browne took turns at the saloon piano, and the stokers emerged from
below disguised as negroes; and there was one, draped in Denis
Browne's cabin curtains and veiled with an antiseptic bandage, who
masqueraded as Queen Elizabeth. Brooke watched for a while, then
went early to bed. Then on the evening of the 17th, led by the
Franconia (the Divisional H.Q.) the transports of the R.N.D.
anchored in Trebuki Bay of Skyros. Here too was an assembly of
ships. But there was room. It was still daylight, and Lister and
Brooke, pacing the deck, remarked on the hot smell of flowering sage
and thyme which came to them from the land.

Next day Brooke stayed on duty aboard, while Lister and the
others explored the coast, rested in the steading of a shepherd whom
they identified as Eumaeus, and ate their fill of goat's cheese. Meanwhile Brooke on board was the first to get the mail.

Marsh enclosed a cutting from *The Times* of April 5, reporting the
sermon given by the Dean of St. Paul's at the Cathedral on Easter
Sunday. The congregation consisted of widows, parents, and orphans
in their hundreds. As the Dean reached the pulpit, a man jumped to
his feet and began a loud harangue against the war. When he was
removed, Dean Inge gave as his text, *Isaiah XXVI*, 19. *The dead shall
live, my dead bodies shall arise. Awake and sing, ye that dwell in the dust.*
He had just read a poem on this subject, 'a sonnet by a young writer
who would, he ventured to think, take rank with our great poets—so
potent was a time of trouble to evoke genius which must otherwise
have slumbered.' He then read aloud 'If I should die', and remarked
that 'the enthusiasm of a pure and elevated patriotism had never
found a nobler expression. And yet it fell somewhat short of Isaiah's
vision and still more of the Christian hope,' for a Christian would
hardly be content to think of the brave man's soul only living on as a
'pulse in the eternal mind'. The report then drew attention to a

recent review of the sonnets in *New Numbers*.[1] 'You will be pleased,' wrote Marsh, 'to have been recited in St. Paul's Cathedral on Easter Sunday, and the Dean is a fine scholar and critic, though a Dean. I suppose in his position he could hardly do otherwise than say that the sonnet would have been better if it had been written by Isaiah.'

As embarrassed as he must surely have been gratified, Brooke said no word of this to his companions of the Latin table. In England the little publishing concern at Ryton Dymock was soon sold out of the current issue and the back numbers as well. There was neither paper nor labour to meet with the demand. Since there was only one packer on the job, and she nursing two children, the impasse was inevitable. Having disposed of its last copy, the cottage enterprise closed down, as though, having made history somewhat sooner than was ever anticipated, there seemed no need to cope with the confusion brought about by such an avalanche of success. There was to be no further issue of *New Numbers*. The editorial office was finally shut down as a mark of respect for Brooke. But that was not yet.

Marsh's letter about the Dean gave news that Brooke's friend Virginia Woolf was also becoming an author of promise. *The Voyage Out* had just appeared. A second communication from Gray's Inn enclosed a copy of a letter to Marsh about the sonnets from Henry James. Surely Rupert would be pleased with 'this lovely letter from the dear old boy'. Henry James was acclaiming their 'happy force and truth', though he found them a little unequal. 'This evening, alone by my lamp, I have been reading them over and over to myself aloud, as if fondly to test and truly to try them, almost in fact as if to reach the far-off author, in whatever unimaginable conditions, by some miraculous, some telepathic intimation that I am in quavering communion with him . . . I take off my hat to them, and to their author in the most marked manner.' He thought 'If I should die' was slightly flawed by what he called the hackneyed rhyme of 'given' and 'heaven', and he would have preferred the line 'And the worst friend and enemy is but Death' to read 'And the worst friend and foe is only Death'. However, he bade Marsh 'tell Rupert of my pleasure and my pride', adding, 'If he shall be at all touched by this it would infinitely touch *me* . . . I think of him quite inordinately.'

[1] It is impossible to shred up this beauty for the purpose of criticism. These sonnets are personal—never were sonnets more personal since Sidney died—and yet the very blood and youth of England seem to find expression in them. They speak not for one heart only, but for all to whom her call has come in the hour of need and found instantly ready . . . No passion for glory is here, no bitterness, no gloom, only a happy, clear-sighted, all surrendering love. *Times Literary Supplement*, March 11, 1915.

It was probably during these long hours alone on board that Brooke finished the letter to Violet Asquith which he had begun at Port Said. He told of the threnody he was working on, 'a very serene affair, full of major chords and larger outlooks, like an English lawn at sunset,' but he couldn't find the necessary detachment to do much writing, not even on 'our world-forgotten, laughing little island'. To Sybil Pye, who had sent her admiration of the sonnets, he remarked, 'It took me an awful long time to hammer them out: you can't think,' and explained more fully his inability to do more. 'I think *reading* in wartime's right enough, but writing requires a longer period of serenity, a more certainly undisturbed subconscious. If our s-c's turbulent one's draught from it is opaque. Witness the first three sonnets.' However, his life was placid enough. 'We read Homer to each other, and drift among the isles of Greece . . . We know and hear and think nothing: only, by the wine-dark sea, over our Samian, sometimes remember faintly that there are men fighting somewhere, and sigh, and laugh and forget.' Marsh too was told of a sonnet or two almost done 'and the very respectable and shapely skeleton' of something more ambitious in scale that would be posted off to him if ever it got that far.

I cannot write you any description of my life. It is entirely featureless. It would need Miss Austen to make anything of it. We glide to and fro on an azure sea and forget the war—I must go and censor my platoon's letters.

My long poem is to be about the existence—and non-locality—of England. And it contains the line—

In Avons of the heart her rivers run.

Lovely isn't it.

Freiburg [*sic*] sends his chin-chin. I've no doubt there'd be other messages, if I could find anyone.

By now the day was drawing in, and a little boat was sighted making for the ship. Lister and Shaw-Stewart, sated with cheese, and each laden with a flapping tortoise, were being rowed back by a Greek fisherman. Brooke hailed them from the deck with 'slight sarcasm' for they had overstayed their leave, and should have been on watch over an hour ago. Next day he went ashore himself and took part in a rather desultory Battalion exercise. The more serious operations were due to take place on the morrow. The hills reverberated with the sound of the stokers shooting adders—a practice which had to be stopped—and one group was discovered trying to set off an intractable row of tortoises in a race. On closer view, the island seemed like an enormous rockery of marble, tumbled white and pink. Here there were patches of the diminutive red poppy, and there the ilex and dwarf holly clung to the slopes, or stunted olives stood about in groves, and hovering everywhere the pleasant scent of thyme and sage and mint. Just off shore the water was so still and clear you could peer fathoms down to its floor of white marble, and shadows, green or cobalt blue, lay gleaming darkly between the rocks.

At dawn next day, Tuesday, April 20, the men were stirring early. It was a Divisional Field Day. For four hours of the previous night Brooke had stood at watch. He was already tired when the exercise began at 8 a.m., his platoon being situated, near Shaw-Stewart's, on the right wing of the Hood Battalion's front. The operations were confined chiefly to the area of a dried up river-bed, a valley lying between the mountains of Pephko and Komaro and overlooked by Mount Khokilas, the highest point of the island, which loomed ahead, some miles further inland. About a mile up this valley, and a short distance from the place of rendezvous for the 2nd Brigade, there was a small olive grove of some dozen trees. Denis Browne had discovered it on his first day ashore, and to this spot, during a lull in the afternoon, Browne took Lister, Shaw-Stewart, and Brooke, and there they enjoyed a respite in the shade of the trees. 'He liked the place and spoke of it,' Browne wrote afterwards, telling how Brooke had remarked on the strange peace and beauty of this valley. There was a rough map of the island which had been duplicated and issued to the officers. On his copy Brooke filled in the heights of the mountains and such other features as he could learn, and he also drew pencil maps of his own, and marked in the names of a few salient points. It was a hot afternoon, a fierce glare rebounding from the rocks; and the operation necessitated much clambering from point to point, so that several of the men tore their boots. By four o'clock, the arduous exercise over at last, Freyberg, Lister, and Brooke, happened to be together on the beach, when someone suggested swimming out to the ship about a mile away. Brooke said he wished he could join them, but he didn't feel up to it. So the others plunged in, and he followed, seated among their clothes in a fisherman's boat.

That evening the Latin Club was giving a dinner to some friends from the *Franconia*. Only two guests turned up, but the occasion was noisy and convivial. They were drinking hock, and Brooke drank with the rest, but he seldom spoke, and when the meal was over he turned to Shaw-Stewart, who was sitting beside him and said, 'I believe it's making my lip swell.' It was only ten o'clock but he made his excuses and went to bed a long while before the party broke up.

Asquith was his first caller next morning. The upper lip was a good deal swollen, and there were pains in his back and head. He lay there for most of the day, evidently in the belief that his only trouble was exhaustion from the field-exercise, but in the evening he reported to McCracken, the Battalion surgeon, who found his temperature was 101 and ordered hot fomentations for the swelling (which was now on the *right* side of the upper lip) but he was not particularly worried.

Next day Shaw-Stewart looked in about noon, and found an orderly applying a hot compress. He didn't say much, lest it should hurt the patient to speak. 'He said he was feeling damnably ill,' wrote Shaw-Stewart in his account. In the late afternoon he went back, and since Brooke had summoned up the strength to hunt up and hand over a letter he had written the night before, he gave the impression of being somewhat better. It was a letter to the Ranee, which must go to the Colonel to be censored. Shaw-Stewart outlined the general idea of some forthcoming feint attack that Quilter had been describing that afternoon in an address to his officers, and he said that Brooke needn't bother to leave his cabin as he could 'demonstrate' equally well by merely 'looking frightful' through the port-hole.

The letter Brooke handed over was written in the small hours of the 20th, having finished his watch before the Divisional Field Day. His main reason for writing was to sort out a muddle. He gathered that Marsh had apparently jumped to the conclusion that the Staff appointment offered at Port Said was accepted, and had then let the Ranee know, only to hear later that in fact the invitation was declined. Brooke explained that at least the offer *was* put to him, 'but I'd made up my mind to see at any rate some of a campaign in my present capacity, and I'm very happy as I am, with several people I like: and it wouldn't be very fair to my company to leave it suddenly at the last moment like this, with a gap it couldn't fill, out here . . . However, I gather we're pretty well as safe as if we were all Staff officers, so all's well. There's no further news. I'd like to hear if Alfred is going to France, or elsewhere. If you have any important piece of news, you might repeat it in two or three letters, as the odds are I shall only get one of them.'

Having parted with his letter to the Ranee, he must have become rapidly worse, for when Browne looked in after dinner and asked how he was (this was Browne's first visit of the day) Brooke said he felt rotten and asked him not to switch on the light. Browne was surprised to find he was really ill, for he had dropped in only to show him *The Times* report of the Dean's sermon which he had just got in a letter from his mother. Having seen it already, Brooke merely remarked out of the darkness that 'he was sorry Inge did not think him quite as good as Isaiah'. He was very drowsy. Browne went straight to McCracken. He said there was nothing to worry about. Earlier in the voyage another officer, who had shared a cabin with Asquith, had been troubled with the same kind of swelling on the lip, and after a poultice or two it had cleared up in three days. But that night Asquith learned that the temperature had risen to 103, and McCracken told him that Brooke was in no condition to resist pneumonia, if that's what it was. Had the surgeon known something of his patient's medical history he would have had small hope. Brooke had no resources to combat infection of this virulence. The coral poisoning at Tahiti had expended them to danger point.

Next day, Thursday 22nd, Browne looked in three times, but on each occasion Brooke was comatose. He found that the surgeon, however, was now gravely alarmed, chiefly because of pains in the chest and back. It was about 11 a.m. when McCracken decided to get further opinions, and sent a wireless message for Fleet Surgeon Gaskell, his assistant, Captain Casement, who was Staff Medical Officer of the Division, and Dr. Schlesinger, Medical Officer to the Brigade, whom Browne recognized when he came aboard as an able man from Guy's. By 3 p.m. these men were in conference on the *Grantully Castle*. There was some disagreement as to the treatment, but they agreed that the place on the lip was originally a mosquito bite. Perhaps it had occurred on the first or second night ashore at Port Said, but anyway it was infected; later it must have responded to the dieting prescribed for mild sunstroke, and at length seemed cured; but the infection was still latent and liable to renew its activity when the system was run down.

By this time a further inflammation had declared itself on the right side of the face and down the neck, as if the infection were spreading, so they decided to make an incision and submit a swab to a Dr. Goodale, a bacteriologist serving as a junior medical officer on board. In a letter to Rugby, McCracken reported that Goodale identified the germ as 'Diplococcus, morphologically resembling Pneumococcus'. They put it to Denis Browne as a case of acute blood poisoning, then owing to Brooke's general state of health being so low, they recommended the patient's removal to a hospital ship. When told of this new plan, Brooke protested, not wanting to be parted from the Hood, but Browne managed to quieten him, assuring him it was for the best. The nearest British ship of the kind was the *Cecilia* at Lemnos. Even if she were signalled to make for Skyros, it would be dangerous to move the patient by the time she arrived, but nearby in Trebuki Bay a French hospital ship lay at anchor, the *Duguay-Trouin*, originally a training ship built in 1878.

At 4.30 p.m. two stokers hoisted the patient, wrapped in blankets, and lowered him over the side into a picket-boat from H.M.S. *Canopus*, where Schlesinger, Asquith, and Browne were waiting to escort him over the mile or so of water to the French vessel. Brooke had said 'Hullo' to Browne as he stooped to lift him into the pinnace, but he soon lapsed into a dazed sleep. From the rail Shaw-Stewart could only see a tuft of hair and a hand come up from under the wrappings to pull them free of one side of his face. There were no other patients on the *Duguay-Trouin*, but no less than twelve surgeons. They gave the English officer one of two airy cabins which stood back to back on the sun-deck, and found an English-speaking male nurse to attend him. Asquith explained that Brooke was 'our best young poet and the apple of Winston's and Sir Ian's eye', then shortly before 7 p.m. he asked Brooke if there was anything he wanted. He said 'Water', no more. Then Asquith took the picket-boat to the *Franconia*, consulted with Gaskell as to the possibility of getting English nurses, and drafted marconigrams to Sir Ian Hamilton at Lemnos and Mr. Churchill at the Admiralty. General Paris signed them. They named the French vessel, and the disease adding *Condition very grave. Please inform parents and send me instructions re disposal of body in case he dies and duplicate them to Duguay-Trouin.* While Asquith was busy on the *Franconia*, Kelly was making an entry in his journal. '. . . I looked into his cabin before breakfast, when I found him very dazed, but I had no idea he was dangerously ill. The doctors made me realize, however, that it was far more likely that he will not live, and I felt very much depressed. I have had a foreboding that he is one of those, like Keats, Shelley, and Schubert, who are not suffered to deliver their full message . . . Oc Asquith went over with him and by the time of writing this (10.15 p.m.) has not returned.'

Next morning, April 23, Marsh was at Raymond Buildings, about to leave for the Admiralty, when he was telephoned by Mr. Churchill.

The First Lord read the message from the *Franconia* and asked Marsh to pass on the news to Rugby. At about midday a telegram was delivered at Bilton Road.

> *I have had bad news admiral telegraphs Rupert on board french hospital ship duguay trouin with septicaemia condition very grave please inform mother and telegraph instructions if anything special end of telegram Churchill is telegraphing for further report is there anything you wish wired I have strong hope Marsh.*

The reply was *If message of love can be sent send it please at once waiting anxiously for the news Brooke.* Some hours before this in Trebuki Bay, the same morning, Asquith and Browne were going back to the French vessel, and they saw anchored near her the great battleships *Le Ville de Carthage*, and in another direction *Canopus*, the *Royal George*, and the *Prince Edward*. The time was 9 a.m. McCracken was with them. They found the French surgeons about to operate, ready to carry out a free cauterization of the infected area. At the same time an attempt was made to establish a focal abscess in the thigh. Both McCracken and Schlesinger approved this as being the only possible chance of drawing off the bacteria concentrated in the neck, in fact they were impressed to know that the French Fleet Surgeons were so up-to-date in their methods as to practise this particular operation. Asquith and Browne took it in turns to watch by the bed. Shortly after midday he regained consciousness. Asquith spoke to him twice, and he seemed to make an effort in his throat, but no words came. A little later, when Schlesinger was alone with him, it seems that he did manage to make himself understood. He 'had had some pains earlier in the morning, but the French had done everything possible for him, and now he was comfortable .

Asquith was on the *Franconia* at that time. When he got back after the midday meal, Brooke was evidently worse and the French Captain, having received a wireless inquiry from Sir Ian, asked Asquith to draft a reply. Oc asked the Chief French Surgeon what he should say. The answer was *Etat désespéré.*

It now became known that this section of the Allied fleet was under orders to sail for Gallipoli at 6 a.m. next morning. So Asquith went off again to make alternative arrangements in case death should occur before or after sailing. He left Denis Browne in charge.

When the last message reached London, Winston Churchill sent a marconigram to Lemnos.

SAILING TO BYZANTIUM

Personal. From First Lord to Major John Churchill. Endeavour if your duties allow to attend Rupert Brooke's funeral on my behalf. We shall not see his like again. W.S.C.

At the same time Sir Ian was writing to Marsh. 'The wording of the message terrifies me. Alas, what a misfortune . . . He was bound, he said, to see this first fight through with his fellows. Ah, well, I pray fervently he may yet pull through . . . We are off ! ! ! unless the weather plays us a scurvy trick we shall be at it on Sunday next and may the best cause win,' and he entered in his Diary, 'War will smash, pulverize, sweep into the dustbin of eternity the whole fabric of the old world; therefore, the firstborn of intellect must die. Is *that* the reading of the riddle?'

At 2 p.m. the temperature was 106; Browne was drawn aside by the chief Surgeon and told that his friend was sinking. One of the few Christians among Brooke's close friends, Browne at once left the ship in haste, and was away for half an hour, fetching the Chaplain from the *Franconia*. A priest could do no more than kneel at the bedside and pray, and he was starting back to his ship when Asquith reappeared and, seeing how things were, immediately left again to make arrangements which would have to be carried out almost at once. Browne stayed behind. He sat in the cabin for another one and a half hours, until he was asked to leave for a minute or two while the orderlies tidied up. It was during this short interval that the French surgeon looked in and coming out to Browne told him his friend was dying. He ran back, and again he waited, 'with the sun shining all round his cabin and the cool sea breeze blowing through the door and the shaded windows,' as he described it for the Ranee. There had been no movement, no sign of consciousness since noon; a little less than an hour after this, he died. Denis Browne looked at his watch. It was 4.46. The French surgeon made out the death certificate and handed it over. The cause of death was entered as 'Oedème malin et septicémie foudroyante'. Rupert Brooke had lived 27 years, 8 months, and 20 days.

Half an hour afterwards Asquith came aboard, and the two men walked up and down in conference. They were sure that Brooke would never have wished for burial at sea; yet if the body were left on board, it might never be reclaimed, for the *Duguay-Trouin* was bound for some remote port on the coast of Asia. They decided to bury him on Skyros that same night and shared out the duties to be done. Asquith remained on board.

It was seven o'clock when Browne, Freyberg, and Lister, in command of a digging party from A Company, stepped ashore and walked inland to the spot near the 2nd Brigade's rendezvous where Brooke had rested, made his sketch map, and found the place very pleasant. Browne marked out an area for the grave which was overhung by one of the twelve olive trees, 'leaning slightly forward with its upper branches, though its stem is straight'. The three officers broke the surface, then their men got down to work.

Meanwhile the Frenchmen aboard their vessel fetched a number of small palm-trees and placed them in a rectangle on the upper deck, and in the middle of them they set down the coffin under a British flag. It was dark by now, and a message was received from the *Canopus*—'Make haste'. There was no time to engrave a plate, so Asquith asked a French orderly for a cauterizing iron, and by the light of lamps brought close he burned deeply into the wood the name and the date. Then they placed the dead man's pith helmet, holster, and pistol, on the coffin where he lay in his uniform, covered them again with the flag, stood back, and saluted.

On the *Grantully Castle*, Colonel Quilter, Myburgh (second in command of the Hood) and a party of about twelve officers of the Battalion climbed into a boat, and then a steam pinnace from the *Dartmouth* with General Paris and some of his Divisonal staff aboard, came alongside and took them in tow to the *Duguay-Trouin*. There the crew presented arms and the coffin was taken aboard Quilter's boat, and a further boat of Frenchmen was added to the tow, and they all made for the shore, with their lights bobbing on the water, like a festal procession.

Twelve bearers, petty officers of the Hood, mostly Australians, and a guard of honour commanded by Shaw-Stewart, were drawn up on the quay. The moon was clouded, the way up the water-course (that would be a torrent in winter) was rough with loose rocks and stones, and men with lamps had to be posted every twenty yards of the way inland to the rendezvous. It took the bearers just under two hours to negotiate a distance of less than a mile. Shortly before eleven o'clock, Lister and Asquith saw a man with a lantern coming slowly up the gorge. Behind him walked Platoon-Sergeant Saunders of No. 4 Platoon, holding aloft a big, roughly put together cross painted white, and along the cross-beam, painted in black, the name of the man they were burying; then came Shaw-Stewart with drawn sword, leading the firing party, then the bearers with the coffin, and General Paris walking behind it.

When Asquith saw the coffin, he asked for a spade and jumped into the grave and lengthened it a little, and he found it all lined with sprigs of olive and flowering sage. When all was ready and the men assembled, Quilter threw in a wreath of olive. The moon remained clouded, and a slight breeze got up, stirring the foliage, as the Chaplain read the burial service of the Church of England. Brooke, surely, would not have scorned to receive the same obsequies as Swinburne. 'The scent of wild sage,' Kelly remarked in his journal, 'gave a strong classical tone, which was so in harmony with the poet we were burying that to some of us the Christian ceremony seemed out of keeping.' Three volleys were fired into the air, Shaw-Stewart presented arms. 'It is strange,' he wrote, 'to think I had been wondering if I should ever use my sword!' The hills reverberated, and startled goats were heard jingling away. 'One was transported back a couple of thousand years,' wrote Kelly, 'and one felt the old Greek divinities stirring from their long sleep.' Then the Last Post.

The parade broke up and they found their way down to the shore, while Freyberg, Kelly, Asquith, Lister, and Browne stayed behind and gathered lumps of the pink and white marble from round about and heaped them into a cairn over the grave. At the foot was a small white cross, three struts nailed together, given by the platoon, and while the rocks were being piled up, the Greek Interpreter (a man picked up by Asquith in Lemnos) inscribed an epitaph in pencil on the back of the larger cross, which by now was driven into the ground at the head. He wrote in his own language:

> ἐνθάδε κεῖται
> ὁ δουλος τοῦ Θεοῦ
> ἀνθυπολοχ αγος τοῦ
> Ἀγγλικοῦ ναυτικοῦ
> ᾽αποθανὼν ῾υπερ τῆς
> ᾽απελευθερώςεως τῦς
> κων · πούλεως ᾽από
> ,τῶν τουρκων [1]

> Here lies
> the servant of God
> Sub-lieutenant in the
> English Navy
> Who died for the
> deliverance of Constantinople from
> the Turks

SAILING TO BYZANTIUM

An epitaph in Greek, and a cairn on the island of Achilles, for the pupil of Walter Headlam, and the Fellow of King's. In a letter to a chance acquaintance met in his wanderings abroad he had written a postscript—'Anyway, King's College, Cambridge, is my address, whatever part of the world I'm in.'

So the survivors of the Latin Table accomplished their task. The chunks of pink and white marble lay heaped in a long tumulus. 'I don't (as you know) set much store by what happens to me or anyone else after my death,' wrote Shaw-Stewart as he watched the bombardment on Gallipoli next day, 'but even I am fired by the extraordinary beauty and aptitude of his grave.' Always more fatalist than the others, he was dimly aware, even then, that he had assisted at the burial of one who had become the symbol of his generation, and Kelly ended the entry in his journal, 'It was as though one were involved in the origin of some classical myth.' As they walked away, one of them said, 'He has it all to himself, except for a few shepherds.'

The steam pinnace was waiting for them at the jetty. Not until they were half-way back to the *Grantully Castle* did Asquith suddenly realize that his birthday had come and gone. Within a few hours they would be sailing up the narrows of the Dardanelles. There was no time to waste. Kelly and Denis Browne went into Brooke's cabin and were sorting and packing all night, and Kelly did not omit to keep his journal up to date. 'For the whole day I was oppressed with the sense of loss, but when the officers and men had gone, and when at last the five of us, his friends, had covered his grave with stones and took a last look in silence—then the sense of tragedy gave place to a sense of passionless beauty . . .' Then, copying the note-book, lest it should be lost on the way to England, it must have seemed as if the man he had left behind on Skyros, foreseeing the event, had himself found words to describe the thoughts of his friends at midnight as they walked away, and written them where they would soon be found.

> He wears
> The ungathered blossom of quiet; stiller he
> Than a deep well at noon, or lovers met;
> Than sleep, or the heart after wrath. He is
> The silence following great words of peace.

Four hours later, at dawn, the *Grantully Castle* was heading for Gallipoli.

Chapter XIV

MAN INTO MARBLE

Kelly and Browne worked fast in the cabin. With devoted care each made a copy of the black note-book containing fragments of verse, drew up an inventory of nine items in the haversack, and sorted the other things into twenty-two envelopes. They found £11. 10s. 0d. in gold pieces, a compass which they gave to Lister, a silver watch, a crystal box, a red amber cigarette holder, and the empty green frame for a locket which he had been wearing round his neck with the identity disc. All this they packed up for Rugby with his clothes, and on the top they placed a letter written by Rupert for despatch to his mother in the event of his death.

Meanwhile Saunders wrote on behalf of No. 4 Platoon, and Colonel Quilter spoke for the Battalion, saying, 'He died for his country. There is no nobler end. Believe me'—shortly before dying for his country himself. He fell in June, as also, in circumstances of conspicuous gallantry, did Denis Browne; Lister died of wounds that autumn; Shaw-Stewart (Welsh Ridge 1917) and Kelly (Beaumont-Hamel 1916) survived another year or two. By the end of June the Hood Battalion alone had lost eleven of its fifteen officers. Brooke was the first Fellow of a Cambridge College to give his life, but already there were heavy losses among his contemporaries. On the day his loss was reported in the *Cambridge Review* his name was only one of sixty-six dead and forty-two wounded. It was the beginning of the end of a generation. Only two of the five men who had heaped the cairn on Skyros lived to see the Armistice: Brigadier-General Arthur Asquith, D.S.O. and Major-General Sir Bernard Freyberg, K.C.B., V.C., D.S.O.

Sooner or later, the national mind, bewildered and striving by whatever means to prevent such a calamity from becoming altogether inconceivable, would have found some focal point or other to represent the magnitude of its loss. But now, on the eve of an historic and bloody campaign, when in any case the world was watching, one man died quietly in his bed, a young poet so eloquent of the hour, that it

514

seemed almost inevitable that Death should single him out as the first instalment of a holocaust. When Henry James was told of the news he merely lowered his head, saying, 'Of course, of course,' and then he wept.

On April 26, *The Times* published an unsigned obituary of a few lines. Written by Marsh, it ended, 'He died before he had fulfilled his own hopes or ours; but either we believe in waste altogether or not at all. And if any seeming waste is not waste, there is none in a young life full of promise and joyfully laid down.' Since all communications with London had to come through the C-in-C in Mudros Bay, for several days it was assumed that the death had occurred at Lemnos, and so it was announced. Marsh's few sentences were only a preface to a valediction published over the initials of the First Lord of the Admiralty. Written at a critical moment in the operations, when the first reports of the Gallipoli landing were hourly expected, the generosity of spirit informing every line began the process of transferring the memory of Brooke from the private to the national plane.

Rupert Brooke is dead. A telegram from the Admiralty at Lemnos tells us that this life has closed at the moment when it seemed to have reached its springtime. A voice had become audible, a note had been struck, more true, more thrilling, more able to do justice to the nobility of our youth in arms engaged in this present war, than any other—more able to express their thoughts of self-surrender, and with a power to carry comfort to those who watched them so intently from afar. The voice has been swiftly stilled. Only the echoes and the memory remain; but they will linger.

During the last few months of his life, months of preparation in gallant comradeship and open air, the poet-soldier told with all the simple force of genius the sorrow of youth about to die, and the sure triumphant consolations of a sincere and valiant spirit. He expected to die; he was willing to die for the dear England whose beauty and majesty he knew; and he advanced towards the brink in perfect serenity, with absolute conviction of the rightness of his country's cause, and a heart devoid of hate for fellow-men.

The thoughts to which he gave expression in the very few incomparable war sonnets which he has left behind will be shared by many thousands of young men moving resolutely and blithely forward into this, the hardest, the cruellest, and the least-rewarded of all the wars that men have fought. They are a whole history and revelation of Rupert Brooke himself. Joyous, fearless, versatile, deeply instructed, with classic symmetry of mind and body, he was all that one would wish England's noblest sons to be in days when no sacrifice but the most precious is acceptable, and the most precious is that which is most freely proffered.

We watch glimpses of the shock which followed this sombre pronouncement: Henry James writing to Marsh, 'If there was a stupid and hideous disfigurement of life and outrage to beauty left for our awful conditions to perpetrate, these things have been now supremely achieved, and no other brutal blow in the private sphere can better them for making one just stare through one's tears . . . What a price and a refinement of beauty and poetry it gives those splendid sonnets—which will enrich our whole collective consciousness'; Maynard Keynes to Duncan Grant, 'In spite of all we have ever said, I find myself crying for him'; and D. H. Lawrence, disgusted with the war, discovering that the shock of Brooke's death only filled him 'more and more with the sense of the fatuity of it all'. He wrote to Ottoline Morrell:

> He was slain by bright Phoebus' shaft—it was in keeping with his general sunniness—it was the real climax of his pose. I first heard of him as a Greek god under a Japanese sunshade, reading poetry in his pyjamas at Grantchester—at Grantchester upon the lawns where the river goes. Bright Phoebus smote him down. It is all in the saga.
> O God, O God, it is all too much of a piece: it is like madness.[1]

The myth-making tendency of a race in anguish, having found its object, was thoroughly astir. In the *Cambridge Review*, five days after the *Times* announcement, Gilbert Murray, deploring the loss to the University, wrote, 'I cannot help thinking that Rupert Brooke will probably live in fame as an almost mythical figure.' The *Sphere* (May 3) declared that Brooke was 'the only English poet of any consideration who has given his life in his country's wars since Philip Sidney received his death wound under the walls of Zutphen in 1586'; an anonymous contributor to the *Daily News* said, 'To look at he was a part of the youth of the world,' and so it went on, gathering momentum. Tributes and proud homilies were appearing everywhere. 'He is the youth of our race in symbol,' said the *Star*. 'The passion in his words is in all our soldiers from the very bottom of the social pyramid to the very top.' Memorial verses of good intent but gruelling sentimentality proliferated in the press. The editor of the *Nation* seems to have been driven distracted. 'I should be afraid to say,' he wrote in his editorial, 'how many poems commemorative of R.B. I have received since his untimely death.' Elegies appeared on all sides, and even a morsel beginning, 'If *you* should die, think only this of me,' somehow found its way into print, beyond which good-natured vulgarity could hardly go. On May 8 de la Mare wrote in the *Westminster Gazette*, 'But once in a way Nature is as jealous of the

---

[1] D.H.L. to Lady Ottoline Morrell, April 30, 1915.

individual as of the type. She gave Rupert Brooke youth, and may be, in these hyper-enlightened days, in doing so grafted a legend.'

Meanwhile the men of the Hood, acquitting themselves with superlative courage, were engaged on sterner business. However, just before the landing, General Paris was obliged to send a memorandum to the British minister for foreign affairs at Athens, explaining why a man of his unit had to be buried on shore. The grove of twelve olive trees, it turned out, was a spot called Mesadhi, the property of a Greek shepherd named Aristides Psairiotis.

On May 18, while another myth was coming into being along with those of Sidney and Byron, and Brooke's especial friends were beginning to grow inured to the hard fact which at first had seemed incredible, the packages from the *Grantully Castle*, now anchored off Gallipoli, arrived in England. For several weeks, Mrs. Brooke could not bring herself to open the box of clothes, but she read the letter. It was dated March 9, approaching Malta. All monies after his debts were paid were to go to the three men whom he now named as his heirs: Wilfrid Gibson, Lascelles Abercrombie, and Walter de la Mare. The capital of his allowance from her was to be distributed among them, and at her death she was asked 'to leave some of the money you would have left to me, to these three'. His reason was—'If I can set them free, to any extent, to write the poetry and plays and books they want to, my death will bring more gain than loss.' He then appointed Edward Marsh as his literary executor. He was to have the manuscripts after her death, 'unless Ka Cox would like some'. Eventually Ka was to have any other papers of his. He specified certain smaller bequests, among them a green jade ornament (for Dudley), an Easter Island image (for Jacques), a Gill stone statue (for Cathleen), and he ended, 'I'm very sorry for you. Be brave. You've always been very good to me. I think of you all the time. With love. Rupert.' In a postscript he put his last injunction—'Be kind to Katharine Cox.'

A separate note arrived for Ka herself, written the following day.

Dear child,

I suppose you're about the best I can do in the way of a widow. I'm telling the Ranee that after she's dead, you're to have my papers. They *may* want to write a biography! How am I to know if I shan't be eminent? And take any MSS you want. Say what you like to the Ranee. But you'd probably better not tell her much. Let her be. Let her think we might have married. Perhaps it's true.

My dear, my dear, you did me wrong: but I have done you very great wrong. Every day I see it greater.

You were the best thing I found in life. If I have memory, I shall remember. You know what I want for you. I hope you will be happy, and marry and have children.

It is a good thing I die.

Good-bye, child,
RUPERT

A week had passed before he wrote the letter which Dudley Ward now received. It was the day before the 'demonstration' off Gallipoli. 'You'll already have done a few jobs for me,' it began. 'Here are some more.' He repeated some of the instructions made to the Ranee; certain groups of letters were to be destroyed. 'If other people, Ka, for instance, agitate to have letters destroyed, why, you're the person to do it. I don't much care what goes.' It went on:

Indeed, why keep anything? Well, I *might* turn out to be eminent and biographiable. If so, let them know the poor truths. Rather pathetic this.

It's odd, being dead. I'm afraid it'll finish off the Ranee. What else is there? Eddie will be my literary executor. So you'll have to confer with him.

Be good to Ka.

Give Jacques and Gwen my love.

Try to inform Taata of my death. Mlle Taata, Hotel Tiare, Papeete, Tahiti. It might find her. Give her my love.

My style is rather like St. Paul's. You'll have to give the Ranee a hand about me: because she knows so little about great parts of my life. There are figures might want books or something of mine. Noel and her sisters, Justin, Geoffrey, Hugh Russell-Smith. How could she distinguish among them? . . . Their names make me pleasantly melancholy.

But the realization of failure makes me *unpleasantly* melancholy. Enough.

Good luck and all love to you and Anne.

Call a boy after me.

The message for Raverat was the shortest and earliest in date, written off Gibraltar.

My dear, I turn to you. Keep innumerable flags flying. I've only two decent reasons for being sorry for dying (several against)—I want to destroy some evils and cherish some goods. Do it for me. You understand. I doubt if anyone else does, almost.

He wrote to Marsh at the same time as he prepared the instructions for the Ranee. 'This is very odd,' it began. 'But I suppose I must imagine my non-existence, and make a few arrangements. You are to be my literary executor.' Once again he duplicated certain points made to his mother, only adding Alfred's name as someone who could have a few manuscripts, if he happened to want them.

If you want to go through my papers, Dudley Ward'll give you a hand. But you won't find much there. There may be some old stuff at Grantchester.

You must decide everything about publication. Don't print much bad stuff.

Give my love to the New Numbers folk, and Violet and Masefield and a few who'd like it. I've tried to arrange that some money should go to Wilfrid and Lascelles and de la Mare (John[1] is childless) to help them write good stuff, instead of me.

There's nothing much to say. You'll be able to help the Ranee with one or two arrangements.

You've been very good to me. I wish I'd written more. I've been such a failure.

Best love and goodbye

RUPERT

Get Cathleen anything she wants.

To Cathleen herself he wrote, 'Thank God I met you. Be happy and be good.'

While Marsh was preparing the volume *1914 and Other Poems* for publication by Frank Sidgwick, Mrs. Brooke set in order her son's affairs. She found an overdraft at his Cambridge bank of about £300, and he was still owing some rent to Mrs. Neeve at the Old Vicarage; but his assets of one kind or another were such that when all debts were settled there was money in hand for distribution to his three heirs. Each received £166. 19s. 8d. as the first instalment of an inheritance that was materially to affect their lives, so considerable were the royalties on the poems throughout the years to come. Luckily these initial transactions on behalf of the creditors and the three poets were all in order by June 18 when Mrs. Brooke could do no more. She heard that on June 14 while acting as Reserve Machine-gun Officer at Vermelles in France, Alfred was killed by a mortar bomb.

After the first fortnight of elegies and newspaper articles, some of Brooke's closer friends began to fear the reality they had known might be lost and forgotten altogether if they did nothing to protest. At Cambridge there was something of a controversy. The first to make himself heard was E. J. Dent in *The Cambridge Magazine* (May 8), where at the end of a long article he complained, 'It is

---

[1] This probably refers to John Drinkwater.

grotesquely tragic—what a characteristic satire he would have
written on it himself—that he should have died (at Lemnos too!) just
after a sudden and rather factitious celebrity had been obtained by a
few poems which, beautiful as they are in technique and expression,
represented him in a phase that could only have been temporary. No
Englishman can ever quite eradicate the national tendency to romanticism, just as there is, according to Romain Rolland, an essential
Massenet that slumbers in the heart of every true Frenchman. In the
first shock of the moment that romanticism he so hated came upper-
most.' John Sheppard in *The Cambridge Review* was more moderate in
his complaint. 'Though it is not easy, we owe it to him not to comfort
ourselves by letting our thoughts dwell on a mythical being who was
not Rupert, and whose loss is therefore the easier to bear.' Harold
Monro, however (*Cambridge Magazine*, May 22), bitterly resented
Brooke being 'advertised' as the soldier-poet. 'One fears his memory
being brought to the poster-grade. "He did his duty. Will You do
yours?" is hardly the moral to be drawn . . . Few people trouble to
know much about poetry—but everyone takes an intelligent interest
in death. It is something definite to understand about a poet, that he
is dead . . . His whole poetry is full of the repudiation of sentimentalism. His death was not more lovely than his life.' Monro also made
a shrewd critical point, saying that to a great extent Brooke's volume
of work was 'a collection of intellectual jokes . . . English people
attach levity to the word . . . A good joke is after all more stimulating
than the best Piece of Advice'. This needed to be said, as also that
Brooke was apt to be 'stimulated to write by the oddness rather than
the intensity of an idea'. But this, of course, could not be applied to
the sonnets. It almost seemed as if they had been written by somebody
else.

On June 16, *1914 and Other Poems*, containing the poems from the
South Seas, was published. Here at last was the best of the more
characteristic work—by a poet unfamiliar to readers who had in-
ferred an image solely from the sonnets. The *New Statesman* put it
plainly. 'A myth has been created: but it has grown round an imaginary figure very different from the real man.' Although readers of the
evening papers were as familiar with the sonnets as with Hamlet's
soliloquy, uncritical admiration was laying them open to more objective comment, and now—here were the poems from Tahiti. 'Some of
the Deans and great-aunts,' wrote the *New Statesman*, 'who picture
Brooke as a kind of blend of General Gordon and Lord Tennyson will

have a jolt when they read the poem on the theology of fishes.' At the same time Gwen Raverat in a letter to Stanley Spencer, was protesting that the numerous articles she had seen 'might have been written about King David, or Lord Byron, or Sophocles, or any other young man that wrote verse and was good-looking . . . they never got the faintest feeling of his being a human being at all. I wonder if we are all as vague as that to our fellow creatures.' All along there had been a curious lack of personal reminiscence. At the end of July a writer in the *Academy* summed up, 'It may well be, as more than one writer has suggested, that in the future he will live as a mythical figure, a legend almost, to which two slender volumes are the only key.'

These protests at Cambridge and elsewhere were as futile and unavailing as a few brickbats thrown in to block the progress of Niagara, for the force they opposed was the national mind fulfilling a nation's desperate need. Normally it requires considerable effort of the sympathetic imagination for any reader to adjust his mind closely enough to a poet's point of view for a real understanding of his poem. But in early 1915 there were tens of thousands of readers, inarticulate themselves, already emotionally conditioned by the times into thinking and feeling alike. Confronted by the sonnets they experienced that agreeable surprise of 'recognition' which so often only belongs to the sophisticated reader in perfect accord with his author. They caught themselves out, as it were, actually responding to a poem, a thing undreamt of, and indeed it would probably never happen to them again. Unwittingly, Brooke had achieved *his* part of this phenomenon, abnormal circumstances assisting, and nothing his pre-war friends could exclaim in protest would alter the fact. So they had to stand by while their Socialist agitator and advocate of the unrefined Elizabethans became the idol of what one would now call the Establishment. It was galling for them to watch ikons being set up to an iconoclast. Of course the Ranee was the last person to share the opposition's point of view. By devious ways Rupert had returned to the man he was born to be. She had lost Rupert, first to the aesthetes, then to the Fabians, then to some obscure emotional distemper, and finally to what she regarded as the 'smart set' in London. Having seen him come back to the fold of conformity at the eleventh hour and win acclamation, she was not minded to let him go again. So the trouble-makers not only failed, they defeated their own purpose, for E. J. Dent's article in particular, which in places was certainly ill-judged, only succeeded in putting the Ranee on her guard against anyone who tried to confuse the grand simplicity of her son's public image with the addition of so-called 'human' attributes. During the summer, having set out to compile a Memoir, Marsh was perplexed to discover that his subject's own parent was much less concerned for the success of the enterprise than he was himself.

It was mid-June when Ka faced going back again to Cambridge, and stayed with the Cornfords at Conduit Head. The Raverats were there too. 'Rupert was quite right as to the effect his death would have on her,' Mrs. Cornford remarked in her notes. 'There was something calm in her deep down, as there had not been for so long.' They all talked of him without the least constraint, exchanging reminiscences, laughing. But one evening Ka entered Mrs. Cornford's room as she was going to bed, 'and cried very bitterly and quietly and said, "You don't know what it is for me, who made him suffer so, when you all only gave him happiness!" I said, "But then you gave him infinitely more than us, who were only friends. If you gave him pain, you gave him far greater happiness too." I prayed it was true.' Ka then showed Frances the farewell note, drawing her attention to the passage beginning 'You were the best thing I found in life', and Frances commented in her journal—'Was this the real truth? He was so determined to leave her every scrap of comfort he could. But indeed I believe it was true. Anyway it was everything to her.' And it would have meant no less to Brooke, could he have seen the next four years go by and Ka become a wife and the mother of a son. 'And I knew quite clearly,' Mrs. Cornford wrote, 'that Rupert thought his death worth while for that alone.' Writing to Maynard Keynes of this same harsh thread in Brooke's life history, Jacques Raverat affirmed, 'I still really think that he died of it, in a way.'

Throughout July all kinds of memorials were contemplated: a bust in the Poets' Corner at Westminster; a symposium of essays, 'just a throwing of our pens into the grave as they did for Spenser,' as Masefield suggested; these had some point, but there were others, and the proposal that the clock at Grantchester should be permanently fixed at ten to three was the silliest. At length old Whitelaw was the first to moot a practicable scheme, a plaque in Rugby Chapel. In February 1916 a committee was formed, which included F. M. Cornford, Marsh, Whitelaw, and the Headmaster; a leaflet was printed and *The Times* announced the project, inviting subscriptions to be sent to Bilton Road. The frontispiece to the recent '1914' volume (Schell's photograph in profile) was to be used as a model for the sculptor Havard Thomas and Eric Gill was engaged to cut the lettering, including the popular fifth sonnet, on a slab beneath the portrait medallion.

In April President Hadley of Yale University wrote to Mrs. Brooke, telling her that her son had been awarded the Howland Prize, and Charles Howland himself, one of the American subscribers to *New Numbers*, gave her the utmost pleasure, by telling her of America's pride in the 'possession of him jointly with Englishmen as one of the Masters of Song in our common tongue, and indeed that he typifies the nobility of sacrifice for a cause that is ours as well as yours'. Nothing gave her such renewal of heart as this gesture of friendship from the United States, not even the Henry James preface to *Letters from America* which had come out the month before. It was the last work of his life, and the grandest of all Brooke's memorials.

In the course of a magnificently convoluted essay, James explained how he saw his subject as 'an unprecedented image, formed to resist erosion by time or vulgarization by reference', and he maintained that 'With twenty reasons fixing the interest and the charm that will henceforth abide in his name and constitute, as we say, his legend, he submits all helplessly to one in particular . . . While he is still in the highest degree of the distinguished faculty and quality, we happen to feel him even more markedly and significantly "modern".' Byron, he said, quarrelled with the temper and accent of his age. To modern eyes he was 'comparatively plated over with the impenetrable rococo of his own day'. Yet he stood apart, 'hugged his pomp', whereas Brooke, though something of a rebel too, accepted so much, taking 'for *his* own the whole of the poetic consciousness he was born to, and moved about in it as a stripped young swimmer might have kept splashing through blue water and coming up at any point that friendliness and fancy, with every prejudice shed, might determine. Rupert expressed us *all*, at the highest tide of our actuality.' In various ways Henry James bore witness to the natural poet. 'No young man had ever so naturally taken on under the pressure of life the poetic nature, and shaken it so free of every encumbrance by simply wearing it as he wore his complexion or his outline.' At least half the value of Brooke's existence, even the half of his poetical value, James argued, was impossible to convey to after ages, since it was manifested 'by the simple act of presence and communication'; and he accounted for the universal acceptance of the popular image in these terms: 'What it first and foremost really comes to . . . is the fact that at an hour when the civilized peoples are on exhibition, quite finally and sharply on show, as they absolutely never in all their long history have been before, the English tradition . . . should have flowered at once into a specimen so beautifully producible.'[1]

It remains the most impressive summary of the effect on the public mind made by the news from Skyros, but in places the mannered coils of gloriously serpentine prose are difficult to follow. Next in importance among the more sober articles, and a good deal more accommodating in style, was the essay by Walter de la Mare in Brooke's own journal, the *Westminster Gazette* (May 8, 1915). Here, corresponding with 'the simple act of presence' which, according to James, posterity would inevitably miss, we find de la Mare's 'He was himself the happiest, most complex, and characteristic of his poems'; and de la Mare pointed out the contrast between the exceptional individual and the relative homeliness of the material he used. 'The vast majority of people are just such workaday creatures as ourselves . . . With him there was that happy shining impression that he might have come—that very moment—from another planet.' But against this 'perhaps no English poet—though all share in the sensuous exaltation—has been so possessed not by the beauty, the endearingness, the symbolism, but the sudden flowering miracle of the ordinary'.

In June the *English Review* published the portrait sketch by Edward Thomas that has already been quoted in part. He testified to the excitement caused by Brooke's audacious appearance on the modern literary scene. 'No poet of his age was so much esteemed and admired, or was watched more hopefully. His work could not be taken soberly, whether you liked it or not . . .' Though he possessed all of the Shelleyan eagerness and the despair, said Thomas, he did not attain the Shelleyan altitude, but 'perhaps no poet better expressed the aspiration towards it and all the unfulfilled eagerness of ambitious self-conscious youth . . . He stands out clearly against that immense dark background, an Apollo not afraid of the worst of life.'

By 1917 the portrait medallion was finished in Chelsea, approved, and sent to Bilton Road where Mrs. Brooke propped it up in the hall. It was reproduced in magazines, and the unveiling became a widely anticipated event. Early in the year *The Times* announced a postponement of the ceremony owing to the Government's wish that the

[1] *Letters from America*. Sidgwick & Jackson. 1916.

railways be kept clear of avoidable travel. A year later the plaque
was still unconsecrated, but it was removed from Bilton Road and set
up in its place. The opposition deplored it, of course, calling it 'a
worthless sentimentalized plaque with an outstretched neck'. If not
true to their idea, it was true enough to something else of importance.
It was the living image of the youth the Ranee had known, lost for a
while, and regained at the last moment. 'I think the mouth is beautiful,' she wrote to Marsh, after first seeing it affixed to the wall, 'also
the general expression and the appearance of pressing forward.
Looking at it was almost too much for me, and I was glad when it
went; it brought what he was back more than any photograph . . .
The fact of it being so very unlike in style to the various bishops in
the Chapel is quite what his ought to be!'

At the end of July, 1918, the *Collected Poems* appeared with a
Memoir by Edward Marsh which soon became renowned. There was
widespread curiosity which it satisfied, and the task was elegantly
done. But appearing at a time when the proper aim of a biography was
still regarded as the memorial of a public reputation rather than the
portrait of a private individual, and being, perforce, a compromise
with all the complexity and suffering smoothed away, it gave an incomplete impression. The *Cambridge Review* declared 'A legend has
been endorsed. This life slips by like a panorama of earth's loveliest
experiences'; the *Oxford Magazine* accounted for Brooke's apparent
slowness to mature by declaring 'He seems to have missed the up-
lifting education that the passion of love would have afforded him';
and Holbrook Jackson in *Today* saw Brooke as the Joy of Life personified. 'There is really nothing to tell of his life but his enjoyment
of it.'

Mrs. Brooke, who herself thought the central figure 'somewhat
attenuated', missed the element of moral sternness, which she knew so
well should be there. Others missed other traits, but there was no
such outcry as there had been in May, 1915. The Memoir, composed
under stress, was an act of love which largely silenced criticism. The
one protest of any substance was couched in subdued terms, but it
carried the weight of authority. From internal evidence which is un-
mistakable the anonymous essay in *The Times Literary Supplement* of
August 8 was the work of Virginia Woolf. After defining the limita-
tions of the Memoir, she told how Brooke was 'consciously and
defiantly pagan' and an originator, 'one of those leaders who
spring up from time to time and show their power most clearly by

subjugating their own generation. Under his influence the country near Cambridge was full of young men and women walking barefoot, sharing his passion for bathing and fish diet . . . He had read everything and he had read it from the point of view of a working writer.' Mrs. Woolf was concerned to establish Brooke's professional seriousness of purpose.

In discussing the work of living writers he gave you the impression that he had the poem or the story before his eyes in a concrete shape, and his judgements were not only very definite but had a freedom and a reality which mark the criticism of those who are themselves working in the same art. You felt that to him literature was not dead nor of the past, but a thing now in process of construction by people many of whom were his friends; and that knowledge, skill, and, above all, unceasing hard work were required of those who attempt to make it. To work hard, much harder than most writers think it necessary, was an injunction of his that remains in memory from a chaos of such discussions.

To support this argument there was the scholarly dissertation on John Webster which was already in print among the posthumous volumes that Marsh had seen through the press, but now the Memoir, reissued separately from the poems, was itself a best-seller, and the long deferred unveiling of the medallion came back into the news.

The celebrations began on March 27, 1919. In the evening de la Mare delivered a lecture in the hall where Brooke had once given his schoolboy talk on the modern poets. Next day Mrs. Brooke gave a luncheon at her home. Dudley and Ka were in Paris; Jacques was an invalid; so Geoffrey Keynes and his wife (the Margaret Darwin of an earlier page) represented the Cambridge friends, and Colonel Freyberg, formerly commanding Brooke's A Company of the Hood, stood for the comrades of the *Grantully Castle*. De la Mare, Gibson, and Abercrombie, the three heirs, were present with their wives; Denis Browne's mother was escorted by Marsh; and the guest of honour was Sir Ian Hamilton who had come to unveil the plaque. De la Mare, seated beside Mrs. Keynes at table, asked her if she would ever have guessed, had she not known, what Abercrombie was. '*I* thought,' she wrote afterwards to a relative, 'he looked much more like a poet than the other two.' The Ranee made Geoffrey sit at the head of the table and carve the chicken, treating him like a son; the C-in-C of the Gallipoli campaign, an unlikely figure in Bilton Road, was in genial vein, and as for the hostess, the letter from Margaret Keynes gives a glimpse of her on her great day.

Mrs. Brooke was very wonderful. It was such a relief to find her so entirely free from the faintest hint of sentimentality. No one had to drop their voices or feel intrusive. She talked about Rupert and Alfred perfectly naturally. Her vitality is simply amazing: she really did thoroughly enjoy having a houseful. She was on the go the whole time, talking hard and obviously liking it all and keeping Rupert as he really was in her mind and not letting the legendary Rupert intrude. Geoffrey and I both felt the actual ceremony in the chapel and the concert afterwards had absolutely no relation to Rupert at all. It was someone else they were commemorating.

After the luncheon Sir Ian spoke at the unveiling. 'His personality? Let me say this of it: I have seen famous men and brilliant figures in my day, but never one so thrilling, so vital as that of our hero. Like a prince he would enter a room, like a prince quite unconscious of his own royalty, and by that mere act put a spell upon everyone around him . . .' Then Mrs. Brooke was hostess of several hundreds to tea in New Big School. A concert followed in the Temple Speech Room. It included the first performance of an Elegy for strings by F. S. Kelly who had begun its composition on the *Grantully Castle* while Brooke lay dying, and there were choral settings of the sonnets by Sidney Nicholson, organist of Westminster Abbey. 'It seemed impossible that neither of the boys could be there,' the Ranee wrote to Marsh next day. 'I longed so very much for Alfred in the Chapel to stand with me.'

Mrs. Brooke had always been rather concerned about the loose boulders heaped on the grave, and as early as 1916 she was considering alternative designs for something more appropriate. She was handling this project on her own, and before the Armistice she had approved a sketch of 'medieval design adapted to Greek surroundings' (no mean adaptation) complete with measurements and angles of blameless precision but melancholy import—a tomb-stone of the horizontal slab variety set within a rectangle of what Keats has called 'black purgatorial rails' to shield it from the nuisance of defiling goats. This orthodox device of bland Pentelican marble was duly manufactured, conveyed to the island when the seas were safe, and then another ceremony took place on Skyros. The stones were scattered and the two wooden crosses brought back to Rugby. The slab lay incongruous in their place. Fortunately its Gothic trespass cannot supplant in the mind the image of a prehistoric cairn.

The sales of the poems, helped by the Memoir, were beginning to challenge the records set up by the publishers of Tennyson and Byron, and these were given yet further impetus in April, 1925, when another memorial was unveiled with one of the sonnets inscribed, dedicated this time in Horse Guards Parade to the honour of the R.N.D. and the speech by Winston Churchill included a tribute to the '1914' series of poems. 'We meet his verses everywhere. They are quoted again and again. They are printed on newspaper, written in books, blotted by tears, and carved in stone. But they belong to us, to the Royal Naval Division.' His words were literally true. The suffering pagan who was also this champion of the Rights of Man was receding almost beyond recall.

But that was not the end of the memorials engendered by the sonnets. During the late twenties a Belgian philanthropist, his motives again as flawless as the marble of the medieval tomb, launched an appeal with the result that in April, 1931, a statue was unveiled on the little hill overlooking Skyros town. To honour the memory of Brooke, the Sculptor Tombros prudently made no attempt to reproduce a likeness, but wrought in bronze the nude figure of a young man symbolizing Youth. Yet again there were mixed opinions. Someone for instance, was put in mind of a poster advertising an embrocation for the relief of rheumatism. Except to make the point in passing, it were ungracious now to be critical of a tribute for missing the mark it was never aimed at. Brooke had become an abstraction.

Early in 1930, in the last year of her life, Mrs. Brooke confessed in a letter to Marsh, 'I can't tell you what I feel when I read of these young men who were his contemporaries going ahead as they do. The one thing that consoles me is Sidgwick's half-yearly account of the sale of his works.' The three heirs were being materially blessed beyond their benefactor's dreams. The statement she was referring to had been coming to her over the last four years, and the first of them had included a summary of the past sales. 'The grand total to the end of 1926,' Mr. Sidgwick wrote, 'is 291,998', but if one had included the cheap edition of the war sonnets sold at 6d. then '300,000 is not picturesque (and then there is America).' This was only the opening chapter of a commercial record and the only one the Ranee lived to see for consolation.

II

As the years passed there was much speculation as to what would have happened if Brooke had lived. E. M. Forster was not sure he would have increased his reputation as a poet. He would certainly have become 'a live wire in public affairs and an energetic and enlightened administrator. He had the necessary mixture of toughness and idealism.' Virginia Woolf thought much the same. She knew of people who had returned Brooke's manifest disapproval. 'In fact Bloomsbury was against him and he against them,' she wrote to Gwen Raverat in 1925.

Meanwhile I had a private version of him which I stuck to when they all cried him down and still preserve somewhere infinitely far away—but how these feelings last, how they come over one, oddly, at unexpected moments —based on my week at Grantchester, when he was all that could be kind and interesting, substantial and good-hearted. (I choose these words without thinking whether they correspond to what he was to you or anybody.) He was, I thought, the ablest of the young men; I didn't think then much of his poetry, which he read aloud on the lawn, but I thought he would be Prime Minister, because he had such a gift with people, and such sanity and force; I remember a weakly pair of lovers meandering in one day, just engaged, very floppy. You know how intense and silly and offhand in a self-conscious way the Cambridge young then were about their loves—Rupert simplified them, and broadened them, humanized them. And then he rode off on a bicycle about a railway strike. My idea was that he was to be a member of Parliament and edit the classics, a very powerful, ambitious man, but not a poet.

She did not share the popular view of the war poems, recalling that they had seemed to her mere 'barrel-organ music', while the earlier pieces 'were all adjectives and contortions, weren't they?'

What did she mean by contortions? By an odd coincidence, one of those lovers whom Mrs. Woolf describes as meandering into the Old Vicarage when she was staying there, was A. Y. Campbell, who had played the Elder Brother in *Comus*, himself a poet with a turn of wit, and there exists a parody of his on Brooke's early manner which illustrates Mrs. Woolf's point. The parody called *The Voice*, was preserved among Brooke's papers. He evidently enjoyed it. 'With festering hearts that yearn for shadowy night,' it begins, 'We will creep out, a very little way.' It transpires that 'they' hope to reach a wan land far from the cruel day. 'God will be there, of course, and tedious Time, And pale Eternity, that long long thing . . .'

> *Occasionally I shall change my tune:*
> *I'll crack the stars, kick God, and splosh the skies.*
> *I'll sing of lute-players Rossetti-wise*
> *Or pull sad faces at the pulpy moon.*

Such was the critical view of some contemporaries, and perhaps in 1925, when Mrs. Woolf was writing her letter, she was too close to her own past, too distracted by the major poetical events around her, to look back and observe how far Brooke in his short span developed and purified his style. By this time a new tradition more proper to the age was gaining ground; pre-war verse, written before Armageddon, seemed even more remote than it was, its concerns uninteresting, its manner dated. Brooke, once such a very 'new-fangled young man', had become un-modern; a movement he was associated with at the start, having lost its first vigour, lay wide open to attack, and the critics who felt in duty bound to discredit it—no very difficult task—succeeded so well that as time passed they went on to accomplish what they never intended. Where the general reader was concerned they confused him and lost him as a poet of any sort whatever. It is easier now to discriminate.

Just as Brooke introduced a new mode of informality among his friends, which gradually spread and became a feature of that general relaxation of manners which the years of war accelerated, so to the poetry of his time he brought a lightness of touch graced by his metaphysical turn of wit. Like the Cavalier poets, he was a man of public affairs with a lyrical gift, and because he was also in some ways what H. W. Garrod has called 'the average nice young man', he won popularity without aiming or even wishing for it, expressing under a guise of levity the deeper emotions of a reticent class. He risked more sentiment than ever they would have dared, but almost invariably he seemed to wear a smile, said little to which the general heart could not easily respond, and by virtue of his wit, succeeded in making poetry out of that light understatement that Englishmen used to reserve for the things they took most seriously. More than anything else, it is this grace of sociability, so natural to Brooke, which makes him seem old-fashioned. The magnanimous view, an evident zeal to win over, communicate, and share, can hardly be said to be characteristic of a modern poet. Perhaps there is good reason, but perhaps, too, it is a loss to poetry.

Brooke's reputation is an untidy one. He would never have been embarrassed with it had he not been a poet, yet it is not for his poetry itself that he is so widely known. He is a writer apt to be 'known' first and read afterwards, the wrong way round for an author of serious pretensions. While still developing, and preoccupied with what we would be able to call a passing phase, had he not himself passed with it, the lot was his to be made a national figure and have greatness thrust upon him. There he remains, fixed in the public mind, caught in the act of making a superb but not very characteristic gesture. His death at once placed his poetical reputation at the farthest remove from that of, say, Housman, whose secure place in literature has always been as tidy as one of his own stanzas. The works of any one man react upon each other, and his life, if in any way conspicuous, reacts upon them all. So Brooke is remembered as the author of the war sonnets, and it is as if one should characterize Wordsworth by *The Happy Warrior*; and the zeal of his less critical admirers has projected on his public image a sentimental gloss. A kind of patina of 'quaintness' has grown over it; but 'quaintness', said Brooke himself, 'which swathes dead books as sentimentality swathes dead people, has little hold on the living.'

'No one that knew him,' wrote Edward Thomas, 'could easily separate him from his poetry.' It may seem at first of small consequence that 'no one ever met him without being sensible that he belonged to the company of the gods', as H. W. Garrod once put it in the course of a lecture at Oxford; yet his comeliness (whether a blessing or a curse) was no less a real factor in the course of his life than if he had been born the heir of a considerable fortune. Thomas was right. One cannot isolate the poems from this adventitious fact, even although we may feel we should. It was the man inseparable from the poems which in the same lecture prompted Garrod to speak of Brooke as 'somehow an unmatched effect in our literature . . . One cannot afford to be cold to the romantic sum of him . . . After all, what an ailing crowd, or what a dull crowd, are most poets!' He goes on to maintain that Brooke was an addition to 'the sum of the world's effects'. So in an effort to evaluate the poems which have been lying around for years, growing hackneyed, we turn and hark back through time, see first the profile of an athlete on a plaque, an anointed runner poised at the ready for some Olympic event in the Elysian fields, and look again, determined to penetrate the marble of a myth. On the further side of a murky fog smelling of cordite, we catch sight of him, stretched out at ease in his Edwardian garden, chewing the end of his pencil on the lawn at Grantchester; and suddenly he jumps to his feet, runs indoors, and is gone again. But he has left behind some poems, and we gather them up, and look them through.

Compiling an anthology of the best sonnets in our literature, an editor would find at least seven of these forty-five sonnets at hand worthy to be considered: War sonnets 4 and 5, *Clouds*, *Psychical Research*, *Haunting*, *Seaside*, and '*Oh! Death will find me*'. For the rest, there are the poems from the South Seas (especially *Heaven*, *Tiare Tahiti*, *Retrospect*, and *The Great Lover*) but also *The Old Vicarage*, *The Fish*, *Thoughts on the Shape of the Human Body*, *The Night Journey*, *The Voice*, *Dust*, *A Letter to a Live Poet*, and *Dining-Room Tea*; these will always be read by those who turn to poetry for pleasure. Brooke exists in literature as a man does in his shoes. He has become a part of the heritage that his young successors at Rugby discover for themselves in the Temple Reading Room, for being young himself, and youth and age his theme, he is eminently accessible to the young. Some of them will remain there, asking no more of poetry, perceiving nothing beyond. The others, whom Brooke himself would most approve, are those who have chanced upon his 'star Lunisequa, steadfastly following the round clear orb of her delight', and responded, discovering their first authentic spark of poetry, and have dimly descried a universe beyond, the land of the major poets; and so they move on, as if following that star, like magi towards a revelation.

There are readers who have recovered from an adolescent 'phase' of Brooke and lived ever afterwards in a state of resentful convalescence. Others, as if riled that he did not live to endure the horrors of the Somme, or have the foresight to see them coming, suppose that he looked at Hell through Georgian-tinted glasses, the victim of a doom of charm he apparently could not escape. Seldom do we find Brooke dispassionately acknowledged as a stage on a personal journey of self-discovery, as in Auden's *Letter to Lord Byron*:

> For gasworks and dried tubers I forsook
> The clock at Grantchester, the English rook,

In October, 1930, a few months after the statue on Skyros was unveiled, Mrs. Brooke died at Rugby. Ka survived her by three and a half years. The Ranee had carried out her son's wishes. Now she was entitled to wishes of her own. Her revoking the appointment of Marsh as literary executor at least did no harm to her son. On the contrary, she simply transferred his affairs from the scholarly hands of an older generation to those of a younger one. Marsh's work was done. Now Sheppard, Ward, Keynes, and de la Mare, became trustees—three of the intimate circle of friends from the halcyon Cambridge days and one representative of the heirs. If Brooke would have deplored her failure to see eye to eye with Marsh, he could never have bettered the alternative. It was Geoffrey Keynes who eventually began to reverse the process we have been following, and setting on one side the popular myth that was now a fact of history, looked round for ways and means of turning the marble back into man before it was altogether too late. Over the years his library became a kind of Sargasso sea through which anything relating to Brooke would gradually drift and come to rest for a while on its way to King's; and in all that accumulation—an extraordinary amount for so short a life—nothing was more precious to his purpose than the letters he managed to call in and copy, for in *them*, more than anywhere else, something of the flesh and blood he knew might still be found.

There are the notes made for Whitelaw at Rugby, for Headlam at King's, pages of chop-logic for the Apostles, bravado for the Fabians, scraps of Marston and Theocritus, the Shakespeare Apocrypha and the Minority Report, many of the books he read, lists of books and of necessaries for the caravan, hotel bills, military manuals and drafts of poems—the relics of a mind habitually on the alert and squeezing the last drop out of the day; such a man as one can well imagine advising a young acquaintance, as once he did, that the secret of a contented life was to 'swim, read, work, and learn to be happy alone'. And from among these disintegrating box-files and bursting envelopes we pick out the notes of one more pugnacious harangue to the Fabians.

He is giving a talk on Shakespeare, and is evidently determined 'to smash some of the silly block notions people have about him'. He quotes the lines where Cleopatra offers gold and 'her bluest veins to kiss' and says, 'The snob and sensualist (as he was) who wrote those lines was a short fat man with sandy hair'. Yet by comparison how matchless his creative art, and how sublime the sphere of Art itself! for there, in Art, things are ends, Brooke says, like flowers and sunsets, and the richness of mortal life comes from our ability to perceive things in themselves, in all the singularity of their nature. 'People "are" more than things, and more at one time than another.' But the workaday eye can only see through a glass, darkly. It is Art alone which can bring men face to face. From Shakespeare, the man among men, to Poetry, from Poetry to Art, the speaker progresses and comes at length to his peroration on the borderline of religion. It was indeed his faith that Art was a Platonic heaven 'where feet to Ambulation fade', and time and again he had found it proven by Shakespeare, Donne, John Webster's lightning flash, all those poets whose pages had given him joy and in whose good company he longed so desperately to be. And so, at the last, he is, having lived abundantly with his whole being and died with honour. 'Here, in this world' he says, reading from the last page of his notes:

Here, in this world we move in, everything is useful. All things are becoming, and influencing, and changing, and being improved. We are full of reforms and renovations, are we not? . . . I beseech you to remember the Kingdom of Art. There nothing is useful nothing changes. All things are taken out of the flux for ever. They are themselves. They intensely are. You shall meet the lover there and the perfect evening and all the faces that did so ludicrously, so pitiably change. *There* is *no* alteration, no growing old or going away. There is no decay.

APPENDIX

Poems, 1911, and the contemporary critics

The only volume of verse published in Brooke's life-time was thought by most of the critics to reveal two aspects of the author's character—his breadth of interest and his dare-devil lack of taste; the one represented by poems on such a variety of themes that some of them, it was suspected, must have been written 'for a wager' (this was not far wrong, since the *Westminster* competitions were deliberately set as a challenge) and the other revealed by the 'ugly' group, which consisted of *A Channel Passage* (often referred to as 'the disgusting sonnet') *Jealousy*, *Lust*, and *Wagner*, a small proportion, but it determined the general impression made by the book on the contemporary reader.

The Times Literary Supplement (August 29, 1912) reviewing Brooke among seven others, reproached James Stephens (*The Hill of Vision*) for his swagger and brutality, qualities which in Brooke were to be taken 'much more leniently; they are so obviously boyish. His disgusting sonnet on love and sea-sickness ought never to have been printed; but we are tempted to like him for writing it. Most people pass through some such strange nausea as this on their stormy way from romance to reality . . . We can endure his "showing off" in this and some other such outbursts, because here is clearly a rich nature—sensuous, eager, brave—fighting eagerly towards the truth. And already Mr. Brooke can show now and then an almost uncanny accomplishment. "The Fish" is as cleverly written as could be.' *The Hill* was picked out as representative of the work more moderate in tone, and the reviewer concluded with a wise observation: 'We shall watch Mr. Brooke's development with high hopes; but he must remember that swagger and brutality are no more poetry than an unripe pear is fruit.'

The *Morning Post* (December 11, 1911) was rather captious. 'Mr. Brooke seems to have been oppressed by the dread of writing prettily . . . What possible excuse is there for a sonnet describing a rough Channel crossing with gusto worthy of a medical dictionary?'

Alone of these reviews it detected the influence of Browning. Since Brooke felt strongly about that poet, and left some account of his views, a digression is justified. Shortly after Christmas 1912, he wrote an article on the poet who first converted him to the art of verse. It was occasioned by the celebrations of the Browning centenary at *The Royal Society of Literature* earlier that year, when Pinero and Henry James each delivered an address. Brooke attributed Browning's popularity with the general reader to the cult of his obscurity. 'It became a favourite pastime for ingenious brains to construe the craggiest passages in Browning, and to read him was for long in England the mark of a taste for nimble intellectual exercise rather than for a love of poetry.' His style was not nearly so difficult as people supposed, but 'His ideas were new, for poetry—and for that reason people thought them at first obscure—but they were quite clear. Only he had as it were a stutter in his utterance.' So far Browning had influenced novelists rather than poets. There was hardly a trace of his manner in *Georgian Poetry*, for instance, and yet it was Browning who had brought realism back into verse, and colloquial speech, and thanks to him the modern poet 'may have and avow emotions of love not only at sunset or just after, but in the most commonplace glare of noon, or even at breakfast time.' It is clear that Brooke considered that it was his sympathy with Browning and Donne which set him apart from his fellow Georgians. Byron, too, like Browning, expressed a relish of real existence. In 1912, so soon after the Pre-Raphaelites, the reappearance of this quality in English verse was something for remark. In the *Spectator* for January 27, for instance, John Buchan who considered Brooke's *Poems* characterized by 'a curious absence of imitation and a strenuous originality', went on to say, 'At his worst he falls into a kind of abusive Byronism, where he mistakes ugliness for strength . . . a book of rare and remarkable promise.' The same article reviewed *The Everlasting Mercy* and took exception to its 'harsh realism'. *The Dublin Express* briefly put all the trouble down to the 'exuberant faults of youth' and censoriously declared that *A Channel Passage* 'were better left unprinted, nay unwritten'. In *The English Review* (February, 1912) Brooke had a short article to himself. His merits illustrated the value of a classical education. On every page there was evidence of a 'delight in craftsmanship . . . which makes us enjoy even his emetic sonnet "A Channel Passage," a satiric masterpiece.' Here was a change of tune! and the first sonnet 'Oh Death will find me' was described as 'like an echo of

Propertius', while the book as a whole was recommended to any reader who would like to be 'charmed by melody and amused by the ironic imagination'. *The New Age* (January 18, 1912) was more critical, though the reviewer was one of the few to remark on the excellence of *Dining-Room Tea*. This new poet was at once 'an unflinching realist' and a 'solemn and sentimental enthusiast'. He was a puzzle, seeming oddly unco-ordinated, his poems of passion were 'frigid and unreal' and 'the appalling narrative of a cross-Channel voyage should never have been included in the volume. It spreads its aroma all round.' The critic of *The Nation* (July 6, 1912) argued that in order to evaluate the book any reader would have to answer the question, 'Does it effect a mere insolent display of acrobatics or a triumphant transformation of the commonplace into the unique?' The poem *Dining-Room Tea* showed that this new poet was well capable of this latter achievement. The secret lay in the influence of Donne who had taught him to be 'not only remarkably skilful, but to be insolently skilful also'. This insolence, at worst, was 'the sign of an energetic and original talent somewhat too determined to be sure of itself', but even this was a good sign. 'Mr. Brooke's talent, in fact, is pugnacious; and that is what a poetic talent should begin by being.'

The poet could have counted on a favourable notice in the *Westminster Gazette*. The issue of January 6, 1912, ended 'If Mr. Brooke can only find the courage to be less startlingly unusual in the future, that future may make for him an enduring place', but before that the 'disgusting sonnet' had marred the effect, for 'the bravest, purest soul that ever saw no harm', wrote the critic, 'would be forced to wince before such a remorseless catalogue of ignoble symptoms . . . For obvious reasons it cannot be quoted here.' The *Observer* said much the same, but tried to account for Brooke's mannerism of ugliness. He was uneasy, self-conscious, and had 'lost his balance in the struggle to break away from convention'. So far so good. 'He will have none of the merely agreeable and pretty, which is a sign of grace, but here and there he merely succeeds in being nasty, as in his continual insistence on the physical unpleasantness of old age. If he must flout the discipline of convention he must exert a sterner discipline of his own. He dares to be a Daniel, however, and it is enormously to his credit that he has managed to stagger free from convention.'

Robert Lynd (*The Daily News*, February 14, 1912) acknowledged the two elements in the book, but for him they had a unity of impression that was to be admired. 'Mr. Brooke has written a new book of the pessimism of the flesh, a new arrangement of charnel-house thoughts and gross imaginings of the horrors of old age, which is juster in phrase and more imaginative in its satiric gloom than anything of the kind that has been written in recent years. There is, of course, just a little of challenge and masquerade in these graveside infirmary woes of Mr. Brooke's, that is inevitable in a poet who is both overcivilized and young.' Lynd tried to point out that Brooke's so-called ugliness was only 'an inverted reverence for beauty'. It was a more gratifying notice than anything Brooke received at the hands of his Cambridge critics. To the *Cambridge Review* (February 8, 1912) it was not necessary to disgust in the process of being realistic, never was a comparison of love and nausea anything other than 'bad art'. This element ruined a promising book. 'There is so much that is beautiful in his poems, that it is nothing short of tragic to have the harmony of the whole spoilt by the presence of a few very false chords.' Mr. Brooke was still young, so there was hope that he would live to discover the function of the waste-paper basket, and to the *Cambridge Magazine* he was 'plain spoken to the point of insincerity. He deals with corruption, with senility, with dirtiness, in a manner more unpleasant than the dear old "macabre" of other days, because it is not merely decoration but is inherent in the *purpose* of the poem' —an odd argument, for one would suppose that, of the two evils, it were more promising in an artist to be dirty of set purpose than wantonly to besmirch what was 'clean' with offensive ornament. The *Manchester Guardian* (April 3, 1912) was no more encouraging, since it informed the poet that his laudable pursuit of detachment and truth had led to a 'dislocation in the mind'. He was too cynical. He would have to come to a clearer understanding of what he wanted to say before his verses could show promise.

Brooke would have paid more attention to the opinions of his friend Edward Thomas, given in the *Daily Chronicle* for April 9, 1912. Of the six books under review his was found the most interesting as 'a symptomatic quintessence of the rebellious attitude today . . . He is full of revolt, contempt, self-contempt, and yet arrogance too. He reveals chiefly what he desires to be and to be thought. Now and then he gives himself away, as when, in three poems close together, he speaks of the scent of warm clover. Copies should be bought by everyone over forty who has never been under forty. It will be a revelation. Also if they live yet a little longer they may see Mr. Rupert Brooke a poet. He will not be a little one.'

APPENDIX

If there was something of the truth in Henry Nevinson's opinion that 'the fear of being petted and fussed over for his beauty, the fear of falling into a flattered literary career, and of winning fame as one more beautiful poet of beautiful themes, it drove him into violence and coarseness for salvation', we know that the reason was both deeper and more complex. It was not only that much of the richness of life that Webster made the substance of his verse had become forbidden territory in deference to a more 'polite' society, it was that society itself, in Brooke's opinion, needed to be shocked into a more honest view of the realities of life. The notorious 'disgusting sonnet' was as much a blow in the cause of Fabian reform as of realism in literature. The reviews of *Poems 1911*, reacting to a new poet who is in revolt against traditional prettiness, are especially interesting in that they enable us to share their image of the man and poet that Brooke was before he came to terms with society, as he did in 1914, and would have been again, when the crisis was over and the time had come to rebuild among the ruins of his Edwardian world.

INDEX

[*Note:* RB stands for Rupert Brooke]

Abbey Theatre (Ireland) at Cambridge, 124

Abel, RB's Fiji guide, 429

Abercrombie, Lascelles, 250, 371, 384, 406, 407, 449, 475, 500, 519; and Catherine Abercrombie, 450, 526; *see also* Gallows Cottage, *New Numbers*

'Afterwards' (RB), 52

Agamemnon, off Mudros Bay, 1914, 493

Aiken, Conrad, 454

Ainley, Henry, 391; introduces Edward Marsh to Cathleen Nesbit, 370

Aldershot, RB at, 67, 68

'Alexander's Ragtime Band', 371–2

Alexandra, Queen, 448

'ambarvalia' poem of RB, 240

Anson Battalion, 463 *et seq.*

'Ante Aram' (RB), 125

Anti-Semitism of RB, 438

Antwerp, fall of (War I), 467

'An Unusual Young Man' (RB in *New Statesman*), 483–4

Apia, RB in, 418

'Apostles', the, at Cambridge, 70, 78, 154–5, 156, 170, 175, 177–9, 222, 223, 348, 386, 450, 533

Appius and Virginia, RB's theory of authorship of, 276, 287–8, 388, 388n

Archer, William: on 'modern poets', 92; on 'social injustice', 242

Arizona, RB visits Grand Canyon in, 439

Arnold, Dr. Thomas, of Rugby, 23, 24, 34, 85

Arts Council, RB foresees, 244

Ashendene Press, Jacques Raverat at, 192, 233

Asquith (parents, family generally, Herbert Asquith), 391, 451, 452, 469, 479, 513; in *The Enchantress*, 403; receives invalid RB in Downing Street, 485

Asquith, Arthur, 'Oc', 1914 comrade-in-arms of RB, 465, 467, 469, 473, 475, 479, 496, 500, 501, 509; in RB's last illness, 506, 507, 508, 509; builds grave cairn, 512; in Cairo, 495; in Malta, 492; as Brigadier-General, 514

Asquith, Cynthia (Lady Cynthia), 380

Asquith, Raymond, and Mrs. R., 391

Asquith, Violet: RB meets, 380; RB's correspondence with, and friendship with, 383, 391, 405, 425–6, 428, 454, 477, 478, 479, 482, 485, 487, 488, 489, 490–1, 499, 504, 519

'As the Wind, and as the Wind' (RB), 497

Atalanta in Calydon (A. C. Swinburne), 75, 76, 102

Atlantic Monthly, The, 399

Auden, W., *Letter to Lord Byron*, 532

Austen, Jane, RB's reading of, 391, 404, 409

Austin, Alfred, at the King's *Comus* production, 163

Bacharach, A. L. (librarian to Cambridge Fabians), 245

Bacon, Leonard, 412, 466

Badbury Rings, 482

Badley, J., headmaster of Bedales, 108

Bakst, Léon, RB's opinion of, 377

Balfour, Arthur, 79, 193, 233, 306, 307

Ballad of the Ridgeway (St. John Lucas), 52

Bank, New Forest, 180

Baring, Maurice, 455, 456, 478

Barrie J. M. (Sir James Barrie), 391, 450, 451

Basileon (King's, Cambridge, magazine), 125, 343, 349

Bastille, The (prize poem by RB), 50, 63, 64, 65, 66, 74

Bath: Richard England Brooke in, 19, 28

Baudelaire, Charles, 43, 86, 94, 97, 252; *Les Fleurs du Mal*, 97; 'The Corpse', 88

Baynes, Godwin, 173, 189, 207, 229, 267

INDEX

Beardsley, Aubrey, 78, 81

Beauchamp, Lord (Lascelles Abercrombie's landlord), 450

Beaulieu, camping at, 229–30

Beaumont and Fletcher, 259, 387

'Beauty and Beauty' (RB), 365n

Bedales, Noel Olivier at, 108, 109, 110, 173, 188–9, 226, 239

Beerbohm, Max, 121, 158, 212, 391

'Beginning, The' (RB), 116, 130

Békàssy, Ferenc (poet), 293

Belgium, the Brooke family holiday in, 128–30

Bell, Clive and Vanessa, 170, 257

Belloc, Hilaire, 46, 47, 102, 413, 484; as influence on RB, 171; *Emmanuel Burden*, 171, 175; *The Four Men*, 482; anti-semitism of, 438; RB's meetings with, 122, 175; debates with Shaw, 374, 384

Belloc-Lowndes, Mrs., 452

Bennett, Mr. and Mrs. Arnold, 306

Benson, A. C., 108, 170, 223, 452; describes RB, 241–2, 364; invites RB to meet Percy Lubbock, 241–2; on King's College Chapel, 104; on RB's first stage appearance, 107; *Men and Memories*, 364

Benson, Frank (actor), 48, 74

Berkeley, Reginald, RB's Suva companion, 428; RB's literary advice to, 428–9

Berlin, 338 seqq., 366

Bernhardt, Sarah, in *Phèdre*, 134

Berry Hall, Great Walsingham, 17, 18

Betteshanger Park, Northbourne estate, 463, 469

Bibury, 351, 358

Bilton Road house, Rugby, 219 seqq.

Binyon, Lawrence, 406; at the *Comus* production, 163

Birrell, Augustine, 391

Birrell, Francis, 196

Björkman, E., 378–9

Black Sea project, RB's interest in, 487

Blackwood, Basil, 391

Blandford, in 1914, 473–8

Bloomsbury group, 154 seqq., 353–4

'Blue Evening' (RB), 199n

Blunt, Wilfrid Scawen, 183, 214

'Bobbieship', 40

'Bobbie Longman', 82, 113; and 'Sarawak', 70, 71–2

Bonnard, RB's travel companion, 299

Booth, General, lying-in-state of, 355–6

Boston, RB visits, 399, 443–4

Bournemouth, 57–63, 97, 120, 125, 126; *see also* Brooke, Aunt Fanny, Grantchester Dene

Bradby, Mr. and Mrs. H. C., 36, 331

Bridges, Robert, 94, 403, 463; at the *Comus* production, 163; RB's opinion of, 361

Brierley, 169

Brooke, Alan England, 19, 477; as Dean of King's, 72, 101

Brooke, Anne, marries John Reeve of Wighton, 18

Brooke, Alfred (RB's brother), 27, 28, 41, 55, 78, 79, 92, 120, 121, 124, 167, 213, 216, 306, 311, 314, 318, 455, 519; and the Fabians, 195; joins the *Carbonari*, 204; in Italy, 50, 258; in Cannes, 300; joins Post Office Rifles, 463; in battle, and death of, in France, 474, 506, 519

Brooke, Arthur, father of Justin, 108

Brooke, Ellen England, 18

Brooke, Fanny ('Aunt Fanny'), 27, 32, 41, 97, 226, 249, 457, 498; working at School Field, 217; sends war woollies, 473; RB's last visit to, 477

Brooke, John Reeve, 18. *See* Reeve, John (father and son)

Brooke, Justin (friend of RB), of Emmanuel, 106, 108, 123, 124, 133, 134, 149, 160, 163, 169, 190, 200, 300, 518; and Ka Cox, 271, 351, 352; buys 'Opel' car, 182; at the Slade School ball, 212; in *Dr. Faustus*, 133; at Drewsteignton, 280–4; in Canada, 226, 391

Brooke, Margaret and Reeve (RB's cousins), 50; on visit to Italy, 54–5

Brooke, Richard England (Rector of Bath, father of 'the aunts', and son of John Reeve Brooke II), 18–19; retires to Bournemouth, 28; daughters of, 28, *and see* Brooke, Fanny

Brooke, Richard (RB's brother), 26, 29, 57, 79, 196; death of, in 1907, 114

Brooke, Rupert: outline of themes and events: birth of, 26; schooldays begin, 28; friendship with James Strachey begins, 29; at Hillbrow, 28–33; at Rugby, 33, 34–95; as freshman at King's College, Cambridge, 96–145; the decision to join Fabians, 146; his life at King's, 146–85; as the Stevensons' lodger at The Orchard, 186–246; at The Old Vicarage, 247 seqq.; from Cannes to Verona, 293–319; on new terms with Ka Cox, 320–50; the break with Ka begins, 351; his London life, *see* Gray's Inn; Marsh, Edward; Thurloe Square; and the *Georgian Poetry* venture, 360, *and see* this entry; meets Cathleen Nesbitt, 370; the enduring regard for Noel, *see* Olivier, Noel;

Marsh takes him in hand, 293 seqq.; social round intensifies, 391; dependence of, on Frances Cornford's advice, 393, *and see* Cornford, Frances; relations with family, *see* Brooke: Arthur, Aunt Fanny, Mr. and Mrs. W. P.; the departure for Canada and the U.S.A., 395, 396 seqq.; his experiences and journeys overseas, 397–447; in the U.S.A., 397–402; to Canada, 402–12; to the South Sea Islands, 413–28; in New Zealand, 428–30; in Papeete and Mataia, 430–7; and Taatamata, 431–7, *and see* ̄aata-mata; his poisoning by coral, 434–5; return to the U.S.A., 437–46; the London social round resumed, 449–54; war is declared by Germany on Russia, 454; his 27th birthday, 455–7; gives readings at The Poetry Bookshop; *see* Monro, Harold, Poetry Bookshop; joins R.N.V.R. with Denis Browne, then the Anson Battalion, 461–3; after the Dunkirk landing, 464–7; an interlude in London, 467–8; his attitude to war defined, 471–2; goes to Hood, 473; writes Flecker's obituary, 479; the letter from Taatamata, 479–80; his war poems are written, 481 seqq.; in the *Grantully Castle*, 489 seqq.; to Byzantium, 490 seqq.; offer of a Staff appointment for, 496; fatal illness begins, 506; course of illness, and death, 506–10; funeral of, 511–14; truths and myths concerning, 514 seqq.; speculations, 528–34; *Poems*, 1911, 535 seqq. For friends, correspondents, works, *see* individual entries; *see also* play titles for roles played by RB and friends

Brooke, William, of Geist, husband of Anne Parker of Berry Hall, 17, 18

Brooke, William Parker, of Fettes and Rugby (RB's father), 19 seqq., 72, 90, 92, 95; marriage of, 21; at Fettes, 19; at Rugby, as master, 21, 22 seqq.; at School Field, 34 seqq.; as 'Tooler', 37; and the death of Richard, 114; on the Clevedon holiday, 195–7; declining health, and death, of, 120, 213, 215–16

Brooke, Mrs. W. P., 'The Ranee' (RB's mother), 19, 20, 59, 63, 79, 132, 232, 239, 454, 527; marriage of, 21; at Rugby School, 22 seqq.; and the move to School Field, 28, 34 seqq.; is named 'The Ranee', 70; and the Olivier sisters, 166, 178, 318; and RB's Fabianism, 177, 195; at the *Comus* production, 163; leaves School Field, 219; gives hospitality to Whitelaw, 263; in Cannes, 298 seqq.; on RB's 'unsatisfactory nature', 375; and Ka Cox's visit to Rugby, 329–33; after RB's visit to the U.S.A., 448; during the war, 473, 475, 477; and the projected Staff appointment for RB, 496, 498; RB's last letter to, 506; receives RB's effects after his death, 517; settles RB's financial affairs, 519; fosters a legendary' impression, 521 seqq.; and the memorial plaque, 525; gives luncheon after Walter de la Mare's lecture, 526; revokes Edward Marsh's literary executorship, 532; death of, 532

Browne, Arthur, 465

Browne, Denis, 65–6, 88, 89, 360, 380, 383, 424, 450, 454, 467, 469, 477, 496, 502; in *Dr. Faustus*, 124; as music critic for *Rhythm*, 375; sees RB off to the U.S.A., 395; hears RB's news from States, 396; meets RB on return, 447; joins R.N.V.R. with RB, 461–3; at Downing Street and Admiralty receptions, 452, 479; goes to Hood Battalion, 470; war service of, 470 seqq.; with Howe Battalion, 473; in Hood again, 488; other mentions, 474, 475, 478, 481; in *Grantully Castle*, 490 seqq.; with RB in Malta, 492; in the 'Latin Club', 497, 498, 501; hears of RB's illness, 496; and Shaw-Stewart's illness, 495; and RB's death, 507, 509, 510, 511, 512, 513, 514; describes RB's death to 'The Ranee', 510; discovers the olive grove, Skyros, 505; dies in battle, 514

Browne, Maurice (director of Chicago Little Theatre), 441, 443, 446–7; describes Lascelles Abercrombie, 449; *Recollections of Rupert Brooke*, 441, 441n, 447, 447n

Browning, Oscar, 106–7, 121, 122; on 'The Evolution of the Family', 183

Browning, Robert, *Sordello*, 97

Brunelleschi, 262

Buckler's Hard (Beaulieu), 229, 275

Bullen, A. H., *Anthology of Elizabethan Lyrics*, 246

Bullock, Mrs., 331

Burns, John, 245, 246

Busoni, 65

Butt, Clara, RB describes, 430

Byron's Pool, 265, 267

Café des Westens, Charlottenburg, Berlin, 339, 341, 342, 367

Calgary, RB visits, 411

Calgary News Telegram, quotes RB, 411

'Call, The' (RB), 15

Cambridge, RB's life at, 96–216

Cambridge History of English Literature, RB's critique of, 241, 258

Cambridge Magazine, The, 365, 378, 380, 519

Cambridge Review, The, 125, 130, 158, 210, 222, 258, 359, 514, 516, 520; RB's introduction to, 115; RB begins reviewing for, 116; RB offered editorship of, 177; on Marsh's memoir of RB, 525

Cambridge University Fabian Society, foundation of, 118

Campbell, A. Y., 158, 196, 529

Campbell, Mrs. Patrick, 451

Canada, RB's impressions of, 403 seqq.

Cannes, RB in, 293 seqq.

Cannan, Gilbert, 385, 391, 423, 424, 477

Canopus, H.M.S., 508, 511

Capponi, la Marchese, 462

'Carbonari', the, of Cambridge, 102, 112, 122, 132, 170, 171, 174, 176, 183, 204; RB addresses: on 'From Without', 207–8; on 'Eggs in Moonshine', 209

Carey, Clive, 173, 454; in *Dr. Faustus*, 124; and RB's singing lessons, 288, 290

Carman, Bliss, 405–6

Carnival (Compton Mackenzie), RB reviews, 392

Casement, Captain (Staff Medical Officer), 507

Cathleen ni Houlihan, and *The Pot of Broth* (Irish Players' repertoire), RB studies, 125

Cedric, RB travels in, 395

Cecilia, hospital ship, 508

'Channel Passage, A' (RB), 213, 221, 279, 302, 535, 536, 537; Edward Marsh on, 293

Chapman, RB reads, 289, 291

Chardin, 284

Charles Oldham Shakespeare Scholarship, RB wins, 177, 204, 235, 240, 241

Charlotte Street, London, RB's room in, 288, 292, 296

Charlottenburg, RB in, 338–44, 367, 368

Chatham Barracks, 369

Chaucer's Mill, Trumpington, 265

Cheshire Cheese, Fleet Street, meetings at, 391, 392

Chesterton, G. K., 451; RB 'reviews' imaginary book by, 201–2

Chicago, RB in, 440–2; the Little Theatre, *see* Browne, Maurice

Childers, Erskine, 430

Children of the Chapel, The (A. C. Swinburne), 68

Christie, the Rev. W., 306

Churchill, Lady Gwendolen, at RB's last social gathering, 488

Churchill, Mrs., 380, 391, 469–70, 479, 487, 488

Churchill, Major John, 510

Churchill, Winston, 391, 410, 454, 462, 479, 480, 486, 487; visiting war fronts, 475, 498; and proposed Staff appointment for RB, 496; hears of RB's grave condition, 508, 509–10; and the fall of Antwerp, 467; his tribute to RB's 1914 poems, 528

'Circular to Freshmen', by RB, 245

'Cities and Thrones and Powers' (Rudyard Kipling), 451

Clark, J. W., 134

Clevedon, Somerset, holidays in, 195–7, 204

Clifford Bridge, *see* Drewsteignton

'Clouds' (RB), 413, 414, 419, 434, 532

Cockerell, Sydney, 183

Coit, Richard, of King's, 117, 118

Cole, E. L. D., 78, 78n

Collected Poems of RB (1918), with Marsh's memoir, 525; sales of, 528

Collijn, Gustave (playwright), 278

Cologne, RB and Dudley Ward in, for Van Gogh exhibition, 346

Comus production, 158–66, 529; RB's role in, 277; reviews of, 164

'Comprehensive irreverence' (Maynard Keynes' phrase), 155, 156

Compton-Burnett, Noel, and RB, in Fellowship rivalry, 380

Comte, Auguste, 147, 148

Conduit Head, the Cornfords' home, 214, 231, 232, 276, 278, 351, 352, 368, 522

Contemporary Art Society, 392

Corelli, Marie, 63, 69, 72

Cornford, Francis M., of Trinity, 107–8, 124, 133, 134, 159, 165, 185; in *Comus*, 159, 160; as Dr. Faustus, 226; engagement of, to Frances Darwin, 168–9; in the Poor Law reform work, 204; and the 1914 war, 457; becomes Sergeant-Instructor of Musketry, 474; on the RB memorial plaque committee, 522

Cornford, Frances (Mrs. F. M.), friendship and correspondence with RB, 190, 213–19, 228, 253–4, 276–8, 285, 303, 347, 348, 356, 360–1, 364, 368, 424, 449, 457, 469; and Ka Cox, 271–2, 277, 348–9, 351, 352, 357, 361, 393, 448; describes Ka, 271–2; describes RB, 277–8; draws RB, 223; and Lady Ottoline Morrell, 392; tells RB of Raverats' engagement, 234; RB tells of 'Old Vicarage' poem, 343; a comment on RB, 354–5, a comment on third of the war sonnets, 472; 'California' scheme of, for

RB, 373; on eve of 1914 war, 458; *Death and the Princess*, 276; RB's opinion of poetry of, 326; the Cornfords at Conduit Head (*q.v.*) and on holiday, 192, 270, 289; plan for RB, 351–3, 373; entertain RB at The Lizard, 372–4; at Cley-next-the-Sea, 457–8, 483; and Cathleen Nesbitt, 452; provide RB with sleeping-bag, 461; Ka Cox stays with, after RB's death, 522

Cotterill, the Rev. Charles Clement, of Fettes (RB's grandfather), 19–20

Cotterill, Clement (RB's uncle), 147

Cotterill, Erica (RB's cousin), correspondence and friendship with RB, 46, 51, 72, 78, 81, 84, 91, 97, 112, 114, 121, 147, 150, 168, 171, 172, 184, 189, 213, 228, 286

Cotterill, Henry, Bishop of Grahamstown, 21

Cotterill, Ruth Mary, later Brooke, Mrs. W. P., 20

Cox, Hester (Ka's sister), 270, 317, 318, 338

Cox, Ka, RB's correspondence with (principal mentions), 190, 217, 225, 229, 247, 248–9, 258, 261–2, 268, 269, 270, 274–275, 279–80, 285–6, 287, 289–319, 327–9, 332, 353, 355–6, 366, 369, 275–376, 381, 392, 293–5, 449, 460, 469, 474, 475, 477, 480, 486, 492, 494, 498, 526; Mrs. Cornford advises 'final' letter to, 393; RB writes this, 401–2; correspondence resumed, 439; RB's last letter to, 517–18; as Fabian, at Newnham, 118, 145; and Poor Law reform, 194, 204; role of, in group, 182, 192; and Jacques Raverat, 179, 189, 204, 234; and the *Comus* production, 160, 161, 163; learns of Clevedon experiment, 197; at the Slade ball, 211, 212; missing from the Lenzerheide party, 212; continues Fabian work, 213; Raverat's and RB's changing feelings toward, 233–4; is invited to Prunoy, 234; RB's growing regard for, 258; described, 270–2; Duncan Grant's portrait of, 273, 365; at the Old Vicarage, 274; her attachment to Henry Lamb, 291, 321–3; Woking cottage of, 280, 327, 328, 329, 335, 338; at Drewsteignton, 280–4; consents to go to Munich, 297; the letters between Munich and Cannes, 296–300, 307–8; to meet 'The Ranee', 329–33; climax of the affair, 336 seqq.; growing difficulties in relationship with RB, 344–6; the discussion at Bibury, 351–2; Frances Cornford's regard for, 361; to receive

Eric Gill statuette, 365; RB feels deeply responsible for, 371, 374; advises Yeats on shirt-buying, 374; decides to leave England, 372; and Geoffrey Keynes, 394; memory of, as 'Retrospect' (RB), 434; continuing uneasy relationship with RB, 445, 453, 458; learns of Constantinople plan, 489; mentioned in RB's will, 517; after death of RB, 522; dies, 532

'Crabbed Age and Youth' (lecture by Jane Harrison), 108n

Craig, Dr., nerve specialist, 298, 312, 313, 332

Craig, Gordon, 377, 424

Crane, Walter: 'Tract on Socialism and the Arts', 241

Creditor Fair, 281–2

Crewe, Lady, 391

Crooks, Will, M.P. (for Woolwich), 195

Crystal Palace, RB's 1914 training at, 462

Curzon, Lord, in *Westminster Gazette*, 171

Daily News, The, reports RB's death, 516

Dalton, Hugh, 118, 119, 120, 150, 166, 167, 182, 183, 189, 196, 213, 241, 336, 405; RB's first meeting with, 102; sponsors RB as Fabian, 157; as Fabian leader, 146, 177; his Fabian Socialism, 117; elected to committee of Fabians, 135–6; stays at School Field, 169; at Fabian Summer School, 192; on National Committee for the Prevention of Destitution, 194–5; writes in *Granta*, 202; quoted, 161–2, 167, 168; father of, 405

Dance of Death, The (Strindberg), 378

Dardanelles, the, strategy concerning, 480; 493

Dartmouth, H.M.S., 511

Darwin, Charles, 45, 110, 147; as a credulous child, 449; centenary of, 183–4

Darwin, Frances, 163, 166, 169, 170–1; describes RB, 159; describes Mrs. Brooke, 163; describes Lytton Strachey, 154; and the *Comus* production, 158–63, 166, 168; engagement and marriage to F. M. Cornford, 168–9, 185. *See also* Cornford, Frances

Darwin, Gwen, 165, 182, 190, 196, 225, 232, 247, 261–2; describes RB, 190, 191; draws RB, 223; and the *Comus* production, 161, 162; on the Clevedon incidents, 196; and the Slade ball, 210, 212; marries Jacques Raverat, 233, 234; *see also* Raverat, Gwen

Darwin, Margaret (later Mrs. Geoffrey Keynes), 158, 163, 165, 182; at the Slade ball, 212; at the luncheon after

INDEX

Darwin—*cont.*
Walter de la Mare's speech, 526

Davidson, John, 94; death of, 206, 206n

Davidson, Thomas, *The Fellowship of the New Life* (lectures), 148, 150

Davies, W. H., 451; RB visits at Sevenoaks, 373

'Dawn, The' (RB), 76, 125

'Dead, The' (RB), 482

'Dead Men's Love' (RB), 326, 366–7

De la Mare, Walter, RB's friendship with, 362, 373, 472, 517; as an heir and literary executor, 517, 532; writes on RB's death, 516–17, 519, 524; *Peacock Pie*, 457; lectures, 526

De l'Isle Adam, 98

Dellefant, Ludwig, 249–50

Del Re, Arundel, 360

Democracy and the Arts (RB), 242–5

Dent, E. J., of King's, 135, 161, 162, 163, 174, 252, 254, 259, 288, 290, 332, 470, 521–2; as music critic for *Rhythm*, 375; on romanticism, 519–20; learns of Old Vicarage's reprieve, 469

'Dew-dabblers' of Cambridge, 108, 182

Diaghilev ballet, 265

Dickens, Charles, 377

Dickinson, G. Lowes, Fellow of King's, 101, 132, 170, 255, 257, 350, 376, 398, 412; and E. M. Forster, 154–5; at the Old Vicarage, 270; at Gibb's Buildings, 358; war outlook separates from RB, 471; visits RB on sick leave, 485

Dickinson Society, 253, 255, 413

'Dining-Room Tea' (RB), 156, 283, 284, 343, 532

Disraeli, Benjamin: *Coningsby*, qu., 96

Ditchling, 373

Dobson, Austin, 94, 325, 350

Dodge, John Bigelow, of 'Hood', 474, 475; in the 'Latin Club', 501; on active service, 495, 496

Dodington, George Bubb, 481

Doll's House, A (Ibsen), 379

Don Juan in Hell, Shaw's, 85

Donne, John, 111, 112; Geoffrey Keynes' work on, 373; RB's work on, 372–3; his opinion of, 260; his debt to, 283–4, 388; *The Anniversarie* of, 468; 'The Extasie' of, 283, 284

Dostoevsky, F., 313, 377

'Doubts (To Cathleen)' (RB), 406

Dowson, Ernest, 44, 47, 53, 65, 123, 181; *Cynara*, 170; RB's opinion of, 94, 95

Draper, Ruth, 450

Dream Play; The (Strindberg), 378

Drewsteignton, camping holiday near, 280–4, 443

Drinkwater, John, 360, 385, 407, 443, 480, 519

Duguay-Trouin, French hospital ship, 508–11

Duhamel, G., death of, 481

Dukes, Ashley, 171

Du Maurier, Gerald, 451; *Outcasts*, 460

Dunsany, Lord, 105

Durnford, R. S., 122

Durnford, Walter, 107

'Dust' (RB), 213, 240, 532

Dymock, Glos. (Abercrombies' home), 406. *See also* Gallow's Cottage, *New Numbers*

Eastbourne, holiday at, 292, 293

'Easter Day Song in Praise of Cremation' (RB), 88

Eckersley, Arthur, 42, 46, 62, 65, 70, 85, 113; on Lucretius, 126

Eden, T. B., 27, 29, 32; Mrs. T. B., 29, 31, 32

Edmonton, RB in, 410

'Eggs in Moonshine' (RB), 209

Einfühlungsästhetik, 367

Elgy, Mrs., at Raymond's Buildings, 358, 455–6

Empress of Ireland; sinking of, 447; RB's letter from Taatamata in, 480

'Endogamy', talk given by RB, 183–4

England, Ellen, 18

England, Richard, death of, 62

English Review, The, RB's appearances in, 199–200, 524

'Eranos', literary society at Rugby, 75, 87, 90, 91, 92, 117

Ervine, Mr. and Mrs. St. John, 373, 374, 380

Everlasting Mercy, The (John Masefield), 371

Eversleigh house-party, 350

Ewald, Frau, 252, 332; RB and Ka visit, 323

Ewald, Paul, 252, 253, 255

Ewing, Mrs. Horatia, 29

Expressionism, RB on, 365

Fabians, Fabianism (and RB's adherence to in Cambridge), 79–80, 117–20, 135–7, 145–51, 156, 157, 176–7, 189, 193–5, 223, 224, 278, 371, 533; RB signs 'Basis' of, 157; as third President, 204; withdrawal from, 246, 379

Falk, Howard, takes RB to Lake George, 408–9

Father, The (Strindberg), 378

Faustus production, RB's role in, 278

Feldberg, RB visits with Ka Cox, 344

INDEX

Feminism, RB's dislike of, 378, 379, 442, 445, 448

Fettes College, 19–20

Ficke, Arthur (poet and editor, Iowa), 441

Fiesole, RB visits, 55

Fiji, RB visits, 420–8

Filippi, Rosina, 370

'Finding' (RB), 199n

'Fish, The' (RB), 252, 261, 283, 341, 412, 532, 535

'Five Knights, The' (RB), 115

Flecker, James Elroy, at Caius College, 45, 131, 174, 223, 228, 365; a letter from RB to, 337; on RB as 'Donne Redivivus', 284; RB criticizes, 188; death of, 479

'Flight' (RB), 240

Flint, F. S., 363

Florence, RB's visit to, 54–5, 120, 121; RB visits Whitelaw in, 260–3

Florio's *Montaigne*, 388

Ford, *'Tis Pity she's a Whore*, 259

Forbes Robertson's 'Hamlet', 383, 392

Forster, E. M., 348, 468; at The Orchard, 203–4, 239–40; and the 'Apostles', 154–5; on RB's possible future, 528–9; biographer of Dickinson, 398; *The Celestial Omnibus*, 155; *The Longest Journey*, 155

Four Men (Belloc), 347, 382

'Fragments of a Poem to be Entitled "The Sentimental Exile" '(RB), 341

Franconia, the, off Skyros, 502–10

Freyberg, Col. Bernard, 473, 487, 488, 485, 526; at RB's burial, 511, 512: survives war as Major-General Sir Bernard Freyberg, K.C.B., V.C., D.S.O., 514

'From the Jaws of the Octopus' (Christmas melodrama at Klosters), 173

'From Without' (RB), 207–8

Fry, Geoffrey, 186–7, 213, 246; sees RB off to the U.S.A., 395

Fry, Roger, 257; on Chardin, 284

'Full Moon' (RB), 199n

'Funeral of Youth, The' (RB), 373

Furniss, Harry, 458

Gallipoli, 513, 515, 517

Gallows Cottage (Abercrombies' home at Dymock), 450; *Gallows Garland, The* (later *New Numbers*, q.v.), 406–7, 450

Galsworthy, John, 412

Gardner, Phyllis, 435

Garnett, David, 189, 190; as member of the Broads party, 267; at the Old Vicarage, 266–7; *The Golden Echo*, 190, 267

Garnett, Edward, 160

Garrod, H. W., on RB, 530, 531

Gaskell, Fleet-Surgeon, 507

Gaudier-Brzeska, RB meets, 450

Gauguin find, RB makes, 441

Gautier, Theophile, 43

Geoffroi (Charles Geoffrey-Dechaume, painter), 471

George, Stefan, 252, 253

Georgians, Georgianism, 362–3, 406; *Georgian Poetry*, 360, 365, 366, 371, 372; RB attempts New York publication of, 402; second volume planned, 449

Gertler, Mark, 451

Ghey, F. L., 73

Gibbons, Dr. and Mrs., of Rapallo, 49, 51, 55

Gibson, Wilfred, 360, 362, 363, 365, 380, 384, 406, 407, 519; RB's first meeting with, 359; visits the Old Vicarage, 364; at farewell party for RB, 394; as one of RB's heirs, 517; with Mrs. Gibson: entertain, RB at Greenway, 450; at luncheon with Mrs. Brooke, 526

Giddings, F. H., *Sociology*, 150

Gide, André, 298, 448

Gill, Eric, 402, 523; RB and the Cornfords' visit, 373; RB's admiration for, 365; the statuettes made: for Ka Cox, 402; for Cathleen Nesbitt, 517

Giotto, 263

Girton, Cambridge, 99, 118, 133, 263

Glencorse (house at Fettes College), 19, 20

'Goddess in the Wood, The' (RB), 221, 240

Goldschmidt, E. P., 258

Goodale, Dr., bacteriologist, 507

Gordon, Cosmo, in *Dr. Faustus*, 124

Gosse, Edmund, 170, 325, 350, 376, 391, 408, 486; at the *Comus* production, 163; RB writes to from the South Seas, 421

Goupil Gallery, a party at, 392

Gow, Andrew, 105, 122, 124, 133, 134, 459–60

Grant, Corrie, M.P. for Rugby, 79, 132, 145, 149

Grant, Duncan, 71, 174, 272–3, 293, 354, 380, 516; at Hillbrow, 29, 30; as art student, 55; in Florence, 67; his portrait of Ka Cox, 273, 365; 'The Dancers', 365; 'The Seated Woman', 365

Grantchester, 184, 202, 203, 339, 341, 345, 346–7, 356, 410–11, 522, 529; RB's devotion to, 207–8, 213, 216; the poem, 'Grantchester', 361; wins prize, 384; 'The Grantchester Grind', 184; Grantchester. Mill, 265

Grantchester Dene, Bournemouth, 28, 62, 97, 477

INDEX

Grantully Castle, 488–9, 507 seqq., 513, 517, 526, 527; the funeral party from, 511

Granville-Barker, A., 168, 385, 451; on *Antony and Cleopatra*, 423; *Waste*, 423

Gray, Thomas, RB's opinion of, 87

Gray's Inn *pied à terre*, 357–8, 373–5, 391, *and see* Marsh, Edward

Great Hampden, Bucks., Masefield at, 355

'Great L ver, The' (RB), 433, 434, 483, 532

Green, Dorothy (actress), 48

Greene, Robert, RB's poem imitating, 201

Gregory, Lady, 124

Grey, Sir Edward, 454

Grierson, H. J. C., edition of Donne by, 372

Guedalla, Philip, as young debater, 77, 80

Guest, Mrs. Henry, RB's last hostess, 488

Guy, the caravan horse, 224, 226

Hadley, Dr., President of Yale, 523

Hague, The, RB visits with James Strachey, 347

Haldane, Lord, 391

Hamilton, Lord George, 193; opposes Minority Poor Law Reform proposals, 245

Hamilton, Sir Ian, 452, 496, 508; offers RB a Staff appointment, 496, 498; and RB's final illness, 499, 509, 510; at the plaque unveiling, 526, 527

Hamilton, Marjorie, 452

Hampden-in-Arden, Rupert and Alfred Brooke visit, 456–7

Happy Profession, The (Ellery Sedgwick), 399n

Hardie, Keir, 118, 309; 'Keir Hardie Night', 118–19, 173

Hardy, Thomas, 228; Frances Cornford visits, 215; at the *Comus* production, 163; at Sayle's breakfast party, 163; *The Dynasts*, 310; *Two on a Tower*, 481, 481n

Hargreaves, Ronald (painter), 446, 447

Harness Prize, Cambridge, 217, 224; RB wins, 235

Harris, John, on RB's lecturing, 377

Harrison, Jane, of Newnham, 108, 124, 160; Augustus John's portrait of, 186; a lecture by, 108n

Harrod, R. F., *The Life of John Maynard Keynes*, 174, 174n

Hartridge, Professor Hamilton, 334

Harvard, RB comments on, 400; RB sees Harvard-Yale baseball match, 400

Hastings, 63

Hathaway, R. H., of Toronto, describes R.B., 406

'Hauntings' (RB), 436, 532

Hawtrey, R. G., 154

Hawtrey, St. John, 444, 445

Headlam, Walter, Fellow of King's, 101, 111, 112, 115, 126, 132, 134, 150, 154, 513, 533; death of, 162–3

'Heaven' (RB), 283, 434, 532

Henley, W. E., 92–3, 102, 120, 472

Herbert, Aubrey and Mary (Cairo), 495

'Heretics', The, Cambridge, RB addresses, 363, 376, 379

Heywood, Thomas, 388, 388n

Hillbrow, RB's first school, 28–33, 77

Hillmorton Road house, Rugby, 25

'Hill, The' (RB), 535

His Excellency the Governor, RB's role in, 158

Hockley, Sabina, 264; Mr. Hockley, 264, 265

'Home' (RB), 341

Honolulu, RB's impressions of, 415–16

Hood, Tom, 244

'Hood' Battalion, 473 seqq.

Hopkins, Harriet, marries Richard England Brooke, 18

Hopkins, Sophia, aunt of W. P. Brooke, 18

Horner, Edward, 196

Horniman, Miss, of the Manchester Repertory, 385

Housman, A. E., 46, 375, 376; appointed Professor of Latin, 250–1; RB's opinion of, 94–5, 102

Howard de Walden, Lord and Lady, 495

Howland, Charles, 523; Howland Prize, 523

Hubbach, W., 206, 229

Hubrecht, Jan, 232

Hullo, Ragtime, at London Hippodrome, 371, 376, 384, 390, 416, 417–18

Hulme, T. E., 362, 363, 369, 384n

Huron, Lake, RB visits, 408

Hutchinson, Eugene (photographer), 441–442, 446

Huxley, A, 45

Ibsen, 379, 380; *John Gabriel Borkman*, 255; *The Wild Duck*, 255; RB's opinion of, 377–8

Imagism, 262

'Impressionist' poets, Monro lectures on, 365

Inge, Dean, sermon by, incorporating RB's 'The Soldier', 502–3, 507

Insurance Act of 1911–12, 245

'In Xanadu' (talk given by RB), 363

Irving, Laurence, death of, 480

INDEX

Isaacs, Rufus, 420
'I said I splendidly loved you' (RB), 240
Italy, three visits to, 50, 84–5, 120–1
'I think if you had loved me' (RB), 213, 240

Jackson, Professor Henry, 124
Jackson, Holbrook, on RB, in *Today*, 525
James, Dr. H. A., 36, 38
James, Henry, 70, 71; as RB's guest or host, 187, 188, 277, 328, 452, 485–6; Preface by, to *Letters from America*, 523–4; Preface to Brooke's *Westminster Gazette* articles, 486; comments on RB's war sonnets, 503; on news of RB's death, 515–16
James, M. R., Provost of King's, 101, 124, 381, 461
Janis, Elsie (actress), 458
'Jealousy' (RB), 535
Jex-Blake, Dr., of Rugby, 21, 22
Joan, Queen of Scotland, 481n
'Joanna', of Munich, 306
John, Augustus, 158, 166, 169, 186, 214, 196; and Ka Cox, 272
'John Donne arriving in Heaven' (Stanley Spencer), 372
John Gabriel Borkman (Ibsen), 250
'John Rump' satire (RB), 175–6
John Webster and the Elizabethan Drama, 386–8; *see* Webster
Johnson, Dr., RB on, 440
'Jolly Company, The' (RB), 170
Jones, A. R., *The Life and Opinions of T. E. Hulme*, 367, 367n
Jones, Llewellyn, patron of letters, 441
Jonson, Ben, 408–9, 420
Jowett, B., 386

Kanai, RB visits, 417
Kandarva island, RB visits, 421
Kastro, RB in, 493
Keats, John, 126, 127, 128, 343; letters of, to Fanny Brawne, 283
Keeling, F. (Ben), 117, 118–19, 147, 167, 168, 177, 449, 459; sponsors RB as Fabian, 157; gives May party, 157; a letter to, from RB, 343; on the National Committee for the Prevention of Destitution, 194; sinks into pessimism, 236; H. G. Wells describes, 118
'Keir Hardie Night', 118–19, 173
Kelly, F. S. ('Cleg') on *Grantully Castle*, and at RB's burial, 490, 497, 499, 501, 502, 508, 512, 513, 514; builds cairn of marble pieces, 512; dies in battle, 514; *Elegy for Strings*, 527
Kettering, RB in, 69–71

Keynes, Geoffrey, 38, 39, 40, 46, 47, 56, 83, 86, 95, 97, 116, 132, 190, 205, 216, 221, 277n, 346, 380, 394, 518, 526, 533; RB's principal correspondence with, 56, 57, 58, 78, 79, 81, 82, 83, 84–5, 86, 96, 97, 98, 113, 126–7, 128, 151, 257, 260, 397; takes Cambridge scholarship examinations, 77, 78; early days at Cambridge, 105; arranges for RB to meet Belloc, 122; buys 'locomotor-bicycle', 128; in *Dr. Faustus*, 124, 133; sends RB a 21st-birthday present, 166; on walking excursion, 179; at May picnic, 182; as host to Henry James, 187; as medical student at St. Bartholomew's, 192, 347; hears RB's news from Cologne, 347; at Slade School ball, 212; helps RB in competitions, 217; camping at Overcote, 223–4; and the Duncan Grant portrait of Ka Cox, 273; at Drewsteignton, 280–4; at Eversleigh, 350; begins his work on John Donne, 373; at farewell party for RB, 394; in R.A.M.C., in 1914, 461; 'A Letter to a Live Poet', 250; as critic of RB's early writings, 51–2; *Henry James in Cambridge*, 187; Preface by, to RB's *Democracy and the Arts*, 243n; as literary executor, 532
Keynes, Margaret, 527
Keynes, Maynard, 69, 77, 187, 196, 213, 293, 336, 341, 349, 450, 522; at Market Lavington meeting, 154–5; as freshman, 156; accepts lectureship at King's, 174; gives a Sunday breakfast, 174; Mrs. Brooke's opinion of, 197; on the 'Carbonari', 209; at Slade School ball, 212; at Drewsteignton, 281; lends RB his Fitzroy Square room, 288; and RB's Fellowship, 336; at Eversleigh, 350; on RB's death, 516
Khokilas, Mt. (Skyros), 505
King's College, Cambridge, described, 103–4. *See* Brooke, Rupert
King's Cross wood-yard fire, 359
Kingsmere, Ottawa, RB visits, 405
Kipling, Rudyard, 451; RB's opinion of, 92
Klosters, the 1908 Christmas at, 173
Kyd, Thomas, 388

Laddie (puppy), 265
Lake Louise, RB at, 442
Lamb, Charles, dinner in honour of, 375–6
Lamb, Dorothy, 158, 182
Lamb, Henry, 158; and Ka Cox, 270, 291, 296–7, 321–2; paints Lytton Strachey, 273; at Lady Ottoline Morrell's, 222; at Parkstone with Augustus John, 296

INDEX

'Latin Club', 501, 503, 505; see also Grantully Castle, Hood

Laurier, Sir Wilfrid, 405

Lawrence, D. H., qu., 187; Sons and Lovers, 446, 450; with Frieda, RB and Edward Marsh meet, 450, 454; on RB's death, 516

Lavery, Sir John, and Hazel, 485

Leeds, Duchess of, 452

Le Gallienne, Richard, 117, 403

Lemnos, RB's illness in, 498

Lenzerheide, Switzerland, Christmas holiday at, 212

Leopold, Prince of the Belgians, at Dr. Faustus performance, 135

Les Papillons, 448

Lester, Alfred, at Coliseum, 458

'Letter to a Live Poet, A' (RB), 532

'Letter to a Shropshire Lad' (RB), 250–1

Leuba, Paul, RB meets in Munich, 252, 253, 257

Levey, Ethel, 371, 372, 384, 390

'Libido', Edward Marsh comments on, 293–4; see 'Lust'

'Life Beyond, The' (RB), 240

Lillo, George (playwright), 340

Limpsfield, the Oliviers' home at, 197, 249, 268, 298, 327, 329, 335, 336, 337

Linder, Estrid, RB's collaborator, 278, 378

'Lines Written in the Belief that the Ancient Roman Festival of the Dead was called Ambarvalia' (RB), 91, 91n

Lister, Charles, officer serving with RB, 495, 496, 498; in Malta, 492–3; in 'Latin Club', 501; and RB's last illness and death, 502; 504, 505, 511, 512, is given RB's compass, 514; dies in action, 514

Lithuania (a play by RB), 340, 343, 346, 374, 378, 380, 385; produced in Chicago, 441

Little Review, The, 442

Llanbedr, Fabian group's Summer School at, 168, 232–3

Lloyd George, David, 245

Local Government Act of 1929, 245

Loftus, Cecilia (actress), 458

Loines, Russell, RB's American benefactor, 398, 399, 401, 402, 404, 412, 413, 439, 444, 474; on 'The Fish' (RB), 412; RB writes to from Mataia, 434

Longman, see 'Bobbie'

Lost Lilies (RB), 74

Lowell, Amy, RB calls on, 399

Lowestoft, visit to with Cathleen Nesbitt, 468

Lubbock, Percy, 107; on A. C. Benson, 241

Lucas, F. L., editor of Webster's Plays, 388n

Lucas, H. F., animal painter, 42

Lucas, St. John Welles Lucas-, as early critic and adviser of RB, correspondence and friendship with, 42–5, 46, 47, 50, 51, 62, 63, 66, 70, 71, 74, 75, 76, 77, 81, 84, 86, 89, 90, 96, 97, 105, 106, 107, 116, 120, 121, 126, 132, 134, 182, 260, 345–6, 359, 395; The Marble Sphinx, 145; waning influence of, 145, 156; Edward Marsh supplanting, 350

Ludlow Castle, 168

Lulworth: reading parties at, visits to, 126, 220, 247, 292–8; Keats in, 128

'Lust' (RB), 286, 343, 370n; as 'Libido', 286, 293–5

Lyndhurst, RB stays at, with Strachey, 335

Lyons Mail, The, a barnstormer performance of, 281

Lytton, Victor and Pamela, 454

Macaulay, G. C., 177

Macaulay, Rose, 134; in Westminster Gazette, 171

Macaulay, W. H. (senior tutor, 100, 177, 222; proposes Shakespeare scholarship entry to RB, 185

MacCarthy, Desmond, 154, 178, 180, 187, 448

McCracken, Dr. (battalion surgeon), 506, 507

MacDonald, Ramsay, addresses the Fabians, 177

Mackay, Isobel, 412

Macpherson, Hector: A Century of Political Advance, 242

Madness (RB essay), 59–60

Magic Flute, The, RB's role in, 290, 291

Mallory, George, 108, 187, 223; in Dr. Faustus, 124, 133

Malory's Morte d'Arthur, 78, 162

Malta, RB in, 491–3

Manaton, Devon, 177–9, 282, 285

Mansfield, Katherine, 362, 373

Manners, Lady Diana, 391; Sir John Lavery paints, 485

Mannucci Capponi, the Marchesa, shows Washington to RB, 442

Market Lavington, 154

Marlowe, Christopher, 83, 388; Marlowe Dramatic Society presentations, 135, 174; Dr. Faustus, 123, 124, 133–5, 225–6, 230, 231–2; The Knight of the Burning Pestle, 258; Richard II, 213, 216

Marne, Battle of the, 463

INDEX

Marrying of Ann Leete, The (Granville Barker), 423

Marsh, Edward, friendship, correspondence, with, 170, 177, 182, 186, 196, 204, 211, 217, 221–2, 223, 260–1, 333, 348–9, 357–9, 361–3, 372, 373, 380, 381, 383, 284n, 391, 392, 394, 404–6, 411–13, 419–20, 424, 435, 436–7, 445–6, 448–51, 460–3, 473–5, 479, 485, 487, 488, 491–2, 528; first meets RB, 107, 108; on St. John Lucas, 260; and Lady Ottoline Morrell, 222, 273, 404; comments on *Poems* (1911), 293–4; as secretary to Winston Churchill, 295 (*et seq.*); and *Georgian Poetry*, 359–60; reviews *Poems* in *Poetry Review*, 324; on 'The Sentimental Exile', 350; offers RB a Gray's Inn *pied-à-terre*, 357; and RB's friendship with Cathleen Nesbitt, 374; as member of *Enchantress* cruise, 391, 403; excerpt from diary of, 454; and D. H. Lawrence, 450; visits war fronts and 'Hood' mess, 488, 498; hears of RB's stokers' pay scheme, 481; RB asks to be his literary executor, 486; on Sir Ian Hamilton's offer of Staff appointment for RB, 496, 506; describes to RB Dean Inge's sermon, 502; reports Henry James's reaction to war sonnets, 503; hears of RB's grave condition from Winston Churchill, 508–9; writes obituary of RB, 515; as literary executor, 517; prepares *1914 and Other Poems*, 519; as member of plaque committee, 522; writes Memoir for *Collected Poems*, 525; Mrs. W. P. Brooke and, *see* Brooke, Mrs. W. P.

Marsh, Professor, father of Edward Marsh, 375

Marshall, A. R., in *Dr. Faustus*, 124

Marston, John, RB's assessment of, 387

Marvell, Andrew, 341; compared with RB, 433; 'Dialogue between Soul and Body', 414

Marx, Karl: the Socialist League and, 149; William Morris and, 147

'Mary and Gabriel' (RB), 365n

Masefield, John, 361, 369, 371, 391, 519, 522; RB stays with, 355; opposes 'California venture' planned for RB, 373; reads RB's *Lithuania*, 380; introduces RB to Duncan Campbell Scott, 404; becomes a corporal, 474; writes to RB on his volunteering, 477–8

Masterman, Charles, M.P., 169; *In Peril of Change*, 146

Mataia (Tahiti), 430, 434, 476

Matisse, Henri, RB's opinion of, 365

Mayne, Jasper, *The City-Match*, 236, 236n

Meach's Lake, Ottawa, 405

Men and Memories (A. C. Benson), 241–2

'Menelaus and Helen' (RB), 130

Meredith, George, 46, 94; *Modern Love*, 167, 230

Meredith, H. O., describes RB, 278

Mermaid Club, Rye, 326

Mesadhi, RB's burial-spot, 517

Meynell, Francis, 389

Middleton, Thomas, RB's opinion of, 387

Milhaud, Darius, *Le Matelot*, 340

Mill, John Stuart, 147

Minority Report of the Poor Law Commission, 193

Modern Language Review, qu., 388n

Moffat, Scotland, RB visits with Norton, 356

Monro, Harold, and Poetry Bookshop, 360, 365, 384n, 402, 468; Monro: lectures at Cambridge, 365; 'Clouds' (RB) sent to, 419; presents RB to American friends, 441; tries to enlist, 459; protests at 'soldier-poet' label, 520

Montague family, of Penton (Crediton), 281

Montague, Paul, at Drewsteignton, 281

Montaigne (John Florio), 185

Moore, G. E., as 'Apostle', and influence of, on RB, 154, 155, 156, 170, 177, 180, 189, 284, 363, 371; on Bergson, 208

Moore, George, 448

Moore, T. Sturge, 384

Mordacq, Sarah, 42

Morning Post, The, on RB, 535–6

Morrell, Lady Ottoline, 222, 273, 322, 392, 454, 516; and Edward Marsh, 222, 273, 404; RB criticizes, 353

Morris, Edmund (painter), 405, 406; death of, 411

Morris, William, 44, 371; at first Fabian Conference, 149; on poet-weavers, 243; *News from Nowhere*, 117, 146, 147, 148; *The Song of Sigurd the Volsung*, 147, 167

Mottram, V. H., 117–18, 118–19

Moulin d'Or reunions, 450–1

Munich, RB visits, 246, 249–58, 261–3, 292, 323; correspondence to and from (RB and Ka Cox), 300–19

Murray, Gilbert, 186, 353, 373, 474, 516

Murray, Rosalind, 353, 373, 472

Murry, Middleton, 373, 375, 381, 391, 394

Myburgh, A., of 'Hood', 511

Nash, Paul, 451

Nation, The: RB's contributions to, 221; on RB's death, 516

INDEX

Neeve, Mr. and Mrs., The Old Vicarage, 203, 246, 263–4, 265, 290, 291, 292, 342, 349, 519

Nelson Battalion, 1914, 472

Nelson, Lieutenant, 495

Nelson, the, off Mudros Bay, 493

Nerval, Gerard de, 123

Nesbitt, Cathleen, 374, 380, 391, 456, 519; RB's meeting with, 370–1; correspondence with RB, 381–5, 389, 396–400, 403–4, 409–18 *passim*, 423–5, 429, 431, 437–8, 440, 443, 446, 449–50, 452–3, 454, 457, 458, 462, 464, 468–71, 493, 498; at the 'Pink and Lily', 391, 449; in *Butterfly on a Wheel*, 473; in *Quality Street*, 430; sees war sonnets, 481; mentioned in RB's will, 517

Neustrelitz, RB and Ka Cox visit, 344

Nevinson, Henry, editor of *The Nation*, 221

New Bilton Adult School, RB addresses, on Shakespeare, 239

Newbolt, Henry, 375, 384n

New Forest cottage (Keeling's discovery), 178, 180

New Inn (Ben Jonson), 420

Newnham College, Cambridge, 99, 118, 133, 182

Newnham Grange, the (George) Darwins' home, 154, 165, 182, 223, 269

New Numbers, 419, 439, 460, 475, 481, 484, 486, 503, 519, 523; Lascelles Abercrombie founds, 449; war sonnets in, 501; closing down of, 503

New Statesman, The, 195; on the 'legendary' aspects of RB, 520–1

New York, RB's first glimpse of, 397; his last days in, 446

New Zealand, RB visits, 428–30

Niagara Falls, RB at, 407, 408

Niagara, R.M.S., RB travels in, 428

'Night Journey, The' (RB), 367–8, 532; Strindberg's contribution to, 378

Nijinsky, 400, 418

1914 and Other Poems (RB), 519, 520, 521

Norton, Harry (a Cambridge 'Apostle'), 78, 174, 293, 356, 450

'Now God be thanked, Who has matched us with His hour' (RB), 467

Noyes, Alfred, 403, 406

'Oh, Death will find me long before I tire' (RB), 77, 532

Old Vicarage, The, Grantchester, 186, 188, 203n, 230, 239, 263–92 (*passim*), 286, 288, 290, 341–3, 349, 482, 532; rumour of demolition of, 469

Olivier sisters, 196; Mrs. Brooke on, 166, 178, 318; *see following entries*

Olivier, Sir Sydney and Lady, 118, 149, 157, 197

Olivier, Brynhild, 189, 206, 229, 230, 318; 361; in Broads, Drewsteignton, and Clevedon parties, 196, 197, 267, 281–2; as Helen of Troy, 232; becomes Mrs. Popham, 468

Olivier, Daphne, 189, 190, 281

Olivier, Margery, 157, 161, 166, 173, 178, 179, 198, 199, 206, 207, 474; at Fabian Summer School, 192; on Fabian committee, 145; in work for Poor Law reform, 204; in the Broads party, 267; as Noel's protector, 247, 249

Olivier, Noel, 157, 158, 161, 166, 173, 178, 180–1, 184, 188–90, 198, 199, 207–8, 226, 229–30, 231, 247, 249, 270, 275, 296, 297, 300, 335, 344, 347–8, 355, 371, 392, 468, 474, 518; invited to Prunoy, 234; at Drewsteignton, 281; declines *Poems* dedication offered by RB, 291; as medical student, 298; and Ka Cox, 275

'One before the last' (RB), 213

'One Day' (RB), 416

Orchard, The (Grantchester cottage), 184, 185, 186–246, 260, 261; RB describes, 204

Osborne, Lady Gwendoline, 452

O'Shaughnessy, Mr., U.S. Consul in Mexico, 443

Our Partnership (Beatrice Webb), 245

Overcote, picnic at, 182

Overstrand, 353, 355

Over's bookshop, Rugby, 23, 41

Oxford Book of French Verse (ed. St. John Lucas), 130

Oxford Magazine, on Marsh's Memoir of R.B., 525

Pacific and South Seas travels of RB, 413 seqq.

Papeete, RB in, 430–7; illness in, foreshadowing final illness, 434–5

Paris, Major-General (later, General), 461, 480, 508, 511, 512, 517

Parker, Anne, wife of William Brooke (married 1761), 17

Parker, John, father of Anne, 18

Parker, Matthew, Archbishop of Canterbury, forebear of RB, 17–18

Pater, Walter, 43, 63, 86; 'Leonardo', 90; *Plato and Platonism*, 283

'Path of Dreams, The' (RB), 51

Patmore, Coventry, 433

Pavlova, Anna, 391

Peguy, Charles, death of, 471, 481

INDEX

Peter Pan, RB's liking for, 117

Petrouchka, 448

Philadelphia, S.S., RB travels in, 443, 446

Philippi, Rosina, 370

Phillips, Stephen, 80, 87

Phoenix, The, RB's contributions to, 57, 59–63, 74; origins of, 48–9, 51

Pigou, A. C., 170, 174, 413–14

Pindar's *Odes*, 115

'Pine Trees and the Sky' (RB), 127

'Pink and Lily, The', Prince's Risborough, 391, 449

Piper of Arll, The (Campbell Scott), 404

Plymouth, Lady, 383, 392

Poel, William, 309

Poetry Bookshop, Harold Monro's, 373, 459, 468

Poetry Review, The, 260, 364, 384

Pole, Reginald, of King's, 174, 391; as Mephistophilis, 230; as Richard II, 213

Poor Law of 1834, 193, 245; Cambridge Fabians' work for reform of, 193–4, 224–5, 227–9; the Minority Report, 245–6; campaign in decline, 245

Popham, Hugh, 229

Popham, Brynhild, 468

Positivism, 147, 148

Post-impressionist painters, 365, 373

Potts, Dr., of Fettes, 21

Pound, Ezra, 262, 263, 365; and Hulme, 363; RB criticizes *Personae* of, 210; RB visits, 373

Praed, W. M., 49

'Prevalence of Earnest Youth, The' (RB), 60

Primmer, Mrs. (Lyndhurst), 335; Mr. and Mrs., 180

Prince Edward (battleship), 509

Prince's Risborough, visits to, 391, 449

Principia Ethica, Moore's, 232, 233, 363

Prunoy, Jacques Raverat's home, 234

Psairiotis, Aristides, owner of olive-grove grave plot, 517

'Psychical Research' (RB), 170, 170n, 413–, 414, 434

'Pudsey, Dawson' (The Orchard bull terrier), 223, 231, 265

Pye, Ethel, 160, 230

Pye, Sybil, correspondence and visits (also with David Pye), 160, 229, 230, 231, 232, 266, 291, 293, 356

Pyramids, the, RB visits, 495

Pyramids, The (RB's prize poem), 66

Queen Elizabeth (battleship), 493, 496

Quiller-Couch, Sir Arthur, 452

Quilter, Colonel, 473, 487, 496, 499, 506, 511; at RB's interment, 512; dies in battle, 514

Rag-time, coming of, 371–2

Raleigh, Walter, 391, 474

Rapallo, Villa Molfino at, 50

Raverat, Gwen (for earlier references *see* Darwin, Gwen), 293, 303, 394; growing reputation of, 374–5; asked to paint The Old Vicarage, 469; protests at RB legend, 521; Virginia Woolf writes to, concerning RB, 529; and Jacques, her husband, as guests, hosts, friends of RB, 233, 269, 271, 289, 298, 335, 364, 374; 452; Gide stays with, 448

Raverat, Jacques, friendship and correspondence with RB, 120, 132, 145, 158, 164, 178, 190–2, 204–7, 217, 229, 247, 255–6, 261–2, 266, 322, 326–7, 345, 348, 356, 376, 383, 391, 424, 438, 440, 455, 458, 462, 473, 476, 486, 492, 518, 526; first encounter with RB, 110–11; in Corsica, 179, 180; after return from illness in France, 188; and Ka Cox, 189 seqq., 522; helps RB with private edition, 204, 240; at Slade ball, 211, 212; draws RB, 247; on RB's poetical method, 280; on the Bloomsbury group, 354; on the Schell photographs, 390; plans to buy Stourpaine House, 481; in RB's will, 517

'Recruit, The' (RB), 484

Reeve, John, husband of Anne Brooke, 18; changes name to John Reeve Brooke, 18

Reeves, Amber, 118

Refugees of 1914, RB on, 470–1

Regina, RB visits, 410

Reinhardt, Max, RB's opinion of, 377

'Retrospect' (RB), 434, 436, 532

'Return, The' (RB), 51

Rhys, Ernest, 384n

Rhythm (edited by Middleton Murry), 362, 375, 391, 392

Ribblesdale, Lord, 493

Rickett, Arthur, *The Vagabond in Literature*, 122

Ricketts, Charles, 160, 451

Robinson, Edward Arlington, 402

Rockies, The, RB visits, 411

Rogers, Dr., in Broads party, 267

Room of One's Own, A (Virginia Woolf), 284

Rootham, Cyril, 291

Rossetti, D. G., 66, 94; example of influence of, 73

Rossetti, William (*The Germ*), 295

Rothenstein, Albert, 158, 212, 391; as designer *for Comus*, 160, 161; as art editor of *Rhythm*, 375; advises RB to buy Augustus John drawings, 169

Royal George (battleship), 509

INDEX

Royal Naval Division, 461 seqq.; Horse Guards Parade memorial to men of, 528

Royde Smith, Naomi, 72–3; and RB's trip to the U.S.A., 391–2

Ruani, New Zealand, RB in, 430

Rugby: in the 1880s, 22–5; RB's father at, 21, 22 seqq.; RB's schooldays at, *see* Brooke, Rupert; *Rugby Elector, The*, 79; Rugby Home Mission Camp, New Romney, 96

Runcton Cottage, Chichester (home of the Middleton Murrys), 362

Ruskin, John, 43–4, 148; on King's College Chapel, 104

Russell, Bertrand, 187; as 'Apostle', 156; at Lady Ottoline Morrell's, 222

Russell-Smith, Hugh, 38, 67, 77, 78, 81, 83, 86, 95, 96, 179, 180; early days at Cambridge, 105, 120, 127; in *Dr. Faustus*, 124; on walking tour with RB, 125, 128; in Munich, 313, 318, 518

Sacharov (dancer) at Wolfskehl's salons, 252–3

Saguenay river, 403, 404

St. Lawrence river, RB describes, 403–4

Saintsbury, Professor, 177

Salzburg, RB and Ka Cox in, 321; memories of, 392–3

Samoa, RB in, 418, 460; RB describes Samoan dancers, 418

Samuel, Herbert, 173

'Sandro' and 'Teragram', 73

Sarnia, RB at, 408

Sassoon, Siegfried, describes RB, 451; discusses Kipling with RB, 451

Saturday Westminster, The, 250–1

Saunders, Platoon-Sergeant, 511

Savile Club, RB's project of joining, 420

Sayle, Charles, 108, 124, 128, 129, 135, 158, 163, 167, 187, 188

Scheldt, German advance to, 463

Schell, S., photographs RB, 384, 389, 523; describes RB, 389–90

Schick, Professor, RB's teacher of German, 249

Schlesinger, Dr., attends RB on deathbed, 507, 509

Schloss, A. D., 91, 132; *see* Waley, Arthur

Scholfield, A. F., of King's, 106, 184, 407

School Field, Rugby, 34 seqq., 64 seqq., 197–202

'School Novel, The' (feature by RB), 60–1

Schwabing, 252

Scott, Duncan Campbell, 404, 406

'Sea, The' (RB), 73–4

'Seaside' (RB), 151–2, 416–17, 532

'Second Best' (RB), 117n

Sedgwick, Ellery, 399, 406

Seneca, RB on, 377

'Sentimental Exile, The' (Old Vicarage), 350, 361, 482

Sex Society, the, of Peterhouse, 223

'Shakespearian Love Sonnet' (RB), 279

Sharp, Clifford, first editor of *The New Statesman*, 195

Shaw, G. B., 45, 371, 448, 451; RB's opinion of, 77, 78; impact of plays of, abroad, 377; joins Fabians, 149; *Candida*, 112; *Getting Married*, 150; *John Bull's Other Island*, 80–1; *Man and Superman*, 112; *Plays Pleasant*, 112; 'Press Cuttings', 188; Mrs. G. B. Shaw, 391; Shaw–Belloc debate, RB attends with Ervine, 374, 384

Shaw-Stewart, Patrick, 475, 487, 490, 495, 497, 498, 499, 501, 502, 504, 505, 506, 508, 511, 512; and RB's scheme for stokers, 481; with RB in Malta, 492; with RB in Cairo, 495; on the aptness of situation of RB's grave, 513; dies in action, 514

Sheppard, J. T., fellow of King's (tutor to RB), 77–8, 101, 111, 112, 115, 132, 174, 450; on the RB myth, 520; becomes a literary trustee, 532

'Shilling Garland' (ed. Lawrence Binyon), 406; *see* Abercrombie, *Gallows Garland*

Shove, Gerald, 167, 174, 177, 180, 196, 197, 204, 293, 450

Shropshire Lad, A (A. E. Housman), 94–5, 102

Sidmouth, holidays in, 179, 181

Sidgwick & Jackson, publish poems of RB, 291; sales, 291n

Sidgwick, Frank, 278–9, 281, 343, 519, 528; on the 'Lust' sonnet, 286–7

Sidgwick, Professor Henry, of Trinity, 104; as Fabian, 156; death of, 156

Sidney, Sir Philip, *Arcadia*, 185

Sierra, S.S., RB travels in, 413–15

Silent Woman, The, RB appears in, 174

Sills, Henry, Fellow of King's, 101, 111, 132

Silver Box, The (Galsworthy), 389

Skyros: described, 504–5; tombstone sent to, 527; statue on, 528, 532

Slade School, 192, 210–12

'Sleeping Out' (RB), 199n

Socialist League, 149

'Soldier, The' (RB), 481–3

Solomon, Simeon, 83

Song of the Beasts, The (RB), 112, 199n

'Sonnet Reversed' (RB), 247

INDEX

'Sonnet Suggested by . . . Psychical Research' (RB), *see* 'Psychical Research'

Sorrows of Satan, The (Marie Corelli), 69, 72

South Seas poems, 450, 520, 532

Sowerby Parsonage, 19

Sowing (Leonard Woolf), 70n

Spencer, Herbert, 233

Spencer, Gilbert, 451

Spencer, Stanley, 202, 372, 451, 452, 455; Gwen Raverat discusses RB myth with, 521

Spender, J. A. (*Westminster Gazette*), 72, 392, 394, 410

Sphere, The, on RB's death, 516

Spielman, Eva, 196, 229

Squire, J. C., 215, 240, 434, 459; as Fabian, 118, 215

Stanford, C. V., 106

Stanford University, RB gives reading at, 412

Starnbergersee, RB and Ka Cox visit, 322, 323, 345, 417

Staten Island, 402

Steer, Wilson, at the Slade ball, 212

Stephen, Adrian, 154, 257

Stephen, Sir Leslie, 154, 379

Stephen, Thoby, 154

Stephen, Vanessa, 222, 257; *see* Bell

Stephen, Virginia (*see also* Woolf, Virginia), 30, 154, 170, 257, 301, 332–3; at Lady Ottoline Morrell's, with Vanessa, 222; at The Old Vicarage, 280, 368; at Drewsteignton, 280–4; *The Voyage Out*, 280, 503; *The Waves*, 156, 284; *A Room of One's Own*, 284

Stephens, James, 384; *The Hill of Vision*, 535

Stevenson, Mr. and Mrs., of The Orchard, 184, 186–246, 291

Stockbridge, Fabians' caravan venture at, 225–9

Stone, C. J., 41

Storrs, Ronald, 452

Stourpaine House, 481

Strachey, James, friendship and correspondence with, 29, 30, 31, 32, 163, 167, 174, 177, 202, 215, 241, 258, 268, 274, 304, 321, 324, 334, 344, 349–50, 450; at St. Paul's School, 55, 66–7; and Bernard Shaw, 188; at *The Spectator*, 192; at Slade ball, 212; revisits Hillbrow, 218; criticizes RB, 218; at Llanbedr Fabian Summer School, 232; at Drewsteignton, 280–4; a night under the stars, 282; on RB's 'Lust' sonnet, 286; at Lulworth, 297; comments on Ka Cox's letter-writing, 318; at the Mermaid Club, Rye, 326–7; with RB, calls on Henry James, 328; with RB at Lyndhurst, 335; helps RB, 338; with RB at The Hague, 347–8; and at the Cologne Van Gogh Exhibition, 347; at Eversleigh, 350; defends Bloomsbury Group against RB, 353; breaks with RB, 354, 394

Strachey, Lytton, 29, 31, 68–9, 70, 78, 156, 174, 177, 420; at Market Lavington, 154; and Virginia Stephen, 154; on the *Comus* production, 164–5; at Grantchester, 202–4, 223, 270; influence of, on RB, 218; at Lady Ottoline Morrell's, 222, 322; Henry Lamb paints, 273; and Frank Sidgwick, 278; at Lulworth, 296; RB quarrels with, 353, 454; on RB, 454; *Landmarks in French Literature*, 282

Strachey, Sir Richard, 29

Strauss's *Rosenkavalier*, 250

Stravinsky, Igor, *Le Rossignol*, RB at first performance of, 449

Strindberg, RB 'discovers', 278, 376–80

Stringer, Arthur, *Red Wine of Youth*, 442, 442n

Studholme family, RB's New Zealand hosts, 430

Superior, Lake, RB visits, 408

'Super-Ski, The' (Christmas show), 212

Suva, RB in, 420, 425

Swift, Stephen (publisher), 215

Swinburne, A. C., 43, 45, 47, 75, 81, 83, 92, 94, 102, 120, 176, 183; funeral of, 180, 181–2

Switzerland, Christmas 1908 party in, 172–3

Symbolist poets, 362

Symons, Arthur: *Studies in Prose and Verse*, 53; *The Symbolist Movement in Literature*, 167

Synge, J. M., *Deirdre of the Sorrows*, 450; *Playboy of the Western World*, 282

Taatamata, Mataia girl ('Mamua'), 431–2, 435, 437, 518; RB dreams of, 476; letter from, in *Empress of Ireland*, 479–80

Tadousac, 403, 404

Tahiti, 430–7; coral poisoning in, as contribution to RB's fatal illness, 507

Tahiti, S.S., RB sails from Papeete in, 437

Taviuni, island of, RB visits, 425

Taylor, Laurette, in *Peg o' My Heart*, 468

Tchekov, *Uncle Vanya*, 384

Tempest, Marie, 451

Temple, Frederick, as benefactor of Rugby School, 66

Temple, William (later Archbishop of Canterbury), 36, 37

INDEX

Temple Library and Reading Room Rugby, 36–7, 78, 532

Tennyson, Alfred, Lord, 52, 58, 61, 87, 110

Tennyson, Charles, qu., 100

Thomas, Edward, 226, 239, 240–1, 384n, 393; meets Edward Marsh, 380; on RB, 524, 531

Thomas, Havard, work on the plaque by, 523

Thompson, Francis, 228, 433

Thomson, James (1700–48), *The Castle of Indolence*, 89; *The Seasons*, 87

Thomson, James (1834–82), *The City of Dreadful Night*, 87, 89–90

'Thoughts on the Shape of the Human Body' (RB), 62, 284, 532

Thurloe Square, RB's flat in, 391

'Tiare Tahiti' (RB), 283, 431, 432, 433, 434, 532

Tilley, A., 222

'Timeless moment', cult of the, 156

Times, The, 515, 522; *Literary Supplement,* 503n, 535

Time's Laughing Stocks (Thomas Hardy), 215

Tinney, Frank, 458

'To My Lady Influenza' (RB), 113–14

'To Two Old School Friends' (RB), 200–1

Tolstoy, death of, 180

Tombros, sculptor of Skyros statue, 528

Torfua, S.S., carries RB to Fiji, 419–20

Toronto, RB in, 405

Torquay, RB in, 146–53

Tottenham, Miss (governess), 27, 28, 32

'Town and Country' (RB), 280, 290, 325, 368, 472

'Treasure, The (Unpacking)', (RB), 483

Trebuki Bay, Skyros, 501 seqq.

Tree, Felicity, 391

Tree, Sir Herbert Beerbohm, 41, 80, 88

Trelawny of the Wells (Pinero), 221–2

Trevelyan, R. C., 154, 348

Trumpington Hall estate, 265

'Ugly poems' of RB, 221, 535

'Unfortunate', 365n

Uncle Vanya, RB quotes from, 348

United States of America: RB resolves to visit, 375; sojourn in, May 1913–June 1914, 396–447; RB on American professors, 400

'Unpacking', or 'Contemplation . . .' (RB), 460

Valetta, RB in, 493

Vancouver, RB in, 411

'Vanitas' (early RB poem), 75

Van Rysselbergh, Elizabeth, 298

Van Volkenburg, Ellen, 441, 446, 447, 482

Vaughan, Professor C. E., 280

Vedrenne-Barker series, at Court Theatre, 80

Venice, RB's opinion of, 84–5

Ventura, S.S., RB journeys in, 417–18

Venture, The (a Rugby School magazine), 74, 82, 83

Verity, A. W., on RB's essay on Puritanism, 235

Vermelles, Alfred Brooke's death at, 519

Verona meeting (proposed), 308, 314, 315, 318–19; RB and Ka Cox meet in, 321

Veronique (musical comedy), 80

Verrall, A. W., of Trinity, 107, 108, 124, 173; Helen, 173; the family, 170

Victory, H.M.S., RB and Denis Browne join, 461

Vienna, RB in, 258–60

Vieux-Dieu, the march to, 464

Ville de Carthage (battleship), 509

'Vision of the Archangels' (RB), 112

'Voice, The' (RB), 181, 532; A. Y. Campbell's parody of, 529–30

Von der Planitz, Annemarie (later Mrs. Dudley Ward), 289, 338, 344

Von der Planitz, Clothilde, 239

Wagner (RB), 535

Wagner, Christian, *Liederbuch der Gottheit,* 116

'Waikiki' (RB), 416

'Waiting for the Robert E. Lee', Ethel Levey's version of, 384

Waley, Arthur, 167, 174, 183

Wallas, Graham, as Fabian, 149

Waller, Lewis, 423

Wallis, Mr., at The Old Vicarage, 290–1

Walmer Castle, 478, 479, 482, 486

Walpole, Hugh, RB and, 373, 448

Wanamakers', RB visits, 398

Wairaki, New Zealand, RB in, 429

Ward, Dudley, friendship and correspondence with, 126, 167, 168, 169, 178, 179, 184, 189, 190, 195, 196, 197, 206, 207, 215, 232, 239, 274, 285, 344, 346, 357, 364, 449, 450, 461, 476, 487, 492, 518, 519, 526; at Slade ball, 212; at Lenzerheide, 212; on staff of *Economist,* 219, 324; as Fabian, 224–5; as 'call-boy' in *Dr. Faustus,* 232; at Stockbridge, 225–9; engagement and marriage of, 289, 338, 344; in Thurloe Square flat, 393; RB describes Samoan life for, 420; mentioned in RB's will; Mr. and Mrs. Dudley Ward, 366, 372, 376, 492

Wartime Sonnets, 467, 468, 471, 472, 475, 478, 532

Warwickshire, RB praises, 456

INDEX

Washington, RB in, 442–3

Waste (Granville Barker), 423

Watson, William, 41–2, 47; RB's opinion of, 93

Watts, G. F., 111

Watts Dunton, Theodore, 94

Waves, The (Virginia Woolf), 284

Webb, Sidney and Beatrice, 80, 149, 167, 168, 193, 204, 228, 232–3, 236, 245; and John Burns, 245–6; and the National Minimum, 192; and Poor Law reform, 193–5; *The New Statesman*, 195; *Minority Report of the Poor Law Commission*, 193; found National Society for the Prevention of Destitution, 194; *Our Partnership* (B. Webb), 233

Webster, John, RB's research and dissertation on, 83, 111, 204, 267, 268, 276, 278, 282–3, 287–8, 290, 291, 293, 369, 385, 526

Wedd, Nathaniel, fellow of King's, 101, 107, 111, 112, 132

Wedekind, Frank, RB's tributes to, 366, 378

Wellesley, Lady Eileen, RB's friendship and correspondence with, 452, 455, 456–7, 459, 461–2, 463, 478, 479, 499

Wells, Professor Chauncy, befriends RB in the U.S.A., 412, 429–30, 431, 437, 439

Wells, H. G., RB meets, 146; as Fabian, 149; at Keeling's party, 157; RB's admiration for, 174; quoted, 118; *New Worlds for Old*, 146

Wendover, 449, 450

Westminster Gazette, 72, 115, 170, 171, 200–2, 265, 279, 398, 403, 407, 410, 412, 413, 430, 486, 516–17, 535; RB's official appointment to, 391, 394; *Westminster Problems Book*, 171

Whistler, J. M., 44, 45, 55

Whitelaw, Robert, master at Rugby, 36, 38–40, 72, 92, 258, 260, 261, 263, 468, 522, 533

Wilde, Oscar, 43, 44, 45, 47, 81, 94, 97, 105, 371; *De Profundis*, 54, 55, 57, 58, 69, 97

William III, RB's essay on, 84, 91

Willison, Sir John, 406

Wilson, Hugh, of King's, 123, 124, 224, 333

Wilson, Steuart, of King's, 224, 450, 452

Wimborne, Lady, 481, 488

Winchelsea, RB and James Strachey in, 327

Winchester Reading Prize, RB and Dalton compete for, 183

Winnipeg, RB visits, 408–10

Woking cottage, Ka Cox's, 301, 327, 328, 329, 335, 338

Wolfskehl, Karl, RB meets, 252, 253

Wollaston, Mrs., 306, 310, 332

Woolf, Leonard, 332; as freshman, 156; on Lytton Strachey, 69–70

Woolf, Virginia, 274, 354 (*see also* Stephen, Virginia); describes Ka Cox, 272; on RB., 529–30; the *Times Literary Supplement* article by (probably), 525, 526; *A Room of One's Own*, 284; *The Voyage Out*, 280, 503; *The Waves*, 156, 284

'Word Book' of RB, 90–1

Working Men's College, St. Pancras, 158

Wyndham, George, 390

Wynne-Willson, the Rev. J. B., 41, 74

Wylrick Station (RB's initial active service), 465

Yale, RB at, 401, 444

Yeats, W. B., 93, 124, 380, 386, 403, 406, 424, 451; RB visits, 373; RB's opinion of, 361; his opinions of RB, 373–4, 442

Yestor, campers' walk to, 282

Young, Hilton (Lord Kennet), RB writes to, 439.